BREAK THROUGH
FROM INNOVATION
TO IMPACT

BREAK THROUGH

FROM INNOVATION TO IMPACT

EDITED BY
HENK VAN DEN BREEMEN
(CHAIR)
DOUGLAS MURRAY
BENJAMIN BILSKI
MAARTEN VERKERK

First published in 2014
The Owls Foundation
P.O. Box 20
6740 AA Lunteren
The Netherlands

ISBN 978-90-823208-0-0

Designed by Martin Colyer
Copy edited by Robert Low

ACKNOWLEDGEMENTS

Coming from a military background, where innovations and breakthroughs are a key part of the culture, I had been thinking about the ideas for this research and book for some time. Three years ago I, together with Paul Baan of the Noaber Foundation and Pieter de Rijcke of De Hoge Dennen, launched The Owls Foundation to accommodate the Owls Project, through which to study and promote innovation. This book is the first result of our work. It is intended to be a contribution to an ongoing discussion on innovations and breakthroughs, and by doing so to help to establish stimulating environments for innovation and a more sustainable society. Over the past three years we have reached out to our immediate and wider networks, and engaged many talented and successful individuals as authors, editors and interviewees. The contribution of nearly a hundred men and women made this book possible. We are greatly indebted to them. We also wish to thank our critical readers Dirk Barth and Colum Gorman; the authors/editors Benjamin Bilski and Maarten Verkerk; the editing team Douglas Murray, Robert Low and Martin Colyer; Theo Bosters for his technical research; the members of the board of The Owls Foundation for their very constructive support; and especially Johanna Noom, who managed this wide-ranging and complicated project.

Henk van den Breemen

CONTENTS

INTRODUCTION BY HENK VAN DEN BREEMEN

This is a book about the secrets of innovations and breakthroughs. The society we live in is the result of many innovations and we will continue to need such innovations today and in the future. In this book we examine a number of innovations and breakthrough processes across an exceptionally wide range of areas in order to understand their underlying mechanisms, and the way they succeeded or failed in making an impact.

An innovation is something new—an idea, method or product—while a breakthrough reflects the extent to which an innovation shapes new developments and makes an impact. But the extent to which an innovation becomes a success or failure depends heavily on the process attached to it and the environment and culture in which it operates. In the international context this means it is essential to create environments where innovation is welcomed, rather than seen as a threat by governments and institutions. If you wish to make such an environment durable it is not merely a technical problem but a human story and a matter of values.

Innovations and breakthroughs involve the process of a continual discussion for improvement, which should be on the agenda of schools, institutions, businesses and governments. The aim of this project is to encourage such a discussion. To that end we have engaged current and former leaders and innovators who were actually involved in breakthrough processes in research, policy, business and philanthropy. There are valuable lessons in their experiences that we look to pass on to future generations. As a result of this engagement and a multi-disciplinary approach, we have written case studies on innovations and breakthrough processes in technology, business, media, diplomacy, tackling child abuse, healthcare, agriculture, the cyber domain, politics, privatisation, energy, international law, climate change, geo-politics and the economy, impact investing, social renewal and logistics. These examples enable readers to compare their own vision to such successes—or mistakes—and see how innovations succeeded.

If you want to change your environment and develop a space that stimulates innovation, then you need to understand the underlying structure of an innovation and breakthrough process. To do this we have described and examined each innovation or breakthrough process stage by stage to success or failure. We assumed that these stages are generic and parallel to the stages of a normal implementation process. We call them generic factors. We have identified innovation and breakthrough, idea and vision, concept (the creative phase), mission and strategy, planning and execution, iterative process (operational phase), to which we have added three further enabling factors in the course of our research: human and environmental factors, and the window of opportunity.

These generic factors are common, recognisable, instrumental, applicable and present in each breakthrough or innovation within the contexts of business and institutions, from small to large in size, right up to governments operating in an international context. These generic factors can also be meaningful attributes for creating impact (values) and a stimulating environment for innovations and breakthroughs. We have found that if we look deeper to study and understand these generic factors, we are in a better position to transfer knowledge and experience and develop cooperation and cross-over activities in stimulating environments to make innovations internationally successful.

This success is not a given, because even though many institutions value innovation, they do not necessarily prioritise the development of a strategy to build innovation into their internal processes. A recent study by Accenture offered a revealing picture. In a survey of 519 executives in British, French and American firms with annual revenues of more than $100 million, 93 per cent admitted that the long-term success of their business depends on innovation, yet only 18 per cent of them had prioritised the development of a strategy for innovation.* Such a strategy for innovation development, acquisition and implementation will have to be developed by the companies themselves. Innovation and breakthrough also have to do with mindset and, connected to that, impact.

Why did we choose the case studies that we did? In the global world of today there is great interdependency. No country, no institution, no company can go it alone. And we cannot ignore the international context. On top of that, no innovation comes on its own. So our approach was broad. First, we sought a diverse and engaging range of subjects. Second, we made use of our own international network. It made a big difference to engage directly with the people who were involved in these cases, either as authors or interview subjects. They all brought their expertise and experience to the studies because they were so directly involved in the processes. There were many possible subjects to focus on, but the subjects we chose were welcomed enthusiastically by the members of our network. They have been very helpful because we have all been thrilled by the idea and also genuinely curious about what the outcome of our study would be.

The active engagement and quality of the leading figures we interviewed is one of the distinguishing features of this project. These remarkable individuals were generous with their time, and thought hard to reflect on their experiences, and on the generic factors of invention, idea, vision, concept, strategy, planning and implementation. They were also asked to consider how these factors were related to each other during the process. In addition, they were asked to reflect on the role of leadership (the human factor), context and the window of opportunity

Each case study was carried out with the creative, operational and enabling factors in mind in desk research, field research and semi-structured interviews, still leaving room for flexibility. We have identified these factors in each study as well as the roles they play. We next supplemented the case studies with qualitative analyses by a group of assessors, with the aid of software. We elaborate on these research methods in the Annex, in which the qualitative analyses are finally brought together. The results are discussed and graphed, and form an extension to the concluding chapter 'Reflections'.

The results are fascinating. We have found that generic factors are present in and play different roles across the case studies, and help to explain successes and failures. They provide a rich bank of data to contribute to the goals of this project and to stimulate an ongoing discussion on innovations and breakthroughs to enter the culture of schools, universities, companies and governments—institutions that can translate these values and principles into reality. In this project the generic factors are recognised and exemplified. They not only play a role as an analytical tool, but can also be used as 'steering buttons' in order to play an important role in the storage and transfer of experience. They point to the great value of being able to work together in a multi-disciplinary way and internationally, and show us how to create an environment that stimulates innovation and from which the future will benefit. .

* W. Koetzier and A. Alon, *Why "Low Risk" Innovation is Costly: Overcoming the Perils of Renovation and Invention* (Accenture, 2013).

CHAPTER 1

THE CREATION AND IMPACT OF THE CYBER DOMAIN

The introduction of digital information and communication technologies (ICT) to the public led to the biggest societal and economic transformation of recent history. These breakthroughs in the cyber domain, mobile space and social media have made a significant impact on society, stability, security and governance. In response to the impact of these technologies and media in these four areas, Western and authoritarian governments are taking very different approaches to the cyber domain domestically and internationally. In this case study, we consider two breakthroughs and their aftermath: the technological breakthrough, the impact of technological change on society, and the responses in governance. On the international level, this has also developed into competition between democratic and non-democratic states about the future of the internet. This is not a technical disagreement, but a fundamental dispute about the core values, structure and governance of the state.

THE QUALITATIVE ANALYSIS FOR THIS CHAPTER
IS ON PAGE 377 OF THE ANNEX

NIGEL INKSTER AND BENJAMIN BILSKI
WITH ACKNOWLEDGEMENTS TO LORD PETER INGE

INTRODUCTION: TWO BREAKTHROUGHS

The groundwork for the original technological breakthrough that would lead to the internet was laid in the 1970s. The Advanced Research Projects Agency Network (Arpanet) created the first packet-switching data transfer system, a digital advance over the circuit-switching systems of the traditional telephone and telegraph. It was created and developed in the 1970s and '80s as a trusted network between engineers among several American national research laboratories. The key political development took place in 1991, when Senator Al Gore Jr succeeded in advancing a bill to privatise Arpanet through the High Performance Computing Act. President George H. W. Bush signed the Act into law and described a vision for the future:

> The development of high-performance computing and communications technology offers the potential to transform radically the way in which all Americans will work, learn, and communicate in the future. It holds the promise of changing society as much as the other great inventions of the 20th century, including the telephone, air travel, and radio and TV. (...) It is no surprise that America holds the lead in high-performance information technology. Our greatest technological strides have been made possible by the unique qualities of American society: Freedom, innovation, entrepreneurial spirit, a combination found nowhere else in the world. And this program will sustain and extend that leadership position. [1]

The first Clinton administration continued the work of the 'Gore Bill' with a number of initiatives including funding the research and development that led to Mosaic, the first World Wide Web browser. Another key development was the deregulation of the US telecommunications sector. However much idealism was expressed in the visions of President Bush and Al Gore in the early 1990s, no one could have foreseen the scale and speed with which the internet would unleash a social and economic transformation in the environment of the free market. The decisive factor that enabled the technological breakthrough was the government's decision to make packet-switched communication technology available to the private sector. Private investment, innovation, idealism and business strategy underpinned the unprecedented market success of the 'dotcom boom'.

The economic success could not have occurred if the technology had been kept under the control of the state. And those states in which the economic benefit was maximised tend to be democratic: states where political power, economic resources and means of communication are shared between multiple stakeholders. This is a fundamental difference in structure and values with those states where all power and resources are concentrated among a small set of elites who are also accustomed to controlling means of communication. As we shall see, in current disputes about internet governance between authoritarian and democratic states, there is a great risk that the democratic world that produced the technological, social and economic breakthroughs may cede the leadership position that President Bush had prophesied in 1991.

Today, more than two decades after the rise of the internet, mobile communications and social media, we live in a world where more and more daily functions are ceded to the cyber domain. We have entered an era of Big Data, where we have entrusted a large part of personal and financial information to corporations based in the United States, which the American government is able to access. This has profound implications for privacy, public trust and concepts of security. The Snowden affair has stirred up a public debate and awoken Congressional scrutiny into the cyber activities of American intelligence agencies. At least the US has this kind of parliamentary oversight. Authoritarian states tend to have very little, and not all supposedly democratic states have anything like the safeguards the US has in place. France is a country with a very wide range of cyber activities, but remains the only Western democracy where there is no parliamentary oversight over the intelligence services. From its military origins to the free market, the cyber domain has undergone a remilitarisation and is now a strategic space where power is exercised.

Some questions that are being asked today, to which there are no satisfactory answers, are: What are governments doing in the cyber domain? How can we distinguish realities and perceptions? How can Western political leadership be adequately informed to set a sensible strategic course?

We will consider, in turn, the impact of technological breakthrough on society, stability, security and governance. In cases where technological change leads to social disruption and structural change, what governance structures are needed and what new technologies should they adopt?

IMPACT ON SOCIETY

After the technological breakthrough was developed in the public domain, the real breakthrough was driven in the environment of the free market. Exceeding all expectations, the increased speed and efficiency in communications and commerce enabled ICT, the internet and social media to make a very deep economic and social impact.

A part of the vision is the view that technology alone is not 'something', but rather an element that is linked to a particular process. What technology is, in other words, depends on what it can become in the process that it is linked to. These can be electoral, policy or business processes. In each of these areas, the impact of technology in the increase of connectivity and accessibility has led to greater efficiency and value. The link between technology and process creates new concepts, and the impact can be measured as a function of this linkage. The crucial question then becomes which technology is being linked to which process and how. In new concepts, technology also changes the substance of process.

Marshall MacLuhan's two ideas of the 'medium is the message' and the 'global village' – concepts formulated to describe the present and future of mass communications in radio and television – have proven very useful when applied to understanding the internet and social media. Technological change with the rise of print and the Gutenberg Bible is the traditional example where a new means of transmission represented a fundamental challenge to traditional authority, and disrupted an established social order in a manner that could not have been predicted.

These two elements – the linkage of technology to process and the change that technology brings to substance – help us to understand the impact of the technological breakthrough on society. Here we consider social interactions, electoral processes, business processes and policy processes.

In social interactions, new media have both the potential to deepen and strengthen existing offline social bonds, but also to lead to atomisation and shallow interactions.[2] There was no fundamental social transformation as a result of technology. It did not change the bonds of family, community, workplace or the university campus, but it may help deepen and widen these, depending on the user. One novelty that did not exist before is that virtual communities of common interest can be formed in real time and at minimal cost. And some of these new virtual communities in turn can have a significant electoral and political impact.

The organic development of the internet has led to the creation of self-selecting virtual communities, which may be extensions of traditional communities, or completely new social groups. New communities that previously could not have been created engage in new sorts of activities online. The broadcasting connecting effect is also an isolating effect when people coalesce in self-selecting, self-isolating communities and reinforce existing perceptions, rather than exposing views to challenge. This phenomenon has been called narrowcasting. This emergence of new social groups, with similar ideas, experiences and perceptions, can also organise online into political movements, leading to success in electoral processes and to political power.

An essential element of the message of Barack Obama's 2008 campaign was that it was about 'you', the voter. The strategic decision was made to take on and defeat Hillary Clinton with use of social media for 'money, mobilisation and message'. This was no small accomplishment against the most popular political brand name in the world. Fundraising was carried out by 'crowd funding', involving the collection of hundreds of thousands of small donations. Without using public money, the Obama campaign turned into an entirely new political phenomenon.

Individuals were involved into the process and brought into the social network of the campaign community. This medium was the message: the campaign was about 'you', and the message was the empowerment of the individual by inclusion in a virtual community. The campaign offered very little substance about Obama himself, his ideas or policy proposals, but the message of virtual inclusion succeeded in bringing electoral success in the world's most powerful nation.

In the case of the Obama campaign, these new and social media complemented traditional media of television and radio. In the Italian election of 2013, Beppe Grillo's campaign created a similar virtual community and its own social network. Those members of Grillo's movement who were running for parliamentary seats were instructed not to appear on television.

In other words, the campaign's use of new media deliberately *was* the message as it sought to highlight the novelty of the movement by rejecting the use of traditional media. A charismatic stand-up comedian with a criminal record succeeded in winning a quarter of the vote, sending 109 inexperienced deputies to the Camera and 54 to the Senate in a time of economic crisis. None of these newly-minted politicians had ever physically met each other or the leader of their movement. What could possibly go wrong?

In both cases, social media was an essential mobilising factor. For Obama it resulted in winning over the Democratic Party and then the Presidency. In the case of Beppe Grillo, nothing much happened. The political establishment outfoxed him and the adults resumed running Italy. This difference in impact reveals that it is not enough for social media to mobilise politically to make a meaningful impact. Unless political and electoral mobilisation is tied to effective political hierarchy and governance strategy, social media mobilisation will not lead to new governance. As we shall see, this has been the biggest problem of the limited positive impact of the Arab Spring, which has been effective in toppling some tyrants, but not in translating this to effective new structures of governance.

In the areas of commerce and government, technology has been an accelerant, transforming the way developed societies operate. E-government in particular has the potential to deliver services to the public efficiently and swiftly at greatly reduced costs. It also offers much-enhanced transparency and correspondingly reduced scope for corruption. On the other hand, the reduction of secrecy in government makes it more difficult to develop long-term policies that may be unpopular in the short term.

Mass online petitioning can help draw attention to problems much like traditional lobbying, but it has not fundamentally changed existing legislative or policy processes. When issues become instant and spread virally, and politicians feel compelled to be seen reacting to them, the result may be that long-term objectives are sacrificed. In the developing world, phenomena such as mobile-phone banking are proving catalytic in promoting impressive levels of economic growth without the need for investment in expensive physical infrastructure.

EFFICIENCY AND VULNERABILITY

In the areas of business, commerce and retail, the process of the globalisation of supply chains that was already under way has been greatly accelerated by communications technologies. On the societal level, the cyber domain has had a very large impact on retail, leading people to conduct their lives differently.

More and more people in the developed world shop online. A customer can obtain information on every facet of retailing in a way that was previously not possible because the information was not available. But a fundamental question remains about the extent to which technology is empowering us or simply freeing us from the burden of making decisions.

As we are moving from an internet that connects people through their devices to a new concept of an 'internet of things', the network will primarily be a system of machines talking to machines. The fridge will tell the supermarket that milk is running low and automatically place an order for delivery, or the car will inform the insurance company whether its owner is driving in a lawful and responsible fashion. Shopping patterns are collected with discount cards, collected in databases and sold on to Facebook, where targeted advertisements are no longer meant to draw in clicks, but the impact is measured in the local shop. What will remain of choice when all preferences are anticipated and taken care of before they are articulated? This is an example of private sector Big Data helping business, and supporting our needs. What else will this detailed information be used for, and who can access it?

How can we measure the impact of information technology, the internet, social media and now, Big Data, on society? Increased empowerment for the individual and virtual communities can lead to greater social and political mobilisation, economic empowerment and also the satisfaction of any desire before it is felt.

The linkage of information technology to common processes of commerce, policy, elections and private life has changed their form and substance, with a deep impact on society. Related to this is the question of stability: what is the impact of technology on the stability of economic systems, of the social and political order? How do these systems and structures – reordered and deeply wired – cope with shocks?

IMPACT ON STABILITY

The question of stability concerns economic and financial systems, as well as political orders. In both areas, connectivity is a form of disruptive technology. The stability of both economic systems and social order can be greatly affected by either the use or the disruption of connectivity.

In the case of economic systems, the nature of trade in goods and services has been transformed by ICT connectivity, reducing the time needed between production and consumption. The distance between the producer and the consumer is minimised or even direct, shortening the logistical chain. A system that maximises efficiency, from tailored made-to-order production to rapid delivery, removes the need for expensive stockpiles. This has an important implication for stability: a supply chain that is maximally efficient is one where redundancy has been eliminated. And a system without redundancy is also the most vulnerable to shocks and disruptions, whether they are natural disasters, acts of terrorism, cyber attacks or spikes in the energy market. In any complex system, there is a trade-off between efficiency and stability. And in this case, a maximally efficient global system can also be maximally vulnerable.

The question then becomes how to ensure that any system or new supply chain is resilient to unexpected shocks. The Japanese tsunami disrupted many supply chains. A primitive local insurgency, such as Maoist rebels descending from Nepal into India and attacking steel mills, can have a deep impact on a complex global logistical chain. On 15 August 2012, the Shamoon computer virus attacked the Windows-based computer terminals at Saudi Aramco, Saudi Arabia's national oil company. This was a deliberate attack by the Iranians, whose oil remained unsold due to sanctions. While the system was restored and 30,000 computer terminals were replaced within two weeks, the attack revealed frightening possibilities. If the virus had spread to parts of the system that controlled production the consequences for global oil prices would have been disastrous. Neither the technology, nor even the means of attack, were new. What was new in this case was the significance of the range of activities to which the connectivity factor applied – both digital and conventional.

On the level of social and political order, the interaction with ICT and social media influences and shapes society – and also affects stability. Mass text messaging to mobile phones played a large part in inciting the Paris riots of 2005 and the Muhammad cartoon riots throughout the Islamic world in 2006, while Twitter was a significant element in the 2011 London riots. Facebook and Twitter are said to have played important parts in the Arab Spring revolutions, but their role should not be overstated. Youth movements trained in organised non-violent conflict according to the principles of the American writer and academic Gene Sharp made use of a whole spectrum of actions of which the social media element was only one.

New levels of connectivity in the 'democratisation of technology'[3] have enabled amateurs to reach new heights of professionalism in command and control. Amateurs improvised war against Gaddafi's regime in Libya, when the rebels Googled weapons instructions and communicated live via Skype, to learn how to use a rocket and determine targeting information.[4]

The Pakistani terrorist group Lakshar-e-Taiba carried out the most audacious maritime and urban terrorist attack in India's history in Mumbai in 2008. Ten attackers were prepared and managed in real time with the help of Google Earth data, GPS devices and mobile phones, moving from target to target. From a safe house in Karachi, a team of attack controllers "monitored the situation by using cell phones and satellite phones and by tracking Twitter feeds, internet reports, and Indian and international news broadcasts.

> Using Skype, SMS text messages, and voice calls, the control room fed a continuous stream of updates, instructions, directions, and warnings to the attackers at each stage of the operation, gathered feedback on the Indian response, and choreographed the assault team's moves so as to keep it from being pinned down by Indian security forces.[5]

While current and former Pakistani officials were involved in managing the attack, it was not an act of state. It was entirely planned, carried out and managed with readily available mobile, internet and social media tools. In 36 hours, 172 people were killed, 304 were injured and $18 million property damage was done. The connectivity factor had empowered determined non-state actors to commit large-scale damage in an urban environment without the use of the capabilities of a state.

TECHNOLOGY AND DEMOCRACY

But while technology is democratised and available to all for good or ill, its democratising power should not be overstated. Twitter was a large megaphone for the 2009 Iranian Green non-revolution, but actual Iranians tweeting in Tehran numbered only a few hundred, and they were easily identified and tracked by the government. Similarly in Egypt, while the book *Tweets from Tahrir* proudly announced the "revolution as it unfolded on Twitter", it also revealed fewer than 100 tweeting activists. In the Arab Spring revolutions, social media played a complementary mobilising role in fomenting social unrest, but did not do anything to transform this mobilisation into effective political hierarchies or governance structures. In the case of the Arab Spring, it was not the video of the self-immolation of the Tunisian fruit vendor Mohamed Bouazizi spreading on social media that triggered the protests, but Al Jazeera's reporting of it.

While social media can play a big role in social unrest, they are unlikely to be either the primary cause or the means of a revolution. The revolutions of 1789 and 1917 occurred without the help of social media. People still take to the streets because they look out of the window and see other people taking to the streets. The role of technology to bring about political change should not be overstated, but unfortunately it remains a widely held view among Western policymakers that when the floodgates of information through ICT technology are opened, democratisation naturally follows. This view is based on a misreading of the Cold War, and reflects the dangers of choosing the wrong analogies.

The view that information technology democratises oppressed societies on its own is based on a mistaken syllogism: communication technologies and radio were used in the Cold War and the Soviet Union eventually fell, therefore the false inference is drawn that communication technologies made the Soviet Union fall. This is followed up with an additional flawed conclusion: to achieve victory again for democracy we must do the same things in digital form.

In political rhetoric, the Cold War metaphor was stretched far beyond its shelf life: the Berlin Wall came down, and so we must echo President Reagan and "Tear down this firewall!" or attack the 'Great Firewall of China'. The Iron Curtain had kept millions from freedom and so we must bring down digital curtains today to liberate others. We supported dissidents in communist regimes and communism fell; bloggers are the dissidents of the 21st century, and therefore one common policy conclusion has been that we, the West, must support bloggers critical of their authoritarian governments. The problem here is that mistaken assumptions and sloppy analysis lead to unserious policy, putting those individuals in danger who should be considered the West's allies.[6]

A serious assessment of the impact of technology and the cyber domain on the stability of an authoritarian state or a democratic society would have to start with a view of the resilience of the system as a whole. This would be a comprehensive evaluation of what authoritarian regimes are doing systemically with ICT, mobile networks, the internet and social media, in which the resilience of a system and its capacity to absorb shocks are understood.

If we were to better understand the totality of forces at play in a complex system created by high levels of connectivity, including its unpredictable and uncontrollable dynamics, then we could gain better insights about what leverage the West could have in the systems and dynamics that it can influence. Above all, technology and connectivity inside a given state cannot be understood separately from their political and social context. A well-organised policy response in a given crisis may be very difficult to carry out, but the starting point should not be a set of faulty assumptions.

Authoritarian states traditionally use communication technology for their purposes in three pillars: propaganda, surveillance and censorship. These tend to be separate activities in old uni-directional media such as radio and television, or the bi-directional telephone. But in a networked system, these three activities overlap and affect each other.

Authoritarian states have rapidly adapted to new opportunities with selective censorship and surveillance of the internet. But because everything is intertwined on the internet, attempts to counter one pillar may strengthen another: for example, blogging freely to counter propaganda and censorship will present a state surveillance apparatus with easy targets. Or conversely, while censorship is harder, propaganda is easier if state-supported bloggers operate alongside independent ones.[7]

The connectivity factor has changed the nature and concept of the relationship between the state, citizen and information – and traditional concepts do not apply any more. In a networked system, the state can invisibly target individuals to an unprecedented degree. States can also penetrate each other's communications to an unprecedented degree, which becomes a matter of security.

Assessing the relationship between connectivity and stability is an analytic challenge, but much can be gained from a systems approach. The maximum efficiency of global logistics and supply chains also reflects a system that is maximally vulnerable to shocks. Connectivity is equally empowering for business, economics, broadening social horizons, revolution and terror. The destabilising effect on political structures is greater than the possibility of using the mobilising force to create effective liberalised governance. The democratisation of technology does not imply democratisation by technology.

IMPACT ON SECURITY

The impact of digital connectivity on security is broad, encompassing government, societal and economic processes. In a pervasive digital environment, there is much new vulnerability in the potential of cyber activism, cyber criminality, cyber warfare and cyber espionage – including commercial espionage.

The processes are connected to systems that were never designed with security in mind. The original engineering concepts underpinning the systems prioritised performance above all else, with the result that the systems are inherently flawed and contain vulnerabilities that can be mitigated but never eliminated short of a fundamental redesign. Knowing and being the only one who knows of a particular vulnerability creates leverage that can immediately be put to use in cyber activism, cyber crime, cyber espionage or cyber war. Each of these areas is currently witnessing activity on an unprecedented scale and sophistication. Approximately 80 million malign events occur every day on the internet.

Our dependence on the cyber domain, with all its vulnerabilities, is overwhelmingly a social and economic problem. With services moved into the domain, a shutdown could have disastrous consequences, because we have left alternatives behind. Improving security is not something either industry or government can do by themselves, but together they may stand a chance developing a spectrum of security measures against this spectrum of threats. This cooperation requires a level of trust that has recently been damaged.

The phenomenon of hacking by the Anonymous network, combined with Wikileaks, represents a new kind of activist threat to states by small numbers of individuals bent on sabotage. Revolutionary leaking in itself is nothing new: Napoleon leaked secret diplomatic agreements by the Bourbons to embarrass them; Trotsky did the same with the Romanovs; and the documents of the ransacked American Embassy in Tehran were published in 49 volumes in the 1980s and are available online. [8] What is new today, however, is the number of actors who can engage in this kind of activity. It no longer requires forcibly taking over a country, just penetrating a network or releasing a large gift brought to you on a flash drive.

In the case of sabotage as cyber war by states, it was a 'zero-day' vulnerability unknown to Microsoft that enabled the US and Israel to develop the sophisticated Stuxnet virus that was designed to specifically attack centrifuges in Iran's nuclear enrichment programme. Similarly, the Aramco attack in 2012 exploited the firm's vulnerabilities with an attempt to manipulate oil prices. Corporate and state-sponsored theft of intellectual property has already had profound consequences, such as the bankruptcy of Nortel in 2009. Maintaining the security of financial systems is also a great challenge.

It is estimated that global money laundering accounted for around 3.6 per cent of global GDP or around $2.1 trillion in 2009,[9] and the largest banks spend nearly half a billion US dollars each a year to counter money laundering, terror finance and fraud. When it comes to cyber crime and cyber fraud, however, many financial institutions try to avoid reporting it, because it would make both government and shareholders unhappy. While there are heavy regulatory requirements, with severe penalties attached, obliging financial institutions to report suspicious activities relating to money laundering, there are no similar regulation and reporting requirements for cyber crime.

Most countries have financial intelligence units whose job it is to receive reports from financial institutions and other regulatory bodies on suspected activity related to money laundering. There are no similar bodies, nationally or internationally, to receive reporting on cyber fraud and cyber crime.

While this is an area that is very difficult to investigate, it would be easier if there were a reporting requirement. If a cyber attack causes physical damage to a financial institution, which is most certainly part of a critical national infrastructure, there is an obligation to report in principle, but there may not be anyone to report to.

The United Kingdom has made some progress towards the establishment of a joint reporting centre to receive reports on cyber attacks, but these will not deal with financial losses. Similarly, the European Union's Computing Emergency Reporting Team (CERT) deals with Europe-wide attacks on infrastructure and the EU's own systems, but it does not deal with people's money.

In many cases of theft, whether it is intellectual property or money, it is often not known or takes a while to discover. Sophisticated hackers will steal money from dormant accounts, where the loss may go undiscovered for a long time. In the case of corporate or state-sponsored cyber espionage, the theft may go unnoticed altogether.

In the case of cyber-espionage, we are now seeing a concentration of espionage activity that is genuinely unprecedented. While we have always had commercial espionage and we have always had state espionage, what is new today is state-sponsored commercial espionage on an immense scale. In security terms, China is the main culprit today, both threatened by the internet while seeing it as very useful. Chinese state-sponsored (or to be more precise, Communist Party-sponsored) intellectual property theft has been described as the "greatest transfer of wealth in history."[10]

Any state today with a national telecommunications company acquires a signals intelligence (sigint) capability that gives it a reach that was previously only available to a small number of intelligence powers. Today, anyone can try to hack into the Pentagon, which was not something that could be seriously contemplated as little as twenty years ago. As ICT has an equalising effect, a new climate of vulnerabilities has emerged. This is forcing not only governments, but also private actors, to develop not only a security culture, but also a counter-intelligence culture.

The vast expansion of the US Intelligence community that followed 9/11 included both expansion of electronic surveillance as well as the development of a large community of private contractors with top-secret (TS) security clearance. The population of "top-secret America" grew to be immense. A 2010 investigation by the *Washington Post* estimated that 854,000 Americans had TS clearance[11], but the actual number was much higher. According to the 2012 report by the Office of the Director of National Intelligence, more than 3.5 million Americans held a secret or confidential security clearance, and an additional 1.4 million held TS clearance – of whom 483,000, or 34 per cent, were contractors.[12] The TS community included 1,271 government organisations and 1,931 private companies working on programmes related to counterterrorism, homeland security and intelligence in around 10,000 locations across the USA.

The Edward Snowden affair has revealed both the secret power and the vulnerabilities of big data: secret power, because we have sleepwalked into a new world without considering the implications for privacy; and vulnerability, because it took a single disgruntled 20-something know-it-all to cause large-scale damage to the United States government, its relations with allies and the hi-tech industry.

The affair has brought to public consciousness what it means to live in a world of big data and it has opened a much-needed debate. Big data alters our relationship to information in the way that the internal combustion engine altered our relationship with the highway. Governments are not driving this process, but are struggling to keep up. The very scale of the NSA programme indicates that while the internet started as a military project, and its social and economic success was a function of its privatisation, it is currently undergoing a process of remilitarisation. In this regard, it was not helpful for public trust that, for a period of time, the same man, General Keith Alexander, headed both the NSA and US Cyber Command.

The case of cyber war differs from cyber criminality and cyber espionage. While espionage and crime are both happening on a large but unknown scale, cyber war is the most talked about, while not very much is actually happening. It is also argued that, in the case of China, corporate espionage and cyber war are blurred.[13]

In the West, critical infrastructure is mostly in private hands, but citizens ultimately hold the government responsible for their security. This presents all sorts of legal conundrums with regard to information sharing, public-private partnerships, and divisions of legal responsibilities between governments and private actors. Debates on these questions are occurring throughout the democratic world.

With regard to the vulnerabilities for cyber war on our critical private or public infrastructure, there have been many alarmist commentators who have painted apocalyptic scenarios.[14] While these scenarios are theoretically possible, cyber war is much more likely to be an addendum to a physical war.

Analysis of cyber war scenarios also suffers from misuse of metaphor – in this case, air war. The idea that massive damage can be done at an early stage of the conflict is an optimistic but not viable concept. In an open conflict, cyber war will be one tool among many, and unlikely to be the most prominent. Electronic warfare, such as knocking out command and control centres with an electromagnetic pulse, or jamming radar signals, is likely to play a greater part on the operational level than cyber war.

Militaries are looking at the cyber domain as a strategic space for both offensive and defensive elements. In a certain sense, the cyber Rubicon has already been crossed. Offensive activities by states are already taking place. The Stuxnet virus and the Aramco attack are examples of creating physical damage. The Flame virus, another US-Israeli computer virus created to attack Iran's nuclear programme, was a more 'traditional' tool of information exfiltration. When electricity grids, hospitals, floodgate systems are targeted or manipulated, deaths will occur and the actions can have the same consequences as war. But without a solution to the problem of attribution, the status of aggression and self-defence in international law will not be clear.

It is more likely that cyber war of this kind will not occur in isolation, in peacetime, or out of spite. It will more likely be one capability to be deployed in a spectrum of instruments in the broader context of a conflict or war.

IMPACT ON GOVERNANCE

The impact of the revolution of connectivity on structures of governance can be seen in several areas. Increased transparency and more direct communication between citizens and their local or central government have enhanced transparency, reduced the scope for corruption and enabled greater efficiency in the delivery of services. New technologies have democratising and flattening impacts on governance, making it harder for governments to conceal or dissemble.

While governments in open societies generally have greater capacity to absorb criticism, they have largely been reactive rather than proactive. If governments are only tactically reactive to events, there is little room left for developing and implementing a long-term strategy. And without a strategy, governance will be more vulnerable. The noise created by extremist or fringe groups, whose online presence may appear disproportionally greater than would be the case if based on traditional support, can crowd out traditional discourse and amplify their political leverage far beyond their political base.

For authoritarian regimes, it is now a lot more difficult to manage information. They are no longer capable of controlling information in ways that they had been accustomed to. But in some cases they have adapted quickly to digital media. In Russia, for example, the central government has shown great tolerance for criticism of corruption at the local level as this can easily be co-opted and turned to strengthen the authority and legitimacy of central government. [15] In China, many sites and subjects are selectively filtered, and blogs and chat rooms are monitored and censored. The scale of operatives involved in the monitoring, censoring and exercising of control over thought and speech is unprecedented in China's history of electronic communications. The Chinese ability to enforce on such a huge scale gives the Communist Party and government a sense that the internet can be controlled. [16] The OpenNet Initiative has carried out a global survey of internet censorship and concluded that 19 countries carry our selective filtering of the internet, and 20 additional countries conduct substantial or pervasive digital censorship. [17]

As discussed above, networked technology can support both democratising trends, as well as strengthen capabilities of repression. Technology alone is morally neutral. Its impact on governance and other possibilities it presents for good or for ill depend on the human, social and political context in which they occur. There is an important difference between the impact on governance, and new responses to this impact in governance. And in domestic governance responses, there are important distinctions between democratic and authoritarian states.

INTERNATIONAL RESPONSES IN GOVERNANCE

On the international level, we are at the end of the beginning of a very broad standoff about the future of governance of the internet – a dispute that will be extensive and protracted, and indeed like the Cold War. According to one observer, the December 2012 meeting of the World Conference on International Telecommunications (WCIT) "may be the digital equivalent of the February 1945 meeting of the Allied powers in Yalta: the beginning of a long Internet Cold War between authoritarian and liberal-democratic countries."

> The battles over Internet governance that surfaced at WCIT are not just about competing visions of the Internet, with one side favoring openness and the other security. They are also about two different visions of political power – one in which that power is increasingly distributed and includes non-state actors, and one in which state power is dominant. [18]

An update of the international telecommunication regulations is badly needed because the last iteration, in 1988, omitted the internet entirely. The dispute between Western and authoritarian states concerns the fundamental difference in governing philosophy between those countries where power is shared between multiple stakeholders – including private actors – and those countries where the state dominates political and economic power. The difference between a 'multi-stakeholder' approach versus the 'cyber sovereignty' advocates who seek to concentrate control of the internet is turning into an international dispute between the West and the Rest, which can lead to fragmentation of the internet in multiple networks – a development that is already under way in some countries and regions.

Similar tensions have emerged in relation to international discussion of security within the cyber domain. In June 2013, a compromise was reached in the sessions in First Committee of the UN General Assembly, where China conceded that existing international law – interpreted by the US and its allies as including the Law of Armed Conflict – applied in the cyber domain, and Western states made concessions recognising the role of national sovereignty. The UN compromise is flexible enough for everyone to interpret as they see fit. The debate is ongoing but it will remain a challenge for Western states to keep the internet open as an instrument of liberty.

EVALUATION

The great revolution of connectivity through ICT technology, the internet and social media has fundamentally changed our relationship to information. The great increase of opportunity, business and prosperity, and the widening impact in social life, society, elections and governance, are juxtaposed with a big increase in risk. Where the internet started as a military project that was privatised, in many parts of the world it is undergoing a process of remilitarisation. The cyber domain is now a strategic space of competition, opportunity and danger, where states are seeking to repatriate a space that was largely widened by private actors.

We have sought to place the technological and societal breakthroughs in a broader historical context, and there are several possible scenarios in the future evolution of the internet. While this topic is a fast-moving target, we can identify several large-scale trends and several possible futures.

With the cyber domain increasingly a strategic space where states compete, most political leadership in the West lacks understanding about it and is ill-equipped to develop long-term cyber policies and strategies. The cyber domain is perceived to be technical and new, but it is neither. Some countries, such as Russia, China and Israel, have long-term cyber strategies. NATO and the EU have fairly well-developed cyber defence capabilities. The United States has published a cyber strategy doctrine, but the sheer size and scale of US bureaucracy and 'top-secret America' makes it very difficult to forge a unified strategic direction. The United Kingdom and France have no published cyber doctrines, although these countries are no less active: the UK has announced its intention to develop offensive military cyber capabilities. France remains the most opaque in this regard, because it remains the only Western democracy without parliamentary oversight over its intelligence agencies. French cyber activities remain unknown and hidden from scrutiny.

We have considered the trends enabled by connectivity and their social, economic and political impact, such as mobilisation, activism, cyber crime and espionage. All of these activities can be expected to grow in the coming decades, especially with the rise of the internet of things. When most everyday household items have IP addresses, their usefulness also presents much new vulnerability.

On a wider scale, depending on how international battles are fought, there are several possible outcomes for the future of the internet. It is possible that the internet remains as it is, with general access everywhere, give or take some local censorship. But if authoritarian governments win the international battles, the future may be a lot grimmer. If all digital communications become subject to sovereignty, then we will witness a balkanisation of several internets, where regions will be isolated from each other's information flow. The technological and social breakthroughs of the past two decades may very well lead to political regression, hand in hand with future technological advances.

CONCLUSION

The breakthrough process to global digital connectivity is a new phenomenon. It is also a classical example of the introduction of disruptive technology that has a large-scale social, political and economic impact. It is comparable to the introductions of print, steel, steam and the radio. The difference today, however, is that the speed of the impact is much greater. The internet and other information technologies have broad and deep disruptive effects on the existing structures in society, stability, security and governance.

The disruptions have happened more quickly than adjustments to new technologies, and we have walked – in some cases sleepwalked – into a new information world we insufficiently understand. We may be aware of the new social and economic possibilities that have been created, but not of the vulnerabilities that go with it. While the social impact is deep, human nature is unchanged and the human qualities of prudence and leadership are needed in this area today.

We can begin to understand the roots of the disruption by looking at past and current structures confronted with new technologies. We can then begin to remind ourselves of the purposes these structures are meant to serve; and what the core of security and governance are meant to achieve. If new technology disrupts existing and familiar structures, the question is forced on us: what structures do we need? This in turn requires us to reflect on how to adapt the governance and security structures we need for prosperous and safe societies.

Unlike in the eras of the British Empire or the Cold War, the security challenges of today are a lot more difficult to understand. Those in positions of responsibility with the power to make decisions are rarely capable of grasping both the technical and political implications of this issue. Younger generations are highly connected today, but have grown up without a sense of threat. Between the young and current leaders, those capable of understanding both technological and political change are rare – but they are needed as future leaders.

We have seen two breakthroughs in this study – and the immediate aftermath in the responses in governance. The factor of the environment was the most decisive in enabling both breakthroughs. In the first case, the technological breakthrough of the innovation of packet-switched information technology occurred in the environment of long-term government-funded defence research and development. The technological breakthrough would not have occurred without long-term cooperation between top research universities, the US Department of Defense and the government.

The second economic and social breakthrough, however, could only have occurred in the environment of the free market. The technological seeds were laid in the closed environment of government-funded research, but innovation proliferated in the open field of the free market. The dotcom boom and bubble were only the first stage of exponential adoption of new technology. What followed was a filtering by companies, whose ideas and innovations mattered for the mainstream.

As public acceptance grew with new levels of familiarity with new technologies, ever more social and economic activities moved online, creating the biggest repository of information the world has ever seen. Today, only after the fallout of the highly damaging Snowden affair do we see a crisis of public trust in governments. We are far beyond the idealistic visions expressed by political leaders in the early 1990s.

We have noted the differences in attitudes to the cyber domain between democratic and authoritarian states, who are competing at the international level over its future. At the United Nations Governmental Group of Experts, a consensus was drafted in June 2013. The consensus was a compromise that conceded two competing concepts: the applicability of existing international law to the cyber domain; and the assertion of the validity of national sovereignty in the cyber domain.

Diplomats and international lawyers deal with assertions of sovereignty all the time, so in that respect this compromise was nothing out of the ordinary. The agreement will also have to be followed up and supplemented with a number of bilateral and multilateral discussions on different aspects of internet security. But the proof will be in the practice.

It is state practice that will determine what the norms are, and where the centre of gravity for a rules-based approach to the cyber domain will lie, between 'international law' and 'national sovereignty'. A draft agreement that concedes something to both sides will not yet tell us how state practice will develop.

When it comes to the behaviour of governments, we should distinguish between the question of control and the question of surveillance. Democratic states, cyber-libertarian idealists and others are all equally scandalised at the manner in which authoritarian states seek to control information flows in the cyber domain.

But when it comes to surveillance, democratic and non-democratic states are equally tempted by the fact that large internet corporations and phone companies – apolitical though they may be – have in their possession more data and surveillance capabilities than states could ever dream of. The temptation to harvest was too great, and led to overreach. The imperative to keep pace – driven largely by fears of the consequences should some important predictive intelligence be missed – led to the development of industrial-scale collection programmes. As the example of cyber narcissist Edward Snowden would demonstrate, secrecy is hard to achieve on an industrial scale.

At the 2013 Davos Summit, the fallout of the Snowden revelations was a big theme, and 'rebuilding trust' was the watchword. This will mean greater security, delivered through stronger and more pervasive encryption. It will also mean the development of laws and process, at national and international levels, to give people control over their data. How this will play out over time, for both security and trust, remains to be seen.

As the cyber domain is moving to the 'Internet of Things', of devices talking to devices, relieving humanity of making many decisions, exposure to a whole new range of vulnerabilities will also increase. Smart appliances will proliferate, but there is a risk of poor code managing their connectivity. Unlike a laptop that communicates security alerts to the user and makes updates, a 'smart fridge' will not tell you it might be compromised. This indeed happened: a fridge was compromised with malicious code and this illegal connection was used to send out spam. The implications of this go much farther than this case, and it is likely that there will be growing pressure for minimum standards for such devices.

The overall breakthrough that created the cyber domain has created a force for social good and prosperity on a large scale. From its military origins to the free market, the cyber domain is being securitised and remilitarised. It is a strategic space where power is exercised, as in other domains. But it remains to be seen what the net effect of that will be. We are only just beginning to see what the manifestations of these trends are. Before we complain about what we don't want to see happen, we need a clearer idea and a debate about what we want our relationship, and our governments' relationship, to the cyber domain to be.

With structures disrupted by new media – and in some cases governments overthrown – the requirements of leadership have not been replaced by technology. The Arab Spring has shown that while social media and the cyber domain can be effective in initiating a revolution they are no substitute for the difficult and boring routine work that is necessary to build stable institutions. The fundamental values of arranging an inclusive, free, prosperous and secure state are not changed by technology – but they will have to adapt to it.

CHAPTER 2

INNOVATIONS IN GLOBAL LOGISTICS

In this chapter we consider the trends and innovations in modern logistics, from its origins in military history to the 21st century, to examine an often-overlooked area upon which civilisation depends. We present a brief historical overview of key developments in modern logistics to the state of the art today. We highlight recent innovations and developments that enable unprecedented levels of value and efficiency in our era of consumer-driven markets. We also focus on three case studies of businesses that reflect these trends.

This book includes several chapters in which logistics plays a key role, agriculture, healthcare delivery and the impact of the cyber domain. This chapter focuses on logistics innovations in general, co-authored with one of its leading experts.

THE QUALITATIVE ANALYSIS FOR THIS CHAPTER IS ON PAGE 378 OF THE ANNEX

ALAN MCKINNON AND BENJAMIN BILSKI

INTRODUCTION

Logistics is the lifeblood and engine of modern civilisation. In this chapter we consider key innovations and trends in modern logistics, and the vital role they play in our age of consumer-driven markets. As in other chapters, we consider the innovations that led to breakthroughs, showing how they are the result of an effective process from vision and concept to strategy and implementation.

Most innovations today are driven by a vision with three factors in mind: business performance, the customer and environmental sustainability. Many stakeholders in logistics industries and services today are unified by this vision to develop innovations that reduce the environmental impact of logistical activities, while serving the customer more quickly and efficiently. As a function of the price of energy, environmental protection goes hand in hand with greater efficiency and good business practice.

Innovations in logistics can be classified as physical, conceptual or related to information technology (IT). Physical logistics innovations are either vehicles or equipment, and include the development and evolution of various modes of transport on land, sea and in the air. Innovations in equipment include the revolutionary rise of the container from the mid-1950s onwards. This basic steel box has transformed logistics worldwide, fundamentally altering the nature and location of ports, facilitating a huge increase in ship size, redefining the relationship between transport modes and, as a consequence, allowing companies to globalise their supply chains.

Conceptual innovations apply to the overall design of a supply chain system or to operational practice. System-design innovations include the development of hub-and-spoke networks by parcel carriers; while innovations in operational practice include the just-in-time concept of replenishing supplies as they are required. Innovations in IT range from the invention of the barcode and the beginnings of digitisation in the 1970s to our present era where cloud computing, big data, GPS and mobile networking are integrated to manage a range of logistics activities in real time. Logistics activities comprise much more than transport, and innovations in logistics are not only innovations in vehicle design. Digital innovations that improve the overall management of supply chains, for instance, can have a greater impact than technical innovations at the level of vehicle design. Logistics activities have both a broad range and a form of hierarchy. Whoever possesses the edge in logistical ability is not only economically stronger; in times of war this can determine the very survival of states. Many early innovations in modern logistics are found in military history, often with civilian infrastructure developing in parallel.

ORIGINS: FROM WAR TO BUSINESS

A contemporary textbook definition of logistics is "the process of strategically managing the movement and storage of materials, parts and finished inventory from suppliers, through the firm, and on to customers."[1]

Logistics is not merely transport, but includes the broader science of moving, storing and managing goods. As recently as 1975, however, the Oxford Illustrated Dictionary still defined logistics as the "science and practice of moving, lodging and supplying troops."[2] Both the original meaning and uses of the word, as well as past innovations and breakthroughs, are found in military history. The necessity of national survival in time of war has historically driven many logistics innovations.

The classical Greek word *logistikē* referred to the "art of calculation, and in a military context, was used to refer to any aspect of strategic or tactical operations that was based on quantitative calculation, whether in connection to movement, equipment, organisation, or fighting."[3] The term reappears in the 10th century, when the Byzantine emperor uses the Greek term to refer to the science of supplying an army.

In the 19th century, the Swiss strategist Henri de Jomini narrowed the meaning of *logistique* to refer only to the organisation of keeping an army moving. The term gradually passed out of use in Europe but was in continual use in the United States, where Jomini's influence was stronger. It was then expanded to refer to "all aspects of supplying an army and to moving the necessary materiel, in the required condition, to the correct place at the proper time." German studies of Roman supply used the term *Logistik* to refer to "the supply of food, its transportation and administration, as well as medical and sanitation services."[4] In the history of war, victory and the very survival of states often hinged on which side had a logistical edge. Attributed to Napoleon is the saying that "amateurs discuss tactics, professionals study logistics."

Napoleon's innovations and victories were the culmination of several developments initiated by military reforms that followed the Peace of Paris of 1763. Napoleon implemented military-logistical innovations that included the improvement of accuracy and mobility of artillery; the universal conscription of the citizen-soldier; and a centralised bureaucracy – all to combine mass manpower with industrial firepower. His most important innovation, however, was to divide his army into corps d'armée, which were complete miniature armies of 20,000-30,000 men led by Marshals who operated independently from each other. Marching along separate routes, the corps could be more self-sufficient in supplies and achieve an element of surprise. In 1806 seven French corps destroyed the Prussian army by falling upon Jena and Auerstädt from multiple directions. The Prussians had nearly double the manpower but were stunningly defeated because Napoleon's conceptual and organisational innovations gave him a logistical advantage.[5]

Civilian innovations in logistics occurred in parallel. The course of the 19th century saw the rise of steam power and the introduction of the first public steam-powered railway service in 1825 between Stockton and Darlington in Britain, and the first steam ships in the following decade. In Britain the canal network drove the industrial revolution whereas in Germany the rail network was more dominant. The first IT innovation—the telegraph—would enable centralised operational command. These innovations increased operational and strategic reach, enabling the Prussians to emerge as the most advanced military power in the 1860s. With new rifle technology, mass movement of troops by rail and centralised communications, the Prussian physical innovations gave them the logistical advantage, when they encircled and stunningly defeated the Austrians in 1866 and the French in 1870.

In the early years of the First World War, the great bloody battles of the Western front, involving massed infantry, machine gun and artillery fire, led to stalemate and exhaustion without affecting the strategic outcome. To evade the battlefield, logistical innovations were introduced from 1917 onwards with military aircraft, the tank and the submarine. In the first year of the Second World War, the Germans possessed a logistical advantage, because of better operational mobility from rapid mechanised warfare in the synchronised deployment of airstrikes, mobile artillery and the movement and supply of troops by truck. In this early Blitzkrieg phase of the war, the Germans succeeded in conquering most of Europe with relatively few military deaths. In both world wars, however, Germany would eventually be defeated because the Allies could out-produce and out-mobilise them on land, sea and in the air. In the post-war period, many wartime innovations in logistics would spread to the world of business.

Commercial applications of logistics, and its later development as an academic discipline, borrowed heavily from the art and science of military logistics. Running and supplying a military organisation with limited resources where lives are at stake can only be achieved by devising a clear strategy and reducing overall aims to smaller intermediate goals. This must be done with full awareness that any planning is constrained by the limits of logistics and communications. This requires a skillset that translates particularly well to business and management.

Until the end of the Second World War, the railways had a near-monopoly on long-distance movement. It was not until the post-war period that the large-scale use of trucks developed on expanded road networks. The post-war period witnessed several major paradigm changes with physical, conceptual and IT-related innovations.

POST-WAR LOGISTICS INNOVATIONS

◎ Physical Innovations

The most significant physical innovation in logistics was the introduction of containerisation in the mid-1950s. The Texas trucking entrepreneur Malcolm McLean converted a Second World War oil tanker and installed steel frames on its deck to stack metal container boxes. On its maiden voyage from Port Newark to Houston in April 1956, it carried 58 containers and 15,000 tonnes of petroleum. Other companies would soon adopt the container and this revolutionised the way goods were moved globally. The container facilitated the trans-shipment of goods between transport modes and transformed the role of the ports. Cargoes were traditionally moved loose, and their handling was very labour intensive. The container enabled a simple mechanical transfer from the ship onto a truck or train with no further need for warehousing at ports. At the time, this reduced the cost of loading and unloading cargo from $5.83 to $0.16 per tonne. Although resisted by dockworkers intent on preserving their jobs, the container offered major advantages in faster handling speed, greater security, lower transport costs and the standardisation of freight movement on a global scale. [6] The container permitted the modularisation of freight movement in standardised loads. It became the top tier of a unit load hierarchy that included at lower levels the pallet, the case and individual product packaging.

Containerisation was also associated with the increases in vessel and vehicle sizes which took advantage of economies of scale in freight movement. Nowhere has the growth been as pronounced as in container shipping. The standard size container, the 'twenty-foot equivalent unit' or TEU, is stackable and has been the main unit of vessel carrying capacity. The early container ships after 1956 could carry 500-800 TEUs; in the 1970s capacity ranged from 1,000 to 2,500 TEUs; from the 1980s to 2000 capacity grew from 3,000 to 8,000 TEUs. [7] This evolution from the 1950s has now culminated in the Maersk Triple-E, the largest class of ship ever made, with a staggering capacity of 18,000 TEUs, and described later in this chapter.

Other transport modes have also enjoyed a substantial increase in vehicle-carrying capacity. In the UK, the maximum truck weight has increased over the decades from 26, 32, 38 and 41 to 44 tonnes today, with significant economic and environmental benefits. [8] In the Netherlands trucks have gone up to 60 tonnes. On the US rail network lengthening trains and double-stacking containers has greatly increased the available payload. In order to maximise efficiency and economies of scale, this expansion of transport capacity developed alongside conceptual innovations in logistics management.

◎ Conceptual Innovations: systems and operations

The 1960s witnessed an important conceptual innovation in the managerial integration of different logistical activities. Before then there were no separate logistics departments within companies. The various functions of order processing, inventory management, materials handling, warehousing and transport were fragmented. Transport would be the responsibility of a production department; orders and inventory would be handled by sales. When all of these activities were brought together, their coordination could be improved and optimised. This conceptual innovation, both systemic and operational, was called the 'revolution in physical distribution management'. It was the birth of modern logistics.

The new logistics management of the 1960s started at the local level with the integration of transport and warehousing operations into physical distribution systems. This process of integrating logistics functions subsequently widened from the distribution of finished products to the management of a full 'end-to-end' supply chain. This integration had three main benefits: first, companies could find the optimal trade-off between the costs of various logistical activities with a 'total cost approach'; second, this optimisation would give distribution a stronger consumer focus; and third, it raised the importance of logistics in the management hierarchy, elevating it from the operational to the strategic level. [9]

> By the late 1970s, many firms had established 'logistics departments' with overall responsibility for the movement, storage, and handling of products upstream and downstream of the production operation. This enabled them to exploit higher-level synergies, share the use of logistical assets between inbound and outbound flows, and apply logistical principles more consistently across the business. [10]

A later big conceptual logistics innovation, from the 1970s onwards, was the development of hub-and-spoke distribution networks principally by express parcel carriers like Fedex, DHL and UPS. Parcels are transported to centralised hubs, where they are sorted overnight and distributed by plane or truck to customers via local satellite depots. This kind of centralised sorting process requires a high level of capital investment—and is amenable to automation—but it reflects the most cost-effective way to process the international distribution of large quantities of parcels in a short period of time. A parcel sent from the Netherlands to Greece will normally not be flown direct, but pass through such a hub. For example, DHL has a massive hub in Leipzig where planes fly in each evening from more than 50 locations. Within a few hours all the parcels are sorted and the planes fly out again. On the national level, smaller hub-and-spoke networks are in place for localised distribution. This mechanism allows for an overnight delivery service almost anywhere in Europe and connection to other hubs around the world.

Another important conceptual innovation is 'just-in-time' (JIT), an operational practice developed by Taiichi Ohno of Toyota in the late 1970s. Just-in-time would grow into a dominant paradigm for manufacturing and supply chain management in the 1980s and 1990s. [11] The aim of the JIT principle is to schedule deliveries to arrive exactly when they are needed, in order to ensure a smooth product flow and remove the need for large inventories. It results in products being pulled into a production or retail operation by actual demand rather than pushed by advanced planning and forecasting. JIT originated as an operational concept but has evolved into a broader management philosophy. The basic approach of JIT was to closely match supply to demand, eliminate waste and reduce inventories to a minimum.

What began as a pull system started within factories has expanded upstream and downstream in the supply chain to pervade all types of logistics operations. But JIT requires a stable environment, and the problem here is similar to one pointed out in the chapter on cyber-security: a maximally efficient system is also maximally vulnerable to shocks. In the years following

9/11 and the Japanese tsunami, JIT has been shown to expose many supply chains to excessive risk. Indeed, some have been so lean, in terms of inventory, that they are anorexic. The question remains today: what level of redundancy and robustness is necessary for logistical systems to be resilient to shocks?

Another major conceptual innovation of the 1970s was the outsourcing of logistics activities. Until then, many companies owned and operated their own vehicles and warehouses. They then started engaging third parties to outsource their transport and the warehouse operations. While transport had been outsourced for a long time, it is only from the 1970s onwards that the whole logistics operation began to be externalised, with companies providing an integrated service comprising transport, warehousing and inventory management. This kind of 'third-party logistics' service would later evolve into 'fourth party logistics' (4PL) during the late 1990s. This concept, which was developed by Accenture, refers to the provision of higher-level strategic support in the planning and management of supply chains. These physical and conceptual innovations have gone hand in hand with innovations in information technology.

◎ IT innovations

Innovations in information technology and digitisation apply today to every level of logistical activity, from the movement and storage of goods to the planning of the supply chain. The telegraph, radio and telephone first established instant long-distance communications; the 1970s witnessed the first steps in digital information technology applied to logistics activities. Among the most important IT innovations during this period were the barcode and the first vehicle routing software packages.

The introduction of barcoding to logistics brought about a standardisation of tracking goods through the supply chain. As soon as the assignment of barcode numbers was standardised through organisations such as the Article Number Association, it spread rapidly down the unit load hierarchy to the product level. The marginal cost was negligible, and barcodes were applied to the container, the pallet, the box, right down to the can of beans checked out at the electronic point of sale (EPOS). The barcode brought several benefits to the wider supply chain: not only were goods tracked down the supply chain but the EPOS also collected information on sales. This would be sent back upstream to the supplier, who could process orders continually adjusted to demand. The proliferation of barcodes and the sensors needed to scan them created product visibility across the supply chain.

In some sectors barcodes have been gradually superseded by radio frequency identification (RFID), though this form of electronic tagging has not yet filtered down to the product level, mainly because its marginal costs remain too high.

The first vehicle routing software packages also emerged in the 1970s to help companies optimise the routing of their vehicles. These first software solutions required mainframe computers, were not very user-friendly and often yielded poor results. Today we have entered a new era that sees cloud computing, big data, GPS and mobile phone apps all integrated into supply chain management packages. An optimal solution can sometimes now be provided by your iPhone.

The digitisation of entertainment, education and messaging has removed the need for large amounts of physical transport and this trend is likely to continue. 3D printing is a new trend that combines digital and physical delivery: while it will still require the movement of materials, it can greatly streamline supply chains and reduce transport intensity at the national and global levels when a design is purchased online and printed locally.

The physical, conceptual and IT innovations of containerisation, increases in vehicle size, integrated logistics management, hub-and-spoke networks, just-in-time, barcoding and digitisation are the biggest breakthroughs of modern logistics in the post-war period. In the same period, logistics has developed into a broad discipline, relating not only to transport but to the whole mix of activities related to the flow of goods, from raw materials to the final point of sale, including the development of the supply chain systems that manage them.

Of course logistics, as an industry, is the servant of other sectors. Logistics activities underpin the development of global markets. Globalisation is a key by-product of these innovations in logistics, with economies of scale lowering production and transport costs. Global value chains are facilitated by logistics and operate synchronously in all domains of land, sea, air, space and information. The seamless integration of all these spaces lies at the heart of the consumer-driven markets of our age.

The coming decades will witness a large expansion of online retailing, which demands adaptation and diversification of logistical solutions comprising ever more sophisticated warehousing solutions and distribution networks. The customer service dimension is central: the overriding goal of logistics managers is to satisfy the customer and to develop the mechanisms to do so most efficiently.

The logistical requirements of the global economy will continue to evolve across a spectrum extending from large-scale long-distance movements in great bulk to localised delivery of small consignments on the so-called 'last mile' to the home. Innovations are constantly being developed to improve quality, efficiency, sustainability and resilience at all these levels. The question is which of these current innovations will become major breakthroughs and game changers in the near future.

LOGISTICS TODAY

◎ Logistics and innovation

A contemporary description of logistics will include four elements: the transportation of goods, the management of inventory, warehousing and related IT systems. But this bundle of activities does not provide a full definition. Logistics as a whole can be conceptualised in different ways, and viewed from four main perspectives: as a function, as an industry, as a service and as a discipline.

As a function, it is the activity of moving or storing products; as an industry and service, it refers to those companies that perform logistics as their core activity on an outsourced basis; and as a discipline, it is an academic subject area, with a body of theory and concepts. As discipline, service, industry and function—how innovative is logistics today?

One study of innovation management in the German transportation industry argued that compared to other sectors logistics service providers (LSPs) score lowest in their implementation of innovations. Within a set timeframe, the study counted the number of companies that had successfully completed and implemented at least one innovation project and benchmarked this against different sectors.

It concluded that on average 60 per cent of manufacturing firms merited the designation 'innovators' and 52 per cent of firms in knowledge-intensive services, but only 30 per cent of transportation firms. The author notes, "To date, there is scant knowledge of innovation management in logistics research in general, and particularly in the transportation industry."[12] Much data was quantified in this study to arrive at this conclusion with a method of counting companies and enumerating single innovations. But is it a fair critique?

This study concerned 'innovation management' and 'innovation implementation', but did not clearly distinguish between the creation and the adoption of innovations.[13] More importantly, when speaking of logistics activity and related innovations, we must be clear about the level of logistics activity in order to place the commentary or critique in its proper context.

Innovations can impact upon logistics at many different levels, as illustrated in Fig. 1, extending downwards from the supply chain, to logistics system design, to vehicle routing and scheduling, to vehicle loading, to operation, and finally to vehicle design. Each of these levels in the hierarchy has its own stakeholders and experiences different kinds of innovation. It is therefore important to specify at which level you are considering innovation.

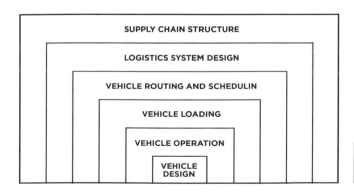

SUPPLY CHAIN STRUCTURE

LOGISTICS SYSTEM DESIGN

VEHICLE ROUTING AND SCHEDULIN

VEHICLE LOADING

VEHICLE OPERATION

VEHICLE DESIGN

FIGURE 1 LEVELS OF LOGISTICAL ACTIVITY AND INNOVATION

On the levels of design and maintenance, the stakeholders are vehicle and equipment manufacturers. The levels of operation, vehicle loading, and vehicle routing and scheduling, are the business of logistic service providers (LSPs). Individual shippers carry out logistics system design. High level of management of the supply chain is carried out by supply chain partners, such as manufacturers, wholesalers and retailers, sometimes with the assistance of 4PL consultancies. It is at these higher levels that some of the newest conceptual innovations are found. In addition, there is much innovation in vehicle design but the rate of uptake can be slow, particularly in the maritime and aviation sectors where equipment has a long lifespan.

In assessing logistics innovations the rate of diffusion and adoption is critical. The study counted the total number of German LSP firms which had implemented at least one innovation, without putting them in the context of their level of logistical activity. It could therefore not account for the scale and impact of higher-level innovations.

The loading and driving of trucks has seen only marginal improvements over the past 20 years. Around the world the road haulage industry is highly fragmented at the operational level, with hundreds of thousands of trucking companies competing intensely and earning narrow profit margins. For example, there are 700,000 trucking companies in China alone. With trucking, the vehicle replacement cycle is about 8-10 years on average, but in aviation, shipping and rail replacement cycles can be 25-30 years. Against this background, vehicle-related innovations are normally gradual and incremental.

A consulting company that applies hi-tech innovations to redesigning and maximising the overall efficiency of a supply chain, will have a much greater impact on the overall system. This is what '4th party logistics' has aimed to achieve and is highlighted later in this chapter by a case study of the company Eyefreight. Innovations in the middle level of vehicle scheduling and routing, as well as driving, will be highlighted by a case study of the company Ecolane. And finally, the culmination of design and economies of scale will be highlighted in a section on the Maersk Triple-E container vessel. An overarching environmental vision drives all these innovations.

◎ The environmental vision

The main driver of logistics innovation has been commercial, but over the past two decades some developments have also been primarily motivated by the need to reduce environmental impacts. Much of this has not been voluntary, as governments have imposed tighter environmental regulations forcing truck manufacturers to be more innovative and find ways to reduce exhaust emissions. There has also been a growing acceptance that improving environmental performance is good business practice. Because logistics is a very energy-intensive sector, carbon reduction and cost savings are closely correlated, so that today there is a convergence between business and environmental interests. In this era of climate change when decarbonising logistics is a central concern, we can distinguish between mitigation and adaptation.

Mitigation concerns the innovations that reduce the environmental impact of logistical activities: in developing better vehicles and equipment that minimise the amount of energy required for moving and storing goods. It also concerns the move to a renewable infrastructure to decarbonise electricity generation, but to build such an infrastructure requires large capital investments and movement of large amounts of materials, such as steel and concrete. In such a development, there is a significant 'carbon payback period' before a net saving in emissions can be made.

Separate from this is our adaptation to climate change: to what extent do we need to redesign our logistics systems and reconfigure our supply chains to reduce their vulnerability to adverse weather effects? With nearly 15 per cent of the world's population living in low-lying coastal areas, adaptation will also concern logistical support for flood protection, climate-proofing of infrastructure and the relocation of populations which live close to the sea.

NEW CONCEPTS AND INNOVATIONS

◎ The problem with predictions

In this section we examine some trends, innovations and developments in contemporary logistics, with all the jargon that comes with it. There has been great excitement in the past few years surrounding 3D printing, the use of drones for delivery and the ambitious concept of the 'physical internet'. Each of these innovations is currently being hailed as transformational in the longer term, but any prediction should always be qualified.

For example, doubts were expressed in the 1990s that online grocery retailing could ever succeed, but it is now a £6.5 billion market in the UK alone. Conversely, it is not easy to tell whether an innovation will in fact lead to a breakthrough, as some innovations in logistics hailed as the next big thing have failed to be as transformational as predicted. These include Radio Frequency Identification (RFID) and Supply Chain Event Management (SCEM).

RFID involves putting an electronic smart tag on items, a step beyond barcoding. The cheapest are the passive RFID tags, which store information that can be read. Active tags, which have a recording capability, can pick up messages and communicate updated information. The most basic tags have a range of around one metre and require specialised scanners. RFID tags have a broad range of applications, including hotel room doors, animal tagging and contactless payments. If RFID tags were universally adopted and placed on individual grocery items, it would be enough for a shopping trolley to pass through a gate to have all its contents scanned instantly. More than a decade ago it was predicted that RFID tags would change supply chain management altogether, that it would be known where everything was at all times. The *RFID Journal* predicted that by 2008 world demand would grow to 30 billion tags, but in 2013 only 5.9 billion tags were actually sold. [14]

Unlike the cheap and universally adopted barcode, the price of the RFID, allowing tags to move down the unit load hierarchy from the container, the pallet load and the case, down to the individual consumer product, has not dropped as dramatically as predicted. The cost of an active tag (with battery life) can range from $25 to $100, while the starting price for a basic passive tag is in the region of $0.07-0.15, [15] which is still too much for individual grocery items. The cost of RFID readers ranges from $500 to $2,000. Another problem was bad publicity.

In 2003, the UK supermarket chain Tesco experimented with RFID tags on the small high-value items that are most frequently stolen: razor blades. Privacy groups were up in arms, claiming the tags would track people to their homes via satellite, although they only had a one-metre range. Protests were held outside Tesco shops and the experiment ended after this PR nightmare. The *Guardian* declared: 'Tesco ends trial of CCTV spy chip on razor blades.' [16] The cost, bad press and lack of consumer understanding have not helped, but the biggest reason that RFID has not taken off as expected is that its functionality is no longer unique or needed: RFID has simply been overtaken by the cheaper combination of the QR-code and the smartphone, where a mobile app directly accesses a supply chain management system.

Another concept that was portrayed as transformational by enterprise resource planning (ERP) companies was Supply Chain Event Management (SCEM). The idea was to break down the supply chain into a series of discrete activities, many of which could be automated. Making this work required a lot of advance planning, as well as complete visibility of supply chain processes. Tolerances had to be defined and contingency plans built in to deal with events falling outside the accepted range. While some IT companies believed that this was the future and a great software opportunity, it has not lived up to expectations.

A SCEM system, coupled with the just-in-time concept, becomes extremely complex as more and more contingencies are factored in. It is not just a matter of a truck driver's extended coffee break leading to a delay in the process flow. The complexity increases exponentially if the SCEM system has to factor in all the things that can go wrong, all the contingency plans that you need with all of the interconnections in the system. A software solution should increase efficiency by reducing complexity. The case of SCEM showed that it is more effective to improve the integrity and reliability of the system, thereby minimising the chances that things go wrong in the first place, than trying to develop elaborate contingency plans to correct them after they have occurred.

These examples illustrate attempts in the recent past to predict the next big thing in logistics that have not been borne out by subsequent events. Nonetheless, major logistics providers such as DHL are exploring the interplay between trends in technology and trends in society and business in order to anticipate which innovations will lead to breakthroughs. In its scenario planning, DHL is experimenting with the provision of Big Data services, 3D printing and 'autonomous logistics'—or drones. [17] But are 3D printing and delivery drones for parcels simply riding the wave of the so-called 'hype-cycle', devised by the US consultancy company Gartner, [18] or will they be genuinely transformational?

3D printing was first invented in the 1980s. Commercial and domestic applications of the technologies have been developing for more than a decade. 3D printing offers a means of drastically reducing the amount of logistical activity, replacing complex supply chains for manufactured products with much simpler chains for the delivery of bulk materials to localised 3D printing operations. It is remarkable how many logistics providers, including UPS, DHL and the US Postal Service, are adding 3D printing to their service portfolios. But how does 3D printing scale up? With a relatively slow process and the cost of the printing material at around $50 a kg, the process is currently very expensive compared to the scale economies of batch production. In order for it to be a viable process, there is a need to attach a high value to customised products. In addition, it is technically difficult to produce anything but simple parts and there is a limited range of possible materials for printing. It is therefore unlikely that 3D printing will replace most conventional manufacturing processes, but rather will split into niche applications such as an enterprise service by logistics firms for the spare parts industry and a consumer market for basic personalised items, such as toys for children. The spare parts industry will be transformed by 3D printing, with inventories sharply reduced and replacement parts simply printed on demand. While the technology is groundbreaking, it will probably not supplant traditional manufacturing.

On the possible use of drones for delivery, we may similarly see some niche applications, but not a large-scale transformation. Amazon and DHL are experimenting with the use of drones for parcel deliveries, but there are several reasons why drone delivery is unlikely to expand beyond a niche application for a limited range of products. As the 'everything store', Amazon carries a vast product range and inventory, whereas the added value of using a drone is in quick same-day delivery, which has to be from a local fulfilment centre. While Amazon has greatly expanded its network of fulfilment centres in recent years, it is impossible to decentralise inventories of its vast online product range. Nor does the drone model permit the scale economies of hub-spoke distribution networks and the consolidation of last-mile deliveries in viably-sized loads.

There are also technical problems: in the absence of a miracle in battery technology, the range of drones is limited to 10 miles; the GPS will require a high level of precision and it is unclear how to standardise household reception; and compared to conventional distribution methods, the energy cost per order is likely to be high. In addition, there are some security and liability risks: people can be injured or killed by drones dropping out of the sky or colliding with aircraft; or they may simply become a new prop for target practice in upgraded clay-pigeon shooting.

It is very unlikely that authorities will approve of this commercial use of drones beyond a niche application for the rich. But Amazon's publicity stunt did achieve one thing: the role of drones in logistics has now become a talking point.

While we must take some predictions for the future and claims about the transformational nature of certain innovations with a pinch of salt, there are at least two interesting conceptual innovations in logistics: 4th party logistics and the 'physical internet'. The former is a type of outsourced supply chain management that has been around for almost 20 years but is evolving into new forms, and the latter is a far-reaching attempt to rethink the nature of distribution.

◎ 4th Party Logistics

In logistics terminology, the first party is the one selling the goods; the second party is the one receiving the goods; and the third party is the intermediary who provides the intervening transport and storage services, ranging from DHL and UPS, down to a small trucking company. In the mid-1990s, Anderson Consulting (now Accenture) argued that a higher-level service was needed, where a company would outsource the management of the supply chain alongside the development of new business models. This 4th party logistics (4PL) service was seen as the culmination of a long-term process of logistics outsourcing that started in the 1970s. During the late 1990s and early 2000s 4PL also followed the hype cycle, when exaggerated claims were made about its likely impact on supply chains, but the number of true applications of the principle fell short of expectations. With some innovations that are over-hyped in their early stages, however, it is the timing and rate of diffusion that is misjudged rather than the value of the new idea. It has taken longer than predicted for the 4PL concept to mature and become accepted. Meanwhile, however, the concept has benefited from major advances in IT and software, which are now critical components in any 4PL offering.

The Physical Internet and Crowd Shipping

There is a great deal of spare capacity in freight and passenger transport systems, which wastes money and energy and generates unnecessary emissions. Two recently advocated concepts aim to reduce this excess capacity. The physical internet concept aims to achieve this by applying the principles of the digital internet to logistics, harnessing spare capacity for economic and environmental benefit. 'Crowd shipping' is its corollary in personal travel: encouraging passengers to use their spare carrying capacity on cars, bikes, buses and planes to carry parcels for other people. Crowd shipping has had an innocent start with a few cheerful websites, [19] but it does raise serious questions about liability and security. The typical questions asked at airports, such as "Did you pack your own bags?" and "Are you carrying anything for someone else?", may start receiving awkward answers on a large scale. When drug traffickers catch on to the business opportunity presented by a generation of unwitting tech-savvy mules, it may well become an air security minefield.

The physical internet, on the other hand, is unlikely to be exposed to these concerns, at least to the same degree. It is based on an ambitious vision that may well enter the logistics mainstream in the coming decades.[20] The idea is to apply the concept of internet hubs to physical distribution. When an email is sent, it may travel through hubs in different countries: its path does not matter as long as it arrives at the appropriate server and email box quickly and efficiently. The idea of the physical internet is to route freight consignments in a way that absorbs spare capacity in transport systems (and other transport modes), ensuring that they get to their destination on time regardless of the route followed.

The Canadian professor advocating this concept, Benoit Montreuil, noted that in the US trucks move around with 40 per cent of capacity unused, and in Europe with around 30 per cent spare capacity. He added that in the US in 2009 the industry average was that 20 per cent of all miles driven were with a completely empty trailer.[21] The presence of a physical internet could significantly raise these vehicle utilisation levels. The digital internet is used as a metaphor to create an "open global logistics system based on physical, digital and operational interconnectivity".[22] In practice, it would mean that a case of Rioja could travel from Spain to Sweden through a number of hubs and countries, where it mattered less what route it actually took because it was piggybacking on vehicles that would be moving anyway. The physical internet is positioned as a separate system, alongside the digital internet and the internet of things, which are described in the chapter of this book on the impact of the cyber domain; the related energy internet is discussed in the chapter on smart grids.

The champions of the physical internet go beyond the email analogy. In their concept, they envisage a standardised, transparent and interacting global network of networks, with the same framework filtered down to each conti-

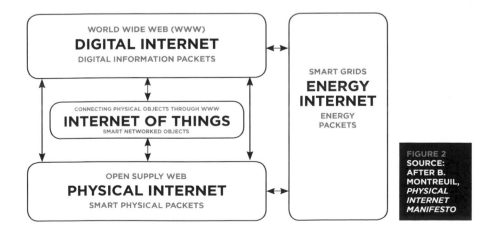

WORLD WIDE WEB (WWW)
DIGITAL INTERNET
DIGITAL INFORMATION PACKETS

CONNECTING PHYSICAL OBJECTS THROUGH WWW
INTERNET OF THINGS
SMART NETWORKED OBJECTS

SMART GRIDS
ENERGY INTERNET
ENERGY PACKETS

OPEN SUPPLY WEB
PHYSICAL INTERNET
SMART PHYSICAL PACKETS

FIGURE 2
SOURCE: AFTER B. MONTREUIL, *PHYSICAL INTERNET MANIFESTO*

nent, country, state, city, facility, centre and processor. Logistics centres will be designed for the physical internet. To make these automated facilities and transport modes compatible worldwide, they also envisage a complete re-modularisation of standard container sizes so that packages of different sizes can be slotted together in a three-dimensional tangram as they are moved across hubs to their destinations.

The operational challenges and costs of making this concept a reality are potentially immense. It is probably for this reason that the physical internet is seen as a very long-term development, perhaps not coming to fruition until 2050 or later. This puts a safe distance between the innovators and those charged with the practical implementation of the concept over the coming decades, should it gain wide enough support.

Potential constraints on the realisation of the physical internet are not only financial and technological—they are also human. Complete visibility and transparency presupposes the willingness of shippers and carriers to surrender tracking information to a decentralised network. These organisations and are known to guard proprietary information very closely, so this will require a big change in mind-set. This 'open distribution web' is to be an 'interconnected set of open warehouses and distribution centres', which could ultimately supplant the hub-spoke networks of existing parcel carriers. Because it envisages a complete re-modularisation of sizes in the unit load hierarchy, it will mean writing off large investments in the handling systems and possibly warehouses in use today. These transformations may encounter more resistance than the innovators currently concede.

Nevertheless, with a physical internet, big data, cloud computing and a new modularisation and automation, technologies could be more effectively harnessed to generate economic and environmental benefits. And while the reader may be forgiven for thinking this project sounds like an IT analogy taken too far and verging on science fiction, the concept has recently gained credibility with the support of the European Union's new European Technology Platform ALICE, which has adopted it as one of its core principles. [23] The support from a big institution like the EU may well see the concept of the physical internet materialise over the next decades. If this institutional support can help to translate the concept into a viable process of implementation, then it has the potential to be transformational.

CASE STUDIES

We now turn to three case studies of innovative companies. They represent three different levels of innovation in the hierarchy of logistics activity (figure 1). Eyefreight provides transport management solutions, and exploits conceptual and IT innovations on the upper two levels of supply chain structure and logistics system design. Ecolane also introduces conceptual and IT innovations but on the levels of vehicle routing and scheduling, vehicle loading and operation. And finally, the Maersk Triple-E represents literally the biggest physical innovation in logistics in recent years, raising the maximum capacity of a container ship by around 20 per cent.

◎ Eyefreight

Eyefreight provides a comprehensive transportation management system (TMS) which provides visibility, optimisation and collaboration in the world's complex shipping markets. Its global transportation management solution supports the "five key processes of multi-modal, multi-leg, international transportation management: order fulfilment, planning and decision-making, transportation execution, cost settlement, and transportation analytics."[24] In other words, its TMS service improves the entire spectrum of the supply chain distribution network from order to delivery, and can be considered an innovation in supply chain distribution strategy. What makes Eyefreight unique from other TMS firms? Two key terms repeatedly emerge: order allocation and visibility.[25]

Together with the University of Eindhoven, Eyefreight developed algorithms to better allocate and fulfil orders. These algorithms provide planning intelligence that includes product location, optimal carrier and shipping mode selection, and route optimisation. According to its CEO Ken Fleming, "No other transportation management system available today provides this level of automated advanced planning optimisation, and different clients take advantage of different benefits the TMS provides."[26] For example, one client, Heineken, has implemented the Eyefreight TMS in Romania, where it has several breweries. Eyefreight's ability to enable the dynamic allocation of orders between these different breweries has led to a significant cost reduction, so much so that Heineken achieved a return on investment in Romania in less than three months.[27]

For another client, Tata Steel, gaining supply chain visibility was the priority. The ability to react swiftly to deviations in shipping plans during the shipping process cut delays. For example, if there is an unforeseen delay in an ocean shipment of steel coils from the Netherlands to the US, Eyefreight's Control Tower functionality provides Tata with visibility over this delay. Tata can then quickly make the decision to partially offload the coils in New York when the carrier arrives and quickly transfer another part of the shipment designated for New Orleans to trucks. Moving the coils overland rather than shipping them via an ocean carrier to New Orleans allows the company to catch up on the delay. There is an extra cost in doing this, but the cost is greater if the just-in-time requirements for the steel coils are not met; after all, the coils may be rendered worthless if they begin to rust.

Today Eyefreight is a growing technology company led by veterans of supply chain management who pride themselves on being a "nimble, adaptable and collaborative partner to their customers." Emerging from Itude Logistics, their success came from the combination of skilled technicians and entrepreneurs. Their patent-pending algorithms aim to create efficiencies in some of the world's most challenging shipping markets. Founded in the Netherlands in 2009, Eyefreight has offices in Chicago and Sao Paulo with regional operations in the UK, France, Germany, Italy and Sweden.

◎ Ecolane

Ecolane is a company that provides personal transport to hospitals along non-fixed routes. As it offers a scheduling and dispatching solution, as well as being a fleet operator, it occupies the middle zone of our 'onion' diagram (Figure 1) relating to operational levels of logistics activity. The fleet management system is continually adaptive. When a call is made for taxi transport for medical needs, the coordinates are inserted into the software. These inputs lead to continual adjustments to routing and scheduling for the fleet.

The origins of Ecolane lie in the ideas of Sami Pöykkö, a Nokia engineer who carried out early research on combining location-based GPS technology with services in the 2000s. While this is commonplace now with a whole range of smartphone apps, it was ahead of its time when originally launched. In his original idea he sought to use algorithms and location technology to create a carpool 'matchmaking mechanism' for a consumer market, not as a professional service provider. The company started in Helsinki and landed its first contract when the government started organising transport for the elderly. The company then transformed the matchmaking system into a scheduling system. The algorithms were developed to find the cheapest solution per movement. [28]

In 2008, the company reached the limits of the small market for these services in Finland, and the decision was made to focus on the United States. The US Congress had passed the Americans with Disabilities Act (ADA) 1990, with amendments in 2008, which included rights for physical access and public transport, as well as requiring the provision of paratransit services on non-fixed routes. [29] The breakthrough came when Ecolane won a $12 million contract in Pennsylvania. It currently carries out all ADA-related movements for that state. Today the company is active in seven US states, has 40 employees and an annual revenue of $6 million. More than 70 systems have been launched and implemented around the country with mostly government clients outsourcing their transport management.

What is notable in this case is that the innovation emerged from within a large company, Nokia, and while it invested in the start-up, it did not carry it forward itself. The dynamic scheduling system only really took off with the rise of the smartphone and tablet. All drivers are equipped with tablets, and the system knows where they are at all times. The main challenges to Ecolane have not been from competitors but gaining acceptance from clients and changing mind-sets. Similar to concerns raised earlier with the physical internet, the constraints on companies like Ecolane may not be technological but human, when complete transparency does not necessarily sit well with all drivers. Nonetheless, this case is a good example of an innovation in dynamic routing successfully implemented by a growing company.

◎ Economies of Scale: the Maersk Triple-E

Within the vehicle design box in Figure 1 lies the Maersk Triple-E vessel, the embodiment of scale economies in the deep-sea container sector. With a length of 400 metres and width of 59 metres, the Triple E is a third longer than the Titanic, longer than the height of the Empire State Building (excluding the top spire) and has as much steel as eight Eiffel Towers. Empty, it weighs 55,000 tonnes and has the capacity to carry 18,000 TEUs. Maersk has ordered twenty units from Daewoo Shipbuilding & Marine Engineering in Korea at $190 million each, of which ten are in service and ten under construction as of mid-2014. At the time of writing, an additional order for a further batch of ten units has been delayed, but may well follow in the future. As Marc Levinson, author of *The Box*, remarked, "When a company like Maersk orders these vessels, it's betting the company."[30]

According to Maersk, 'Triple E' stands for 'Energy efficiency, Environmental performance and Economies of scale'.[31] Energy efficiency and environmental performance are improved by the hull design and low fuel consumption. With engines specially adapted to the now widespread practice of 'slow steaming', the vessel travels at 16-19 knots, rather than the 23-26 knot average of container ships before 2008. This combination of greater size, hull redesign, higher engine efficiency and slow steaming results in a 50 per cent reduction of CO_2 emissions per container. The economy of scale speaks for itself: with a capacity of 18,000 TEUs the cost of moving a container is reduced by 20-30 per cent compared to other vessels on routes between Asia and Europe.

Not that all this is without qualification. Shippers tend to make large investments like this in good times but demand for the Triple E's capacity is not assured given the cyclical nature of the business. Maersk Group CEO Nils Smedegaard Andersen admitted that achieving equilibrium between supply and demand is "not an immediate thing", and the industry will have to live with overcapacity for some time.[32]

The sheer size of the ship restricts its access to a limited number of ports with the necessary capacity and draught. The Triple E is too wide to traverse the locks of the Panama Canal, even after widening to handle larger ships is completed in late 2014. The width of the Triple E allows it to carry an extra row of containers but no North American port has cranes with that reach. These factors limit the so-called 'string' of ports that can be visited on global trade lanes.

The Triple E represents the latest stage in the evolution of containerisation and economies of scale. Maersk has taken very large risks to make this move. The overall utilisation, rate of return and payback period for Triple E's will be highly sensitive to future trends in world trade and market conditions. The environmental benefit, however, is already here.

CONCLUSION

This chapter has provided an overview of the major developments and innovations in modern logistics. Unlike many of the other chapters, it does not focus on a single breakthrough but rather on a whole range of innovations that have had a profound impact on national survival, war, peace and global prosperity. A recurring lesson is that the impact of innovations is maximised when tied to an effective process of implementation—and when this achieves a marked improvement over the previous situation.

Sometimes a physical innovation can bring about a major paradigm change, such as the introduction of the container in 1956. Thereafter, the growth of the container ship has been an evolutionary process over six decades that has culminated recently in the Triple E. Other modes of transport have seen similar development: a revolution followed by evolution driven by the desire to secure increasing economies of scale. Other physical innovations such as drones and 3D printing are unlikely to transform logistics on a large scale any time soon

Among conceptual innovations, we argue that the biggest impacts have been achieved by integrating management, deploying the JIT principle, adopting the hub and spoke model and elevating the outsourcing of logistics to the 4PL level.

IT innovations overlap with both conceptual and physical innovations and have extended from the telegraph to the era of cloud computing and Big Data. The physical internet represents a daring and ambitious vision that essentially combines physical, conceptual and IT innovations. The recent support of an influential European Union committee gives it added credibility though there is a risk that the promoters and supporters of the concept underestimate the level of capital investment and cultural change needed to make it a reality.

While logistics is an industry in its own right, it is also the servant of other sectors. Partly for this reason, the science, art, scholarship and business of logistics is underappreciated and its role in circulating the lifeblood of our civilisation demands greater recognition. Given the critical role of logistics in creating a prosperous, sustainable and secure future for mankind, it needs a healthy flow of innovations and enlightened management capable of implementing them.

CHAPTER 3

THE SILENT REVOLUTION IN AGRICULTURE

This chapter is about the national, regional and global influence of the concepts of agricultural optimisation developed at the University of Wageningen in the Netherlands. This concept, known as the 'Law of Wageningen', combines key insights from 19th-century German agricultural science with Dutch traditions of cooperation and research. It is a scientific concept that has been developed and continually refined since the 1960s, where the key insight is that the optimum of a biological process is also the economic optimum per unit of production. If your goal is to feed a planet, with minimum input, maximum output, minimal pollution and minimal animal pain, then the Law of Wageningen is the only way. This concept of agricultural optimisation has evolved in changing environments and the silent revolution is the breakthrough of its deep influence and impact. The story of the universal science of Wageningen emerges from the Dutch experience.

THE QUALITATIVE ANALYSIS FOR THIS CHAPTER
IS ON PAGE 379 OF THE ANNEX

GERT VAN DIJK AND BENJAMIN BILSKI

INTRODUCTION: HISTORICAL CONTEXT

◎ The Netherlands' unique agriculture

After the United States, the Netherlands is the second largest exporter of agricultural products in the world. How is this possible for a country that has only 0.48 per cent of the world's used arable land and 0.23 per cent of its population?

The Netherlands has a unique history of agriculture and horticulture. A large part of arable land has been reclaimed from the sea and lakes. For more than a thousand years alluvial land was surrounded by dykes, lakes were reclaimed and swamps were drained. The floodplains along the major rivers were dyked and drained in the last century, and even a large estuary was sealed off to turn the Zuyderzee into a freshwater lake, the IJsselmeer, where the entirely new province of Flevoland was subsequently reclaimed from water. The initiative for these large-scale projects came from landlords, large investors and governments. However, daily management was largely in the hands of settlers, either tenants or buyers of newly-dried land who were largely farmers.

In the Netherlands farmers are used to cooperating with each other, as well as with landlords and government, because they have a common interest. Farmers are principally autonomous and responsible for their own piece of land. But if a farmer's land, along with his neighbour's, is below sea level on the other side of the dyke, there is a shared interest. To keep the land dry, they had no choice but to work together. Both landlords and farmers were very conscious of a need to cooperate, which resulted in the Middle Ages in semi-public and public-legal governance structures (*waterschappen*) to control the water.

The Netherlands lies in the delta of north-western Europe, where the three great rivers of the Meuse, Rhine and Scheldt meet the sea. This has had important cultural and economic consequences: the country is pre-eminently a trading nation. Commerce got an extra boost in the colonial era, when many adventurers from Amsterdam enthusiastically participated in explorations and conquests. The success of the colonial expeditions went hand in hand with the abovementioned 'polder-tradition' of cooperation. When a ship was fitted out to make a risky voyage to a place like India, ordinary citizens could invest and participate. This was also a common interest because not only the ship owner or regent but also a large number of citizens had a stake in the expedition's success.

The Netherlands was the first country in the world to cross the urban population threshold of 50 per cent as early as 1622, something which did not happen globally until 2007. Trade and regular contact between the city and the countryside were well developed early, which meant two things for farmers: the urban areas and the coastlines of the great rivers created access for farmers to reach other markets, and the possibility of exporting by sea came into the picture very early.

The potential for high levels of surplus production was also there: much land was easily irrigated and fertile from sea and river clay. For less fertile land, the farmers had to rely on scarce animal manure, because artificial fertiliser did not yet exist.

◎ Agricultural crisis and breakthrough

Halfway through the 19th century, Dutch agriculture was showing a mixed picture. Large farmers who benefited from soil rich in clay were very prosperous, and in some regions dairy farmers and horticulturalists were making good money from exports to England. But elsewhere many traditional farms did not rise above their own subsistence. Towards the end of the 19th century, however, a broad crisis erupted across the whole European agricultural sector.

In 1880, the market was flooded with very large amounts of grain coming simultaneously from the endless plains of the American Midwest, Canada and Ukraine. Domestic tobacco was crowded out by American varieties, and rising industrialisation also led to the development of products that competed with traditional agriculture: petroleum and gas replaced vegetable lamp oil; synthetic dyes supplanted *Rubia tinctorum* madder; and butter faced increasing competition from margarine.

This crisis led many European countries, especially Germany and France, to respond with the weapon of protectionism and closing their borders to all this grain. Newly modernising European states wanted to maintain domestic agricultural production at any price, for they did not wish to be dependent on others for their domestic food supplies. It is an argument that prevails to this day around the world. The United Kingdom and the Netherlands, however, did not engage in protectionism.

In the Netherlands the government convened a commission to focus on these problems, and concluded that it was not in the interest of a trading nation to carry out measures to restrict trade. Any such measure would provoke countermeasures, which the Netherlands could not afford. The commission admitted that much work had been done, and much had been accomplished, but more had to happen. Farmers had to keep themselves afloat with assistance from the government, but not with subsidies. They were advised to cooperate fully in the Dutch polder tradition, in which the government would participate. In addition, legislation, regulation and the encouragement of research and education were to make Dutch agriculture and horticulture strong enough to position themselves in the world economy and compete internationally.

In this way, the basis was created for a sort of self-governance of the sector, to which the government would be strongly committed throughout the next century. A large number of agrarian organisations were formed very rapidly, varying from local dairy cooperatives and Christian goat-breeding associations to banks and broadly distributed state organisations.

Cooperation in the old polder tradition was carried on in a new form. In the past, without cooperation the farmers would literally drown under water. Now they cooperated to modernise their production and distribution processes to avoid drowning economically. Everyone started working together to make the whole supply chain 'from farm to fork' more efficient: maximising output, improving efficiency of production and distribution, and also refocusing on transforming raw materials such as grain into products for which there was demand from wealthy consumers. That is the moment when the Netherlands took the lead in managing a major breakthrough — from agriculture to agri-business.

Another feature of the response to the 19th-century crisis was a new focus on investment in knowledge and research. The National Agricultural School was founded in 1876, which would later become Wageningen University. Following the crisis, knowledge was collected from all over the world and this led to the development of areas of study that would grow into new academic disciplines, including the studies of soil, fertilisation, and minerals, as well as Mendelian genetics.

◎ German agricultural science

The breakthrough from agriculture to agri-business in the Netherlands in the 1880s was made possible by the combination of the Dutch tradition of cooperation with the application of systematic scientific knowledge. In the country, each region had its own local customs for building farms, treating soil and raising animals; regional variability grew out of imitating past local successes. This would dramatically change with the scientific revolution and systematic knowledge applied to agriculture.

Local farming traditions were supplanted by impersonal calculations about the fertility of soil, input-output relations and the general aspiration to maximise production. The most important part of this new revolution originated in Germany, where the founders of modern agricultural science were Justus von Liebig (1803-1873), Georg Liebscher (1853-1896) and Eilhard Alfred Mitscherlich (1874-1956). These men developed the concepts that Professor C. T. de Wit (1924-1993) and his successor Professor Rudy Rabbinge would further develop into the concept and paradigm that is now known as the Law of Wageningen.

Justus von Liebig was a pioneer in agricultural science, biological chemistry and organic chemistry who first introduced laboratory-oriented teaching methods for chemistry at university. He discovered that nitrogen was an essential element in fertilisation, and famines have been averted thanks to his innovations. The most important concept that he developed was known as Liebig's Law of the Minimum, which stated that plant growth is not controlled by the total number of resources available but by the scarcest necessary resource. The limiting factor of growth is determined by the least abundant resource. Liebig's law was the general qualitative principle that enabled quantitative models to be developed for the application of fertiliser in modern agriculture.

Georg Liebscher built on Liebig's work and formulated the concept of the Law of the Optimum, which stated: "The closer other production factors [*editor's note:* like nutrients and water] are to their optimum, the better plants can use a production factor in minimum supply in order to reach a higher production." Eilhard Alfred Mitscherlich would complement these insights with mathematical equations, where the key principle can be understood as follows: in agriculture we are dealing with biological processes that occur according to fixed schedules. The closer you approximate the biological maximum – in either vegetable or animal production – the closer you approach the economic optimum, providing that all nutrients and productive inputs are fine-tuned. Liebig's law was often illustrated by a wooden barrel: the shortest vertical stave determines how much water the barrel as a whole can hold.

To equate maximum economic efficiency in terms of maximal biological production means that scientific evidence and understanding lie at the heart of the social, cultural and economic factors that affect agriculture.

◎ Concept: the Law of Wageningen

From the late 19th century onwards, when Dutch industry started to develop, there was an unprecedented intimacy between it and the agricultural sector. Because of close proximity and intensive communication between country and city, there was never a great mental or cultural distance between them. It is one of the reasons that the Netherlands never really had a feudal system. With short physical distances and an abundance of water, industry started paying attention to the agricultural sector, providing it with resources — such as tractors, greenhouses and electricity — that helped it modernise rapidly.

The main principles of modern agricultural science, as developed in Germany in the 19th century, were studied and applied around the world. Wageningen University would be both the focal point where these concepts were studied, and the place where they would be developed and crystallised further. The university became the nexus between agriculture, industry and government.

In the post-war period it became the national mission of Wageningen to focus on continually pushing Dutch agriculture forward. The 1950s and 1960s saw the rise of multi-disciplinary approaches to agriculture. Many areas of academic research that interacted with agriculture were developed at Wageningen. This period saw the introduction of agricultural economics, agricultural politics, rural sociology, agricultural education (and extension education), agricultural machinery and mechanisms, and biological systems theory.

This period also saw improved public communications in a new process where the triangle of research, education and public information campaigns directed at farmers was formalised in mechanisms developed by Wageningen together with the government. Initially the information campaign concerned basic up-to-date education about the theory and meaning of plant food, the quality of seed, and the possibility of replacing human labour with machines. In later years, until the present day, the focus shifted to fine-tuning fertilisation, genetic manipulation and computerisation. All these measures would lead to the lowering of production costs and increases in efficiency and value.

The later 1960s through to the 1980s witnessed a transition from practical questions to more theoretical ones, such as crop science and plant ecology. With the rise of computing, the German concepts were combined with systems theory. In this period, C. T. de Wit started developing computer models refining Mitscherlich's equations, Liebscher's Law of the Optimum and Liebig's Law of the Minimum to determine the optimally efficient use of nutrients to maximise crop yield.

Building on their German predecessors, Professors de Wit and Rabbinge developed the concept now known as the Law of Wageningen, which can be summarised as follows: each crop or animal has an optimal level of production, and the aim is to achieve this optimum in the most cost-efficient and least polluting way per unit of production. If you achieve a maximal production with optimal conditions, then you also use the least amount of land, the smallest amount of inputs and minimal pollution. This insight has continuously been tested and refined, and is ultimately the basis of the great economic successes of Dutch agriculture and horticulture.

It is notable that key elements of optimisation theory contradict common ideas about marginal returns. We are accustomed to thinking in terms of diminishing returns: we can add more manure and water to our garden, but after a while this will not increase the yield. While this is true, it is necessary to look at the whole as a system. Increasing some inputs makes sense only if other inputs are balanced to an optimal level as well. Stated the other way around: if you produce optimally, then holding back any single input will hold back production as a whole. Only such a systems-theoretical approach considers the whole.

To illustrate: a typical cow can reach a maximum production of 8,000 litres of milk per year. If it is underfed and produces half of that amount, milk will be more expensive, and the ratio of pollution to return will also be higher. For this reason, modern agriculture should strive to achieve the biological maximum if it is to reach optimal economic output. As Professor de Wit once put it, low-input agriculture is like burning down a forest in order to catch a pheasant.

The earth's surface is 70.8 per cent water and 29.2 per cent land, or nearly 149 million square kilometres. Of the total land surface, 13.31 per cent represents total arable land, of which only 4.71 per cent is in use today supporting permanent crops. There is such a thing as a global theoretical optimum, which is high enough to feed double the present world population with less land than is currently being used. Perhaps this reveals why the aim to achieve a maximum level of production in the Netherlands was so popular. Land was scarce and expensive, and the focus was on increasing production per acre.

◎ The concept in practice

In the period from the 1970s onwards, the Law of Wageningen was tested by scientists and on farms. Theoretical insights and discoveries were immediately tested for validity by academics working with farms and going out into the field to observe theories in practice. Results came back very quickly. Despite its small size, the Netherlands has great variability in soil composition, leading to a varied set of results being recorded by Wageningen on the basis of one concept. This enabled researchers to quickly discover the main elements of the concept that had universal validity, which would not have been possible in a bigger country with less variation.

This was the iterative process in action: the concept was tested in the field – to the point where academics would come out throughout the year to see how things were going – and the feedback loop of results, trial, error and new evidence would lead to continual refinement of the concept, which would expand and grow more robust. Professor de Wit had accomplished a scientific breakthrough with the Law of Wageningen and it grew into a new paradigm.

New disciplines attached to his way of thinking as the concept was expanded and refined. The concept next achieved a policy breakthrough after Professor de Wit was invited to join the Netherlands Scientific Council for Government Policy in 1985. This was an important breakthrough, as his scientific concept achieved the status of a new norm and policy paradigm for the whole country.

As the main elements of the concept of the Law of Wageningen were tried and tested in the Dutch context, the concept would be refined to its universal elements. This in turn would lead to its global influence and breakthrough – the silent revolution and global impact of the Wageningen concept.

EVALUATION

◎ Global influence

How can we assess the global influence of Dutch agricultural production theory? While Wageningen is not the only agricultural university in the world and C. T. de Wit was not the only one who worked on developing this concept, he was a leading figure whose influence helped shape the university as it is today, and whose influence is spread through his students. Professor de Wit supervised 30 PhD dissertations, and his students have established faculties at other universities modelled on Wageningen or hold positions of international prominence. Professor Rudy Rabbinge serves as a senior adviser on African agriculture at the United Nations, among other functions. Louise Fresco was director of research of the Agriculture Department at the Food and Agricultural Organisation.

Today, Wageningen University is a thriving research and education institute with more than 3,800 BSc students, 3,700 MSc students, 1,900 PhD candidates, 6,500 permanent staff and an international student body representing 106 countries. No other agricultural university in the world works on this scale, nor do any comparable institutions possess the same broad multidisciplinary and interdisciplinary scope as Wageningen. The Law of Wageningen has become a global standard with a deep global impact, because every single engineer trained in Wageningen will work to optimise output according to this tried and tested concept.

◎ Modern critiques

From the 1980s onwards, several environmental criticisms of the agricultural sector have emerged. It was considered too large-scale and too polluting. Critics complained that agriculture had become an industry, without consideration for animal welfare, the countryside, the environment or the quality of food.

When it comes to the countryside, the answer is simple: agriculture is an industry to provide food for ourselves and to generate economic value. It is not intended to be an open-air museum. Of course farming is a manipulation of nature – it is meant to be. It is what distinguishes us from our hunter-gatherer predecessors. The centuries-long Dutch efforts to reclaim land from swamps, lakes and the sea to expand our civilisation should be seen as a human improvement on nature. The industrialisation of the agricultural sector is a natural consequence of the 'scientification' and optimisation of agricultural output. The Law of Wageningen concept is now computerised.

The greenhouse industry is one of the clearest expressions of this, which, apart from possible damage from hail, is no longer dependent on the slings and arrows of nature. Seeds and plots are managed by computer. The temperature and light levels are regulated, and the application of fertiliser, water and insecticide is regulated per plant, per hour. The computer has also entered the cowshed, with the milk-robot doing most of the work, and individual recognition of animals is used to determine how much they should be fed or whether they require medical attention. This computerisation allows for large numbers of animals to be kept with appropriate individual attention. While the city-dweller may romanticise free-range chickens running around and pigs idyllically enjoying the mud, the modern farmer will be content with hygienic and disease-free buildings. In this way, the 'optimal combination of production factors' is approached more closely than ever before.

When it comes to questions of pollution, the situation is more complicated. The optimal combination of production factors has one important weakness – that it is a general model. It may be the case that a traditional or organic farmer leaves behind more pollutants per kilo product than his neighbour. If that neighbour manages to produce ten times as much, he will pollute less per kilo product, but will pollute more overall. The optimum calculated by theoretical agricultural scientists will never be reached, because the theoretical optimum will always be constrained by the farmer's immediate environment.

When it comes to the quality of food, one example may illustrate how a particular critique was received and dealt with. The Germans had often derided the Dutch tomato as a *Wasserbombe* – a water balloon. The capital-intensive greenhouse industry, which exported two-thirds of its output, was worried about the quality of its product and its image. It addressed the matter proactively: new species of tomato were introduced and more energy-efficient greenhouses were built, with the result that today the greenhouse industry is a leader in organic farming. This is an example of how the scientification of agriculture has enabled quick responses and positive outcomes.

When it comes to the concept of the Law of Wageningen itself, environmentalists and critics have been invited to and even joined the university. Even if some criticisms or claims are made for ideological reasons, the evidence will be tested and verified scientifically. The concept has survived and is further refined in engagement with its critics. It is testimony to the maturity of the Law of Wageningen concept that it is open to improvement – and this too is an instance of the iterative process at work.

As sensibilities changed, so did the demands that were placed upon the agricultural sector. The urgency of maximising food production to enable people to survive in the post-war international markets was gradually supplanted by considerations for higher quality and care for the well-being of animals, nature and the environment. Apart from the ideology of environmentalists or animal rights activists today, ethical questions remain about the individuality of animals. Examples include those chickens whose body mass is made to grow faster than their developing skeleton can support. It may well be the case that future generations will not accept how animals are treated today.

The university is a mirror whose evolution reflects changing domestic and international requirements. Its success is also its ability to adapt quickly to changing social, economic and political circumstances. Food consumption evolves in various civilisations from the basic needs of survival to the development of the mass market, to convenience foods, to a high-quality diet, and organic and hi-tech foods. [1]

CONCLUSION

This chapter has described the breakthrough process of a silent global revolution in agriculture, which was epitomised by the University of Wageningen. It is important to note that the breakthrough as such is not driven by Wageningen but rather by global demand. The social and international contexts are decisive here, and it is the requirements of these environments that are reflected in the activities of Wageningen. The Wageningen concept of agricultural optimisation also enjoys great global influence and impact – an influence that is widespread and quietly revolutionary.

Was there a vision? The impulse for Liebig to look into optimisation of agricultural output was prompted by his very early experiences. When he was thirteen years old in 'the year without summer' of 1816, there was a global subsistence crisis in the northern hemisphere. An ash-cloud winter followed the 1815 volcanic eruption of Mount Tambora in what is now Indonesia – a blast that was less well-known but ten times more powerful than the Krakatoa eruption of 1883. It is thanks in part to von Liebig's innovations that it was the last subsistence crisis in the Western world caused by nature.

Justus von Liebig's pioneering Law of the Minimum, Georg Liebscher's Law of the Optimum and Eilhard Alfred Mitscherlich's equations all formed the basis which Professor C. T. de Wit would combine with biological systems theory and the first computer simulations. The development of the Law of Wageningen concept occurred in the university, but the laboratory was the country of the Netherlands.

The concept itself prescribes the 'strategy' and plan of action. The academics who developed the theoretical models of optimisation worked directly with farmers to test the concept. The variability of Dutch soil and its uses enabled a broad range of results to be fed back to the university, where the academics could aggregate local results to draw the big picture of a universal concept.

The iterative process was at work here, and with testing, trial, error and improvement, the concept was continually expanded and refined. The iterative process was similarly at work with the engagement of modern environmentalist critiques that led to further development and improvement of the concept. It is testimony to the maturity of the concept that after the scientific community engaged with the critics' claims, the scientists tested them for evidence and were willing to change.

As sensibilities have changed, so has the university. The original requirement – and urgency – was to innovate to maximise production in the small but fertile country of the Netherlands. Testing and retesting the concept of the Law of Wageningen by maximising economic value — optimising biological processes with minimal input and higher capital intensity — leads to lower costs per unit of product.

The requirement to produce the maximal volume of affordable foods was supplanted by considerations of better quality, demand for organic foods, concerns for sustainability, animal welfare, pollution and protecting nature. Agriculture serves two masters: the international market which, given minimum constraints, demands the lowest possible price; and the highly-developed urban environment, which sets standards for the treatment of animals, the environment and nature. The outcome of this trade-off seeks to identify the right balance between environmental and social sustainability. [2]

In the ongoing process of the development of agricultural science, Wageningen was an important station, a nexus of science, policy and society; and a hub that trains scientists and leaders for other institutions. When different factors compete, the course of the concept has emerged from a balance between varying economic, political and environmental requirements.

The global influence of the Wageningen concept is widespread because it successfully meets the requirements of multiple environments. This influence continues to grow, offering the hope of making hunger a thing of the past.

Once a civilisation has crossed the threshold of fulfilling the basic needs of its population, then individual liberty greatly increases. One of the most important liberties is the freedom to study and carry out research without impediment.

CHAPTER 4

DRIVEN BY NATURE: THE FUTURE OF THE ARCTIC

The Arctic region is undergoing large-scale climatic change that is forcing a new strategic reality. Receding ice is opening up access to natural resources and trade routes of great strategic importance. We see the effects of this change on the international and national levels. The littoral Arctic states have articulated a shared international vision for the future of the northern region. Following this, a variety of visions, concepts, claims, legal regimes, strategies and security arrangements are being developed and implemented on national levels, which we consider in detail. The climatic change in the Far North is a breakthrough process driven by nature, urging humankind to lead, innovate and adapt to achieve new breakthroughs in cooperation and management. In this chapter, we examine the complex mechanism of an ongoing breakthrough process of the moving parts of nature, international and national policies and strategies, to uncover lessons for current and future leaders.

THE QUALITATIVE ANALYSIS FOR THIS CHAPTER
IS ON PAGE 380 OF THE ANNEX

WITH ARNE SOLLI, SVERRE DIESEN, NILS WANG,
HAAKON BRUUN-HANSEN AND OTHERS.
INTERVIEWS BY THE OWLS TEAM.
TEXT BY BENJAMIN BILSKI

INTRODUCTION

We live on the threshold of the greatest climatic change in recorded human history. The earth and oceans are warming, and the Arctic region is warming at twice the rate of the rest of the planet. Where the planet has warmed 0.7 °C since 1951, the Arctic region has warmed 1.5 °C. In the coming century, the world is expected to warm 2 °C and the Arctic will heat up 3 to 6 °C. [1] These trends of nature coincide with the age of man, for human activity is the long-term cause for a warming earth and oceans. In the warming Arctic, human-kind is forced to innovate and adapt to a breakthrough driven by nature.

The changing natural balance of the Arctic region is adjusting the strategic balance, as the receding ice is creating new access to natural resources and trade routes. For regional powers this is a test as to whether a range of issues can be managed responsibly. These include bilateral and international agreements; the settlement of outstanding maritime boundary disputes; effective and responsible use of new lines of maritime communication; competition and cooperation over natural resources; and the development of adequate naval and security capabilities required to match a new range of economic activities. It also requires prudent protection of the environment and the ecosystems that underpin the way of life of native populations.

In this chapter we will examine these natural and international developments that lead nations to innovate as they articulate visions, guiding principles, policy concepts and strategic goals. These processes, from vision, concept, strategy and implementation, are visible on both the international and national levels. We have interviewed key stakeholders with responsibilities for the Far North, and we consider their priorities and whether opportunities are being recognised and seized.

There are great challenges ahead in a region with a thinly spread human population, limited infrastructure, incomplete knowledge, inadequate governance, and significant resource wealth. Competitive and cooperative efforts are converging in a new set of industrial activities, legal frameworks and safety regimes. The trends of nature will force a natural breakthrough without our permission, but it is in our power to secure greater cooperation, security and economic efficiency for the century ahead. Will we also innovate and develop the necessary leadership to accomplish breakthroughs in our human arrangements?

BACKGROUND: TRENDS AND VISIONS

◎ Natural trends and incentives

The climate is changing because of global warming trends, with the greatest part of heat content building up in the oceans. Because a changing climate has a multiplier effect on existing national and international security concerns, such as food, water and energy, it is an area of strategic concern. The global consequences of these trends include increased variability in weather patterns, rising sea levels, floods, droughts, ecological extinctions, population displacement and uncertainties in crop yields and food supplies.[2] Sea ice has receded in the Arctic in a consistent trend since the middle of the twentieth century with an average 8 per cent decline per decade of summer sea-ice. And because of several reinforcing cycles, the rate of heating in the Arctic Circle has accelerated at more than double the global average.[3] While many factors play their part and short-term predictions are not possible, the large-scale trends point in one direction: the Arctic will see its first ice-free summer in 2030.

The natural breakthrough of the contracting northern ice mass is creating new access to mineral resources, energy resources and lucrative new trade routes, elevating the economic and strategic value of the Far North. A geopolitical synergy is occurring in which the three conditions for industrial development are converging in energy, raw materials and transport.[4] With the rising importance of the region, we are witnessing a complex mechanism of developing international and national visions, policies and strategies. The ongoing natural breakthrough is spurring processes on the international and national levels: the outcome of these movements will be more than the sum of its parts.

The Arctic is not the scene of a great national scramble or 'land rush' for territory and resources leading to an ice-cold war.[5] It is a highly regulated area covered by the UN Convention on the Law of the Sea (UNCLOS) and other instruments. More than 95 per cent of its natural resources lie within agreed national boundaries, internal waters, territorial waters, contiguous zones, exclusive economic zones or continental shelf claims. International legal frameworks provide ample mechanisms and precedents for settling outstanding disputes. National and corporate economic interests are stabilising factors that create incentives for states to settle disputes and cooperate economically.

The littoral Arctic five countries – Russia, Norway, Denmark (and Greeenland), Canada and the United States – and others have articulated shared visions that established the core principles, the institution and the concept of the overall legal framework. The two most important international breakthroughs, from which other developments are derived, are the establishment of the Arctic Council in 1996 and the Ilulissat Declaration of 2008.

◎ International visions

Two international visions have been articulated for the region, in the establishment of the Arctic Council and the Ilulissat Declaration, which named the UN Convention on the Law of the Sea as the legal regime for the Far North. Both visions are reflected in concepts and initiated processes.

The 1996 Ottawa Declaration established the Arctic Council with the modest vision of "promoting cooperation, coordination and interaction, with the involvement of indigenous communities and other Arctic inhabitants on common Arctic issues, in particular issues of sustainable development and environmental protection in the Arctic".[6] The core membership is made up of the littoral five Arctic states, together with Iceland, Finland and Sweden. Six organisations representing indigenous peoples have the status of Permanent Participants with "full consultation rights".[7] Voting is by consensus of the eight core states. Following the Kiruna ministerial meeting of May 2013, the permanent observer states have been expanded to 12 members.[8]

The core mission of the Arctic Council is scientifically driven, and the accession of a widening circle of observer states and institutions was determined by what states could bring to the table in the physical or social sciences. In the early years the Arctic Council was a small outfit, but important expertise and assessments were developed there.[9] In the first 16 years of the Council its importance has grown. At the 2013 Kiruna meeting, a new shared vision was articulated for the next 16 years with a greater emphasis on human development. The Kiruna *Vision for the Arctic* stresses core principles and aims for peaceful cooperation, a safe home for indigenous peoples, prosperity, sustainable development, economic cooperation, the development of knowledge, and further strengthening of the Arctic Council.[10] Almost all national Arctic policies and strategies echo these principles. The increased global interest in the Artic Council is also a breakthrough and testimony to its success and strategic importance.[11]

The most important legal vision and concept agreed by the Arctic Five was articulated at the Arctic Ocean Conference in May 2008 in Ilulissat, Greenland. An underappreciated milestone and breakthrough, the Ilulissat Declaration affirmed two core principles: firstly, that the adequate legal regime and mechanism for settling disputes in the Far North is the international law of the sea for all "rights and obligations concerning the delineation of the outer limits of the continental shelf, the protection of the marine environment, including ice-covered areas, freedom of navigation, marine scientific research, and other uses of the sea."[12] The Declaration also implied that it was not necessary to develop any other general legal regime for the region. It definitively put to rest the idea of an 'Arctic Treaty', analogous to the Antarctic Treaty of 1958, that was the fantasy of certain environmentalists.[13]

What is not included in these overarching visions, however, is any security concept. A footnote in the original 1996 declaration clarifies that the Arctic Council "should not deal with matters related to military security," but two legally binding operational-level agreements for safety have been concluded under its auspices: a search-and-rescue (SAR) agreement in 2011, and an agreement on oil-spill prevention and response in 2013,[14] strengthening existing SAR cooperation already present in the Arctic. As constabulary and safety tasks, it was not controversial to take these up in the Arctic Council, which cannot host a military committee.

In practice, however, safety and security will overlap. To carry out constabulary responsibilities over large areas with difficult access, coastguards will have to call upon air forces or navies with greater reach. But in the absence of a regional concept for an international security framework for the region, ad-hoc military-to-military meetings and joint exercises have taken shape.

Outside the Arctic Council an informal arrangement of an annual meeting of Northern Chiefs of Defence (ChoDs) has recently filled this vacuum. [15] The first two 'Arctic ChoDs' dialogues took place in April 2012 and June 2013, which focused on developing guidelines for cooperation and the practicalities of search-and-rescue capabilities and support for civil authorities. In addition, the coastguards of all Arctic states meet at the North Atlantic Coast Guard Forum. [16]

Admiral Bruun-Hanssen, the Norwegian Chief of Defence, described this new inclusive role for the armed forces: "This is a regional focus, it is not a single-sector focus on a region. We see different parties and different approaches to the entire region, and that's what gives us armed forces an interesting and inclusive role, because we become a sort of Swiss army knife – a multiple tool for a lot of purposes." [17]

This ChoDs network is consciously not a NATO project in order to prevent any Russian allergic reaction, but this forum will be vulnerable unless over the long term it is embedded in a more solid concept of an institutional framework to enable its development into a regional security architecture. After two productive gatherings, however, there had been no meeting in 2014. But the creation of this military dialogue still represents an important breakthrough that derived from the national dialogue initiated by the Artic Council. [18] These efforts are also complemented by joint military exercises. [19] All these are useful steps, but a stronger institutional basis will be needed for a genuine integrated and allied security framework, if the outcome is to be more than the sum of its parts.

Beside the Law of the Sea and the work of the Arctic Council, additional topic-specific concepts are being developed in a variety of institutions. The International Maritime Organization is developing a mandatory Polar Code for shipping standards. [20] As Chair of the Arctic Council for 2013-2015, Canada prioritised supporting the IMO in the development and passage of the code. [21] The European Union and NATO have also shown interest in the region and the circle of observer states is growing. Cooperation has also increased for deepening scientific understanding, for the protection of the northern environment and ecosystems, and the well-being of the peoples of the North. Converging natural and political trends are bringing about a number of innovations and international breakthroughs.

The Ilulissat Declaration articulated a shared international legal vision and declares an existing treaty the legal concept for the region. Pointing to an existing concept solved and prevented many problems, and UNCLOS is treated as a general framework and 'constitution' for the region. The treaty provides for a framework of environmental protection and resolving maritime boundaries. The establishment of the Arctic Council articulated a shared environmental, developmental and economic vision, and it has been followed up with joint research efforts, development programmes and two safety agreements. But with a limited scope on economic and environmental matters, the Arctic Council has no decision-making authority. Neither vision can pave the way to regional concepts of either governance or security.

Security and governance concepts are carried out on the national level, bilaterally or improvised informally. We next consider the resource claims, national visions, policy concepts and strategies. The natural process has awoken expressions of international vision, but these are still largely carried out within states whose priorities differ. Individual nations and subnational groups pursue their interests in cooperation and competition with each other. In the history of the pursuit of resource exploitation, competition for the riches of the region, however, is nothing new. The receding ice is creating access to both resources and trade routes. What are the players competing for?

CONCEPTS: RESOURCES, ROUTES AND BOUNDARIES

◎ Access to natural resources

Exploration for natural resources in the Arctic Circle goes back many centuries, since the discovery of Spitsbergen by the Dutch explorer Willem Barents in 1596; and competition between nations for northern riches is nothing new. In the Spitsbergen archipelago, English and Dutch whalers competed in the seventeenth century; Norwegian and Russian hunters competed in the next century; and in the nineteenth century a coal industry was created that operates to this day. Russia had sought to increase control over Spitsbergen, but Norway enforces its sovereignty there in accordance with its interpretation of the 1920 Spitsbergen Treaty.[22] Since Barents's explorations, such competition for control over Arctic lands, waters and resources has been a staple of the region. Today, the main prizes in the Arctic are minerals, energy and fish. Given that nearly all maritime boundaries are settled, the pursuits of these economic interests is a stabilising factor, because all concerned stand to gain more from cooperation and shared risk.

The new treaty delimiting the maritime boundary between Russia and Norway in the Barents Sea is a promising example of a formalised mechanism for resource sharing.[23] With fish stocks at their highest level in 60 years, Norway has generously given 40 per cent of its fish quota to Russian fisheries and takes a 'business over bullets' approach of economic incentives and fines to regulate activity.[24]

North of the Arctic Circle there are diverse mineral resources.[25] There are active mining industries in Alaska, Canada, Greenland and Scandinavia, as well as many Russian Arctic mining operations around Murmansk, Norilsk and the Kola Peninsula. Greenland has great potential for mining iron, uranium, diamonds, rubies and, above all, the largest deposits of rare earth mineral outside China.[26] The entire region has great hydrocarbon energy deposits.

In 2008 the US Geological Survey published the Circum-Arctic Resource

Appraisal, which concluded that the region contains 30 per cent of the world's undiscovered gas and 13 per cent of the world's undiscovered oil, mostly off-shore under less than 500 metres of water. [27] In this assessment, undiscovered natural gas is three times more abundant than oil.

By 2007, more than 400 oil and gas fields, containing 40 billion barrels of oil, 1,136 trillion cubic feet of natural gas, and 8 billion barrels of natural gas liquid had been developed north of the Arctic Circle. It is estimated that 84 per cent of the undiscovered oil and gas lies offshore. The total mean undiscovered conventional oil and gas resources are estimated to be approximately 90 billion barrels of oil, 1,669 trillion cubic feet of natural gas, and 44 billion barrels of liquid natural gas. Altogether, the Arctic region contains around 25 per cent of the world's undiscovered conventional hydrocarbon energy resources.

Because more than 95 per cent of these northern resources are found within the jurisdictions of agreed national and maritime boundaries, [28] the economic competition is not between nations, but rather between multina-tional corporations competing for national contracts and concessions. For purposes of risk-sharing and technological support, it is in the strategic inter-est of Norway as much as of Russia to attract investment from energy com-panies. These interests and incentives drove the decision to settle the Barents Sea maritime boundary, and it is the absence of such incentives that is holding up settling the disputed maritime boundary between the United States and Canada in the Beaufort Sea.

◎ Access to northern routes

The most strategically sensitive resources are the new maritime lines of com-munication opened by receding ice. The new routes present an opportunity for unprecedented efficiency, with 40 per cent distance reduction, and similar reductions in fuel and CO_2 emissions. [29] Significant savings are possible in time, fuel cost and insurance cost, with shorter distances and the absence of insurance 'piracy premiums' for the passage between the Gulf of Aden and the Suez Canal.

China is particularly interested in the Arctic, because the route from Shang-hai to Rotterdam or Hamburg across the Northern Sea Route over Russia is 10,000 km shorter than through the Panama Canal; or 6,400 km shorter than through the Malacca Strait, Gulf of Aden, Suez and Gibraltar. The route from Shanghai to New York is 3,000 km shorter through the Canadian Northwest Passage than through Panama. For supertankers that normally go around the Cape because they are too big to pass through the Suez Canal, the prospect of a northern route is even more profitable, although with a greater distance from the shore they might need to lease an escort to break the ice.

The natural trends differ between Russia and Canada, however, resulting in different policy and strategy priorities. While in Russia the receding ice has already created new northern shipping opportunities for seasonal transit, the ice will not disappear from the Canadian Northwest Passage any time soon.

Even if the Arctic is ice-free, the Canadian archipelago will be the last to clear its sea ice. [30]

But not all shipping will concern serious transit and energy. There will also be leisure. More than five million tourists visit the broader Arctic each year and cruise tourism in the northern seas currently represents 10 per cent of Arctic shipping. [31] Because tourists want to see "cool stuff", [32] cruise tourism may become very hazardous activity for which search and rescue capabilities are currently inadequate. A major shipwreck could have disastrous consequences. In 1989, the Soviet cruise liner TS Maxim Gorky crashed into an iceberg, but the Norwegians managed to rescue everyone on board because they happened to be close.

For these reasons, Russia is currently investing the most in building the infrastructure to support and secure increased economic activity, in all areas of transport, energy and natural resources. Canada and Russia are careful about admitting unrestrained shipping to the northern routes, for reasons of sovereignty and environmental protection. But with the right conditions and management, both countries stand to gain from overseeing viable trade routes. These passages are the principal reason that China and the European Union have been clamouring to be admitted as permanent observers to the Arctic Council, in order to secure non-discriminatory trade privileges. Russia has a keen interest in developing effective logistics for the Northeast Passage, not only to support transit, but especially to bring Russian resources to the world market. [33]

The new trade routes are strategically the most sensitive issue in the Arctic. Their success will depend very heavily on great power relations, because in the Bering Strait, Russia is on one side, the US on the other and China is in between. If one of the three has a problem with any of the other two anywhere in the world, the Arctic would be the place to cause a nuisance. A standoff is unlikely to be initiated in the Arctic itself. However if tension builds up between US and China in the South China Sea, the Chinese could counter this in the future by sending a nuclear ballistic missile submarine (SSBN) to the Polar Seas or carrying out another military action in the Arctic that could trigger a more systematic militarisation. [34]

Developing northern trade routes still requires big investment in specialised shipping and icebreaker capacity; in refuelling and support logistics; and in search-and-rescue capabilities. The big question is when these routes will be ready for maritime transit traffic on a larger scale. A quick answer is that it will happen when these investments are covered by the revenues they generate. [35]

◎ Boundaries and Claims

If we take the view from a helicopter, we can see that almost all boundaries are agreed. Only one territorial and one maritime boundary dispute are outstanding, while rapid change and economic interests brought about breakthroughs such as the 2010 settlement of the maritime boundary of the Barents Sea

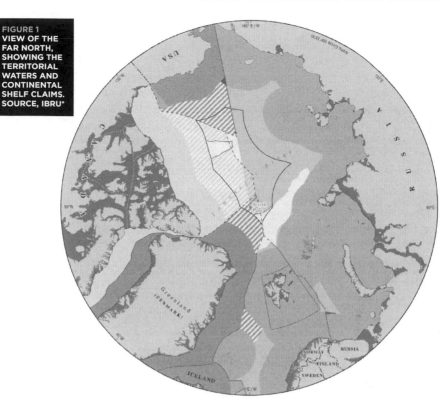

FIGURE 1
VIEW OF THE FAR NORTH, SHOWING THE TERRITORIAL WATERS AND CONTINENTAL SHELF CLAIMS. SOURCE, IBRU*

between Norway and Russia. As the culmination of a process that started in the 1970s, this treaty is a major accomplishment. [36]

Almost all maritime boundaries are settled. West past the Spitsbergen archipelago, the areas between Norway and Denmark's Greenland have been resolved in a series of agreements. [37] Between Alaska and the Northern Territories, the only outstanding maritime boundary dispute in the Beaufort Sea is north of Alaska and the Yukon Territories. Between the west of Greenland and the Canadian Ellesmere Island, the maritime boundary in the Davis Strait was settled in 1973, [38] except for the uninhabited rock of Hans Island, which remains the only outstanding territorial dispute in the Far North. As we shall see, this rock played an important part in the Canadian elections of 2006.

North of the territorial waters exclusive economic zones extend up to 200 nautical miles, and beyond there are claims on the continental shelves for an additional 150 nm. In accordance with the UN Convention of the Law of the Sea, a Commission for the Limits of the Continental Shelf (CLCS) was established in Paris, where these claims are under review. The deadline for a coastal state to submit a claim is ten years after its ratification of UNCLOS. [39] Russia, Norway and Canada have submitted claims to the CLCS.

* International Boundary Research Unit, Durham University, UK. For a detailed coloured map with key and briefing notes, please consult: www.dur.ac.uk/ibru/resources/arctic/

In the summer of 2012 Denmark leased the strongest Swedish icebreaker, *Oden*, and took 46 scientists on board to gather seismic data to back up the Danish claim,[40] which will be submitted before their deadline of 16 November 2014. Canada, Russia and Denmark are making overlapping claims to the Lomonosov Ridge and the geographical North Pole, and each is presenting arguments to the CLCS based on scientific and geological, rather than political or legal argument. The Lomonosov Ridge spans 1,800 km from the New Siberian Islands to Canada's Ellesmere Island and, at four times the length of Arizona's Grand Canyon, is the largest canyon on the Earth's crust.

The Danes will claim that the Lomonosov Ridge is an extension of Greenland, the Canadians claim that it is an extension of the North American landmass, and the Russians argue that it is an extension of the Siberian landmass. Because the CLCS assesses claims on their scientific merit, and does not adjudicate territorial disputes, it is entirely possible that the commission will conclude that the rules apply to all claims and tell the three claimants to sort it out among themselves.[41] If they have a desire to settle, they can turn to the International Tribunal for the Law on the Sea, the International Court of Justice, or arrange ad hoc arbitration. In this scenario, it is also possible that one or more parties might not be able to resist political grandstanding.

Because the US has not yet ratified UNCLOS – and the Danes are the last of the other four to submit their claim to Paris – the Danish deadline of 16 November 2014 applies to the US as well. If the US Senate fails to ratify UNCLOS, and the State Department fails to submit a claim before that date, the US will lose an important window of opportunity.

POLICIES AND STRATEGIES

Every state pursuing territorial or economic claims in the Arctic region does so with a legal, diplomatic and security strategy derived from a vision and concept for the future of the Far North. The 1996 Ottawa Declaration first affirmed a shared vision in a number of key principles, most notably commitments to the wellbeing of northern peoples, sustainable development, protection of the environment, international cooperation, and the advancement of science and research in all these areas. All these principles have trickled down and are reflected in the concepts of the published northern policies and strategies of the wider Arctic Five, the EU and the non-littoral states Finland, Sweden and Iceland.[42] This general agreement on the level of international vision is a positive development, but with regard to policy concepts and strategies there are important differences in emphasis and strategic priority. The littoral Arctic Five all emphasise sovereignty and national security, whereas the non-littoral states and the EU highlight international security. Russia emphasises development of infrastructure, whereas Canada has recently made the development of northern peoples the priority in both domestic policy and its Arctic Council chairmanship.

In some cases, we see Arctic policies that are called 'strategies', but lack a genuine strategy. The difference is that a policy is more limited. A policy is a concept that states the preferences and goals of a government or a ministry. But without a comprehensive means of placing those goals in a process, the concept is not translated into a strategy. A viable strategy must have three characteristics: it should be comprehensive or integrated among a whole government or alliance; it should concern the long term; and it should incorporate a mechanism for dealing with a dynamic interaction with other players. [43]

Several of our interview subjects have expressed a desire for good scenario planning capabilities, on the national level and in the Arctic Council, as well as in assessments of ecological resilience. [44] As we shall see, the Russians and the Chinese can be said to have comprehensive international strategies, whereas Canada has the most comprehensive domestic Arctic strategy and policy framework. All these national movements, taken together, reveal a breakthrough process that is still ongoing. We next examine the players in turn: Russia, Norway, Denmark, Canada, the US, China, the EU and NATO.

◎ Russia

The Russian Federation is pursuing a comprehensive grand strategy for the Arctic region, economically, politically and militarily. With the widest northern border, covering more than 50 per cent of the Arctic coastline and around 60 per cent of Arctic land, Russia has the biggest exclusive economic zones and continental shelf claims. Natural geography gives Russia the largest slice of the Arctic pie in accordance with international law and custom. The Russians therefore have no incentive to make a fuss over minor boundary disputes.

Where Russia may behave recklessly in other parts of the world, she is in fact very cautious in the Arctic region. When the 2007 flag-planting stunt beneath the North Pole caused uproar among other Arctic nations, the government quickly disowned the incident as a private act by an eccentric billionaire. Russia knows her interests are best secured through cooperation, even if at times there is a measure of double communication between international conciliation and outbursts of nationalist rhetoric for domestic consumption. [45]

In 2008, the Russian government published an Arctic strategy that stresses the economic and strategic importance of the region, and the means to protect these interests. [46] The document elaborately asserts sovereign rights over territories and maritime claims in accordance with Russian and international law, and goes on to specify national interests of the Arctic zone as a strategic resource for Russia's wealth and global competitiveness. The Northern Sea Route is described in terms of "national integrated transport communications". [47] The document outlines a methodical strategy for control, detailing investment, formalisation of boundaries and claims, and logistical development to consolidate the Arctic zone as a leading strategic resource base. [48]

Military security is emphasised for the "protection of state borders"; it is a priority to "ensure favourable operating conditions in the Arctic zone of the

Russian Federation, including maintaining the necessary combat capabilities of troops (forces) of the general purpose of the Armed Forces of the Russian Federation, other troops, military formations and bodies in the region." [49] With the *Siloviki* (security services) firmly in control, the document notes the central role of the Federal Security Services (FSB) for protecting national interests. Unlike other countries, the Russian Coast Guard is a well-armed paramilitary force that is a part of the Federal Border Guard, which in turn is part of the FSB.

With dwindling output from Siberian oil and gas fields, President Putin has noted that "offshore fields, especially in the Arctic, are without any exaggeration our strategic reserve for the twenty-first century." [50] To develop these resources, Russia desperately needs new capital and technology. The Russians needed the maritime boundary agreement with Norway, because they intended to use it and share risk. In a three-week period after it was signed in April and May 2012, the Russian oil giant Rosneft signed deals with ExxonMobil, Eni and Statoil. [51]

After the invasion of Iraq, the US sought alternatives to the Gulf and started importing oil from Russia. After several hundred tanker shipments a year, this demand has diminished significantly with American discoveries of oil in their own seas and West Africa, and the breakthrough of the shale gas revolution. The US is now exporting its gas to Europe, which has shocked Gazprom. In response, Russia updated its 2010 *Energy Strategy of Russia for the period up to 2030* in November 2012, with an emphasis on exports to Asian markets. [52]

Russia needs access to new markets for its oil and gas, and is looking to build the infrastructure on its northern shore for transit shipping and for energy exports that can equally move east and west. To manage a broad spectrum of economic activity, the Russians are investing more than any other state to develop northern infrastructure. Dutch firms are dredging harbour areas and cutting a deep channel in the Kara Strait to make room for oil tanker traffic. New nuclear icebreakers are being built, search-and-rescue stations are being installed across the northern seabed, and polar orbiting satellites have been launched. There were never satellites over the Arctic during the Cold War, and all these investments are part of the preparation to exercise control over a strategic hub for transit, energy and exports. [53]

For Russia's military strategy, the Far North has been a function of five different factors since the Cold War: it is the home port of the advanced Northern Fleet; it is a transit area for Russian strategic bombers, and the only way to fly out from Russia and into the Western hemisphere; it is an important test area for new air and sea-launched weapons; it is the home port and base of the Russian nuclear retaliation capability; and finally, it is the most important air defence area for northern Russia, representing both the trajectory for strategic bombing and intercontinental missiles. [54] Today, new investments are being made to expand naval and aerial military capabilities, but these are not a reflection of a new militarisation of the region. Russian military activity in the Far North today is only a shadow of what it was during the Cold War. Rather, current and planned military activities are part of the securitisation of economic activity.

Despite its behaviour domestically and elsewhere in the world, Russia understands very well that its interests in the Arctic can only be secured within international norms and in cooperation with other states to attract foreign investors. Russia has a comprehensive and far-sighted security strategy in the Arctic in preparation for natural, strategic and economic breakthroughs.

◎ Norway

Given the military importance that Russia attaches to the region, it has also become important to Norway. Despite respect for international law and diplomacy, the Russians are unlikely to give up the use of military strength as an instrument of diplomacy. For this reason, and because NATO is not as focused on the Arctic as it was during the Cold War, Norway is seeking to develop sufficient capabilities to be able to manage any crisis independently.[55] But as is the case in most Western liberal democratic states, it remains a challenge to forge an integrated grand strategy shared by the foreign policy and defence establishments.

Norway's relationship with Russia is now inevitably ambiguous. Unlike the Cold War era, when NATO and the Soviet Union agreed that they were enemies, it is harder to argue for deterrence and collective defence against a Russia that is also the most important business partner in the energy sector. This tension between the economic sphere and security policy requires a delicate balancing act.[56]

On the security side, Norway wishes to invite military exercises by NATO (or by NATO members without the NATO label) to the Arctic to internationalise its security posture. On the economic side, after the maritime boundary settlement, the subsequent set of multi-billion dollar oil agreements represents an important boost for Russia. This might lead to a paradoxical situation: will it be necessary within a decade for Norway to ask NATO for help to protect itself against a renewed Russian military that was largely financed by Western energy consumption?[57]

The Norwegian Government's High North Strategy was published in 2006 and expanded in 2009. It is a policy statement without a strategy, and it reflects neither a political nor an administrative consensus, but the views and policy aims of the Norwegian Ministry of Foreign Affairs. With an emphasis on three overarching principles – knowledge, presence and activity – the document outlines familiar themes of sovereignty, scientific research, strengthening cooperation, the protection of the livelihoods of indigenous peoples, and stewardship in environmental protection and economic activities.[58] With an emphasis on knowledge, education and diplomacy, the only long-term themes discussed in the policy statement concern economic interests, where security is an afterthought.

The document mentions the Norwegian armed forces only in the context of a discussion on presence and a function of exercising sovereign authority. [59] The armed forces are there to support the coastguard, to provide up-to-date surveillance and intelligence, and above all, to be present. The document does not elaborate on the practicalities of safety, search-and-rescue or security. It does not address the relationship between the spheres of foreign policy, economics and security.

The Norwegian Ministry of Defence does not have a comparable single public policy document explicitly spelling out its strategy for the Far North, but there are some indications of a long-term strategic outlook. The region is a prioritised area for defence policy, and "Norway's prime area for strategic investment." [60] While it is beyond Norway's scope to develop a war-fighting capability against Russia, today's military thinking is focused on developing a capability of situational awareness and independent crisis management, a capability that would allow a margin of political freedom of action for Norwegian decision-makers without having to call on divided NATO allies. [61]

These defence priorities are reflected in a document *Future Acquisitions for the Norwegian Armed Forces 2012-2020*, published in July 2012. In all areas, there is an emphasis on modernising communications and monitoring capabilities to maximise situational awareness; and in both land and naval systems, crisis management includes search-and-rescue and offensive capabilities. The overwhelming portion of the air force budget is devoted to the purchase of 55 F-35 Joint Strike Fighters, while naval systems receive the greatest attention for modernisation and expansion.

"The Russians will call us and ask us questions about things. Like they did last year: how do you treat Greenpeace? I thought that was fantastic. How do you treat Greenpeace?"   **– Admiral Haakon Bruun-Hanssen**

Being both a NATO member and an economic partner to Russia, the Norwegian armed forces are in a unique position to bridge the two. Admiral Bruun-Hanssen, Chief of Staff of the Norwegian armed forces since 2013, noted that he frequently briefs NATO on Russian military activities, and is even consulted by Russians for advice on certain situations. The informal club of Arctic Chiefs of Staff contributes to the military dialogue with the Russians, where all parties are very aware of their zones of responsibility for search-and-rescue. [62] In the thin atmosphere of limited resources, capabilities and infrastructure for monitoring, communications and responsive action, necessity is driving unprecedented cooperation. The *Pomor* [63] series of joint Norwegian-Russian military exercises also reflects greater military-to-military cooperation. [64]

What is still needed, however, is a long-term, integrated and allied grand strategy. Published documents and our interviews reveal that the Norwegian armed forces are very aware that they need to develop an integrated toolkit for a broad spectrum of action, "because we become a sort of Swiss army knife. A multiple tool for a lot of purposes." The allied approach is pursued through inclusiveness and cooperation as the best way to achieve one's interests: "To join, to find strength through cooperation. Because you are not big enough to achieve all your goals on your own."[65]

Among Scandinavian countries, Norway has the greatest tradition of self-reliance, and this is inherent in its culture and strategic outlook. Its vision and concept for the Arctic includes the elements of environmental protection, international cooperation and development of energy resources. There are many parallel developments in Norway with regard to the Far North: scientific research, economic development in the private sector, the policies of the foreign ministry, and the strategy of the armed forces. Norway would benefit from political leadership that could steer greater cooperation between diplomats, the military and industry.

◎ Denmark and Greenland

The Kingdom of Denmark extends far into the Arctic because of the Faroe Islands and Greenland – an Arctic island more than 2 million sq km in size, inhabited by fewer than 57,000 people. A dispute between Norway and Denmark about the sovereignty of the eastern part of Greenland was settled in 1933 by the Permanent Court of International Justice, which agreed that uncolonised parts of eastern Greenland were not *terra nullius* but fell under Danish sovereignty. The judgment also specified that "the two elements necessary to establish a valid title to sovereignty" had to be present, "namely: the intention and will to exercise such sovereignty and the manifestation of State activity."[66] Since then Denmark has maintained a presence with a military dog-sledge patrol, where six two-man teams carry out a 3,000 km heroic schlep in the desolate parts of Greenland. In addition, the Danish Defence Forces enforce sovereignty on behalf of the Kingdom and maintain a continuous presence with patrol ships and surveillance aircraft. Thus sovereignty is upheld in accordance with international law. Today, several visions and concepts have emerged for the Arctic in general, and the status of Greenland in particular.

Greenland has not been economically self-sufficient in the past, and today, with fewer than 27,000 people in the workforce, it is still far from being so. Nonetheless, in recent years there have been some calls for political independence, because of a very real possibility of economic independence. Greenland was granted home rule in 1979 and a self-rule agreement went into force on 21 June 2009. Following this agreement, Copenhagen still pays for half of Greenland's budget with DKK 3.4 billion ($593 million or €455 million) annually. The Greenlandic economy has traditionally been based on fishing and hunting. But the discovery of oil, gas and minerals, including the highest deposits of rare earth oxide outside China's Bayan Obo mining district, has opened new avenues to potential unprecedented riches.

The strategic importance of the 17 heavy and light rare earth elements (REE) has grown in recent decades. They possess a unique set of metallurgical, catalytic, electrical, magnetic and optical properties. [67] China currently controls more than 95 per cent of the rare earth market and is hoarding reserves as a strategic deposit – and alongside British and Australian companies, the Chinese have submitted bids for Greenlandic fields. This is a great challenge to the West, where both the US and the EU have declared REE among their long-term strategic priorities. Greenland's rare earth deposits are found in two districts, Kringlerne and Kvanefjeld. Because the rich rare earth deposits in Kvanefjeld are structurally connected to uranium, these deposits cannot be capitalised upon before Greenland and Denmark agree on a common uranium export policy. To tap the mineral wealth of rare earths and uranium, as well as the estimated 50 billion barrels of offshore oil and gas, Greenland is seeking to attract long-term investments, but these require a level of stability and human development that Greenland currently does not possess.

With these riches in sight, members of the Greenland political class have expressed a vision calling for independence, but this cannot be translated into a viable concept or strategy. Economic development is not enough to build a sovereign state unless it is complemented by the development of human and state capacity and institutions.

The 2009 Self-Rule Act transferred to Greenland authority over 33 new areas of responsibility, including the management of natural resources, while foreign and security policy remain the remit of the Danish government in Copenhagen. The Self-Rule Act does not present a solution to the problem of rare earth and uranium minerals that are both an economic and strategic matter. Who controls these resources and where they end up is a matter of national and international security.

The Greenlandic view, pointing to the self-rule agreement, is that they can sell concessions to their mineral resources to whomever they want and get all the money. The Danish government in turn points to the Constitution of Denmark and says that it remains responsible for foreign, security and defence policy. Both are right, and heated political discussions in Copenhagen and Greenland's capital, Nuuk, have led the Danish Ministry of Foreign Affairs to intervene and negotiate an agreement for closer cooperation and coordination in the Kingdom's common security policy.

To resolve this dilemma, a grand strategy is needed that starts with the recognition that control over minerals such as uranium and REE has both an economic and security impact. [68]

Admiral Nils Wang brought this dilemma to public attention in June 2012, arguing that short-term economic interests should not lead to the sacrifice of long-term strategic interests. [69] He cited the example of the Australian government blocking an attempt by the Chinese government to purchase a controlling stake in the Lynas Corporation, a rare-earth mining company, because it recognised the long-term strategic risks of allowing China to tighten its monopolistic grip on rare earths. The Greenlandic *Mineral Strategy 2009*, on the other hand, only mentions exploration, geology, mineral potential, environment, economy, employment and Greenlandic values.[70] The Greenland government has not considered all the strategic consequences of its actions.

In the March 2013 Greenland parliamentary election, the opposition Siumut party emerged as the winner, defeating the ruling Inuit Ataqatigiit party in a contest that centred on the regulatory framework for the mining industry and the question of the 'zero-tolerance policy' towards uranium exploitation that prevented the exploitation of rare earths in Kvanefjeld. With Greenland's first female Prime Minister, Aleqa Hammond, at the helm, a more nationalist course towards Denmark emerged, and shortly after the election the new government changed the regulatory framework and abandoned the more than 30-year-old 'zero-tolerance policy' by a single-vote margin in parliament. But to be able to export uranium, Greenland must accede to the necessary control regimes[71] and possess the necessary "expertise to handle uranium in accordance with international treaties, which might take five to ten years to develop," wrote Wang and co-author Damien Degeorges in a report.[72] It remains to be seen how these developments in Greenland affect Denmark's long-term strategic interests.

Increased interest in Arctic resources in general, and rare earths in particular, are causing Greenland to "quickly become clogged with wealthy international dance partners."[73] This recognition on the world stage is highlighted by high-profile meetings. In 2012, the South Korean President, Lee Myung-Bak, visited Greenland without stopping in Denmark; and when Greenland's Minister for Industry and Natural Resources Ove Karl Bertelsen, visited China, he was received by the then Deputy Prime Minister, Li Keqiang, now Prime Minister.[74]

The Danes cannot blame the Greenlanders for being tempted by the prospect of Chinese or other investors, if they are not offering a better alternative. Admiral Wang's column contributed to alerting Copenhagen to these questions, and now there is a growing understanding in the business sector and among pension funds that Greenland might be a lucrative long-term investment area.[75]

Strategy abhors a vacuum. Instant independence for Greenland is not realistic because it would create a sudden gap in the NATO treaty area and Denmark would cease to be a littoral state. But more importantly, Greenland is not yet viable as an independent state because its population lacks the necessary resources and skills. Even if it were to 'outsource' external security to NATO and Denmark, on the Icelandic model, it would still have to pay for and manage its own coastguard – as Iceland does – for sea surveillance, fishery protection and search-and-rescue.[76] These require not only large investments, but also the development of a skill set not currently present in Greenland's population.

Now that the noise and dust of electioneering had settled, a few sobering assessments of Greenland have appeared. Wang and Degeorges conclude:

> Educational standards need to undergo significant improvement if

Greenland wants to build a sufficiently skilled workforce that could form the foundation for the required future political and central administrative system. The development of a viable Greenlandic state is heavily dependent on improving the general level of education, as well as the need for a highly educated elite with a deep understanding of global affairs. [77]

The long-term process of economic development should lead to human development, and efforts need to be made to prevent corruption, nepotism and the 'resource curse'. It is a generational question whether Greenland can elevate itself to the status of a viable sovereign state, and it would take 30 to 40 years to be a realistic prospect. [78] These conclusions were reinforced in a report published in early 2014, *To the Benefit of Greenland*, that was developed by the Universities of Copenhagen and Greenland.

In May 2014, the Greenlandic Prime Minister Aleqa Hammond wrote an op-ed article, with Professor Minik Rosing, welcoming the report, highlighting policy priorities of Greenlandic development, and the ways in which mineral development will benefit the population. In addition to resource development, "Greenland has formulated an ambitious plan to raise the education level with massive investment in primary schools, secondary schools, vocational schools and the university." [79] These are welcome signs of long-term realism replacing the short-term nationalism that characterised the elections of the previous year.

On the international level, Denmark does not have a fully integrated Arctic grand strategy, but progress has been made in the scientific, legal, diplomatic and defence spheres. As mentioned, Denmark dispatched a scientific expedition in the summer of 2012 to collect seismic data in preparation of its claim to the Commission on the Limits of the Continental Shelf before 16 November 2014. The Danish Ministry of Foreign Affairs published the *Kingdom of Denmark Strategy for the Arctic 2011-2020*, a mildly worded document that covers a familiar spectrum of themes in international cooperation and security, sustainable development, environmental protection and maritime security. It is slightly more comprehensive than its Norwegian counterpart, but its tenor is similar and it has a more assertive conclusion. In a brief section on exercising sovereignty the bottom line emerges: while cooperation with the Arctic Ocean's coastal states is close, "there will be continuing need to enforce the Kingdom's sovereignty, especially in light of the anticipated increase in activity in the region." [80]

The *Danish Defence Agreement 2010-2014* white paper specifies several overriding initiatives for the Arctic. The North Atlantic command structure will be streamlined, by bringing Greenland Command and Faroe Command into a single joint service structure, the Arctic Command Headquarters, which was inaugurated on 31 October 2012. In addition, an Arctic Response Force has been established, and an extensive new risk analysis in and around Greenland is being conducted on the future tasks of the armed forces beyond 2014. This analysis is ongoing, and will be finalised by the end of 2014. [81]

Denmark is the smallest Arctic country but is responsible for the largest land mass. A variety of visions has been expressed by Copenhagen and Nuuk, but neither the published Danish Arctic strategy nor the defence agreement provide satisfactory answers for the grand strategic implications of Greenland's resource wealth. It appears, however, that both Copenhagen and Nuuk have woken up to the implications of these matters with prudent assessments and policy concepts, where long-term strategies for investment, resource development and human development are converging

◎ Canada

"The North is part of our identity as a nation and people feel very passionately about it, but very few Canadians have visited the North, because it is so expansive and so remote. So it is an imagined connection, but there isn't necessarily a lot of in-depth knowledge among the Canadian population at large about the specifics of Canada's North. It is a little bit of a paradox." [82]

Canada is the most passionate player in the Arctic and the one country where international policy and strategy are most derived from domestic priorities. These priorities are now focused on the economic and human development of the indigenous peoples of the North. Canada was shocked into action by a 2005 United Nations report on the development of its indigenous peoples, which noted:

Economic, social and human indicators of well-being, quality of life and development are consistently lower among Aboriginal people than other Canadians. Poverty, infant mortality, unemployment, morbidity, suicide, criminal detention, children on welfare, women victims of abuse, child prostitution, are all much higher among Aboriginal people than in any other sector of Canadian society, whereas educational attainment, health standards, housing conditions, family income, access to economic opportunity and to social services are generally lower. [83]

The report added: "Canada has taken up the challenge to close this gap."

Canada's new determination to focus on the human and economic development of the peoples of the North is manifested in its domestic political priorities, as well as the chairmanship of the Arctic Council, in which it has placed human development at the top of the agenda. The process of Canadian deliberation serves to maximise the inclusiveness of all stakeholders. Because the Far North is a very emotive subject for the Canadian people, seasonal political grandstanding for electoral purposes is to be expected. More important, however, is the vision and concept described in Canada's new Northern strategy, which many Canadians we spoke to consider to be an integrated strategy.

Canada is a federation with ten provinces and three Northern Territories: Yukon, Northwest Territories and Nunavut. Out of a population of 33.5 million, a mere 100,000 live in the Northern Territories, the majority of whom are indigenous. Because Canada is not a unitary state, there are always many players involved in each issue, where the federal government departments negotiate with provincial governments, territorial governments, municipalities, native peoples and other stakeholders. With the overall aim to make the North economically self-sufficient, any initiative requires a policy of outreach. This consultative approach is inherent in the country's structure and culture. The Canadian government has made a point of including Northerners as much as possible in the development of the new Northern strategy, and also named the Inuit Minister of the Environment, Leona Aglukkaq, as the representative to the Arctic Council during Canada's chairmanship from 2013 to 2015.

The vision and policy concepts were translated into *Canada's Northern Strategy*, published in 2009, which aims to be an overarching policy framework, to be used as a guideline and umbrella for all government departments, although each department remains accountable to its minister. The colourful trilingual document, written in English, French and Inuit, heralds the four pillars of Canada's Arctic strategy: sovereignty, governance, economic and social development, and environmental protection. Each of these pillars carries equal weight, and international policy derives almost as an afterthought from these domestic priorities. We spoke with members of the Department of Foreign Affairs, the Department of Aboriginal Affairs and the Department of National Defense. How does the strategy translate into their policy processes?

In the Department of Foreign Affairs, Trade and Development, Jeanette Menzies heads the Canadian International Center for the Arctic Region. Her portfolio includes formulating Canada's Arctic foreign policy; bringing coherence to the work by missions and embassies; working on the Arctic Council chairmanship; conducting outreach to foreign embassies in Ottawa; managing a leading role in scientific research; and encouraging business and investment in Canada's North.

The Department for Aboriginal Affairs covers policy towards the three Northern territorial governments of Yukon, Northwest Territories and Nunavut. This geographical area of more than 3.9 million sq km is 40 per cent of Canada's landmass and faces three oceans. In Nunavut the indigenous population is 85 per cent, in the Northwest Territories about 50 per cent and in the Yukon 20 per cent. The overarching policy aim is "development of the North for Northeners" politically, economically and socially, but overcoming the challenges of remoteness and isolation is hard.

There are more than 50 isolated communities in the Northern Territories with around 1,000-2,000 people in each, living in conditions of six months light, six months darkness and -40°C winters. Over 50 per cent of the Northern population is under 25, and they have great potential to connect via new media, both in social media and broadcasting. While economic development is slow, this new connectivity is an important enabling factor. Each of these communities has its infrastructure requirements in housing, schools, hospitals, energy, ports and airfields. The Inuit there have independence in issuing contracts and choosing whom to do business with. And with the consultative approach, the DAA organises large advisory boards with all stakeholders involved in order to coordinate this development at all layers of government, federal, territorial and municipal. It should come as no surprise that the primary theme of Canada's chairmanship of the Arctic Council from 2013-2015 is the 'Development of the Peoples of the North'.[84]

And what about the level of defence? The military and defence mandate derives solely from the government strategy outlined above, and helping to deliver that mandate. Necessity is driving this integrated approach.[85] In 2007, Prime Minister Stephen Harper declared, "'Canada has a choice when it comes to defending our sovereignty in the Arctic. We either use it or lose it. And make no mistake, this government intends to use it."[86] But despite this bellicose language, the military and security presence of Canada's north remains modest, with no more force additions than reinstating a presence that was removed after the Cold War.[87] With a fleet of 15 icebreakers, the Canadian Coast Guard has greater capability of operating in ice than the Royal Canadian Navy, and is called upon to escort an average of four vessels through the ice per day.[88]

On the question of transport and traffic, it is notable how little the Canadian Northwest Passage is discussed as an international strait in any of the policy documents or by the policy practitioners we spoke to. This is in contrast to the emphasis the Russians are placing on the development of the Northern Sea Route. The political class, however, caused a stir in 2009 when a motion was passed in the Canadian House of Commons to rename the Northwest Passage, the Canadian Northwest Passage.[89] This was an effort to 'nationalise' a passage considered an international strait by the US and the EU,[90] but both the move and the reactions to it were largely beside the point. While the sea ice is melting north of Russia, it will not disappear from the Canadian archipelago for a long time to come. While human activity is expected to increase in the North, Canadian civil servants noted to us, "In our analyses the Northwest Passage is probably not going to be open for the next 20 years."[91]

This explains why transport is barely discussed. The question of natural mineral and energy resources is also mentioned very little. While there is recognition that there is going to be an increase in resource-based human activity, the Northern strategy does mention the preparatory scientific research needed for resource exploitation. The government will stimulate this research, but the private sector is expected to take over from there and stimulate employment:

> The Government of Canada announced a significant new geo-mapping effort – Geo-Mapping for energy and minerals – that will combine the latest technology and geoscientific analysis methods to build our understanding of the geology of Canada's North, including in the Canadian Arctic Archipelago. The results of this work will highlight areas of mineral and petroleum potential, lead to more effective private sector exploration investment and create employment opportunities in the North.[92]

In Norway and Russia, energy, fish and mineral resources, and their surrounding logistics and instruments of international cooperation, are all considered central to their Northern strategies. For Canada, international co-operation is peripheral to the domestic considerations of social development. While Canada is developing the Alberta tar sands, it matters little if the buyer is the US or China. Neither of those countries seems interested in resolving the maritime delimitation of the Beaufort Sea, quite possibly because there are no joint exploration agreements in the pipeline for oil and gas. The biggest increase in traffic will be driven by domestic resource development.

As a corollary to the emphasis on domestic priorities, international interest in Canada's Arctic policy also focuses on domestic developments. Sometimes the view from Denmark can be strange, when domestic politics, rather than policy, takes centre stage.

In 2005 Harper's Conservatives put the Arctic at the centre of the election campaign, attacking the Liberals for weakness in their emphasis on diplomacy. They argued that if there is insufficient investment in military hardware, Canadian inherent rights to the Arctic will be challenged by other players. [93] In response, the Liberal defence minister Bill Graham flew to Hans Island, the disputed barren rock between Greenland and Ellesmere Island, and hauled down a Danish flag that had been planted there in 1984 and replaced in 2003. [94] Graham took the flag and delivered it to the Danish Ambassador in Ottawa, stating that a Danish flag had been found on a Canadian island, and would he take it back to Copenhagen and inform the Ministry that Canada would not accept this? The result was a period of diplomatic turmoil. [95] But the stunt was to no avail. The Conservatives won.

Given the emotive importance that the Arctic holds for the general population of Canada, this kind of grandstanding can be expected every five years. Other Arctic states should not worry too much about the double communication between posturing for a domestic audience and the outreach that Canada makes to international partners. The politics is part of the game, but the policy is quite serious.

All in all, Canada has a fairly comprehensive and integrated *domestic* Arctic strategy. It is natural considering the geographical, social and governance structure of the country. It is admirable that Canada has prioritised the geographically challenging task of the development of its indigenous peoples. With its national and international attention focused on this question, it may well be possible to create a meaningful breakthrough to dramatically improve the lives of the peoples of the north. But Canada would benefit if it were also to develop an integrated international strategy with planning that looks further ahead than the next election cycle.

◎ United States of America

Of the Arctic Five, the United States government has been the slowest to move on Arctic affairs. In the very last days of the George W. Bush Administration, the *Arctic Region Policy* was announced on 9 January 2009 as a Presidential Directive,[96] which was reaffirmed by the Obama administration in the National Security Strategy of 2011. This is a policy concept, not a strategy.

The directive enumerates familiar Arctic themes: emphasising the question of sovereignty that the US holds in the Arctic; urging protection of the environment and environmentally sustainable resource management; protecting and involving indigenous communities; and enhancing scientific research. On the legal front, the directive acknowledges the Beaufort Sea dispute with Canada and seeks consultation with the Senate to ratify the UN Convention on the Law of the Sea.

What sets the American view of the Arctic apart from other states is that it is viewed solely as a security and homeland defence challenge. The melting ice opens a back door to the American continent, and this has to be secured. Whereas the Arctic strategies of Norway and Denmark are largely diplomatic pamphlets written by diplomats for international consumption, and Canada has an integrated social development strategy, President Bush's 2009 *Arctic Region Policy* and the Pentagon's 2011 *Report to Congress on Arctic Operations and the Northwest Passage* treat the Arctic solely as a security matter. And if it is only a security challenge, then it competes for attention and money with the Middle East, the South China Sea, Afghanistan and Iraq.[97]

It is therefore very difficult to finance even the modest ambitions that these documents contain. Although Hillary Clinton attended the 2013 Kiruna session of the Arctic Council, the State Department under her and her successor John Kerry did not take any initiatives on the Beaufort Sea dispute or the Law of the Sea. With such little attention and guidance coming from the White House, the Pentagon and the State Department, the US Navy and US Coast Guard chose to develop their own Arctic policies and strategies. Not to be upstaged, the White House and Department of Defense did eventually produce two short Arctic strategy documents of their own.[98]

The US Navy's department of Energy, Environment and Climate Change established the Task Force on Climate Change in 2009. This office, until recently headed by Rear Admiral David Titley, the chief oceanographer and navigator of the US Navy, has carried out the most innovative work on the Arctic in the American government. The TFCC's remit included research on the changing Arctic, rising sea levels, changes in storm patterns, assistance to vulnerable nations and increases in humanitarian assistance and disaster response.[99] In October 2009, the TFCC published the *US Navy Arctic Roadmap*, which provided a comprehensive overview of investments in capabilities the Navy requires, as well as new methods of strategic and operational planning. The roadmap in the document describes three phases of navy action, from assessments to developing capabilities and their implementation. This work was followed up in May 2010 with the publication of the *US Navy Climate Change Roadmap*, which includes a similar phased plan, calling for education on climate change in the Naval War College curriculum and implementation of climate change assessments in training and in strategic and operational planning.[100] Rear Admiral Titley and his successor Rear Admiral Jonathan White, with their staff, have shown valuable leadership in laying the intellectual and organisational foundations for the US Navy's future activities in the Arctic.

In May 2013 the US Coast Guard took the lead and published its *Arctic Strategy*, the only constabulary agency in the world to do so. This is the most comprehensive document produced by the American government, covering its vision, policy concept and long-term strategic objectives, which are defined as improving awareness, modernising governance and broadening partnerships. Each of these objectives is tied to a strategy for long-term success.

In the same month the White House released its first *National Strategy for the Arctic Region*, a rushed 11-page document that aims to be an overarching framework. It describes a set of policy preferences, with an emphasis on security, responsible stewardship and international cooperation. The document lists objectives in a familiar range of areas: energy security, domain awareness, freedom of the seas, environmental conservation, integrated management, and to "increase understanding of the Arctic through scientific research and traditional knowledge."[101] While it states all these goals, the document says very little about how they are to be carried out. Despite its title, the objectives are not tied to clear processes, which are left for other departments to figure out. This document can therefore not be considered a serious strategy.

Six months later, the Department of Defense issued its own first *Arctic Strategy*, another brief document of 14 pages. The Pentagon defines the "desired end-state of the Arctic" as "a secure and stable region where US national interests are safeguarded, the US homeland is protected, and nations work cooperatively to address challenges."[102] In an improvement over the White House, the Pentagon document connects these goals to processes and means to achieve them, including multilateral security collaboration, preparation for a wide range of contingencies, engagement with private and public partners for domain awareness, and support for the Arctic Council. The emphasis of this document is on the exercise of sovereignty and the protection of the homeland.

With this relative inattention from the highest levels of executive authority in the American government, it is not surprising that the US Navy and Coast Guard took the lead in developing their own comprehensive strategies. In the 2011 *Report to Congress on Arctic Operations and the Northwest Passage* – reiterating the *2010 Quadrennial Defense Review* – the Pentagon urged both the development of necessary capabilities and the ratification of the Law of the Sea:

> The QDR highlighted the need for DoD to work collaboratively with interagency partners to address gaps in Arctic communications, domain awareness, search and rescue, and environmental observation and forecasting capabilities to support both current and future planning and operations. It also reiterated DoD's strong support for ac-

cession to the United Nations Convention on the Law of the Sea (LOS Convention) to protect US interests worldwide and to support cooperative engagement in the Arctic. [103]

There is a slightly tragic sense in this report, in which the urgency and need for capabilities is recognised, but the limitations in the present fiscal environment are also acknowledged. The appeal to ratify the Law of the Sea is sensible, but has not moved the Senate to action. If the US fails to ratify the UN Convention on the Law of the Sea in time, it will not have access to the Commission on the Limits of the Continental Shelf (CLCS) to submit its claim before 16 November 2014 (the Danish deadline) despite the fact that the US recognises its guiding principles as international law.

This is an egregious oversight, not least because it was President Truman who first declared US sovereignty over its continental shelf in his Proclamation of 1945, initiating a custom that has matured into an established rule of international customary law. It is remarkable that in a situation where the international legal community, the defence establishment and the White House are all in agreement about the necessity for ratification, the US Senate remains incapable of pulling together 60 senators to overcome the threat of a filibuster. The US has wasted several great opportunities already and risks being left behind in the Far North if the Senate doesn't take the region more seriously very soon.

On the political level, the US is a bystander in the big developments occurring in the region, and has no overall vision for the Arctic. Nonetheless, there have been some important positive moves. When Secretary of State, Hillary Clinton did attend the Arctic Council sessions, and expressed support for its growth and development. The US Navy's Task Force on Climate Change has done the most important intellectual groundwork and policy for the future of the Navy. This is the only part of the US government where an innovative vision, concept, strategy and phased plan are being carried out to a genuine breakthrough transforming the US Navy on the whole spectrum from its curriculum and research to its activities. The US Coast Guard also developed a comprehensive vision, concept and strategy for the long term. At the highest level, however, the two short documents published by the White House and Pentagon reflect their inattention. The Senate's failure to ratify the Convention on the Law of the Sea is the greatest oversight, but it is not necessarily the greatest obstacle for regional governance, which can still be developed on the basis of international law and agreements.

◎ The European Union and NATO

Not to be outdone, a memo from the European Commission cheerfully announced to the European Council and Parliament that the "European Union is inextricably linked to the Arctic region (...) by a unique combination of history, geography, economy and scientific achievements." [104] With Denmark in the inner circle, and Finland and Sweden in the next echelon, the EU is vying for a greater role and a permanent observer seat in the Arctic Council. EU members Finland, Sweden and Denmark are full members of the Arctic Council; and the Netherlands, United Kingdom, Poland, France, Germany and Spain have the status of Permanent Observers. But the EU itself has not yet succeeded in upgrading its status of ad hoc observer. Finland campaigned the strongest on behalf of the EU, and Norway supported the EU's application.[105] Their application was approved at the Kiruna session of the Council in May 2013, but a final decision has been deferred until the EU lifts its seal trade ban.[106] With Canada's Environment Minister Leona Aglukkaq as Arctic Council chair, the EU will be pressed to reverse a policy of immature and emotive environmentalism that has caused great harm to the way of life of the Inuit.

The Arctic holds precious resources for the EU, and the EU in turn is a huge consumer market for Arctic produce. Half of the fish caught in the waters above the Arctic Circle are consumed in the EU, and more than a quarter of Arctic oil and gas flows to the EU. More than €200 million of European funds has been invested in Arctic scientific research. As the world's largest trading bloc and most profitable consumer market in control of 40 per cent of the world's shipping, the EU has a natural interest in securing nondiscriminatory access through the Northern Sea Route and the Canadian Northwest Passage, when it opens. But while Canada is decisively turning east in its trade orientation, the EU has yet to secure its strategic interests.

The NATO alliance has also taken note of the security requirements for the Arctic. In January 2009, Secretary General Jaap de Hoop Scheffer convened a NATO seminar on the Far North in Iceland. He spoke about the importance of securing new routes of Arctic navigation, and also the development of adequate disaster relief capabilities. Concerning natural resources, he envisaged five areas of NATO involvement in energy security: "Information and intelligence fusion; projecting stability; advancing international and regional cooperation; supporting consequence management; and supporting the protection of critical infrastructure." And finally, he took note of territorial claims, the UN Convention on the Law of the Sea, Exclusive Economic Zones and continental shelf claims. In all these areas, he noted that the NATO-Russia Council could play a role, both on the political level, and on the operational level for coordination of search and rescue, and disaster relief operations. All in all, he noted that there are many opportunities for NATO to play an active role, but the approach was decidedly modest, referring only to making use of existing mechanisms. NATO's low-key approach to the Arctic was continued by his successor as Secretary General, Anders Fogh Rasmussen.

The Russians will not accept any role for NATO in the Arctic. As the dominant Arctic power, inviting a greater power in would have a destabilising effect. Given that the entire Arctic Circle from Alaska to Norway is already covered by Article 5 of the North Atlantic Treaty (whereby an attack on a NATO member state is considered an attack on all members), it is not necessary to cause unnecessary confrontation. NATO members, without a NATO flag, participate in the Arctic ChoDs meetings and Coast Guard forums, and NATO members should conduct ad hoc exercises and operations in a manner that could strengthen Norway without antagonising Russia. But without a solid institutional basis, it will be very difficult to elevate the Arctic ChoDs meetings to a genuine concept of regional security architecture.

◎ China

China is the fastest-growing great power in the world, and as the world's greatest exporter of goods 50 per cent of its GDP is related to shipping. China has a great economic and strategic interest in the Far North, both for access to natural resources and trade routes. Not only does the Northern Sea Route over Russia to Rotterdam mean a 40 per cent distance and fuel reduction, but the very possibility of an alternative route could greatly increase China's freedom of action. At the moment, the passage west through the Malacca Strait is a bottleneck that can easily be corked by an American carrier battle group in time of dispute.[107] The Bering Strait could become a strategic chokepoint between the three great powers.

China stands to gain the most from both the Northern Sea Route and the Northwest Passage, and is making generous overtures to Nordic countries and Canada with these interests in mind. China attempted to buy a large swathe of Iceland's territory, but was rebuffed. In Norway, China has invested heavily in Elkan, an electrochemical conglomerate. And China has recently shown interest in the Greenlandic rare earths, bidding alongside two Australian companies, Tanbreez and Greenland Mineral and Energy. What the Far North has not yet seen from China, however, is systematic buying of entire industries.

With about $4,000 billion in foreign currency reserves, of which approximately $3,000 billion is available for shopping around, there is no reason to believe that China may not decide at some point to engage in systematic acquisitions in the Far North.[108] Chinese investment tends to be more risk-averse in that it seeks out common stock of companies that are already publicly traded and scrutinised by markets and regulatory bodies. In its investment strategy, China does not appear to be venturing to explore and create new industries and markets.

China does appear to have a grand, if as yet unpublished, strategy for the region: there is clearly a long-term commercial strategy with the development of a substantial icebreaker fleet; and there is Chinese investment and integration into the scientific community.[109]

There is also a concerted diplomatic strategy, reaching out to Iceland, Greenland and others. The Chinese are connecting to far corners, such as the Norwegian ice-free port of Narvik, in order to develop an overland rail connection, for shipping to the American East Coast. These elements taken together reveal a grand strategic approach without a military component. China also sought to achieve permanent observer status at the Arctic Council in 2008; the application was approved in the Kiruna session of May 2013.

All in all, China is the wild card in the equation, but it seeks to secure its interests in a non-confrontational manner. With the prospect of Chinese shipping creating a situation in the Bering Strait where Russia is on one side, the United States on the other, and China in between, stability in the region will depend on the relations between the three great powers. While there is very little risk that the Arctic itself would become the source of tension, it is not unthinkable that a standoff caused in another part of the world, such as the South China Sea, Taiwan or the Senkaku Islands, could lead to retaliation in the Arctic. The effect of connecting China through the Far North to the West means that the polar region will be exposed to the potential risks and dangers that surround China's ambitions in Asia's warmer waters.

EVALUATION

We have considered the large-scale natural trends and a range of international and national initiatives that seek to catch up with innovations to adapt to a breakthrough process driven by nature. We can see that the natural breakthrough has spurred processes at the international and national levels. The Far North is a moving target and in recent years there has been a large number of new publications, policy statements and strategy documents by national and international actors. The Arctic reveals surprising cooperation between rivals, and at times an equally surprising lack of cooperation within governments and among allies.

The race for resources and access is ongoing, but we do not see the hostile competition of the time when Spitsbergen was *terra nullius*. While there is good reason to believe there will be no open conflict, it remains an open question as to whether capabilities will be matched to requirements in safety and security, and whether some countries will fail to grasp the opportunities available to them.

Despite many positive developments, we should not forget that the situation today is still far from desirable. There are still great shortcomings in technology, access, logistics, communications, governance and scientific knowledge about environmental trends, both in climate and in the resilience of ecosystems.[110] There is also a lack of high-detail geographical data publicly available. This sort of proprietary research is privately held by energy and shipping companies, but without a wider availability there is a greater risk of cruise ships running into trouble, or running aground as happened in 2010.[111]

The Arctic Council is an important success story, and a part of this success was its relative unimportance in the early years since 1996. Bernard Funston, the Chairman of the Canadian Polar Commission who has been a part of the first 16 years of the Arctic Council's evolution, noted that "its weakness was its strength. It was non-threatening. It was consensus. It required people to get along. Issues percolated."

In the first decade, the Arctic Council operated below the radar and worked on developing scientific expertise and a series of very important assessments. Today with the greater interest in the Arctic Council, the policy community is taking over, and the centre of gravity has shifted from science to national interests. [112] Nonetheless, the Arctic Council admits new members on the basis of what they bring to the table, and this is often measured by their scientific contributions.

The Arctic is a complex mechanism and efforts are being made to synchronise its many components to create a new and stable future. We have seen that the stabilising factors which lead to greater cooperation have been economic interests. Another important stabilising factor is that all parties recognise that they cannot meet the responsibilities they have for security and safety on their own, and they are working to cooperate. The informal Arctic ChoDs dialogue, while not a part of the Artic Council, is very much its offspring.

CONCLUSION

The Arctic region is in the midst of a natural breakthrough process to an ice-free future, in which great economic development and political cooperation are possible. It is an excellent example for the purposes of our book of an ongoing breakthrough process, but unlike other chapters, this breakthrough is in the near future.

These changes create a new environmental balance and new levels of human access. This access, in turn, creates opportunities for business, economic and human development. On the national and international level, we can identify visions, policy concepts, strategies and plans for implementation. We can identify innovative new mechanisms and cooperation in logistics, markets, safety and security. This natural breakthrough process at the macro level is leading to human breakthroughs at the international level, which in turn are driving breakthroughs at national levels. Which of the process elements are the *most* decisive? It appears to be the international vision.

◎ The international and national visions

The most decisive human responses to macro-level environmental change are the international declarations that have expressed a large-scale vision. The international visions expressed in the Ottawa Declaration, Ilulissat Declaration and Kiruna Vision for the Arctic affirmed a number of key principles that are reflected in all national policies and strategies.

The Ilulissat Declaration is an expression of an international legal vision, which pointed to an existing international concept that declared the law of the sea the 'constitution' for the Arctic region. No new treaties were needed, and the innovation of this brilliant and simple declaration was not to innovate, but to settle the most important questions of international law and legitimacy at a stroke. This opened the door to moving forward on all other dealings in the region. At the international legal level, we therefore had a clear progression from vision to overall legal concept.

With the vision of the Ottawa Declaration, which established the Arctic Council in 1996, we similarly see a transition from vision to a concept of cooperation on a range of issues in development, scientific research and environmental protection. The Council has also succeeded in developing two binding safety agreements for search-and-rescue and oil-spill prevention.

These two visions do not, however, form a basis for comprehensive concepts of a regional governance structure or regional security architecture. The law of the sea is limited to the sea, and the Arctic Council explicitly excludes matters of military security and cannot host its own military staff committee. These international visions can therefore not be translated to comprehensive concepts and strategies at the international level. Governance and security matters have therefore been devolved to the national level, which is largely positive but also fragmentary.

The ad-hoc 'Arctic ChoDs' round table was created out of the necessity to develop the capabilities and cooperation needed to meet the obligations of the Arctic Council's safety agreements. In that respect, this dialogue is also a breakthrough that is forcing innovation to develop integrated and allied mechanisms and strategies. The shared recognition that no nation can handle the responsibilities and challenges alone is driving cooperation, and this too is an important breakthrough. Nonetheless, without a solid institutional basis, it will not be possible for international visions to develop into genuine concepts and a strategy for regional governance and security.

The national levels that we discussed at length are separately moving parts that differ in emphasis and strategic priority. Among all the participants, we can see the process flow of international visions into national policy concepts and strategies. The international visions are therefore the most decisive of the process elements at all levels. At the national level, the international visions mixed with domestic priorities to create a diverse set of concepts – some of which are more comprehensive than others.

But if we want to see an international vision for governance and security of the Arctic translated into genuine international concepts and strategies, then leadership and innovation at the highest level will be needed.

◎ Leadership

For the Arctic Council to become a genuine intergovernmental organisation, rather than merely a high-level talking shop, a new kind of Arctic Treaty would be needed. It would transform the organisation into one with a structure modelled on a regional group like the European Union, with an executive authority, a military staff committee, and other departments covering a broad spectrum of activity. But such a daring international move is beyond what is achievable today, and could upset the existing equilibrium. For a meaningful and genuine international breakthrough, innovative and courageous leadership would be needed – a leadership that can inspire a large-scale vision for a large number of people. It requires leadership to articulate a vision for the future that can inspire change. It takes leadership to see beyond what is being done to what might be possible.

The breakthrough driven by nature is forcing human innovations and breakthroughs. These national movements, with breakthroughs at national or subnational levels, are collectively driving breakthroughs at the macro level, to an outcome that will be more than the sum of its parts. The natural breakthrough is creating a new regional and strategic balance, and with varying levels of urgency a flurry of smaller innovations and breakthrough processes, ranging from ministries to national governments to international organisations. On the whole, these developments are very promising.

But what we have not yet seen is an inspirational leader like President John F. Kennedy, who articulated a large-scale vision, inspiring and challenging his nation to innovate in order to accomplish a seemingly impossible task within a decade.

> But why, some say, the moon? Why choose this as our goal? And they may well ask why climb the highest mountain? (...) We choose to go to the moon. We choose to go to the moon in this decade and do the other things, not because they are easy, but because they are hard, because that goal will serve to organise and measure the best of our energies and skills, because that challenge is one that we are willing to accept, one we are unwilling to postpone, and one which we intend to win. [113]

After Kennedy's speech, industries were mobilised, and innovations sprang up in textiles, metals, plastics, aviation and many other areas. An entire generation was inspired to take up science, with global benefits that have reached into every industry and field of science, and endure to this day. The discoveries of science can lead to policy outcomes, but genuine leadership inspiring innovation can be more enduring. If a great leader emerged and challenged his nation to innovate on a large scale, the impact could last deep into the century. Will a leader emerge in the coming decade to inspire us to innovate in the same way in the Arctic?

CHAPTER 5

EUROPE'S ENERGY IMPASSE

Energy is the cornerstone of daily life and industrial activity. Industrial development has always been based on proximity and access to energy sources: Britain's Industrial Revolution was driven by coal, while China's industrialisation was kicked off by the availability of hydrocarbons in the Daquing region. Today, Western economies and China are both dependent on energy imported from countries with unstable regimes. To prevent such dependence, France developed its own nuclear energy, which today supplies most of its domestic and industrial electricity. But Europe as a whole, and France in particular, may be overtaken by circumstances and events leading to an energy impasse. The explosion of demand, awareness of climate risk and emissions targets, the US shale gas revolution, the impact of the Japanese tsunami and the Fukushima disaster and the impact of the global financial crisis have all contributed to political division and indecision across Europe. The only way forward is by technological innovation and commitment to research and development. The author considers the role of smart grids, electricity storage, offshore wind, CO_2 recycling, carbon capture and storage technology and hydrogen technology in overcoming this impasse.

THE QUALITATIVE ANALYSIS FOR THIS CHAPTER
IS ON PAGE 381 OF THE ANNEX

FRANÇOIS CHABANNES
WITH THE ASSISTANCE OF JACQUES LANXADE

INTRODUCTION

Energy is not a product or activity like any other. Energy acts as a cornerstone of national economies. The control of energy determines an economy's efficiency.

Since prehistoric times, humans have had unrestricted access to abundant free energy from the sun, wind, water, etc. Those who first understood this potential innovated and gradually came to control their environments, their prey, their predators and their fellow humans. First it was fire, through burning wood in the oxygen provided by air, which gave people access to cooked food, heating, light and safety. In the ashes of their fireplaces, they discovered metals from which they forged weapons and tools.

Then, after several millennia, chemical energy was developed from powders, propulsives and explosives. Those who first mastered these techniques constructed firearms and artillery, sweeping away the equilibrium of belligerents in Europe and destroying empires in America. Then came the discovery of thermodynamics, transforming the power of fire into mechanical energy. Over the last two centuries, coal used to power steam engines and hydrocarbons used to fuel combustion engines have played a decisive role in global confrontations between nations by determining the mobility of their armed forces. Finally, just a matter of decades ago, humans discovered nuclear energy, embraced nuclear deterrence, mastered light energy from lasers and discovered the infinitely small quantum where mass and energy are one and the same.

In order to master energy, you have to have the means to deliver it. When the Industrial Revolution started at the end of the 18th century, Britain's carbon resources in the form of coal were of the same order as Saudi Arabia's oil reserves discovered in the mid-20th century. Carbon was the means of conveying energy that made Britain great and allowed it (temporarily) to dominate the world. Its coal resources would start to decline by 1918 together with its political power. It was only in 2000 that the United Kingdom rediscovered energy from oil and gas in the North Sea, which by 2014 was again heading towards depletion.

Comparable analyses can be conducted for other countries in Europe, in particular France and Germany, and also extended to the United States and the Soviet Union. By the end of 1945 the latter two nations were the largest oil producers in the world. They managed to bring Germany and Japan to their knees by blocking access to oil reserves (in the Caucasus and Indonesia) that were vital to their war efforts. The US's progress in this respect is particularly significant. In 1945, aware of having started to exhaust domestic reserves (in Texas) by supplying US armed forces deployed virtually all around the world, President Franklin D. Roosevelt signed a global agreement with King Ibn Saud of Saudi Arabia on the way home from Yalta.

Since that time, the US's dependence on its oil suppliers from the Middle

East and OPEC has continued to grow and requires an enormous permanent military commitment in the Middle East to secure its supply. The two Gulf Wars, in Kuwait and Iraq, are an illustration of this. The vast US debt, a consequence of an annual deficit that is practically the same as the country's military expenditure, has resulted in a dramatic loss of competitiveness when compared to emerging economies. We will consider below how the shale gas revolution, starting in the early 2000s, will probably quickly re-establish the US as the number one oil and gas producer in the world, becoming an exporter while other developed and emerging countries will still be major importers over the coming decade at increasingly high prices. Once again, geopolitics will be turned upside down by energy. In particular, why would the US, which has played a policing role in the Gulf for some sixty years, maintain its powerful but costly military deployment in the Middle East if it is no longer directly involved, unlike Europe and Asia?

The example of China is also just as instructive. The discovery of huge hydrocarbon reserves in the Daqing region in 1959, some 16 billion barrels, allowed China to launch its extraordinary industrial development. But the Daqing reserves, from which 11 billion barrels have already been extracted, had entered into decline by 2007. As was the case with the US, China is now dependent on the Middle East for over half of its oil consumption (9.4 million barrels/day). However, also similar to the US, China has enormous reserves of shale hydrocarbons (3,600 trillion cubic metres), ahead of the USA (24,000), Canada (11,000) and France (5,200).

One can see from these examples that countries, or more precisely economic entities, that benefit from abundant cheap energy, can develop. A lack of energy leads to recession and conflict.

It was this logic that led France, in reaction to the first oil shock of 1973, to devote itself to building up its nuclear generating capacity, ultimately accounting for three-quarters of its electricity needs with the remainder coming from hydroelectric generation. This has allowed France to reduce its dependence on oil and coal, energy sources that were threatening to strangle French economic development, to a minimum. It is this abundant electricity supply that has allowed France to pursue considerable development of industries that have high energy requirements (such as cement and aluminium). But France has remained largely isolated in its initiative. By the end of the 20th century, at the beginning of the major transformations which we will now describe, the majority of global energy came from the fossil resources coal, oil and gas (85 per cent), and the majority of developed countries are highly dependent (UK 90 per cent) on foreign, often politically unstable, suppliers (Iraq, Iran, Libya, Venezuela, etc)

However in the space of a decade, the situation has fundamentally changed, with Europe, and France in particular, letting itself be overtaken by new circumstances. Nevertheless, technological breakthroughs have the potential to offer an escape from this situation.

2000-2013: THE TURNING POINT FOR GLOBAL ENERGY

◎ 2000-2013: The explosion in demand

In 2000, the global population was 6 billion, rising to 7 billion by 2012. The forecast population for 2025 is 8 billion, a figure that is predicted to rise to 9 billion by 2050. In 2013, some 1.4 billion people, in other words 20 per cent of the world population, still did not have access to electricity, while 3 billion people depended on wood and coal as their main fuel. Globally, humanity's requirement for primary energy may increase from 13 Gtoe [billion tonnes of oil equivalent] to between 26 and 36 Gtoe in 2025.

Furthermore, the lightning development of information technologies has made access to electricity a need that is perceived as a priority, ahead of issues that are perhaps more pressing for daily life. The digital economy consumed some 10 per cent of global electricity in 2013. Decentralised approaches using renewable local sources of energy are appearing but remain limited. These may offer a solution for Africa.

◎ 1995-2013: The realisation of climate risk

The greenhouse effect caused by the unrestricted release of CO_2 and other greenhouse gases into the atmosphere from the combustion of fossil energy in the form of coal, oil and gas has been clearly identified since the turn of the century. Between 1800 and 2000, the level of CO_2 in the atmosphere rose from 280 to 360 ppm (parts per million). It is now 400 ppm (May 2013) and this level will continue to rise as a result of the massive global consumption of coal (in Europe, particularly in Germany).

It should be recalled that humanity emits approximately 30 gigatonnes of CO_2 a year, of which 15 Gt can be absorbed by the environment (by forests and oceans) and 15 Gt is added to the 1,500 Gt already produced by humans since the Industrial Revolution.

In 1995, the United Nations (163 countries) launched a vast negotiation procedure at Kyoto, with a protocol eventually being signed in 2005. The overall objective was, between 2008 and 2012, to reduce the emissions of greenhouse gases (CO_2, CH_2, NO_2, etc) of all industrialised countries by 5.2 per cent in relation to 1990 levels.

During the long and complicated negotiations, three major blocks of international consensus formed. One was led by the European Union, driven by renewable energy lobbies and environmental NGOs who identified the absolute priority as ceasing CO_2 emissions in the shortest time possible. Another, led by the US, considered that the commitments by major emerging countries, and China in particular, were insufficient as they were the main emitters of greenhouse gases. The US signed the protocol but the US Congress did not ratify it.

The third group, bringing together major emerging countries, recognised the urgency of the climate situation but ascribed historical liability to Western countries. They wanted to maintain their priority for economic development which required the massive consumption of fossil energy in the short term. They undertook to launch ambitious programmes for low-carbon energy in the medium term, in particular nuclear generation, an option they described as renewable energy.

In 2014, nearly twenty years later, it can be said that the intense and interminable negotiations of Kyoto did at least result in the reality of global warming as a result of human activity being very widely accepted. The negotiations also identified the need to economise on the use of exhaustible resources that belong to the whole of humanity and not just to current generations.

◉ 2000-2013: The shale hydrocarbon revolution in the USA

Traumatised by the attacks of 11 September 2001, President George W. Bush's US, after having launched a punitive offensive in Afghanistan, invaded Saddam Hussein's Iraq (March 2003) as a preventative war against supposed weapons of mass destruction. It was in fact a conquest that had the strong scent of petroleum (and Texas) about it, the objective appearing to many to be the securing of energy supplies for an American economy that had become increasingly dependent on a hostile Middle East.

It was around this time, from 2000, that small and medium-sized US drilling companies began exploring the possibility of extracting gas and oil held in impermeable bedrock. This development particularly sparked interest because, in geological terms, oil is most frequently held in impermeable bedrock. Alluvium containing organic material slowly sinks into the Earth's crust under the weight of subsequent layers and ultimately, at a depth of 1,500 metres, the pressure and temperature conditions are such that the organic material is transformed into kerogens and then into hydrocarbons. If the surrounding alluvium, known as the bedrock, is impermeable, the gas and oil remain trapped and fracturing would be required for extraction. If, on the contrary, the bedrock is permeable, the hydrocarbons, being lighter than water, escape their bedrock and migrate towards the surface. They are then trapped in natural geological reservoirs and can be extracted using contemporary conventional techniques.

This means that as impermeable bedrock is more common than permeable, much larger amounts of hydrocarbons can be released if efficient *in situ* fracturing can be conducted.

Although they were not originally developed for shale hydrocarbons, the oil industry has separately mastered two relevant key technologies. The first is directional drilling that was developed from offshore technology, allowing horizontal drilling through alluvial layers that have not been inclined by tectonics. The second is hydraulic fracturing, which was used for several decades to extract remaining petroleum resources from conventional wells reaching depletion. The breakthrough innovation has been to combine these two technologies that have been used for decades to fracture and then extract hydrocarbons from impermeable bedrock.

The pioneers of shale gas extraction very quickly discovered huge reserves (in Texas, Pennsylvania, Ohio, Alabama, Wyoming and Colorado). However, these pioneers have often been far from exemplary in terms of their respect for the environment and have given rise to a wave of "green" condemnation that portrays shale extraction as using huge amounts of water while presenting a major risk to groundwater. In the US, these pioneer companies were quickly acquired or eliminated by much more powerful and influential drilling companies. Production became considerable from 2005: 5 million barrels/day in 2008, 6.2 million in 2009. The US is now self-sufficient in natural gas, and prices are a third of those in Europe. The US is set to regain its position as the world's largest oil producer by 2017, a position it held a century ago.

Beyond the figures, the essential fact is that the US has rediscovered abundant cheap energy. The competitiveness of US industry has improved in comparison with emerging nations, and in particular with regard to its main rival China, whose export economy is closely linked to oil.

◎ Fukushima disaster

On 11 March 2011, a massive magnitude 9 earthquake hit north-eastern Japan. It was the most powerful earthquake ever recorded in the country. The epicentre lay in the sea some 300 kilometres off the coast. The consequent tsunami arrived at the coast about an hour later. The tsunami wave reached 30-40 m in places and ravaged nearly 600 km of coast as far as 10 km inland, devastating many towns and port areas. As the warning had been given 54 minutes earlier, much of the population managed to take refuge at high points. Nevertheless, 18,500 people were killed or went missing and approximately 100,000 were injured.

In contrast, the earthquake itself caused only minimal damage to infrastructure and buildings, in particular in Tokyo, which largely stood up to the tremors although buildings were tested to the limits of their anti-seismic capacities. In particular, 18 nuclear power stations and their 54 reactors all shut down at the time of the earthquake with reactor core control rods deployed to stop chain reactions.

However, the tsunami flooded the Fukushima power plant. The tsunami wave exceeded 15 m in height while the protective barrier was only 6 m high and designed to withstand earthquakes of magnitude 8. The equipment designed to cool the four reactors in operation (out of a total of six), after the automatic shutdown when the earthquake hit, was swamped as well as the emergency diesel units. As the cooling of the nuclear cores failed, temperatures exceeded the limits beyond which fuel pellets fuse. Fires and explosions of the hydrogen released by superheated water devastated installations that had been commissioned in 1970-74 from designs dating back to the 1960s.

The details of the tenacious battle by the authorities and the Japanese people to control the situation, with the evacuation of an area of 20 km radius around the power plant, have been the subject of many accounts and analyses. Crucially, favourable winds blew the radioactive cloud that formed after the explosions over the Pacific Ocean instead of over the land mass and possibly Tokyo.

In technical, industrial and environmental terms, the main lessons have now been drawn from Fukushima and its impact on the Japanese economy has been assessed. However, the effort to stem the infiltration of radioactive water and decontaminate soils continues.

As usual in the case of nuclear issues, arguments have raged between those who want to consider Fukushima a global catastrophe that should conclusively condemn nuclear power and those who see the accident certainly as a major incident, but who wish to put things in perspective in view of the human drama of a Japan that has once more suffered an extremely violent seismic event but which, overall, has dealt with it effectively. Beyond the arguments, we should simply focus on the facts.

Fukushima showed that nuclear installations must be protected against all adverse events, even if "totally improbable" such as a magnitude 9 earthquake. Consequently, in the current industry, "hard core" facilities must guarantee the evacuation of the residual energy of an affected reactor in all circumstances. Alternatively, the sector must change and adopt reactors that extinguish themselves naturally if temperatures rise. This technology exists.

Fukushima has shaken up nuclear policy in Europe alone, even though detailed safety analyses have been conducted all around the world. In the USA the Nuclear Regulatory Commission (NRC), the regulatory authority, gave the green light after Fukushima to the construction of two new reactors for the first time since 1978, the date of Three Mile Island. India, China and Russia conducted additional safety evaluations but relaunched their programmes, with China intensifying development. In Europe, Fukushima has been the subject of powerful media and political/ideological campaigns orchestrated by green lobbyists to make the incident a "Chernobyl II", with the result that without any consultation at European Union level, Germany, Italy, Belgium and Switzerland quickly announced that they were abandoning their nuclear programmes.

France displayed indecisiveness, maintaining its EPR programme while announcing the closure of the Fessenheim reactor and the reduction of its generation of electricity through nuclear means from 70 per cent to 50 per cent by 2030. Only the United Kingdom remained steady, with a diversified energy mix including nuclear and large offshore wind farms. Fukushima appears to have thrown light on the divide in Europe on the role of nuclear power in its energy future.

◎ 2000-2008: Upsurge in intermittent renewable energy (IRE)

With the momentum of Kyoto, started in 1995 and signed in 2005, and against the background of a global consensus in the fight against greenhouse gases, IRE suddenly appeared on the scene around 2000 as the major weapon against climate change. Systems of subsidies for IRE were established in most developed countries from 2000, featuring advantageous purchase tariffs, financed by the consumer, and accompanied by priority access to distribution grids and investment aid.

Rather belatedly (2008), the European Union adopted an action plan known as the "Climate and Energy Package" that set "20-20-20" targets for common European energy policy by 2020 by raising the share of renewable energy in the European energy mix to 20 per cent; by reducing CO_2 emissions in EU countries by 20 per cent; and by improving energy efficiency by 20 per cent.

Germany appeared as the champion of IRE during this decade. The country tripled the contribution of IRE to its electricity consumption in just a few years. It established a photovoltaic solar power industry that developed rapidly (Qcells, Solarwatt, Siemens), employing 125,000 people by 2008. Wind power also took off: in the space of a few years, 19,000 wind turbines have been constructed to provide generation capacity of 23 GW. A solid export industry has been established (Enercon, Nordex, Ostwind, Repower) that had captured 50 per cent of the global market by 2007.

The US wind power industry, also benefiting from subsidies, developed rapidly in this period. In 2013, the US was the country producing most energy from wind power, installing 35.3 GW that year (with a cumulative capacity of 318.1 GW), and is projected to reach 64 GW annual installed capacity by the end of 2018, with a cumulative capacity of nearly 600 GW. The industry is led by General Electric Energy, an exporter and leader of some 15 good-sized companies. Although the feed-in tariff offered is only some 20 per cent of the French tariff, tax breaks in favour of wind power have been effective in promoting the development of this industry, although it remains vulnerable as a result.

China has come late to this sector, but has mobilised its considerable resources with a view to creating an export industry. It was still far behind the US and Europe in both the wind and solar power sectors (6 GW) in 2008 but had already launched its solar panels and wind turbines onto the global market. Its practice of export dumping has started to destabilise Western production centres, but its household equipment objectives will ultimately also make it the leading global market.

In France between 2000 and 2008, it was a case of "more haste, less speed" behind the shelter of its nuclear programme, which supplies some 70 per cent of the country's electricity without producing CO_2, giving it the leading position in Europe in terms of carbon cleanliness. It does not have any land-based wind industry. Its solar power industry (Photowatt) has not taken off at all. As for the British, similar to the Danes in turning their attention to the sea, they have favoured offshore wind generation in a very varied energy mix. However, by 2008, the country only had a limited IRE capacity.

◎ 2008: The financial crisis: impact on European energy

The American bank Lehman Brothers was declared bankrupt on 15 September 2008 and the US authorities decided not to rescue it. Stock market prices tumbled. Interbank credit dried up. Central banks had to inject massive amounts of liquidity to avoid meltdown.

In Europe, in the earlier credit crisis, the ECB had to refinance banks and released over €200 billion in a single week in August 2007. After the Lehman collapse, European states introduced measures to avoid panic by savers and were obliged to assist their banks by recapitalising them. Dexia was temporarily saved by funding of €6.4 billion from France, Belgium and Luxembourg. Germany injected €50 billion to save one of its biggest banks, and the United Kingdom announced a rescue package of £50 billion for its banking sector. In the US, the House of Representatives passed a $700 billion rescue package. These actions restored confidence but did not have the effect of relaunching economic activity.

One consequence was that Europe reduced its subsidies to renewable energy. The bubble of the green economy, generously subsidised from 2000-2008, deflated at the end of 2008. The German photovoltaic industry, also under attack from Chinese overproduction, was devastated. In Europe, where solar electricity cost up to ten times the price of fossil fuel energy, the bankruptcies mounted up. It was only in 2010 that the EU decided to inject €4 billion into new energy, of which €1 billion went into smart grids. In the intervening time, investment in IRE had been reduced by half. Growth only returned in 2011, and at a slow pace. Meanwhile, CO_2 emissions had started to rise once again.

During the crisis, Asia increased its investment in energy capacity in all sectors—nuclear, renewable and fossil—and rapidly caught up with Europe and the US in terms of capacity. China has even overtaken the US in wind power and India is close to Europe in terms of nuclear generation.

EUROPE FACING AN ENERGY IMPASSE

Despite fifteen years of effort, Europe remains profoundly dependent on fossil fuels, oil and gas in particular. Every year it spends 500 billion euros importing hydrocarbons. This dependence has recently been heightened by the decision of six countries to renounce nuclear power. This has had the immediate effect of Germany increasing its coal imports, in particular from the US where there is a surplus due to the boom in shale gas.

Europe does not seem to acknowledge that not only is its population among the most densely packed in terms of the number of people per square kilometre, but it also has the highest energy consumption in terms of KWh per person. The German dream of meeting 100 per cent of its energy requirements from intermittent renewables (IRE) cannot be achieved on its territory which is too confined and too densely populated. Beyond its lack of space, Europe also does not seem to be aware of the cost of the intermittent nature of IRE, which requires colossal investment in transport and distribution networks (smart grids) and the storage of electricity in order to satisfy peak user demand.

As a result, unless it chooses an energy mix using the currently available technology, associating spatially hyper-dense nuclear power plants with low-carbon intermittent renewable energy spread out over large sites, Europe is condemned to dependence on fossil fuel and pollution from greenhouse gases. But beyond environmental considerations, the European energy impasse is basically political and economic in nature. While the US will have abundant cheap oil and gas available in the short term and China, India and Brazil will have optimised energy mixes ranging from nuclear to wind power, how can Europe, mired in a battle between the climate and technology lobbies, hope to remain globally competitive?

Without a return to an energy mix incorporating balance and common sense that alongside the use of IRE embraces the risk of nuclear power and the opportunity of shale hydrocarbons, and is reasonably compatible with environmental concerns, Europe is condemned to a deindustrialisation that will not even leave it with the resources to subsidise the intermittent renewable energy that would be its root cause.

◎ France's indecision

Although it has a well-developed nuclear sector, France has destroyed its export credibility in this industry by revealing the uncertainty of its political commitment to this source of energy to the whole world. How can exports be made under these conditions when it is clear that in the nuclear sector partnerships between suppliers and clients must be able to be guaranteed for at least a decade? And how can it do without an export industry which represents, together with aeronautics and luxury goods, one of France's last chances to restore its balance of payments, in a country in the throes of full deindustrialisation and which is being bled white by fossil energy imports to the extent of €70 billion a year?

Furthermore, in order to develop IRE and offshore wind power in particular—the only approach that offers the enormous space required—production must be subsidised while the sector is still uncompetitive and very heavy investment made in infrastructure to adapt networks to the unpredictability of generation (smart grids). France's financial situation may very soon prevent it from being able to do this.

CAN TECHNOLOGICAL BREAKTHROUGHS RESOLVE EUROPE'S ENERGY IMPASSE?

Intermittent renewable energy (IRE: wind and solar power) is different from permanent renewables (hydroelectricity, biomass, geothermal, etc). In addition to being unpredictable, IRE is limited in Europe by its poor spatial-temporal density (wind power: 2.5 W/m^2 for 2,000 h/year; solar PV: 5 W/m^2 for 1,000 h). Western Europe does not have the available space nor the wind or sun necessary to produce an essential part of its energy requirements from IRE.

Without state subsidies, IRE is not competitive. The solar power bubble burst when initial subsidies declined. Wind power may follow a similar path, in particular in European countries affected by the ongoing severe budgetary crisis (Spain, Italy, France, etc). Although supported politically by parties with green credentials, IRE facilities are often violently opposed locally by environmental groups who accuse them of ruining the landscape.

While given priority, the "forcing" of IRE is not always welcomed by the current distribution grids that favour demand over supply. Any halting of fossil fuel or nuclear generation to give priority to "green" supplies entails an increase in the hourly cost of electricity and substantial line losses.

◎ Intelligent networks (smart grids)

Traditional electricity transport and distribution grids are optimised to respond to demand by immediately adapting to preserve the network's stability.

The major innovation of smart grids consists in acting on demand to stabilise it (intelligent meters, off-peak) as well as, in particular, on generation to optimise it by integrating the random nature of IRE with the variable reactivity of energy sources used to compensate for it (nuclear is slower than gas and hydroelectric power plants).

Although the productivity of photovoltaic solar power is relatively easy to anticipate, with uncertainty limited to the intensity rather than the timing, location or duration of generation, it is not the same for wind power. Wind speed, even if supposedly well-established, experiences considerable random fluctuations that are difficult to predict even over the very short term (<1 hour).

Smart grids that integrate wind power generation must thus have access to continuous forecasts of fluctuations and the impact of these on each turbine's production capacity. This involves the manager of each wind farm accurately adjusting the modelling of that wind farm's production to local weather conditions. This new approach involves a great many parameters such as the energy production differential between wind turbines according to their position within the wind farm and the direction of the wind (shelter effect), resulting in fluctuations in electricity generation, load drop-outs and out-of-service equipment. The introduction of wind power into a smart grid thus requires a considerable amount of data to be provided in real time.

The models currently used to simulate airflows in wind farms are unsatisfactory because they do not take into account the possibility of turbulent gusts of wind and resonance. The prediction of these factors is required to allow the speedy disconnection of wind turbines at risk in order to ensure safety and avoid dangerous fluctuations of voltage.

New modelling combining probability and fractal mathematics is being developed and will profoundly change current grids by improving their global efficiency, in particular in terms of CO_2 emissions, but will also greatly increase costs. Considerable investment in digital sensors, processing equipment and developing hypercomplex software is required and may take up to ten years before being fully operational. The development of smart grids is one of the conditions necessary if the progress of intermittent renewable energy is to meet a substantial proportion (maybe 30-40 per cent) of electricity generation in Europe (and perhaps globally).

◎ Electricity storage

IRE poses the acute problem of how to store electricity on a large scale. The unpredictable peaks and troughs of wind power, and to a lesser extent the maximum generation of photovoltaic units, occur several hours before peak demand at the end of the day. This makes it necessary to store electricity from IRE generation in order to supply it to meet demand. The stability of grids and their productivity depends directly on this factor. The only technique for storing electricity on a large scale that has currently reached maturity is pump storage. Water is pumped to an elevated reservoir when excess electricity cannot be fed into the grid. This water is then returned to a lower reservoir to generate electricity to respond to peaks in demand. Pump storage systems have efficiency of approximately 80 per cent. Globally, such schemes can store 140 GW, of which 45 GW is in Europe and 5 GW in France. However, the number of sites still available is limited and new projects generally encounter hostility from local residents. Thus innovation is required in the field of electricity storage. There are se veral candidate technologies at present.

Mechanical solutions have been identified for some time but remain at the experimental stage. These consist of flywheels turning in a vacuum, brought up to speed by an electric motor supplied by peaks in electricity generation. The system then returns energy to the grid when the wind dies down or the sun sets. Another solution consists of storing electricity in the form of compressed air injected into natural large-scale enclosed spaces (caves, aquifers, etc). Efficiency of 40-70 per cent can be obtained with the recovery of the compression heat (pump storage efficiency is 80 per cent).

Electrochemical solutions using accumulators and batteries for large-scale storage have, up to now, only been developed for military applications (submarines). The first innovations to store intermittent renewable energy have been based on large sodium sulphur accumulators developed in Japan (NGK). With modular power of 1-2 MW, they can store 80-100 WH/KG. This technology uses readily available, inexpensive materials. It is already used in the control of output from gas power stations during off-peak hours for resale during peak hours (80 MW). It may represent a solution for smart grids using IRE.

Lithium-ion, from the automotive sector, may offer an alternative to the sodium sulphur option. Furthermore super capacitors, condensers used in transport to recover braking energy, could be adapted to smooth out additional voltage from wind turbines submitted to gusts of wind.

Finally there is hydrogen, which is easy to produce by electrolysis. It can subsequently be used to produce electricity by means of a fuel cell. However, the overall efficiency is low (35 per cent) and fuel cells are still expensive. Hydrogen is not an ideal solution to smooth out the unpredictable voltages of wind and solar power. In summary, systems to store and then return electricity will be essential to deal with intermittence in grids when, after subsidies and prioritisation have dwindled, market realities are imposed to optimise the inclusion of wind and solar power in smart grids. There are several solutions in existence; their costs will be the determining factor in the forthcoming competition.

◎ Offshore wind power

Offshore wind power is gradually gaining pace in Europe in contrast to onshore wind power, which suffers from inefficiency due to the dispersion of wind in areas of high human density and severe pressure because of environmental concerns. Offshore offers stronger, more constant winds (30 per cent load factor offshore compared with 20 per cent onshore), more space and fewer constraints, accommodating higher, more powerful and more efficient wind turbines (7-8 MW).

On the other hand offshore suffers from the gigantic scale necessary for turbines weighing 6,000-7,000 tonnes which require enormous foundations to anchor them to the seabed. Although opposition is not as strong as it is from local residents to onshore developments, many people are still against offshore wind farms as they consider them an intrusion on coastal landscapes, and in particular detrimental for fishing and amateur sailors.

Thus the interest in farshore projects in deep water. The wind turbines are no longer anchored to the seabed but are semi-floating and held in position by several anchors. This could allow larger units to be constructed that offer a considerably improved performance (possibly 10 MW) while remaining mobile to minimise losses from interference. Farshore turbines have more space, benefit from regular winds and cannot be seen from the coast. Much of the technology developed on oil production platforms in the North Sea is applicable. Companies in the sector are already offering "wind float" solutions for depths of 30-1,000 m at over 30 km from the coast.

Farshore offers a semi-breakthrough technology that could open up access to wind power for electricity generation on the scale required by European demand, replacing fossil fuels and without emitting CO_2 or affecting landscapes. But a major uncertainty remains in the shape of the maintenance costs of these units which may turn out to be prohibitive.

◎ Recycling anthropogenic CO_2

In 2013, the 500 million inhabitants of Europe consumed 1,700 Mtoe (million tonnes of oil equivalent) of primary energy, in other words 15 per cent of the energy produced in the world. This represents 3.6 toe (tonnes of oil equivalent) per person per year (France 4.2 toe, USA 7.2 toe). Some 56 per cent of this energy is imported, namely 80 per cent of oil and 65 per cent of gas. Coal is the main ingredient of domestic energy. The result: Europe emits some 4,500 million tonnes of CO_2 a year.

Unless there are technological developments, this Europe, currently 80 per cent dependent on fossil fuels, will not achieve its greenhouse gas reduction targets set for 2050. Overall, emissions are currently stagnating due to the economic crisis but continue to rise in Germany, which has called a halt to its nuclear programme and is consequently importing American coal and opening lignite mines. Emissions are set to rise when the expected return to growth materialises. What technological breakthroughs could shatter this downward spiral?

◎ Carbon capture and storage (CCS)

This procedure consists of recovering the CO_2 from production sources and storing it in underground repositories to avoid its release into the atmosphere with the consequent contribution to the greenhouse effect.

The first stage separates the CO_2 from other elements (water vapour, oxygen, nitrogen, etc) present in gaseous emissions from industrial processes or in exhaust gases. Because of the cost of the capture process (two-thirds of the total), it is reserved for major industrial units that are sources of significant, concentrated emissions (cement, steel, petrochemical and fertiliser plants, refineries, etc). Depending on the type of emission, CO_2 is captured by pre-combustion, oxy-combustion or post-combustion. The second stage consists of transporting the CO_2 (via gas pipelines) to a natural underground cavity (former gas or oil fields, deep saline aquifers, coal mines). At the planned depth, CO_2 takes on a quasi-liquid state occupying a very small volume.

Some projects are already under way. Since 2010, TOTAL has been testing LACQ, a complete chain of capture/transport/storage of industrial CO_2 using a depleted gas deposit at a depth of 4,500m. Two other major projects are being conducted in Norway, the CO_2 being separated from natural gas and stored at 1,000-2,600m in two saline aquifers. According to estimates by the Intergovernmental Panel on Climate Change, the planet's geological storage capacity lies between 1,000 and 10,000 billion tonnes for annual emissions of some 30 billion tonnes. While the capture of CO_2 is an attractive solution in the short term to reduce the threat of fossil fuels to the climate, the results of storage have already turned out to be disappointing and present the problem in Europe of acceptance by the public of the geological confinement of a gas that may become dangerous over the very long term. CCS does not thus provide the desired breakthrough.

◎ Giving value to atmospheric CO_2

Rather than trying to bury CO_2 forever, why not seek a breakthrough for this curse of fossil fuels by giving value to its potential richness, the carbon atom? The initial objective may be to use CO_2 directly, either as a refrigerant fluid over a wide temperature range, or, in its supercritical state (at its triple point at high pressure at 74 bar, where CO_2 can be gas, liquid or solid) for applications in the food and pharmaceutical industries, for sterilisation, deodorising, etc. However, the volumes involved would be far too low to be really useful.

The real breakthrough would be to create a carbochemical sector by combining CO_2 with hydrogen ($H_2 + CO_2 \rightarrow C_X H_Y O_Z$) replacing petrochemicals and capable of the industrial synthesis of the gas and oil currently extracted from fossil reserves.

A hydrogen/CO_2 carbochemical sector could produce intermediate chemical products such as ethylene (C_2H_4), propylene, multiple fuels, polyurethanes and acrylates that are ingredients of several plastic materials widely used in the textile, automotive and construction industries. It could also produce fuels such as methane (CH_4) and methanol (CH_3OH) which could be utilised by the current distribution network and used to fuel vehicles.

A carbochemical sector involving the massive recycling of anthropogenic CO_2 by combining it with hydrogen would genuinely represent a major breakthrough allowing humanity, and Europe in particular, to extract itself from the "fossil fuel trap" in which it is caught.

But hydrogen does not exist naturally, it has to be manufactured. For industrial use, it is currently re-formed from natural gas:

$$CH_U + H_2O \rightarrow CO + 3H_2 \text{ then: } CO + H_2O \rightarrow CO_2 + H_2$$

However, this process produces significant amounts of CO_2. As the objective is precisely the reverse, other carbochemical processes that make use of carbon-free hydrogen must be found.

◎ Production of carbon-free hydrogen

The first solution is the electrolysis of water, already described as a way of absorbing peaks of IRE generation. In order to supply a carbochemical sector, wind and solar power would specialise in the production of hydrogen. The work of smart grids would be simplified. They would simply direct green IRE electricity to the electrolysers. Attractive in qualitative terms, implementing this type of solution, which would integrate chemistry and the generation of electricity, should be studied and practical examples developed. There should also be analysis of the storage of the hydrogen produced by IRE and its distribution to CO_2 recycling units. However, a genuine solution representing a significant breakthrough would be the production of hydrogen by the dissociation of water using heat or light. Two research strands are currently the subject of considerable attention around the world.

The first of these uses direct dissociation of water at a very high temperature. Heat is produced by the nuclear fission of uranium 235 in a generation IV reactor known as VHTR (Very High Temperature Reactor) which uses heat transfer fluid at over 1,000°. VHTR functions on the principle of generation III+, as does EPR, with thermal neutrons, and differs from other generation IV reactors with fast neutrons such as Superphénix and ASTRID. VHTR has been identified for its aptitude for electricity/hydrogen cogeneration. Hydrogen is produced by the thermal dissociation of sulphuric acid which results directly in oxygen and hydrogen at over 1,000°.

Benefiting from the experience of water reactors, VHTR already operates in the form of helium-cooled prototypes which can be used directly (Brayton cycle) with an electricity turbo-generator and/or passing through an exchanger outside the nuclear containment to supply heat to the chemical process producing hydrogen.

Currently, to the detriment of the environment, the production of hydrogen (50 million tonnes/year) is achieved by steam methane reforming resulting in massive emissions of CO_2, while VHTRs are at the experimental prototype stage (General Atomics GT-MR). If hydrogen is to become a major energy consideration in the campaign to reduce CO_2, production must be reorganised. Dozens of VHTRs would have to be commissioned in Europe.

The second solution is inspired by nature with the imitation of photosynthesis. This low-energy process dissociates water using solar energy to form hydrogen and oxygen.

Many teams in France, including the Atomic Energy Commission (CEA) and the National Council for Scientific Research (CNRS), and around the world, are researching how microorganisms can produce hydrogen and oxygen naturally from water and sunlight. They are seeking to synthesise enzymes, known as hydrogenases, that act as catalysts for the dissociation. Specific attention has been paid to the mechanisms used by plants and algae.

Publications on this research have increased in recent years. Very recently an announcement was made (Virginia Tech) of a process that would allow large quantities of hydrogen to be produced from a vegetable sugar, xylose, which is present in most plants, at ambient temperature and pressure.

The innovation consists of synthesising enzymes, discovered in microorganisms surviving at extreme temperatures, which are biocatalysts that release hydrogen at outputs far higher than from photosynthesis. Other publications (Rochester) describe high-output photosynthesis from catalysts consisting of nanoparticles, associating nickel, cadmium and selenium.

It is clear that the global energy situation, which is so unfavourable to Europe, would be completely transformed if the continent was the first to develop large-scale industrial production of hydrogen at low cost and without greenhouse gas emissions, from renewable biomass. It is therefore essential that European researchers lead the way in pioneering this breakthrough.

CONCLUSION

Energy is currently a major problem for humanity. Demand is set to triple by 2050 while the atmosphere is already saturated with CO_2. Fossil fuels account for more than 80 per cent of the total primary energy used and there is no carbon-free alternative in the short term. Since Kyoto (1995), humankind has recognised climate risk as a major issue and fossil CO_2 has been identified as the enemy to be fought, although there is no consensus on the urgency of its elimination.

Since 2000, the European Union has focused on intermittent renewable energy (IRE) to replace fossil hydrocarbons without resorting to nuclear power. At the same time, the shale gas revolution in the US has completely overturned the geopolitics of fossil resources and pushed the expected depletion of oil and gas to beyond 2100.

The financial crisis of 2008 severely affected the European economy, depriving it of the considerable financial means necessary to subsidise transition towards full IRE generation.

Fukushima in 2011 reinforced the divide between Europe, where the media has portrayed the accident as a global catastrophe that means the end of nuclear power, and the rest of the world which, after having drawn the appropriate lessons, has relaunched major nuclear programmes, in particular in China and India. The EU, driven by the withdrawal of six countries from nuclear development, including Germany, has used Fukushima to emphasise its commitment to IRE. However, the EU has not acknowledged the limits of IRE or the unsuitability of its territory for the production of green electricity on a major scale. It has, though, changed its focus to offshore wind power, which is more efficient but requires greater investment.

France continues to vacillate within a divided Europe. The country has an efficient, exportable nuclear programme, but it is threatened by a particularly virulent green lobby which during election campaigns has achieved spectacular closures of facilities (Superphénix, Fessenheim, etc). This has cast doubt on France's commitment to the future of the nuclear programme that it has pioneered.

France has shale oil and gas reserves that are probably considerable, but their exploitation may involve environmental risks. Under threats from the same green lobby, the country has rejected even assessing this wealth even though it is ruining itself by importing hydrocarbons costing €70 billion a year.

France has substantial wind and solar power resources, in particular in terms of offshore wind power, but these are not (yet) competitive and their subsidisation on a case-by-case basis is driving the disastrous collapse of many small terrestrial installations with fewer than ten turbines that are often imported and unprofitable.

The result is that, in 2013, green energy objectives were far from being achieved. Europe has never before emitted so much CO_2 and is spending 500 billion euros a year importing hydrocarbons. Germany has never consumed so much coal, importing it even from the US. As for France, it can no longer balance its foreign trade, dragged down by imports of fossil energy which have reached record levels and have accelerated deindustrialisation. For these reasons, Europe, and in particular France, is headed towards a ruinous energy impasse.

In the short term, not disregarding the global economic downturn, the effects of which have already been felt in the South, Europe, and France and Germany in particular, will have to re-evaluate their energy mix on the basis of new principles, including, as the United Kingdom has done, embracing nuclear and shale oil and gas in a pragmatic and above all economic approach.

In the medium term, a coordinated, powerful research effort must immediately be launched on a Europe-wide basis to encourage advances and achieve the technological breakthroughs that are required to get out of the current impasse.

A first focus of efforts is to improve the effectiveness of IRE. There are three approaches to explore. The first approach is the real-time connection of bidirectional smart grids to solar and wind farms, in order to permanently optimise the input of their green but intermittent energies. Domestic consumers of electricity could thus also become producers from wind and sun, and sell their electricty back to the smart grid. The second approach is the storage of intermittent electricity in order to smooth out its usage. Several different technological solutions must be evaluated (pump storage, mechanical inertia, electrochemical solutions, electrolysis). The third possibility is farshore wind power, which could offer a solution for the production of significant amounts of green electricity using large-scale floating wind farms anchored in deep water in windy locations without causing environmental harm.

Another strand of effort is much more ambitious: to transform the CO_2 that is poisoning the atmosphere into an economic asset. The capture of CO_2 is in the course of development but its storage remains problematic. Beyond this, CO_2 combined with hydrogen could become the basis of a new carbochemical sector, replacing the current petrochemical sector, for the production of fuels and composite materials that are consumed by modern economies on a massive scale. The desired breakthrough would thus be achieved.

But how can hydrogen be manufactured on an industrial scale without emitting CO_2? There are two possibilities worth examining. Because water dissociates directly into hydrogen and oxygen at very high temperatures, it may be possible that generation IV nuclear reactors (VHTR) that are still in the research stage, could be adapted and designed to accommodate the industrial production of hydrogen. The second option is to explore the possibilities of photosynthesis. In nature, photosynthesis dissociates water using sunlight. Around the world, researchers are hard at work reproducing this phenomenon in the laboratory. Recent papers have reported results that could lead to the production of hydrogen in large amounts. This would be the best solution and a huge breakthrough.

Only determined, coordinated action on a European scale can get us out of this energy dead-end into which utopian national ambitions, impatient to the point of blindness, have taken us. In this respect, the imperative for France is first to address the financial circumstances of its energy sector by using the advantages it has in the short term. It would then be in a position to finance the enormous innovation effort required to change the energy sector, an effort to which it must dedicate itself using all the considerable strength of its researchers and enterprises.

CHAPTER 6

SUSTAINABLE ENERGY AND SMART GRIDS
BREAKTHROUGH IN THINKING, MODELLING AND TECHNOLOGY

By 2020, some European Union energy and climate policies will expire and discussion of a post-2020 policy needs to be initiated. One of the fundamental issues is related to the portfolio of energy sources which can provide the most environmentally-safe, cost-effective roadmap. In this chapter we discuss the challenges of electric energy systems of the future with regard to the integration of sustainable energy resources and smart grids developments. In our view, such a system requires innovation in three related fields: development of sustainable energy sources; development of smart grid technologies for generation of renewable and intermittent sources and storage devices, transmission and distribution controls, and the development of new models to understand the complexity of these types of systems. We discuss the state of the art and the future expectations for these related fields.

THE QUALITATIVE ANALYSIS FOR THIS CHAPTER IS ON PAGE 382 OF THE ANNEX

MAARTEN VERKERK, HENK POLINDER AND PAULO F. RIBEIRO

THE CHALLENGE

The supply of sustainable energy is one of the greatest challenges modern society faces. On the one hand traditional sources like oil, coal, and gas are limited and polluting, and contribute to the heating-up of the earth. On the other, nuclear energy remains disputed, because of safety concerns and the problem of radioactive waste (even if nuclear is sometimes termed, by China, "renewable"). Governments, universities and industries are cooperating intensively to develop sustainable energy sources that will meet future requirements.

Many sustainable sources, such as sun, wind and hydro energy, produce energy in the form of electricity. A great advantage of electric energy supply is that it can be transported easily over large distances. It is widely recognised that the development and integration of sustainable resources also requires innovation in the electrical grid and associated technologies for generation, transmission, distribution and energy storage systems. The present electrical system is based on a model of large and centralised electricity generators (large-scale plants based on fossil fuels) whereas the future electrical system will be based on a large amount of smaller, local generators (solar panels, wind turbines). Changes in renewable energy generation will induce big changes in the management and distribution of electrical energy because of their unpredictability. The present electrical system has to be made smarter in order to accommodate and balance supply and demand on the local, regional, national and transnational levels.

The International Energy Outlook 2013 reports that the world's net electricity generation could increase by 93 per cent from 20.2 trillion kilowatt hours in 2010 to 39.0 trillion kilowatt hours in 2040 (EIA, 2013). Electricity supplies an increasing share of the world's total energy demand and is the world's fastest-growing form of delivered energy. World electricity delivered to end users is projected to rise by 2.2 per cent per year from 2010 to 2040, as compared with forecast average growth of 1.4 per cent per year for all delivered energy sources. In general, projected growth in OECD countries is slower than in non-OECD countries, where at present many people do not have access to electricity.

Beginning in the early 2000s, high fossil fuel prices in combination with concerns about the environmental consequences of greenhouse gas emissions provoked interest in developing alternatives to fossil fuels. The long-term global prospects for generation from renewable energy sources continue to improve, making them the fastest-growing sources of electricity with forecast annual increases averaging 2.8 per cent per year from 2010 to 2040 (see figure 1). In particular, non-hydropower renewable resources are predicted to be the fastest-growing sources of new generation in both OECD and non-OECD regions. Non-hydropower intermittent renewables, which accounted for 4 per cent of the generation market in 2010, could increase their share of the market to 9 per cent in 2040 (EIA, 2013).

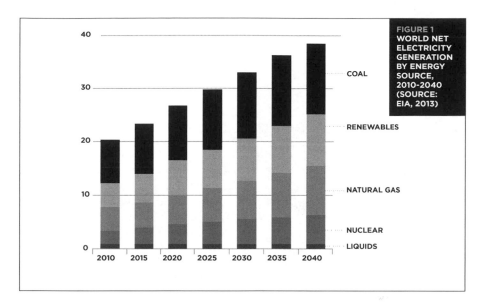

FIGURE 1
WORLD NET
ELECTRICITY
GENERATION
BY ENERGY
SOURCE,
2010-2040
(SOURCE:
EIA, 2013)

The successful integration of renewable energy sources and implementation of smart grid technologies will require a holistic analysis and design process. Grid project investments in Europe currently amount to more than €5 billion and are estimated to reach €56 billion by 2020 (Pike Research, 2011). An evaluation by the European Commission of European smart grid projects showed that it is very difficult to grasp technological and non-technological key characteristics of this complex system: the difficulties encountered during the data collection process; the lack of quantitative data to perform analyses; the recognition of the higher complexity of the system and the lack of proper integration; the difficulties with the setting of business models; the lack of consumer involvement; the need for proper ICT infrastructure; the need for better data protection and security; and the need for a legislative framework to ensure proper division of responsibilities (EC, 2011). The EC report highlights that "a scan of the collected projects seems to suggest a lack of specific attention to the social implications of Smart Grids." (EC, 2011)

In our view, a sustainable energy system needs innovation in three basic areas:

(a) development of sustainable energy sources;

(b) development of smart grids to accommodate production and consumption of energy under market signal incentives;

(c) development of models to understand the non-technological aspects of the production and consumption of energy, e.g. social and ethical questions. In addition, these non-technological aspects have to be integrated in the design of sustainable sources and smart grids.

In this chapter we will focus on the smart grid as an innovation. To understand the importance and the main characteristics of these grids we will give an overview of the most important sustainable energy sources. After that, we will discuss what is required with respect to the electrical infrastructure. Finally, we will examine theoretical models to understand the complexity of sustainable energy and electricity systems in general and smart grids in particular.

SUSTAINABLE ENERGY SOURCES

As renewable electricity generation increases, additional transmission infrastructure is required to deliver generation from cost-effective remote renewable resources to load centres, enable reserve sharing over greater distances, and smooth output profiles of variable resources by enabling greater geospatial diversity. **NREL - Renewable Electricity Futures Study, 2013**

	ENERGY PER YEAR (2012)	AVERAGE POWER
GLOBAL ENERGY CONSUMPTION	158000 TWH	18 TW
GLOBAL ELECTRICAL ENERGY CONSUMPTION	20148 TWH (13%)	2.3 TW

FIGURE 2 ESTIMATES OF GLOBAL ENERGY CONSUMPTION AND GLOBAL ELECTRICAL ENERGY CONSUMPTION IN 2012

Figure 2 gives estimates of global energy consumption. This table shows that about 13 per cent of total energy consumption is used in the form of electrical energy. This percentage will grow in the future, with the Internal Energy Outlook 2013 expecting that in the period 2010-2040 world energy consumption will grow 56 per cent whereas world electricity consumption will grow 93 per cent (EIA, 2013).

Figure 3 gives estimates of the most important sustainable energy sources. There are some other sustainable energy sources, such as energy from ocean currents, ocean waves and the salinity gradient between salt and sweet water. However, these sources are in such an early stage of development that they do not yet make a significant contribution. Most sources produce electrical energy (hydro, wind, solar) and other sources produce heated water (solar, geothermal) or fuels (biomass).

Comparison of figures 2 and 3 shows that until now only 3 per cent of our energy consumption is produced in a sustainable way (sun and wind: 0.04 per cent). In other words, at the moment we are still far from being a society based on renewable energy.

Of course sustainable intermittent energy sources present an additional challenge, not least because there is a limited amount of electrical energy storage devices in the grid. The Sandia Report (2013) presents the most comprehensive analysis of the technologies, current and future applications, and uses

	ACTUAL ENERGY PRODUCTION (2012)	INSTALLED CAPACITY (END 2012)
1. NON-INTERMITTENT RENEWABLE SOURCES (NIRE)		
HYDRO ENERGY	3500 TWH	800 GW
GEOTHERMAL ENERGY	67 TWH	11 GW
BIOMASS ENERGY	900 TWH	
TOTAL NIRE: 44467 TWH (22% OF WORLD ELECTRICITY PRODUCTION)		
2. INTERMITTENT RENEWABLE SOURCES (IRE)		
WIND ENERGY	525 TWH	282 GW
SOLAR ENERGY	115 TWH	100 GW
OCEAN WAVE ENERGY	SMALL	SMALL
TOTAL IRE: 640 TWH (3% OF WORLD ELECTRICITY PRODUCTION)		
3. TOTAL RENEWABLE SOURCES (NIRE + IRE)		
5107 TWH (25% OF WORLD ELECTRICITY PRODUCTION, 3% OF WORLD ENERGY PRODUCTION)		

FIGURE 3 ESTIMATES OF THE USE OF SUSTAINABLE ENERGY SOURCES IN 2012 (BASED ON WIKIPEDIA, IEA WIND 2012 ANNUAL REPORT). FOR COMPARISON: THE AMOUNT OF ELECTRICITY GENERATED BY NUCLEAR SOURCES IS 2620 TWH

of energy storage systems in electric grids. Through fast control techniques and technologies, production has to be equal to consumption (the power balance has to be kept) in order to maintain the frequency and stability of the grid. In the current system, this balance is kept by automatic control systems mainly via thermal power stations, where the consumption of electrical energy is automatically balanced by the production of electrical energy by adapting the consumption of coal, oil or gas to demand (see figure 4). In possible future power systems, with fewer thermal power stations, this power balance must be kept via energy storage devices, because most of the sustainable energy sources (such as wind, solar, ocean wave, and tidal energy) have an intermittent nature. This means that they are not continuously available: if there is no wind, there is no wind energy. To keep the power balance in these grids without thermal power stations, it may be necessary to have forms of energy storage and to control the loads.

To understand the characteristics of the various forms of renewable energy we will discuss the most important sources in more detail. We will focus on hydro, wind and solar energy. We also will discuss one new source with a high potential: ocean wave energy.

◎ Hydro energy

Hydro energy or hydroelectricity is the production of electrical energy by using the gravitational force of falling or flowing water. The best-known form of

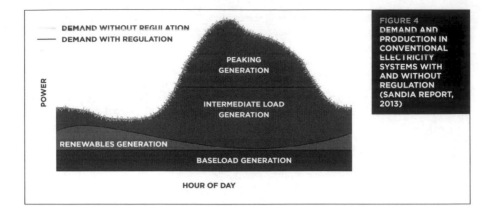

FIGURE 4
DEMAND AND
PRODUCTION IN
CONVENTIONAL
ELECTRICITY
SYSTEMS WITH
AND WITHOUT
REGULATION
(SANDIA REPORT,
2013)

hydroelectricity is the energy produced in turbines driven by the water from a reservoir behind a dam in a river. However, on a smaller scale, hydroelectricity can also be generated by putting turbines in a river with flowing water. Hydroelectricity is still the most widely used form of sustainable energy. The growth of this source is limited (to roughly 3 per cent per year), probably because of worries about the environmental impact of building dams in rivers and because the most attractive locations are already being used. However, in emerging economies like Africa and South America, a big increase in hydroelectricity is possible because many rivers have not yet been exploited.

The power from a flow of water can be expressed as

$$P = Qgh$$

where Q is the mass flow (in kg/s) of the moving water, g is the gravitation constant, and h is the height difference between the water behind the dam and the location of the turbines. This shows that the growth of hydroelectricity is mainly profitable at locations with a large height difference and with a large mass flow of water. Among the attractive properties of hydroelectricity from a dam are the fact that hydroelectricity can be well-controlled and that the reservoir can be used to store energy. These reservoirs can also be used for pumped storage, using energy to pump water when more energy is available than is needed and using this energy when necessary. These properties make hydroelectricity a very suitable generation source for smart grids.

◎ Wind energy

Wind energy is the production of electrical energy by using the kinetic energy of moving air (wind). Nowadays, wind energy is mainly generated with three-bladed horizontal axis wind turbines. Wind energy is the third-largest source of sustainable electrical energy (after hydro energy and biomass). From 1980 to 2010, wind energy grew at roughly 30 per cent per year. Since 2010, growth has been lower because of the economic crisis, but its potential is still very large. In densely populated countries in Western Europe, there is a trend to place wind farms offshore. The power produced by a wind turbine can be expressed as

$$P = \frac{1}{2} \rho_{air} C_p \pi r_r^2 v_w^3$$

where ρ is the mass density of air, C_p is the aerodynamic efficiency, r_r is the rotor radius, and v_w is the wind speed. From this expression a few important conclusions can be drawn. The fact that the power is proportional to the cube of the wind speed has a number of important implications.

If there is no wind or the wind speed is low, the turbine produces no or little power. On average, a wind turbine operates at a capacity factor (average produced power divided by maximum power) in the order of 30 per cent offshore and 20 per cent onshore. And while it is mainly attractive to develop wind farms at locations with high wind speed, the very low spatial efficiency of wind farms requires huge areas covered by widely spaced wind turbines to avoid negative wake turbulence effects.

Thus to obtain significant electricity production hundreds of square kilometers are needed (example: London Array Installation on 100 km² for 600 MW, i.e. a very low ratio of 6 MW/Km²). This drawback is severely threatening the expansion of large ground wind farms in highly populated developed countries, especially in northern Europe (such as Germany and the Netherlands).

A less attractive property of wind energy is that there is hardly any energy storage. Some energy is stored in the rotating mass of the blades. That is enough to filter power pulsations with frequencies above around 1 Hz, but lower frequency power variations have to be compensated for in another way.

◎ Solar energy

Solar power is the production of electrical energy from solar radiation. The best-known form of solar energy is probably photovoltaics, the direct conversion of solar energy into electricity using solar cells. A less well-known and less used form of solar energy is concentrated solar power, where solar energy is concentrated to heat steam and drive a steam turbine. Solar energy is also used directly for heating. During the past decade, the growth of solar energy has been in the order of 50 per cent per year, which is larger than the growth of wind energy.

The potential for growth is enormous: the amount of solar energy reaching the earth is four times larger than the planet's total energy consumption. The production of solar energy varies with the day and night cycle and depends on the weather. The global formula to estimate the electricity generated by a solar panel is E=A*r*H*PR, where E is the generated energy (kWh), A the total solar panel area (m²), r the solar panel yield (%), H is the annual average solar radiation on tilted panels, and PR is the performance ratio, where the coefficient for losses ranges between 0.5 and 0.9. This formula shows that the amount of energy produced by solar panels depends heavily on the sunshine

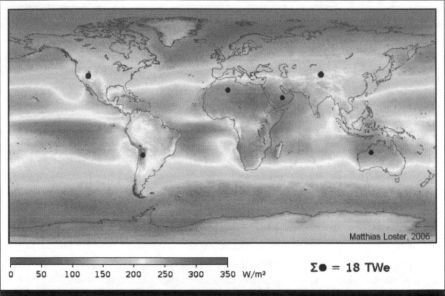

$$\Sigma \bullet = 18 \text{ TWe}$$

0   50   100   150   200   250   300   350 W/m²

FIGURE 5 THE THREE-YEAR AVERAGE OF SOLAR IRRADIANCE, INCLUDING NIGHTS AND CLOUD COVERAGE. SUNLIGHT HITTING THE DARK DISCS COULD POWER THE WHOLE WORLD: IF INSTALLED IN AREAS MARKED BY THE SIX DISCS IN THE MAP, SOLAR CELLS WITH A CONVERSION EFFICIENCY OF ONLY 8 PER CENT WOULD PRODUCE, ON AVERAGE, 18 TW ELECTRICAL POWER. THAT IS MORE THAN THE TOTAL POWER CURRENTLY AVAILABLE FROM ALL OUR PRIMARY ENERGY SOURCES, INCLUDING COAL, OIL, GAS, NUCLEAR, AND HYDRO (LOSTER 2010)

at the location of the panels: the panels have the highest energy production in countries around the equator (see figure 5). Unlike large-scale hydroelectricity and wind energy, an important part of solar energy is produced with small-scale solar panels connected to the local distribution grid throughout the power system.

◎ Ocean wave energy

Ocean wave energy is the production of energy from ocean waves. In deep water, where the water depth is larger than half the wavelength, the power available in waves is given by

$$P = \frac{\rho g^2}{64\pi} H_{m0}^2 T_e$$

with P the wave energy flux per unit of wave-crest length, Hmo the significant wave height, Te the wave energy period, ρ the water density and g the acceleration by gravity.

There are many different concepts for generating energy from ocean waves, such as floating buoys reacting against the sea bed, floating buoys reacting against each other, oscillating water columns, and overtopping devices. The technical challenges in this field are huge: the mechanical forces of waves during storms are extremely demanding, and the salty and humid environment is very aggressive to the (electrical) components. Ocean wave energy is still in a very early phase of development and is barely exploited commercially.

However, the potential is very large. The variations in output power of this renewable energy source are larger than for other forms of renewable energy because of the irregularity of the waves.

◎ Sustainable energy and smart grids

The large-scale introduction of renewable sustainable intermittent and non-intermittent energy generation requires the development of new grid technologies. Most of the sustainable energy is produced and transported in electrical form. It is not necessarily produced where it is also consumed. This means that the transport capacity of the future grid must probably be much larger than it is now. Currently, variations in power consumption and in power generated from intermittent sustainable sources are instantaneously compensated by variations in generated power in conventional power stations. If conventional power stations are abolished in a sustainable system, it is necessary to adapt the load to the available power or to use large-scale energy storage. Therefore, the distribution grid has to be adapted to enable the large-scale use of small-scale solar power in a safe way and also considering the bi-directional flow of power on distribution circuits.

◎ The future of sustainable energy

High renewable electricity futures can result in deep reductions in electric sector greenhouse gas emissions and water use. Direct environmental and social implications are associated with the high renewable futures examined, including reduced electric sector air emissions and water use resulting from reduced fossil energy consumption, and increased land use competition and associated issues. **NREL - Renewable Electricity Futures Study, 2013.**

Changing to a sustainable intermittent or non-intermittent energy source is not a trivial matter. It has taken generations to build up the current energy system; it will probably also take decades to change to a completely renewable and sustainable power system. Figure 6 presents the vision that renewable energy sources are mainly harvested where they are available (hydro energy in mountainous regions, solar energy closer to the equator, wind energy more offshore) and that a smart super grid is used to connect everything.

◎ Nature, structure and complexity of smart grids

In the last few years the steady growth of distributed generation and the expected higher penetration of renewable energy sources, together with policies on electricity distribution supporting the need for a "smarter grid", have begun to change the structure of the sector. It is within this context that the concept of smart grids has surfaced and certain significant technological developments are taking place.

In the near future, electric energy supply systems will change further. It is likely that large-scale power plants will be complemented by a large num-

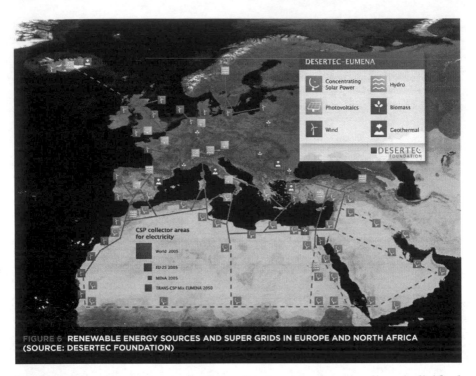

FIGURE 6 RENEWABLE ENERGY SOURCES AND SUPER GRIDS IN EUROPE AND NORTH AFRICA
(SOURCE: DESERTEC FOUNDATION)

ber of small-scale energy generation units. Among other suppliers, individual households will generate solar or wind energy. Intelligent systems will be used to communicate, control, protect and balance the supply and demand of energy more comprehensively. The whole system of central and local energy generation, transmission and distribution, enabling intelligent control and information systems, is called a smart grid. Smart grids will integrate micro grids (local systems) and super grids (high-voltage transmission and bulk generation systems).

Figure 7 illustrates the new concept of smart grids and the functional relationship among the different subsystems and technologies. The bulk generation, transmission and distribution to customers are directly and electrically connected and are themselves linked via communication systems with the Markets, Operations and Service Providers.

The ultimate goal is to create not just a smart grid but a smarter one. By applying technologies, tools and techniques currently available, as well as those under development, the goal is to make the grid work more efficiently by ensuring its reliability to degrees not possible before, while maintaining its affordability. It would reinforce global competitiveness, while accommodating renewable and traditional energy sources and potentially reducing our carbon footprint. But it requires introducing advancements and efficiencies that are yet to be envisioned.

The grid of the future, according to the US Department of Energy (LSC, 2010), needs to satisfy the requirements of being more reliable, more secure,

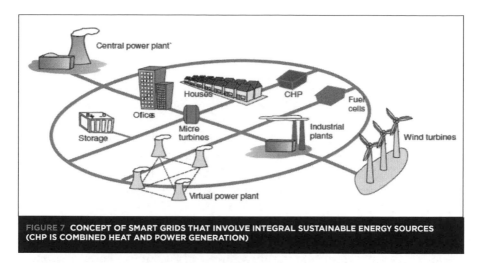

FIGURE 7 CONCEPT OF SMART GRIDS THAT INVOLVE INTEGRAL SUSTAINABLE ENERGY SOURCES (CHP IS COMBINED HEAT AND POWER GENERATION)

more economical, more efficient, friendlier to the environment and safer. To realise this from an architectural perspective, the grid needs to have the following attributes: an evolved energy supply mix, enhancements of the transmission grid, the co-existence of many grid configurations and the activation of the end-user as producer. These can be realised by further advancements in enabling technologies and control methods.

In addition, the following aspects on the supply side, demand and systems design should be considered. On the supply side, there needs to be a higher penetration of renewable resources, improvements in energy storage and balancing and the integration of isolated 'islands' with renewable energy grids. On the demand side, utility control systems needs to respond to local demand with aggregated local energy storage and the use of privately-owned energy storage, and to transport this energy efficiently. Managing supply and demand in these ways requires an architecture of complex autonomous adaptive systems with an effective cyber security.

The architectural concepts depend on a number of new functionalities that will be supported by future technologies that include power electronics, communications and computer science disciplines. In their fields of research new and detailed definitions need to be developed for cyber security and systems engineering, as well as for enabling functions, such as communications networks, visualisation and data management, and markets and economics. Performance will be monitored by new operations and control systems, as well as by planning, analysis and simulations.

Besides the physical components, the technological and computational concepts will involve a new distributed systems architecture, which connects the world of people, devices and systems. This requires new approaches in self-integrating systems, multi-agent systems, virtual computing architectures, and the messaging-oriented middle (software or hardware infrastructure for distributed systems).

The computational aspects will also involve the development of new computer applications to address smart grid areas. This includes control systems that respond to the market, tools that monitor and control as well as model and simulate. Such systems will carry out signal processing, protection, performance monitoring, state estimation, contingency analysis, stochastic analysis, and prognostics and asset management. Advancements in many areas of computer science are still needed to make smart grids a reality, including the information science for visualisation, artificial intelligence, data analytics, high-performance computing, internet for real-time systems. Finally, these system require high levels of cyber security technology to reduce damage from potential attacks, and to protect the integrity and privacy of information.

◎ Conclusion

What will be the architecture of the future electric grid? We know that micro grids will minimise the demands on the transmission and bulk generation systems and manage production and consumption of local energy. We know that super grids have to be adjusted to meet the generation of sustainable energy at the distribution level. We also know that smart grids will connect micro grids and super grids to accommodate and balance demand and supply at the local, national and supranational level. Finally, we have a much more complex set of requirements that have to be met by all agents and sub-systems in order to operate the electric grid of the future in a stable and sustainable way.

Despite all this know-how, the best answer to the question "What will be the architecture of the future?" is: nobody knows which is the best model or framework. Another more probable and adequate answer to this question will be: the architecture of the electrical system of the future will not be designed at once but will evolve over many years from today's infrastructure through the deployment and integration of intelligent systems, through the development and implementation of new devices and components, and through political decisions and actions.

It may be that the key decision parameter in the development of smart grids is the perception of the climate risk. A global awareness of the threat of increasing CO_2 in the atmosphere could facilitate the development of renewable sources and the enormous possibilities of energy saving. If so, smart grids should be adapted to the new habits of the population.

DEVELOPMENT OF NEW MODELS

Experience with the dynamic operation of large and time-varying sustainable energy systems is limited, so the need for a theoretical framework is significant. Research institutions and companies have developed detailed and comprehensive frameworks for the research and development of complex electrical systems.

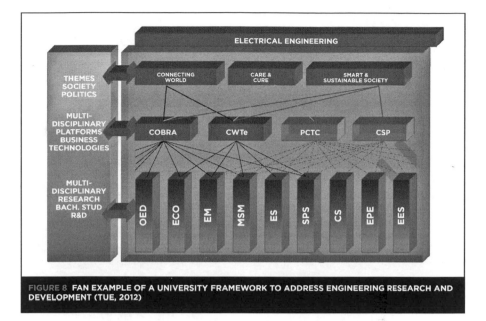

FIGURE 8 FAN EXAMPLE OF A UNIVERSITY FRAMEWORK TO ADDRESS ENGINEERING RESEARCH AND DEVELOPMENT (TUE, 2012)

◎ Model of the Technical University of Eindhoven

Figure 8 (TUE, 2012) illustrates the structure of the electrical engineering programme at the Technical University of Eindhoven. The diagram shows three levels of complexity: society and politics, multidisciplinary business platforms, and multidisciplinary technical research.

At first sight, this model seems to be quite complete. It involves technology (first layer), business models (second layer) and society (third layer). However, on further inspection the model shows a lot of shortcomings. Let's first focus on the technological layer. It shows a lot of different electrical systems that focus on the micro grids (local system), smart grids (regional systems) and super grids (international systems). However, this layer does not include any traditional or sustainable energy sources. The model seems to express the idea that these sources are unproblematic and do not have to be taken into account. In addition, it presents a view of technology from within. The view of engineers on technology and the view of society on technology are not highlighted.

Business models come in on the second layer, which describes the technological aspects of business platforms. The model suggests that for an engineer only the technological aspects have to be taken into account and that the business aspects can be ignored. But every technological product has to serve customers and has its price. The model does not invite engineers to think about these elements.

In the third layer society is addressed. It specifies a connecting world, care and cure, and the idea of a smart and sustainable sector. In the first place, the explicit attention for these societal sectors ought to be welcomed. The ideas of a

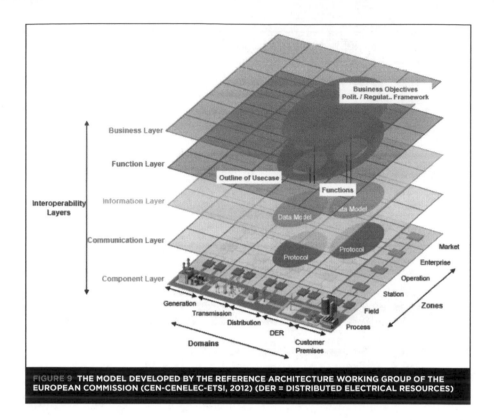

FIGURE 9 THE MODEL DEVELOPED BY THE REFERENCE ARCHITECTURE WORKING GROUP OF THE
EUROPEAN COMMISSION (CEN-CENELEC-ETSI, 2012) (DER = DISTRIBUTED ELECTRICAL RESOURCES)

connecting, healthy and sustainable society are key to guiding the development
of a technological society. However, the model is both too abstract and too general to consider many of the complexities of an electric grid design and operation. It covers general ideas but does not give the engineer enough information
to identify which parties are relevant and what interests are justified. It does not
address the fact that society consists of quite different actors who have different
interests. In addition, it does not address different dimensions of sustainable
energy and smart grids, or social, legal and ethical considerations.

In conclusion, the model presented in figure 8 accurately reflects the technical and systemic world of the engineer and needs further development to
fully account for the complexity and normativity of sustainable energy and
smart grids. In other words, this model shows engineers working with reduced
models in which they address a reduced reality.

◎ Model of the European Commission

Figure 9 presents the model developed by the Reference Architecture Working Group of the European Commission (CEN-CENELEC-ETSI, 2012). This
model spans three dimensions: domains, zones and interoperability layers.
The domains cover the complete energy conversion chain from energy generation to the end users. The zones represent the hierarchical levels of the power

system management. The interoperability layers highlight the interoperability between components and systems. In this simplified model five different layers are distinguished. The advantage of this model is that it urges engineers to take into account the whole energy conversion chain, the whole power system and the relationship with business models. This model has a technological and economical spirit.

◎ Triple I model

A quite different model has been given by Ribeiro et al. (2012), shown in figure 10. This model states that designers have to use three different perspectives to specify new technologies: integrality, inclusiveness and idealism. The idea of integrality refers to the different aspects that have to be taken into account; the idea of inclusiveness to the different stakeholders whose interests are at issue; and the idea of idealism to the ideals, value systems, or basic beliefs that underpin the development of smart grids. This model is based on the ontology as developed by the philosopher Dooyeweerd (1969) and the practice model developed by the philosophers Hoogland, Jochemsen, Glas, Verkerk and others (Jochemsen, 2006; Verkerk et al., 2007).

The first 'I' refers to the different aspects that have to be analysed. In total fifteen different aspects are identified, varying from the numerical, physical, social, economic and juridical to the moral dimension (see figure 11). Each aspect has its own nature, dynamics and normativity. Consequently, these different aspects cannot be regarded in isolation but every aspect has to be analysed in detail.

◎ Different aspects or dimensions

The second 'I' refers to the different stakeholders and their justified interests. Based on a philosophical analysis Ribeiro et al. argue that the interests

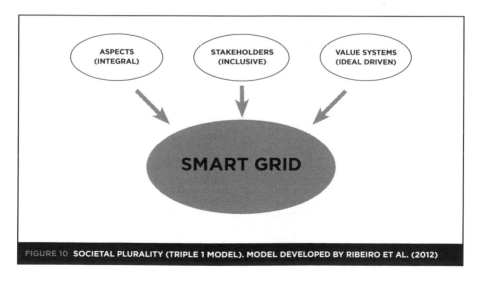

FIGURE 10 SOCIETAL PLURALITY (TRIPLE 1 MODEL). MODEL DEVELOPED BY RIBEIRO ET AL. (2012)

of stakeholders are different. For example, this comes to the fore when we analyse how different stakeholders will cope with a widespread blackout of the electrical system. Industrial enterprises will balance the risks, potential losses and prevention costs on economic grounds, hospitals will always choose back-up installations to prevent harming patients, and citizens will accept the

ASPECTS	ELECTRIC GRID	SMART GRID
ARITHMETIC	NUMBERS	MEASURABLE QUANTITIES: VOLTAGE, CURRENT AND POWER
SPATIAL	USE OF SPACE	TRANSMISSION AND DISTRIBUTION NETWORK
KINEMATIC	MOVING	ROTATING GENERATORS, ENERGY FLOW
PHYSICAL	MATERIALS AND PROPERTIES	CABLES, TRANSFORMERS, GENERATORS
BIOTIC	INFLUENCE ON ANIMALS, HUMAN BODIES, ENVIRONMENT	INFLUENCE OF ELECTROMAGNETIC FIELDS AND WAVES ON LIFE
PSYCHIC	FEELINGS OF SAFETY	INTERMITTENT RENEWABLE SOURCES LEAD TO FEELINGS OF UNCERTAINTY
ANALYTICAL	DISTINCTION BETWEEN DIFFERENT TYPES OF GRIDS	DIFFERENT TYPES OF GRIDS: MICRO, NATIONAL, SUPER, SMART
FORMATIVE	CONTROL	CONTROL OF POWER GENERATION, DISTRIBUTION AND CONSUMPTION, SMART METERS
LINGUISTIC	MEANING OF TERMINOLOGY	TERM "SMART" CHOSEN TO PROMOTE TECHNOLOGY? SHOULD IT BE "SMARTER"?
SOCIAL	INFLUENCE ON HUMAN BEHAVIOUR	LEADS TO MORE SUSTAINABLE HUMAN BEHAVIOUR?
ECONOMIC	COPE WITH SCARCITY OF ENERGY AND HIGHER DEMAND	PRICE DIFFERENTIATION DEPENDING ON MOMENTARY SUPPLY AND DEMAND
AESTHETIC	AESTHETICS OF BUILDINGS & SYSTEMS	BEAUTIFUL V2G CONNECTION POINTS?
JURIDICAL	LIABILITY, OWNERSHIP OF NETWORKS	WHO IS LIABLE FOR A FAILING SMART GRID?
MORAL	CARE FOR THE ENVIRONMENT, HUMANS AND ANIMALS	HOW DO SMART GRIDS HELP IN CARING FOR HUMANS?
BELIEF	TRUST IN SYSTEMS	SOME PEOPLE TRUST THAT SMART GRIDS WILL IMPROVE LIFE

FIGURE 11 OVERVIEW OF THE DIFFERENT ASPECTS OF SYSTEMS DESIGN FOR SMART GRIDS

risks as long as their normal life is not unduly hampered. So, "inclusiveness" requires the analysis of the interests of all the stakeholders. In this analysis the lists of interests will be very helpful.

The third 'I' refers to the ideals, values and basic beliefs that underpin the search for sustainable sources and the design of the energy system of the future. It has to be noted that in Western culture different value systems are present. Some people believe that economic considerations have to be dominant (the neoliberal approach), others believe that the present system can be adapted to meet environmental and sustainability requirements ("shallow ecology"), while others state that we not only need technological innovations but also radical societal reforms ("deep ecology") (Naess, 1973). It is important to make this third 'I' explicit in order to discuss the "why" of sustainable energy and smart grids and to prevent these fundamental questions being suppressed by technological and economical perspectives.

The approach of Ribeiro et al. is summarised in figure 12. It shows that for every (sub-) technology an extensive analysis of the three I's is required. On the one hand, it is a tough job to do this kind of analysis, especially because engineers will run into many "we don't knows" that will urge them to do additional research. On the other hand, failures in this field are so costly that no organisation or institution can permit them.

◎ Comparison of models

The model of the TUE – as concluded above – faces a lot of shortages and is dominated by the technological perspective. The model of the European Commission supports engineers to think over the whole energy conversion chain, hierarchy of power systems and relation with business models. This model is dominated by a technological and economical spirit. The Triple I model is quite different because it highlights technological and non-technological aspects, the different interests of various stakeholders and the ideals or values that underpin the design of the electrical system of the future. We conclude that a combination of the model of the European Commission and the Triple I model will be most fruitful.

CONCLUSIONS

The development of a sustainable energy system requires innovation in three basic areas; in sustainable energy sources; in smart grids to integrate production and consumption; and in the development of models to understand the non-technological aspects of the production and consumption. This includes the markets, but also an understanding of the social and ethical questions. These non-technological aspects have to be integrated in the design of sustainable sources and smart grids. The development of sustainable energy sources is under way. The most important contribution to sustainable energy will be from hydro, biomass, wind and solar energy. We suggest that renewable en-

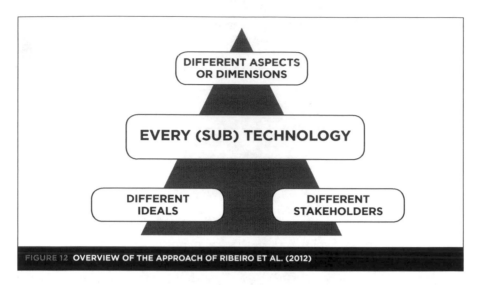

FIGURE 12 OVERVIEW OF THE APPROACH OF RIBEIRO ET AL. (2012)

ergy sources are mainly harvested where they are available (hydro energy in mountainous regions, solar energy closer to the equator, wind energy more offshore).

The development of sustainable energy sources will radically change the electrical infrastructure of the future. Micro grids will be necessary to minimise the demands on the transmission and bulk generation systems and to manage production, transmission, distribution, storage, and consumption of local energy. Super grids are required to meet the generation of sustainable energy at a global level. Additionally, smart grids will connect micro grids and super grids to accommodate and balance demand and supply at local, national and supranational level. Despite all this know-how, the question "What will be the architecture of the future?" cannot yet be answered.

The most probable and adequate answer to this question will be: the architecture of the electrical system of the future will not be designed at once but will evolve over many years from today's infrastructure through the deployment and integration of intelligent systems, through the development and implementation of new devices and components, and through political decisions and actions.

The electrical infrastructure of the future will be very complex, so an adequate model to understand this complexity and its normative aspects is of the utmost importance. We conclude that a combination of two models is required to integrate technical, societal and ethical considerations: the European Commission model and the Triple I model. The European Commission model supports engineers to think over the whole energy conversion chain, hierarchy of power systems and relation with business models. The Triple I model developed by Ribeiro et al. highlights non-technological aspects, the different interests of various stakeholders and the ideals or values that underpin the design of innovations.

Innovations in the field of renewable energy sources are driven by ideas about a sustainable future. This chapter shows that the production of electricity from renewable sources will grow considerably. However, the growth in total global energy consumption exceeds the growth in production by renewable sources. As a consequence, the use of traditional sources like oil, coal and gas and disputed sources like nuclear energy will still grow in the coming decades. In other words, the idea of a sustainable future is still utopian and so more radical choices will have to be made to meet the requirements of the future.

Innovations in the field of smart grids are also driven by ideas about a sustainable future. New technologies are being defined and standards agreed. Despite all these efforts there is not yet such a thing as a smart grid. The smart grid is an innovation that will be shaped by the efforts of many actors like engineers, energy generation enterprises, energy distribution enterprises, technology firms, governments and consumers. Only in a couple of decades from now will we know what smart grids really are.

CHAPTER 7

A POSTSCRIPT ON THE FUTURE OF ENERGY
WITH JEROEN VAN DER VEER

The former CEO of Royal Dutch Shell Jeroen van der Veer spoke with us about the future of energy. We asked him about his views on renewable energy sources, the possibilities of reducing the consumption of fossil fuels, and energy policies and strategies for the future. He argues that what is needed, above all, is a shared international vision and realistic domestic priorities to bring governments and industry together to manage innovation processes and make renewable energy commercially viable. Van der Veer considers the lack of an international vision for energy today and the leadership required to develop genuine innovation for energy sources and systems.

THE QUALITATIVE ANALYSIS FOR THIS CHAPTER IS ON PAGE 383 OF THE ANNEX

INTERVIEW BY HANS HILLEN, HENK VAN DEN BREEMEN AND MAARTEN VERKERK

"I have given various speeches where I always go back to when I joined the industry. It was in the early 1970s. At any moment in time, the energy industry assumed something about ten years ahead, which ten years later proved to be completely wrong." — **Jeroen van der Veer**

THE SCALE OF THE GLOBAL ENERGY SYSTEM

The Energy Information Agency in Paris publishes the annual *World Energy Outlook*, which projects future trends in energy demand and consumption up to 2040. According to the 2013 report, global energy consumption will grow 56 per cent, and world electricity consumption will grow 93 per cent. Because this growth of demand is much faster than the growth of renewable energy sources, the ever-increasing challenge for the coming century is to satisfy demand while reducing carbon emissions to meet the targets set in the Kyoto process. If it is said that we need to reduce carbon emissions by 40 per cent by 2030, while global energy consumption will double, then what is really being asked is that CO_2 emissions need to be cut by 80 per cent.

There are no easy answers to this challenge, especially since renewable energy sources are not yet able to compete commercially with fossil fuels. Even if Europe and the West conserve the maximum amount of energy possible, this would have little effect on the growth of energy demand and consumption, especially in India and China.

We asked Jeroen van der Veer, the former CEO of Royal Dutch Shell, to share with us his thoughts about the future of energy: what visions and ideas for innovations and breakthroughs there are for overall energy systems; what processes these should be attached to; and how innovations should be managed to support the development of a viable energy future.

Addressing three factors—transitions in energy, the redesign of our energy system, and the increase in the use of renewables—van der Veer says: "It is relevant for all three factors that people simply don't realise the size of the world's energy system," both now and in future.

With the present energy system, van der Veer argues that one cannot simply identify a current problem with fossil fuels, and "do something intelligent in the desert, where we can develop solar energy and then we put some money into it and that solves the problem in ten or twenty years. That is nonsense, because in about forty years the energy system is going to double in size."

The world's population is set to grow from 7 billion to 9 billion with a growing middle class. "Whatever the middle class does—think about Asia—they will use more energy. And in that estimate of the system doubling in forty years, the assumptions of better energy conservation and improved energy efficiency are already included. If you don't assume that, then the energy system will more than double.

"So the first point is that the world energy system is huge. And to change that system will always take time. If you have a huge system, you can't change it in one day. You simply lack the investment capacity. Even if you agree on the vision, concept and execution, it will take decades before you see material change."

The underestimation of the scale of the global energy system is only one part of the problem. At the international level, there is no shared vision on the future of energy.

"There is no consensus in the world about what the right solutions are. I am talking about the right mix of energy sources. Take for instance the World Economic Forum in Davos, where I chaired a session on the New Energy Architecture. They are now looking ahead to the year 2050 to help decide on the right energy mix. But there is absolutely no consensus about it today. And if there is no consensus about such an important question, what do you do?

"Then you have to go one abstraction level higher. Because there is no point in arguing if you can't agree. You can argue for ever but you will never convince the other side."

ACCEPTABLE, AVAILABLE, AFFORDABLE

"Why is it so difficult to reach consensus at the international level? The answer is that individual countries differ in perspectives on three criteria: I call them the three A's—the *acceptability* of different energy sources (such as nuclear energy); the *availability* of energy in their own territory; and *affordability*.

"First, is this form of energy *acceptable*? These are very often environmental concerns. Think about CO_2 emissions and coal. Think about nuclear energy and nuclear waste. Think about space: the huge windmill next to your house. All that has to do with the word acceptable.

"Second, is it *available*? The easy one is solar energy, which is only available in daylight. Gas may or may not be in the ground. This question includes the very interesting debates surrounding shale gas. And within availability you have a sub-category of questions: maybe it is available but not in your own country. That is typically the Middle East. If you use it in the United States, it raises all kinds of geopolitical questions. So is it available under your own feet, or in your own neighbourhood, or not?

"Third, is it *affordable*? This is simply the price: can people pay for it? In this way you can describe every form of energy, including renewable energy.

"Now you can see why people don't have the same vision, because the three A's work out differently according to country and region. For example, if you have a lot of gas, you will be more relaxed about other forms of energy. If you have a lot of sun in the middle of Algeria then you may prefer that.

"It was probably initially a political choice, but the French developed second-generation nuclear energy and they think it is acceptable. They built many of those nuclear power stations themselves. So far so good and that is the French perception.

"So you balance those three A's all the time, which is basically a political decision based on national thinking."

THE DIFFICULTY OF LONG-TERM PLANNING

The problems of perception with regard to the global energy system begin with the questions of scale. Given the differences of the three A's, the objective differences of availability combined with the subjective differences of acceptability, one consequence is the lack of a shared international vision. But it doesn't end there. "For politicians," van der Veer notes, "it is not their natural habit to think in decades."

Because energy is one of the most vital interests of a state, he says, "the political system has part ownership or full ownership" of its energy industries in most countries. Today we witness frequent protests by large crowds, celebrities and retired politicians in Western capitals taking to the streets demanding immediate action on climate change. The European Union seeks to impose unrealistic targets on its member states. The political classes are inclined to relieve these pressures from above and below by doling out generous subsidies for renewable energy sources as a short-term political gesture, with little consideration for the physical limitations, future trends or economic viability of doing so. The priority of subsidies for current technology over investment in research and development reflects this short-term thinking.

Van der Veer goes on: "The problem is that they are in too much of a hurry to develop a certain form of renewable energy. What is the best example? Building an offshore wind industry could be attractive for a country like the Netherlands, because we have wind, we have an offshore industry and we like to do things in the sea. So we have a lot of support industry to operate there. But offshore wind is in fact very expensive today. What is our government's reaction? We put huge subsidies into it. [Former Environment Minister] Jacqueline Cramer poured €4 billion into it. Now we have the *Dutch Energy Agreement for Sustainable Growth*,[1] which has announced another €4 billion. And you don't even get that many kilowatt-hours out of it.

"So I disagree with that. People may think, 'Oh, he comes from Shell, so he will disagree with renewables.' That is nonsense. I do agree that offshore wind can be attractive for the long term. What you have to do is carry out a lot of research and development to get this form of energy to produce kilowatt-hours at a lower cost."

TOWARDS A SMARTER INNOVATION POLICY

At technical universities we make use of the learning curve, or cumulative learning, which is used in all industries. The economics of a learning or experience curve are reflected in a lowering of cost for successive generations as technology improves and production increases in scale. The learning curve of 'Henderson's Law' found an average of 15 per cent cost reduction for every doubling of output. This is an empirical law based on averaged findings without a firm theoretical basis. It was found useful for developing cost projections in a variety of industries, including cars, aviation, televisions and high technology. Both the economies of scale and the innovations of new generations factor into cumulative production output to enable an average learning curve of 15 per cent cost reduction per cycle.

Instead of misguided innovation policies promoted by central government, van der Veer points to the dynamics of the learning curve as instructive for the development of the renewable energy industry, especially offshore wind farms, which are currently not market-viable.

"With this kind of technology, it is reasonable to estimate that if you build the first generation, then the second generation probably already has a lower cost of 15 per cent. And then the third generation is 15 per cent lower than that figure, and so on. A learning curve for 15 per cent is not unreasonable." In this iterative process, four such cycles, leading to a fifth generation, could halve the price per unit of electricity.

Rather than blow an entire budget on merely subsidising the manufacture of an expensive first generation, a smarter innovation policy focuses on research and development according to the learning curve, bringing industry on board for new public-private partnerships. This way offshore wind energy could be developed into a genuinely market-viable industry, rather than a way of meeting regional targets in a wasteful manner.

"So you have to build not too many expensive wind turbines, but you have to build a few. You do a lot of development and research and you put a target there: the price per unit of electricity should be much cheaper.

"Now if you do that seven times, and if one cycle takes two years—that is pretty fast, by the way—then in 14 years offshore wind may be roughly commercial. That is very important, because if it is commercial it doesn't need subsidies. And the industry wants to build it, because you can make money on it.

"To fund that or to contribute to that kind of research with public-private partnerships with the government will cost much less money than the large sums of money that the Netherlands is currently putting into it. So they have a wrong model. I can't be more straightforward. They are really on the wrong track.

"Now if you explain that to the minister, as I did at the time to the Minister of Economic Affairs, you'll see that they are not deaf. So why did they pursue the policies that they did? It's quite interesting. They will say, we have agreed targets in Europe: by 2020 we have to have so much renewable energy and we are a country which, if we agree something, likes to adhere to that. And within all the alternatives we have, while this may be waste in your view, it is the lowest waste. Now you may have an intellectual debate on whether that was the best choice, but I think they should have turned back.

"The planet will not be saved by having 20 per cent renewable energy in Europe in 2020. You can help the world in a much better way, but maybe some years later by applying more commercial technology. Then you can discuss how many years later, when you have unsubsidised commercial forms of renewable energy. That is what the debate should be. But there was simply not enough momentum in Europe to go back to Brussels to adjust the 2020 targets."

"So, you have first to achieve a lower cost per unit of electricity before you build a lot of wind farms. Development targets should be based on the cost per kilowatt-hour without subsidy. That is what should have happened. And, by the way, this applies to other renewables as well, not only offshore wind."

Is the Dutch wind farm policy an example of politics without vision that is focused on the short term and leads simply to the wrong decision?

"Yes, exactly. By imposing too strict targets too early, you get sub-optimisation, because you do the wrong things."

Do subsidies slow down innovation?

"I think in general if you subsidise research in early development, especially if you do it in public-private partnerships, it can be a good thing. Take those wind farms. Before you say that offshore wind is too expensive, look around to see how it can be done cheaper. You go to Boskalis and Van Oord, who will say, we are dredgers and work on the normal tariff, but if the order is big enough, we can build special ships. Then you can go to Heerema for construction, and so on. All these industrial players like to make money, but no one wants to invest in research and development. Now they have their eyes on a huge pile of short-term government money. That is the wrong approach.

"What you could have done together with the top industrial sector is to form a new public-private partnership, to go through the first three or four cycles in the learning curve. My estimate at the time was that the cost to make wind energy commercially viable is about €800 million, and we could create a fund. We invest €400 million in stages, subject to achievements, and leave €400 million in a fund. Then you form a consortium with Boskalis and Van Oord, with Heerema and other firms, who fund the other €400 million to match the investment by the government. And you can use that money especially for the early phases of the research and development, of going through those learning curves."

As we saw in our case study on the cyber domain, the early stages of the development of the technology happened entirely inside the US government, and it was a political decision by President George H. W. Bush to bring it to the market. In this case, Jeroen van der Veer and former Defence Minister Hans Hillen agree that the investment should come from both parties, with both government and industry sharing responsibility. When the development process succeeds, then industry can take over.

"Or to put it more directly: in the first round, the government funds the wind farms to the tune of about 65 per cent. But in the second round, we go down the learning curve, and the government pays 58 per cent. In the third round we are already below 50 per cent, and so on. For the industry this can be quite attractive, and for the government results can be achieved at a relatively low cost.

A EUROPEAN ENERGY POLICY?

"What then can we do—apart from complaining about what we can't do?

"If I focus on Europe, we come back to the previous point, because every country has different perceptions for the 'three A's': in Germany they are closing nuclear power stations, in Finland and in France they like to build them. We say about Kyoto that we have to reduce CO_2 but we now use more coal in Europe than when we agreed Kyoto—and in the United States less, by the way. But it shows that if we continue with an energy mix policy country by country, we will end up nowhere.

"We will not achieve the A of acceptable. Even if we do it for one country, its neighbour will think that it's not acceptable. I think we will probably end up with more expensive electricity for our industry and our consumers than for instance in the States. So it is not only the A of acceptable, I don't think we will achieve the A of affordable either.

"So the first thing we need is a real European energy policy.

"You need to have an overall energy policy. Now there are two remarks about that. You can't have an energy policy if you don't have a European foreign policy, because for a European policy you have to decide how much to import from Russia, how much from Algeria and how much from the Caucasus. How do we do that? Do we have a pipeline through Russia or around Russia as with the Nabucco pipeline? Or do we use liquefied natural gas (LNG) ships from the Middle East? For a European energy policy, you need to have this kind of foreign policy thinking. That is only the A of availability, which includes the security aspect.

"But if we decide for instance that we would like to have it as a kind of insurance against an uncertain future, we need to have nuclear energy in the basket, because nuclear is in itself very interesting as it is the only large-scale solution with basically no CO_2. If that is part of an energy policy, then you need a process on how to decide where to build this nuclear energy capacity. Because the Germans will say: put it in the Netherlands. And the Dutch will say, put it in Belgium. And they say put it in France.

"I think that nuclear energy is part of the solution for Europe. Suppose a European Commissioner produces a great policy result, backed by good research—but then I think it will get stuck in the process to decide where it should go. I think that will be very tough.

"You will get a lot of manoeuvring, but it is better than no European energy policy. You have to start somewhere. So the first step is to map the overall picture for Europe on the three A's, and then to initiate the processes to allocate what to do where. Then it is very helpful in my view if Brussels doesn't make life difficult for itself by having too tough energy targets for 2030.

"Because 2020 is near, the Commissioner (Günther Oettinger) said we would like to have targets probably for 2030, but these are not yet agreed. The present proposals, supported so far by Dutch civil servants, is that by 2030 we should have a 40 per cent reduction in CO_2 since 1990, which is the reference here for Kyoto. Now I always like simple calculations. By 2030 our GDP has doubled compared to 1990, in fact I hope it is a bit better. So if we save energy by 40 per cent vis-à-vis 1990, then per unit GDP we have to reduce our CO_2 emissions by 80 per cent. Is that achievable?

"I am not against the Greenpeaces and all kind of environmental thinking, but we should understand what we are doing. The new target may be more disruptive than the 2020 target was.

"I always go back to central energy policy, funding research and the processes of allocation. That is the way to accelerate the energy transition."

In other words, a target that is too severe will in fact take us farther away from it if it leads to subsidies of inefficient and suboptimal outcomes, ignoring both economic viability and economic growth.

A GLOBAL ENERGY POLICY?

While it would be a big step to have a European foreign policy, energy remains a global foreign policy issue and an expression of global power. Beyond national interests and processes we are currently unable to develop a coherent European energy policy, but to do so globally is even more difficult. Does van de Veer agree that the global political field of energy is often underestimated?

"There are two strong global aspects to energy. The first is the IPCC report on climate change.[2] The second is the IEA, the International Energy Agency in Paris, which is more focused on availability and its effect on the political dimension. The IEA updates its *World Energy Outlook* annually, and the IPCC revisits its assessment report every six years. If you use those two as a basis, then you have enough overall, let's say think tank, capability in order to form a real European policy.

"On the matter of climate change—what would be the outcome if we were super-clean here in the Netherlands? Imagine that on the A of acceptable we do a perfect job, but our electricity prices have become so high that we can't compete. Then we are out-competed by products from China based on coal-fired power. That is one extreme.

"The problem is that we now have a country policy, and we need to get it to a regional policy. For that you need new Kyotos, new kinds of agreements, to solve this second problem.

"But don't underestimate the Chinese. While they still build a lot of power stations and they still build new coal-fired power stations, many of the new ones are running on gas. So they do react and of course very much helped by all the problems they have, especially in Beijing with the air pollution that brings it pretty close to home for them.

"So to take one step back—for climate change we need global coordination to a certain degree to do something about that CO_2. If you take it to a higher abstraction level, then coal should eventually be left in the ground, because per kilowatt-hour it generates by far the highest CO_2. So if you look from a global perspective, it is probably the lowest-cost solution to minimise the use of coal.

"Now in all projections over the last 10 years, the use of coal has grown more than all the renewable energy sources. And that may happen again. So coal production is still on the increase. And every additional ton of coal ends up in CO_2 as well. So the first challenge is to stabilise the use of coal or even to force a reduction. These are large problems that require large-scale solutions. With all due respect, wind turbines next to your farm will not solve that.

"What then are your options? Your options are nuclear and gas. Gas is not perfect but there is a lot of it, it is relatively easy to extract and quick to distribute. Shale gas in the US is driving out coal there. But in Europe the problem is that the price of our gas is much higher than coal. What is then your option? There is the ETS, the European Trading System, or a tax on CO_2, or a tax specifically on coal. But that can only work if you do it within at least a European context. Otherwise one doesn't have a level playing field for the industry.

"If you look at Availability, you come to the role of the Middle East. There are still huge gas reserves in the Middle East, e.g. in Iran and Qatar. They are huge and will be for many, many decades. When I started to work for Shell, we thought that the world's gas reserves would last for 20 to 30 years. Now we think they may last 200 years. Nobody knows.

"But gas is not evenly spread. So you cannot avoid geo-political thinking. And that is why it is not up to the industry to choose the energy mix for a country. In the end, it is always a political choice."

ALTERNATIVE ENERGY SOURCES

Will severe emission targets make a country uncompetitive if the price of energy remains too high? Is solar energy a solution?

"Solar energy is, thanks to the Chinese, already commercial available: decentralised solar for domestic use. The question arises again, what should a government do? Should we subsidise solar, as the Germans and the Dutch do? Or do you say as a government: if you build a new house with a roof on the south, you are allowed to do that, but it should be a solar roof. So basically do you use the power of government to set rules?

"I think that is much more powerful and in the end costs less, not only for the government but for society as well, to do it that way. Now maybe solar technology is not developed enough to say that every roof that has to be built should be a solar roof. But then government can say something else: in Europe, we can say that by 2024 every roof facing south should be at least 50 per cent solar. And by 2030 it should be 75 per cent. If you set those rules, then companies will start to do research because they are assured of a market. That is a much better incentive than subsidy.

"But when it comes to large-scale projects, such as solar farms in the desert in Algeria, can they work? I think so. But are they commercially viable? No. Is Algeria a country where you feel comfortable to have a very large investment sitting there for over 30 years? I'm not so sure.

"So there is a form of solar energy which may over time become commercial as well. It is here that you need smart grids. You have to connect grids, which is not easy, the difficulty being that you have to transport electricity over long distances, so you need special investment to go from one type of current to another.

"Solar energy can play a big role in this, but not soon. That is my message on those factors. It is important to continue to do some experiments, but it doesn't solve the equation.

"Then you have onshore wind, which can cost less than offshore wind. But nobody wants to have it next to their home, so you have a problem of space.

"With energy from ocean waves, you have the same problem as with large-scale solar plants—technically possible but not commercial as yet. Over time, you still have to do research in that area.

"And you have all kind of alternative solutions. You can say, OK, what do I do with solar? I generate electricity and I transport it to Europe. Or you can say, in Algeria we have a lot of sun. I generate electricity and with the electricity I make hydrogen, and hydrogen is much more flexible to transport than electricity. So you have different pathways.

"Research and development are also needed for traditional gas as well as shale gas. While shale gas is not ideal, I find it strange that this country [the Netherlands] doesn't like to do exploration. We need exploration to see whether we have commercial shale gas or not. If I were the government, I would like to know that, because later it could be an alternative to Russian imports.

"In the Shell scenarios shale gas was mentioned but as unconventional and with a minor role. Nobody had foreseen the major role that shale gas now plays for the US, so that they are substantially reducing their imports of oil and gas and they have electricity prices which are substantial lower than in Europe—40 to 50 per cent lower, in that order of magnitude. Nobody had foreseen that. Some of today's forecasts will be wrong in ten years."

Despite the difficulty of long-term predictions, and the impossibility of forecasting the role of new technologies that may emerge, some generalisations are possible about larger trends.

"There are two likely scenarios. One is that after 2060 you will see a real major contribution from solar energy, but much more decentralised. This is not so much the Algeria desert scenario, but one where solar-based technology becomes a part of everything you build, with solar roof panels, walls and windows. And the other scenario is basically gas, with natural gas and shale gas as the big breakthroughs that will drive out coal.

"In both scenarios you can help the overall system by imposing a penalty on coal. There is then the disaster scenario in which you fail to drive out coal, but I think that is unlikely. Because if you continue to increase coal, people will notice. Either you get local air pollution as in China, or you get completely unacceptable climate change, and coal will be seen as the culprit."

With a major role for gas in the present and future, and despite the role of shale gas, Europe will continue to have to rely on Russia for supplies. Taking a global view of energy politics, there will be a great deal of interdependence. Is the way Europe and Russia are currently behaving towards each other in light of the Ukraine crisis helpful for a global energy policy?

"No, it is not. But first, to be fair to Gazprom, they have so far, even in the Cold War, supplied Western Europe with a track record of 100 per cent. That is incredible. They have never failed, not even technically. So the first reality is that they have perfect contract compliance. And, they will bend over backwards to keep that record.

"People say Ukraine's supply was interrupted. But that is a different story, about non-payment and gas siphoned off that was not measured."

LEADERSHIP AND INTERIM SOLUTIONS

Of all the interim solutions, however, neither solar energy, nor offshore and onshore wind energy, nor ocean wave energy provides in the shorter term a commercially viable alternative to fossil fuels at present. This leaves nuclear energy, which has a very minimal carbon footprint, but may not be acceptable to many societies in the West, especially since the Fukushima disaster.

The dilemma has come to the fore as decision-makers are unable to resist the political will of electorates protesting at nuclear energy, or directives from the European Union. It is becoming ever more difficult to exercise leadership because a confluence of forces is driving reactive policies and compromises in which long-term national, regional and global interests are sacrificed. After the Fukushima disaster, nuclear energy became unacceptable and a nuclear phase-out started in various European countries, especially in Germany, which plans to shut down all its reactors in 15 years or so. Austria and Spain have passed laws to cease production of new power stations, and other European countries are debating phase-outs. These short-term reactions are not in their long-term interest, either economically or environmentally. Nuclear energy remains a viable interim solution to reduce carbon emissions on a large scale, but in the public mind it no longer passes the test of the first A—Acceptable.

Van der Veer comments: "Mind you, Angela Merkel could have said: we will close all old nuclear power stations, but we will create a European task force that will look into how we can build safe nuclear energy for the future. That would have been a much better stance in my opinion than simply: I'm shutting down nuclear energy, full stop."

The challenge for leadership is immense. To be able to exercise leadership effectively in this area requires solid intellectual foundations and public support that does not exist. As our case study on the Responsibility to Protect doctrine shows, the ground was prepared over a long period before the diplomatic breakthrough occurred. To articulate a vision at the political level, and to gain traction with genuine public support, requires a broad campaign. It may be better to start from the bottom, General van den Breemen noted, to develop an integrated policy across the whole of government, rather than merely in one ministry. At this point in the conversation, former Defence Minister Hans Hillen interjected, "Don't overestimate politics."

Or would a top-down approach be more effective? "I think top-down," says van der Veer. "You first have to agree in Brussels that the goal in the end is to get an European energy policy. So, our heads of state can say: this is our common policy. But that will take years of preparation, because people are all over the place at the moment."

IN CONCLUSION

In this conversation, Jeroen van der Veer has provided us with valuable insights about the realities and possibilities of our energy future, and the requirements of leadership and management for genuine change. First of all, people are generally unaware of the scale of the global energy system and the fact that it will nearly double by 2050, with serious environmental, economic and geopolitical consequences. The higher abstraction level of the 'three A's' of Acceptable, Available and Affordable of every form of energy works out differently in different countries. There is a lack of consensus, within countries and at the regional and global level, which makes it impossible to articulate a shared vision. Nuclear energy is a viable interim solution until renewables are commercially viable, but it is generally not acceptable to the public.

The availability of inexpensive fuels in the West is partly because different countries have different cultures, and there is no consensus on the right energy mix for Europe. The shale gas revolution has a great chance to strengthen Europe's strategic position if European states were more proactive in shale gas exploration. A genuine pan-European vision, energy policy and energy strategy are required, which includes the role of Russia's energy strategy.

Renewable energy sources are largely unaffordable without subsidies at present. Most politicians' short-term horizons lead to a rush to subsidise renewables that are not commercially viable. On this last point, van der Veer proposes a very interesting challenge to us to spend less but achieve more by investing in the research and development of new generations of offshore wind energy, according to the principles of the learning curve. This is a good example of a long-term strategy where an iterative process can lead to a genuinely sustainable and viable solution. For that we need to move beyond the ideas stage.

"We don't have consensus. We have the ideas, but we don't have a common or shared vision, or a shared concept, or a shared strategy. So here we are stuck. Take the example of nuclear—there are huge problems with planning and execution.

"To achieve it you need a common vision. That in the end is leadership. I think leadership is helped by a very strong Energy Commissioner in Brussels with this as the main item on the agenda. And then it will still take some time.

"But the window of opportunity is there. The CO_2 problem is huge, but if we solve it one day earlier or one day later doesn't make any difference. So we have a very long window. That sometimes works to your disadvantage, because then you go too slowly. You can always delay it for a day, because the window isn't closing—unless you live in Beijing!"

CHAPTER 8

THE POWER OF IDEAS: RESPONSIBILITY TO PROTECT AT THE UNITED NATIONS

The Responsibility to Protect (R2P) is an international concept that aims to protect civilians from mass atrocities. In a short period of time, the R2P concept developed from a philosophical theory on sovereignty into a new norm in international relations. This chapter considers the gradual acceptance of the concept at the United Nations, where it has brought about a paradigm change in thinking and language regarding prevention, protection, intervention and rebuilding in situations of possible mass atrocities. We examine the substance and stages of development of the R2P concept. A conceptual breakthrough led to a diplomatic breakthrough because of the power of ideas and determined leadership by key players in delegations, the UN Secretariat and NGOs. While the concept now enjoys wide acceptance, its implementation still remains uneven. In this chapter we examine how an idea can break through to the status of an international norm.

THE QUALITATIVE ANALYSIS FOR THIS CHAPTER
IS ON PAGE 384 OF THE ANNEX

WITH HERMAN SCHAPER, FRANCIS DENG AND OTHERS.
INTERVIEWS BY THE OWLS TEAM.
TEXT BY MARTIJN DADEMA AND BENJAMIN BILSKI

I am respectful of your sovereignty – an important international concept.
But I don't see it negatively. I don't see it as a concept of barricading yourself
against the world. I see it as a very positive concept of a state's responsibility
for its people. And if you need help from the international community, call
for help, and at least be receptive for help. Given international concern for
human rights and humanitarian issues, if you do not discharge your
responsibility, and your people are suffering and dying, the world is not
going to watch and do nothing. They will find one way or another of
interfering, or intervening. So the best way for you to protect your
sovereignty is to discharge the responsibilities of sovereignty, and indeed,
to be seen to do so.   **– Dr Francis Deng**[1]

THE VISION OF FRANCIS DENG

The concept of the Responsibility to Protect has several parents[2], and a story
of origin that is both simple and remarkable for its deep impact and ongoing
development. It is a philosophical and conceptual breakthrough that became
a diplomatic and political breakthrough. It succeeded, because the concept
provided an answer to questions the international community was asking
after the massacres in Rwanda and Srebrenica. It provided a solution to an
institutional crisis of the United Nations. The concept matured from theory
to a diplomatic breakthrough at the highest international level because of determined advocacy and cooperation by key thinkers, delegations and NGOs,
who seized a unique opportunity with the support of the UN Secretariat. It is
all the more remarkable because the breakthrough from idea to international
norm occurred in a relatively short period of time.

The vision and precursor concept of R2P was 'Sovereignty as Responsibility' as formulated by Dr Francis Deng, who had established the Africa Project at the Brookings Institution in 1989. With his colleagues, Deng prepared
studies of African conflicts placed in their proper regional and national context. Until then, the continent had been viewed through the lens of Cold War
proxy wars.[3] In the 1996 book *Sovereignty as Responsibility*, a philosophical
chapter on the nature of sovereignty authored by Deng and Roberta Cohen
redefined sovereignty according to its underlying principles.

Deng wrote *Sovereignty as Responsibility* at a time when the number of
refugees in the world had risen to 20 million, 7 million of whom were African.
Globally, the number of internally displaced persons (IDPs) was 30 million, 16
million of whom were African. In cases where wars were between states and refugees crossed international borders, they became the concern of international
humanitarian law. But with internal conflict and internal displacement reaching unprecedented levels in the 1980s and 1990s as the Cold War was coming to
an end, Francis Deng fought to make IDPs an international humanitarian issue.

Responses by the international community, whether strategic or humanitarian, "nearly always evoke a reaction that is both appreciative and hostile

to foreign intervention."[4] The problems of refugees and IDPs are rooted in, and exacerbated by, crises of national identity. According to Deng, leaders and movements who claim legitimacy as the custodians of identity must assume concomitant responsibilities. This applies not only to the state but to every party involved:

> This is an important message for Africans to heed, whether they are governments, rebel leaders, militia leaders, civil society, or the general population. If they fail to discharge the responsibilities of sovereignty, whether through the state or alternatives to it, they cannot legitimately complain against international humanitarian intervention or against its withdrawal or neglect.[5]

The crises of identity in Africa have to be addressed by a constructive management of identity and viewing internal and external sovereignty as responsibilities, rather than privileges. Internal sovereignty is derived from a government meeting its responsibility in providing its citizens with physical security, basic services and respect for human dignity. External sovereignty is derived from a legitimate and accountable internal sovereignty: "In other words, by effectively discharging its responsibilities for good governance, a state can legitimately claim protection for its national sovereignty."[6]

Francis Deng next delved deeper into the question of internal legitimacy. Sovereignty traditionally derives from three sources: "The degree of respect merited by an institution, the capacity to rule, and the recognition that the authority acts on behalf of and for the benefit of the people."[7] When these sources become linked more specifically to the responsibilities of good governance, such as management of internal affairs, including ethnic relations, the economy, and foreign policy, then sovereignty is conditional. As a result, responsibility and accountability will become good objective measures of good governance and sovereignty. Scholarly opinion was "rallying behind a radical reassessment of the place and value of sovereignty in the contemporary world."[8]

When sovereignty is established as conditional and a government manifestly fails, the legitimacy to act to resolve a large-scale humanitarian crisis falls to the international community.

> Living up to the responsibilities of sovereignty becomes in effect the best guarantee for sovereignty. (...) Governments could best avoid intervention by meeting their obligations not only to other states, but also to their own citizens. If they failed, they might invite intervention.[9]

In a clear precursor to the three-pillar approach that would later be developed by UN Secretary-General Ban Ki-Moon,[10] Francis Deng concludes *Sovereignty as Responsibility* with a description of a strategy consisting of three phases of responses, from early warning, to diplomatic intervention, to international action:

> What is envisaged is a three-phase strategy that would include monitoring the developments to draw early attention to impending crises, interceding in time to avert the crisis through diplomatic initiatives,

and mobilizing international action when necessary. The first step would aim at detecting and identifying the problem through various mechanisms for information collection, evaluation, reporting and early warning. If sufficient basis for concern is established, the appropriate mechanism should be invoked to take preventive diplomatic measures to avert the crisis. (...) If diplomatic initiatives do not succeed, and depending on the human suffering involved, the Secretary-General may decide to mobilize international response, ranging from further diplomatic measures to forced humanitarian intervention sanctioned by the Security Council. [11]

This book established the theoretical basis and most important principles of what was to become the Responsibility to Protect, a concept that would turn the sacred cows of sovereignty and non-interference on their heads. What was originally conceived of for an African context had universal application when it provided an answer to an acute intellectual and institutional crisis at the United Nations, following the failure to act in Rwanda and Srebrenica, and after the successful campaign of prevention in Kosovo that took place without permission from the Security Council.

ILLEGAL BUT LEGITIMATE: TOWARDS A NEW CONCEPT

The Responsibility to Protect is a deceptively benign-sounding concept. In fact, (...) it represents a deep and disturbing challenge to those leaders who wish to treat their people with impunity. — **Kofi Annan** [12]

The impetus and moral outrage that would lead to the development of the Responsibility to Protect came following the Rwandan genocide in 1994 and the massacre at Srebrenica in 1995. In both cases the international community and United Nations manifestly failed. There was an overwhelming sense among many in the international policy community that *something* had to be done to prevent such crimes from happening again. [13] When in 1999 the crisis in Kosovo led to a successful NATO intervention that left the Security Council behind, it was clear that there was a deep structural problem for the United Nations when legality of sovereignty and legitimacy of protection were diametrically opposed. The Kosovo Commission, established by the then UN Secretary-General Kofi Annan, concluded with unprecedented wording, that

the NATO military intervention was illegal but legitimate. It was illegal because it did not receive prior approval from the United Nations Security Council. However, the Commission considers that the intervention was justified because all diplomatic avenues had been exhausted and because the intervention had the effect of liberating the majority population of Kosovo from a long period of oppression under Serbian rule. [14]

Kofi Annan made an important conceptual contribution to resolving this impasse shortly before the 1999 General Assembly convened. He argued that there are two kinds of sovereignty enshrined in the UN Charter and international humanitarian law, sovereignty for states and for individuals: "When we read the Charter today, we are more than ever conscious that its aim is to protect individual human beings, not to protect those who abuse them."[15]

In the context of a general awareness of this crisis of credibility, the Canadian Foreign Minister Lloyd Axworthy and former Australian Foreign Minister Gareth Evans were the individuals who next made real progress on the concept. They captured the mood of the time and combined it with the intellectual groundwork laid by Francis Deng. Axworthy claims he got the idea for the Responsibility to Protect after meeting Deng, who had come to Ottawa in his new capacity as Special Representative of the Secretary-General on Internally Displaced Persons to argue for a commitment by the international community for the protection of IDPs. As a result of this meeting, Axworthy saw in Deng's theory on sovereignty as responsibility a way to navigate the United Nations out of the intellectual and institutional post-Kosovo crisis that was fresh in his mind.[16]

The international community has the right to intervene in a crisis if a government fails in its primary responsibility to protect its citizens. This concept not only applied to IDPs but had a universal application. Deng's concept of sovereignty as responsibility gained traction, above all because it provided an answer to questions that were being asked at the time. Axworthy and Evans succeeded in translating these combined visions into a clear concept.[17]

Axworthy and Evans gathered a team of former officials to create the International Commission on Intervention and State Sovereignty (ICISS). Axworthy chaired the advisory board and the commission worked for a year. They presented the pamphlet *The Responsibility to Protect,* a term coined by Gareth Evans,[18] to Kofi Annan on 17 December 2001.

The pamphlet outlines the vision and concept of the Responsibility to Protect, establishing the basic principles of responsibility, the criteria for sovereignty, the criteria for evaluating a crisis, threshold criteria for military intervention that draw on the classical Just War tradition, and finally, the responsibility of the interveners to rebuild the country they acted to protect. The focus of the report was not yet on the four specific crimes of R2P, but on the much wider notion of "populations suffering serious harm."

"Building squarely on Deng's formulation,"[19] the first step was to recharacterize sovereignty "from *sovereignty as control* to *sovereignty as responsibility* in both internal functions and external duties."[20] The criteria of responsibility are not just respect for human rights, but include provisions for human security, such as "physical safety, their economic and social well-being, respect for their dignity and worth as human beings, and the protection of their human rights and fundamental freedoms."[21] This shifted the terms of the debate from a 'right to intervene' to a 'responsibility to protect'.

Where sovereignty as responsibility drew on natural law traditions of justice and governance to define the legitimacy of public authority, *The Responsibility to Protect* describes natural law principles from the tradition of Just War to spell out the criteria for military intervention. And while these threshold criteria are set high, the concept implied military intervention in states for the way they mistreat their own citizens, rather than for any international misdeed affecting the vital interests of an intervening state. [22]

On the operational dimension, the *Responsibility to Protect* pamphlet called upon coalitions to match capabilities and resources to the requirements set by the aims of the operation. [23] It also elaborated on the obligations of the responsibility to rebuild, which include the need for a post-intervention strategy for security, institution building, economic development and a national reconciliation between the parties. [24] To address the problem of a Security Council deadlock, the pamphlet suggests that its permanent members should "agree not to apply their veto power, in matters where their vital state interests are not involved". [25] Sidestepping the question of Security Council reform, the pamphlet couldn't do much more than offer this 'code of conduct' for the permanent members.

The new terminology of *Responsibility to Protect* and its shorthand 'R2P' placed military intervention amid a broader continuum of responsibilities, from prevention to rebuilding, based on Francis Deng's positive approach to sovereignty.

TOWARDS A DIPLOMATIC BREAKTHROUGH

How was it possible that a 100-page pamphlet proposing a new concept of responsibility turned entrenched notions of sovereignty and non-interference on their heads, and achieved a diplomatic breakthrough within four years by international consensus? And how did this concept evolve in record time to achieve the status of an emerging international norm?

The 2005 breakthrough in the World Summit Outcome was the result of determined leadership by key players, with a willingness to take the long view in a diplomatic strategy that included the formation of new coalitions, systematic work by NGOs, UN Secretariat support, tacit support from the Security Council, strong support from Africa, and a mixture of persuasion, courage and diplomatic sleight of hand, to overcome obstacles and brinkmanship by opponents.

In the first two years, however, there was little indication that the R2P concept could ever receive international support through a General Assembly resolution, let alone a consensus document. The only state championing R2P at that time was Canada. In 2002, Canada circulated a draft resolution to debate the ICISS report, but was promptly thwarted by the Non-Aligned Movement.

After one of its officials observed that a "small but determined and influential group of rejectionists was capable of swaying the majority opinion," Canada concluded that the majority could still be won over, and was encouraged to plan and carry out a long-term diplomatic strategy. [26] The target would be the 2005 World Summit, a once-in-five-years event that would produce a unanimous Outcome document that could anchor R2P firmly into the UN system, rather than a mere General Assembly resolution, of which over 300 are produced each year.

The overall aim of achieving a breakthrough in international recognition for R2P was broken down into sub-goals on several levels: targeting the UN secretariat and like-minded governments, and engaging NGOs and civil society. Specific diplomatic strategies were developed for each track, approaching these players in parallel.

In so doing, Canada succeeded in persuading Kofi Annan's sixteen-member High Level Panel to endorse R2P and add Gareth Evans to their ranks. Canada also reached out to other governments to create a 'Friends of R2P' coalition, and also worked on the ground level in operationalising R2P in practical measures – either by creating new initiatives or placing existing policies and activities into the R2P framework. This was a very pragmatic part of the process that a Canadian diplomat referred to as the 'just do it and don't call it a doctrine approach'. [27] Canada laid the groundwork to enable R2P to become a movement with genuine momentum. These activities created a buzz around the concept that enabled a breakthrough from theory to practice.

Canada also reached out to the NGO community, most notably to William Pace's World Federalist Movement (WFM), which planned and carried out its own diplomatic strategy. The WFM approached governments and NGOs, organized roundtable discussions and sought advice on how to advance the R2P agenda. WFM led global consultations and created a civil society coalition for R2P, bringing many NGOs on board. [28] It was the only NGO doing systematic full-time work on R2P in the period from 2003 to 2005. [29]

WFM carried out a three-track strategy: to persuade decision-makers of the moral imperative and importance of the adoption of the language of R2P; to create political will within governments to support the R2P concept; and to focus on operational questions and international capacity building. An additional reason that this approach was successful was that it recast existing policies under the new R2P label. [30] In the wake of the Iraq war, which was not a R2P intervention, there was renewed hostility to humanitarian intervention, and the advocates of R2P sought to create a consensus by embedding the concept as much as possible into the existing legal, institutional and customary framework of the United Nations. [31]

The High Level Panel published their report *A Secure World: Our Shared Responsibility* in December 2004, the first document to embed the language of R2P into UN discourse. The pamphlet discussed R2P in the context of collective security, placing all UN activities in a framework defined by R2P. It begins with a discussion on sovereignty and elaborates on the importance of prevention. It continues with collective security, the use of force, the question of legitimacy and finishes with post-conflict peace building. Kofi Annan endorsed almost all of its recommendations, paving the way for the inclusion of R2P in the World Summit. Annan became a very strong supporter of R2P, both as a matter of principle and because he saw in the concept the best means to carry out much-needed UN reform.

On the diplomatic front, there were two main obstacles to R2P that had to be overcome. First, there was the reluctance of permanent members of the Security Council, especially the United States (who rejected limitations on freedom of action), and Russia and China (who were wary of unauthorised humanitarian intervention). Second, there was determined opposition by several countries who viewed R2P as a 'right to intervene' and sought to sway the Non-Aligned Movement and G77 to keep R2P off the agenda.

American, Russian and Chinese reluctance was overcome by dropping any reference to a 'P-5 code of conduct'[32] and leaving the last word on intervention in the hands of the Security Council. Russia and China had also learnt an important lesson from Kosovo. If they opposed action to prevent mass atrocities too often, the legitimacy of the Security Council would be called into question and their own influence would diminish. The 1990s were marked by atrocities, paralysis and a loss of faith in the UN system. It was in their interest to keep *this* Security Council relevant and prevent Kosovo from turning into a norm.[33]

Within the United States, a constructive bipartisan new report by George Mitchell and Newt Gingrich fully endorsed R2P in the context of exploring the alignments between *American interests and UN reform*.[34]

Finally, the big obstacle of opposition by the Non-Aligned Movement was overcome by the creation of a new African consensus. After the Organization of African Unity became the African Union (AU) in 2002, its Constitutive Act listed a set of core principles that had absorbed the lessons of Rwanda. An important qualification was added to the familiar notions of sovereign equality, independence, prohibition of the use of force, and non-interference: Article 4(h) codified a principle of non-indifference, embedding in AU policy,

> the right of the Union to intervene in a Member State pursuant to a decision of the Assembly in respect of grave circumstances, namely: war crimes, genocide and crimes against humanity.

The fact that the AU contains, among its core principles, a duty to protect populations in case of three of the four major crimes listed in R2P (including ethnic cleansing) was an important source of common ground for African leaders to support R2P as a matter of principle. The stature of Francis Deng and respect for his wisdom was also a factor that helped shape the African consensus.

African leaders also saw in R2P a means to strengthen regionalism. Because the relationship between the AU and the Security Council could be problematic, the non-indifference clause also served the purpose of encouraging African states to step up to solve African problems and not rely on undesirable Security Council interventions. In a valuable international convergence of principles and interests, the notion that states must be seen exercising a responsibility to protect their populations was only controversial for Zimbabwe and Libya at that time.[35]

The African consensus was the strongest argument against those states in the Non-Aligned Movement who sought to portray R2P as a Western concept and appealed to tired clichés of conflict between 'the West and the rest'. R2P was recognised as a universal concept that represented a consensus of small and medium-sized democracies. Great powers were wary of R2P for the obligations and constraints it could impose, and dictators feared having their populations forcibly protected. The African consensus, informed both by principle and the interests of strengthened regionalism, paved the way for global consensus.

THE WORLD SUMMIT

In September 2005, world leaders arrived in New York for the United Nations World Summit. The preparatory work throughout 2005 had produced a fairly comprehensive draft outcome document, which included R2P as a substantial part of Kofi Annan's reform agenda. But disagreements remained on several critical issues, such as the status of the Security Council and the threshold criteria for intervention. The G77 were reluctant to support it, but were willing to compromise in exchange for concessions in development aid.

A fragile preliminary consensus had taken shape in the months ahead of the summit, but it would be upset by several interventions. US ambassador John Bolton intervened on 5 August by presenting several hundred amendments to the outcome document. [36] While many were unobjectionable, he didn't seek common ground with allies and the tactic threw the negotiations into disarray. The Russian ambassador next turned against R2P with an endless barrage of technical objections but was confronted by the Canadian ambassador, who persuaded him to back down. The Indian ambassador launched an anti-colonialist broadside against R2P, but would be overruled by President Singh. US Secretary of State Condoleezza Rice similarly overruled John Bolton, after she was made aware of a secret parallel outcome document. [37]

Simultaneously, Kofi Annan and President of the General Assembly Jean Ping worked with American UN official Robert Orr on a secret draft outcome document that preserved the preparatory work and incorporated main points of consensus of the summit. The R2P provisions were included with a specific focus only on four major crimes (genocide, war crimes ethnic cleansing and crimes against humanity). It was partially watered down, with the exclusive purview of the Security Council reaffirmed, without specifying its obligations. The responsibility to rebuild was left out. Kofi Annan and his small circle kept a tight lid on the parallel document until the last moment when they approached world leaders directly. The secret document was presented two days before the outcome was voted on. At this point, no world leader was willing to embarrass their country by spoiling the proceedings. The diplomatic breakthrough for R2P occurred on 24 October 2005 when the World Summit passed it unanimously.

A BASIC CONCEPT

Paragraphs 138 and 139 of the Outcome document[38] of the 2005 World Summit are the formal articulation of the international breakthrough of the R2P concept.

Responsibility to protect populations from genocide, war crimes, ethnic cleansing and crimes against humanity

138. Each individual State has the responsibility to protect its populations from genocide, war crimes, ethnic cleansing and crimes against humanity. This responsibility entails the prevention of such crimes, including their incitement, through appropriate and necessary means. We accept that responsibility and will act in accordance with it. The international community should, as appropriate, encourage and help States to exercise this responsibility and support the United Nations in establishing an early warning capability.

139. The international community, through the United Nations, also has the responsibility to use appropriate diplomatic, humanitarian and other peaceful means, in accordance with Chapters VI and VIII of the Charter, to help to protect populations from genocide, war crimes, ethnic cleansing and crimes against humanity. In this context, we are prepared to take collective action, in a timely and decisive manner, through the Security Council, in accordance with the Charter, including Chapter VII, on a case-by-case basis and in cooperation with relevant regional organizations as appropriate, should peaceful means be inadequate and national authorities are manifestly failing to protect their populations from genocide, war crimes, ethnic cleansing and crimes against humanity. We stress the need for the General Assembly to continue consideration of the responsibility to protect populations from genocide, war crimes, ethnic cleansing and crimes against humanity and its implications, bearing in mind the principles of the Charter and international law. We also intend to commit ourselves, as necessary and appropriate, to helping States build capacity to protect their populations from genocide, war crimes, ethnic cleansing and crimes against humanity and to assisting those which are under stress before crises and conflicts break out.

Article 138 affirms that each state "has the responsibility to protect populations from genocide, war crimes, ethnic cleansing and crimes against humanity", including their incitement; and that the international community should assist states to exercise this capability, and establish an early warning mechanism. Article 139 elaborates the role of the United Nations to use appropriate peaceful means to protect populations; for the Security Council to take collective action in accordance with the Charter; and for the General Assembly "to continue consideration of the responsibility to protect", continuing the development of the concept.

The phrase "through the Security Council, in accordance with the Charter, including Chapter VII, on a case-by-case basis" means that the application of R2P action is not automatic, and the veto of the permanent members remained in situations of mass atrocities.

These two articles, although relatively short in appearance, opened the door to an ongoing flood of activity that is reshaping the United Nations. The articulation and formalisation of the political and moral concept of the responsibility to protect enabled its champions to formulate sub-goals and plan strategies to implement these into the United Nations structure and in global action.

STRATEGY AND IMPLEMENTATION

Paragraphs 138 and 139 represent the basic concept that specifies the overall goals of the responsibility to protect. In the remainder of this chapter, we examine the efforts to develop and refine the concept, its strategic substance and brief history of implementation. For the champions of R2P at the UN today, four specific aims flow from the general concept: to advance further conceptual development of R2P; to increase political acceptance; to embed R2P in the UN structure; and to support R2P-related activities, missions and interventions in country-specific situations. These four aims each have respective diplomatic, political or operational strategies. In the context of these four aims and their strategies, we will also address obstacles and opposition to R2P that remain today, both political and institutional.

◎ Conceptual Development

> Recognizing the fledgling nature of agreement on the responsibility to protect, the Special Adviser's primary roles will be conceptual development and consensus-building. [39]

After Ban Ki-Moon assumed the office of Secretary-General in 2007, he brought a renewed institutional commitment to R2P. In a letter to the Security Council in August 2007, he described creating two positions at the Under Secretary-General level, of a Special Adviser for the Prevention of Genocide and Mass Atrocities, [40] and a Special Adviser on the Responsibility to Protect, to be held by Francis Deng and Edward Luck respectively. [41] They shared an office and staff, and under Deng's supervision, Luck went to work on developing the concept for the UN system. The results of his advisory work are a series of annual Reports of the Secretary-General on R2P that refine and develop the concept and explore what it means in practice – both for the UN's structure and its activities.

In January 2009, the first Secretary-General's report was presented to the General Assembly. *Implementing the responsibility to protect* brought a very substantial elaboration and refinement to the R2P concept, and building on paragraphs 138 and 139, it introduced a strategic dimension in the three-pillar approach.

Pillar one: The protection responsibilities of the State (sect. II)
Pillar two: International assistance and capacity building (sect. III)
Pillar three: Timely and decisive response (sect. IV)

The report has many practical recommendations for states in Pillar I, elaborates on improving research and analysis mechanisms of new information of an ongoing crisis – and connecting such an early-warning mechanism effectively to decision-making and operational mechanisms. The report also discusses how R2P connects to international criminal law. The second pillar includes important references to defusing conflicts in their early stages:

> Those contemplating the incitement or perpetration of crimes and violations relating to the responsibility to protect need to be made to understand both the costs of pursuing that path and the potential benefits of seeking peaceful reconciliation and development instead. [42]

According to the report, developing the mechanisms and capacities for an early intervention could prevent large-scale atrocities. This reflects an international consensus (supported by the lesson from Rwanda) that the cost of a late intervention after atrocities have already been committed is many times greater than the cost of early intervention.

The third pillar, pertaining to international response, covers a spectrum of activity from diplomatic interventions, to coercive measures such as sanctions and military action, and work through regional organisations, all in accordance with Chapters VI, VII and VIII of the UN Charter. While this may not change many UN activities, the overall R2P concept helps place existing programmes, such as peace-building missions or conflict-prevention work, into a broader strategic framework. With this framework in place, it becomes much easier to identify gaps in capabilities.

The Secretary-General has since released reports annually, including the July 2010 report *Early warning, assessment and the responsibility to protect*, which identified capability and capacity gaps in order to develop an effective early warning mechanism for the UN.

With painful memories of General Roméo Dallaire's urgent missive warning of an impending genocide in Rwanda – a message that was never passed on to the Security Council – the second report stresses that, in order to improve early warning capacity, "the institutional weakness in the analytical capacity of the United Nations" needs to be addressed. Improvements are needed in the UN's capacity to analyse and react to information, and in the flow of information within the UN system, and between the UN and the Security Council. [43]

In a follow-up speech, Ed Luck stressed that "early warning should not be the beginning of the UN's engagement in a situation of concern", where the UN is merely waiting for bad news while the human toll rises, and options to intervene are increasingly limited and unattractive. Rather, there should be a system-wide response mechanism that includes preventive mechanisms of early understanding and early engagement. [44] Creating an effective early warning system linked to actionable policy options remains the biggest challenge of the implementation of R2P today.

In June 2011, the Secretary-General presented *The role of regional and sub-regional arrangements in implementing the responsibility to protect* to both the General Assembly and the Security Council. This third report explores the role of regional organizations, and clarifies their relationship to the UN with regard to the implementation of R2P in accordance with Chapter VIII of the Charter. Regional organizations are uniquely placed for a whole spectrum of activities that can be placed in the R2P framework in order to make use of local expertise to identify where the international community should focus its capacity-building efforts:

> Often, neighbours and subregional and regional organizations have the keenest sense of when trouble is brewing in the neighbourhood and of where and how the international community can be of greatest assistance. They can identify capacity gaps and serve as conduits for the two-way flow of information, ideas and insights between stakeholders at the local and national levels and those at the global level. [45]

Incorporating regional organizations into the information-flow and the three-pillar structure of R2P means building systems that can provide a measure of 'structural prevention'. These systems will be operating effectively when they have incorporated their local strategies into the grand strategy of R2P.

In July 2012, the fourth report *Responsibility to Protect: timely and decisive response* was released, further refining the strategy for implementation according to the three pillars with available tools and partners. The report also provides a respectful commentary on 'responsibility while protecting' – a concept on transparency and accountability during military interventions that was proposed by Brazil in the wake of the Libya campaign. (We will return to 'RWP' below in the discussion on Libya.)

The 2013 report concerns Pillar 1 of R2P and focuses on *State responsibility and prevention*. It elaborates on the risk factors that could lead to mass atrocity crimes and on state responsibilities in addressing and preventing possible atrocity crimes. The report describes possible policy options for atrocity prevention, including for building resilience and promoting and protecting human rights. It also articulates targeted measures to prevent atrocity crimes. This last report is a practical refinement of the concept for domestic policymaking and provides an agenda for the prevention of mass atrocity crimes.

Professor Jennifer Welsh, formerly of the Oxford Institute for Ethics, Law and Armed Conflict and now Professor of International Relations at the European University Institute in Florence, prepared the next report. She has devoted much of her recent scholarly work to Pillar 2, and in her capacity as the new Special Adviser succeeding Edward Luck, this work is now reflected in the 2014 Report to the Secretary General, *Fulfilling our collective responsibility: international assistance and the responsibility to protect.*

This document is both principled and very practical. After restating the nature of the atrocities covered by R2P, the report elaborates on the principles and approaches that can help guide states to fulfil their protection responsibilities, while naming those actors who could contribute to the responsibility to assist. The core of the document elaborates on three main forms of Pillar 2 support: encouragement, capacity-building and protection assistance, with examples of good practice on the national, regional and international levels.

These reports represent an ongoing breakthrough process that is changing the United Nations for the better. The entire process of conceptual development, from 'sovereignty as responsibility' to the state of R2P today, has been a gradual one.

Gutta cavat lapidem, non vi, sed saepe cadenda. (The drop hollows out the stone, not by force but by constant dripping.) It has proven successful for the advancement of the R2P concept, strategy and implementation in the UN mainstream, to make a routine out of annual reports. The battle of ideas on the levels of vision and concept has been won, though pockets of resistance remain. Developing strategy and implementation, both inside the UN system as well as in R2P-related programmes or interventions, therefore requires continual attention and effort. The next challenge is to increase the acceptance of the concept, not just in theory, but also in practice.

INCREASING POLITICAL ACCEPTANCE

During the Libya intervention, when Robert Mugabe spoke out in the General Assembly, complaining that it was an incorrect application of R2P, it was evident that a breakthrough and paradigm change had occurred.[46] The argument was no longer whether R2P should be put into practice, but *how* it should be practised. Rather than attempting to return to the mind-your-own-business tropes of 'sovereign equality' and 'non-interference', the discussion had turned to what R2P really means and how it should be applied. While this battle of ideas has been won, vigilance and courage remain necessary to keep the vision alive. Sometimes the courage of one man is enough to make a great difference.

There was a moment when the life of R2P hung in the balance. In 2009, the President of the General Assembly (PGA), the Nicaraguan Sandinista Miguel d'Escoto Brockmann, held very conspirational ideas about R2P. He surrounded himself with sixteen special advisers, including Noam Chomsky, who was not chosen for his theory on syntax. They sought to bury R2P. If Articles 138 and 139 could not be repealed, then the next best thing was to shut down any discussion of it. The PGA attempted to block any response from the General Assembly to Ed Luck's first report.[47]

This was a violation of standard procedures. Normally, the Secretary-General makes a proposal and governments react by applauding, complaining or passing resolutions. It was not the business of the PGA, who represented a distinctly militant and negative minority view, to speak on behalf of the entire international community or to dictate their responses.

When Guatemalan Ambassador Gert Rosenthal approached the Group of Friends of R2P to address the threat that the PGA presented, he found them unwilling to fight the case. The Group of Friends coalition at the time was chaired by Canada, the first champion of R2P, but the Liberal government that had financed the ICISS report and played such a key role in making the 2005 breakthrough possible, had since been replaced by the Conservative Harper government. They had doubts about R2P, which in their eyes was associated too much with their domestic political opponents. When Rosenthal found the coalition unwilling to challenge the PGA, he assumed the role himself. [48]

Rosenthal's diplomatic strategy was to create an 'alliance of reasonable people' to take on the PGA on procedural grounds by defending the integrity of the General Assembly's relationship to its President. Starting with developing countries, including some who had opposed R2P, Rosenthal patiently succeeded in gathering support for a modest GA resolution that was passed in October 2009.

The resolution had only two clauses in the preamble, one reaffirming respect for the principles of the Charter, and the other recalling the 2005 World Summit Outcome, especially Articles 138 and 139. One operative clause took note of the Secretary-General's first report on R2P, and it ends with: "Decides to continue its consideration of the responsibility to protect." [49] This doesn't seem like much on paper, but it was an important victory in keeping the concept alive when a determined enemy in a position of authority came very close to burying it. Later that year, the Canadians handed the chairmanship of the Friends of R2P coalition to the Netherlands, which shares it with Rwanda. [50] They continue to champion the concept in New York.

'Groups of Friends' are informal vehicles of countries that support a particular cause within the UN system. Within that definition, this particular Group is unique in that it has countries from every region, showing cross-regional support for R2P. They work on several tracks: to ensure conceptual development; to enhance the political acceptance of R2P among UN delegations and organisations, governments and civil society; and to further embed R2P within the UN system. In addition, the Group has occasionally focused on the application of individual country situations.

To support these processes, the Group made use of various diplomatic instruments, including ambassadorial and expert meetings, public statements, coordination on negotiation processes on resolutions and other statements. This includes targeting Security Council members to include R2P language in resolutions. The Group also provides input for the annual SG-reports and its member States fund R2P-related organizations.

Another important element is to provide political and financial support for the Special Advisers of the Secretary-General for the Prevention of Genocide and the Responsibility to Protect. This support was especially needed in the

Fifth Committee, the budgetary committee of the GA. The first showdown occurred in December 2010, when the opponents of R2P, the so-called ALBA group that includes Cuba and Venezuela, sought to exclude all language on R2P from the budget of the special advisers, and to ensure that no funding was made available for R2P-related matters.

The Group of Friends of R2P has supported the Joint Office in preparations for the debates in the Fifth Committee with experts, and has lobbied hard with all regional groups to ensure that the amendments of the ALBA group would be defeated. Thanks to hard work and strong lobbying by the Group of Friends, the votes in the period 2010-2012 in the Fifth Committee were increasingly in favour of the Joint Office and R2P, and only very few countries retain fundamental problems with the concept.

The fundamental political opposition towards R2P is restricted to a few hardliners, in particular Cuba, Nicaragua, Venezuela, Syria and Iran. They have been trying to block progress on R2P on various fronts, beside the Fifth Committee and GA, but also in other arenas whenever the opportunity arises. For the Group of Friends, these open enemies can be dealt with. They are easy to defeat rhetorically and politically. The real challenges for advancing political acceptance in the UN arise when theory and practice contradict in the actions of permanent members of the Security Council, especially Russia and China.

China and Russia were formally in favour of R2P and have never voted against the concept. But they have been hesitant to include R2P in Security Council deliberations, both in thematic debates as well as in specific country situations, especially with regard to Syria. During their tenure as the Special Advisers on Prevention of Genocide and R2P, Francis Deng and Ed Luck have not been invited to brief the Council on issues of concern. Deng's successor, however, the Senegalese jurist Adama Dieng, did brief the Security Council twice in 2014 on atrocities in South Sudan and the Central African Republic. This could be seen as a reflection of a gradual trend of growing acceptance.

Nonetheless, we have seen progress in 2013 with the adoption of much more progressive language on R2P in two statements by the President of the Security Council on the protection of civilians in armed conflict,[51] and peace and security in Africa.[52] The latter states:

> The Council underlines the importance of raising awareness of and ensuring respect of all applicable international law, including international humanitarian law and human rights law, stresses the importance of the responsibility to protect as outlined in the 2005 World Summit Outcome Document, including the primary responsibility of Member States to protect their populations from genocide, ethnic cleansing, crimes against humanity and war crimes. The Council further underlines the role of the international community in encouraging and helping States, including through capacity-building, to meet their primary responsibility.

This more progressive language was partly possible because ten members of the Security Council in 2013 are members of the Group of Friends of R2P.

Although progress has been made in increasing acceptance in New York, much remains to be done in capitals and other UN headquarters around the world. In the Human Rights Council in March 2013, many countries of the Global South, including African and Latin American countries, rallied against the inclusion of R2P language in a resolution on the prevention against genocide. So while acceptance increases in New York, outreach to bring change in other UN capitals is still needed.

EMBEDDING R2P IN THE UN STRUCTURE

Apart from the political acceptance, the struggle for implementation also concerns the administrative side, and the challenge to embed the R2P concept in the structure of the United Nations. The United Nations system is formally very supportive of the concept of Responsibility to Protect. In his Five-Year Action Agenda, Secretary-General Ban has identified "advancing the responsibility to protect agenda" as one of the main priorities for his second term. Mainstreaming R2P within the UN system is an important element of this agenda, but progress has been slow for several reasons.

The three pillars of R2P provide strategic direction for the prevention of mass atrocities. This creates a conceptual and causal link between existing concepts, institutions, and programmes of the UN system. R2P should therefore be relevant to many entities within the UN and not only to its Special Adviser. The R2P concept, with its three pillars, is the best opportunity the United Nations has ever had to bring a grand strategic direction to the whole spectrum of its institutions and activities.

UN institutions have activities with regard to development, conflict prevention, mediation, reform of security apparatus, implementation of human rights conventions, managing diversity in government policies, protecting civilians in peacekeeping operations, and providing humanitarian aid. All have a direct link to the prevention of mass atrocities, and therefore to R2P. These connections are not always recognised or built upon, and most UN entities do not frame their existing activities according to the concept, although their practice without theory also contributes to the concept.

Inside the UN structure, there has also been substantial institutional opposition. R2P can be an unsettling doctrine, especially if it is politically sensitive or forces large organizations to change their habits. There are two main types of opposition to R2P inside the UN: from the humanitarian community, and from the political and development community.

The humanitarian community, including the UNHCR, the ICRC and the OCHA, worries about the politicisation of protection of civilians, which is an established requirement in international humanitarian law. This community has argued repeatedly that protection of civilians is distinctly different from R2P. This was especially apparent in the last SG report on *Protection of Civilians*, which distinguished the legal concepts of the protection of civilians, as codified in international humanitarian law, from R2P, which is primarily a moral and political concept:

> I am concerned about the continuing and inaccurate conflation of the concepts of the protection of civilians and the responsibility to protect. While the two concepts share some common elements, particularly with regard to prevention and support to national authorities in discharging their responsibilities towards civilians, there are fundamental differences. First, the protection of civilians is a legal concept based on international humanitarian, human rights and refugee law, while the responsibility to protect is a political concept, set out in the 2005 World Summit Outcome. Second, there are important differences in their scope.
>
> The protection of civilians relates to violations of international humanitarian and human rights law in situations of armed conflict. The responsibility to protect is limited to violations that constitute war crimes or crimes against humanity or that would be considered acts of genocide or ethnic cleansing. Crimes against humanity, genocide and ethnic cleansing may occur in situations that do not meet the threshold of armed conflict. I urge the Security Council and Member States to be mindful of these distinctions. [54]

This distinction is conceptually correct, and there are legal and normative differences. There are however also many similarities, especially in conflict situations where mass atrocities occur. In these situations, the Protection of Civilians (PoC) and Responsibility to Protect concepts do overlap substantially. In general, the overlap between these concepts is much larger than the differences. The humanitarian community however is very careful to distinguish between the concepts to avoid a backlash against PoC, due to the highly politicised debate on R2P in Libya.

The development and political community (UNDP, DPA, DPKO) [55] also have difficulty seeing the added value of R2P for their existing activities in good governance, conflict prevention, security sector reform and human rights. The prevention of mass atrocities is often equated with prevention of conflict. The former head of DPA remarked:

> Whether we are talking about R2P, protecting civilians, or trying to retrieve failed or failing states, the international community essentially has three instruments to achieve its aims. One involves the political arts: mediation, negotiations, international political support or censure, election support, etc. We usually sum these tools up under the rubric of preventive diplomacy. A second lever we have is often clothed as a development or economic issue, but its essence is our effort to help countries improve governance and develop some modicum of the rule of law. These are, of course, also essentially political in nature. The third, and most difficult, lever we have is the use of coercion either through sanctions or military action. [56]

These institutions have no political objections to R2P, but fail to see the relevance or added value to their day-to-day work. They also do not recognise that

R2P and the three-pillar approach provide a framework strategic priority for their own work within the UN system as a whole. But they believe it is easier to not bring R2P into the mainstream of existing UN programmes. The important and practical 2013 SG report on Pillar 1 will play an important part in realising this mainstreaming, and lays the groundwork for a bigger report in 2014, considering what the international community can do according to Pillar 2.

A clear example of relevance of a mass atrocity perspective for both humanitarian as well as development and political actors within the UN system was the last few months of Sri Lanka's civil war in 2009, when as many as 40,000 civilians were killed. The UN system did not respond as it should have done, and the Secretary-General established an internal panel to review the UN's response to this crisis.

The panel's report concluded that events in Sri Lanka marked a grave failure of the UN to adequately respond to early warnings and to the evolving situation during the final stages of the conflict and its aftermath. To the detriment of hundreds of thousands of civilians, this failure was in contradiction of the principles and responsibilities of the UN.

The investigative panel, led by Charles Petrie, a former United Nations official, criticised what it called "a continued reluctance by UNCT institutions" and staff members in Sri Lanka at the time "to stand up for the rights of the people they were mandated to assist." Many "senior staff did not perceive the prevention of killing of civilians as their responsibility." The failure of the UN mission to confront the government about "obstructions to humanitarian assistance," the failure to "address government responsibility for attacks that killed civilians, and the tone of UN communications with the government on these issues, collectively amounted to a failure by the UN to act within the scope of institutional mandates to meet protection responsibilities." [57]

STRATEGY AND IMPLEMENTATION IN SPECIFIC CASES

In this section we briefly consider several additional crises where R2P was pertinent, called for, applied or not applied. The record so far is mixed: the crises in Sri Lanka, Darfur and Syria represent the biggest failures of the international community to protect civilian populations from deliberate mass atrocities and large-scale displacement. Nonetheless, there have also been important successes in Kenya, Guinea, Kyrgyzstan, Yemen and Libya. While risks remain in some of these countries of relapsing into crisis, preventive action has helped avert bigger atrocities. These instances of R2P in practice reveal the strategic sequence that the three-pillar approach entails, with mixed success.

◎ Darfur

Darfur in Western Sudan has seen the worst mass atrocities of the 21st century. In an extreme conflict of identity between the centre and periphery, similar to South Sudan, proxy militias were unleashed on the civilian population backed by the state's air power. Over 4.2 million Darfuris were affected by the conflict, of whom 2.5 million have been internally displaced, 240,000 have fled to neighbouring Chad and the Central African Republic, and over 400,000 have been killed.[58]

The UN Security Council, the African Union and European Parliament have each passed resolutions on Darfur, referring to responsibility to protect.[59] The African Union's small peacekeeping mission was endorsed by the Security Council, and grew from 150 to 7,000. The 2006 Security Council resolution 1706 referred to R2P and sought to bolster the AU's mission, but the lack of consent from the Sudanese government prevented the force from being made operational. In 2007, the Council passed resolution 1769, which authorised a joint UN-AU force of 26,000 – a mission that was extended in 2010.[60]

In addition, the European Force in Chad and Central African Republic (EUFOR), was deployed to protect refugees crossing the border. Finally, the International Criminal Court (ICC) issued a warrant for the arrest of Sudan's President Omar Al-Bashir, on counts of war crimes and crimes against humanity in 2009, and a second warrant in 2010 that included a charge of genocide.[61] However, none of these missions had the mandate to end the mass atrocities "in a timely and decisive manner" as called for by paragraph 139.

Geopolitical interests, lack of political will and logistical difficulties, and support for President Bashir from Arab and African states as well as Russia and China, have all led to a stalemate, where violence continues at a lower intensity. The bulk of the discussion inside the United Nations had been focused more on whether it represented genocide rather than on what to do. The crisis of Darfur includes the some of the worst crimes carried out with the greatest impunity in recent years, and is one of the international community's greatest failure to protect.

◎ Kenya

Following a rigged presidential election in 2007, violence flared up in many parts of the country, leading to over 1,000 deaths and 500,000 displacements. Clashes were both politically and ethnically motivated; the international response came quickly. The French Foreign Minister Bernard Kouchner appealed to the UN Security Council to react "in the name of the responsibility to protect", to "choose dialogue or bear responsibility for human catastrophe."[62] Secretary-General Ban Ki-Moon expressed concern, and UN High Commissioner for Human Rights Louise Arbour called on the Kenyan government to respect its international obligations.[63]

After initial mediation attempts had failed, former Secretary-General Kofi Annan led a panel of respected African leaders who successfully mediated the crisis and brokered a power-sharing agreement. Three commissions were established to review the post-election violence, and the conflict has been successfully defused. This rapid diplomatic intervention represents a model of successful action under the responsibility to protect.

◎ Guinea

Following a violent crackdown committed by government forces on a peaceful protest in a stadium in Conakry on 28 September 2009, alongside evidence of other systematic killings, rapes and other abuses by security forces, the international and regional communities responded rapidly. The regional organization ECOWAS led mediation between the government junta and the umbrella opposition group, which has since led to positive efforts towards a national unity government.

On 15 January 2010, the Joint Declaration of Ouagadougou was signed, establishing a national unity government, with elections to be held in six months. On 27 June, three million Guineans voted in the country's first free, fair and democratic elections, although the opposition alleged fraud. The opposition candidate would eventually win the presidential run-off election, and this represented an important transition from a coup to a democratically elected president. The crisis of Guinea represents a successful preventive R2P application, although risks along ethnic lines remain.

◎ Kyrgyzstan

Kyrgyzstan witnessed ethnic violence between Kyrgyz and Uzbeks in the southern part of the country in 2010, leaving hundreds dead and 300,000 displaced internally and across the border to Uzbekistan. The international response came relatively quickly, with both the OSCE and the UN engaging politically to stop the violence and engage political dialogue. Both Special Advisers Francis Deng and Edward Luck engaged the parties and called for international support. A number of programmes were launched which largely defused the violence. The international community acted decisively, and elections led to a successful peaceful transition, although the Uzbek minority remains threatened.

◎ Côte d'Ivoire

The presidential elections of 2010 led to a political stalemate, when the incumbent President Laurent Gbagbo refused to accept and honour the outcome that declared his opponent Alassane Ouattara the winner. Clashes ensued, and over 1,000 people were killed and 500,000 forcibly displaced, of whom 94,000 fled to Liberia. The elected President Ouattara fled to a hotel in Abidjan, where he was protected by a UN peacekeeping operation. Initial mediation efforts by the UN and ECOWAS failed. Mandated by Resolution 1975, a combination of French forces, UN peacekeepers and forces loyal to Ouattara defeated Gbagbo's troops and arrested him. Over 20,000 people were killed. President Outtara immediately called for the establishment of a truth and reconciliation commission, which Secretary-General Ban Ki-Moon supported. While it took a military intervention to resolve this crisis, and while the greatest efforts are being made towards reconciliation, Côte d'Ivoire still runs the risk of relapsing into ethnic violence.

◎ Libya

The implementation of United Nations Security Council Resolution 1970 and 1973, which led to a military intervention in Libya, has been hailed by R2P supporters as the ultimate R2P application, but also caused much controversy. R2P was an important aspect of the considerations in the Security Council's response to President Gaddafi's violent crackdown on protesters in February 2011. Several global leaders expressed enormous concern about the plight of the population of Libya, and in particular that of Benghazi. Both resolutions were timely and focused on the protection of civilians. Resolution 1973 explicitly

> Authorizes Member States that have notified the Secretary-General, acting nationally or through regional organizations or arrangements, and acting in cooperation with the Secretary-General, to take all necessary measures, notwithstanding paragraph 9 of resolution 1970 (2011), to protect civilians and civilian populated areas under threat of attack in the Libyan Arab Jamahiriya, including Benghazi.

NATO implemented this mandate proactively and in August 2011 the Gaddafi government fell after opposition forces acting under the National Transitional Council advanced towards Tripoli and other major cities. However, over the course of the period between February and August, the debate regarding the meaning of the resolutions and their implementation became increasingly bitter. Some complained that the Libyan intervention was no longer focused on the protection of civilians, but resulted in 'regime change.'

The alternative view was that "all necessary measures" of which the resolution spoke were being used by the NATO-led alliance to prevent atrocities and protect civilians – nothing more, but certainly nothing less. The case of Libya continues to impact the conceptual debate on R2P and the relation between R2P and regime change, and the role of military intervention in furthering the objectives of R2P. It also has an impact on the position of some Security Council members. In particular, Russia uses – or one might say, abuses – the Libya experience as an argument to block any Security Council R2P action of any nature.

The Brazilian intervention in this debate introduced 'Responsibility While Protecting' as a complementary concept to R2P that demanded greater clarification and transparency at a time of military intervention. While this was very much an outsider's complaint about NATO, it would ultimately be welcomed, because it helped restore the support for R2P in the developing world.

◎ Syria

Syria currently represents the biggest ongoing failure and crisis for the responsibility to protect, with any decisive action by the United Nations being blocked by Russia and China. By November 2014 more than 191,000 had been killed in the civil war, 7.6 million civilians have been internally displaced and 3.2 million refugees are registered in neighbouring countries – together, over half of the Syrian population. The regime of Bashar al-Assad has probably added the use of chemical weapons against its population to its list of crimes, in addition to torture, starvation and murder on a large scale in the prison system of the regime, where 85,000 are estimated to be arbitrarily detained. The rise of the Islamic State terrorist group has also led to increased ethnic cleansing and cruelty, especially against Kurdish, Yazidi and Christian minorities in Syria and neighbouring Iraq. It was not the atrocities of Bashar al-Assad, but those of the Islamic State that have awoken the international community and the United States to carry out air strikes against the terrorist group. The Syrian regime enjoys strong support from Russia and Iran, and is not being held accountable by the international community for its atrocities. Where Libya revealed the risks of action, Syria represents the deep and severe perils of inaction.

EVALUATION

On balance, the concept of the Responsibility to Protect has achieved a remarkable breakthrough at the United Nations, though the process is gradual and ongoing. The first great accomplishment was in Francis Deng reformulating sovereignty in terms of responsibility, and articulating a clear and powerful vision that laid the foundation for a universal framework which provided the solution to the institutional crisis of the UN in the 1990s. There should never be a dilemma between the paralysis of legality and the legitimacy of humanitarian action.

The champions of the concept showed foresight and leadership by seizing the window of opportunity offered by the World Summit of 2005. In the early years, the Canadian diplomatic corps and William Pace's World Federalist Movement were the only bodies promoting R2P and doing systematic work on it, reaching out to civil society, the media, religious organizations and the UN Secretariat.

This diplomatic breakthrough sets the R2P concept apart from other comparable concepts, doctrines or theories, and represents the biggest victory yet in the battle of ideas. It was followed up with other smaller victories that would not have been possible without key delegations planning a long-term strategy and the determined support of the UN Secretariat. Changed language reflects the fact that mainstream discourse has shifted to a new paradigm. But despite these successes, much fragility and opposition remains in both the political and administrative spheres of the UN.

On the political level, battles have been won in the World Summit, the Fifth Committee and the General Assembly, and several Security Council discussions and resolutions. However, challenges of implementation remain to R2P, both within the United Nations system and institutions. The actual application of R2P to specific crises remains as uneven as the Security Council's priorities, decision-making process and outcomes. The concept will not solve the problems inherent in the Security Council's structure, but it may insert itself into the conversation more often.

From a diplomatic point of view, it was never realistic to expect R2P to become the sole driving force of deliberations and decision-making. Many factors are weighed in political and international decisions, and the aim of the diplomats who champion R2P is to increase its weight as a factor in UN deliberations and decision-making.

Another necessary and missing element for effective political-military decision-making in the Security Council is the controversial question of military advice. It is crucial for the Security Council to have adequate military advice about the feasibility and practicality of the missions it orders. When a country, an ad-hoc coalition or another organization implements a decision of the Council, it is not unreasonable to expect that the country or coalition in question, or NATO, has a more developed relationship with the Council.

There is no tradition of reliable military advice to the Security Council. Articles 46 and 47 of the UN Charter called for the creation of a Military Staff Committee, composed of Chiefs of Staff of the permanent members of the Security Council, to advise on the application of armed force. But these clauses were never implemented. With the onset of the Cold War, military advice fell to the regional and alliance level, and in the more than two decades since the end of the Cold War, Articles 46 and 47 have never been revived. Planning for war still remains a taboo subject in a UN culture that prides itself on being a culture of peace – even in peacekeeping operations. Whenever the Council orders an operation, the execution of the mandate is basically delegated to the commander in the field.

Another problem for the effectiveness of Security Council on military affairs is the large gap between the political decision for an intervention and those who carry it out. When the Council orders an operation, its permanent members do not contribute much themselves. Suppliers of troops for international peace-keeping operations such as Bangladesh, India, Pakistan and Ethiopia attach great importance to classical peacekeeping on the basis of neutrality, consent of the host nation and use of violence only for self-defence. With such an inter-pretation of a mandate, they are much less attracted by any idea of engaging in active combat. They have difficulty with concepts that straddle both peacekeep-ing and the waging of war, such as 'peace enforcement', 'robust peacekeeping' or other actions that might be necessary for the protection of civilians.

Many of these structural problems inherent in the UN system, both politi-cal and administrative, explain the mixed record of R2P in practice. The R2P concept has not solved these problems, and the intervention in Libya did not cause these problems either. But Libya did bring many inconvenient truths to light. The intervention renewed fears that it was a doctrine of regime change – although it should have been clear by now that if a government is bent on committing crimes against humanity against its own population, an effective intervention to protect the civilian population can imply regime change if it is the only way to put an end to major crimes.

For the Responsibility to Protect to be effectively implemented across the

United Nations system, however, means not only overcoming political opposition in whatever political arena discussions are held. It also means overcoming barriers that are present in the structure and culture of the UN as a whole – both political and administrative, particularly in the Security Council. The Responsibility to Protect has provided a concept, doctrine and brand that could be driving change effectively if pursued with vigour and leadership both within and outside the UN system.

CONCLUSION

The Responsibility to Protect is a good example of a breakthrough process, where the story of its genesis from vision and concept to strategy and implementation is clearly identifiable. It also contains many valuable lessons about breakthroughs in general. The path from the ideas first formulated in the mid-1990s to the diplomatic breakthrough in 2005 is not an obvious one.

The first stage of ideas and vision – Francis Deng's clear articulation of the precursor concept of Sovereignty as Responsibility – would become the most important seed for the Responsibility to Protect. The environmental factor is crucial here for traction – it caught on in part because it provided an answer to questions that were being asked. At a time of a crisis of credibility for the United Nations, with a conflict between legality and legitimacy of action during a succession of humanitarian disasters, Francis Deng's ideas were the answer to those questions. The process starts when ideas catch on, but the ideas alone would not lead to a conceptual breakthrough.

It required the initiative and leadership of Lloyd Axworthy and Gareth Evans, with the imprimatur of the Canadian government, to take the ideas and organise a series of roundtables that led to the *Responsibility to Protect* pamphlet of 2001. Credit goes to Gareth Evans for the daring coinage, introducing the term of the 'Responsibility to Protect' and shifting the debate in a new direction. It was no longer about more effective action in this or that crisis, but about reframing the intellectual and moral foundations of the United Nations.

The result was an intelligent, clear and principled document, which was presented to the highest levels of the United Nations and its delegations. The *Responsibility to Protect* document was oriented towards the UN from the beginning, and was the first comprehensive articulation of the concept. But a pamphlet and a press ceremony are not enough to accomplish a genuine breakthrough that changes a key institution for the better.

Ideas circulate and prompt discussion and debate. But to prepare for a diplomatic breakthrough, or any breakthrough at all, it is necessary to have a dedicated and organised group of people to work to prepare the audience – whether it is the general public, a parliament or a General Assembly – and create a buzz.

The buzz is the necessary fuel in the preparation of a breakthrough, and can circulate for many years without result. The spark is leadership acting fast in a window of opportunity, igniting a breakthrough that is suddenly a new norm in an institution. A paradigm change occurs, and like a revolution, it is never predicted but considered inevitable after the fact.

How was the buzz created? It required a dedicated effort to champion the concept by the Canadian diplomatic corps and William Pace's World Federalist Movement – the only people in the early years doing systematic intellectual work on the concept and promoting it. Their championing of R2P created momentum and mobilised many other institutions and delegations to support the concept. This kind of work may seem a fruitless process for a number of years, until the tide turns, and a breakthrough is made inside a major institution.

It is not possible to change a major institution in a short period of time. To achieve a diplomatic breakthrough for R2P like the World Summit would not have been possible without the elements of the context of a crisis, a solution in a concept, the momentum of activism by states and other organizations, and above all, determined support from institutional leadership – in this case, from Kofi Annan. All these factors came together to make the breakthrough possible: context, ideas, momentum and the leadership to recognise and seize the best window of opportunity.

Another crucial factor for the success of the breakthrough, and many stages of follow-up inside the United Nations, is that the same people were involved in the various stages: Francis Deng, Lloyd Axworthy and Gareth Evans all contributed to creating the vision and concept of R2P, but they are also still involved in further stages of strategy, planning and implementation. The iterative feedback process from strategy and implementation back to vision and concept – driven by the same people – ensures that the integrity of the vision is maintained, and helps drive the breakthrough forward in practice.

On the political level, the champions of R2P in the Group of Friends currently form a strong phalanx in defence of the concept. The 2009 episode with the Sandinista PGA revealed that if vigilance drops, and the enemies of the concept assume positions of high authority, pushback is very possible. Any vision and concept that forces established institutions to do better is likely to cause discomfort. Without the determined leadership of champions keeping a vision alive, a breakthrough has no chance of succeeding, and may even be reversed. The real challenge and difficulty is in reforming institutions. Old habits and inertia will resist change, but if an institution's structure, lines and systems of communication are improved, new habits can quickly fall into place. But we are faced with some institutions that will be incredibly hard to reform, especially the UN Security Council, and without these reforms implementation might remain difficult.

The impact of the Responsibility to Protect is testimony to the power of ideas and the ability of a few individuals to drive a breakthrough process with an enduring global impact.

CHAPTER 9

AN UNEXPECTED SUCCESS:
THE RAPID UNIFICATION OF GERMANY

The unification of Germany in 1990 was a breakthrough that occurred with unexpected speed. While economic and social challenges remain to this day, it is still considered a miracle that it was possible to unite two countries politically, legally, monetarily, economically and militarily in such a short period of time. The eventual outcome of a Germany united and fully integrated into the West, the EU and NATO was not obvious at the time, when a variety of competing concepts on the future of Germany were circulating. Events would take over and the most decisive factor was the role of leaders who seized opportunities when they presented themselves – and succeeded in producing a good outcome. Does this case hold lessons for other divided nations?

THE QUALITATIVE ANALYSIS FOR THIS CHAPTER
IS ON PAGE 385 OF THE ANNEX

BY KLAUS NAUMANN WITH HORST TELTSCHIK

Our first priority was not territorial unification. Our first priority was freedom − freedom for the people of the GDR. Because if we got freedom in the GDR, I was absolutely sure that in the end we would get unification.   **− Horst Teltschik**[1]

For me, the Cold War ended when the Soviets accepted a united Germany in NATO.   **− Brent Scowcroft**[2]

BACKGROUND

When the Berlin Wall crumbled in November 1989, almost nobody thought that within a year the world would change more dramatically than at any time since 1945. A process was set in motion that overcame the artificial division of Europe enforced by the Soviet Union through its occupation of Eastern Germany in 1945 and Communist dominance in the Warsaw Pact countries since 1948. It was a breakthrough process in which political leaders' instincts, courage and willingness to take risks played a decisive role. The coincidence that like-minded leaders in the three decisive countries—the United States, the Soviet Union and West Germany—trusted each other was also very important. The process triggered an avalanche which would bury the Soviet Union and lead to the peaceful disintegration of the Soviet empire that had reigned from the river Elbe to the Pacific coastline at Vladivostok.

The process of German unification also meant doing something for which no textbook was ever written: the merging of a market economy with a social-ist economy that was centrally planned and state-controlled. Simultaneously, close to 18 million people who had never in their lives known individual free-dom or the rule of law had to be familiarised with the basic principles of a free democracy.

Those who were involved in the events of 1989-1990 witnessed momen-tous change that is worth recording and studying. In my capacity as Chief of Staff of the German *Bundeswehr* I was responsible at the time for most of the planning for the military issues of German unification. In autumn 1991 this included disbanding the *Nationale Volksarmee* and overseeing the retraining and integration of East German non-commissioned officers and personnel into the new *Armee der Einheit*, which came to an end when the *Bundeswehr* forces in Eastern Germany were assigned to NATO in January 1996. We highlight this challenging, but ultimately successful experience of the armed forces. The unification also occurred constitutionally, politically, economically and ultimately socially. Nevertheless, it should be noted that although there could be lessons for other divided countries that are still wait-ing for unity, the German experience was probably unique. In this study, we consider the military situation, the political and international developments, the key personalities and their leadership, and the many practical aspects of a breakthrough process leading to the unity of two countries in a window of only three months. It is testimony to some daring leadership which recognised and seized this window of opportunity when it presented itself. Both preparation and chance played important roles in this success.

THE MILITARY CONTEXT

During the Cold War political realities were to a large degree determined by the military situation between the two opposing camps, NATO in the West and the Warsaw Pact in the East. Today, two and a half decades years later, few people remember the harsh realities and the nature of the threats which existed until 1989.

Berlin, a city of three million inhabitants, was artificially and brutally divided by a wall, barbed-wire fences, anti-personnel mines, automatic machine-guns and border guards who repeatedly shot and killed their own fellow citizens whenever they tried to escape to West Berlin. Germany, a country of 82 million, was cut into two parts by a 1,200-kilometre fence, armed with anti-personnel mines and booby-traps and guarded by border forces numbering 60,000 men in an adjacent five-kilometre-deep zone. No citizen of the German Democratic Republic was permitted to enter these zones without a (rarely issued) entry permit. Similarly, the borders of the former Czechoslovakia and Hungary were sealed off against any attempt by their own citizens to leave what the Communists called "the paradise of workers and farmers". It was indeed, as Winston Churchill termed it, an Iron Curtain that divided Europe.

Militarily the region saw the highest concentration of armed forces any part of the world had ever seen in peacetime. One could describe it as a period in which war was absent but possible at any time. Taking the military situation as an example, there were nine combat-ready Army Corps from seven NATO countries stationed in West Germany. These were supported by two Allied Tactical Air Forces, as well as by the bulk of the NATO navies whose mission was to defend the vital lines of maritime communication between North America and Europe, and to prevent any breakthrough by the Soviet Navy through the Greenland-Iceland-United Kingdom gap into the North Atlantic. There were around 10,000 tactical nuclear weapons in Germany and thousands of tons of American chemical munitions. The French Army stood ready as NATO's operational reserve.

Similar arrangements, although not as highly concentrated, existed throughout Eastern Europe from the North Cape to Eastern Anatolia. In East Germany there was a Soviet-dominated 500,000-strong force that also included 160,000 East Germans, kept at 48 hours' readiness to attack through West Germany and seize the Atlantic coastline from Rotterdam to Cadiz. They were supported by the Polish armed forces, who had to take control of Schleswig Holstein and Denmark, and by two Czech armies, who had to attack through northern Bavaria in order to protect the flank of Soviet armies who would attack through neutral Austria south of the Danube, aiming at the encirclement of all NATO forces to the north of the river. These forces would enjoy the support of the bulk of the Soviet and Warsaw Pact air forces. In addition, they probably had plans to deploy hundreds of tactical nuclear weapons in support of the advancing armies *in the first hour of war*.[1] This was the truly unpleasant and gruesome reality of 1989, which all the NATO countries hoped would end when Mikhail Gorbachev became General Secretary of the Soviet Communist Party in 1986.

INTERNATIONAL AND POLITICAL BACKGROUND

During the whole year of 1989 I could closely see the changes in Poland. Peaceful changes from a Communist government to a democratic one, without any political or military interference from the Soviet Union. And this was very encouraging. — **Horst Teltschik**[4]

German reunification was never near the top of the list of realistic expectations. East Germany was perhaps the last state to come to mind when considering the possibility of political liberalisation. Thus, at the beginning of 1989, reunification seemed to us as distant a prospect as it had been in the previous forty years. — **President George H. W. Bush**[5]

As early as 1988 West German Chancellor Helmut Kohl, his Foreign Minister Hans-Dietrich Genscher, the head of the Chancellery Wolfgang Schäuble and behind the scenes Kohl's national security adviser Horst Teltschik began to see a mid- to long-term possibility of ending the division of Germany.

In those early stages, however, several different visions for the future of Germany existed among the different political parties. While Kohl and Teltschik, of the Christian Democratic Union (CDU), would recognise a historic opportunity for reunification, Genscher's Free Democratic Party (FPD) was more reluctant to engage the "nationalist" problem and hoped the Germanys would become closer in the context of European integration. The opposition Social Democrats and Greens, for their part, opposed any "nationalist" reunification on ideological grounds and hoped for harmony with a reformed socialist East Germany.[6] Kohl's challenges included overcoming these domestic political differences.

Kohl and his cabinet saw the enormous economic difficulties of the Soviet Union, which was suffering terribly from the fall in oil and gas prices since 1986 and from its overblown military budget. In 1986 it became increasingly difficult for the Soviet Union to sustain its ambitious armaments programmes or to honour the barter trade arrangements with its allies on which the entire Comecon Eastern Bloc economic partnership was based. This was the economic context that compelled Gorbachev to launch his programme of reform of the Communist system called perestroika, paired with the policy of transparency and openness called glasnost. Kohl saw this situation as an opportunity in which he could help his fellow Germans in the GDR, which depended financially and economically entirely on the USSR.

At the same time, he saw the chance of winning Gorbachev's confidence through economic aid. But Kohl and Teltschik, his main envoy, knew that they could not achieve a change for the better without the consent of Germany's many neighbours. East Germany was viewed as a part of Germany and therefore a part of domestic policy. As Teltschik was responsible for international affairs in the Chancellery, he was sent as the Chancellery's main negotiator to Poland, Hungary, Czechoslovakia and Bulgaria.[7] Kohl and Teltschik tried to convince West Germany's East European neighbours that it could be trusted. They conveyed the message that no attempt to overcome the division of Germany would be directed against them, and that a united Germany would never exploit its greater power to enforce its will upon its neighbours.

To this end Kohl and Teltschik, as well as the entire Chancellery led by Wolfgang Schäuble, established a tight-knit network of contacts from 1984 onwards. This network enabled confidential consultation and the keeping of neighbours in the loop, first and foremost Poland but also Hungary. Supporting these efforts, the Foreign Ministry and the Defence Ministry were instructed to work along the same lines.

These efforts were supported by very close personal contacts between the Chancellery and the George H.W. Bush Administration, flanked and supported by excellent contacts between the two defence ministries. The huge advantage was that President Bush's foreign policy team, consisting of his National Security Adviser Brent Scowcroft and Secretary of State James Baker, supported by very able policy staff including Condoleezza Rice, Robert Blackwill and Robert Zoellick, saw the opportunity to end the division of Europe and were prepared to grab it. It was also of great importance that Kohl's Defence Minister Manfred Wörner would become NATO's Secretary General in 1988.

Nevertheless, the Kohl government did not see unification as a short-term option. Until mid-1989, the common view in the government was that German unity should be seen as a long-term objective but that the time was not yet ripe to pursue this objective proactively. From the beginning of the Gorbachev period the Bonn government focused on building trust and confidence, often based on warm personal relationships between the leading personalities. For example, Horst Teltschik and Brent Scowcroft had developed excellent contacts with one of Gorbachev's closest advisers, Nikolai Portugalov. The German issue was not high on the agenda in the Soviet Union and this created an opportunity.

When Gorbachev took office, he quickly concluded that the Soviet Union would not be able to sustain its foreign policy for economic reasons: it was a foreign policy primarily based on military power. Since there were no resources to modernise in the same way as the Americans were doing during the Reagan Administration, he concluded that he had to reform the Soviet Union – but he never intended to give up control over Eastern and Central Europe. His objective was never to abandon Communism. He wanted to reform it and he hoped to secure continued Soviet dominance. He understood that he could not call for a Common European Home if the inhabitants were not permitted to move freely from room to room, admitting that the Europeans should get some leeway. In order to reduce the enormous burden of the Soviet armaments programme, he launched his major arms control initiative in a speech at the United Nations in 1988.

This message was well understood in the West German government. Foreign Minister Genscher was quick to see that there was an opportunity for change, and Rupert Scholz became the first German Defence Minister to speak of German unification as a long-term option. But there was no tangible evidence that Gorbachev was willing to consider German unification until the end of 1989. The only Western government that saw German unification as an achievable short- to mid-term option was the Bush administration.

It saw that the time had come to place the issue on the agenda and moved cautiously in this direction. But the Bush team was also very aware that the issue of German unification would be highly contentious among West Germany's NATO allies. The opening position of the Bush administration on the issue was a pragmatic management of the status quo which would evolve into proactive support. President Bush was not just the first leader of an American Administration but the first Western leader to publicly and unequivocally support reunification, something which Kohl would never forget. Brent Scowcroft observed of Bush: "His leadership and personal diplomacy emerged as key factors in preparing the way for German unity amid the larger questions of the transformation of Europe, issues such as security and changes in the strategic balance between East and West."[8]

The first step was to indicate that the time would come to bring the Cold War to an end. In 1988 the US had defined what would constitute the end of the Cold War, and stated the three conditions that had to be met. First, the US-Soviet nuclear confrontation must be stabilised and reduced. Second, tensions and competition in the Third World must be reduced. And finally, Moscow must be persuaded to respect the fundamental human rights of its own citizens.

When President Bush took office in 1989, he began to move beyond containment, expressing sweeping visions for the future. In May 1989 he spoke of a commonwealth of free nations and later added his vision of a "Europe Whole and Free" to NATO's new mission. In 1989, three political strands in Germany, the US and the Soviet Union were converging: for the Soviet Union, the economic need to reduce its self-imposed armaments burdens paved the way for more and closer East-West cooperation; for the US, the desire prevailed to move beyond containment and to bring the Cold War to an end; and Chancellor Kohl was determined to seize a once-in-a-lifetime opportunity to unify Germany.

Competing German, European, Soviet and international visions about the future of Germany and Europe led to competing concepts, policies and strategies. President Bush's concept of a "Europe Whole and Free" competed with

Gorbachev's concept of a "Common European Home", but pointed to the same situation: a collapse of the Soviet Union's economic and military hegemony over Europe, to be replaced by a dynamic and economically integrated continent. A remarkable precursor to the unexpectedly rapid developments that followed the fall of the Berlin Wall happened earlier that year, in the joint declaration of 13 June 1989, when Kohl and Gorbachev affirmed "self-determination" and the mutual reduction of conventional as well as nuclear forces. The reference to self-determination – twice – echoed principles of the OSCE's 1975 Helsinki Final Act, which includes the freedom of states to choose their own alliances. It also mentioned the dignity of the individual and the role of international law in domestic affairs.[9]

In the process towards unity between the fall of the Berlin Wall on 9 November 1989 and the formal agreement on unification of 3 October 1990, we can point to Kohl's daring ten-point speech as a key concept, and also the strategies of the "Two-plus-Four" diplomatic framework. But neither of these prepared anyone for the speed at which events would overtake any planning. For the unification of Germany was not a single concept which had been carefully drafted and meticulously executed. As so often in history, it was the coincidence of independent developments that achieved fundamental change when they were channelled in one direction. It was, above all, the determination and courage of the statesmen who were at the helm at the same time: Chancellor Kohl, President Bush and President Gorbachev.

THE ROAD TO UNITY

If you look at when the changes in the Warsaw Pact had started – without those fundamental changes, without Gorbachev in office – nothing would have happened. Therefore it was important that there was a peaceful transition in Poland, and Solidarność had started in 1980. It was important that Hungary opened its borders. And nothing was done by the Soviets. No reaction. When the changes started in the GDR there were still 340,000 Soviet troops there. They could have closed the border immediately. But they didn't. And then Gorbachev's perestroika and glasnost – if he had not started changing the Soviet Union, then forget about German unification. All these things belong together.   **– Horst Teltschik**[10]

As the political and economic crisis mounted in the GDR, more and more educated East Germans fled to the West – more than 200,000 in the course of the year, of whom 50,000 crossed over in the first week of November 1989. This led to the key event that accelerated the process of change in Europe: the opening of the Berlin Wall on 9 November 1989. We know today that it happened more or less by sheer accident and that this step was not intended to permit more individual freedom. It is one of the ironic footnotes of such a historical sea change that the entire East German military leadership had been summoned to their headquarters at Straussberg on the evening of

9 November in order to receive orders for ending the spreading unrest. But they were instead ordered to wait and watch the freshly imported movie *Dirty Dancing* until the necessary coordination with the Soviet leadership had been completed. While they were watching and probably enjoying the "time of their life", the Wall opened and crumbled. It was an incredible event, which I had never expected to see in my lifetime, but at the time nobody in Germany or Europe expected a united Germany within a year.

There was no planning for the complex task of uniting two countries, which had a few commonalities—the same language, and apart from the past 50 years, the same history. And despite four decades of socialist education and indoctrination of 18 million East Germans there were elements of a common culture. Moreover, there was no clear-cut political objective to achieve unity at short notice. The first public statement on the side of the West German government was the statement of Chancellor Kohl in the *Bundestag* on 28 November 1989 on which he elaborated a week later at the NATO summit in Brussels. These two speeches were politically very daring, both domestically and internationally.

Shortly after the crumbling of the Wall—on 21 November—Horst Teltschik met with Nikolaj Portugalov, a former Soviet diplomat to Germany, a leading expert on Germany, senior counsellor in the all-powerful Communist Central Committee, and, as it happened, also a KGB General.[11] They had known each other for ten years. Because Portugalov always adhered strictly to the official line, Teltschik considered him a useful weathervane to gauge the mood in Moscow. They met at a time when mass demonstrations were occurring in major East German cities (250,000 people on the streets in Leipzig, 50,000 in Halle and 40,000 in Chemnitz, as well as additional tens of thousands in Schwerin, Dresden, Cottbus and East Berlin), with the socialist slogan "we are the people" being replaced by the chant "we are one people."[12]

Portugalov admitted that in Moscow they knew early on that the most recent developments in the GDR were caused by the "first glimmers of perestroika". This clue meant that they took responsibility for the developments, but he added that "concerns were expressed that the development of German-German relations could take a dangerous and undesirable direction, which would lead to many questions for the Chancellor."[13] Portugalov elaborated with questions on Kohl's priorities, on European integration and security—and what about a peace treaty? "You see," he said, "on the German question we think about all possibilities, including the nearly unthinkable." He could imagine, he added, that the Soviet Union could give a green light to a sort of German confederation. Learning of this window of Russian consent, Teltschik memorably wrote in his diary, *Ich war wie elektrisiert*. ["I was electrified."] He carefully added that these considerations should lead to a meeting between the Chancellor and Gorbachev.[14] In the context of all the ongoing dramatic changes in Eastern Europe, this meeting with Portugalov was a turning point, insofar as it was "*der Tropfen der das Fass zum Überlaufen bringt*" ["the straw that broke the camel's back"[15]].

Teltschik immediately reported to Kohl, and in the space of a few days he and his team wrote a speech for the Chancellor which he delivered to the *Bundestag* on 29 November. In a masterful political move, no one outside the Chancellery was informed of the speech ahead of time, not Foreign Minister Genscher, who might claim its ideas as his own, nor European allies, who would have tried to prevent it. Kohl's ten-point speech, while later overtaken by events, represented the first public articulation of a policy concept, strategy and plan for the reunification of the Germanys. In the speech Kohl offered economic aid in return for political and economic reforms, including free elections. He also proposed a treaty community to work on inter-German issues, to be followed by East German elections, a confederal structure and eventually a federal system for the whole of Germany.[16] The speech did not include a timetable for these developments but the internal perception was that it could be gradually implemented over the course of a decade.

Before this speech, there were several other concepts of the future of Germany floating around. In a dinner earlier that month, on 13 November, Henry Kissinger offered the US President two scenarios. While he considered reunification inevitable, he envisaged a united neutral Germany between NATO and the Warsaw Pact. The other scenario was to disband both alliances.[17] The British Prime Minister, Margaret Thatcher, met President Bush on 24 November at Camp David and emphasised that democratisation should be a bigger priority than reunification. "The overriding objective is to get democracy throughout Eastern Europe," she told me. "We have won the battle of ideas after tough times as we kept NATO strong." But it would take time, for democracy was not just setting up elections. "It's a political way of life," Thatcher wisely observed. "Only then is it irreversible."[18]

Between these competing visions and concepts, Kohl's ten-point speech was decisive in bringing about a change in the policy of the Bush administration. President Bush had become increasingly outspoken on the matter. "It appeared he had firmly made up his mind," wrote Scowcroft[19]. When we asked Horst Teltschik if they felt confident of American support before the ten-point speech, he answered without hesitation, "We were absolutely sure that Bush would support us. And he did so from the very beginning."[20]

The Chancellor's statement at the NATO summit in Brussels on 4 December 1989 revealed that, apart from the US, Spain and Turkey, none of the allies was in favour of a united Germany. The first to speak was the Italian Prime Minister Giulio Andreotti, who voiced his concern that uniting the two Germanys could trigger a wave of *pan-germanismo*, as he called it, which would orchestrate a new Anschluss swallowing Austria and South Tirol, the Italian province of Alto Adige. Most allies were either fearful that German unification would start the 20th century all over again, or had simply not thought through the notion that such a reunification could happen any time soon. Nobody said "We love Germany so much, we want two of them" but it was the sentiment one could feel in the conference room.

The leader who came closest to that position during this meeting was Margaret Thatcher. She opposed Kohl's ideas in very clear and occasionally harsh words, triggering a blunt reaction from the German Chancellor, who did not avail himself of diplomatic language when he reminded the allies of their countless commitments to German unification. Mrs Thatcher was extremely exercised by this reaction and turned to her neighbour, President Bush, hoping that he would help her in rejecting Kohl's push for unification. To her surprise, Bush supported Kohl and not her. The exchange was caught on an open microphone, and everyone understood.

Experiencing occasionally stiff resistance from allies who had agreed time and again that German unity was a common NATO goal was a development that the Kohl government had not expected. The fact that French President François Mitterrand did not speak at all on the issue during the summit was a deep disappointment for the Germans. Their disappointment grew when they learned of Mitterrand's strenuous attempts to convince Gorbachev that he should resist all attempt to advance German unification.[21] His last attempt was an unscheduled trip to Kiev on 6 December during which he tried very hard to convince Gorbachev to do all he could to prevent German unification. Nevertheless, based on the US's strong backing, NATO also declared its support. NATO Secretary General Manfred Wörner reminded President Bush of the historic window of opportunity that these events presented.

"This is a unique opportunity. This is a decisive moment," Wörner told Bush. "In weeks or months, you personally will have to make decisions that can decide the future of Europe." There was only one critical issue: whether Germany would be neutral or remain in NATO. "The answer to this question will decide future decades of European history." He added that "a demilitarised Germany would repeat the mistakes of the Versailles Treaty. It would not be tied to any safe structure. The most natural reaction then would be for the British and French to try to control the new Germany. The Germans will react, forming their own alliances." Wörner was frightened by the possibility of a regional balance comparable to the situation before the First World War. His solution was that a united Germany could *only* be stable when fully integrated into NATO—and that the Russians would have to accept it. He reminded the President: "If Germany is out of the integrated NATO structure, the United States will be out of Europe. This will lead to the destabilisation of Europe. If you leave now, you will be leaving at the decisive moment." Wörner helped dispel any doubts in the American administration that the goal should be a united Germany, fully embedded in NATO. This goal was worth fighting for, while alternatives could still be forced by domestic German politics, the East German elections or international pressures.

A diplomatic mechanism was next established, between the Four Powers (the US, the Soviet Union, the UK and France) together with the two Germanys. The so-called "Four-plus-Two" mechanism placed the priority on the powers, and was promptly changed by Genscher and Teltschik's team to

"Two-plus-Four". The talks that started in February 1990 concerned not only unification but also the thornier security and military issues of the reduction of nuclear weapons and conventional forces in Europe. Following President's Gorbachev's visit to Washington in May 1990, an important breakthrough would be achieved when Chancellor Kohl and Gorbachev met for a bilateral meeting in July 1990 in Shelesnovodsk in the Caucasus region. There they formally agreed that a united Germany would remain a NATO member.

They set a limit of 370,000 for the manpower of the German armed forces and agreed on a number of conditions aimed at assuring the Soviet Union that the expanded NATO treaty area would not be exploited to the geo-strategic disadvantage of the Soviet Union, for instance through the siting of NATO nuclear weapons. They also agreed on the withdrawal of all Soviet forces from Germany by the autumn of 1994. The issue of NATO enlargement was not mentioned at all, since both the Soviet Union and the Warsaw Pact still existed. However, the speed with which Germany achieved unification in the course of 1990 was not driven by the skill of diplomats but by the force of events. A rapidly deteriorating political and social crisis in the GDR created the opportunity for early elections, and the outcome accelerated the settlement between the "Two", creating the window in which the "plus Four" could complete their international tasks. The international Treaty on the Final Settlement with Respect to Germany, the so-called 2+4 agreement, was signed in Moscow on 12 September 1990, and on 3 October 1990 Germany became a fully sovereign united country. On that day the division of Europe came to an end and the long, and still unfinished, road towards a whole and free Europe began.

CONSTITUTIONAL FRAMEWORK AND POLITICAL DEVELOPMENTS

West Germany had no blueprint for unification at hand and could not take advantage of any historic example. Domestically two very different models of society had to be merged: the socialist system of the GDR and the free market economy of a Western democracy. Many volumes have been written dealing with the transformation of a capitalist system into a socialist one, but there were very few papers on the reverse of that process. The two German states negotiated and agreed a treaty on unification. This was a historic achievement by Wolfgang Schäuble, and the parties agreed that the legal basis of the united Germany should be the *Grundgesetz*, the constitution of West Germany. This meant that unification would not establish a new state but that the German Democratic Republic would ask to become a part of the Federal Republic of Germany.

There were two possibilities for unification under the *Grundgesetz*. Under Article 146, new all-German elections would select delegates to a new constitutional assembly, which would create a new political state with a new form of government, laws and constitution. The second option of Article 23 allowed for "other parts of Germany" to join the Federal Republic. In this scenario, the East German state would dissolve into its *Lander*, which would be absorbed into the FRG with its system intact. Kohl and the American government strongly preferred the Article 23 option and they succeeded in this. The danger was averted that via Article 146 the SPD East and West could send united Germany with a new political order down a neutral or socialist path.[22]

Yet even before the first "Two-plus-Four" negotiations started, the crisis of events took over. The East German government had made a few positive steps in December 1989, planning for free elections in May 1990. But shortly after, in response to calls for the dreaded State Security Organisation, or Stasi, to be disbanded, they fell into old habits by staging incidents such as defacing a Soviet war memorial, to which the Stasi would respond, thereby reasserting its "authority". Realising that the game was up, members of the Stasi started destroying its vast files. The rumour that this was happening led to thousands of demonstrators flooding the streets of Berlin on 15 January 1990, breaking through the Stasi headquarters gates, storming and plundering the building.[23] Brent Scowcroft observed that by "January 26, when President Bush spoke to him about our new CFE proposals, Helmut Kohl no longer believed that East Germany could or would reform itself. It was on the verge of total collapse."[24]

In that meeting Bush recalled "a plainly tired" Kohl relating the accelerating developments: "The East German government was having problems, but not because they did not want to make reforms, he said: 'They just *cannot* do it right'." While Havel had moral authority in Czechoslovakia and Mazowiecki in Poland, Hans Modrow, the GDR's last prime minister, had hardly any influence at all among his people.

"I myself am pushing necessary reforms forward piece by piece," explained Kohl. "There is some success in the economic field, but things that should take one day take weeks. The result: the confidence of the population in the administration is catastrophic. People are leaving in their thousands, and the rest are sitting on packed suitcases. Since 1 January, 43,000 people have come over. In the long term, this is unsustainable. They are good people, doctors, engineers and specialists. They cannot be replaced."[25]

The reality of the crisis overtook the gradual phased implementation of Kohl's ten-point plan. A window of opportunity had opened with Russian consent to unification, although it must be said that when James Baker persuaded Gorbachev to support the "Two-plus-Four" mechanism in February 1989 he reiterated that "there would be no extension of NATO's jurisdiction for its forces one inch to the east."[26]

In the morning the Chancellor was depressed. The polls on Monday had given SPD-East a clear majority of 44 per cent against CDU-East. The SPD have already started talking about the possibility of an absolute majority.
                                              – Horst Teltschik diary, 14 March 1990[27]

The feeling is perfect. In the first free election of the GDR in 58 years, the 'Alliance for Germany' is celebrating an overwhelming election victory. After an impressively high turnout of 93 per cent, the Alliance won 192 seats, while the SPD only won 88. Who had expected that?
– Horst Teltschik diary, 18 March 1990[28]

The next turning point was the surprisingly good outcome of the East German legislative election of 18 March 1990. The American administration had also been nervous about the outcome, because while the East Germans would probably dump the Communists, an SPD victory could still be an impediment to moving the process of unification and integration forward. With the election of Lothar de Maizière as interim prime minister, the new East German government immediately committed itself to unification in accordance with Article 23.

With the "Two" settling their internal matters so rapidly, the effect on international diplomacy of the "plus Four" was dramatic. "They definitely ended any Soviet hope to slow the drive for unification through an obedient Eastern Germany," wrote Bush and Scowcroft. "Instead, Moscow was confronted with a new East German government that enthusiastically embraced speedy absorption into the Federal Republic."[29] Diplomacy focused next on the borders and claims issues with Poland, and on overcoming the last obstacle: Soviet consent to a united Germany in NATO.

President Gorbachev visited Washington with much fanfare on 31 May 1990. The Soviet Union was desperate for loans, wanting $15-20 billion. Through many officials, they often repeated the same position: that a united Germany should be neutral, and not in NATO, or should even join the Warsaw Pact. It was ultimately a simple legal argument, and an appeal to the principle of self-determination in accordance with the Helsinki Final Act, with which Bush persuaded Gorbachev to drop his objection.

Bush recalled, "I tried a new tack. I reminded Gorbachev that the Helsinki Final Act stated that all countries had the right to choose their own alliances. To me, that meant that Germany should be able to decide for itself what it wanted. To my astonishment, Gorbachev shrugged his shoulders, and said, yes, that was correct. The room suddenly became quiet. [Marshal Sergei] Akhromeyev and Valentin Falin [secretary of the Central Committee] looked at each other and squirmed in their seats. Bob Blackwill slipped me a note asking whether I thought I could get Gorbachev to say that again. I nodded to him. 'I'm gratified that you and I seem to agree that nations can choose their own alliances,' I said."[30] Scowcroft noted, "I could scarcely believe what I was witnessing, let alone figure out what to make of it."

In the third Two-plus-Four ministerial meeting on 17 July, agreement was reached on the Polish-German border as well as an outline of the final settlement. Formal unification took place on 3 October, with the Federal Republic absorbing the five East German *Lander* in accordance with Article 23.

Bush reflected on the breakthrough: "For the United States, and ultimately for Europe, reunification was an astonishingly successful achievement. Was there an element of luck? Absolutely, considering how fortunate it was that the personalities involved worked as cooperatively as they did. But our sensitivity to legitimate German concerns, along with those of the French and British, as well as the Soviet stake in the outcome, kept the process alive and moving in the right direction."[31]

MILITARY UNIFICATION

On the military side, unification meant that the armed forces of East Germany, the *Nationale Volksarmee* (NVA), would cease to exist on the day of unification, and its personnel would be put under the command of the West German Minister of Defence, Gerhard Stoltenberg. To dissolve the armed forces of a country, while integrating some of its personnel and at the same time reducing the armed forces of West Germany from 490,000 to 370,000 for a united Germany, was a challenge of a complexity and magnitude that no NATO force had seen before.

I was closely involved as I was initially responsible for all military aspects in all negotiations leading to unification, including the withdrawal of Soviet forces and the stationing of NATO forces in a Germany that achieved full sovereignty on the day of unification. When I was appointed Chief of Defence in October 1991, I assumed the military responsibility for the establishment of the *Armee der Einheit*, and for the *Bundeswehr*'s assistance to the Soviet-Russian forces withdrawing from Germany until September 1994.

In addition, Germany had to negotiate quite a few international agreements dealing with military issues such as airspace control, status of forces agreements for allied as well as Soviet forces, and most importantly, the agreement covering the withdrawal of Russian forces from Germany until the autumn of 1994. It was a truly busy time for the Ministry of Defence. Historians may one day see its results as an incredible achievement, because all of these issues had to be dealt with in little more than a month.

The GDR turned out to be a deeply militarised entity. One third of its territory was used by either the Soviet or the East German armed forces. These areas were off-limits to civilians and included an 11,000 km road network reserved solely for military use. The *Bundeswehr* had to take control of 900 garrisons and 28 major training areas. The barracks were dilapidated and did not come close to matching West German hygiene and health standards. There were no shower facilities for the soldiers and the heating system did not produce more than 12°C in the barracks in wintertime. In order to accommodate the *Bundeswehr* in the eastern part of Germany, some 590 military facilities were expected to be renovated and used at a cost of DM1 billion a year from 1992 onwards. The remainder of approximately 1,800 military facilities, constituting a book value of DM55 billion, was transferred to the Ministry of Finance.

The materiel of the NVA turned out to be substantially greater than the numbers the GDR had declared at the Vienna Conference on Conventional Forces in Europe (CFE). When counting came to an end in October 1990, there were 8,317 main battle tanks and other armoured combat vehicles, 3,400 artillery pieces, 479 combat aircraft and attack helicopters, 71 navy vessels, 250 surface-to-surface missiles, 10,600 anti-aircraft missiles, 46,000 anti-tank missiles, 70,000 trucks, 1.2 million small arms and 300,000 tons of ammunition. We retired the NVA's senior military staff and gained their cooperation, without which we would not have found all its weapons caches. The *Bundeswehr* destroyed most of this materiel, averting the possible destabilising effects that other large post-Soviet caches have had. Only a small portion was given to allied or friendly countries.

The *Bundeswehr* also noted and shared with the allies a few technical surprises, after the Soviet-made materiel was examined. By way of just two examples: nobody had expected a laser beam-rider round to be fired by Soviet T-55 main battle tanks against armed helicopters; nor the ship-to-ship missiles which were capable of homing in on the radars of Western surface ships. In addition, the *Bundeswehr* had to dismantle the Berlin Wall (126 km long), the border fence of 1,200 km along the former inner-German border, and 818 observation towers, and to clear some 1.3 million anti-personnel landmines.

To complete the picture of the magnitude of the task, it ought to be mentioned that the *Bundeswehr* had to monitor the withdrawal of Soviet forces from Germany and to assist the Soviet, later Russian, authorities wherever necessary. There were some 550,000 Russian citizens in Eastern Germany, 338,000 of whom were military personnel. The Soviet Western forces had 4,209 main battle tanks, 3,682 artillery pieces, 8,209 armoured vehicles, 691 combat aircraft, 683 helicopters, 3 million tons of materiel and 677,032 tons of ammunition.

We understood very well what it meant for the Soviets to withdraw and therefore the order had been issued to do all the *Bundeswehr* could possibly do to ensure that the withdrawal was dignified. We knew that the Soviets had never really tried to win the hearts and minds of the people of the German Democratic Republic. They had always been occupation forces. We tried to give them the impression that we did not see them as enemies and that we wanted them to remember that they were leaving a country that hoped for friendship between the Russian and the German peoples. We believed this would help heal the wounds of a terrible war.

But the material aspects were only one element of the task and probably the easiest one. The *Bundeswehr* had to integrate personnel of the former enemy, who had indoctrinated the NVA to hate the West German "enemy of the workers' class". Moreover, the NVA had never been a people's army but the army of the Communist Party. The senior officers and most of the non-commissioned officers (NCOs) were party members. The generals, admirals and the officers in charge of political indoctrination had all been retired before the day of unification. Nevertheless, there were 23,354 officers who came under the command of Minister Stoltenberg on 3 October 1990. Some 11,500 of them applied for service in the *Bundeswehr* of the united Germany. They had to agree to a two-year probation period and had to accept that they would be fired immediately if they had collaborated with the Stasi.

In 1991 some 6,056 of them were admitted to the two-year probation period. This meant that the same number of West German officers had to be retired earlier than planned, since there were no additional slots and the overall size of the German armed forces had to be reduced to 370,000 men by 1994. In 1993, at the end of the probation period, 5,662 officers of the former NVA applied to be enlisted in the *Bundeswehr*.

After careful evaluation 3,575 officers were accepted, 600 continued to serve as NCOs, and 1,600 were transferred to the civilian *Bundeswehr* administration. The inclusion of the NCOs was more difficult because the NVA had followed Soviet career schemes, which did not foresee these NCOs integrating into Western armed forces. They became assistants who did not have their own responsibilities.

Including them meant training them more or less from scratch and this was done from 1991. The success was limited and did not match the input, but the motto had been that they should be given the chance to succeed. The order that had been issued for the *Bundeswehr* at the beginning of this unprecedented experience was: we are meeting as Germans, there are no winners and there are no losers, we want to be one nation and we will establish the armed forces of the united Germany.

Twenty-four years later one can say with hindsight that the armed forces and the Roman Catholic Church were the only two German organisations that acted in that spirit and were the only ones who really succeeded in bringing about unification. For the *Bundeswehr* it was a mission without any precedent and it was a unique opportunity for the German military, whether of Western or Eastern origin. Both sides stood the test and they contributed immensely to the success story of German unification. The *Bundeswehr* soldiers, airmen and sailors went east in a spirit of sincere patriotism, committed to a task, which they saw as a once-in-a-lifetime opportunity. The former NVA military personnel in turn accepted the chance they were given and most of them served with a morale that deserved respect.

But it was at the same time a mission which had a much wider dimension than the purely national. We understood very well that our Western allies were watching attentively to see whether the united Germany would stay the course of being a reliable ally. At the same time, the new partners of the former Warsaw Pact countries and the former Soviet Union, including the successor states after the break-up of the USSR, were following with close attention how the former NVA military were treated by the "winners" of the Cold War. They saw it as a test of the extent to which we Westerners really honoured the principles we were preaching of the rule of law and human rights. When they saw that we were trying hard to treat former enemies in a fair and balanced manner, many of them concluded that they could trust the West. Thus the military part of the process of unification played a supporting role in bringing about a Europe whole and free. This had been the vision in 1949 when NATO was founded and it became NATO's new mission after the end of the Cold War.

EVALUATION: IS GERMAN UNIFICATION A MODEL?

Looking back, it still seems as if what occurred in 1989-1990 and thereafter was a miracle. The achievements were gigantic: the huge empire of the Soviet Union, with its sphere of influence reaching from Vladivostok to the banks of river Elbe, disappeared with a whimper – and not as had so often been the case in mankind's history, with a bang. The map of Europe was altered more profoundly than at any moment since the Westphalia Treaty of 1648, and this happened peacefully and not as the result of a war.

And last but not least, Germany, one of Europe's youngest nation states, which had been at the centre of the three big wars fought in Europe in the 20th century – the First and Second World Wars and the Cold War – was united with the consent of all its neighbours and of the countries that had been victorious in the Second World War. This paved the way for a wider and deeper European integration, leading to the enlargements of NATO and the EU, and the creation of a common European currency.

Today, with hindsight, it is a tragedy that the instrument that was conceived on the margins of German unification and which was supposed to foster Europe's cohesion, the Euro, now seems to jeopardise this cohesion. Indeed, while Germany was prepared to give up the Deutsche Mark, France did not honour the agreement to transfer some national financial sovereignty to the EU when the decision on the common currency was taken.

But was the breakthrough and miracle of 1989-1990 a result of innovative thinking? There was one element which could be called innovative as far as international diplomacy is concerned: the idea of Chancellor Kohl and Horst Teltschik to win the trust and confidence of Germany's neighbours and of the Soviet Union through a patient, skilful and almost unnoticed process of establishing friendly relations and building a network. It was this quiet approach, with an eye on the long-term, that would make a deep impact, rather than loudly heralded political successes. The network was advanced and had produced its first tangible results when the opportunities of 1989 emerged, but its work was far from complete.

What happened then was the result of courageous risk-taking and of a determined political instinct to seize opportunities. It was also the result of the coincidence that the political leaders at the helm in Germany, the US and the former Soviet Union understood that there was a chance to bring about a peaceful end to the biggest confrontation Europe had ever seen in its long and bloody history; and it was also the result of accidental events such as the opening of the Berlin Wall and the factor of luck.

I therefore conclude that the events of 1989 do not provide a pattern which could be applied elsewhere, but there is every reason to study them carefully and in depth.

As there are other divided countries in this world and so many nationalities spread over the territories of two or more states who wish to live in a state of their own, one may ask the question whether there is any pattern they might wish to follow. I am doubtful that the German experience can be copied elsewhere. Local and regional factors are most decisive, and historical memories weigh heavily in such processes. For these reasons I believe that the process of German unification and the German achievement of merging two very different societies deserve careful examination by all who might be confronted with a similar challenge in the future. But the lessons learnt from such an examination need to be applied in a way that is tailored to match prevailing local circumstances.

CHAPTER 10

THE OSLO BREAKTHROUGH

The Oslo agreement between the State of Israel and the Palestine Liberation Organisation (PLO) is a breakthrough in which we can examine the process elements of vision, concept, strategy, planning and execution. It was an unlikely and tumultuous historical breakthrough that led to successes which persist to this day, but also remained incomplete. We piece together a Rashomon of perspectives that emerge from memoirs, histories, and new interviews we conducted with key players, to show which visions made the concept of the Oslo Declaration of Principles possible, what went right, and what went wrong.

THE QUALITATIVE ANALYSIS FOR THIS CHAPTER
IS ON PAGE 386 OF THE ANNEX

WITH SHIMON PERES, AMNON LIPKIN-SHAHAK,
AHMED QUREI AND OTHERS.
INTERVIEWS BY THE OWLS TEAM.
TEXT BY BENJAMIN BILSKI

INTRODUCTION: REGIONAL CONTEXT

◎ Shifting Visions and Concepts

The famous handshake between Israeli Prime Minister Yitzchak Rabin and PLO chairman Yasser Arafat on 13 September 1993 marked an agreement and breakthrough. It shifted the paradigm from a zero sum conflict between two peoples who made maximal claims over one land, to a serious attempt to divide the land between them.

It was a real accomplishment to transform a state of open conflict into the beginnings of a working relationship. Both parties travelled a long distance to reach this point, but it was only a preliminary political step initiating a very fragile process. It was made possible by key individuals who seized opportunities, and by the chemistry and goodwill between negotiators, whose link to officials turned a secret agreement into official policy. Without a combination of global, regional and political enabling factors this process could not have started.

A geopolitical realignment in the region followed the end of the Cold War and the defeat of Saddam Hussein's Iraq in the first Gulf War. Between the 1967 Six Day War and the first Oslo agreement of 1993, there were shifting visions and concepts of peace and war. The vision for Israel to pursue an agreement with the PLO, and for the PLO to shift from terrorism to political peace negotiations with Israel, were not givens. This was partially the result of a measure of political maturity on both sides after they had exhausted the alternatives.

Following Israel's stunning victory in June 1967 over the combined armies of Egypt, Syria and Jordan, the Arab League issued its infamous non-vision of 'three no's' that set the tone of Arab rejection and a continuation of a zero-sum mentality. [1]

In November 1967, the United Nations Security Council's ceasefire resolution 242 provided the first articulation of the concept of "territories occupied in the recent conflict", in exchange for:

> Termination of all claims or states of belligerency and respect for and acknowledgement of the sovereignty, territorial integrity and political independence of every State in the area and their right to live in peace within secure and recognized boundaries free from threats or acts of force. [2]

This basic concept of 'land for peace' was reiterated in UN Security Council Resolution 338 following the 1973 war and formed the basis of the 1979 peace treaty between Egypt and Israel. At the time, it was accepted by Israel, but rejected by Arab states and the PLO. With regard to the Palestinians, the formula of 242 did not necessarily imply a two-state solution, with Israel alongside an independent Palestinian state.

In the 1980s, Israel and Jordan explored a different vision for peace. As prime minister and foreign minister, Shimon Peres pursued secret contacts with King Hussein and came close to an agreement that would restore most of the West Bank to Jordanian sovereignty in a confederation with three parliaments. A memorandum of understanding was agreed upon, but Peres failed to win support from prime minister Yitzchak Shamir and resigned shortly afterwards.[3] After a Palestinian-Jordanian arrangement fell apart because of the PLO's opposition to 242, the three players parted ways. It was the end of the vision and concept known as the 'Jordanian option'.[4]

The first Palestinian intifada uprising started in 1987, to the surprise of the PLO in Tunis, where its headquarters were at the time, adding pressure on King Hussein. Because attempts to sideline the PLO would put his reign in danger, the king deflected Palestinian violence by supporting the intifada publicly. In the summer of 1988, he relinquished Jordan's claim over the West Bank and 'gave' the claim to the PLO and West Bank leaders. While this was a harsh move on the ground,[5] it elevated the possibility for Palestinians to seek political independence without competition from, or integration with, another Arab state.

In the interest of preserving his kingdom, Hussein created a territorial division between Jordanians and Palestinians because the 1974 pan-Arab formula of treating the PLO as the "sole and legitimate representative of the Palestinian people" had always been a challenge to his own legitimacy.[6] When he disengaged himself from Israeli interests, the pre-condition were created for the Israeli-Jordanian peace agreement of 1994.

While the PLO had never publicly defined the range and limits of its territorial goals, the Jordanian move created new possibilities for international recognition. A few changes in policy were announced in the Palestinian National Council (PNC) meeting in Algiers in November 1988. Arafat proclaimed the independence of the 'Arab state of Palestine' and himself as 'President of Palestine'. In the same session, the PNC accepted the 1949 General Assembly resolution 181 as a basis for a two-state settlement and, following pressure from secret American contacts with the PLO, the acceptance of Security Council resolutions 242 and 338.[7] While an important turning point, the PNC outcome also included vagueness of the territorial claim, a glorification of terrorism, and a call for escalation of the intifada;[8] Israel could not take it seriously as a vision for peace.

The next day, the Israeli Foreign Ministry issued a statement in response to the PNC decisions, complaining that "ambiguity and double talk are again employed to obscure its advocacy for violence."

> No unilateral step can substitute for a negotiated settlement, no gimmick can mask the tragedy inflicted on the Palestinian people time and again by the absence of reasonable, realistic and peace-seeking leadership. As it continues to shoulder its responsibility for tranquility in the territories, Israel remains committed to the pursuit of a just, comprehensive and lasting peace with all its neighbours, first and foremost, Jordan and the Palestinians. Israel's policy remains equally

firm in its adherence to an insistence upon UN Resolutions 242 and 338 as the only commonly accepted basis for peace negotiations. [9]

PLO decision-making thrives on vagueness, and support for peace is presented alongside support for violence. As the Palestinians' chief negotiator at Oslo and later prime minister of the Palestinian Authority Abu Ala'a admitted to us, PLO decision-making will be "more vague than in a very stable state, or Israel, or any other country," because there is much competition between many ideas. [10] The vagueness speaks to the broad and varied support for the PLO from a mix of states, radical movements and fellow travellers. The survival and legitimacy of the PLO leadership includes, as part of the game, public statements that include something for everyone. For this reason, while the 1988 PNC outcome includes the first call for a two-state settlement, in addition to a call for intensification of violence, it could not be considered to be a serious concept for peace.

GEOSTRATEGIC CHANGE AND AN AMERICAN VISION

In the period from 1989 to 1991, large-scale geopolitical changes — the end of the Cold War, the invasion of Kuwait by Saddam Hussein's Iraq and his defeat by an international coalition, and the dissolution of the Soviet Union — decisively shifted the geo-strategic map in Europe and the Middle East in America's favour. With both the new Russian Federation and China weak, the American government was in a position to capitalise on these gains.

In an address to Congress on 6 March 1991 after the cessation of the Gulf War, President George H. W. Bush articulated a vision of a 'new world order', and described four challenging goals for the Middle East: the creation of new regional security arrangement; halting the proliferation of weapons of mass-destruction; an Arab-Israeli peace process; and fostering economic development "for the sake of peace and progress."

Concerning the Arab-Israeli conflicts, President Bush noted:

> We must do all that we can to close the gap between Israel and the Arab states and between Israelis and Palestinians. The tactics of terror lead absolutely nowhere; there can be no substitute for diplomacy. A comprehensive peace must be grounded in United Nations Security Council Resolutions 242 and 338 and the principle of territory for peace. This principle must be elaborated to provide for Israel's security and recognition, and at the same time for legitimate Palestinian political rights. Anything else would fail the twin tests of fairness and security. The time has come to put an end to Arab-Israeli conflict. [11]

The United States wished to enlist the support of other powers, and after intense diplomatic preparation by James Baker and his team, compel regional actors to get on board. As the last joint-venture between the USA and the Soviet Union, the letter of invitation to the Madrid conference stressed that the international community "will have no power to impose solutions on the parties or veto agreements reached by them" but stressed the vision that "the objective of this process is real peace." [12]

Prime minister Shamir was reluctant to attend the conference, but sent low-level delegates who were instructed not to come to any meaningful conclusion. [13] As long as the Israeli Law of Association that forbade contacts with PLO officials remained in place, Israel refused direct engagement. On the other side, the PLO had been embarrassed and weakened for their overt support for Saddam Hussein's conquest of Kuwait and Scud missile attacks on Israel.

After Saddam's defeat, the Saudis and Gulf States withdrew their financial and political support for the PLO, and Kuwait expelled nearly 450,000 Palestinians. The unreliable patronage of the Soviet Union dwindled. Violent resistance was no longer an option for the Palestinians in their weak position. They had no choice but to use diplomacy. In Madrid they were eventually represented by a joint Palestinian-Jordanian delegation, and all parties could focus on satisfying the Americans.

With a broad undefined vision, reluctant parties with no authority who wished only to please the Americans, and an absence of any strategy or plan, the Madrid Conference failed to produce a meaningful result. Madrid did not produce any agreements, but did accomplish a few things, such as the revocation of the notorious UN resolution 3379, and it created a negotiation framework: four bilateral tracks—between Israel and Jordan, Israel and Syria, Israel and Lebanon, and Israel and the Palestinians—and a multilateral track with regional actors and members of the international community about broader issues, such as water, the environment, arms control, refugees and economic development.

The creation of the multilateral track at the sub-ministerial level was the most useful product of the Madrid Conference. For the first time a forum was created for formal discussions on less controversial subjects, and, more importantly, an informal venue was formed for a club of rivals where meetings of greater substance could take place. [14] These informal connections helped members of Israel's new government to establish a secret negotiation track.

ISRAEL'S FOUR VISIONS

I heard from Rabin in a private meeting, one week or two weeks after the elections, after a dinner, when he was very open. There were no politicians around the table. It was a small group. (...) Rabin said: "I'm going to make a breakthrough with the Palestinians. We have to have an agreement and I'm going to make a breakthrough with the Palestinians." At that time, it was coming from nowhere.
— **Amnon Shahak** [15]

The 1992 Israeli general election brought political change and a potential peace camp to power. Yitzchak Rabin defeated Shimon Peres for the leadership of the Labour Party, and won the general election of 23 June 1992. He became prime minister and Peres minister of foreign affairs. Peres and Rabin were life-long rivals who were thrust into the limelight beside each other many times in Israeli political history. Now they were now forced to cooperate as never before.

The manner in which the government functioned and communicated, during the peace negotiations and after, was affected by their rivalry and the factions they represented. Rabin came from the security establishment and made sober analyses of long-term strategic trends in the region. Peres had held positions in the Ministry of Defence, as well as the prime ministership, but was an idealist compared to Rabin. With an eye on the long term, but focused on science and economic affairs, he surrounded himself with young ideologues whom he brought in to the foreign ministry.[16]

Four visions came together into the new Israeli government: Rabin's strategic outlook, Rabin's diplomatic outlook, Peres's economic idealism, and the ideology of the young leftists who joined Peres in the foreign ministry.

Rabin formed his new strategic outlook during and after the Gulf War. According to him and the security establishment, the main threat to Israel's national security had moved from the inner circle of states to the region's periphery. Terrorism, Rabin noted in a 1991 lecture, was the weapon of the weak and not an existential threat to Israel.[17] The Gulf War introduced a missile threat against which troop mobilisations, natural obstacles and battlefields were meaningless. The real existential threat, to which Israel would have no credible response, was the combination of a ballistic missile threat, nuclear weapons and Islamic fundamentalism.[18]

Although such threat assessments seem more commonplace now, Rabin's was met with incredulity in the United States. Iran was viewed as the principal threat, as were Iraq and even Algeria. In practice, this meant Israel started to develop capabilities for preemption by acquiring long-range bombers and began to invest in more effective missile defence systems.

To prepare Israel for a future confrontation with the 'outer circle' of threats, it was important to neutralise the 'inner circle' of threats. Close dangers such as the Palestinians could be dealt with through routine security management, and did not reflect a national security threat. Therefore, Rabin believed Israel needed to create a buffer through a coalition with adjacent Arab states, by improving relations with Egypt, deepening secret contacts with King Hussein of Jordan, and initiating a concrete process to resolve the Palestinian issue. It was a regional grand strategy that drove Israel's initiative on the Palestinian issue, reversing Rabin's earlier reluctance to deal directly with the PLO.[19]

The second vision concerned Rabin's diplomatic outlook and his awareness that there was one relationship on which Israel's security depended most. The United States was the only country with the ability to impose solutions in the Middle East. For Israel it was therefore essential to maintain a good relationship with Washington in order to preserve Israel's qualitative edge and support for its strategic deterrence. [20] This meant accommodation on two issues the Americans cared a lot about: Palestinian self-rule and peace with Syria. Both Rabin and the United States considered the strategic imperative of peace with Syria more important, on which much time and effort would be spent throughout the 1990s to no avail.

The third vision was the idealism of Shimon Peres. His ideas took shape in the 1960s when he realised there was a worldwide revolution going on, that land and agriculture were no longer the dominant factors in human organisation. For more than 10,000 years land determined economic output and required both civilian and military administration. Competition over land and resources was the principal rational reason for war, shaping discipline, investment in arms, nationalism and ideology. Peres realised that the world was moving away from the land thanks to modern science, which has no borders, no administration and cannot be conquered by armies. [21] He turned state policy towards investment in scientific research and development, pioneering nuclear research in the Dimona reactor, which brought great strategic and economic benefit to Israel. But Peres also realised that Israel cannot remain an island of wealth in a sea of Arab poverty. In order to have healthy economic relations with the Arab world, there was a need to resolve the Palestinian issue, both politically and economically.

Shortly after the first Oslo Agreement had been signed, he published *The New Middle East*, which stressed the necessity of accompanying agreements with a solid economic component: "I have always believed that political victories not accompanied by economic benefit stand on very shaky ground." [22] In this book, Peres argues that peace in the Middle East will change the ideological climate and institutions, foster political stability, economic relations, democratisation and regional security. War economics will be replaced by peace economies, and new sources of investment, the desalination of water, growth in agriculture, linking transportation and communications, and the development of tourism, will all contribute to a rising tide of prosperity. [23] With such an idealistic vision for the economic future of the region, it is not surprising that when Abu Ala'a inserted economic components into the earliest drafts of the Olso agreement, Peres read them with great interest.

The fourth vision was the ideology that Peres's young entourage brought to the foreign ministry. This was the awareness that a democratic state cannot sustainably rule another people, and that in the interest of maintaining a Jewish and democratic state, it is necessary to end the dream of a 'Greater Israel' and to resolve the Palestinian issue. And in order to resolve it, negotiations had to take place with political decision-makers, who were the PLO in Tunis. These ideas originated on the left and became the government's view with Labour's election victory. [24] Despite Rabin's Mapai roots, he was not a left-winger, but would support Uri Savir and Yossi Beilin's pursuit of a secret negotiation track with the PLO, based on his own strategic vision.

The minimal international requirements of Resolutions 242 and 338 were successfully applied in the Egyptian-Israeli peace agreement. The Arab League, however, had no collective vision for peace since it set the tone of rejection in the Khartoum Declaration; and the PLO had issued statements in favor of both peace and violence.

In the new Israeli government, four distinct visions and concepts came together, which were crucial for enabling the next step of a secret negotiations track. The idealists, ideologues and economists around Shimon Peres in the foreign ministry were the men of vision who would negotiate the Oslo agreements. This would happen without involvement of the army, the defence ministry, the intelligence agencies or anyone from the security services who reported to Rabin. The competition between Peres and Rabin affected the extent of communication and cooperation between the foreign ministry and the security establishment, and would affect how the negotiations were conducted and the agreements implemented.

When the low-level bilateral track with the Palestinians initiated by the Madrid Conference had moved to Washington, it became a media circus of daily recriminations. Low-level Israeli officials, who were not authorised to make meaningful decisions, argued with low-level Palestinian officials from the West Bank and Gaza: they had to check every detail by fax with Yasser Arafat, who refused to delegate. It was clear to Peres that serious negotiations would not be possible through the Washington track.[25] This posturing continued until a secret back channel was initiated with help from the Norwegians.

THE OSLO BREAKTHROUGH

This was the golden era between Rabin and Peres, who were very hostile during their whole history to each other. They really worked together.
— **Amnon Shahak**[26]

But then there was something which was very problematic, which was the hatred between Rabin and Peres. They had a real hatred between them, until the end of Rabin's life. — **Yossi Beilin**[27]

◎ Establishing the Oslo Back Channel

Rabin sought to restrict Peres's role in several ways. He took responsibility for all the bilateral negotiation tracks initiated after Madrid, leaving only the multilateral track to Peres. And because that track was conducted at the subministerial level, where the delegations were led by Deputy Minister Yossi Beilin, the arrangement further restricted Peres's role.[28] It also led Beilin to take the initiative, leaving Peres in the dark.

Beilin was connected to the Norwegian sociologist Terje Larsen, whose NGO ran projects in the territories and who had already offered to set up a back channel to help the Washington negotiators. Also close to Beilin were

Professor Yair Hirshfeld and his student Ron Pundak. They operated as Beilin's long arm in the Palestinian community. [29] They also took initiatives and kept Beilin in the dark to some extent.

In November 1992 Hirshfeld and Pundak approached Hanan Ashrawi, a prominent Christian Palestinian leader from the West Bank who had served as spokeswoman for the Palestinian delegations in Madrid and Washington. They asked her to recommend a Palestinian counterpart if there was to be a secret back channel. She suggested Abu Ala'a (Ahmed Qurei), who was the PLO's principal economist and not a politician.

Ashrawi then approached Abu Ala'a and convinced him to do what he had never done before – to meet with an Israeli. Professor Hirshfeld is a good man, she said, an academic who wants to discuss economics. [30]

During the multilateral meeting in December, Abu Ala'a and Hirshfeld were in London and a secret meeting was arranged. It was still illegal for Israelis to meet PLO members, but Hirshfeld left the detail of the meeting out of his report to Beilin. By coincidence, Terje Larsen was also in London, and when Hirshfeld told him about meeting Abu Ala'a, Larsen immediately realised the opportunity and offered to assist in follow-up. [31]

In the meeting with Abu Ala'a, Hirshfeld stressed that the meeting was unofficial and that he was speaking as an academic and private citizen. He did not discuss economic affairs, nor the issues of the multilateral track, but turned instead to the political issues that concerned the Washington negotiations. Above all, he wanted to discover whether or not the Palestinians were serious. Abu Ala'a filed a report of this meeting to Arafat, who passed it on to PLO official Abu Mazen (Mahmond Abbas), and it was he who seized the opportunity for a secret channel. He concluded that Hirshfeld could not possibly be acting on his own initiative, that he must have received authorisation from Peres or Beilin. [32] The Palestinians took the opportunity seriously. As it happened, Hirshfeld *was* acting on his own accord. The official blessing only came later.

Hirshfeld told Beilin about the meeting and received permission for a follow-up meeting. While this was still illegal at the time, Beilin and others pushed for the Law of Association to be repealed, which happened on the night of 19 January 1993. In a synchronised arrangement with Larsen, Hirshfeld and Pundak boarded a plane to Oslo the next morning. The first Oslo meeting was a track-II secret negotiation by private citizens. Yossi Beilin was the only person in the Israeli government aware of it.

A series of chance encounters, and three levels of chutzpah on the Israeli side – Hirshfeld keeping some things from Beilin, Beilin keeping some things from Peres, Peres not telling everything to Rabin; and a clever Norwegian seizing a rare opportunity – all made the initiation of the secret track-II talks possible. All our interview subjects agree that Yossi Beilin was the man of vision who initiated the process.

Given this fragile and coincidental sequence of events, there was nothing inevitable about the process starting like this. But if it hadn't started this way, it might have started another way because a measure of political maturity on both sides enabled them to reach out and make concessions. [33] The combination of the four strategic and idealistic visions that were brought into the new Israeli government, and the pragmatism on the part of key PLO figures, were decisive in enabling this breakthrough.

The track-II negotiation later became an official secret track-I. Good chemistry and humour between the negotiators played an essential part, as did the ability of the negotiators on both sides to negotiate with their superiors. Abu Ala'a was crucial in this regard because he was one of the only Palestinians who knew how to negotiate with the elusive Arafat. Above all, the Oslo process succeeded because it was initiated by the parties themselves, and not imposed by outside pressure. [34]

◎ From Track-II to Secret Track-I

At the first meeting outside Oslo, Yair Hirshfeld and Ron Pundak met Abu Ala'a; Hassan Asfour, secretary of the negotiations committee from Abu Mazen's office; and Mahel El-Kurd, one of Abu Ala'a's former economic advisers from Arafat's office. During the first two meetings, preliminary proposals were discussed on a number of issues, [35] and only Yossi Beilin on the Israeli side was aware they were taking place. Israeli military intelligence later found out as well, and reported it to Rabin, but since it appeared to be one seminar among many, Rabin did not attribute any importance to it. [36]

After the second meeting, Hirshfeld and Pundak produced a 'draft zero,' an unsigned paper that listed the points of consensus so far. The basic outlines of the Declaration of Principles had already been agreed upon. Hirshfeld and Pundak presented their draft to Yossi Beilin, who casually passed it on to Peres. Since it looked like just another academic paper, it went unread for a few days, but Peres did finally read it and realised its importance. He told Beilin that it was very interesting – and problematic. After Hirshfeld and Pundak were brought in to explain it to Peres, it had to be shown to Rabin. To everyone's surprise, Rabin shrugged and said, if they want to talk, let them talk. [37]

Rabin had probably not yet realised the potential of the secret track, but he allowed it to go on while the Washington circus continued, having failed to initiate any meaningful bilateral track himself. [38] Peres became very supportive because his staff had brought him back into the bilaterals – a victory of sorts over Rabin. [39] He was impressed with Abu Ala'a, observing that:

> In their reports to me, the two Israeli academics stressed that Arafat's eventual instructions that the Palestinian delegation return to Washington were attributable, in large measure, to the existence of the Oslo back-channel. (...) I formed the distinct impression that Abu Ala'a was a man of his word, a man with whom we could do business. [40]

In the next few meetings, a revised 'draft zero' with comments by Peres was discussed, and the draft Declaration of Principles was developed further.

But Hirshfeld and Pundak felt they could not progress further with their current mechanism. In their weekly meeting on 13 May 1993, Peres and Rabin decided to make the track official, and Peres proposed himself as the head of the Israeli team, which Rabin promptly vetoed. [41] They agreed to send Uri Savir, the Director-General of the Israeli Foreign Ministry. From May onwards, it entered its second phase and became an official negotiation track with the PLO. And shortly after, they were joined by Yoel Singer, the foreign ministry's legal adviser.

No one in Israel knew about it — not the cabinet and not the army. Inside the foreign ministry, only a very small circle was involved. And in the prime minister's office, only Rabin knew. He did not trust his own staff, and did not involve anyone from his own offices. Systematic work was being done only in the foreign ministry, but not in the prime minister's office, which some considered an unforgivable shortcoming. [42] No one from the Israeli security establishment or the army were involved in the negotiation process, but the tables would be completely turned in the process of implementation when the army took over both negotiation and implementation.

With regard to the Palestinians, the Israelis realised that the Palestinians were serious about the Oslo track because they too kept it secret. What happened next was a remarkable bit of manipulation on the part of Arafat and Abu Ala'a — for every solution that was offered in Washington, they would find a problem, and for every problem that the Oslo negotiators encountered, they constructively offered solutions. [43] It was clear that the Washington negotiations now served only as a cover, and that Oslo hosted the only decision-making track.

◎ The Breakthrough: Two Agreements

The Americans eventually learned of the Oslo track. It was remarkable that the hundred or so people involved — including Israelis, Palestinians, Norwegians and Americans, as well as Tunisians, Egyptians, Moroccans and Russians who knew about it — all managed to keep a lid on it. A single leak to the press could have derailed the whole process. [44]

Not without difficulty and intermittent crises, the negotiators achieved a breakthrough with two agreements: the Declaration of Principles and an exchange of letters. Once these agreements were reached in Oslo, and when both sides gave it their support, the Americans went all-in to become the great facilitators. The personal chemistry between Uri Savir and Abu Ala'a saved the agreement when it was on the brink of collapse near the end. Eventually, they settled on a draft of the Declaration of Principles of Interim Self-Governing Arrangements, which spelled out a step-by-step approach describing the transition to Palestinian self-rule. A crucial factor in saving the process was a move by Shimon Peres, who went farther than the negotiators had dared. He said that for self-government, Arafat himself should come to Gaza. [45] It took a statesman to view another man as a statesman, and this helped seal the deal.

Even after the Declaration was signed between the negotiators on the night of 19 August 1993, their work was not yet done. The news of the signing was made known to the Americans, who embraced it and agreed to host a signing ceremony at the White House. Shortly thereafter, it exploded in the press and became world news before the approvals had even been made on the domestic front. Rabin had no difficulty getting the Declaration approved by his cabinet on 30 August, but it remained controversial in the Knesset and among the Israeli public.

After the White House signing ceremony, on 23 September, a motion of no-confidence was raised in the Knesset that was narrowly defeated, by 61 votes to 50, with eight abstentions. For most of the PLO, the Declaration was a surprise and a shock, and Arafat struggled to get it approved by the PLO Executive Committee, with six out of eighteen members resigning in protest over what they considered capitulation. To maintain some consistency with the language of his past, Arafat would later embrace the Declaration by portraying it as a 'first step to victory' and ignoring its details.[46]

For the chief negotiators Uri Savir and Abu Ala'a, work remained. The Declaration of Principles had been agreed upon, but the terms of the mutual recognition had not. Uri Savir notes:

> We were thus at the point of declaring an end to the Israeli-Palestinian conflict and transforming our ties into permanent political relations. They might be good or bad, but they would no longer be all or nothing. We therefore demanded that the PLO recognise the State of Israel, accept Security Council Resolutions 242 and 338, renounce and combat terrorism, end the intifada, and rescind the clauses of the Palestinian Covenant that denied Israel's legitimate right to exist. Only then would Israel recognise the PLO as the representative of the Palestinian people.[47]

The Palestinian representatives had a hard time accepting this. Abu Ala'a argued that the PLO Covenant hadn't been 'operative' for years, and that it was no longer taught in Palestinian schools. Savir replied that it was not enough to recognise Israel merely as a fact of life, but that is must also be recognised as legitimate. After some back and forth and three days and nights of deliberation by the PLO's Executive Committee, they eventually arrived at the formula of mutual recognition. The Palestinians agreed that, from a practical point of view, the relevant passages from the Covenant were null and void,[48] and this was eventually tepidly formalised in a resolution at the 21st session of the Palestinian National Council in April 1996, which "repealed the articles of the Charter that declared the armed struggle to be the sole way to liberate Palestine".[49] Four letters were exchanged — the PLO's recognition of the State of Israel; Israel's recognition of the PLO; Arafat's call to his people to end violence; and a secret letter from Peres, where Israel promised not to close non-PLO institutions in Jerusalem.[50]

The exchange of letters was a bigger breakthrough than the Declaration of Principles. It represented the most important paradigm change, turning a state and non-state relationship defined by violent conflict into a working relationship to resolve their differences peacefully. While the level of mutual recognition was minimal, it was as far as they could go.

The State of Israel and the PLO agreed to attempt to divide the land between two peoples even if they couldn't recognise the legitimacy of the identity and political aspirations of the other side. The Palestinians could not recognise the facts of Jewish history and claim to the land, nor could Israel recognise the legitimacy of the Palestinian national movement. That impasse persists to this day. It was the limited and practical extent of the mutual recognition that made the interim agreements possible, and this was deliberate.[51] Moving beyond a zero-sum mentality was itself a significant breakthrough, but translating the goodwill between negotiators and leaders into goodwill between peoples remained a challenge.

THE DECLARATION OF PRINCIPLES AS CONCEPT

It was an empty frame. Some people will tell you this was the disadvantage. But it was a process, this was the aim. It was not done by mistake. Maybe it was a mistake to do it this way, but it was not done by mistake. It was done on purpose, because the problems were too big. It was not possible to solve the problems of refugees, Jerusalem, borders, security. None of them. They knew that if they are going to try to touch these problems, they wouldn't be able to reach an agreement. They wanted to create a framework, and build the picture piece by piece.
– Amnon Shahak[52]

◎ An Agreement to Agree

How can the Oslo Declaration of Principles be considered as a concept? For this project, we define a vision as the first structured ordering of an idea. The concept is defined as the concrete translation of the idea and vision into a general aim, and broken down into a set of sub-goals. A comprehensive concept should be true to the vision and reflect the strategies as the means to attain these goals. A good concept bridges vision and strategy, and a strategy guides the process of execution of specific actions to meet the set sub-goals of the concept.

The integrity of a properly implemented concept is ensured by an iterative process, in which each stage of execution is continually measured against the vision and concept. This keeps the implementation of a strong concept and strategy on rails in order to realistically attain the general aims set forth in the vision.

The Declaration of Principles is a shared concept, the product of negotiations between adversaries. It was not a peace treaty. Rather, it was the first step towards peace. In order for it to work, each party had to share the same vision, speak the same language, and translate ideas into words on paper that reflected joint conceptual thinking. With these criteria in mind, what kind of a concept was the Declaration of Principles?

The Declaration contained the outline for the interim period during which limited Palestinian self-government, combined with a continuation of negotiations, would ultimately lead to a 'permanent settlement based on Security Council Resolutions 242 and 338.' It granted sovereignty to the new Palestinian Authority over Gaza and the city of Jericho, called for democratic elections, established a police force, and contained many specific requirements of process. But it had very little substance.

The framework for the interim period described elections for the Palestinians, created Palestinian jurisdiction over Gaza and Jericho, and described the transfer of authority over these areas. Four annexes were added to the agreement describing the conditions for Palestinian elections, the withdrawal of Israeli forces, economic cooperation, and regional development. The bulk of the Declaration, however, tackled the negotiating process and was an agreement to reach future agreements. The Declaration mentioned both the intention to negotiate a list of unresolved issues of a permanent status agreement, as well as the intention to negotiate an agreement for the interim period that the parties were about to enter. The Declaration described the intention to negotiate the establishment of Palestinian self-governance in the interim period, and the intention to make agreements on economic cooperation. But the Declaration did not yet contain any of these agreements.

The Declaration deferred the 'remaining issues' to a later date, "including: Jerusalem, refugees, settlements, security arrangements, borders, relations and cooperation with other neighbours, and other issues of common interest." It was principally an agreement to reach future agreements, and as such, a lot of trust was placed in trust. It was an empty canvas that the parties had merely agreed to start painting together.

For this reason, and in retrospect, the great White House signing ceremony oversold an extremely fragile and tentative agreement as if it were a peace treaty. Rabin and Arafat's handshake became an iconic image, and the fanfare created unrealistic expectations. The Declaration as a concept was deliberately limited on substance and deliberately emphasised process. The paradigm shift between a process of conflict to one of negotiations was significant, but it was very thin on substance. [53] The Declaration's language was imprecise, and it would soon become clear how differently the two parties interpreted the agreement.

But the Declaration was also an important breakthrough in other respects. Israel became more fully integrated into the international system. The end of the Cold War, the Madrid Conference and the Oslo Process led to 56 countries establishing or restoring diplomatic relations with Israel between 1989 and 1995. [54]

◎ The Declaration as Strategy and Plan

The Declaration of Principles has no strategic content beyond forming various committees to carry on the negotiations and discussions on a number of issues. It did contain plans to make successive agreements, and on the diplomatic level these were carried out between 1994 and 1995 in three agreements that would be bundled in 'Oslo II' on 28 Septemper 1995.[55] But while big issues were absent from the Declaration, there also was no meaningful substance on security arrangements, economic issues, the question of incitement or the role of culture and religion. The economic annexes were also agreements to agree rather than matters of substance. The end state remained undefined, while the Declaration did call for a wholly unrealistic five-year time span to reach this permanent status settlement.

The Declaration mandated elections so that "Palestinian people in the West Bank and Gaza Strip may govern themselves according to democratic principles,"[56] and it stipulated that the elections take place no later than nine months after the agreement was signed. Annex I was an agreement to agree on the manner in which the elections were to be campaigned for, televised, and monitored. These minimal clauses were not tied to plans to implement democratic principles in any meaningful way, which should apply to culture and society as much as to governance, the separation of powers, a fair market economy and the rule of law. With all of this left out the concept, it wouldn't be long before they were defied with impunity.

The negotiations prior to the first Oslo agreement were conducted entirely by foreign ministry idealists and academics in a private capacity. As noted, Rabin was the only one in the prime minister's office involved in the negotiation process. Without his own staff involved, no one reached out to the army or security services, so Rabin left a wide gap between the idealists around Peres and the defence establishment. The lack of communication between the two sides greatly affected the manner and success of implementation on the Israeli side.

Implementation of policy in Israel is carried out by two powerful ministries, Treasury and Defence. They were entirely absent from the visionaries' negotiation stage. Yossi Beilin, the main visionary and ideologue behind the Oslo agreement, distanced himself completely from the manner in which it was implemented by the army.[57]

If we examine the sequence from vision, concept, strategy, planning and implementation, several gaps are apparent. A combination of idealistic visions, strategic pragmatism and common interests led to the initiation of a secret negotiating track where a preliminary concept was developed. But the concept lacked substance, had fundamental ambiguities, specified only a few sub-goals, had no strategic content, deferred all the difficult questions, and left the end-goals undefined. The opening positions of the first follow-up negotiations revealed how far apart the Israeli and Palestinian interpretations of the Declaration really were.

The period between the signing of the Declaration and the assassination of Yitzchak Rabin on 4 November 1995 was the crucial early period, which is our focus in this case study. Afterwards, there was a breakdown of the Oslo process in a rapid succession of events: Hamas suicide bombings, the electoral defeat of Shimon Peres and a general collapse of trust. The situation intermittently improved and worsened until the whole thing collapsed with the beginning of the murderous second intifada in 2000. Was this failure inevitable? Was it planned? Or was it an unintended consequence of circumstances? What can the period of implementation during the early Oslo years between 1993 and 1995 tell us about what was to come?

We can divide the early period of implementation into two parts: the follow-up negotiations and the Palestinian implementation following Israeli withdrawals.

IMPLEMENTATION

◎ Follow-up Negotiations

The die had been cast and the region produced mixed reactions to the Declaration. It was supported by Jordan, Egypt and Saudi Arabia, but bitterly opposed by Syria and Iran. The extremists of the region, Islamic fundamentalists and the remnants of old Arab nationalism, considered the Oslo Declaration an existential threat. They sought to undermine it at every opportunity. Iran intensified its support for Hamas and Islamic Jihad, in parallel to the global euphoria and hard work of refining and implementing the agreement.

Arafat welcomed the Declaration without troubling himself much about its details. His first priority became the consolidation of his own power. The Palestinian men of vision behind the agreement were removed from the process of implementation. As soon as the signing ceremony in Washington had taken place, Arafat felt that Abu Mazen and Abu Ala'a had received too much international attention, so he removed them from the centre of decision-making.[58]

Similarly, on the Israeli side, Yossi Beilin irritated Peres when he overstepped his station by portraying himself, Pundak and Hirshfeld as the heroic pioneers of Oslo, rather than the decision-makers.[59] Beilin would have no place in the negotiations that implemented the Declaration, but he would later pursue the secret Stockholm channel that led to a first draft of a final status settlement, the ill-fated Beilin-Abu Mazen agreement of 31 October 1995, agreed four days before the assassination of Rabin.

The Israeli decision-makers carried on after the White House signing celebrations. New negotiation teams were assembled in which the army played a prominent role. Deputy Chief of Staff General Amnon Shahak became the new head of the Israeli delegation, which included Yoel Singer from the original Oslo team, as well as Generals Uzi Dayan and Danny Rothschild.

On the Palestinian side, the negotiation team was led by the American-educated Dr Nabil Shaath, who had chaired the PLO's political committee and was a member of the Madrid delegation. A week after a formal meeting between Rabin and Arafat in Cairo on 6 October 1993, negotiations on implementation began in Taba. While Shahak and Shaath were both well regarded and admired in the press, and while they respected each other, the honeymoon ended abruptly when the gaps became apparent.[60]

In their opening positions at Taba, Israel stressed limited and gradual transfer of authority to the Palestinians while maintaining control of the border crossings between Gaza and Egypt. The Palestinians demanded a full withdrawal from Gaza and Jericho and a complete transfer of civil powers. Yoel Singer told Peres that what was going on in Taba "was not negotiations, but endless soapboxing." The common concept of the Declaration was already torn by diverging language, interpretation and strategies. Without a common vision, language and interpretation, a productive process was impossible.

On the Israeli side, negotiations and implementation had been taken over by the army and all political decisions became subordinated to short-term security needs. There was a lack of vision or long-term strategy in this approach, and the foreign ministry had misgivings about it, but it did not express them publicly. The lack of coordination between the foreign ministry and the army was reflected in both the negotiation and the implementation stages.

The head of the foreign ministry's policy planning unit, Harry Kney-Tal, [61] pointed out that Israel's attention was focused on day-to-day affairs whereas the Palestinians had long-term strategic goals. The zero-sum game returned as the Palestinians sought both complete disengagement alongside full economic access, while ignoring Israel's vital security interests. While the Oslo negotiators had created a genuine partnership that led to the first shared concept, it wasn't possible to find common ground in the shared interest of developing a joint strategy against violent opposition. "Thus," said Kney-Tal, "contrary to the guiding principle of the Oslo negotiations, each side wanted to extract the maximum from the other, rather than exploit the advantages of partnership." [62]

When the Taba talks between the negotiators stalled on the question of border crossings, the leaders were soon at odds themselves. It became clear to Peres and Rabin that Arafat did not understand what was meant by the Declaration's term 'external security'. And the Palestinians pressed for full sovereignty over the crossings to Egypt and Jordan, which meant Israel would lose effective control over who entered the country. This could have killed the peace process before it took off, but a reunion of the Oslo teams — and difficult marathon follow-up negotiations in Oslo, Paris, Davos and Cairo — re-established some common ground. Savir observed that there was a great gap in what each side considered important: "For Israel it was security; for the Palestinians, it was national and political pride." [63] Eventually an agreement was struck with a 180-page annex on border passages. Then the first violent tragedy struck that nearly derailed the process.

On 25 February 1994, a Jewish settler, Baruch Goldstein, entered the Tomb of the Patriarchs in Hebron and killed 31 worshippers. The news reverberated in the territories, Israel, the Arab world, and the international press. For crisis control, delegations were despatched to Tunis in order to plead with Arafat, who had been branded a traitor by his followers. In a second delegation on 20 March, General Shahak succeeded in convincing Arafat not to throw away all that had been accomplished. Arafat made a difficult and unpopular decision to continue with the fragile negotiation process. [64]

The preparations continued, and Arafat and the PLO elite moved from Tunis to Gaza in May 1994 for the first-ever experiment in Palestinian self-rule, to implement the Declaration and follow-up agreements. The sense of euphoria was great, and Rabin, Peres and Arafat were awarded the Nobel Peace Prize in 1994 — an award for a concept with little substance, before its implementation was even tested. What did Arafat do next in these early years in Gaza?

◎ Implementation: the PLO Moves to Gaza

Shortly after the Oslo accord was signed, Yossi Beilin asked Arafat why he never changed out of his uniform into civilian clothes now that he had entered the political phase. The answer was silence. [65]

In a ceremony in Cairo on 4 May 1994 for the Gaza-Jericho agreement, Arafat made a scene in front of the world's press. The negotiators had worked around the clock to hammer out the final wording and details during the night, and it turned out that Arafat had not signed the maps. And he refused to acknowledge the details of the agreement made the night before. It almost led to a scuffle on stage, until Egypt's President Hosni Mubarak bluntly demanded that Arafat not embarrass his hosts, and made him sign. [66]

According to the terms of the Declaration, "direct, free, and general political elections" would take place within nine months of signing so the Palestinians could "govern themselves according to democratic principles." [67] While the elections were originally planned for July 1994, they were pushed to January 1996 when Arafat won a landslide victory of 87.3%. In the intervening time, he worked around the clock to consolidate and 'election-proof' his position.

The Palestinian population had previously enjoyed a free press, human rights organisations, a familiarity with democratic processes, power-sharing, free trade, and access to the independent Israeli judiciary and appeals process. Arafat had not set foot in Palestine since 1967, and after having ruled the PLO from Jordan, Lebanon and Tunis, he was out of touch with the Palestinian population. Gaza at the time had high unemployment and few institutions. Israel and the United States, working with the World Bank and International Monetary Fund, convened a donors conference to support building economic institutions, but Arafat, accustomed to accepting suitcases filled with cash throughout his entire career, had difficulty with the concepts of transparency and accountability. [68]

There was only a two-month window between Arafat's arrival in Gaza in May 1994 and the election originally scheduled for July. With control over two-thirds of Gaza and Jericho, Arafat's jurisdiction extended to 750,000 residents, but not to the 1.1 million additional West Bank residents. The Declaration deliberately stipulated that Israeli security forces would not redeploy "until the eve of the elections." [69] He first succeeded in pushing the elections back to January 1996, expanding the window of opportunity from two to twenty months, and next turned his attention against all sources of independence and potential opposition: political rivals, the judiciary, the free press, human rights organisations, and then the law itself.[70]

Arafat's first executive order after signing the Declaration was a decree from Tunis on 20 May 1994 that restored all laws that had been in effect on 5 June, 1967, illegally cancelling all Israeli legislation since 1967 in direct violation of the Gaza-Jericho Agreement that he had signed two weeks earlier.[71] But many regulations instituted under the occupations were in areas where Ottoman, British, Jordanian, Egyptian, Israeli and case law had formed distinct and complex layers. The result was that it was left up to the arbitrary conduct of a weak and dependent judiciary, often appointed for political loyalty and without knowledge of the law, to decide which rules applied to whom and when.[72]

The Declaration and the follow-up agreements created the Palestinian Authority and introduced the new layer of a Palestinian Basic Law that was meant to be in accordance with democratic principles.[73] But the Soviet-trained Arafat implemented the PLO revolutionary penal code that had regulated its members over the decades. This revolutionary Marxist code introduced the death penalty and created military courts which would be used to try civilians – and is in place to this day.[74] This deliberate legal chaos created room for arbitrary reign and led to a de-facto abolition of the rule of law.

When Arafat moved to Gaza, the Gaza-Jericho Agreement authorised him to appoint a 24-member cabinet that served as both an interim legislature and executive, and he was permitted a 9,000-strong police force.[75] But he ignored this limit and rapidly expanded the police force to 13,000 by December 1994 and to 22,000 by August 1995. The process of cooption began quickly, with top officers brought in from the 'outside' who reported directly to Arafat. Also chosen for its political loyalty, the force was systematically deployed for political and financial ends – threatening political opposition; intimidating NGO leaders, human rights activists, journalists, academics and other critics; censoring the media, shutting down independent newspapers; carrying out spurious arrests, imprisonment and torture; and protecting business monopolies.

In 1995 a prominent academic named Abdel-Sattar Qasem wrote a scathing column attacking the dictatorial style of Arafat and his newly-established Palestinian Authority. He soon received death threats. A month later, he was shot point blank in his legs and hand. The small, left-wing paper *al-Umma*, set up in early 1995, mocked Arafat with caricatures and criticised the Palestinian Authority police. In response, agents raided the office, confiscated equipment and burnt the building to the ground. This led to an enormous amount of self-censorship among Palestinian journalists.[76]

The seeds of democracy were quickly uprooted and the human rights community was the next target in the intimidation campaign. Some groups were shut down while others were forced to subordinate their principles to nationalist aspirations. Self-censorship soon pervaded the human rights community as well as the media. Human rights activists either ceased documenting viola-tions or refrained from publishing their findings.[77]

Arafat was inoculated against criticism from independent sources. He was in firm control of the executive, legislative and judicial branches of Palestinian power. Dominating the media and having beaten everyone into submission, he rewarded himself with a landslide victory of 87.3% in the January 1996 election against a 72-year old women's rights activist.

This episode between 1993 and 1996 is less appreciated and known than what followed, but it was the prelude for the further degradation of Palestinian society as a preparation for the war, the second intifada, that was underpinned by a religious culture of death. While the second intifada was started by oth-ers, like the first, Arafat was a leader who felt compelled to follow the mob. He both lit and fanned the fires that would burn out of control.

EVALUATION

◎ Internal and External Factors

Israel had made a number of mistakes in the negotiation and implementation processes, and was exposed to greater vulnerability. The lack of communica-tion and coordination between the army and the foreign ministry was one shortcoming, as was the fact that other than Rabin himself, no one from his office was involved in the negotiation stage. The idealistic visionaries of the foreign ministry turned a basic ideology into a very limited concept that was not resilient enough to withstand the mistakes and mismanagement by the players, and the deliberate sabotage by external actors – especially the terror-ism of Hamas, and the Jewish 'lone wolves' Goldstein and Yigal Amir, Rabin's assassin. A vision without a substantial concept, tied to a process without a clear strategy and plan for implementation, is but a wish.

Palestinian violations of the Declaration and follow-up agreements ex-posed grave uncertainties around Arafat's style of governance that kept eve-ryone off-balance. With a 'Noah's Ark approach' to divide and conquer, he created two of everything: two police forces, two intelligence agencies, two finance ministers, two private militias – letting them compete with each other.[78] While seeking to control every decision, he never stabilised the ca-pacities of his government, and remained ambivalent to violent opposition to the peace process. His energy went into the expansion of security services and the expansion of personal control in a way that undermined democratic institutions and principles. A handful of Tunis loyalists became the new eco-nomic elite, monopolies were enforced, and corporate contracts were awarded and rescinded erratically.[79]

Nothing undermined support for the peace process among the Palestin-ians more than the lack of economic benefit for ordinary people. The socio-economic disparity between the wealth of a corrupt Tunis elite and those in the Palestinian refugee camps nurtured a radical and violent political opposition.[80]

The Islamic resistance movement Hamas, an offshoot of the Muslim Brotherhood, viewed the Oslo accords as an existential threat to its organisation. The accords ended the first intifada, and with that, its relevance. It adopted a strategy with three elements – a continuation of violence against Israel; a public confrontation against the Palestinian Authority, focusing on its corruption and mismanagement while keeping the lines of communication open; and the building of grassroots social and political support. [81]

The Goldstein massacre in Hebron on 25 February 1994 provided a boost to Hamas, which launched suicide bomb attacks inside Israel in Afula and Hadera in April, in Tel Aviv in October, and in Ramat Gan and Jerusalem in the summer of 1995. The lack of action by the new Palestinian Authority against terrorist activity led to Israeli road closures, which in turn led to greater economic hardship for Palestinians and enabled further radicalisation of the Palestinian population.

Terrorism and the style of Arafat's reign greatly undermined support for the Oslo process among the Israeli public. Nevertheless, Arafat used Hamas to keep pressure on Israel. [82] He came to a tacit understanding with Hamas in talks in December 1995 and agreed that Hamas could continue its armed struggle against Israel as long as it did not do so from territories the Palestinian Authority controlled. [83] After this green light, a string of four suicide bombings in February and March of 1996 led to the surprise election victory of Benjamin Netanyahu, who had opposed Oslo. [84] The new Israeli government would abide by agreements that had already been made, but it was in no rush to move the process forward, choosing instead to focus on exposing PLO violations. [85]

Following strong pressure from the United States and Israel, Arafat gave the green light to Mohammed Dahlan, the head of Preventive Security in Gaza, to pursue Hamas. Dahlan crushed the organisation by pursuing both its militants and its charitable institutions. It would not recover until the start of the second intifada. The irony is that for the Israeli public, the governance of Rabin and Peres was associated with uncertainty and violence, while Netanyahu's prime ministership was associated with a drop in terrorism. But in this case, it is Dahlan, rather than any Israeli leader, who deserves the credit. [86] Within a space of six months, Arafat had given the green light both to Hamas terrorism and to a severe crackdown on the organisation.

Many of these details were unknown at the time, and many remain unknown to this day. Despite the chaos and intermittent violence, the period from 1994 to 1995 until the assassination of Rabin was marked by euphoria and great hope for new beginnings. But as Shimon Peres noted to us, no Palestinian leader had the stature and legitimacy of Arafat. The process could not be started without him, but it gradually became clear that the peace process could not be completed with him. [87] And yet, despite all this, some enduring successes remain. How can we assess the Oslo accords as a breakthrough?

CONCLUSION

The Oslo accords represents a breakthrough process, in which the presence and absence of the elements of vision, concept, strategy, plan and implementation are visible. It was both an important initial success, a Nobel Peace Prize-winning concept with little substance, followed by chaotic implementation of a process that remains incomplete to this day.

With the background of the large-scale geostrategic realignments of the early 1990s, a combination of new American and Israeli visions and the maturity of the parties created the initiative to move forward. For the initiation of the secret negotiations, chance, misinterpretation, chutzpah and individuals seizing opportunities all played their part to make it the Oslo process, rather than the London or Amsterdam processes that had been attempted before.

The success of the negotiations themselves, the process of translating a vision into a concept, was made possible by the good chemistry between the negotiators and their ability to negotiate effectively with their superiors. This trusted line to political leadership upgraded the academic exercise of a track-II negotiation to an official act of state. The secret negotiations led to a shared concept and genuine diplomatic breakthrough in the Declaration and exchange of letters. To seal the deal, it took a statesman like Peres to view Arafat as a statesman – but the test remained whether he was to behave like one.

The concept itself, thin on substance, was a concept of process that did not define its end state. In the next stages, the gaps in interpretation and the removal of the men of vision from the implementation led to the return of a zero-sum mentality. Corruption and terrorism undermined public support. And in both Arafat's reign and new political leadership from the Israeli opposition, new strategies were implemented that did not derive from the concept. Despite important political, diplomatic and economic benefits that endure to this day, the connection between the elements of vision, concept, strategy and implementation would be lost.

◎ Lessons

In our other case studies, we see that succesful breakthrough processes are made possible by the fact that the same people who formulate the vision are involved in the follow-up stages. On the Israeli side, the separation of camps around Peres and Rabin, diplomats and soldiers, affected communication, and cooperation within the Israeli government, leading to a severance of the process elements of vision and implemenation. On the Palestinian side, many violations of the letter and spirit of the agreement undermined trust and public support. Between the two sides, the shared concept had many ambiguities, leaving wide gaps in interpretation from which it was impossible to develop a shared strategy.

The strategies of the parties that followed, Arafat in Gaza and later Netanyahu's strategy after 1996, did not derive from the concept.[88] They were separate political strategies combined with creative reinterpretations of the minimal agreed concept.

On both sides, support and legitimacy for political leadership comes from a number of sources. With competing sets of ideas, it becomes more difficult for leaders to express a unified view on one side, let alone between both sides. It is a difficult balancing act to maintain support from political bases and the general public, and leaders under pressure are more likely take the path of least resistance in order to hold on to their position. With ambiguous support from political leadership, it is not surprising that the momentum can easily be lost, the window of opportunity overrun, and the process not completed. Many of the successes and failures in this regard do come down to leadership.

It is hugely important that anyone in an official capacity seeking to change a situation for the better does not rely purely on an ideology for the end state. A process cannot be initiated without a vision, but it also cannot be meaningful unless it is understood as a comprehensive process with all its stages. It was a telling moment in our interview with Yossi Beilin when he told us he had difficulty understanding what we meant by 'translating a vision into a concept'. As an ideologue who is not a process-thinker, he preferred to move straight from the idea to the end state, and innocently distanced himself from the messy way in which the army had implemented the agreements.

When asked what lessons he had for for future generations, Shimon Peres noted to us that "It is not enough to have a good, brilliant idea." He went on: "Brilliance is the enemy of leaders. A good leader must have the talent to be average. If he is too brilliant, he raises too many expectations. So everybody admits he is brilliant but what can you do with that?"[89]

CHAPTER 11

CHINA IN THE AGE OF ACCELERATING CHANGE:
A POSITIVE APPROACH

After China's astonishing advances in the past three decades, its economy is now the second largest in the world and could overtake that of the United States within 15 years. Contrary to popular belief, China's new leaders are characterised by mental agility and a willingness to experiment and innovate. They see globalisation not as a threat but as an opportunity. The US and the West have two choices in dealing with the Chinese challenge: competition or collaboration. A collaborative approach, particularly in the military and information technology sectors, would yield a rich harvest in terms of international peace and prosperity.

THE QUALITATIVE ANALYSIS FOR THIS CHAPTER
IS ON PAGE 387 OF THE ANNEX

BY WILLIAM A. OWENS, JAMES BLAKER AND
MARTHA BEJAR

If you were one of the 60 million or so first-time visitors to China in the last ten years, you probably thought you had entered a cauldron of exuberant modernity and dramatically accelerating change. The scale of change is indeed almost incomprehensible. Over the last three decades, China has produced the largest and most rapid growth in human material well-being in history.[1] The country's population increased over the last decade by about 100 million people, while its gross domestic product roughly tripled to over US$7.4 trillion, moving China's economy past the rankings of the UK, France, Germany, and Japan and second now only to the United States. China's per capita purchasing power more than tripled. It took the United States a century to rise from the lower third to the world's second largest economy. China accomplished an analogous rise in a little more than twenty years. China's economic rise seems tectonic: a shift that significantly alters the global economic and political systems – a sharp curve in the pathway of human history. Our conceptual framework provides some insight as to how this occurred.

Despite differences among them, China's governing elites since the formation of the People's Republic of China have sought to build national power, welfare, and international influence as rapidly as possible. Two potential paths emerged, one which roughly followed the model the Soviet Union had pioneered in the first half of the century: essentially a communist autarky. The other path, while also incorporating socialist aspects, was less dedicated to autarky and more oriented towards global foreign trade with and investment by the United States and Western Europe. These became competitive concepts through the 1950s and into the 1960s. The stakes of the debate were very high, not only for the party factions that supported one view or the other, but for Chinese society as a whole.[2]

Of course this broad summary of one of the truly great changes in recent history – the rise of China in world affairs – suggests that big changes may *always* begin with inherently contradictory ideas and controversy. That ignites (and conditions) the process of change from vision through to execution. A logical corollary of this is that "big changes and radical innovation don't come quickly" – the greater the change, the longer it takes to become orthodoxy.

But in the case of China and US-China relations the *rate* of change is accelerating and will continue to increase in the years ahead. I'll sketch a speculative forecast of how the rise of China will change the world over the next decade. Just to reveal the bottom line: China will not rule the world, but the world will be very different in 2023 because of how the Western world deals with its rise.[3]

China has had a thousand years of non-intervention in other countries. Five hundred years ago, during the Ming Dynasty and before the explorations of Columbus, when China was the true superpower of the world, Chinese Admiral Zheng set sail for the markets of south-east Asia, India, the Middle East and Africa. There was no plundering, no heavy-handed dominance, and no acquiring of territory. He demonstrated China's products and the opportunities of trade with China, left money and ideas for the development of the countries he visited—and then he went home.

China today has many problems in which it is absorbed. Its border challenges are certainly one. Taking care of an ageing population is another. The move towards a more participating society, not least by giving more voice to the Chinese people, is a priority. Indeed, the "right to rule" of the Communist Party is at stake in this. Beneath China's real growth is the need to eliminate corruption, a core, well-articulated priority of the current President, Xi Jinping. In our view, the Chinese are unlikely to be involved in fostering a military or national security challenge to the US or the world.

THE EMERGING AGE OF ACCELERATING CHANGE

Consider the earlier contention that the last three decades of change in China were "tectonic" – that they have greatly changed the country's economic and political terrain, but have also altered the world as a whole, raising both new mountain ranges of challenges and new tranquil seas of opportunity in the course and history of mankind.

Most projections postulate that China will have the world's largest economy within 15 years, and could, should it choose to do so, supplant the United States as the world's most potent military power in about the same period. What could that mean to mankind and how would we navigate such a change?

Two paradigms guide the thinking in and outside China about the answer. The first is the "competitive model". This reflects the superpower relationships that evolved between the United States and Soviet Union from the mid-1960s to the early 1990s. That was an era driven by a mutual assumption that armed conflict between the two powers would benefit neither while devastating not only both players but the rest of the world along with them. Its modern version posits an expansionist China confronted by a containing US, a tension reflected in a bifurcation of economic spheres of influence and competition – a situation captured by the pundit's description of "the United States seeking to keep China down, and China seeking to keep the United States out (particularly out of Asia)". The second paradigm is the "collaborative model". This is less familiar, perhaps less obtainable, but has the potential to be more mutually beneficial. It presumes a mutual priority of cooperation and collaboration between the two powers not just to prevent armed conflict but to promote common values of human rights and opportunities, globally. These two models are caricatures of reality; the real world has aspects of both and of neither. Yet they help frame the necessarily tricky discussion of the future.

Consider what China's rise to power means to those Chinese who are between the ages of, say, 35 and 70 years old. That is the age group from which most of the individuals who – because they hold most of the power, wealth, status and authority – will create China's future. To them, big changes that come fast are not surprises. They have lived with such change all their lives. The younger members of this group have no personal memories of the Japanese occupation, the civil war, the establishment of a communist state, the Korean War, collectivisation, communisation, the Great Leap Forward, or the 100 Flowers Campaign. Their parents would, however, and most of this age group has gone through the Cultural Revolution, Sino-Soviet antagonism, the one-child policy, the opening to the United States, the economic reform, the Tiananmen confrontation, and the current social networking revolution. These were all first-order political, social and cultural wrenches. Living through them may have inculcated a deep desire for "stability" and a belief in some golden Chinese age that never really existed. But it also builds resilience, agility, flexibility – and willingness to innovate, if only to survive in a tumultuous world.

We in the West associate modern China with dogma, conformity, routine and bureaucratic repetition. But I see these as outer dress, costumes that cloak a willingness to change, to adapt more quickly to opportunities and surprises. The core strengths of a new breed of Chinese leaders (especially the private sector, but increasingly part of the state-owned sector as well) are mental agility, willingness to experiment, and an inclination to innovate. What distinguishes them from their revolutionary predecessors is their recognition of the dangers of attempting to change things too radically, too rapidly. But they are dedicated to pushing out the edges of the current envelopes of political, social, economic, scientific and military affairs – not unilaterally, but in concert with like-minded partners. They tend to embrace globalisation, because they know it is inevitable and because it is imperative to a growing China.

Beneath the ubiquitous phrase of "globalisation" things are different – fundamentally different – from two decades ago. The core of this difference is the expanding recognition that interdependency comes with increasing globalisation. It is imperative that the emerging economic relationship between Europe, Japan, the United States and China is not competition but mutually beneficial collaboration.

For example, beginning in the late 1980s, the synergy of the US-China economic relationship increasingly flowed from rising consumer expenditures in the US, backed by increasing savings in China. Americans increasingly bought goods manufactured or assembled in China because the quality of the goods was getting better and the prices remained low. There were exceptions – some of the pet food from China to the US killed the dogs that ate it; some of the toys had too much lead in their paint. But for the most part these were eddies in a rising river of better-quality and lower-price goods. In 2008 James Fallows described the mainstream of the relationship:[4]

> Let's say you buy an Oral-B electric toothbrush for $30 at a (drugstore) in the United States ... Most of that $30 stays in America, with (the drugstore), the distributors, and Oral-B itself. Eventually $3 or so—an average percentage for small consumer goods—makes its way back to southern China.

That was a good deal for American consumers, the drugstore, and Oral-B. And it fitted well into China's economic planning, for although most of the dollars Americans spent on goods coming from China stayed in the US, there were so many similar exchanges that they filled China's sovereign wealth coffers. Again, Fallows's description clarifies how it worked:

> When the Chinese factory originally bid for Oral-B's business, it stated the price in dollars: X million toothbrushes for Y dollars each. But Chinese manufacturers can't use the dollars directly. They need Chinese currency – RMB – to pay the workers their 1,200-RMB ($160) monthly salary, to buy supplies from other factories in China, to pay taxes. So they take the dollars to a local commercial bank. After showing receipts or waybills to prove that they earned the dollars in genuine trade, not as speculative inflow, the Chinese manufacturer trades them for RMB.

China's laws require the local bank to turn them over to the People's Bank of China – a kind of central bank – in exchange for RMB at the official rate of exchange. The People's Bank transfers the dollars to another arm of the central government, the State Administration for Foreign Exchange, or SAFE. It is then SAFE's job to figure out where to park the dollars for the best return: so much in US stocks, so much shifted to euros, and the great majority left in the boring safety of US Treasury notes. So, writes Fallows:

> And thus our dollars come back home. Spent at the drugstore, passed to Oral-B, paid to the factory in southern China, traded for RMB by the local bank, "surrendered" to the People's Bank, passed to SAFE for investment, and then bid at auction for Treasury notes, they reenter into US money supply and are spent again—ideally on Chinese-made goods.

Until 2008 both nations found this a pleasant arrangement. For America, it meant cheaper iPads, lower interest rates, reduced mortgage payments, a lighter tax burden, and a strong dollar. For China it allowed the government to impose a very high savings rate on its people by, in effect, keeping the buying power earned through Chinese exports out of the hands of Chinese consumers (other than some of the Chinese entrepreneurs). China, as a whole, has been spending little of what it earns.

But the arrangement also contributed to instability. Americans have been living on credit driven by the macro-economic fact that the nation's total consumption is greater than its total production. The value of the dollar over the last decade has been unnaturally high and the value of the stock market and real estate rose continuously. Interest rates – for mortgage loans, credit card debt and commercial borrowing – stayed low. Taxes did so, too, in large part because foreign lenders – including China – held down the cost of financing the national debt and federal deficit. In marked contrast, China had been consuming only about half of what it produced. Because of this, the overall living standard in China has been not rising as rapidly as it could have except for the diversion of wealth into loans that helped the Americans to cover their federal deficits.

Enter the global recession. The effects of the recession have been hard on both China and the United States and both have taken steps to reverse them. China has shifted some of the wealth it has accumulated towards internal expenditures (largely on infrastructure) and development programmes abroad (largely in Africa). Meanwhile the US has used resources to avoid a financial meltdown which would have pushed the recession into a much more severe global depression. China has begun to address its savings overreach while the US government has begun to correct some of the causes of the recession. Both recognise the unstable economic balance between them and both governments are working to correct it. Most importantly, both accept that their national goals depend on them working together. The US faces a debilitating deficit if China pulls its billions out of US Treasury bonds. China faces political fragmentation if it does not extend the benefits of its export-driven wealth beyond its urban El Dorados. Both these outcomes are likely unless the two governments cooperate economically and in other policy areas. They both stand to benefit from de facto coordination and both stand to lose from unbridled competition.

Meanwhile, China's economic relationship with other Asian nations has also been moving towards closer integration. The production of manufactured goods is increasingly disaggregated geographically in Asia. That is, different parts of the production process migrate to different countries where their competitive advantage is greatest. Higher-income, more technologically advanced countries (e.g. Japan and South Korea) specialise in producing high-value-added parts and components, while China, Vietnam and Indonesia increasingly become the countries where final assembly of the product occurs, before being shipped to the US, Europe and elsewhere.[5] However, there is an awareness that "the next China is China" as many new factories and opportunities move to the far less developed and very needy western regions of China, where there is a dramatic need for jobs and development.

With all of the promise of the New China, there are many challenges for it. Minister Liu He, vice-chairman of the National Development and Reform Commission, told the delegates at a Summer Palace Dialogue (a conference of high-level economists from the US and China which he and I have sponsored over the last three years): "China is an emerging nation. We have many problems, and we do not have the ability of a developed nation. We will not have [that] for many years." I will mention just a few of these many challenges.

First, for example, resolving the issues of the State Owned Enterprises (SOEs) is of immense importance. These SOEs are some of the largest companies in the world and account for about 35 per cent of China's total GDP and 40 per cent of its tax revenues. These numbers are changing little as China's economy expands. The companies and financial structures are bureaucratic and very structured. Gao Xiqing, the director of the China Investment Corporation (CIC)—a $500 billion sovereign wealth fund—and a graduate of Duke University, said: "We were destined from day one ... to be a bureaucracy. We're going to be very cumbersome. We're going to be constrained by government interference. We try very hard to stay away from that. Not totally successful but to some extent. But because we have been successful in what we've done, we have antagonised a lot of government agencies." These "government agencies" and SOEs sap the Chinese economy of resources and while central planning can take credit for much of China's growth there are many issues with the immovability of the SOEs. For example they take a dramatic percentage of China's total capital (over the last decade often more than 50 percent), making credit very difficult for the entrepreneurial enterprises that generate most of the new jobs and portend the future of the Chinese economy in terms of new industrial and digital opportunities.

"Planning", meanwhile, is often inefficient. An example is the shipbuilding industry, which has been dramatically expanded to dozens of large facilities. While this expansion has occurred world demand for ships has dramatically dropped. While Japan has consolidated and brought new technologies and cooperation to its shipyards, the Chinese shipyards are wallowing in a market competing with lower-quality ships and selling them at dramatically lower prices. Central planning often fails.

For the last decade, then, globalisation has generated mutual economic benefit, cooperation and political amity. The current economic arrangements are not stable, however, because they foster certain moral and political thorns. Low labour costs, for example, may give China an advantage in the labour-intensive aspects of the global manufacturing process, but they carry internal political costs along with them, not least aggravation of wealth disparities inside the country. These disparities are increasingly visible, and they pose serious challenges to the Communist leadership, which bases its authority on the promise of equal access to economic benefit.

Over the last two decades, the Chinese government has, among other things, made heavy investments in education, science, and technology – and probably in industrial espionage – in a concerted effort to supplement the economic return it gets from labour-intensive manufacturing. The quality of products coming out of China is high and getting better. And the Chinese are now challenging, and in some areas surpassing, the long-assumed US/ Japanese/European edge in innovation, technology, and science. Meanwhile, lingering unemployment in the US and Europe and a growing recognition on the part of enterprises there attest to the fact that they are losing out to the Chinese in research, engineering, technology and science. This inevitably fuels demands for protectionism.

Dominance in several entire industries has essentially moved to China. In some cases the transition is hard because of the inefficiencies of China's SOEs. But it is happening. One could make a case that in the telecoms equipment industry (Huawei, a non-SOE), in the high-speed rail industry (CSRC, CNRC and

CRCC), and in the major construction industry (CSEC, CCCC), we have already seen the rise of the most important technologies and companies in the world. And in many other industries there is a movement – strongly supported by the Chinese government – to become the world's leaders. For example, COMAC will one day compete strongly with Boeing and Airbus, and CCB and ICBC will play a major role side by side with Citibank, JP Morgan and Deutsche Bank.

All of this raises the spectre of a Chinese threat to US national security, analogous in some ways to the Chinese leadership's tendency to raise suspect similar strategic challenges on the part of the United States, Japan and Europe to China's security. Representative of this is a comment from CIC director Gao Xiqing: "The US is telling China's $500 billion sovereign wealth fund to 'go away'." During the financial crisis, "we were sort of welcome" but since then "somehow we've become stigmatised," he said, adding: "There have been quite a few cases where the US says 'go away'."

In 2010, I saw some of these phenomena up close. Sprint-Nextel, at the time the third-largest wireless communications company in the United States, had put out a request for bids to upgrade the quality and range of its wireless equipment. No US telecommunications equipment manufacturers submitted proposals, but a number of foreign companies, including Amerilink using Huawei equipment, did. As the founder and chairman of Amerilink, I worked with Huawei, advising them on how to overcome concerns that Chinese-manufactured equipment might pose a security threat to the US. To ensure that there would be a trusted interface between Huawei and Sprint, I established the 100 per cent American-owned company Amerilink, which would have a dedicated patriotic American board, including Dick Gephardt, Gordon England and Jim Wolfensohn. We offered to open this board and all deliberations and technology to the National Security Agency, and Huawei would not be involved in any way in Amerilink. Equipment and services would be delivered to Amerilink, tested, quality-controlled and delivered to Sprint. There would be no direct Huawei-to-Sprint interface.

I was familiar with the issue of cyber security and threats from my military career and from having chaired a then-recent study and assessment by the National Academy of Sciences on the issue. I understood – perhaps better than most – what to worry about in cyber security, how to alleviate the legitimate concerns, and which of the burgeoning mythologies regarding "threats" were largely baseless. Huawei provided complete details of their proposal and of the equipment they would use in meeting Sprint's requirements and to a team of American first-rate cyber experts I had brought in to help with my evaluation.

Two aspects stood out from the material the company provided. The first was that it would not jeopardise the security of the Sprint wireless network or of the communications carried on it. The second was what the Huawei "solution" to the Sprint request for bids would provide. The technology they offered was far superior not only to what Sprint required; it was, I believe, at least two years ahead of anything any of the other companies – including Ericsson (at the time the world's leading telecommunications equipment company), Alcatel-Lucent, Samsung and others – could offer. I was convinced that from technical and security standpoints, Sprint would award the contract to Huawei. We had no awareness of what the bidders would propose on costs, but it certainly seemed that from a value perspective (to the bottom line of Sprint), Huawei would have a compelling offer (we were later to discover the Huawei bid was also the lowest in cost).

But we were also conscious of the strong prejudices against Chinese participation in US telecommunications equipment – and of the lobbying by Cisco and other US manufacturers against Huawei. So, partly from my discussions with their executives, Huawei proposed to provide an unprecedented transparency to their equipment and operating codes and other security assurances as a means of alleviating concerns. To me, this carried much more potential than simply a win for Huawei and Sprint; it also could build a new, mutually beneficial, trusted, transparent economic and security bridge between the two nations, one that could help check the *mindless* descent into greater distrust and acrimony regarding the emerging issue of cyber attacks and cyber war between the United States and China. In many ways for those of us who witnessed the phases of the Cold War, this new trust and transparency could be an inoculation against the factors which led to the mistrust and craziness of that long confrontation.

Not everyone saw it that way. *The Wall Street Journal, Washington Times,* right-wing bloggers, and cable pundits pushed hard against entertaining the Huawei bid, darkly alluding to dangers of disabling attacks on the United States. Senators and representatives picked up the scent of a new opportunity to make some point for the upcoming 2010 elections, and joined the baying. Letters were written to the Federal Communications Commission, Secretary of Commerce, and the President demanding the rejection of the Amerilink/ Huawei bid. Articles in the Chinese press began to call attention to "another American effort to keep China down".

With demands from the US government delivered by then Secretary of Commerce (now US ambassador to China), Gary Locke, Sprint rejected the Amerilink/Huawei bid. The Huawei CEO and founder, Ren Zhengfei, had told me at the start of this project that we would not succeed because of forces in the American government, and I told him I thought we would. He was right.

Naturally, the single largest hurdle to continued amity and cooperation between the two nations lies in military policy. The balance of military power currently favours the United States. But China has the capacity to ramp up her military expenditures rapidly, and that capability will almost certainly grow over the next decade. As US military operations in Afghanistan and Iraq come to an end, potential Chinese military capabilities increasingly figure in US military planning. Yet there is widespread agreement at the US and Chinese policy levels that we must find a way to a nurturing military-to-military relationship. When I brought a group of very senior US/Chinese "Sanya" generals to the US in 2011, during a meeting with Hillary Clinton, then Secretary of State, she told us: "There is no more important relationship in the world, and the military-to-military relationship is the most important part of that."

Both the Chinese and US military planners think about what a future military conflict between the US and China might entail, where it might occur, and what their opponent might attempt to do. In short, when it comes to military relationships, both military establishments tend to gravitate toward the competitive model, pulled towards it from time to time by various "incidents". The US bombing of the Chinese Embassy in Belgrade in 1999 (still a deep-set issue); the Chinese fighter aircraft crash with the US EP-3 reconnaissance plane in the South China Sea near Hainan Island in 2001; the Chinese destruction of a weather satellite in 2007 and the American interception and destruction of an inactive surveillance satellite the following year, followed in 2010 by a Chinese anti-ballistic missile test; the fairly recently announced US military "pivot" toward Asia and various other incidents have all added to mutual mistrust. The Chinese view held by many in Beijing (and a growing number of the 500 million Chinese bloggers) that there is a new "US containment strategy" portends a growing movement to a "more than competitive" view throughout China.

Military cooperation in anti-piracy, personnel exchanges, visits and regular discussions offset some of the competitive gravity, and over time, official dialogues have established some areas where common agreement and operational cooperation grow. But concern on the part of some senators and congressmen over this has grown also, and the constraints they impose on the substance of the official dialogues have restricted the official discussions of military cooperation and collaboration between the US and China. For the most part the official, formal dialogue on the Chinese-US military relationship has slipped towards ritual, gauged by the rank of the participants rather than the substance of what emerges from what they say to each other and in their public communiqués.[6]

That does not necessarily mean, however, that the military establishments of both nations single-mindedly welcome greater competition, plan only for conflict, and are uninterested in developing a more cooperative and collaborative relationship. I say this for two reasons. First, the US military is entering a period of accelerated doctrinal and operational change, driven by the combined pressures to reset after the last decade of conflict, the implications of the US strategic "pivot" towards Asia, and the prospect of an extended period of declining budgets. It does not want a conflict with China, particularly as it enters a multiple-year reset effort. Second, the Chinese do not want a conflict with the US. This second point is worth another supporting anecdote.

Nearly a decade ago I helped establish something called the "Sanya Group". It is a private, unofficial group whose members are retired three and four star military officers from both the US military and the People's Liberation Army (PLA) devoted to bringing our militaries closer at the "level 2". I believe that it is the most senior continuing set of dialogues we have ever had at a level involving the most senior military officers of both countries (in general ex-members of the US Joint Chiefs and the most senior members of the PLA). We have been meeting twice a year, alternately in China and the US, for about a week at a time. The meetings are informal, unscripted, unrecorded, without attribution, free-flowing and evolving. As you might expect, the early sessions were stilted and the discussions largely socially ritualistic – interesting how speculating about the weather appears to be a universal, if limited, ice-breaker. But the members of the group have been pretty much the same, and over time the discussions have grown in breadth and depth. They have expanded to include individual "war stories", past experiences, and, more recently, the future faced by our children and grandchildren. (The Chinese participants more often include observations on the world their *great*-grandchildren will face.) The observations are generally optimistic.

We talk of scientific developments that will solve diseases, and of technology that will end pollution, poverty and energy constraints, and of the potential of conflict to prevent these possibilities. We have found general agreement that excessive money that goes to build, sustain and use military forces would be far better spent elsewhere, so far as the future of our offspring are concerned. We have not agreed on what to do to allow our nations to shift resources, money and the effort that goes to military affairs to other, more productive undertakings. But we increasingly speculate about what might and what would have to exist for our military successors to do so.

These are the ramblings of men who no longer command military forces, and for whom their grandchildren do not always do what they tell them to do. They committed most of their lives to military affairs, believe their commitment was honourable and their purpose just, as was the recognition and power their institutions accorded them as they rose to its highest levels. But they sense huge changes in the world and a need to recognise the significance of the changes, to adjust and to innovate for the sake of those who will follow.

I find this somewhat surprising and quite significant. The Sanya Group is hardly composed of Pollyannas, and military professionals don't often express the view that there are more important things than national security and maintaining the military capacity to ensure it. Perhaps their willingness to do so in the confines of the group hints at the potential significance of their view: namely, that we humans are entering a new age in human affairs and that they don't mean by that term something that is a temporary deviation from a commonly understood and accepted historical evolution – it's not a "fad". Rather, they see us today in the midst of an accelerating shift from one set of human institutions to another, akin to the transition into the industrial age. That last "new" age was not confined to economics. It wrought huge changes in broader human affairs including their governmental, global and military dimensions. This is, of course, not a new perspective. Allusions to a new information age have been around for the better part of the last two decades. Some point to structural and institutional changes of the same magnitude, and claim that the rate of the changes will be much faster than any previous transition from one age to another. We see this today in the growing potential of bandwidth everywhere, the "cloud", "big data", "big data analytics". And it could be in these arenas that we will live and collaborate or compete.

If this turns out to be an accurate prediction, how might it play out? If the changes are analogous to those associated with the emergence of the industrial age, would there be a race for the means of information? Would military affairs shift towards the problem of cyber defences and offensives, data and corrupted data? Would the affairs of nations be conducted in the form of alliances, blocs, bilateral agreements and the other residues of past ages? Or will the new age give fundamental new meanings to and understandings of what we already commonly refer to as globalisation? And will it, in the process, replace the paradigm of competition with that of collaboration?

My great hope is that this new world will truly be flat, and that this will be the new existence. Recognising that shifts in the ages of mankind have been hugely complex, that it is hard to recognise when and why they began, and even more difficult to forecast their outcomes, my sense is that the transition we are now undertaking is different. It is occurring more rapidly, affecting more populations much more swiftly than any of its predecessors. It is mankind's first nearly simultaneous global age shift. It is rightly referred to as the emerging information age because its central resource is information, and unlike the resources and commodities that drove past "new ages" its effects are essentially not constrained by time, distance, geography or political institutions. It is too early to see it as a new golden age, for access to information is not equal to understanding what it means or the same thing as wisdom in choosing what to do with and about that understanding.

The challenge – and it is at least as hard a challenge as any mankind has faced – is to reach a common understanding and consensus on how to obtain mutual benefit from that understanding. Meeting that challenge will mean changing institutions, particularly those institutions which seek to prevent the flow of information and intellectual interaction. The institutions that will seek this are powerful, and they see greater information flow, wider and deeper intellectual interaction, and accelerated change as serious threats to their particular institutional goals and orthodoxy. I'm convinced, for example, that Huawei's effort to expand into the US telecommunications market was stymied largely by US telecommunications technology-oriented companies' concerns, not with the ability of the Chinese company to charge less for its products, but by the better technology Huawei is increasingly able to provide to its customers.[7] I believe that two or three US technology companies perceived the threat to their markets and to their business plans; more specifically, that to compete successfully they would have to find ways of matching the capabilities and speed at which the Chinese company could produce better information technology. Likewise, I am aware of, have been deeply involved in, and fully understand the institutional military belief that "accurate information is power – as long as we have it and our enemy does not."

But the information technology, research, science and economics that drive and reflect the new information age are eroding the disparities and discrepancies of awareness and understanding that protect human institutions from more rapid change. We live in a new global system of growing transparency and accelerating change. I believe in many of the precepts being taught at Singularity University in Los Angeles, that we are moving to an age in which the profound changes of machine-to-machine interfaces among machines that approach human knowledge will lead to solutions of some of our greatest challenges: healthcare, education, energy and peace. And I believe that while we humans tend to plan linearly, these changes and opportunities will progress exponentially. This poses a great opportunity for China and the world.

This disparity in the use of information could be one of China's great challenges. As the US proceeds down this path there is evidence that in China the progress is not as fast or deliberate. Given the impact ICT has in transforming a country, there continues to be a pressing prerequisite to define, and track the Networked Readiness Index (NRI). NRI "measures the propensity for countries to exploit the opportunities offered by information and communications technology". The NRI takes into account four sub-indexes: the environment for ICT, the readiness of the community/country, the usage of ICT, and the impact of ICT (Economic and Social). China's NRI position fell seven places in the rankings in 2013. See the chart below:

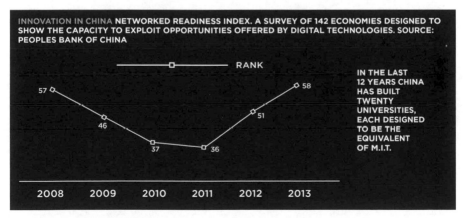

The sooner mankind recognises these profound opportunities, the sooner we will resolve the clash of ideas, passions and beliefs that threaten us all. Doing this, of course, will not be easy. But here are some steps that are worth considering.

At the most general level, two concepts come to mind. One has American precedents from a period when there was much talk of a "new age". In 1957, the launch of the first man-made satellite to orbit the earth – the Soviet Union's Sputnik – spawned a surge of US federal spending for education, associated with the National Defense Education Act of 1958. A few years later, President Kennedy established the Peace Corps. Both were products of their time; both were formed in a competitive context. The National Defense Education Act sought to create a surge of mathematicians and scientists to "help America win the race to space and the Cold War". The Peace Corps sought to "help people outside the United States understand American culture and help Americans understand the cultures of other countries". Both helped to create a generation of 20-to-30-year-olds that contributed understanding to and resolution of what was then the central problem facing mankind. Why not internationalise the notion of equipping the next generations of men and women with the scientific, technological and cultural understandings of the new information age and apply them collaboratively rather than competitively? If 10 per cent of the world's military expenditure (about $300 billion a year) were focused on that enterprise, instead of the fundamentally competitive character of military affairs, wouldn't it make the world better and faster?

The other general concept stems from the grand experiment of the European Union. This social, political and economic endeavour grew from the central question of how to convert the competitive forces which had proved so devastating in wars of the 20th century to collaborative, productive undertakings. It is still a work in progress, but how can the experience and approaches under way in Europe be applicable to globalisation and the rapidly emerging information age?

I believe the greatest danger mankind faces over the remaining years of the first quarter of the 21st century is slipping back to military confrontations, particularly between the United States and China. Among the steps we ought to take to prevent this are (1) an international No First Cyber Attack Agreement; (2) greatly expanded "real" military exercises and other military collaborative interactions involving the forces of the US, China, Japan and Korea; and (3) the creation of a global information umbrella that provides faster and much clearer transparency about military operations and situations that could escalate to military confrontations (and which could be immensely important in humanitarian disaster situations).

Globalisation and the information age will not grind down all the cultural, political and economic differences among the world's nations. They will not eliminate stupidity, hatred, fear of "the other", jealousy, miscalculation or evil. But the most profound change they might make possible is a shift toward real collaboration. And if we realise the full potential of this we will have a truly new kind of world with China.

CHAPTER 12

OPENING A NATIONAL DEBATE:
ISLAM AND THE NETHERLANDS

Political leaders generally do not like broaching controversial or difficult questions, but Frits Bolkestein in the Netherlands is an important exception. In his capacity as leader of the Liberal Party, he argued that the subject of immigration in the Netherlands was a broad and fundamental issue that required a nationwide debate. After an initial storm of protest, this debate did indeed happen. This is a case study of a breakthrough in making a difficult issue debatable. When governments force through large-scale policies in the absence of a national debate, it can lead to a backlash from the voters and undermine the legitimacy of the government. Frits Bolkestein, a former government Minister and European Commissioner, articulated a clear vision and pioneered a debate that continues to this day. The very initiation of the debate was a breakthrough, but the policy changes that followed the debate have averted large-scale social problems. A true statesman, Frits Bolkestein describes the events in his own words.

THE QUALITATIVE ANALYSIS FOR THIS CHAPTER
IS ON PAGE 388 OF THE ANNEX

BY FRITS BOLKESTEIN.
EDITED BY WIM POST AND BENJAMIN BILSKI

On Queen's Day 1990 I became head of the Liberal Party (VVD) in the Dutch parliament. Until then there had been only a small number of speeches, articles and books on the subject of the integration of Islamic minorities in the Netherlands. Some had sought to broach the subject, but had been blocked. Yet the newspapers I read at that time were full of articles about inter-ethnic friction. In September 1990, a Dutch parliamentary delegation travelled to Almaty, the capital of Kazakhstan, then part of the Soviet Union. We had to wait for a few hours for our transportation, so I invited my three colleagues one by one for a walk. I told them the same thing: that the growing number of non-western immigrants in the Netherlands would present problems that were too large for any one political party to deal with. Collective action was needed.

The members of the Liberal D66 and Christian Democratic parties listened sympathetically, but only the Labour party member responded. He said that integration was the only solution, although a member of his own party had said on an earlier occasion: "It is an illusion to think that you can both integrate into a new society and unconditionally retain your old identity." I concluded that integration remained a controversial subject because of the tension between it and the preservation of cultural identity.

THE SPEECH

Back in the Netherlands, my parliamentary work continued and I let the subject rest for a while. The VVD was in opposition at that time, but during the winter and spring of 1990-91 the party leaders took no initiatives on what we had discussed in Almaty. What to do? In the summer of 1991 I decided to write an article myself. But before this was published in *de Volkskrant* on 12 September 1991, I had to deliver a speech at the Liberal International in Lucerne, Switzerland, on 6 September. My speech concerned the collapse of the Soviet Union and European foreign policy.

In the speech, I discussed the deteriorating economic situation in the Soviet Union, the forthcoming independence of the republics on its periphery and the complete absence of traditions of democracy in the region. I argued that the sooner the countries in Eastern Europe joined the European Community (EC), the better, since that would increase their prosperity, as was the case with Greece, Portugal and Spain after they entered. I discussed the prospects of an enlargement of NATO. I concluded with a discussion on refugees and immigrants. Germany had absorbed many refugees from the East, and pressure was growing on the Netherlands from people who wanted to settle there. I continued:

"Prominent among recent immigrants in the Netherlands are people from Morocco and Turkey. Many of them settled in my country in the Sixties when labour was scarce. These two communities have continued to grow through natural increase and also because marriage partners have been brought in from their countries of origin. It is an influx such as we have never before had to absorb. What should government policy be towards these people who come from a different culture and who speak little or no Dutch?

"Our official policy used to be: 'Integration without prejudice to everyone's own identity.' It is now recognised that this slogan was a bit too glib. If everyone's cultural identity is allowed to persist unimpaired, integration will suffer.

"And integration there must be, because the Turkish and Moroccan immigrants are here to stay. That is now recognised by all.

"If integration is officially declared government policy, which cultural values must prevail: those of the non-Muslim majority or those of the Muslim minority?

"Here we must go back to our roots. Our history has produced some fundamental political principles, such as separation between church and state, freedom of expression, tolerance and non-discrimination. We maintain that these principles hold good not only in Europe and North America but all over the world.

"In many parts of the Muslim world these principles are not honoured. Islam is not only a religion, it is a way of life. In this, its vision runs counter to the liberal separation of church and state.

"In many Islamic countries there is little freedom of expression. The case of Salman Rushdie may be extreme but still indicates how far apart we are on this issue.

"The same goes for tolerance and non-discrimination. The way women are treated in the Islamic world is a stain on the reputation of that great religion.

"I repeat that on these essential points there can be no compromise. These principles have a value that is not relative but is fundamental. But anyone who rejects the theory of cultural relativity may very well at the same time accept cultural pluralism."[1]

Reactions to my speech in Lucerne were mixed. One critic accused me of 'facile populism', another said I want to submit Muslims to 'cultural brainwashing'. The mainstream daily *NRC Handelsblad* argued that they could not consider that I was right while at the same time being sympathetic towards Moroccan children who spent months away from school. I tried to defend myself by saying that my comments were just common sense: "It should not be possible that our constitutional principles apply only to those born Dutch and not for immigrants." I wanted a "big and open national political debate."

The Minister of the Interior, Ien Dales, wanted that too. She added, "I pick up the glove of Bolkestein's challenge. I will organise a forum for a national debate about integration."

THE ARTICLE

I published a more detailed version of these views in *de Volkskrant* on 12 September 1991. The article started with a reflection on civilisations. When we look at history "everyone agrees that Classical Athens, Renaissance Florence and pre-revolutionary France in the eighteenth century represent the heights of Western civilisation. And when we speak of 'heights' we imply there are levels of civilisation. By a lucky constellation of talents and circumstances these periods were focal points of intellectual and artistic creativity. They stood above those which they succeeded and those which came after.

"If we wish to raise the level of abstraction and compare entire civilisations, we must be clear about which period is being considered. Japanese civilisation of today differs from the Tokugawa era. Islamic civilisation in the period of the renowned Caliphates was superior to the European Middle Ages. How do things stand today?

"As I noted in Lucerne, after some black pages in our history, rationalism, humanism and Christianity have produced fundamental political principles, such as the separation between church and state, freedom of expression, tolerance and non-discrimination – principles to which we attach universal validity and which cannot be bargained away. This is our political vision. It means that a civilisation that honours these principles stands above a civilisation that does not. We cannot afford to treat these principles as relative without betraying them.

"What is the status of these values in the world of Islam? In most countries religion and the state are intertwined. Islam is more than merely a faith in God. It fully regulates Muslim lives.

"In countries such as Pakistan and Sudan, sharia law, the criminal law of the Koran, is applied. Islamic fundamentalism, a reaction to the frustrations of modernity and the antithesis of liberalism, wants to increase the extent to which religion and the state are intertwined." [2]

I expanded on the status of the principles I had outlined at Lucerne. The Rushdie affair revealed attitudes to freedom of speech. I noted also that a 1983 conference on the status of democracy in the Arab world had to be held in Cyprus, because no Arab state was willing to permit it on its soil.

"And tolerance? On 5 October 1990 a religious leader said in a radio programme of the (subsidised) Turkish Broadcast Association in Amsterdam: 'Those who resist Islam, the order of Islam or oppose Allah and his prophet, you have permission to kill, hang, slaughter or banish, as it says in the Sharia.'

"Non-discrimination? The treatment of women is a stain on Islamic civilisation. An outsider is endured in Saudi Arabia, but no more. 'We are less than animals for them,' an Indian taxi driver complained. Homosexuals are persecuted in the Gaza Strip.

"According to some, these are excesses – phenomena at the edges that should not interfere with the relationship between Western European civilisation and the world of Islam. The fact remains that the world of Islam has a tense relationship with its surroundings.

"In the Indian subcontinent this has led to a division, an apartheid. In Sudan there has been a longstanding civil war between the Islamic north and the Christian and Animist south. In Transcaucasia and in Nigeria there are similar tensions. The problems that the Islamic world has with Israel are well known.

"Maybe these tense relations are due to the fact that Islam is a relatively young religion. Islam is about fourteen hundred years old. How was Western Europe around the year 1400 with regard to the separation of church and state, freedom of expression, tolerance and non-discrimination?

"About as bad as the Islamic world today. Maybe that world will develop in the coming six hundred years as Western Europe has. But we cannot wait that long, because a large-scale immigration from Islamic countries to Western Europe has occurred. The Netherlands has never before absorbed such a large population transfer.

"Where an interface with Islamic culture used to be far away, today it is around the corner. How should the Islamic minority and the non-Islamic majority relate to each other? The same question also applies to other minorities.

"One thing should be clear: the four fundamental political principles we mentioned are not up for negotiation. Not even a little bit. Everyone in the Netherlands, both Muslim and non-Muslim, should adhere to the laws that are derived from these principles.

"The 1979 report *Ethnic minorities* by the government think tank WRR formulated it as follows: 'Very important aspects of our Western culture, such as individual freedom and equality, are often militantly opposed by other cultures. In those cases of confrontation where in practice no compromise is possible, we have no choice but to defend the achievements of our culture against those who attack them.'[3]

"Therefore there are limits to our multicultural society, where the above-mentioned political principles are threatened. But anyone who rejects cultural relativism can still accept cultural pluralism. Everyone in the Netherlands can do what they wish, say what they want, eat their own food, wear their own clothes, and practise their religion.

"The French High Court said that on matters of integration it bases its reasoning on a 'logic of equality' and not a 'logic of minorities'. The first implies equality of individuals before the law, the second implies institutional recognition of minorities as such. The first logic, the court continued, is also applied in Belgium and Germany, the second by the Netherlands and the United Kingdom. The court is not only referring to the formal channels of dialogue that minorities have, but also to certain aspects of our education. The Dutch Constitution recognises freedom of education. And there are a few subsidised Hindu and Muslim schools. Dutch legislation on education provides for schooling in [minorities'] own language and culture.

"In the Netherlands, just like in France, government policy is aimed at integration. Where the French court speaks of 'institutional recognition of minorities', we would use the word 'pillarisation'. (In England, they would call it 'communitarianism'.) It is clear that Islamic schools, and education in [minorities'] own language and culture, strengthen the cultural identity of the

Muslim minority. Does this strengthen or weaken the inclination to segregation? To put it differently, what supports integration the most: emancipation by pillarisation, which is separate development, or emancipation by shared development?

"Emancipation through pillarisation has a good reputation in the Netherlands. A century or so of pillarisation, it is claimed, led to the emancipation of Catholics and the Reformed '*kleine luyden*' (common people). On this basis we should also prefer emancipation through pillarisation for the Islamic minority. But perhaps the Catholics and *kleine luyden* would have been emancipated without pillarisation. Indeed, perhaps they would have been emancipated more quickly away from the oppressive environment of their own pillars.

"The problem is that we cannot afford to be wrong. Developments that are set in motion today will be deep-rooted and irreversible. Freedoms that are demanded in law today will have consequences for decades and possibly much longer.

"The fact that 'black schools' exist is very regrettable. Separate schools are a precursor to a divided society. Will Islamic schools strengthen segregation? Which Islam will be taught there: the broad-minded or the fundamentalist version?

"Because of these considerations, the WRR recommends that education in minorities' own culture should be voluntary and kept outside regular school hours. But wouldn't extra support to learn Dutch be even better?

"We used to believe in 'integration with preservation of identity'. Now we know that they stand in tension with each other. All policy should be aimed at integration. That's why the WRR sees the duty of a certain basic education not only as a matter for unemployed immigrant recipients of welfare, but also for their young women. [4]

"The fact that there is much resistance to overcome may be seen with the experience of the subsidised 'Step-up' programme. This programme is targeted at four- to six-year-old children belonging to a minority, to provide them with a more successful start in the Dutch education system.

"We had hoped that children's education would be stimulated by their mothers. But unfortunately it turns out that Turkish and Moroccan mothers do not attend group meetings. One of the advisers of the programme, an internationally well-regarded female professor at the University of Istanbul, indicated that this problem does not exist in Turkey, because participation at this kind of meetings is mandatory. But when a Dutch adviser proposed introducing the same requirement here for parents who participate in the programme, it led to protests by a Turkish-Dutch colleague. Taken aback by this fierce reaction, the leadership of the programme did not make the group meetings mandatory as long as it could not be proved that this attendance had a positive impact on the development of the child. The programme therefore remained dependent on the voluntary participation of the mothers, that is, the permission of their husbands."

I concluded the article with the exhortation:

"The integration of minorities is such a difficult problem that it can only be solved with courage and creativity. We can afford neither permissiveness nor taboos. What is needed is a wide debate in which all political parties participate, about what is allowed, what is possible, what might be, and what might be the consequences otherwise."[5]

My article was ready when criticism of my speech in Lucerne had already started, but after it was published all hell broke loose. The Dutch Ministry of the Interior collected nearly a hundred responses which ranged from critical to very critical. Prime Minister Ruud Lubbers called it 'dangerous' and another Minister called it 'insulting to the Muslim community'. A pundit called it 'anti-Islamic and it even fans racist sentiments'. A representative of the Turkish community said I was orchestrating 'impure thoughts'.

But why was the reaction to the article such a great shock, when it did not say much more than the 1979 report *Ethnic minorities* by a government think tank? I have often noticed that preconceived ideas – such as ideologies – can get in the way of observation. One looks, but does not see. Or better: one does see, but doesn't permit oneself to. As Kant wrote, "The Enlightenment is the elevation of man from the immaturity that he has himself to blame for. *Sapere aude* – dare to think. That is the essence of the Enlightenment." It is the battle between preconceived ideas and traditional authority.

With us, traditional authority consisted of a cartel of experts who believed in an ideology of 'integration with preservation of cultural identity' and fiercely resisted my views. Then there was the alleged superiority of Western civilisation to the Islamic world. Here I would say: look at the facts. Why do so many people from the Middle East want to live in Western Europe? At the very least because they think life is better here than there? And why is it better here? Why do so many Arabs want to send their children to study in the United States? Why do they seem to say: 'Yankee go home, but please take me with you'?

The United Nations Development Programme (UNDP) first published the Arab Human Development Report in 2002, written by the Egyptian political scientist Nader Fergany. This report explains the 'backwardness' of the Arab world. The most important causes of this backwardness compared to the Western world are: lack of freedom, lack of knowledge, and lack of female empowerment. Are these not questions of culture?

Why do we have so much difficulty in acknowledging the accomplishments of our culture? In the Christian gospel of Matthew we learn that one should not judge lest one be judged. But in a broader sense, the reluctance is a symptom of a shrinking self-confidence in our own culture. This is a complex question to which I devoted the closing chapter of *The Intellectual Temptation*, a book about the relationship between intellectuals and politics. I concluded the book with the following:

"In its modern form, the noble Western tradition of self-criticism has often been corrupted into mere sentimental self-flagellation, without a genuine openness to learning. (…) So who actually shares in this lack of self-confidence? Is it just the intellectual elite? It started with the elite, but has now trickled down into the general culture. After all, it was the intelligentsia that encouraged secularisation and invented multiculturalism. They were the first to be what we all have since become." [6]

THE BREAKTHROUGH

I spoke about what happened in 1991. What has happened since? The answer can be brief: *'polderen'* (consensus). [7] The Minister of the Interior, Ien Dales, got her conference. Other conferences followed, such as one on policy for big cities in Rotterdam on 16 February 1996. In a sombre speech, the director of the Netherlands Institute for Social Research warned: "In fifteen years, half of the city population will be immigrants." He spoke about "high unemployment among these groups, an integration problem that immigration can't keep up with, interethnic animosity, black schools, white flight, criminality and decay." He concluded: "There is a broad sense in Europe that policy cannot cope with the decline of big cities. Earlier such policies in the United States failed." [8] Prime Minister Wim Kok shared this sombre tone. I will return to the question of whether this negative vision came true.

In the decade that followed my article, the national debate did occur in several areas. Several widely-read articles appeared in the 1990s and my own parliamentary work was devoted to these questions. Paul Schnabel published *The Multicultural Illusion* in 1998, with the subtitle *A plea for adaptation and assimilation*. Schabel wanted to "depart from a fruitless and ultimately unacceptable multiculturalism, which wishes to make distinctions but not differences." He pleaded "against the hope that a multicultural society will be viewed as an equal opportunity for other cultures to determine our own culture." [9] Others joined in the public debate in this vein, and I published two books on the subject. [10]

In parliament, I had to develop policy for my party, and fast. Together with my spokesman, we decided on the following three elements: limit immigration, combat discrimination, and promote integration. On the first point, I was impressed by the positive influence on integration that limitation of immigration had in the United States in the 1920s. The second point resulted in a joint motion with parties on the left, seeking a law promoting equal work opportunities for immigrants. That law would eventually be passed, and the motion is framed on a wall outside parliament. On the third point, that of integration, nothing promotes it as well as paid work. For this reason I entered the 1994 elections with the slogan: 'Work, work and more work.'

Today, in the second decade of the new millennium, we live in a new era in which we commemorate 9/11. That was a horrific event, because three thousand people met their death, many of them burned alive. What was the cause of this attack? In the Belle Epoque they also dealt with terrorism. No fewer than six heads of state were assassinated in the two decades before 1914 [11]— only then it involved the few and not the many, as in New York, Madrid and London. In the Belle Epoque the cause was anarchism, and now it is Islamist resentment. How did this happen? In the time of the great caliphates, the Umayyads and Abbasids, the Islamic world was powerful and prosperous. That is clearly no longer the case. How come? For Islamists there are two possibilities. Either Arab rulers have left the path of the faith, or the West, led by America, has in some way confiscated this power and wealth unfairly. Either way, the decadence of the Islamic world will not be reversed any time soon, and the resulting resentment will accompany us for some time to come.

Therefore I do not see these attacks as a sign of strength, but of weakness. This is my answer to those who argue that Islam is a threat to Europe. This is not the case. Islam is not a threat to the West. On the contrary: it is the West, with its ideas about democracy, individualism and pluralism, that is a threat to Islam.

What is the state of the terrorist threat in the Netherlands today? In a 2009 report, the Dutch intelligence service AIVD noted that "the growth of the Salafist movement in the Netherlands is stagnating. (...) Violent sounds are slowly disappearing from Salafi mosques. (...) A part of the breeding ground for radicalisation has disappeared." [12] This sounds reassuring, but we should keep an eye on the possibility of things spilling over from abroad. For example, today there is a risk of radicalisation from the Syrian civil war with the return of radicals to the Netherlands and other European countries after they have fought in Syria.

What is the situation with Muslims today? In 2006 Statistics Netherlands published its Integration Map. It was a sobering piece of work. It concluded: "The difference in performance between non-Western immigrants and native pupils has not narrowed. The number of welfare recipients among most foreign ethnic groups is high. When it comes to crime, the second generation aren't doing much better than their parents. The second generation often seek a marriage partner in their country of origin. Dutch culture is often considered as inappropriate or even threatening to their culture."

In January 2010, the Netherlands Institute for Social Research published a report on ten trends of integration that gave a more nuanced view of the picture of 2006. The most important part of this is demography. The number of children per Moroccan woman of the second generation is only slightly above the average of native women – and that of Turkish women is below it. This is a positive development that belies the claims of a 'tsunami' by one politician, and counters the pessimism expressed at the 1995 conference.

The Institute also describes several other positive trends. In education, children of non-western immigrants are still behind native children, but the differences are narrowing. More and more migrants are studying in higher education. More non-western migrants speak Dutch. Fewer migrants get a marriage partner from their country of origin. More migrants can be counted as belonging to the middle class. [13]

These trends are positive. But there are also unfavourable developments, especially in crime and unemployment. More improvement is needed. The Moroccan-Dutch politician Ahmed Marcouch argued that the Moroccans need to step up and fight criminality emerging from their own community. [14] He is right.

One politician after the other has proclaimed the death of multiculturalism. The German Chancellor Angela Merkel has. The French President Nicolas Sarkozy did. The British Prime Minister David Cameron eventually did as well. The question remains, of course, what they mean by the concept of multiculturalism. If they mean that everyone should respect the fundamental norms of a society – Cameron pointed to forced marriages – then we can all swiftly agree. When it comes to non-essential norms, I believe in the importance of the law and defer to it. Publicly, the law of the land is the mother of all our freedoms.

EVALUATION

The text above has been adapted from earlier articles, speeches and books. For this volume, I am asked to consider my starting a public debate as a breakthrough process, according to the elements of vision, concept, strategy and implementation. I called for a public debate and we got one. When my 1991 article was published, I was surprised by the intensity of the negative reaction, but these could be seen as the birth pangs of a new paradigm. This storm was in fact the beginning of the debate. It is important to resist pressure that seeks to impose silence, and during and after the storm the debates and work continued. After my article, books on the subject and work in parliament, important public intellectuals have picked up the subject. Policies have been implemented and we have seen some larger trends showing signs of improvement. Without a debate, the grim projections of the 1995 conference might well have become reality. Let us examine this breakthrough according to the framework of this book.

Was there a vision? Yes, my political vision is in the tradition of classical liberalism, which concerns the individual and the state and has always opposed the group rights that led to the 'pillarisation' of society. In the 19th century Dutch society was divided into three pillars: Catholic, Protestant, and Socialist. These pillars meant separate schools, associations, trade unions, newspapers, hospitals, radio, television and political parties. No single pillar of Dutch society could politically dominate any of the others, and this pillarisation was the basis of Dutch toleration, but also great cultural differences between cities, and between the city and countryside. In the social upheavals of the 1960s, the pillars were shattered. For example, Catholic and Protestant political parties merged to form the Christian Democratic Party, and Dutch society was more united by similar trends.

The problem arose when the integration of Muslim immigrants meant in practice that they were placed in their own pillar, and any political negotiation happened through designated representatives. Muslim citizens were cut out of the political process in this way. The outcome of multiculturalism was not integration but segregation. As I noted repeatedly, our democratic rule of law is based on the separation between church and state, freedom of expression, tolerance and non-discrimination – founding principles that are not up for negotiation and to which we assign universal validity.

The preservation of these principles in our society was my vision. But I also realised that the challenges posed by large-scale immigration from the Islamic world and by other non-Western migrants was too much for one political party to handle. It was a matter of public and national interest, and my concept was to address these questions in an open national debate that involved all political parties.

Was there a strategy for this concept? Yes and no. My speech at Lucerne and article in *De Volkskrant* were meant to initiate this national debate. In my work in parliament, the three-part policy strategy of limiting immigration, combating discrimination, and promoting integration was consistent with these principles, as was the election campaign of 1994. But neither I nor my party directed the national debate. Many joined in and organised conferences and discussions, at the political level, in the media and in academia. I continued speaking on the subject, and wrote books and articles during the 1990s. The policies in question were all implemented.

Was there a breakthrough? Yes, without a doubt. We succeeded in making a difficult question openly debatable. Taboos were broken and a hidden industry with entrenched interests was challenged and eventually dismantled. We cannot predict with certainty what the positive social outcome has been of initiating this debate. But we can take as a yardstick two measurements that we have seen in this chapter: a comparison between the pessimistic projections made in a 1995 conference on city policy, and the reality following the 2010 report by the Institute for Social Research. In 1995 we saw a grim prediction of urban decay, and social and economic segregation. In 2010, the reality revealed many improvements compared to what could have happened. We have succeeded in adjusting the course of the country for the better – and that too is a breakthrough.

LESSONS

What lessons are there for future generations? Governments should not impose large-scale policies on their people without their consent and without considering the consequences. When large questions are to be considered, it is best to prepare the people for it in a national debate.

The absence of a national debate on big issues can lead to a backlash from the people, which may include violence. We only need to look to France for a recent example, when the government passed a law in 2013 permitting gay marriage. This was done in the absence of a national debate, and there were violent reactions around the country. The electorate had never been prepared for it with a national debate, revealing that many taboos still exist. We had no such backlash in the Netherlands, because it is a subject that had been openly debated for some time. Regardless of what one's position is on this subject, this is a recent example of what can happen in a free democratic state when no one dares to initiate a national debate on a big issue.

When I initiated the debate, I did so as leader of my party and was in a position to do this with a measure of authority. It is not a matter of breaking taboos for their own sake, but of reminding a country of its core values. This is the moral responsibility of public intellectuals and those in positions of public authority.

CHAPTER 13

PRIVATISATION AS BREAK-THROUGH?

Privatisations of major industries in the UK, Western Europe and the former Soviet Union over a period of two decades since the 1980s represent a set of breakthroughs that have produced mixed results. We examine the political decisions that led to these privatisations, their consequences, and the manner in which they have served the public interest. We will further consider the relationship that privatisation has to innovation: to what extent does a privatised economy stimulate innovation? We conclude that an innovative economy is not a factor of proportions of public or private ownership but also a matter of culture and liberty. Innovation is served when there are well-balanced and integrated institutional arrangements between all stakeholders of government, private enterprise, academia and society who share ownership in the public good.

THE QUALITATIVE ANALYSIS FOR THIS CHAPTER IS ON PAGE 389 OF THE ANNEX

ROEL KUIPER

INTRODUCTION

Politicians often ask themselves what the best conditions are for sustained economic growth and how to foster innovation. Ruchir Sharma, the head of Emerging Market Equities at Morgan Stanley, wrote a book about this topic that became a bestseller: *Breakout Nations, In Pursuit of the Next Economic Miracles*.[1] His point of departure is the "boom" that started around 2003, featuring countries like Brazil, Russia, India, China and South Africa—the BRICS. In the following years many observers noticed a shift in economic power from the West (the United States and European Union) to these newly industrialised countries. But a decade later, these observers are no longer so sure about this prospect.

The economic growth of the BRICS countries is slowing down. China's growth dropped from above 10 per cent in 2010 to below 8 per cent in 2013. Some economies are built on natural resources, like Russia; others on cheap labour costs, like India and China. But domestic investment remains poor and domestic consumption has not overtaken declining exports, because of the financial and economic crisis in the West. Moreover, these countries do not act as a united bloc, because their political elites are all focused on domestic issues. Sharma asks which nations will continue to have sustained high-level economic growth over the next decades. This is the group that he calls the 'Breakout Nations', and it includes countries like Turkey, South Korea, Indonesia, Nigeria, the Czech Republic and Poland.

Whereas BRICS countries made good use of the tailwinds of favourable global circumstances, the breakout nations propel themselves. There are no fixed rules, because economic success is not just a question of getting the mathematics right, but about matters of society, education and culture. The "rules of the road" that Sharma offers include these general lessons: stabilising debts and inflation at home; keeping currency and interest rates low; creating surplus value abroad; and having an educated and hard-working workforce. Sharma does not include privatisation as one of the "rules of the road" and points to the intervening and guiding role of governments. In South Korea and Taiwan governments "started on the path of success with unconventional policies that defied the usual free-market prescriptions."[2] They subsidised and protected their industries, limited free trade and provided investment guarantees.

This contradicts the ideas that have been promoted in the US and Europe to limit the government's role in economics. The assumption had been that such a role is a hindrance to innovation and economic growth; the real economic breakthrough comes from markets, which can do better than governments. The policies that promoted privatisation of public services and economic activities flowed from these assumptions. Various types of privatisation were implemented in the United Kingdom, the European Union and in different countries of the former Soviet Union and Eastern Europe. What was the economic gain for nations who followed these policies of liberalisation and privatisation?

In this chapter we consider these large-scale privatisations and examine the relationship between privatisation and innovation. We consider the underlying vision, concept and goals of privatisation policies and the manner in which they were carried out in various countries. The question of privatisation, however, is related to innovation in two distinct ways: first, to what extent were the privatisation policies innovative? Second, what are the right policies to foster in an innovation-based economy?

Innovation is defined as the creation of new inventions or inventive designs. In the context of this chapter, an economic theory can be innovative and lead to innovative policies. But for our purposes, innovation also refers to the presence of innovation in an industry, where new discoveries in technological change can lead to greater efficiency and improve lives. In this chapter, we consider both sides of privatisation: the extent to which it was innovative, and what innovation it produced in an economy. We also ask what lessons there might be for future policymakers who wish to stimulate economic growth and foster innovation.

While large-scale privatisations can be seen as breakthroughs, privatisation or liberalisation in itself – the transfer of ownership of goods or industries to private hands – is an old idea. The question of whether privatisation policies in a particular country or region are innovative depends heavily on the context of circumstances, regulatory framework, the rule of law, and other political, cultural and economic factors. There have been major differences between countries that went through this experiment, especially between Eastern Europe and the EU. In Russia, Ukraine and some other countries of the former Soviet Union, unregulated privatisations helped to create a class of wealthy oligarchs, owning the businesses once held by the state. The legal framework and economic policies of these states were too weak to make liberalisation economically beneficial for the general public, even if there was a desire to do so. The liberalisation of markets in countries like Poland and Hungary seemed also to follow this road, but their economies were soon integrated in the internal market of the EU and its legal framework.[3]

In Western Europe, many countries followed the "British experiment" of the 1980s, although with less vigour and consequence than British Prime Minister Margaret Thatcher proposed. In fact, many European leaders were not adherents of free-market liberalism and it was their intention to retain a regulating role for the state.

Nevertheless, the tides were in favour of the liberalisation of markets and the privatisation of former state-owned companies. The British experiment became the example for a wider European experiment once the European countries decided to build one single internal market. The European Commission tried hard to create a "level playing field" and this proved to be the real game-changer. National governments were prohibited from supporting their national industries any longer and public services in EU countries were to be integrated and reconstructed beyond national control.

Thirty years later there are more mixed feelings about these policies than ever before. There are critical evaluations not only of economic profits and consumer prices but also of the public outcomes of privatisations. Privatised firms are not being taken back into public ownership, but their operations are more closely connected to a rediscovered public interest or common good.[4] What does this entail for the idea of privatisation as an innovation and breakthrough? Can we, after all, do without governments to attain sustained economic development? I will begin with the history of the idea, and then provide some examples of privatisation policies and their consequences. Finally, I evaluate privatisations as innovations and the institutional conditions that should be considered to make them work.

THE UNDERLYING VISION AND CONCEPT

After decades of post-war economic growth, the Western world faced a deep economic crisis in the 1970s. Western economies, dependent on oil from the Middle East, had to cope with a very dark scenario when oil prices went up, including, though not limited to, rising unemployment, inflation and state debt. The Keynesian consensus prescribed an increase in public expenditure to stimulate consumption, but this now proved to be counter-productive. Increased public expenditure stimulated inflation and disrupted public finances, interest rates and savings. Governments were already loaded with heavy obligations and had to meet the social costs of mass unemployment. The welfare state was proving to be a financial burden. In these circumstances, Western governments were forced into more austerity as they searched for new answers. A new approach was offered by economists of the University of Chicago and their leading monetarist Milton Friedman (1912-2006).

Friedman had offered a brilliant analysis of the 1930s crisis and emphasised that governments could play a decisive role in aggravating economic crises. Governments had to care for balanced public finances in order to prevent inflation, and should provide guidance and regulation but stay out of economic activities. Markets should do the economic job and should therefore be as free as possible.

These ideas were translated into economic policies by Ronald Reagan, President of the United States, 1980-1989, and in an even more profound way by Margaret Thatcher in the UK from 1979 to 1990. Thatcher was clear in her first speech as Prime Minister: she would advocate free enterprises in free markets. This meant an end to what she called "socialism".[5] The British government should withdraw from sectors and industries that could be run by the market. Clearly, she wanted more private ownership and a smaller public sector: "It needs reducing." Soon she would embark on a policy of privatisation and denationalisation, wherever possible.

Nigel Lawson, Chancellor of the Exchequer 1983-1989, explained what these policies were to achieve: "No industry should remain under state ownership unless there is a positive and overwhelming case for it so doing."[6]

Privatisation, of course, means selling state property, and shares in public companies and services, to private owners. In the most rigid way it meant the end of state protection or state support for certain industries. In the UK this was illustrated by closing down state-owned coalmines and shipyards.

For Thatcher, free enterprise should take over and the market would produce the necessary public goods and services whenever possible. Along these lines she privatised British Steel, British Telecom, British Gas, British Airways, British Aerospace, British Rail, and many more major national industries and public services. Rolls Royce was partially privatised, and while this was painful for some it is a company still focused on some public services. The British government would claim that it brought the economy back into the hands of the market and that the general public would gain more by free-market policies than by state intervention. Between 1983 and 1990 the British government gained £23 billion by transferring state-owned industries to the private sector.[7]

Although many European countries were suspicious about these economic experiments, most of them would also carry out policies that limited the government's role and promoted economic liberalisation. They followed what seemed to be new economic wisdom and a new international mindset, expecting that free trade and new markets would help to overcome the economic crisis of the 1970s and 1980s. One of the remarkable achievements of these years was the establishment of the internal market among the member states of the European Union. Even more remarkable was that this idea was shaped in Brussels by one of Margaret Thatcher's former ministers, Lord Cockfield.

He modelled the concept of the internal market on the British approach. In order to keep the UK on board, in 1985 the EU's member states accepted the European Commission's White Paper and road map for implementing a free-market strategy for the union. The internal market would favour big industries and companies. It envisaged a Europe with open borders and minimal influence by member states on public services. Soon the European Commission would issue guidelines for further liberalisation for all kind of services conducted by national governments. This is how privatisation policies became part of the DNA of the European market. The aims of European regulation included liberalised markets in public transport, the production and distribution of electricity and gas, telecommunications and postal services.

Today economists are surprised by the lack of empirical data for these proposed policies. Other than the "Chicago Boys", the Chilean students of Milton Friedman who were tasked with carrying out privatisation policies under President Augusto Pinochet from 1975, there had been no empirical testing of these theories and their consequences. Decision-makers had no long-term empirical evidence of the success of the policies they advocated; they were truly an experiment. There was a need to limit the government budget and here were some new monetarist ideas.

However, what everyone did know was that open, globalised markets would stimulate trade and economic activity. Globalisation became an important idea after the fall of communism and the opening up of Eastern Europe and Asia. All over the world countries began to open their stock markets to the outside world: Taiwan in 1991, India in 1992, South Korea in 1993 and Russia in 1995. But internationalisation and globalisation offered insufficient reasons for governments to privatise public services or network industries like gas, oil, railways, telecommunications and public utilities. Yet privatisation became an element in this worldwide "new capitalism" that created wealth for some and meant a dismantling of post-war bureaucratic and societal structures in Europe.

Although overall aims shifted over time, governments had several main objectives in embarking on policies of privatisation. Of course, not every government was inclined to follow these policies and in many countries the political culture was not especially open to such policies. Nationalisation and economic protection have long been part of the game of serving the national interest. In some cases governments do not want to lose their "national champions". It takes a certain economic mindset to give due weight to arguments in favour of privatisation. Given such a mindset, privatisation has been presented as a breakthrough process, serving some of governments' main objectives.

The first objective is a negative one: to reduce the load in terms of budget and governance. During the 1990s this negative impulse was turned into a positive idea: reinventing government by making its functioning more efficient. The second objective was built on the assumption that privatisation, in combination with liberalisation of markets, would bring economic growth and prosperity. In many countries old industries and factories had to be replaced by more modern facilities. A third objective derived from this assumption: better services, better-quality products and freedom of choice would result, satisfying consumers and the general public. Citizens would be better off as result of these policies. We can see these three main objectives as criteria for a breakthrough, with privatisation leading to greater innovation in the economy.

OUTCOMES: PRIVATISATION AND INNOVATION

The transition that politicians had in mind were undoubtedly meant to be innovative and to lead to greater innovation. Privatisation would enable innovation in industries and companies that were formerly owned or directly steered by governments. They would also bring indirect innovation to governments, stirring a new interest in improving public services. According to the standards of this concept, termed "New Public Management", governments should become more efficient, "entrepreneurial" and "managerial", and therefore business models were applied to government services.[8] Many of those were now turned into more or less independent agencies. The broader underlying assumption and the justification of privatisation policies were that they would improve public services, economic performance and stimulate growth and prosperity. But it is not easy to measure this general assumption.

In some countries like the Netherlands these policies were embraced.

They gave short-term relief from the pressure on public finance and formed a part of economic recovery. At the same time, however, former state-owned companies went bankrupt in free-market-circumstances, creating mass unemployment. In Britain the privatisation of British Rail in combination with a liberalised market in public transport brought more than twenty new companies into competition, creating upheaval in rail transportation. Today, rail in Britain consists of several regional monopolies, with a fragmented and confusing price structure. Many former state companies were sold to foreign owners with global interests, who would cut the number of employees or shut down factories. The formula was one of downsizing and using the subsequent savings for the next acquisition.

But counter-productive results were drawing the attention of the general public. It is not even clear how the general public itself benefited from these policies. Prices of energy and public transport in private hands certainly did not go down. Only telecommunications became cheaper, but this was also due to the rapid introduction of new technologies. The economist Massimo Florio, who investigated the effects of privatisations on consumer prices, concluded that "privatisation per se does not lead to lower prices for consumers".[9] The accumulated result in terms of consumer welfare is a "zero-sum game".[10]

For politicians privatisations were especially helpful in reducing budgetary problems, but the economic result for countries as a whole proved difficult to measure. What about the innovative impulse that was to follow from privatisation? Did it create better companies, better government organisation or better services and products? The claim was that state-owned companies were rigid and slow in their functioning, offered poor quality and were neither skilled nor swift enough to adapt to changing circumstances in order to create greater added value. In many ways this was true, and there were indeed reasons to stimulate them to achieve better results. While the state was necessary in post-war circumstances to set up new industries, fifty years later there was no need for governments to remain owners of companies or industries which served only an economic function.

It seemed fair that the state would reduce its share in chemical industries, steel, mines, aviation, pharmacy, and so on. But was this also true for public goods provided by network industries (railways, telecommunications), public services and utilities (mail, water, electricity)? The modernisation of these industries and services could offer a strong reason to privatise them. In that case the "common good" would be better served by private companies. What were the actual innovative merits of these privatisations of networked industries and utilities?

As could be learned from unregulated privatisations in the former Soviet Union and Eastern Europe, innovation does not automatically follow as a consequence of privatisation. The tragedy of Russia is that talented and well-educated sections of the population find little chance to express their potential and skills – their innovations are developed in Israel and Silicon Valley.

What is needed are economic drivers (consumer demand, industrial capacity and energy resources), research capacities, technological development, a highly educated workforce and government regulation in order to facilitate businesses and fair competition. An important factor is also the diffusion of economic power: by definition, giant corporations are rarely economic drivers of innovation. Many companies that used to be public monopolists became private monopolists after a process of liberalisation. While delivering utilities and services as necessary goods for consumer households, privatised companies still try to dominate the market by reducing competition. This happened in both the former Soviet Union and in the liberalised European market, for instance in the area of energy supply.

Innovation of public services and utilities by privatised companies is not a given. This is especially true in the sector of network industries with high costs of rails, grids, pipelines and cable facilities. In private companies there is a natural tendency to keep the costs of these investments as low as possible, or to shift them to users or to other parties. In the UK this has led to the alarming conclusion that twenty years after the privatisation of the electricity industry, a radical change in energy policies was needed to replace ageing plants, to meet the government's objective to achieve 15 per cent renewable energy, and to keep consumer prices under control. A 2011 White Paper from the British government stated that "current market arrangements will not deliver the scale of long-term investment needed, at the required pace, to meet these challenges. Nor will they give the consumers the best deal."[11]

In this area privatisation will not automatically bring innovation of production and services. What in fact happened is that the shareholder value of these companies improved and private owners profited most from privatisation. This was especially true for energy industries (like gas), utilities and public transport. But privatisation in itself is not a strategy to foster innovation in an economy. Privatisation can even hinder it. The decisive factors for innovation are market circumstances, education and helpful government regulation.

If privatisation was designed as a gateway to innovation the results have been modest. Privatisation as such does not produce innovation. However, in some sectors privatisation has made industries more apt to facilitate new technologies. In the sector of telecommunications, innovations were the result of technological developments. Transferring state-owned companies to private hands made them stronger and swifter to adopt and implement these innovations. Government regulation helped to bring about this result and to let consumers profit from technological innovations. But, again, this is not due to privatisation as such, but to markets and government stimuli.

The best results occur when these factors come together and cooperate to bring about a culture of innovation. The Dutch Scientific Council for Government Policy recently issued a report about how to foster such a culture of innovation, *Towards a learning economy*. It pointed to four factors: human capital (which requires education), infrastructure for knowledge (research and development), regulating institutions (governments) and a spirit of cooperation (governance). Economies cannot innovate without such a culture and institutional structure to support innovation. Results will follow when this potential is there and is correctly used. Innovation is a common enterprise and needs coordination and a lively idea of the public interest.

The development of the "breakout nations" illustrates these connections. Another illustration is offered in Israel by the way that country is fostering a culture of innovation through the creation of institutions that are meeting-places between academia, the armed forces, government and business. The Advanced Technologies Park in Beer Sheva was recently inaugurated, in order to promote the commercialisation of hi-tech and biotech innovations that were developed either in the armed forces or academia.[12] Governments can play an important role in stimulating this culture of innovation by establishing and maintaining these bridges between sectors, and by subsidising business incubators without being the primary economic agent.

Public administration in Western countries achieved a lot in realising better management, smarter work processes and higher levels of productivity. New Public Management produced another mentality and new attitudes in civil services. But it should not be forgotten that the mindset and mentality of the civil service should be oriented towards the common good. Governments should serve public interests and not their own interests or the interests of small governing elites. A spirit that helps to promote a culture of innovation should be alive in a civil service that is oriented towards the common good of the general public. We need closer relationships between stakeholders in the common enterprise of economic innovation, and therefore responsible governments that bring partners and the people together.

The last decade has shown the emergence of a more critical attitude towards privatisation. No one believes any longer that free enterprises in free markets will automatically produce the best economic results. On the contrary, since many industries and companies have been sold off or outsourced, mass unemployment and inefficient use of the labour force illustrate a unbalanced economic landscape. After the 2008 crisis new moral attitudes emerged. Jeffrey Sachs, one of the leading economic spirits of recent decades, concerned about the inability of governments to oversee private contractors, stated: "The proper approach is to rebuild public management, not to turn it over to voracious private firms."[13] Indeed, new ideas are emerging about the role of economic institutions and the need for steering mechanisms to shape better conditions for economic and social development.

EVALUATION

In 2011-2012 the Dutch Senate, in which I serve, held a parliamentary inquiry into thirty years of privatisation. The committee, which I chaired, concluded that privatisation and liberalisation were designed to solve some urgent financial problems of public finance. Initially this was the most important objective of the Dutch government in the 1980s. In many countries privatisation is indeed one of the first measures that governments take when they are confronted with immediate financial problems. It was part of the "shock doctrine" in Eastern Europe when they had to adopt a market system, and today it remains one of the recommendations to EU countries like Greece which are struggling with their budgets. The Dutch considered, for better and worse, the "British experiment" to be an important signal of the future condition of globalising markets.

Over the last thirty years, throughout Europe there has been a strong political vision favouring privatisation, but the consequences were not thoroughly and properly considered. Now many evaluations and even parliamentary inquiries are being undertaken to get a closer insight into the considerations and decisions behind these policies. The conclusion of the parliamentary inquiry of the Dutch Senate was that the Dutch followed European guidelines without a clear plan and without making clear how privatisation would serve the public interest. There were no definitions, no descriptions, no concepts. Decision-makers operated only with the general idea that privatisation and liberalisation would improve the performance of companies, public services and products. Major and far-reaching decisions were based on political and ideological reasons, driven by expectations of profits but not by empirical evidence.

For this chapter and in my parliamentary work, I have examined privatisation from the perspective of political decision-making. I should add that it was beyond the scope of this chapter to support it with empirical evidence for the best balance of public and private organisation of an economy, but I would encourage more research in this area. It appears, however, that the best balance will differ per country. Societies are often measured by their economic indicators; but decisive human factors, such as education, culture, civil society and the rule of law, are harder to quantify. In fact, they are key factors for any culture of innovation and sustainable economic development. It is important to recognise that economically reductionist approaches to society will omit its most valuable qualities.

Because of the long-term public damage of privatisation, in terms of companies that were stripped or closed, underinvestment, loss of quality and lack of public control, there is now a movement, at least in Western countries, to reconsider privatisation. After three decades of globalisation and liberalisation, the newest economic ideas are concentrating on the role of economic and political institutions that should be in place to get the economic system right. Nobel prize winner Douglas C. North has helped to clarify this point: "The major role of institutions in a society is to reduce uncertainty by establishing a stable (but not necessarily efficient) structure to human interaction." Niall Ferguson took up this message in his book *The Great Degeneration: How Institutions Decay and Economies Die*. There he poses the alarming question:

could it be "that the economic, social and political difficulties of the Western world today reflect a degeneration of our once world-beating institutions?"[14] This question is one of the most important ones in our world today, and Ferguson is a conservative who argues for strong state institutions that work together with a vital civil society.

Ferguson draws a picture comparing stagnating states with "breakout" states. The difference is not that the former have regulated economies and the latter do not. They all have. Rather, it is the total picture of all institutions working well to stimulate economic development, which goes hand in hand with social justice, a free society, proper legislation, honest governments, and so on. The breakout nations are those whose public institutions produce stable and functioning social and legal systems. According to Ferguson, a growing economy is accompanied by a big civil society, equal treatment of citizens, the rule of law, competition, scientific discovery and a strong decentralised government.

So governments are needed, not to take over but to steer and to guide. Governments should safeguard public interests when private enterprise is tending to undermine them. Private and public interests must be harmonised from a broader perspective. These ideas can be added to the "rules of the road" Sharma is talking about.

The lesson to be learned is that free-market policies can cause disarray in economic institutions when they are needed for sustained economic growth. Short-term gain can lead to long-term failure of the system. This makes governments today less ready to embark on massive programmes of privatisation. It means that they lose control of their domestic economies. Of course, this does not mean that privatisation cannot contribute to innovation or better economic results and products. Privatisations should be tailor-made. Whether privatisation can serve economic strategies depends on the particular circumstances. Too much "economic reductionism" was hidden in the approaches of the past, leaving out the effects on the economic structure as a whole or the common good.

Unfortunately, this general blindness influenced clear and fair decision-making and many unintended harmful consequences were among the results. This is partly due to the fact that the project was not evidence-based, but ideological. It represented visions and promises rather than balanced concepts. The way ahead is to restore an institutional environment to steer and guide economic processes more precisely. The breakout nations, as Sharma points out, are all doing this. They don't believe in totally liberalised circumstances, but they do believe in the way they are shaping their economies. They don't rely on globalising markets.

They count on what fits and suits their society best. To a certain extent, the state is back.[15] The future seems to be for those economies that bring out the best mix between the market, government and civil society. And that is also an old lesson.

CHAPTER 14

THE AL-JAZEERA BREAKTHROUGH

"When we talk about the idea, when it started, we don't have solid proof of who was the first to think of Al Jazeera. When you have a success story, everybody claims that it was his idea. (...) So I don't know for 100 per cent whose idea was this. So it might be the Emir himself, of the country. And many people believe that it was his idea or at least he was thinking along these lines. Other people think it was some of his advisers, executives in the media industry here who thought about something like this and then it moved until it got to the Emir and the Emir adopted the idea. He liked the idea and went along with it. (...) Many people now when they look into the history of media in the Arab world, they think about before Al Jazeera and after Al Jazeera."

— Dr Mostefa Souag

"The present Arab Spring would not have happened if Al Jazeera hadn't been there. If Al Jazeera hadn't been there, it would have happened eighteen years later from the moment we are living in. Eighteen years. It is this age of Al Jazeera which we have to use as a yardstick to measure the impact of free media on the Arab world."

— Ahmed Sheikh

THE QUALITATIVE ANALYSIS FOR THIS CHAPTER
IS ON PAGE 390 OF THE ANNEX

WITH JOHN GROFFEN, MOSTEFA SOUAG,
AHMED SHEIKH AND OTHERS.
INTERVIEWS BY THE OWLS TEAM.
TEXT BY BENJAMIN BILSKI

INTRODUCTION

If the history of media in the Arab world is divided between the eras of 'pre-Al Jazeera' and 'post-Al Jazeera', we have witnessed a breakthrough. The rapid emergence of a modernising Qatar and Al Jazeera in the past two decades has shaken the media world and the Arab world, and continues to upset the status quo which the wider region had been accustomed to. There is no doubt that a successful breakthrough has occurred, and we will examine the extent to which this process was planned, and also the role that chance has played. In the whirlwind of rapid developments that surround the rise of Al Jazeera, not all of its impact, consequences or successes could have been predicted.

If we examine Al Jazeera in the context of the emergence of modern Qatar, we can identify the role played by the vision, a concept, a political strategy, and a business strategy. Above all, the breakthrough is a result of a principled determination to introduce a new kind of journalism to the Arab world. The Owls team spoke with key figures in Al Jazeera and Qatar who explained the main principles, decisions and actions that created this media breakthrough, which in turn enabled social and political breakthroughs in the Arab world.

BACKGROUND

◎ The first idea: BBC Arabic and Qatar

The history of media in the Arab world reveals that nearly all of the press has traditionally been an extension of the interests of elites who have concentrated political and economic power in their hands. The character of Arab media tended to be set by a Ministry of Information, and varied in ideological flavouring from the nationalist and tribal to the religious. As technology evolved, the reach and impact of radio and television increased.

When the main interest of broadcasting and newspapers was serving the government and its leaders, the outcome was that the public greatly distrusted official media. Islamist and other political opposition, when barred from broadcasting, would spread their messages through decentralised media such as audiocassettes, DVDs or audio files on the internet. In a region with illiteracy rates of more than 50 per cent in many countries, television would become the most important source of information.[1]

In 1994 the first modern attempt to create a pan-Arab news channel of a higher standard was a joint venture between a Saudi prince and the BBC. With an office based in Rome, BBC Arabic was a paid service that reached Arabic viewers via a Saudi TV station, the Orbit Communication Company. "Even though this was a Saudi company, it was forbidden in Saudi Arabia, because its dish was not allowed," according to Ahmad Rachidi, later Al Jazeera's station chief in Morocco.[2] The only regular viewership of BBC Arabic was in Qatar, because the state paid for the service from Orbit and gave it free to all Qataris via cable. BBC Arabic was largely unknown in the rest of the Arab world because almost no one could pay $10,000 for the required decoder, except government departments and large businesses. But the channel fascinated the new Emir of Qatar. "So that was the first idea."[3]

From 1867 until 1971, the Emirate of Qatar was part of a British protectorate. With independence, and the discovery of one of the world's greatest natural gas reserves, North Field, Qatar's wealth skyrocketed. Sheikh Khalifa bin Hamad Al Thani seized power immediately after Qatar's independence and oversaw the development of its infrastructure into a modern state. The economy jumped from relying on pearl fishing and a modest oil income to the third-largest proven natural gas reserve in the world, with over 25 trillion cubic metres.[4] Compared to other Gulf States, the development of Qatar came later, but at a faster pace.

Sheikh Khalifa bin Hamad Al Thani was deposed by his son Sheikh Hamad bin Khalifa in 1995 after he "managed to convince the major stakeholders in Qatar and also the member of the ruling family that it would be better if his father was replaced by himself," says the former Dutch ambassador to Qatar, John Groffen. Sheikh Hamad had "ideas about what Qatar should be like. He had views of a modern, independent, economically active Qatar. And those views did not really go parallel with his father, who had very strong links with the conservative Saudi ruling family."[5]

Shortly afterwards a conflict emerged between the BBC and their Saudi partners about the Arabic channel. While in the original agreement the BBC insisted that the Arabic service had to reflect the same values as the World Service, the differences in culture and attitude to press freedom led to a collapse of this arrangement. The 'cultural sensitivities' that the BBC had agreed to "turned out to mean editing anything with which the Saudi royalty disagreed."[6] The conflict was irreconcilable with regard to human rights in Saudi Arabia and the partnership collapsed. BBC Arabic was abruptly switched off on 20 April 1996.

The newly-crowned Emir, enthused by BBC Arabic, seized the opportunity and offered the BBC-trained Arabic staff a new opportunity. Both he and the staff happened to be in London on the day after BBC Arabic was shut down. The calculation and decision were made very quickly to bring this journalistic talent home with him to Qatar. "He met all the people there, all the journalists, all the presenters, all the producers, to say: you are not going to be unemployed. We offer you a very good job in Qatar. And it was decided," said Dr Mostefa Souag, Acting Director General of Al Jazeera.[7]

VISION AND MISSION

"I think this idea of having a BBC World Service, in the sense of a Qatar World Service or an Arabic World Service was something that appealed very much to His Highness." — **Ambassador John Groffen**

"When we heard the Emir planned to abolish the Ministry of Information, we said to each other, this has got to be a joke. This could not happen in the Arab

world. When we first heard about Al Jazeera, we thought this is another joke."
— **Dr Mostefa Souag**[8]

"The vision was that it would be a free, independent media organisation that is financed by the Qatari government without interfering with its operations as such. (...) And it was really a crazy idea in the beginning, because nothing showed that the Qatari leadership was well prepared or well placed to be the one to launch this channel." — **Mohamed Krichen**

With the right mixture of a good idea, financial means and great luck of timing with BBC-trained talent becoming available, the decision was made to create Al Jazeera as a pan-Arabic world service. It was not to be a traditional megaphone and echo chamber of state propaganda, but something new altogether. The starting conditions were a radical departure from anything the Arab world had ever seen.

The Emir had a vision for the future and a grand strategy from the beginning of his reign, which was most recently refined and expressed in the Qatar National Vision 2030, covering domestic, economic, developmental and international ambitions. An important part of the media strategy was to let it be free. The concept of Al Jazeera was modelled on the BBC, not only for its journalistic standards, but also for its relationship to the government. It received a start-up payment of $137 million, and it was tasked with becoming financially independent within five years. In 1998, the Emir abolished the Ministry of Information, ending censorship of press, radio and television. All government-owned media became independent public institutions and the freedom of the press was codified in the constitution.[9]

Could this have happened elsewhere in the Arab world? No other country had this combination of resources and will, nor, above all, the courage to step back and risk entrusting genuine freedom of expression to a talented professional group of journalists.

Al Jazeera's former Editor-in-chief Ahmed Sheikh, who joined the station at its inception, compared the unique decisions in Qatar to other Arab countries: "Why didn't it happen in other Arab countries? Now we come back to chance. You need someone who is really open-minded to accept innovation and to accept new thinking. I wouldn't expect the Saudi rulers to do something similar to Al Jazeera. It is true that they launched Al Arabiya TV, but their parameters are different and to this very day they are different, totally different. They are there in the field, they sometimes do some good reports but they are different. They are limited by the Saudi way of thinking."[10]

It could not happen in Egypt either, because the government, whether military or Islamist, would not be willing to take the risks which the public accountability of an independent free press would expose them to. It was never a question of money: "The Egyptians were criticising Al Jazeera all the time, attacking us. I used to tell them: You have 80 million people and you have so many journalists and you have the money. It doesn't cost that much, by the way. People didn't realise at that time that it was costing us only $50 to $60 million a year. What is that? Nothing! To this day, Al Jazeera doesn't cost that much. So money is not an issue if a government wanted to establish similar operations. And I was asking myself: why don't the Egyptians launch a similar service to fight Al Jazeera, to compete with Al Jazeera instead of attacking it verbally all the time and doing nothing to limit its activities? Or to thwart, to ward off its impact in their country? I wouldn't expect Hosni Mubarak to launch a similar service, it is just, you know, the Arab world ... I wouldn't even expect Morsi to do a similar thing." [11]

Qatar remains the only Arab state without a minister of information. The concepts of the new Qatar and of Al Jazeera are related. The station was not to be micromanaged. The freedom of the press was to be a genuine right and one that the state could not take away. So what would the principles of Al Jazeera itself be?

"Freedom of speech is a principle to defend in the Arab world," reflected Ahmed Sheikh. "Yes, that was the law code behind the whole thing. It originated from our understanding that we are free. We are defenders of freedom of expression. And the law code that we put this [under] was 'an opinion and the other opinion'. That is still our motto. Because we believed at that time, if you want to be authentic and if you want people to trust you, then you have to give people the opportunity to listen to different points of view." [12]

Dr Souag noted that the concept of Al Jazeera was a combination of substantial financial backing, independence, a high standard of journalism, and the defence of freedom of speech and freedom of information. [13] Ahmed Sheikh recalls the amazement of arriving at the nascent station and asking: "What are our limits? Where do we stop?" And the chairman answered, "There are no limits. This is going to be a freewheeling service. No taboos. Except professional limits. Limits that are imposed by the spirit of the profession itself. You have to be transparent, you have to be impartial, you have to be objective. If you exceed these things, if you violate these principles, then there is a limit." [14]

This independence allowed the station's new leadership to discuss and define Al Jazeera's vision and core mission: "It was decided in our meetings and deliberations at that time, that our mission, the vision and the mission, is to establish a freewheeling media organisation that promotes human rights, democracy, freedom of speech and expression, and defends the rights of the people to learn and know what is happening about the world. The vision was that it is a free, independent media organisation that is financed by the Qatari government without interfering in its operations." [15]

JOURNALISTIC CONCEPT AND STRATEGY

The next step would be to translate these starting conditions and principles into a concept and strategy. How would Al Jazeera distinguish itself? Would it look like the BBC or CNN? "At that time it was decided that the concept should be based on our understanding that we are part of Arab and Muslim culture," said Ahmed Sheikh. "And as long as we speak in Arabic, then this brings into question that we belong to this culture, to this civilisation, and even in our discussion, there were different opinions. Are we going to talk about civilisations or even one civilisation, about different cultures? And at the end of the day we said it is one human civilisation, but different cultures." [16]

But in order to really make an impact, the emphasis would be on distinguishing themselves with originality "whether in pictures, whether in news, the way you look, the way you deal with things, the way you cover stories. And also we decided that we must not limit ourselves. It is true that we are part of Arab and Muslim culture but this doesn't mean that we have to limit ourselves to the boundaries of this culture." Special importance would be attached to environmental, human rights and poverty issues. [17]

These elements of originality, coverage of the whole world and not being limited to Arab culture, all became embedded in the concept. "Unfortunately we didn't write these things down until very late. When I became the Chief Editor, we wrote them down—the code of ethics and the code of conduct. We decided that this is the code, these are the principles that we are going to follow in our coverage, in our work. There were ten points and I used to call them the 'Ten Commandments'. It was something new in the Arab world as a matter of fact. No one had ever attempted to put in place a similar code of ethics and code of conduct, to govern his newsroom." [18]

The 'ten commandments' in this code are published on the website and emphasise journalistic professionalism and integrity. [19] They include adherence to "the journalistic values of honesty, courage, fairness, balance, independence, credibility and diversity, giving no priority to commercial or political over professional consideration;" to tell the truth "unequivocally"; to "present the diverse points of view and opinions without bias and partiality;" to "recognise diversity in human society... so as to present unbiased and faithful reflection of them"; to "acknowledge a mistake when it occurs"; to "observe transparency"; to "distinguish between news material, opinion and analysis to avoid the snares of speculation and propaganda;" and above all, to "stand by colleagues in the profession and give them support when required, especially in light of the acts of aggression and harassment to which journalists are subjected at times."

The focus of Al Jazeera was very much on this last point. Despite many controversies and shattered taboos that followed reporting on Israel-Palestine, Iraq, Osama bin Laden and the Arab Spring, the real mission has been to represent a new kind of journalism inside the Arab world, and stand up to established forces that seek to suppress it. Hassan Rachidi, Al Jazeera's station chief in Morocco, was arrested in 2008 for reporting that deaths there had occurred as a result of clashes between Islamist protesters and the police. It was reported by various sources, and published by various media, but the Moroccan government decided to use this opportunity to pursue only Al

Jazeera, demanding an apology and pursuing Rachidi in a politicised trial for "publishing false information with the intention to disturb public order." Ahmed Sheikh stood by Rachidi and firmly stated that there would be no apology to Morocco, because in quoting and naming multiple sources, Rachidi had not made any mistakes in his reporting.[20]

With the 'ten commandments' together with the three basic elements of the concept of originality, Arab and Muslim culture, and universality all in place, they stepped into a market competing with big rivals.

As noted, the Qatari grand strategy included allowing Al Jazeera to be genuinely independent. The strategy of the news organisation in turn derived from the principles in the vision and concept, and the journalists had the courage to stick to them. The staff of Al Jazeera carry a strong sense of responsibility and ownership of the mission with them in their work, and this is also reflected in the willingness of Al Jazeera reporters to take personal and physical risks to report on the ground, alongside the most courageous of their profession.

A point was made to develop a presence on the ground in each and every Arab country.[21] The willingness of Al Jazeera to report on corruption and human rights abuses has been a threat to the governments in the region, who have retaliated by taking action against Al Jazeera's journalists and offices, against advertisers, and against Qatar itself. Governments in Egypt, Jordan, Kuwait, Syria, Iran, Saudi Arabia, Libya, Tunisia and Morocco and the Palestinian Authority have all lodged protests with Al Jazeera and Qatar – and some even severed diplomatic relations. (Saddam Hussein only complained about a report on his lavish birthday celebrations.)[22] "Arab ambassadors in Doha said they spent so much time complaining about Al Jazeera that they felt more like ambassadors to a TV channel than ambassadors to a country."[23]

Individual reporters, however, have taken great physical risks. According to the Committee to Protect Journalists, since 2000 four Al Jazeera reporters and freelancers have been killed in war zones or areas of social unrest, and ten were imprisoned in this period. In June 2014 three Al Jazeera journalists were sentenced to up to ten years in prison in Egypt for allegedly aiding terrorism and endangering national security. Local producer Baher Mohamed received ten years, while reporter Peter Greste, an Australian, and Mohamed Fahmy were sentenced to seven years each. A fourth Al Jazeera employee, reporter Abdullah al-Shami, who was arrested at the same time, was released on medical grounds after going on hunger strike for more than four months.

The concept formed and crystallised over time, mistakes were made, and as the organisation grew rapidly and spread globally, challenges remained over staying true to the original concept. Nonetheless, its success was also very much a function of seizing opportunities when they presented themselves, and connecting them to a large-scale vision and strategy. In other words, success derives from openness to risk and opportunity, which can be realised because it is linked to an adequate budget, goals, planning and executive determination.[26]

WORK: PROGRAMMING

"When the Americans started targeting Bagdad and bombing, and the cruise missiles fell on the city, I was in the newsroom, the old one. I went to the satellite room and talked to them: get onto the roof, set up the camera. We had correspondents there, they came up in a tie and a suit to talk to the viewers. We had to tell them off. Change your clothes. And CNN used our pictures. That was our debut. And everybody started saying: just who are those people who did it before anyone else?" **– Ahmed Sheikh**

"We came to the question of Israel. Are we going to allow the Israelis to express their point of view? And there was a heated discussion. Some people were against it. And some people, like myself, said: well, whether you like them, whether you hate them – I hate their guts because I'm Palestinian, you know – they are there and they have a point of view. And they are part of the equation. You have to give them a chance to speak up, to put their point of view. And we were the first to allow them to come on the air." **– Ahmed Sheikh**

"It's a pan-Arab team. We have people from everywhere, and of course, we have people with different ideologies. I am liberal, maybe there is my colleague who is Islamist, there is another colleague who is communist. Sometimes this can be a good point for the life of a newsroom team, and sometimes it's negative. There are a lot of people saying we are pro-Israel. Others treat us as pro-American. And there are people who treat us as Islamist." **– Hassan Rachidi**

Programming started modestly with six hours of broadcasting a day in 1996, expanded to twelve hours the following year. Luck played another important role in 1997, when a French satellite channel accidentally broadcast a pornographic film instead of an educational children's programme. They were kicked off the satellite, and a slot opened up on a more powerful transponder where viewers could receive a clear signal with a small satellite dish. [27] Al Jazeera again seized the opportunity and acquired the lease for the slot. Now with their reach greatly extended, their programming could have maximum impact. The programming included new reporting, but Al Jazeera also pursued sensation where they found it.

◎ Taboos

Serially breaking Arab taboos was a particular sport for some programmes, like the flagship talk show 'The Opposite Direction'. The first episode of this programme was devoted to the Gulf Cooperation Council (GCC) and its member states, "and it was a heated discussion. Someone was attacking two guests, one of them was pro-GCC and the other was against it. Everything was put in it. Jaws fell ... throughout the Arab world. Someone just criticising the GCC and their rulers. Nobody believed it! Because the Arab world was a blackout at the time. Who could ever think of criticising these idols?" [28]

On talk shows, guests were often selected to be as controversial as possible. Liberal dissidents from countries in the region were put up opposite members of the regime and corruption was discussed openly. Israelis were invited and spoke Hebrew on an Arab station, which most Arabs had never seen before. Programming was dedicated to women's issues in the region. Talk shows were deliberately staged for dramatic effect, and taboos were "being broken almost every week. Guests debated whether Islam was an obstacle to social progress, whether the House of Saud was corrupt, whether Kuwait was really a part of Iraq and whether Arab countries should really allow America to station troops on their territory. One particularly scandalous episode about Islam had guests questioning the existence of God and comparing the Koran to the Declaration of Human Rights."[29] The audience was scandalised and heckling was common in the studio. But they could not look away.

◎ Liberals and radicals

But for all the liberalism of pursuing truth and creating an open space that allowed a multitude of opinions, illiberal individuals and movements also found their voice on the station. One of the most popular regular shows on the channel features Sheikh Yusuf Al-Qaradawi, a spiritual leader of the Muslim Brotherhood. He has passionately defended the whole spectrum of what one might call Arab conventional wisdom, ranging from supporting women's participation in democracy to encouraging suicide bombing. Opinions are divided on whether he is "a moderate, conservative or even a force for good at all."[30] A contradictory character, attacked by extremists for his liberalism and in the West for his extremism, he remains one of Al Jazeera's figureheads. When we asked Hassan Rachidi about the allegation that Al Jazeera promotes Islamism, he responded: "If you have one weekly programme on Islam, it's a small percentage of the programming. Also, this programme presented by Sheikh Qaradawi is very famous. But it is kind of 'light Islam'."[31]

One example well illustrates where Al Jazeera stands on the question of political Islam. With 'giving a voice to the voiceless' and reporting the news truthfully as key principles, there was an interesting case of a radical in Morocco. In his capacity as Al Jazeera's station chief in Morocco, Hassan Rachidi wanted to report on the man, who was the target of state propaganda:

"Between 2003 and 2007, the big players in Morocco were the Islamists, because they were in opposition. On Moroccan state TV, it was forbidden for the Islamists to appear and explain their opinions. Every day we had riots and activities, done by the Islamists. As a journalist, I have to cover what is news for me. And when I covered these activities, this is the only professional way to be, fair, credible and objective. Because this is news.

"There is a big radical Islamist in Morocco. I read a lot about him, but the first time I saw him, it was on one of our programmes on Al Jazeera. For me, what I read about him, it has nothing to do with what I understand from his speech, his way of thinking. That means that what I read about him doesn't give me a global idea. Because when I saw him, he was more radical than what I read. And I think that for me, and for other people, other viewers, this is the best way to be credible, to be objective, and to give everybody the chance to [enjoy] free speech."[32]

As it turned out, the radical was a lot worse than he was depicted in state propaganda. This discovery was not an act of sympathy or agreement with the man, but a journalistic victory nonetheless. A truth was determined objectively and revealed to the public, rather than dictated by the state. The acts of independent journalism are all acts of defiance to states where freedom of speech does not exist and television is merely an organ of the state.

Al Jazeera's reach within the Arab world also led to extremist movements and friendless tyrants choosing it as their medium of choice. The Palestinian movement Hamas seized the opportunity to make policy statements and threats on the channel. Colonel Gaddafi used the station for publicity stunts, while connections to certain Ba'ath party officials led to exclusive scoops and interviews from Iraq. While still unknown in the West, Osama bin Laden was another person who adopted Al Jazeera early on in order to reach the broadest audience possible for his threats, ideological soapboxing and even an interview. These unique leads were newsworthy, but they would also invite suspicions about the nature of Al Jazeera's relationship to such regimes, individuals and organisations.

◎ Al Jazeera and the Arab Spring

Al Jazeera's reporting would play a pivotal role in the Arab Spring, the biggest regional social revolution in recent decades. "The present Arab Spring would not have happened had Al Jazeera not been there," says Ahmed Sheikh. The video of the Tunisian fruit vendor Mohammed Bouazizi whose wares were confiscated by the police and who set himself on fire on 17 December 2010 reached the Arab and wider world in an Al Jazeera broadcast.

Ahmed Sheikh recalled that the video was already on the social networks. "We were a bit reluctant to use it, because we could not verify it. If you are in the newsroom, you don't let your adrenaline run high all the time. High adrenaline will get you in trouble. A single mistake will cost you your credibility for years to come. All the great things you do just disappear if you make a single mistake. So, they were reluctant for two or three days before to use it. Then they decided, let's do it. Put it on air.

"And it just ignited the whole Arab world. It was Al Jazeera's report on Bouazizi which ignited the revolutions in other countries, because the circumstances in Egypt and Tunisia were similar. People were tortured. People were being killed in police prisons. So now those who are, who were and are still against the Arab Spring, and those who were with the old regimes started directing these accusations against Al Jazeera, saying that Al Jazeera is actually pro-Muslim Brotherhood. No, that is untrue. We were in Tahrir Square in Cairo. It was the Egyptian masses, in their hundreds of thousands, who put the Al Jazeera screen there. Not us. Al Arabiya, the other news organisation, they were afraid of change. Al Jazeera was not afraid of change and it is still not afraid of change."[33]

◎ Al Jazeera and Qatar

The independent media pursues news where it occurs, even if it has had a role in shaping it. It was not Al Jazeera that created the starting conditions for the Arab Spring revolts, nor was Bouazizi's immolation the only spark of the uprisings. Non-violent protest movements had been preparing for some time. Nonetheless, the role of Al Jazeera in initiating the Arab Spring, and the active role of Qatar in the overthrow of Gaddafi, led to renewed questions about the nature of the relationship between the station and its sponsor.

Because Arab television stations had always been organs of the state, many would still assume that the same was also true of Al Jazeera. Rather than appreciate the extent of Al Jazeera's independence, the American and Arab governments alike lodged protests with the Qatari government, asking them to rein the station in. They continually had to be reminded that Al Jazeera really is independent. However, the parameters and extent of Al Jazeera's independence were not a given. The incoming staff had to fight to establish them.

Ahmed Sheikh notes: "It is true that the Qatari government is the financier of this operation but if you want to succeed, you have to be independent. Otherwise don't venture into this field. We told them this from day one. And, honestly, they were offended about it. I was in the newsroom from day one and we never got a call from the Sheikh or from anyone else saying, tell him this, do this, don't use that interview. Don't interview this. Don't interview that. Never, ever.

"The relationship was based on the similar relationship of the BBC to the British government. And even at certain times, we are even more disassociated from the Qatari government than the BBC and the British government. I still remember that in the Falklands war, the BBC was there defending the British.

"But we never took that position, even when Israel invaded South Lebanon in the July war in 2006. I was the chief editor and the Hezbollah rockets fell on houses in Haifa and old women, Israeli women, went into the streets wailing and crying. And I went to the editor and said: Put these pictures on the air. And he was so angry and said: Why do you want to do that? They are killing the Lebanese! And I said: And the Lebanese are killing them and they are all human beings. We have a similar case here and there. Put it on air. And he did, of course."[34]

But the complete financial dependence on the Qatari government means that keeping the concept of complete media independence alive is a challenge, especially as the organisation is growing, with a proliferation of dedicated and international channels. Ahmed Sheikh stresses that "I still believe that Al Jazeera is maintaining that concept of independence. It is still trying. That spirit of independence from the Qatari government, who finances it so graciously, is still alive there. And it is still a driving force behind its operations."

But is this combination of dependence and independence not difficult in practice? "It can be difficult in practice, but it also has its own benefits, if you are free from the burden of commerciality. To keep running the operation you have to have commercials on the screen. We do not worry about that, and that is an advantage in itself. We have the money. The mistakes that might take place these days are part of the operation itself, and those who are responsible for them are the ones who have the strings in their hands. It is not something that comes down to them from the top."

On the question of independence, Al Jazeera senior presenter Mohamed Krichen adds a qualification over the degree of variability in the station's independence when the state itself is involved in ongoing political developments: "There is no way that Netherlands TV or CNN or BBC or anyone can be really completely free from any influence from business. In the Western world it is the big company, in our world it is the government.

"But I think despite this, Al Jazeera still has its own particularity. What I mean is that it is not completely at the order of the government so that we are not like any official television in the Arab world. We are not the Saudi Arabian TV, or the Tunisian, or the Egyptian. But also we are not completely free, we are something in between. And this level of independence is completely related to political events. Sometimes there is no real challenge in politics so that you can have 90 per cent [independence]. But when there is something moving and they who sponsor you are involved, you can have this 90 per cent going [down] to 70 or to 65 per cent.

"In my experience, I can say that the dream of being completely [independent] and always to work independently as a journalist, is going to be a dream. And you should manage with realities and be more realistic. It is a struggle but ... you can never dream to be always independent and work... in a very professional way like you dream. That is my conclusion after many years." [35]

This may also explain a measure of self-censorship when dealing with Qatari subjects, either positive or negative, in order to emphasise the pan-Arab character of the station and to counter the perception that Al Jazeera is merely a mouthpiece for the government. [36] Although the explanation may be more mundane: how much news is really there? Hassan Rachidi disputes this criticism:

"Some people – some critics – will say that we are not covering enough what is happening in Qatar. Qatar is a small country. There is nothing much. If you want, we can do some features on traffic accidents. But this is a good example. We will cover something that needs to be covered, for instance: [in December 2012] Human Rights Watch published a report on Asian labour conditions in Qatar. And it was very critical of Qatar. The manager of HRW came to Qatar, and held a press conference. We covered that. It was broadcast directly, and we did two reports, in English and in Arabic." [37]

But others have also questioned the extent to which Al Jazeera is truly independent from Qatar, when editorial independence fluctuates by Krichen's admission from 90 to "65 or 70 per cent" when "they who sponsor you are involved."

◎ The business

The seed capital of $137 million was meant to enable Al Jazeera to become financially independent within five years. This never happened. Because Al Jazeera's reporting was not suffused with that flattery which Arab regimes were accustomed to, they took steps against the channel. Unable to block its reach on their territory, the Saudis began to use their economic clout to undermine the financial basis of the station, coercing advertisers to take their business elsewhere. Other governments would follow suit, because Saudi Arabia dominates regional commercial interests.

Although Al Jazeera was estimated to have over 35 million viewers each night in the early years, it was impossible to glean accurate viewer statistics with any precision. For these reasons, the station had not managed to achieve financial independence when the initial stake of $137 million from the Emir was spent. Hugh Miles noted in 2005 that "its annual running costs were estimated at about $25 million, but being blacklisted by the Saudis had cost the network a hefty $10-13 million."[38]

With the rise of specialised channels for sport, children's programming and expansion to America, the annual running cost today is closer to $50-60 million per year. But this is still a relative bargain given the impact the stations have. The entrepreneurial growth strategy is ambitious and broad, even if the target is not so much to make profit as to widen and deepen the network's impact. While this rapid growth remains directly financed by the Qatar government, however, the challenge remains to stay true to the principles of the original concept. The financial security that Al Jazeera enjoys also means that they are able to develop a long-term strategy for the next decade, and to systematically carry it out.

And what about the backlash that the government of Qatar has to endure due to Al Jazeera's impact? Ahmed Sheikh had the best answer to this question: "This is life. You have to grow up!"

EVALUATION AND CONCLUSION

"The question you asked at the very beginning: was [the breakthrough] an accident? Or innovation? I think it was both." — **Ahmed Sheikh**

"I am convinced that Al Jazeera would not have happened in any other country in the Gulf. The unique environment for Al Jazeera was in Qatar. You have a unique environment like you have a garden. Some seeds fall and some seeds will grow into flowers and some won't. This was the right spot for the seed to fall." — **Ambassador John Groffen**

"I am giving you the two sides, I am not telling you it was or it was not planned but certainly I have the feeling that it was planned. How successful would Al Jazeera be from the time it was created? I don't think many people believed that it was going to be this successful. They thought it was going to be successful for a certain region or the Arab world, but not to become an international phenomenon."
— **Dr Mostefa Souag**

◎ Innovation and the media breakthrough

There is no doubt that Al Jazeera represents the biggest breakthrough that the media in the Arab world has ever seen. But none of the elements that comprise Al Jazeera are innovative in themselves: there have been groups of courageous and principled professional journalists before; there have been satellite television and Arab television before. The breakthrough was no accident, although luck undoubtedly played an important part. The breakthrough was achieved by the combination of principles, standards, risks, leadership, courage, timing, resources and luck.

Al Jazeera could not have come about without the accident of the sudden availability of BBC-trained staff and then the sudden availability of a slot on a powerful satellite transponder. In both cases, leadership played a part by way of seizing an available opportunity quickly. And thereafter, a new paradigm was created in which work could take place at a high level and with deeper impact.

It was possible because an idea and vision could thrive in the only Arab state that was willing both to finance the operation of a pan-Arab station and risk the blowback from regional states. But bringing about a genuine breakthrough means overturning the status quo. Authoritarian regimes always live in fear of their own populations, and no other Arab state was willing to risk creating this much room for freedom of speech.

As Dr Souag observes of the stark contrast with traditional state-based Arab television, "Many people now when they try to look into the history of media in the Arab world, they think about before Al Jazeera and after Al Jazeera. So pre-Al Jazeera there had been many, many television stations. This is the mother ship we are on here, Al Jazeera Arabic. When it started, there were many television stations. Most of them, but not all, were owned by government. Most were used to promote government policies and propaganda, as well as some social and economic programmes. Maybe some entertainment, especially movies. But they were doing what the government told them to do. Or they wanted to impress the government and say: look, we are doing even more than you tell us to!"

As Ahmed Sheikh noted, "Al Jazeera was not afraid of change and it is still not afraid of change." The willingness to deliver news reporting in a revolutionary way means that they are unafraid of the consequences of their reporting, which includes revolution. It was not the video of Bouazizi's self-immolation spreading on social media that triggered the Arab Spring revolutions, but the video broadcast as part of a verified Al Jazeera report. Events took over, and Al Jazeera was there on the ground to report in every state – and it has lost journalists in Libya and Syria.

According to Mohammed Krichen, it is part of the spirit of the station to support democratic change: "Al Jazeera, since the beginning, was seen as a channel that gives a voice to the voiceless. It is the channel that supports everybody under oppression. It is a channel that supports human rights and defends them, in Tunisia, Algeria, Morocco, Saudi Arabia. If Al Jazeera did not support the revolution in Tunisia or in Libya or in Egypt or in Syria, it would not be Al Jazeera any more. The spirit of Al Jazeera was democratic change for the Arab world so that when these uprisings came, the right place of Al Jazeera was against governments. Let's say, for example, if Al Jazeera had supported the Mubarak regime, or supported the Gaddafi regime, or supported the Ben Ali regime, or the Assad regime. For our audience it would not be Al Jazeera. They would be finished with Al Jazeera. You cannot try to promote liberty for many years and then say no, I have nothing to do with your revolution."

One gains a fuller perspective by understanding not only how Al Jazeera views Qatar and the region, but from the role Al Jazeera plays in Qatar's grand strategy – and how this strategy is viewed in the region. Al Jazeera and Qatar have played a central role in the Arab Spring. Al Jazeera has regularly opened its programming to host civil society protest leaders, whereas Qatar assisted the uprisings politically, financially and, in the case of Libya, even militarily.

Qatar developed a good reputation as a mediator in the years 2000 to 2010, bringing together parties in conflict from Lebanon, Eritrea and Darfur. After the United States and the United Kingdom persuaded Qatar to participate in the United Protector actions in Libya, Qatar became more activist and evolved from mediator to regional player.[39]

Egypt, Saudi Arabia and Iran are all centres of Islamic religious authority beyond their borders. For Qatar to extend its religious influence, it has found allies in the Muslim Brotherhood. Perhaps the prominence of Sheikh Al-Qaradawi on Al Jazeera can be seen as an expression of this alliance and an aspiration to greater religious authority. Qatar openly supported the rise of the Muslim Brotherhood in Egypt and Tunisia, rather than liberal figures whom they considered too weak. The subsequent fall of the Muslim Brotherhood in both countries weakened Qatar's influence and has also led to a backlash against Qatar by other regional powers.

It has even been suggested that the abrupt abdication of Emir Sheikh Hamad bin Khalifa Al-Thani in favour of his son Sheikh Tamim bin Hamad Al-Thani in July 2013 was a result of overreach in this failed strategy. Others suggest that perhaps there is not much more to Qatar's grand strategy than simply an impulse to seize opportunities when they present themselves.[40]

By March 2014, tensions between Qatar and other countries in the Gulf Cooperation Council reached a new pitch when in an unprecedented move,

Saudi Arabia, Bahrain and the UAE simultaneously announced the recall of their ambassadors, seeking to compel Qatar to fall into line with the GCC and, above all, the policy of Saudi Arabia. [41]

◎ Looking ahead: a battle for the truth

Al Jazeera's staff started with BBC-trained journalists, who brought their education and standards with them. For the long term, however, this was still a form of running on reserve fuel. Ahmed Sheikh has been involved in establishing a training centre, which is now growing into something bigger: "Now we have our own training centre and we are in the process of turning it into our college, a media college. We hope that in the future it will issue its own certificates It originated from this understanding that you have to have all the time, if you want to keep the impact that you have, to have the driving force, it is [through] your people." [42]

A training centre would be the best way to keep the original principles and concept by passing them on to future generations of employees. There is a risk that the criticism that Al Jazeera has faced with regard to its reporting on extremists is attracting extremists for the wrong reasons. If the station is to grow rapidly in the coming decade, yet stay true to its 'ten commandments' of professionalism, its founding principles and its support for democratic change, then these values have to be upheld and taught. The station will also need to continue to attract people who hold these values strongly, rather than base their long-term engagements on momentary political agreement.

When it comes to reporting, it is always a challenge never to let rumours, conspiracy theories, or any other political or financial temptations interfere with the core principles of independence and objectivity. This challenge will become greater with the proliferation of television stations and the expansion of staff and contributors. In this growth phase it is crucial that the founding concepts are kept alive: "Al Jazeera has to keep that spirit alive, has to maintain its independence," says Ahmed Sheikh. "That is very crucial. Once you lose your independence, once you become an organ of a party, an ideology or the state, then that is the end of it." [43]

In an age of social media, where unverified rumour circulates with equal force and intensity alongside truthful reporting, news organisations have a particular responsibility not to report news unless it has been properly verified by multiple objective sources. In the coming decade, however, Al Jazeera has an ambitious strategy, spanning television and digital media, to be not only a dominant reporter of news, but also the arbiter of facts. This is a part of a broader responsibility of news organisations in the age of social media: to fight the battle of who is telling the truth, and to be the institution that is trusted to validate the truth.

Ambassador John Groffen commented: "Basically the world is a big marketplace. And not everything that people say in the marketplace is immediately true. We would not publish everything that is being said in a market in the newspaper as a fact. That seems to happen with a lot of things that are being said on the new media. Because if you link to a site that links to another site you get the idea that this is a sort of communed opinion, a shared truth, which in fact it is not: it is, rather, an untruth which has been reported repeatedly. So I think indeed, like Al Jazeera said, we always have to check what is being said. I think that is indeed a responsibility that these major networks have."

◎ Lessons: the age of processes

We asked our interviewees what lessons they have to pass on to future generations of leaders:

Ahmed Sheikh: "You are in the age of ideas, you are in the age of mass communication, the internet age where the world has become a global sort of village, and don't think that those who are credited with innovations are superhuman beings. No, you can be like them. Ideas are there. Well, build on them. You have got to dig deep and find them.

"Today is the age of processes, the age of planning. Be courageous, you can do better if you just understand this process of thinking, of planning, of putting a strategy, of having a vision, of conceptualising that vision, of dissecting it into elements—and each element should have a strategy, a plan of execution. You follow these rules and it is all available. Just look at it. Even the Taliban people these days can hack US computers."[44]

Ambassador John Groffen: "We don't like something happening which we cannot explain. We always have to find a theory. We always have to find a line that was there that we couldn't see and then we try to re-interpret happenings so that they make sense.

"I think with Al Jazeera, the danger you may have is that you start thinking that this was a set-up from the beginning. There was a big idea and there was money. And there was ambition. Each step that was being taken was a step that was well considered and well thought out.

"What I get from all these interviews is that it was a combination of two things. There is a broader environment in which things happen and it is like a river: it goes from a higher part to a lower part. That is something that will always happen. But which path that river will take, you cannot explain or predict at the beginning. I think it is the same with Al Jazeera."

Above all, Ambassador Groffen notes, the role of chance, luck and seizing opportunities should not be underestimated in the intertwined stories of Al Jazeera and Qatar. All played their part—the crisis in British-Saudi cooperation that put a cohort of talented journalists on the street, the sudden availability of a powerful satellite transponder, and the events in Iraq: "The ball was rolling in the direction that Qatar wanted to go."

CHAPTER 15

HIGH-VALUE HEALTHCARE FOR ALL:
INNOVATIVE APPROACHES IN THE UNITED STATES AND THE NETHERLANDS

Although the healthcare industry is notorious for market inefficiencies and systemic waste, our analysis of 21 organisations across the US and the Netherlands shows that innovation and high-value healthcare for all are not only feasible but achievable goals. What is needed is a way to rapidly disseminate the lessons learned from these innovations, realign the healthcare payment system, and provide adequate legislative actions to ensure such innovations can spread through the system.

THE QUALITATIVE ANALYSIS FOR THIS CHAPTER
IS ON PAGE 391 OF THE ANNEX

BY DENIS A. CORTESE, AB KLINK
AND NATALIE LANDMAN.
WITH J. COLT COWDELL, ROBERT K. SMOLDT
AND OTHERS

INTRODUCTION

◎ A nation in need of resuscitation: The current state of US healthcare

Like a person suffering from a debilitating disease, healthcare delivery in the US is ailing. The US spends significantly more per capita and a higher percentage of GDP on healthcare than other developed nations, yet patient outcomes (mortality, safety, access to medical care) are disparate and inconsistent. Moreover, the rapidly rising cost of healthcare delivery is making medical care increasingly unaffordable to the average citizen. This in turn threatens the financial viability of the country. This confluence of issues requires immediate attention and action. The American healthcare delivery system needs to be fixed. It is not sustainable in its current form.

How did we get here? Unhealthy lifestyles are obviously one factor, but so are the growing and ageing population, the payment/financing structure of the US healthcare system and the corresponding incentives it creates for the various system participants.

◎ Consumers are insulated from the full cost of care

Until the 1930s US healthcare providers functioned as a simple fee-for-service and had the flexibility to adjust prices based on the patient's ability to pay. However, with the advent of third-party payers in the 1940s and further coverage expansion in the 1960s through the creation of Medicare and Medicaid, the direct relationship between the provider and the patient has been effectively cut off. Although the US still lacks universal coverage, a recent Commonwealth Fund report states[1] that in 2010 nearly 84 per cent of the US population was covered either through private, primarily employer-based plans (56 per cent) or public programmes like Medicaid, Medicare, and the military health programmes (27 per cent). The remaining 16 per cent were uninsured Americans and undocumented immigrants (who are generally not eligible for public assistance).

While health insurance benefit packages vary by type of insurance, low cost-sharing requirements and lack of price transparency significantly limit patient exposure to the true cost of care. Not surprisingly, consumers with health insurance coverage have little to no incentives to limit their utilisation of healthcare services. This propensity for unchecked utilisation is further exacerbated by the incentive for physicians to provide more service and procedures for patients (supply side), especially in a fee-for-service payment model. Doing more for patients is profitable, even when the outcomes are not improved and the results are worse. So in a fee-for-service environment for physicians, where the patients are insulated from the costs of care, all the incentives are aligned for doing more, even when the results are not improved. In addition to driving higher healthcare costs, this constellation of incentives has also been cited as one of the key barriers to higher effectiveness and scaleability of new models of care.

◎ Serial nature of health insurance coverage reduces incentives to manage public health

Although the precursor to the first health insurance plan (Blue Cross) was created in 1929, third-party health insurance coverage really took off in the 1940s, when (as a result of wage and price controls) health insurance benefits became the primary way for employers to compete for scarce labour. Further coverage expansion occurred in the 1960s with the introduction of Medicare and Medicaid, government programmes that aimed to address the needs of the elderly and the disadvantaged respectively. These historical developments resulted in a "serial" rather than a "birth-to-death" structure of healthcare coverage in the US, with private payers insuring the employed (younger, healthier, wealthier) population and the government stepping in to take care of the elderly and disadvantaged. Since private payers do not need to manage the risk of their members once they become eligible for Medicare or Medicaid, nor are they likely to reap the economic benefits of early prevention and care coordination, they have limited incentives to manage the health of their members and invest in new models of care.

In this regard self-insured employers are an exception because they not only bear the full brunt of the rapidly increasing employee healthcare expenses, but also sustain significant productivity losses as a result of an unhealthy workforce. Unsurprisingly, a number of payer-driven healthcare delivery innovations in the US were initiated by self-insured employers.

◎ Reimbursement for healthcare services is fragmented and primarily volume based

But perhaps the biggest barrier to organisational innovation in US healthcare is the provider compensation system. The tone here is set by the government payers, Medicare and Medicaid, which account for nearly 40 per cent of physician and hospital services[2]. Since their inception in 1965, both programmes have primarily paid providers on a fee-for-service basis without any reference to the quality (outcomes, safety, service) of care received. Moreover, the already low levels of reimbursement and per-unit-of-service price controls imposed by government payers have created a system that incentivises the overuse of services and procedures.

In addition to emphasising volume over value, payments for most healthcare services are negotiated and distributed in silos. Hospital payments are based on Diagnostic Related Groups (DRGs), while nursing homes receive per diem payments, and most physicians are in fee-for-service arrangements. In fact, a patient admitted to the hospital for a specific procedure (e.g., knee replacement) will likely be billed separately for labs and other diagnostic procedures, physician services, hospital, rehabilitation services, etc[3]. As a result of this fragmentation in reimbursement there are no financial incentives for the various parts of the care system to work together and create better value. Finally, federal and state regulations not only dictate the scope of practice for healthcare providers, but also the settings in which they could be reimbursed. Not surprisingly, a number of innovations in US healthcare delivery have either focused on the uninsured (where government oversight is limited) or required providers to risk an insurance plan to create better system alignment and provide flexibility to test new models of care.

◎ In need of value-based competition and comprehensive care: The Dutch healthcare system

Unlike the US, which is just beginning the roll-out of the key elements of the 2010 healthcare reform legislation, the Dutch healthcare system underwent a sweeping reform in 2006. Prior to that reform, healthcare in the Netherlands was characterised by an inefficient dual insurance system and strong government regulation. Specifically, before the reform, individuals with an income below a certain threshold were eligible for the public system, and paid a mandatory, income-based premium into a sickness fund. Those who did not qualify for the public system could choose to insure themselves through the private market (which had no duty to accept them).

In turn, healthcare providers received a fixed operating budget, defined by the government and dependent on the characteristics of the population in their region. Until 1995 this type of cost-containment functioned well, but gradually the system proved to be unsustainable. Waiting lists became a burden for patients and politicians alike, as providers had to implement strict budget controls and had no incentives to be innovative. Given the fact of an ageing society and the growing numbers of people with chronic conditions, the lack of health sector productivity promised to create even bigger access issues in the future.

The 2006 reform resulted in significant changes in the Dutch curative care system.[4] Introducing competition into the market, so the policy-makers reasoned, would incentivise provider productivity. But market elements had no chance in a system where premiums for the majority of the population were income-dependent and where the government dictated prices for healthcare services. To address these issues the government instituted mandatory health insurance for all Dutch citizens and required private insurance companies to compete on the level of flat (community rate) premiums. The government also gradually liberalised healthcare provider prices, in order to create room for negotiations between insurers and providers. Premiums could reflect the negotiating powers and strategies of insurers.

In order to safeguard social justice the government introduced the obligation on the side of insurers to accept every applicant for their policies, to offer everyone a basic package with a defined set of benefits and to work with a community rate (no premium differentiation or relation to health status or age). The government provides an income-related subsidy to those who cannot afford the flat-rate premium. A risk equalisation fund compensates those insurance companies that insure people with high risks and a higher than average health consumption because of their social-economic status or age.

For curative care, the combined individual premium, the premium employers pay and out-of-pocket expenses amount to about $2,300 on an annual basis.

Despite significant progress on several fronts, like the reduction of the waiting lists and more efficiency (prices went down), a number of issues that contribute to the continuing growth of healthcare costs in the Netherlands remain. This is largely driven by the reimbursement system[5], the incentives for supply-induced demand and the fragmentation of the provider organisation. Because co-payments are relatively low there is a tendency for unchecked utilisation of healthcare, incentivised by the assumption that the more care you get, the better off you are. Fragmentation in healthcare provider organisation and reimbursement draws additional parallels with the US system.

The curative care system in the Netherlands can be divided into three tiers. General Practitioners (GPs) — *huisartsen* — comprise the largest part of the first tier. Access to the other tiers — hospitals and specialty care — requires GP referral (except in emergencies). Nearly all specialist care (including outpatient services) is hospital-based. With the exception of bundled payments for select chronic conditions introduced in 2007 and 2010, providers are also paid in silos and primarily for volume. GP reimbursement combines a capitation fee per registered patient with fee for service components. Hospitals negotiate with insurers on the basis of Diagnosis Treatment Combinations (DTCs), while specialists are either salaried or paid fee-for-service within the constraints of a fixed budget.

Thus, payment mechanisms and contracting strategies that better align providers across the system and promote value over volume are warranted. If the problem of fragmentation isn't solved, upfront investments (e.g., coordinated care for the chronically ill, medication reviews by the pharmacist, improvement of therapy-adherence, the gatekeeping role of the GP) will not result in more appropriate downstream utilisation or lower total costs. On the contrary, they are likely to result in higher costs due to upfront investment in the innovation plus the ongoing costs across the rest of the care continuum. The effect is crippling: on the one hand we see fee-for-service that incentivises over-diagnosis and overtreatment; on the other we see that potentially promising innovations make healthcare more expensive instead of cheaper because of fragmentation.[6] So why should a government or insurer want to invest in innovations?

◎ Innovation and Breakthrough Process: Vision and Concept

The success of any new endeavour strongly depends on having a shared goal/vision that unites the interest and activities of all the participants. A shared vision brings focus and moves the various participants beyond misdirected forms of competition toward a common goal. In contrast, lack of clarity often leads to divergent and duplicative approaches, as well as slow progress in performance improvement[7] and accountability. So is there a shared vision in healthcare? What do the innovators strive for? We propose that all have one overarching goal: to achieve high-value healthcare, where value is defined as *quality (patient outcomes, safety, service) divided by the total cost per patient over time.* This goal not only addresses the needs of the patient, but also has the potential to promote and sustain healthcare innovation over the long term.

Although pursuit of value-based healthcare is the latest fashion in the US, the lack of systematic knowledge about the meaning of high-value care, the lack of awareness of healthcare initiatives that have better results at lower costs, the current reimbursement system, the current organisational structures designed to maximise operations in a fee-for-service environment, and the state of information technology (IT) systems have made it difficult to measure, deliver, and pay for high-value care. These same issues also appear to plague the Dutch healthcare system.

As a result of these limitations, quality has been largely equated with a compliance with process (e.g., giving patients antibiotics one hour before surgery), while cost often reflects the cost of individual services. While both process and line item costs are important, achieving high-value healthcare begins with a focus on true outcomes of care and looking at long-term costs. Recognising the need to measure, report, and compare meaningful data, successful innovations have relied strongly on the introduction of novel IT systems and similar tools. But data-gathering data is just the first step. As the innovations below highlight, achieving high-value care also requires shared accountability for value across all providers, as well as more involvement of informed patients in the decision-making process. This in turn requires changes in organisational structure and the nature of reimbursement for services.

Although each of the 21 innovations analysed utilised a different set of tactics to achieve the overarching vision, two key concepts emerged: service line innovation and network facilitators. In the pages that follow eight case studies that fall into the two categories are presented in detail, while the thirteen remaining innovations are summarised in figure 1 on page 284. The characteristics of all case studies are tabulated on page 288, and the contact information of these first eight innovators can be found at the end of this chapter on page 289.

SERVICE LINE INNOVATION CASE STUDIES

Service line innovations can be defined as the (re)design, organisation and management of a distinct area of a healthcare enterprise to create a service of greater value. These innovations can be focused around a particular condition (e.g., mental health, orthopaedics) or population (e.g., frail elderly).

CASE STUDY 1: MOLEMANN MENTAL HEALTH, NL

◎ Introduction

The Dutch mental health landscape has undergone a dramatic change over the last 30 years. Significant consolidation within the health insurance sector created pressure on hospitals and community mental health centres to level the playing field in payer-provider negotiations, and set off a wave of mergers among mental health providers. This resulted in the formation of large-scale mental health provider organisations with fixed treatment programmes that are very much provider- rather than patient-needs driven.

MoleMann Mental Health was founded in 2004 by two psychiatrists, Nico Moleman and Ronald Mann, as an alternative to the existing system. Mole-Mann wanted to offer care that addressed the needs of the patients, their families, general practitioners and ultimately insurance companies, who purchase care in the Dutch healthcare system on behalf of the patient. The aim was to set up a top-level mental health organisation that would elicit a positive answer to the question: would we refer our own family members there? At the time of writing, MoleMann operates in 24 locations (primarily urban areas in the centre of the Netherlands), providing care for 8,000 adults and 6,000 children annually.

◎ Innovation and Breakthrough Process: Vision and Concept

The MoleMann vision is best characterised by patient-centric, small-scale mental health treatment facilities that work in close collaboration with general practitioners, other medical professions, social workers, and community nurses. A key distinguishing feature of the MoleMann approach is the close involvement of the family, other caregivers, and the social environment in patient treatment. This prevents social isolation, enhances the success of the treatments, and offers the family the opportunity to support their loved ones. The "MoleMann perspective" is also characterised by a flat management structure. The lead provider (consultant psychiatrist) in charge of each MoleMann centre has full accountability for both its clinical and financial operations. Each centre director in turn reports directly to the CEO of MoleMann, who is also a psychiatrist.

Strategy

Defining patient needs is the first and most important element of the Mole-Mann strategy. As a result, the organisation is in constant interaction with key stakeholders — patients, family, caregivers, and other providers — to assess the effectiveness and efficiency of care delivered. This concept of a continuously learning organisation generates the other defining element of MoleMann — its culture. Employees at MoleMann must meet a somewhat different profile from that typically expected of mental health professionals. They should be involved, innovative, enterprising, and willing to cooperate with others in the course of a patient's treatment.

Planning and execution

MoleMann entered the mental health sector in 2004, taking advantage of a window of opportunity that came about as a result of legislative changes that allowed patients to connect directly with providers. From the start, Mole-Mann aimed to create a sustainable business model by opting for a small-scale, horizontal organisation with minimal administrative overhead. One of the key enablers was the development of an in-house IT infrastructure that included electronic health records (EHR) as well as business intelligence modules.

Although the primary purpose of the EHR is to support the treatment process, it can also be used for evaluation and internal benchmarking, both within and across clinics, as well as for administrative tasks (e.g., appointment scheduling). The business intelligence modules centralise administrative functions (further reducing overhead) and provide insight into the true cost of care for each patient, thus also enabling informed negotiations with payers.

Other components of the model include a thorough diagnostic process and treatments by highly educated professionals. At least 15 per cent of the MoleMann staff consists of general psychiatrists; other therapists are either psychologists or psychotherapists, and most have qualifications as family therapists. During the intake and diagnostic process all patients are assessed by a psychiatrist, who advises on the treatment plan.

During the treatment process patients have a dedicated therapist. Co-therapists are involved every fifth session to assess whether goals are set properly and if they are being met. Staff meetings regarding patients require the presence of the patient being discussed.

Finally, MoleMann strives for a close alignment with community and patient organisations, making them co-creators in the delivery of care. This not only further lowers operating costs (as some of the activities within the Mole-Mann centres are run by community volunteers), but also creates a high level of patient engagement that leads to MoleMann's superior results in delivering high-value care.

Results

MoleMann is now widely recognised in the Netherlands as a high-value (high-quality/low-cost) mental health provider. Patient satisfaction is very high, with 97 per cent responding that they would recommend MoleMann to family or friends, while treatment costs are at 70 per cent of traditional mental health providers. It is also one of the few high-value providers that is actually profitable and whose staff report high job satisfaction.

A number of new programmes are currently in development, including the establishment in 2011 of "ZorgLab", an innovations incubator and a space for public debate on the future of Dutch healthcare. A new initiative to provide Assertive Community Treatment for the most disadvantaged patients (including the homeless) was recently launched in Amsterdam, and a national network of community-based mental healthcare is in the planning stages.

Challenges and lessons learned

Although MoleMann is currently profitable, reimbursement for mental health services remains a key issue. Mental health operates in a fee-for-service environment, with initial diagnostic interviews paid at a higher rate than follow-up visits. Not surprisingly, many providers opt for four to eight diagnostic interviews, while MoleMann (which strives for high-value care) does only one or two diagnostic interviews. This leads to significantly lower healthcare costs for insurers, but also reduced revenue to MoleMann. Moreover, providers are paid for treatment at the end of the treatment process (typically eight months in length).

Changes in reimbursement resulting from government lobbying by "conventional" mental health providers present another potential challenge. Traditional providers have come to expect their share of the funds that an insurer spends on mental care. This expectation makes it difficult for payers to negotiate lower payment rates. Payers worry that their reputation may suffer if traditional providers run into financial problems under the new (lower) reimbursement schemes.

Employee engagement and preservation of the MoleMann culture present additional challenges. Relentless focus on the needs and best interests of patients and caregivers is not the standard practice in mental health. Thus, to keep employees involved and inspired requires a constant investment of energy on the part of the leadership to keep the overarching vision alive.

CASE STUDY 2: GERIATRIC TRAUMATOLOGY CARE, NL

◎ Introduction

Hip fractures, often as a result of a fall, are one of the most common causes of hospitalisation among the elderly and are associated with both high morbidity and high mortality. [8, 9] Between 2000 and 2004, the annual number of hospital admissions for hip fractures in the Netherlands stood at 17,000. This number is expected to rise in the coming years as a result of increasing life expectancy. [10,11] It is therefore essential to optimise the treatment of these patients in order to prevent physical deterioration, attain social functioning, and to minimise (social) costs.

Research has shown that intensive geriatric care of frail elderly with hip fractures reduces the number of deaths and complications. In addition, multidisciplinary treatment shortens the length of stay in hospital [12]. So, in 2010, the Departments of Orthopaedic Surgery, Traumatology and Geriatrics of Rijnstate Hospital in Arnhem initiated a novel care pathway in Geriatric Traumatology.

The main objective of this pathway was to optimise the care for the frail elderly with hip fractures. Prior to the initiation of the care pathway, the median length of stay for frail elderly with hip fractures at Rijnstate Hospital was a costly 12 days, with clinical mortality at 10.7 per cent.

◎ Innovation and Breakthrough Process: Vision and Concept

The Geriatric Traumatology care pathway aims to provide holistic and patient-centred care for the frail elderly with hip fractures. Specifically, the intervention incorporates multidisciplinary and intensive geriatric care into the standard hip fracture treatment plan to substantially reduce hospital mortality, morbidity, and functional decline in these patients. The new care pathway closely integrates the medical care provided by surgeons and geriatricians, and is supported by a team of nurses specifically trained in the care of elderly patients.

Strategy

Understanding the unique needs of the geriatric population and a team-based approach to patient care are at the heart of the Geriatric Traumatology care pathway. Continuity of care and the recognition of early warning signs are particularly essential in this patient population to ensure optimal treatment and patient outcomes.

Planning and execution

The planning for the new care pathway began with the formation, in 2009, of a working committee of providers, including physicians, nurses and care managers from the geriatric and orthopaedic/traumatology wards. This committee had a clear objective: to develop a care pathway that would better address the needs of the frail elderly with hip fractures.

The committee began its work by analysing the current care pathway for the target population, which showed that the care occurred in three phases (preoperative, operation and postoperative) and across multiple settings (emergency ward, emergency admittance ward, operation room, recovery, medium care and traumatology ward).

Because of this complexity, a step-by-step approach to transforming existing medical care processes into senior-friendly care was chosen. The first step was to organise a Geriatric Traumatology ward in the postoperative phase of the care pathway. This required an increase in geriatric staff, which was realised by introducing a new Diagnostic Treatment Combination in order to have a regular code for the remuneration of extra geriatric fellow treatments.

Integration of medical care was achieved by establishing daily combined visits by the (orthopaedic) surgeon and the geriatrician. This was followed by a joint outpatient clinic six weeks after discharge and a joint discharge letter to the general practitioner or nursing home physician. The collaboration between specialty care (orthopaedics/traumatology) and the more holistic and structured approach of geriatrics allows for earlier detection of complications and increases the chances of recovery for the patient.

Continuity of care was achieved by a newly appointed nurse practitioner who enhanced communication between physicians and nursing staff. Since the majority of daily patient care was provided by the nursing staff, significant effort was dedicated to front-line empowerment. Specifically, the traumatology nurses underwent geriatric training, including spending time on the geriatric ward to gain the skills necessary to care for elderly patients. In turn, geriatric nurses spent time on the traumatology ward.

The quality of postoperative care was also improved by promoting early patient mobility since lack of daily activity tends to disrupt patient sleep patterns and slows the recovery process. To address this issue a dedicated occupational therapist works with patients on a daily basis to help them become more active and prepare them for living at home again. Finally, the physical plan of the traumatology ward was also redesigned to meet the demands of care for frail elderly patients (e.g., use of smaller rooms, with only two patients per room; larger toilets; more comfortable chairs).

Results

Implementation of the Geriatric Traumatology care pathway resulted in a significant decrease in mortality during hospitalisation (from 10.7 per cent to 3.9 per cent), as well as a significant reduction in the median length of stay (from 12 to 9.5 days) for frail elderly with hip fractures. Additional improvements in the quality of patient care included a reduction in the number of patients with serious delirium and lower use of freedom-limiting constraints.

Moreover, the multidisciplinary nature of the intervention transformed the culture of the traumatology ward to one with greater affinity for the elderly. Although additional research is warranted with regard to the cost-effectiveness of the intervention and long-term quality of care (e.g., long-term complication rates, return to normal function, and patient satisfaction), a number of other hospitals in the Netherlands are currently in the process of developing geriatric traumatology wards modelled on the Rijnstate example.

Challenges and lessons learned

Successful implementation of the care pathway is highly dependent on the availability of funding for capital expenditures required to convert a hospital ward into a senior-friendly environment. The financial case for the intervention is complicated by the lack of adequate reimbursement for the intensive level of services provided by geriatricians within the care pathway. Another external barrier is the inadequate rehabilitation bed capacity of nursing homes, which delays the discharge process from the hospital and necessitates the increase in bed capacity of the geriatric traumatology unit. A key internal lesson was that the success of the endeavour is highly dependent on the quality and engagement of the staff. The original nursing traumatology team was very resistant to the new focus on the frail elderly and it took substantial staffing changes to move forward with the new intervention.

CASE STUDY 3: HOSPITAL AT HOME, PRESBYTERIAN HEALTHCARE SERVICES, US

◎ Introduction

Albuquerque-based Presbyterian Healthcare Services is a private, not-for-profit healthcare system and the largest healthcare provider in the state of New Mexico. Employing more than 500 physicians across 30 locations, Presbyterian is an integrated system that also includes eight hospitals and the state's largest health plan. An organisation whose central focus over the last 100 years has been on "improving the health of the patients, members, and communities we serve", Presbyterian is continuously looking for opportunities to improve the quality of care it delivers.

In 2007, faced with an imminent bed capacity shortage as a result of hospital closures and unfavourable demographic trends, Presbyterian decided to launch the Hospital at Home® (HaH) programme, a model developed in the mid-1990s by Dr Bruce Leff and other investigators at the Johns Hopkins University Schools of Medicine and Public Health. Available to Medicare Advantage and Medicaid patients with common acute care diagnoses, the programme provides patients with hospital-level care within the comfort of their homes by leveraging highly skilled staff supported by advanced technology. Patients within the programme show comparable or better clinical outcomes and higher levels of satisfaction when compared with similar hospitalised patients.

◎ Innovation and breakthrough process: Vision and concept

As a subset of Presbyterian Healthcare, HaH offers an alternative to in-hospital care that is affordable, high-quality, and patient-centred. HaH aims to ensure adequate access and to provide care that is comparable or superior to the care that patients would otherwise receive in a regular hospital setting. Moreover, the model aims to be functional at a cost that is lower than standard hospital care and to create broad-level support of providers and patients throughout the community.

Strategy

Presbyterian chose to utilise the foundation developed by Dr Leff and his team at Johns Hopkins to create an outline that would allow implementing the new programme within a year. The key components of the strategy included identifying the right patient population, hiring a lead physician, and working with the health plan to develop a reimbursement contract for the new service.

Planning and execution

The HaH programme was approved in December 2007 and launched in October 2008. To accomplish this task, Presbyterian established 12 multidisciplinary teams (including over 150 people across a range of departments), each tasked with developing a specific component of the project. Concurrently, the leadership team searched for a lead physician for the programme. They sought a physician who was flexible and would be comfortable seeing patients in their own homes without all the resources available in an actual hospital. This proved to be difficult as many physicians who met these criteria were nervous of taking on this novel method of treatment and worried about being on call 24/7. After three rounds of interviews, they hired Dr Melanie Van Amsterdam, an internist who had previously worked with indigent patient populations.

Next came the need to define the right patient population. The team decided to begin by utilising Dr Leff's illness-based medical eligibility criteria, which included the diagnoses of community-acquired pneumonia, congestive heart failure exacerbation, chronic obstructive pulmonary disease, and cellulitis.

Over time the list of eligible diagnoses grew to include complicated urinary tract infections, dehydration, nausea/vomiting, deep vein thrombosis, and stable pulmonary embolus. In addition to having one of these particular diagnoses the patient also had to be a member of the Presbyterian health plan, needed hospital-level care, lived within 25 miles of the hospital, and could be treated at home. Patients were identified across the care continuum including emergency rooms, urgent care, primary care and specialty clinics, or the hospital floor itself.

To accelerate programme approval, the team proceeded to build its reimbursement structure based on existing home health fee-for-service payment arrangements. This lasted approximately 18 months before they realised that HaH would not be able to survive under such a payment structure. So, to ensure long-term financial sustainability of the programme, the team developed a bundled payment schedule that was offered to the health plan at a discounted rate (75 per cent) of the corresponding Diagnosis Related Group.

Finally, the HaH team collaborated with Presbyterian physicians and Dr Leff to modify the care pathways established at Johns Hopkins to work within the Presbyterian setting. When patients are admitted into HaH they are discharged from their current healthcare delivery location to their residence with all the medical equipment they will need. Within one hour a provider is at the home to go over the reason for admission and to outline a care plan. "Admitted" patients are seen by a physician at least once per day and by an HaH-dedicated nurse once or twice per day (depending on the needs of the individual patient).

For further support, the programme uses telehealth services such as blood pressure or oxygen level monitoring, and a shared staffing model by cross-trained nurses to ensure that patients have 24-hour care. Throughout the "admission" the patient is kept apprised of their transition plan and when the appropriate time comes, the patient is "discharged" with proper medications and educated on warning signs. Continuity of post-discharge care is assured by direct communication between the HaH provider and the patient's primary care physician.

Results

Since its launch in 2008, Presbyterian's HaH programme has been shown to be safe, effective, and efficient. Patients within the programme show comparable or better clinical outcomes (a 76 per cent reduction in the incidence of delirium; 38 per cent reduction in mortality at six months) and higher level of satisfaction (90.7 per cent vs. 83.9 per cent) when compared with similar hospitalised patients. The programme also achieved cost savings of 19 per cent, predominantly derived from a lower average length-of-stay (3.3 days vs. 4.5 days) and use of fewer lab and diagnostic tests compared with similar patients treated in the standard hospital setting.

Challenges and lessons learned

Lack of standard reimbursement for HaH services in the fee-for-service Medicare realm limits the scaleability of the model. Currently, neither Medicare part A nor part B have a payment mechanism for HaH, and CMS has yet to move forward with payment reform for HaH despite multiple proposals by HaH founders. Moreover, recent CMS regulations have prevented Presbyterian from advertising the HaH model as a benefit of its health plan. Another challenge for the saleability of the model is addressing the perception of both patients and providers that the hospital is a superior place to receive care.

CASE STUDY 4: CAREMORE, US

◎ Introduction

In the late 1980s, under pressure from employers and government agencies to curb the rapidly rising costs of healthcare, health maintenance organisations (HMOs) intensified their efforts to reduce costs. Their short-term fixes, which included restricting patient access to care and denying coverage for healthcare services, often resulted in worse patient outcomes, increasing frustration for providers, and over the long term, higher overall medical expenses.

To address the problem at hand in a more comprehensive and sustainable manner, Dr Sheldon Zinberg, a practicing physician in Southern California, envisioned a network of healthcare providers who coordinated care to improve patient health while protecting the financial resources of seniors and the Medicare programme. He specifically gravitated toward the senior population, having recognised the fact that "seniors are the most in need and account for 50-60 per cent of the nation's healthcare expenses." He spent two years recruiting like-minded physician affiliates and finally opened CareMore in 1993. CareMore is based in Cerritos, California, and currently operates more than 25 care centres across the Southwest, providing care for over 50,000 Medicare Advantage patients. [13]

⊚ Innovation and breakthrough process: Vision and concept

Dr Zinberg envisioned a system where practitioners could work cooperatively to provide comprehensive, proactive, and high-value care for the frail elderly. The key aims of CareMore are still to "provide focused and innovative healthcare approaches to the complex problem of ageing; to serve our members by prolonging active and independent life; to serve caregivers and family by providing support, education, and access to services; to protect precious financial resources of seniors and the Medicare Programme through innovative methods of managing chronic disease, frailty, and end of life". [14]

Strategy

The key components of the CareMore strategy included a focus on the high-need/high-cost patient population (the frail elderly) and a reimbursement model that provided flexibility to innovative care processes and rewarded providers for keeping patients healthy. To that end, CareMore contracted exclusively with a Medicare Advantage plan and under a full capitation arrangement.

Planning and execution

The first step toward the establishment of the CareMore model involved securing physician buy-in. This was a two-year process that required charisma, persistence, and professional credibility to convince providers to forgo the antiquated system of fee-for-service reimbursement. Eventually, Dr Zinberg was able to recruit physicians across 28 individual medical offices and they officially opened CareMore in June of 1993. Under the leadership of Dr Zinberg, the new entity contracted exclusively with Care America, a Medicare HMO plan, and was unique in taking full medical risk for the HMO patients (capitation). This arrangement allowed CareMore to experiment with delivery innovation, improving both the effectiveness and efficiency of care. In 2001-2002 CareMore started its own health plan to ensure that it would not be at the mercy of changing health plan contracts/ownership and could maintain the flexibility to innovate the delivery model.

In 1995, CareMore introduced two key initiatives to better address the needs of its patient population. The first aimed to improve care coordination for patients recently discharged from hospital or skilled nursing facilities by expanding the role of a core group of employed hospitalists to include post-discharge care. These "extensivists" split their time between hospitals, outpatient clinics and skilled nursing facilities. Having a smaller patient load (six to eight per half-day) allowed physicians to spend more time with patients, families and other caregivers, as well as ensure proper follow-up care. The extensivists are supported by a sophisticated IT infrastructure and additional CareMore resources, e.g., a social service "SWAT" team. [15]

The second CareMore initiative focused on improving care for patients with chronic conditions by opening nurse practitioner (NP)-led clinics. Full-time NPs operate these clinics and teach self-management techniques to patients with specific chronic conditions (e.g., diabetes). They also perform necessary disease maintenance tests/exams such as haemoglobin A1c for diabetic patients. Patients are referred to these clinics by a primary care provider (PCP) or extensivist before seeing a specialist, which helps keep costs down. To ensure continuity of care NPs are responsible for keeping the PCP updated, through a process known as Touch points. Each clinic is supported by electronic medical records and home monitoring systems.

Over time CareMore introduced other "common sense" solutions to optimise patient care. To help reduce post-op complications, CareMore started a pre-surgical clearance clinic to ensure patients were in the best possible condition for proposed surgery. CareMore also offers one-hour Healthy Start visits to new enrolees. During this visit new patients complete an extensive health questionnaire, go through appropriate screening exams (dementia, depression, falls, etc.), have their medications reviewed, and are triaged into appropriate clinics. This same process is repeated annually throughout their Healthy Journey programme. Patients are offered specialised services at home such as blood pressure and weight monitoring. All of this is available to them at no extra cost.

Results

The CareMore model clearly shows that coordinated care focused on prevention can result in higher-value healthcare and that a capitation payment structure provides incentive for deriving innovative ways to keep patients healthy while reducing utilisation. When compared with Medicare fee-for-service (FFS) beneficiaries, CareMore patients have lower hospitalisation rates (24 per cent below average), shorter hospital length of stay (3.2 days vs. 5.6 days for Medicare FFS), and a lower 30-day readmission rate (13.8 per cent vs. 19.6 per cent for Medicare FFS).

Moreover, CareMore risk-adjusted total per capita healthcare spending is estimated to be 15 per cent below the regional average. Condition-specific results show a significantly lower rate of amputations in diabetics (78 per cent lower than national average) and a 56 per cent reduction in readmissions for congestive heart failure.

As the latest "stamp of approval" for the CareMore model, in 2011, WellPoint, one of the nation's largest health benefits companies, purchased CareMore with the intent of expanding CareMore's proven system of providing Medicare recipients with high-quality, personalised care that improves their lives and well-being".[16]

Challenges and lessons learned

To achieve flexibility to innovate and ensure the sustainability of the new model, Dr Zinberg had to seek out an alternative to the standard fee-for-service payment arrangement. Moreover, this antiquated payment scheme was very difficult to give up for many providers, and required significant effort to overcome and bring providers into the CareMore model.

NETWORK FACILITATOR CASE STUDIES

Network facilitators are innovations that rely on the formation of a network of patients or providers which results in higher-value care. These entities might take the form of an IT platform or a forum for patients and/or providers to come together to improve the effectiveness of care delivery and compliance with therapy. A network facilitator model may require a more formal business structure, either at the outset or a new business may eventually evolve.

CASE STUDY 5: BUURTZORG, THE NETHERLANDS

◎ Introduction

In the Netherlands, home care is a national benefit funded by tax revenue and administered by health insurance companies. Initially home care nurses had considerable autonomy and worked closely with other community providers, but over the past two decades home care has become highly regulated, with defined levels of services and nursing 'products' subject to different reimbursement rates. This has resulted in the fragmentation of care, less time with patients, and increasing job dissatisfaction among home care nurses.

Jos de Blok, a home care nurse with a business administration background, envisioned a new system in which nurses provided community care in self-directed teams, supported by information technology infrastructure and a small administration. After years of planning and testing various models, De Blok and colleagues Gonnie Kronenberg and Edith Molenkamp started the first Buurtzorg (meaning 'Neighbourhood Care' in Dutch) team in 2007 in the city of Amelo.

In a few short years, this small grass-roots movement has grown into a national benchmark of care excellence as a result of the enthusiastic response of its nurses throughout the Netherlands. Today there are approximately 6,000 nurses within 500 Buurtzorg teams throughout the Netherlands. In October 2012, a national survey named Buurtzorg the best employer in the Netherlands for the third year in a row.

◎ Innovation and Breakthrough Process: Vision and Concept

Buurtzorg aims to provide community-based, integrated care for patients in need of home care, hospice and dementia care, and to champion autonomous professional nursing (key to being able to recruit sufficient nurses in a tight labour market). Community-based care involves family, primary care providers and community resources, and includes complete patient care, from bathing, medications and treatments, to simple meal preparation. Nurses strive to return patients to independence as quickly as possible.

Strategy

Buurtzorg is based on the principles of trust, autonomy, creativity, simplicity, collaboration, and the conviction that integrated care is the key to high-value care. At the heart of the Buurtzorg strategy is the concept of front-line empowerment. Instead of Buurtzog imposing top-down management, nursing professionals are given the opportunity to learn how to self-manage, through an organisational philosophy that invests in collective ambition, inspires, observes, communicates, and has an attitude of service. To help teams tackle various management issues, Buurtzorg employs 12 coaches who are available to work with each team at their request. Buurtzorg teams also strive to connect with patients, families, other healthcare providers, local community services and political leadership to jointly create an integrated network that supports good health.

Planning and execution

Buurtzorg teams receive home care referrals through primary care providers and hospitals, and compete for patients with other home care agencies. Autonomous teams comprise up to 12 nurses, with a typical patient load of 50-60 elderly, disabled, and/or terminally ill home care patients.

The nurses within each Buurtzorg team schedule and provide all patient care, together deciding the optimal set of services for each patient. Teams self-monitor their productivity and share information to enhance professional development.

They also decide where to rent a team office (often choosing a central location near other healthcare providers to foster positive relationships within the community), as well as how best to creatively meet the needs of elders in communities (e.g., a weekly radio show, 'Radio Support Stockings', or a community-assisted walking device race event). Prior to the initiation of care, an external assessment of each home care patient is conducted by an independent government agency to establish the approved number of service hours and the cost of care for the patient.

The difference between "care approved" and "care delivered" is measured and reported to determine cost savings. Teams self-monitor productivity and efficiency, always looking for creative solutions to keep care efficient and bring patients to optimal function as quickly as possible. Cost savings are passed along to nurses, who earn the highest salaries of any home care agency in the Netherlands.

Nursing care quality is key to the success of the organisation and Buurtzorg therefore strives to employ nurses with bachelor's degrees. Currently, 70 per cent of the Buurtzorg nurses have a bachelor's degree and some of the teams include nurses with advanced degrees. The Buurtzorg Academie, a professional continuing education resource, is available online and at meetings throughout the Netherlands to respond to the education needs of nurses and support continuous care quality improvement. Buurtzorg also embraces evidence-based nursing care and encourages nurses to creatively apply solutions suggested by evidence in each patient situation. The Buurtzorg clinical record uses the Omaha System as a foundation for applying evidence-based practices to individualised patient care plans, documenting care and reporting outcomes.

Information technology is also being successfully leveraged to replace much of the administrative layer at Buurtzorg. The web-based information system includes scheduling, education and electronic health records, and was designed to support professional autonomy, networking and communication. As a result, only 35 "administrators" oversee all 500 teams (some 6,000 nurses).

From the beginning, Buurtzorg has emphasised the need to measure the outcomes of the model, specifically efficiency, cost savings, and the satisfaction of patients and nurses. Internally, efficiency and cost savings are measured at the team level and the organisation level through use of simple metrics: care approved vs. care delivered, while national polls measure employee satisfaction. Buurtzorg has also solicited external validation of the model as described below.

Results

In 2009, Ernst & Young conducted a structured cost and outcome analysis of Buurtzorg through the National Transition Programme, Long-term Healthcare. Ernst & Young found that when compared with other home care organisations, Buurtzorg's productivity was 6.4 per cent higher while overhead costs were some 50 per cent lower. Patients also recovered in half the usual time and had a third fewer ER visits than those being treated by other home care organisations. Finally, there was a 50 per cent lower staff turnover and 50 per cent less sick-leave taken, suggesting an increased level of job satisfaction for the nurses.

In October 2012, a national survey named Buurtzorg the best employer in the Netherlands for the third year in a row. Similar results were found by the Research Institute at the University of Groningen in a 2008-2010 study measuring patient satisfaction. Average reported patient satisfaction scores for Buurtzorg were 9.1 out of 10. The Buurtzorg model is now under consideration for being deployed in other countries, including Sweden and the US.

Challenges and lessons learned

The competiveness of Buurtzorg is hindered by a reimbursement system in which a regional authority and monopoly pays for all the long-term care (usually a payer which in this field also functions as an administrative body). This group has no incentives to be efficient because if it saves money the savings have to be returned to a national fund. Moreover, recent government regulations (2012) that aim to dissociate nursing and non-medical care (e.g., bathing) carry the risk of care fragmentation.

CASE STUDY 6: POZOB, THE NETHERLANDS

◎ Introduction

In 2002, the Dutch Ministry of Health decided that in order to cope with the increasing demands for chronic care, every General Practitioner (GP) would receive the services of a Primary Health Care Practitioner Nurse (PHCN) for 16 hours per week. In addition to the PHCN salary budget, every GP also received a 30 per cent budget to manage this PHCN. As a result of this development, groups of GPs (varying in size from 10 to 200) brought their PHCN management budgets together to increase cost-effectiveness and formed Primary Health Care Groups (PHCG).

There are currently about 100 PHCG operating across the Netherlands. PoZoB is one such (large) PHCG in the south-east region of the Netherlands, around the city of Eindhoven. PoZoB was set up as a strategic coalition to involve all healthcare providers and use well-defined protocols to promote optimal care for patients with chronic conditions (including mental health) as well as the frail elderly. 160 GPs and 150 PHCNs are currently part of the PoZoB network, addressing the needs of patients across five different care streams.

◎ Innovation and breakthrough process: Vision and concept

The overarching aim of PoZoB is to improve the provision of primary healthcare using multidisciplinary teams, care coordination and care protocols that clearly define the provider, location and type of care for a given patient. The key words that define the PoZoB vision are transparency and high-quality care. PoZoB also realised that to achieve these goals there might be "strength in numbers". In place of many individual care providers, one strong Primary Health Care Group would be more successful in working with (local) government authorities and different hospitals in the area, as well as the insurers.

Strategy

Implementation of this new strategic coalition required a high level of organisation supported by adequately qualified staff. Thus, a key component of the PoZoB strategy was the decision to retain experienced business administrators to help set up a properly managed organisation. In turn, one of their first strategic moves was to bring together a small group of provider leaders with an open mind about the future of primary care to help define the vision and mission of PoZoB, and put it into operation. This approach ran contrary to the usual practice of trying to achieve consensus across all participating providers before moving forward with a new initiative.

Planning and execution

The planning process for PoZoB began with an expert group of two GPs and business administrators who defined a vision and mission for the organisation. This brainstorming process took about three months to accomplish. The expert group then proceeded to bring together GPs who were willing to invest time (and money) in new approaches to chronic disease management. This step in the process lasted about six months and involved informing the various small groups of GPs located in the area (some 10) about the new initiative and evaluating their willingness to participate.

The next step was to involve the payment organisations most relevant to the region and define a clear step-by-step plan for both the short term (within two years) and the long term (within five to ten years). These steps were helped by the fact that in 2002 several initiators of PoZoB had been involved in the successful establishment of a large 24/7 GP call centre financed by the payment organisations. The reliability of this call centre led to insurance companies adopting a positive attitude to PoZoB's new initiative.

Finally, PoZoB selected the two conditions to focus on (diabetes and asthma/chronic obstructive pulmonary disease, or COPD) and identified key strategic partners in making these new initiatives a success. Conditions were chosen based on their prevalence in the patient population and the availability of standard treatment protocols.

Following a six-month pilot, the final programme addressing the two conditions was rolled out broadly in January 2005. Building on the success of the diabetes and asthma programmes, in 2010 PoZoB proceeded to roll out additional primary care programmes that focused on mental health, cardiovascular risk and the care of the frail elderly.

PoZoB operations are supported by a web-based IT infrastructure (Care2U), developed in-house and addressing the needs of all healthcare providers involved in each individual care programme. Unlike most IT systems that focus primarily on registration/billing data, Care2U has been developed to manage and evaluate the processes and outcomes of care.

Results

Nearly 160 GPs and 150 PHCNs (with a patient population of 410,000) are now part of PoZoB. The coalition has set up five different healthcare chains across a large number (with overlap) of patients: diabetes (15,000 patients), asthma/COPD (10,000), mental health (3,000), cardiovascular risk management (41,000), and finally the vulnerable elderly in general (1,000). These care pathways have shown significant improvements in patient outcomes. For example, in the case of asthma the number of patients with no exacerbation increased from 70 per cent in 2010 to 85 per cent in 2011. This was mirrored by the fact that the number of patients using inhalation corticosteroids decreased from 85 per cent in 2010 to 60 per cent in 2011.

In the cardiovascular risk group the number of patients with appropriate systolic blood pressure has increased by 8 per cent and the number of patients with appropriate lipid profile has increased by 10 per cent between 2010 and 2011. PoZoB is now preparing to take care of patients who are being admitted to hospitals, effectively substituting for hospital care.

Challenges and lessons learned

The dual reimbursement structure for GP services reduces provider incentives to participate in the coalition. GPs participating in the newly developed integrated healthcare model are rewarded by the payers for clearly described reports and analyses of the impact of care. At the same time, non-participating GPs are still able to bill health insurance companies without any demands for accurate reporting of outcome and process results.

The fragmented nature of Dutch healthcare financing also makes it very difficult to set up integrated healthcare programmes. A substantial part of chronic healthcare costs is paid by insurance companies while other types of care (e.g., mental health and nursing home care) are financed by numerous other financial authorities (including community, local and governmental bodies). Moreover, while the Ministry of Health promotes the formation of large healthcare organisations, the Ministry of Finance is very strict in applying antitrust law.

CASE STUDY 7: INSTITUTE FOR CLINICAL SYSTEMS IMPROVEMENT (ICSI), US

◎ Introduction

The Institute for Clinical Systems Improvement (ICSI), originally the Institute for Clinical Systems Integration, was founded in 1993 in response to a request by the Business Health Care Action Group (BHCAG), a coalition of self-insured employers in Minnesota. Frustrated by escalating healthcare costs and high variation in quality across providers, these payers came together and decided to collectively apply their purchasing power to reform the healthcare market.

The BHCAG looked to purchase consistent high-quality, cost-effective, evidence-based care for its employees from a preferred network of healthcare providers throughout the state. At the time of the bid, no single healthcare system in the Minneapolis/St Paul area had the capabilities to successfully meet the needs of BHCAG. So, three competing provider organisations (Group Health, Mayo Clinic, and Park Nicollet) and a health plan (HealthPartners) made the decision to cooperate and a new organisation, ICSI, was conceived. Since 1993, the organisation has grown to include 55 medical groups representing about 85 per cent of Minnesota physicians, and Minnesota became the first state in the nation where medical care was built around the systematic use of evidence-based best practices.

◎ Innovation and breakthrough process: Vision and concept

Since no single system had the capacity or geographic reach to serve all of the BHCAG covered lives, three competing, yet philosophically aligned multi-specialty group practices came together to respond to the bid. To meet BHCAG requirements, an idea for an "Institute of Quality" that would promote virtual integration across participating groups was put forward. The overall aim of the ICSI collaborative was to standardise and improve the value of care (defined as better quality at lower total costs) across the entire participating healthcare provider network. Thus, ICSI's primary role was to develop practical, evidence-based care guidelines and help physicians implement those guidelines in their practices.

Strategy

In return for a "preferred provider" status with the employer/payer coalition, and thus the potential to gain market share, membership in ICSI required each participating medical group to be involved in the development and implementation of evidence-based guidelines. ICSI also appealed to providers' sense of professional pride by giving them the opportunity to develop innovations that aimed to improve patient care and reduce waste. Participating in ICSI became a sort of seal of approval for providers and, with time, other health plans began to set the expectation that their contracting providers participate in the collaboration.

Planning and execution

Although the participating organisations had similar philosophies and a history of collaboration on clinical research projects, there was little to build upon in terms of broad organisational collaboration. In mid-1992, 70 representatives of participating organisations came together and began a five-month planning process to establish ICSI.

The planning phase culminated with a business plan and a clear definition of the scope of activities for the new organisation. ICSI was set up as an independent, non-profit organisation with initial funding of $2 million coming from HealthPartners. The ICSI governing board was composed of physician leaders from the medical groups, as well as customer representatives, i.e., BHCAG and the health plan. Board members had enough authority and seniority in their organisations that their vote at ICSI effectively committed their organisations to action.

ICSI has evolved over the years in four phases: (1) development of evidence-based guidelines; (2) support for clinical quality improvement; (3) development of multi-provider collaborations; (4) provider-health plan joint initiatives to address appropriate healthcare utilisation. The change in focus was driven at least in part by the eventual return of the market to the "business as usual" employer-health plan-provider contracting arrangements.

This was the result of employers' focus shifting away from value to simple cost containment and also the continuous lobbying by health plans who claimed that they would be better at driving down costs on behalf of employers than employers themselves through direct contracting. This change in the market dynamics resulted in the eventual disappearance of the "preferred provider" status and thus the business reason for provider participation in ICSI. The fact that ICSI has endured over the years, despite these changes, highlights the importance of professional motivation for collaboration.

Results

Today ICSI is a leading healthcare collaborative, comprising 55 medical groups and hospitals representing more than 9,000 physicians, and is sponsored by five non-profit Minnesota and Wisconsin health plans. Since 1993, ICSI has developed more than 60 evidence-based guidelines, as well as 20 order sets and protocols (standardised instructions for the management of a particular disease, condition, or procedural intervention and step-by-step statement of a procedure routinely used in the care of individual patients, respectively). Starting in 2002, many of the measures specified in ICSI-developed guidelines were adopted by a Minnesota Community Measurement for use in public reporting of medical group performance.

ICSI-driven initiatives have also resulted in significant improvement in patient outcomes across the state. The DIAMOND program (Depression Improvement Across Minnesota, Offering a New Direction) is one such example. The programme is now offered through 73 primary care clinics with over 6,500 patients to date. DIAMOND is getting five times the number of depressed patients into remission by six months vs. clinics that provide typical primary care. Finally, medical groups involved in the ICSI high-tech diagnostic imaging (HTDI) pilot have contributed to a zero increase in HTDI claims from 2007-2010, improved clinic efficiencies, reduced patient exposure to unnecessary radiation, enabled provider-patient shared decision-making, and saved $84 million for the Minnesota health community.

Challenges and lessons learned

One of the barriers to guideline implementation was created by the BHCAG itself. To get away from having to comply with state insurance regulations and maintain its self-insured status BHCAG insisted on a fee-for-service payment arrangement with participating providers. Under this reimbursement scheme, implementation of best practices would result in practices losing substantial revenue. Eventually, BHCAG and ICSI were able to persuade state legislators to pass a new law that allowed BHCAG to enter into capitated arrangements with providers. Other insurers also took every opportunity to undermine the ICSI and the direct contracting arrangement between BHCAG and providers, since it exposed the fact that insurers were not value-adding members of the healthcare ecosystem. Finally, the lack of common IT infrastructure across participating organisations posed significant implementation and measurement challenges.

CASE STUDY 8: INTEGRATED CARE COLLABORATION, US

◎ Introduction

Increases in the number of uninsured, as well as underinsured patients, along with reductions in funding for care are placing a considerable strain on the US healthcare system. Highlighting the need for a collaborative approach to healthcare for this population is the fact that patients frequently access similar services from multiple providers. This tendency for disjointed and inefficient healthcare also carries significant implications for the health outcomes of this population.

Compared to the US average, Texas has the highest percentage of people without health insurance coverage (24 per cent versus 16 per cent in 2011), and ranks in the bottom 10 states with regard to the percentage of non-elderly people covered by employer-based health insurance. In the spring of 1997 (and with the healthcare provider Seton Healthcare Family taking a lead role), the healthcare safety net providers in Travis County came together to form what was initially known as the Indigent Care Collaboration (ICC) to address access and financing issues of providing care for low-income and uninsured residents of Central Texas. In 2000 the ICC extended its membership into Williamson, Caldwell and Hays Counties. ICC now counts among its members a wide variety of organisations, including hospital systems, healthcare networks, community health centres, clinics, government agencies, nonprofit organisations, individual providers and others.

◎ Innovation and breakthrough process: Vision and concept

The primary aim of the collaborative was to create a proactive system that would improve access and quality of care for the underserved, while having a direct positive effect on the bottom line of providers. Although participation in the collaborative was driven by a variety of reasons (e.g., non-profit mission, economics, the need to maintain competitive edge), all of the organisations came to the table with a shared vision of improving access and quality of care for these vulnerable populations.

Strategy

To achieve its goals and create a more coordinated and integrated system, the ICC established a regional Health Information Exchange (HIE) to identify the needs in the Central Texas healthcare system and design intervention programmes to improve health outcomes for the above populations. The HIE also provides information at the point of care, which has the potential to reduce duplication of services and improve the quality of care for a given patient. As the ICC began to develop programmes, it became necessary to create a more formal structure to improve data and resource-sharing across participating organisations. To that end, the ICC was organised as a Texas Uniform Unincorporated Nonprofit Association, a structure that allows for the formation of public-private partnerships that have more operational flexibility than strictly public entities.

Planning and execution

As a starting point for the collaborative, Diana Resnik helped convene a group of provider leaders chaired by Charles Barnett (then CEO of Seton Healthcare Family), who challenged all the participants to come together and collaborate in an effort to coordinate care and reduce costs for everyone. The ICC was established as an independent non-profit organisation, governed by a Board of Directors composed of representatives from each of the member organisations. The concept for the collaborative was further solidified as a result of grant funding received from the Health Resources and Services Administration and the Robert Wood Johnson Foundation. The requirements of these grants, namely that the funds had to go to a collaborative of organisations rather than be "owned" by a single organisation and that the funds be used for the development of healthcare infrastructure, served as a forcing mechanism to bring the participating groups together around the concept of a health information exchange. Participating organisations also held brainstorming sessions to define guidelines for ICC implementation. The key requirements were that the structure of the HIE had to guide and support the development of programmes and treatment protocols that address the needs of the underserved population. Moreover, ICC projects had to support and benefit all members of the collaborative.

As a first step toward better coordinated care the ICC built a data repository (iCare) to track patients across the various entry points into the healthcare system. Billing data from participating organisations, including patient and diagnosis information, was fed into the repository on a daily basis, and physicians at the point of care were encouraged to check this data to identify "frequent flyers" and reduce the potential for duplication of services. In addition to point-of-care interventions, the ICC also rolled out a number of population-based interventions that focused on improving the quality of care for specific conditions (e.g., asthma), as well as overall access to care (e.g., Medicaider, PAPP). To create buy-in from the leadership of participating organisations and ensure its financial sustainability as a member-supported organisation, the ICC also created value metrics and began estimating the potential impact of reducing unnecessary utilisation on the providers' bottom line.

Results

The ICC has been providing Health Information Exchange services since 2002 and is now the state-designated regional HIE for 47 counties in Central and East Texas. The iCare platform is now its second generation and continues to provide private, secure and reliable HIE services to all of the region's patients and providers. Along with ICare 2.0, the ICC also offers HIE services in the form of a secure and direct messaging system called Texas Direct. Through a number of programmes, the ICC has enabled patients to access care through federal, state and local funding programmes. Additional community-wide care coordination initiatives focus on providing a coherent, standardised approach to patient care and disease management. The asthma programme alone has seen some impressive results in reducing healthcare utilisation (37 per cent reduction in ED visits, 63 per cent reduction in admissions), while improving quality of life and producing an estimated net annual saving of $2,400 per patient. Finally, the ICC has helped 11 counties in Central Texas create their own collaboratives and continues to provide them with the analytics to identify the needs of the patient populations they serve.

Challenges and lessons learned

The lack of a standard reimbursement mechanism for the HIE and the initiatives that arise from analyses of the HIE data has hindered the scaleability of the model. Initial funding for the ICC came from the Health Resources Service Administration's Community Access Program, the Robert Wood Johnson's Communities in Charge Program, and from Ascension Health. Currently, the ICC receives more than two-thirds of its annual budget from a tiered membership dues model, with contributions scaled to the size and resources of member organisations. Physician culture/engagement and utilisation of the HIE data present another challenge. Despite the value the ICC brings, physician compliance with HIE use is not 100 per cent, as it does not currently fit into the regular physician workflow.

SUMMARY AND CONCLUSIONS

Analysis of 21 innovations across the Netherlands and the United States revealed 10 innovation enablers and three major barriers. It should be noted that while not all of the observations listed apply directly to each innovation, most are true for all of the innovations analysed.

Moreover, the analysis and observations presented are not meant to be prescriptive – in fact, regulatory over-prescription is often a barrier to innovation. Instead, what we hope to provide are some examples and general principles that may be taken into consideration by groups aiming to establish new models of care. The list presented below is by no mean exhaustive, nor should it be followed to the letter in order to achieve high-value healthcare.

◎ Key enablers

1. Shared vision: The existence of a clear, shared vision helps organisations strive toward innovative care that is patient-centred, safe, effective, efficient, timely, and equitable. The "shared" component ensures that this aim for high-value care permeates all levels of the organisation and creates alignment across all of the care providers.

2. Provider leadership: All but one of the innovations profiled were initiated by an individual provider or a group of providers, and the success of the remaining one (ICSI) was highly dependent on strong provider leadership. A clinician leader benefits from clear visibility into the care processes and organisational dynamics, and commands the respect of other providers (more so than a non-clinician leader).

3. Front-line empowerment: Studies show that engaged employees tend to be more productive and more likely to contribute toward achieving greater organisational goals. The innovators profiled (e.g., Buurtzorg, MoleMann)

Country	Innovation/ Organisation	Contact	Innovation Summary	Innovation Type
NL	CONNECTING HEALTH AND WELFARE (NIEUWAGEIN)	JAN JOOST MEIJS MD	In 2011, the primary care centre 'the Roerdomp' and social centre 'MOvactor' in Nieuwegein initiated a collaborative model to address the high incidence of mental illness and the large strain this put on primary care. The model offers social services by prescription, for example a patient suffering from loneliness will receive a prescription to deal with loneliness. Participants can chose from arrangements, such as "Nature", "Discover", "Do", and "Culinary encounters". These interventions seeks to improve wellbeing by discovering and tapping into each patient's traits and drivers. Impact on wellbeing, quality of life and use of care are being evaluated.	SERVICE LINE
NL	DIABETER	HENK VEEZE, MD; HENK-JAN AANSTOOT, MD	Founded in 2006, Diabeter is the first independent care clinic for medical specialist care aimed at a chronic disease, delivering full and continuous diabetes care to more than 850 patients from across the country. A specialized, focused and experienced team of pediatricians, diabetes educators (specialized nurses, dietitians) and psychologists provides diabetes care and support. Parents and patients also have direct 24/7 access to their physician. The Diabeter approach has resulted in substantial reduction in hospital admissions (one of the most costly items in chronic care) and high patient satisfaction.	SERVICE LINE
NL	DUTCH INSTITUTE FOR CLINICAL AUDITING (DICA)	E.H. EDDES, MD	DICA is a platform set up to measure the quality of care for all stakeholders. It started with colorectal malignancies and currently covers 4 registries. In one system, it measures three important aspects of the health care system: quality, costs and patient satisfaction. Results along these three dimensions are communicated via the web. The resulting visibility has already resulted in care improvements, lower costs and higher patient satisfaction.	NETWORK FACILITATOR
NL	KSYOS	LEONARD WITKAMP, MD	KSYOS TeleMedical Centre is a leading TeleMedicine Health Institution in The Netherlands that develops, investigates and implements TeleMedicine services as part of regular healthcare. TeleConsultation enables general practitioners to consult medical specialists in their region through a safe internet portal instead of physically referring the patient, with proven faster and better care at lower costs. With the use of the Health Management Research model, KSYOS has been able to provide over 60,000 TeleConsultations in 2012.	SERVICE LINE
NL	MIJNZORGNET	JAN A.M. KREMER, MD; BAS R BLOEM, MD	In 2009 two Dutch medical specialists (Bas Bloem and Jan Kremer), founded MijnZorgnet, the social network for Dutch healthcare. MijnZorgnet offers a secure online environment where patients and providers can connect and collaborate safely. Patients can build their own Personal Health Communities and can become members of communities built by providers (digital clinics). At this moment about 12,000 patients and providers have an online profile and are active in more than 500 PHC's and digital clinics.	NETWORK FACILITATOR
NL	PAL4 (FOCUS CURA HEALTHCARE INNOVATION	DAAN DOHMEN, PHD	With a clear mission to help the elderly, (chronically) ill and disabled to stay in their own homes as long as possible, Focus Cura developed the Personal Assistant 4 Life (PAL4) application. PAL4 facilitates social networks for the elderly and enables telehealth interventions for homecare providers. Results show higher efficiency of care (saving about 20 hours per nurse each month), while patients can remain in their homes longer and/or can be discharged from the hospital earlier.	NETWORK FACILITATOR
NL	ZIO	GUY SCHULPEN	ZIO stands for "Care in Development" in Dutch and is a collaboration between 90 GPs, 180 physical therapists and dietitians to provide integrated delivery of primary care in the South of The Netherlands. Specifically, in this region providers and insurers have agreed to work under full capitation, including: hospital care, primary care, prescriptions. Part of the projected savings will be reinvested into quality initiatives like public health programs.	NETWORK FACILITATOR
USA	CAMDEN COALITION OF HEALTHCARE PROVIDERS	JEFFREY BRENNER, MD	In 2002, a small group of primary care providers in Camden, NJ began meeting to discuss problems practicing in the city and quickly realized that issues raised were common to all. The Camden Coalition of Healthcare Providers was established as an independent non-profit organization with a mission to improve the quality, capacity, and accessibility of the healthcare system for vulnerable populations in Camden, NJ. Guided by the Camden Health Database, the Coalition was able to launch several health initiatives to improve healthcare value.	NETWORK FACILITATOR
USA	ROCKY MOUNTAIN HEALTH PLANS	MICHAEL J. PRAMENKO, MD	In 1974 a small group of Grand Junction physicians founded the Rocky Mountain Health Maintenance Organization (HMO) to ensure that Medicaid patients would not be denied care because of the low Medicaid payments. The HMO, now part of the statewide Rocky Mountain Health Plans, enrolled both Medicaid members and others, and through a system of cross-subsidies, paid physicians standard fees regardless of the insurer. Once established, the plan partnered with the physician group to ensure quality and access to all members.	NETWORK FACILITATOR
USA	ICARE (BANNER HEALTH)	DEBORAH DAHL, MBA	Banner Health is deeply committed to its mission of excellent patient care and routinely invests in technology, people, and processes to achieve that. One such investment is iCare Intensive Care, which acts as a high-tech patient safety net that provides proactive ICU care. If an adverse change is detected, iCare specialists communicate with bedside ICU teams to help determine what the patient needs. The timely responses have improved patient outcomes (ICU mortality down 31%) and reduced resource use (ICU days down 30%).	SERVICE LINE
USA	MARKETPLACE COLLABORATIVES (VIRGINIA MASON)	ROBERT MECKLENBURG, MD	In 2004, Virginia Mason Medical Center (VMMC), an integrated healthcare system in Seattle, was approached by self-insured employers seeking a solution to rising healthcare costs. Recognizing an opportunity to apply the Toyota lean delivery model, they established what is now known as the Marketplace Collaboratives for various diagnoses, e.g., low-back pain, headaches. VMMC has seen unnecessary imaging decrease by > 20% and a 91% patient satisfaction rate.	SERVICE LINE
USA	PHYSICIAN GROUP PRACTICE DEMONSTRATION (DARTMOUTH-HITCHCOCK)	BARBARA A. WALTERS, DO; STEPHEN J. LEBLANC, BS	In April 2005, the Centers for Medicare and Medicaid Services initiated the Physician Group Practice demonstration, which offered 10 practices the opportunity to earn performance payments for improving the value of care delivered to Medicare fee-for-service beneficiaries. Participating groups were eligible for up to 80% of any savings generated if they were also able to demonstrate improvement on 32 quality measures. All organizations met quality benchmarks and a few achieved savings to receive bonus payments (in part because some were efficient providers prior to initiation of demonstration).	SERVICE LINE
USA	SANDLOT SOLUTIONS (NORTH TEXAS SPECIALTY PHYSICIANS)	KAREN VAN WAGNER, PHD	North Texas Specialty Physicians (NTSP) is meeting the demands of today's medical environment thanks to a decision in 2006 to create a health information exchange (HIE), Sandlot Solutions. The idea was simple, a physician-centric electronic medical record that allowed physicians to "follow patients in real time, make fast, safe decisions, eliminate redundancy, and improve care quality". A recent survey demonstrated costs savings due to increased efficiency, decreased redundant testing, reduced medications errors, and lower cost of care for chronic care patients.	NETWORK FACILITATOR

are clearly attuned to the key drivers of employee engagement, having one's ideas valued and understanding how one's work contributes to the overarching mission of the organisation. Employees are given ample opportunities to lead, identify areas in need of improvement, and are supported by a variety of tools to help them translate their ideas into reality.

4. Focus on a defined population of patients: Nearly all of the interventions profiled began with a focus on a given subset of high-need, high-cost patients (e.g., ICU patients, frail elderly). This focus allows rapid and significant improvements in patient outcomes as well as overall costs. It subsequently frees up resources to maintain or improve not only the health of the original patient population, but also other patients under the care of a given organisation.

5. Patient-centredness: The focus on the need of an individual patient is a cultural aspect and a professional attitude that cannot be underestimated. It is a key characteristic of all the innovators and often dictates both the structure and the business model of the organisation/innovation. A number of innovators interviewed stated that the litmus test for their innovation was a positive response to the question: Would I want this type of care for my family members?

6. Co-creation with the customer: Successful implementation of an innovation is highly dependent on a clear understanding of who the "customer" is (e.g., the patient, the provider, the payer), their needs, preferences, and constraints. Engaging the "customer" throughout the innovation development process not only leads to a better product/intervention but significantly improves the odds of long-term success.

7. Information technology infrastructure: Information is key to providing safe and effective ongoing care for all patients, and it is mandatory if we are to generate knowledge. As highlighted by Banner Health, hospitals that invest in IT systems can improve quality by reducing adverse trends while lowering overall treatment costs. The key is the development and use of IT systems that do not simply re-create an electronic version of paper-based records, but rather help streamline business operations while providing meaningful clinical decision support both at the point of care and across the patient population served.

8. Culture of learning and continuous improvement: In all of the organisations analysed, professionals are expected to go beyond mastering a basic body of knowledge, completing an apprenticeship, and then practising. They are expected to expand their knowledge through perpetual education, pass on the knowledge through teaching or mentoring, and add to the wider body of knowledge through research.

9. Presence of an active and willing payer: As a result of their purchasing power, payers, whether in the guise of a self-insured employer (e.g., ICSI, Virginia Mason), an integrated payer-provider organisation (e.g., CareMore) or the government (e.g., PoZoB, PGPD), are in a key position to significantly affect the quality and productivity of the delivery system.

10. Clear business case: All of the innovations analysed were started under the premise that the new tool/model of care will result not only in improved quality of care, but also in improved efficiency and effectiveness, thus offsetting the cost of the innovation. Some of the business cases are based on a cost-avoidance model by providing an intervention that reduces downstream (and more expensive) care, but are only viable under a payment model that rewards higher-value care.

◎ Key barriers

1. Reimbursement for healthcare services: The fragmented and primarily fee-for-service (FFS) structure of reimbursement found in both countries tends to penalise innovators for increasing efficiency and does not recognise improved effectiveness. As a result of this structure, the major financial upside of providing higher-value care tends to accrue to the payer, which can therefore affect provider motivation to participate in an innovative care model. For example, even if a provider organisation receives a bonus for participation in a high-value network and achieving specific outcome goals, if the improvement results in lower demand for services, the FFS incentives have the potential to undermine or neutralise network incentives (e.g., PoZoB).

Moreover, since providers are paid in silos, downstream providers have the opportunity to "backfill" any services initially reduced by the innovation and thus drive overall costs even higher. To circumvent these issues providers have had to either "pace" the roll-out of an innovation until reimbursement become more favourable (e.g., ICU moving from a per-diem to a capitation payment or redefining the product and the corresponding reimbursement), establish own health plans (e.g., CareMore) or seek out capitation arrangements (e.g., Diabeter, ZIO). Insurance companies should learn from this. They are in the position to reward innovations and to give an advantage to the innovators by selective contracting with them based on higher-value care. In the Netherlands insurers could align this selective contracting with referral policies of general practitioners.

2. Provider culture: Current medical school training tends to emphasise individual achievement, rather than teamwork, leading to "if it wasn't invented here it must not be true" syndrome as well as "turf wars" around a given patient. Organisations that find themselves in network arrangements often feel as if they are competing for the same patients, while in the case of service line innovations there are internal organisational conflicts around limited resources. Providers are also often resistant to change, especially if it requires the redesign of existing process flows.

Thus, the more successful innovations are often embedded within the existing processes, rather than redefining them. This can be changed by leaders who convince their organisations of the importance of healthcare improvement, understand the redesign of processes, and are able to manage internal budgets in order to accommodate and encourage these new policies.

3. Government regulations: US federal and state regulations not only dictate the scope of practice for healthcare providers but also the settings in which they could be reimbursed, which significantly hinders the opportunities to use lower-cost yet more adequate personnel within a given model of care. Moreover, in both the US and the Netherlands legislative action which aims to promote more integrated care is often in conflict with existing anti-trust regulations.

Although the healthcare industry is notorious for market inefficiencies and system waste (nearly one third of medical spending in the US is not associated with better outcomes, and the Netherlands shows similar trends), our analysis shows that innovation and high-value healthcare are not only feasible but achievable. Moreover, a number of innovations in the US (e.g., ICC, CareMore) have been in place for 30-plus years having found ways to successfully address existing system barriers.

Therefore, what is urgently needed is a way to rapidly disseminate the lessons learned from these innovations, a realignment of the healthcare payment system, and adequate legislative actions to ensure that such innovations can more easily scale across the system. For example, the current fee-for service (FFS) model promotes volume over value, and when combined with price controls creates a vicious cycle of ineffective and inefficient care. The fragmentation in care created by this system also reduces the effectiveness of upstream innovations, if providers find ways to "backfill" downstream services in the care continuum. Instead of FFS, new payment models should provide incentives for both improved effectiveness and efficiency, allow for sufficient delivery system flexibility (e.g., settings, provider types) to promote innovative models of care and reduce care delivery fragmentation through increasing bundling of payment and contracting across the patient care continuum. If we continue to ignore the opportunities presented by these innovations to provide high-value care for all, the rising costs of healthcare will continue to burden national finances, while the fragmented, FFS, price-control approach to reimbursement will result in decreased access and poor outcomes for patients.

◎ Lessons for key players

The government has a key role to play in redesigning the reimbursement system to promote value-based contracting, supporting the diffusion of knowledge, and creating mechanisms that result in a learning healthcare system. As an enabler of innovation, the government should foster competition based on quality (patient outcomes, safety, service), not volume, and overall spending. This will require standards for healthcare quality, patient engagement (for instance, shared decision-making), transparency, and vocabulary. Government must take the lead in requiring both connectivity and interoperability of information technology systems as a condition for government subsidies. As government focuses its efforts on building an infrastructure to support high-value healthcare and paying for high-value care, these efforts will create the necessary incentives for providers to quickly adopt safety and quality improvements. This in turn, will improve outcomes, reduce unneeded service use, and develop new models of care, all with the goal of improving value by reducing healthcare spending and/or improving quality.

In turn, payers have a key role to play in the adoption and roll-out of value-based contracting. Under the current FFS structure, better care often leads to substantial revenue losses by the highest-value providers. So, payers should develop contracting strategies that reward high-value providers (who develop and adopt initiatives that result in better patient outcomes, the reduction of overdiagnosis and overtreatment, and lower resource utilisation), and provide motivation for less effective/efficient providers to move toward higher-value care. Payers also have the opportunity to reduce system fragmentation by em-

FIGURE 2 CHARACTERISTICS OF THE CASE STUDIES OF CARE PROVIDERS AND NETWORK FACILITATORS

INNOVATION/ ORGANISATION	SHARED VISION	PROVIDER LEADERSHIP	FRONT-LINE EMPOWER-MENT	DEFINED POPULATION	PATIENT CENTREDNESS	CO-CREATION WITH CUSTOMER	INFORMATION TECHNOLOGY	CULTURE OF LEARNING	WILLING PLAYER	BUSINESS CASE
BUURTZORG	X	X	X	X	X	X	X	X		X
CONNECTING HEALTH AND WELFARE	X	X	X	X	X	X				X
DIABETER	X	X	X		X		X	X	X	X
DICA	X	X		X	X	X	X	X	X	X
GERIATRIC TRAUMATOLOGY CARE PATHWAY	X	X	X	X	X			X	X	X
KSYOS	X	X	X	X		X	X	X	X	X
MOLEMANN	X	X	X	X	X	X	X	X		X
MIJNZORGNET	X	X	X	X	X	X	X	X		X
PAL4	X	X	X	X	X	X	X			X
POZOB	X	X	X	X	X	X	X	X	X	X
ZIO	X	X		X	X	X	X	X		X
CAMDEN	X	X	X	X	X		X	X		X
CAREMORE	X	X	X	X	X		X	X	X	X
HOSPITAL AT HOME	X	X	X	X	X		X	X	X	X
ICARE	X	X	X	X	X		X	X		X
ICC	X	X	X	X	X	X	X	X		X
ICSI	X	X	X	X	X	X		X	X	X
ROCKY MOUNTAIN HEALTH PLANS	X	X		X	X		X	X	X	X
VM MARKETPLACE COLLABORATIVES	X	X		X	X	X	X	X	X	X
PHYSICIAN GROUP PRACTICE DEMONSTRATION	X	X	X	X	X	X	X	X	X	X
SANDLOT SOLUTIONS	X	X	X		X	X	X		X	X

ploying more coherent contracting across the continuum of care (especially for chronic and elderly care). Without a significant shift in payment mechanisms, initiatives and investments that aim to improve the quality of care will not result in lower overall resource utilisation (due to supply-induced demand, overtreatment and higher complications).

Finally, healthcare providers need to look inward to ensure that internal structures and incentives are aligned with the organisation's overarching vision of high-value, patient-centred care. Getting there may require shifts in the structure of the organisation, its governance, budgeting process, etc.

As we have previously stated, the success of any new endeavour is strongly dependent on having a shared vision that unites the interests and activities of all participants. But these initiatives can only survive and persist if the institutional framework and incentive structures created by the government policy, payer and providers are aligned. In the absence of such alignment, innovations will continue to be fragmented, one-off developments driven by intrinsically motivated professionals, rather than being a key strategic component of the Saving Lives, Saving Costs agenda.

CONTACT INFORMATION FOR CASE STUDIES

Service line innovations
- Case study 1: MoleMann Mental Health, the Netherlands. Contact: Nico Moleman, MD; nico.moleman@molemann.nl; Eerste Weteringplantsoen 6, 1017 SK, Amsterdam, the Netherlands.
- Case study 2: Geriatric Traumatology Care Pathway, The Netherlands
  Contact: Hugo Wijnen, MD; hwijnen@rijnstate.nl; Wagnerlaan 55, 6815 AD Arnhem, the Netherlands.
- Case study 3: Hospital at Home, Presbyterian Healthcare Services, US
  Contact: Bruce Leff, MD, founder of Hospital at Home®; bleff@jhmi.edu; Melanie Van Amsterdam, MD, lead physician; mvanamste@phs.org
- Case study 4: CareMore, US
  Contact: Sheldon Zinberg, MD, CareMore founder; sheldon.zinberg@niftyafterfifty; Donald Furman, MD, former CareMore CMO & executive advisor; donaldsfurman17@gmail.com

Network facilitators
- Case study 5: Buurtzorg, the Netherlands
  Contact: Jos de Blok, CEO of Buurtzorg Foundation; j.deblok@buurtzorg.com
- Case study 6: PoZoB, the Netherlands
  Contact: Arnold Romeijnders, GP, medical director of PoZoB; A.Romeijnders@pozob.nl
  Victor Pop, MD, PhD, professor of Primary Care, Tilburg University, scientific adviser to PoZoB; v.j.m.pop@uvt.nl
- Case study 7: Institute for Clinical Systems Improvement (ICSI), US
  Contact: James L. Reinersten, MD, former CEO of Park Nicollet and first chair of ICSI; jim@reinertsengroup.com
- Case study 8: Integrated Care Collaboration, US
  Contact: Diana Resnik, B.S., President and CEO Shoal Creek Hospital and Community Care; DResnik@seton.org

CHAPTER 16

THE MAYO CLINIC IN THE 21ST CENTURY:
REINVENTING A HEALTHCARE ICON

In the mid-1880s, Mayo Clinic created the group practice of medicine, an innovative practice style in which experts shared information, pooled expertise and worked together to provide the best care for patients. Now, 150 years later, the healthcare icon is building on this defining innovation by systematically generating, integrating and delivering its extensive knowledge to people all over the world.

THE QUALITATIVE ANALYSIS FOR THIS CHAPTER
IS ON PAGE 392 OF THE ANNEX

WITH JOHN H. NOSEWORTHY AND SHIRLEY WEIS.
TEXT BY SHELLY PLUTOWSKI

INTRODUCTION

Mayo Clinic developed gradually from the medical practice of a pioneer doctor, Dr William Worrall Mayo, who settled in Rochester, Minnesota, in 1863. His dedication to medicine became a family tradition when his sons, Drs William James Mayo and Charles Horace Mayo, joined his practice in 1883 and 1888 respectively.

A devastating tornado in 1883 brought the Mayo family and the Sisters of Saint Francis of Rochester together. The tornado destroyed one-third of the town, killing at least 37 people. A temporary hospital was set up to treat the injured. Afterwards, Mother Alfred Moes, OSF, founder of the Sisters of Saint Franci, asked Dr William W. Mayo to open a permanent hospital. The 27-bed Saint Mary's Hospital opened in September 1889. Attending staff were Dr Mayo and his sons.

From the beginning, innovation was their standard, and they shared a pioneering zeal for medicine. As the demand for their services increased, the Mayos asked other doctors and basic science researchers to join them, forming the world's first private integrated group medical practice.[1] The founders believed that the combined wisdom of peers was greater than that of any individual, and they worked with one another to solve practical problems for patients. In 1907, Henry Plummer, MD, an early partner of the Mayo brothers, developed a unified patient record. This shared record gave all providers easy access to a patient's critical health information and led to improved, integrated care for patients. The organised group practice was a revolutionary way to practise medicine and in retrospect, one of the most significant healthcare innovations of the twentieth century.

In a 1910 commencement address at Rush University, Dr William J. Mayo detailed some of the circumstances that fostered this movement toward the group practice of medicine:

> "As we grow in learning, we more justly appreciate our dependence upon each other... The best interest of the patient is the only interest to be considered, and in order that the sick may have the benefit of advancing knowledge, union of forces is necessary."[2]

This statement forms the foundation of Mayo Clinic's primary value – the needs of the patient come first – and also reinforces the importance of team-based care. Crucially it also foreshadows the importance of harnessing knowledge, a key element in Mayo Clinic's current strategic direction.

In 1919, the Mayo brothers established Mayo Foundation as a humanitarian, not-for-profit organisation to operate for the health and wellbeing of humanity. In partnership with administrators, the organisation was led by physicians in order to ensure that the patient remained at the centre of decision-making. All physicians were salaried and all proprietary interests ceased.

Today, that mission continues. Mayo Clinic remains physician-led with salaried staff and operates in six states (Minnesota, Florida, Arizona, Iowa,

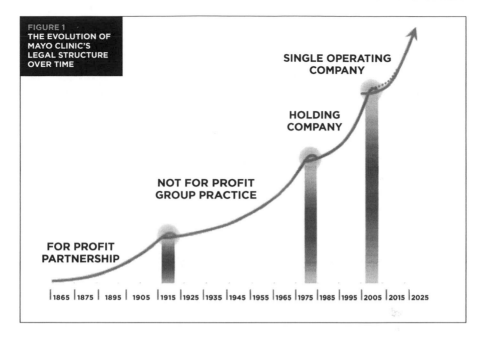

FIGURE 1
THE EVOLUTION OF MAYO CLINIC'S LEGAL STRUCTURE OVER TIME

SINGLE OPERATING COMPANY

HOLDING COMPANY

NOT FOR PROFIT GROUP PRACTICE

FOR PROFIT PARTNERSHIP

|1865 |1875 | 1895 | 1905 |1915 |1925 |1935 |1945 |1955 |1965 |1975 |1985 |1995 |2005 |2015 |2025

Wisconsin and Georgia), employing nearly 60,000 people and caring for 1 million people each year. It is a nearly $9 billion enterprise that reinvests about $400 million annually in medical education and research that will benefit patients. Mayo Clinic is governed by a 33-member Board of Trustees.[3]

In its 150-year history, Mayo Clinic has weathered many storms – the Great Depression, the deaths of the Mayo brothers, various forms of government healthcare reform, price controls, the recession of 2008, new competition and the looming threat of increasing regulation, including implementation of the Affordable Care Act (ACA). However, the organisation has emerged successfully from each challenge, growing and expanding to new locations. But more recently Mayo Clinic's primary business model – destination medical care, where patients with complex conditions travel for diagnosis and treatment – has become dated and vulnerable, causing Mayo's leadership to rethink its vision for what Mayo Clinic will evolve to become by the year 2020.

In 2007, Hugh Price, former president of the National Urban League and a public member of the Mayo Clinic Board of Trustees, asked Mayo Clinic leadership if it had a strategic plan that outlined how the organisation would continue to thrive in an environment of increased competition and constrained resources. In response to this question, Mayo Clinic's Board of Governors – the organisation's internal governing board – created the Mayo Clinic 2020 initiative. The goal of Mayo Clinic 2020 was to develop a tangible construct to describe the organisation's aspirations for the year 2020.

In 2007, Mayo Clinic president and CEO Denis Cortese, MD, commissioned the group, and John H. Noseworthy, MD, the current president and CEO of Mayo Clinic, led the planning effort. Mayo Clinic 2020 group members included physician leaders in clinical practice, education and research, as well as administrative colleagues in business development, marketing and planning.

"Even successful organisations need to reinvent themselves periodically," says Dr Noseworthy. "The strategic plan that grew out of the 2020 initiative defines how Mayo Clinic will be relevant, competitive and accessible in the future. Our goal is to provide hope and solutions for people everywhere – especially for those with complex medical problems – and to protect, preserve and strengthen Mayo Clinic so that it can serve people for generations to come. We want to transform Mayo Clinic and, in the process, we hope to have an impact on US healthcare in general."

Although Mayo Clinic approached 2020 planning from a position of strength and a legacy of humanitarian achievement, careful examination of the external environment revealed challenging trends that would most certainly affect the way the organisation fulfilled its mission in a new century. These include:

◎ Ageing Populations, Declining Resources

People in developed countries are living longer with multiple chronic diseases. These demographic trends will continue to stress the financial underpinnings of social services in these countries, including healthcare. If no changes are made, the US Medicare Trust Fund will be depleted by 2026. Combined with the rising costs of healthcare, diminishing reimbursement from all payer types and the advent of value-based purchasing, Mayo Clinic and other providers will be faced with the perfect storm of reduced revenue and increased costs.

◎ Disruptive Technologies

Advances in science make healthcare diagnosis and treatment more powerful but also more complex. This will continue as genomic medicine becomes commonplace in addressing patients' individual needs. Other disruptive technologies – ranging from regenerative medicine to remote monitoring devices – will alter the healthcare delivery environment profoundly. As people have more access to and dependence on technology, healthcare will also become more available through social media and Web tools.

◎ Workforce Issues

The healthcare workforce faces the convergence of several issues: rapid technological advancements, vast amounts of new healthcare knowledge, new care models and reimbursement methods, and unprecedented growth in demand for healthcare services. To accomplish this, all professionals must work at the top level of their expertise and licensure. Mayo Clinic must also increasingly develop specialised workforces that address new care-delivery models, cultural diversity, and flexible telework models for staffing hard-to-hire positions and optimising use of space.

◎ Consumerism and Commoditisation

The public will expect transparency from US healthcare, leading to value-based purchasing of healthcare products and services. Consumer research demonstrates that ageing baby boomers have an interest in wellness, leading to more demand for these kinds of services. The consumer movement – facilitated by the internet and social media – will also increase the demand for retail medicine, validated health information and lower-cost delivery methods.

◎ Government and Other Environmental Factors

Healthcare insurance reform will advance with the implementation of the Affordable Care Act. The ACA will affect the structure and function of both the public and private healthcare marketplaces, and will have significant impact on payer behaviour, resulting in both reduced reimbursement rates and narrower provider networks available to patients. Similarly, mid-size employers are likely to shift their health benefits to a defined contribution model as the insurance exchange marketplace matures and the "Cadillac" tax on richer employer-sponsored health plans takes effect. Other unpredictable factors that could shape the future healthcare environment include energy costs and global market volatility.

During the planning process, the 2020 team envisioned ways to overcome these significant external challenges while remaining true to the organisation's primary value: the needs of the patient come first. They also affirmed that Mayo Clinic must be held accountable for the value of care it provides – both quality and cost. The group worked on the project for 18 months – conducting more than 100 interviews with internal stakeholders and benchmarking with selected companies outside the healthcare sector – before presenting their recommendations to the Mayo Clinic Board of Trustees in August, 2008. The trustees approved these plans, and the Board of Governors then began work to put the 2020 concepts into a new strategic plan for Mayo Clinic. But a month later, Lehman Brothers collapsed and the world entered the worst recession in 70 years.

INNOVATION AND BREAKTHROUGH PROCESS

Initially, significant challenges in the external environment interrupted Mayo Clinic's progress towards a 2020 vision. The world had entered a global recession. One headline after another reported employee layoffs and companies closing or struggling to survive. Many in the United States lost both their jobs and their health insurance during this downturn. As a result, people started to delay necessary healthcare because of economic uncertainty. Meanwhile, more baby boomers entered the federal Medicare programme, whose payments were lower than the cost to provide care.

This confluence of events led Mayo Clinic to barely break even financially in 2008, and it began 2009 with serious concerns about its ability to meet minimum goals. As a not-for-profit, excess revenue is invested in the research and education missions of the organisation. This is typically between $300-400 million each year. In 2008, however, there was nothing left for reinvestment. For the first time since the Great Depression, Mayo staff worried about keeping their jobs. In late 2008, however, Mayo Clinic leadership responded swiftly and aggressively to turn things around, charting a course to weather the significant financial downturn by relying on dedicated and innovative staff members to change the way they worked to drive out waste and inefficiencies.

"The Mayo Clinic staff is our most precious resource," Dr Noseworthy says. "We engaged the staff to address our financial challenges and asked for their ideas and their flexibility. We also gave them our word that we would do everything possible to preserve their jobs during uncertain times."

The staff response was overwhelming. Chief Administrative Officer Shirley Weis described the strategy as driving costs out of the system by improving patient safety, satisfaction and access while eliminating redundancies and waste.

For example, William Rupp, MD, vice president of operations, had recently been appointed to lead the Mayo Clinic campus in Florida. Dr Rupp decided that one of his first tasks was to spend half an hour with more than 200 staff members working on the frontlines to identify ways to improve patient care and financial performance. Soon, he said, patterns emerged from those discussions, pointing to new opportunities: fix coding so that all services rendered are billed, change appointment rules to reserve slots for more acutely ill patients and examine all medical processes to make sure each step adds value.

"It was and is a multifactorial problem," says Dr Rupp. "That's why many people contribute to making an organisation better. It's not one person, and it's clearly not me. I collected 72 suggestions for improvement from my half-hour meetings, and 71 of them came from the frontlines."

Using an IT tool, leaders also conducted sessions in which all Mayo employees were invited to offer ideas on how to maintain excellence and reduce costs. The implemented ideas resulted in millions of cost reductions

As a result of such efforts taking place across the Mayo Clinic enterprise, expenses in 2009 were more than $313 million below plan, revenues increased by nearly 5 per cent, and one year later, Mayo Clinic ended 2009 with a 4.5 per cent margin – slightly above the organisation's normal target.

The ensuing years have been positive from a financial perspective. The social contract with employees remains in place, and staff continue to offer ideas and innovations about how to continue serving patients in an environment of permanently constrained resources.

◎ Mayo Clinic's 2020 Vision

As finances stabilised in 2009, Mayo Clinic leadership refocused on the future direction of the organisation. In its environmental review, the 2020 planning group completed an internal assessment, which described several organisational challenges, including a cumbersome decision-making process, alignment of limited resources and deepening the pool of talent. Then the group brainstormed what Mayo Clinic *might* look like in 10 years. Highlights include:

- Continued thriving of Mayo Clinic campuses in Arizona, Florida and Minnesota. Mayo Clinic will continue to provide an unparalleled patient experience. The system will be fully integrated.

- A Mayo Clinic Health System, (i.e., a wholly-owned provider network) will surround each of the Mayo Clinics. These will be fully integrated with each other and with the three clinics.

- Beyond the borders of the health system will be a national Affiliate Care Network. Mayo will provide support services that enhance patient-centred, integrated care outside Mayo Clinic regions.

- Mayo's activities will be a highly differentiated, personalised and consumer-driven integrated Web experience for consumers and patients worldwide. Components will include services for patients, referring physicians and specific groups such as benefactors, students, researchers and healthcare consumers in general.

- All of Mayo Clinic's sites, health systems and affiliates will provide appropriate levels of electronic visits (e-visits), e-consults and remote monitoring.

- Mayo Clinic will partner strategically with a few major organisations that will provide a broad network of distribution channels for Mayo Clinic's products and services to a large number of people. These relationships will enable Mayo Clinic to meet some of the healthcare needs of many people without requiring a physical visit.

- Mayo Clinic will have a more dynamic and active public presence, not only through its website but through partnerships with key, large media organisations. It will collaborate in the creation of content across the spectrum of media channels including film, television, gaming, documentaries, mobile applications and consumer products.

- Mayo Clinic will grow its international presence, using technology to deliver its expertise to people around the world.

The group reviewed the current vision statement – *Mayo Clinic will be the premier patient-centred academic medical organisation* – and acknowledged that it no longer reflected the full range of Mayo's aspirations and intents. Instead, they suggested the following statements as a starting point for a new vision:

- Mayo Clinic will broaden and strengthen its position as the world's premier integrated, patient-centred health care institution by providing an unparalleled patient experience for those it serves.

- Mayo Clinic will adapt to evolving patient needs through an innovative, comprehensive platform of services that can be scaled to individual needs and locations over time.

- Mayo Clinic will lead the world in compassionate care delivered through a variety of modalities, delivering value to patients and fulfilling Mayo Clinic's mission of contributing to the general good of humanity.

The final language of Mayo Clinic's new vision emerged after significant input: Mayo Clinic will provide an unparalleled experience as the most trusted partner for healthcare.

◎ Concept: Health Care, Health Guidance and Health Information

The 2020 report proposed a three-pronged conceptual framework for accomplishing this vision. Firstly, with regard to healthcare Mayo Clinic must rededicate itself to delivering an unparalleled patient experience to people travelling to a Mayo Clinic campus for care. Given the fragility of destination care in a more regulated and competitive environment, Mayo must affirm, strengthen and refine its core business proposition – providing patients with superior outcomes, safety and service while reducing costs – through iterative continuous improvement activities and investment in translational science.

With regard to health guidance and health information, the second and third portions of the framework recommended developing platforms for Mayo Clinic to generate, integrate and deliver knowledge that creates meaningful, ongoing relationships with patients, referring physicians and people everywhere – some of whom may never visit a Mayo Clinic site.

◎ Governance Changes

Meanwhile, significant governance changes were under way to allow Mayo Clinic to execute a new, transformational vision that was emerging from the planning process. Dr Cortese directed Ms Weis and Chief Legal Officer Jon Oviatt to begin the work of changing the organisation's bylaws to move Mayo Clinic from a holding company model – in which sites were required to meet financial targets but operated independently – to a single operating entity. The Board of Trustees approved the new bylaws in May 2009, and key legal changes took effect on January 1, 2010:

- Mayo Clinic and Mayo Clinic Rochester merged so that the Rochester campus leadership structure was fully integrated with system-wide leadership. This change created a single president and CEO, a single CAO, and a single governing board, with executive operations teams supporting management at each campus.

- Site CEOs were renamed "Vice President" in support of a single president and CEO.

- Key internal governing boards were replaced by operating teams so that members were responsible for specific components of the operational plan rather than representing a specific site or constituency (education or research, for example).

- The organisation created a single strategic and operating plan that would aim to standardise medical practices and reduce variability across all campuses.

"In the previous model, Mayo Clinic sites in Arizona, Florida and Rochester had their own strategic and operating plans," says Dr Noseworthy. "Even medical departments had their own plans. But there was no uniting force apart from our primary value of serving the needs of patients. So we decided to return to our past and regroup as a single organisation and operating company: one organisation, one vision, one strategic plan, one operating plan and one funding model. Making this transition has allowed us to align all of our activities and take advantage of opportunities for leverage and scale."

The process of "putting the organisation back together again" was difficult, Ms Weis acknowledged. However, successful implementation of the 2020 planning recommendations compelled Mayo Clinic leadership to recognise and remedy internal constraints, conflicting missions and sometimes incompatible priorities.

Work began with integrating the administrative function and continued with Mayo Clinic's clinical practice. During this time of significant organisational change – appointing a new CEO, establishing new roles and titles for leaders, eliminating longtime governing boards, establishing new reporting structures, and embracing a bold new strategic direction – leaders reminded staff that Mayo Clinic's values and core principles would continue to be the organisation's compass as it moved into new territory.

These values – respect, compassion, integrity, healing, teamwork, excellence, innovation and stewardship – guide Mayo Clinic's mission to this day. They are an expression of the vision and intent of Mayo Clinic's founders – the original Mayo physicians and the Sisters of St Francis.

◎ Strategy and Missions

The 2020 report prompted an in-depth strategic planning process that refreshed Mayo Clinic's vision, mission and core business statements:

> **Vision**: Mayo Clinic will provide an unparalleled experience as the most trusted partner for healthcare.
>
> **Primary Value**: The needs of the patient come first.
>
> **Mission**: To inspire hope and contribute to health and wellbeing by providing the best care to every patient through integrated clinical practice, education and research.
>
> **Core Business**: Create, connect and apply integrated knowledge to deliver the best healthcare, health guidance and health information.

"The strategic planning process made it clear that we needed to preserve Mayo Clinic as a destination medical centre, but that we also must manifest our vision in new and different ways," says C. Michel Harper, Jr, MD, Executive Dean of the Practice and chair of the Mayo Clinic Clinical Practice Committee.

"Rather than people always travelling to a Mayo Clinic site for care, we began to look at our core business as delivering our knowledge to people regardless of location. We want to have meaningful relationships with patients and people – not simply rescuing them when they're very ill, but anticipating their healthcare needs before they are aware of them, keeping them well, helping them understand their risks and how we can diagnose and treat them earlier."

That meant defining and executing new methods of healthcare delivery – both physical and virtual. Mayo Clinic's Center for Innovation (CFI), headed by Nick LaRusso, MD, was key to giving form to these ideas. Several years earlier while chairing Mayo Clinic's Department of Medicine, Dr LaRusso and colleagues developed the group's strategic plan, which included a focus on innovation.

"We didn't know a lot of about innovation back then," he recalls. "But over a period of time, we educated ourselves, became aware of the discipline of design thinking and heard about IDEO, which is the premier design company on the planet. So we decided to develop an initiative in which we could apply the principles of design thinking to healthcare. It had never been done before."

Dr LaRusso and team built a SPARC (See Plan Act Refine and Communicate) laboratory to fuse traditional science and design thinking. It was a Skunk Works initiative done *sotto voce*, he said. As they recruited design professionals and ramped up projects, SPARC garnered national visibility for its healthcare work. Then Mayo Clinic leadership asked Dr LaRusso and team to apply the innovation concepts throughout the entire enterprise. CFI – a giant incubator for nurturing new ideas and enabling them to grow and mature until they're ready for patients – was born.

"Mayo has had a legacy of innovation, starting with the group practice of medicine," notes Dr LaRusso. "But innovation is now a discipline within the organisation. Innovation doesn't happen by chance. In order to be successful at innovation, which is extremely difficult, you need a structured programme. That's the role of CFI." Through CFI's innovation curriculum, symposia and small competitive grants available to all employees who want to launch a novel project, CFI and its partners have produced tangible results to help make the 2020 vision a reality.

For example, using the approach of "think big, start small and move fast", CFI has worked with co-creators throughout Mayo to pilot asynchronous internal e-consultations, to support stroke telemedicine work that provides Mayo expertise to rural stroke patient throughout the country, and to launch the Healthy Ageing & Independent Living (HAIL) Lab to support seniors by "ageing in place" — at home, healthy and independent.

◎ Healthcare: The DMC Model

Dr Noseworthy made a defining statement early on in his tenure as CEO: "At Mayo Clinic, the practice is the main thing." This assertion reaffirmed that all activities would be built around what has differentiated Mayo Clinic since

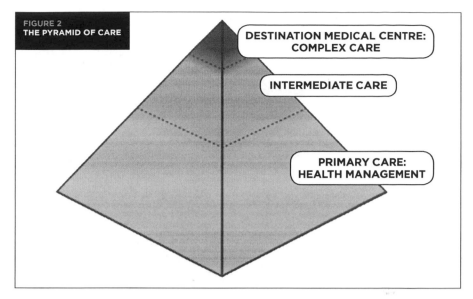

FIGURE 2
THE PYRAMID OF CARE

DESTINATION MEDICAL CENTRE:
COMPLEX CARE

INTERMEDIATE CARE

PRIMARY CARE:
HEALTH MANAGEMENT

its inception – the integrated group practice of medicine. This integrated care is delivered in many different settings to best meet the needs of the individual patient.

The pyramid of care: Healthcare is delivered along a spectrum to meet the needs of individuals at times of great sickness – complex care – and at times of relative health – population health management. Mayo Clinic is best known for its long-standing excellence at providing efficient and safe care for patients with complex diagnostic and treatment issues (the top of this spectrum or pyramid), where integration of practice, research, education; integration of care disciplines (pooling knowledge to a single patient); and integration of care delivery (coherent diagnosis and treatment plan within a few days rather than several weeks) has proven to be a unique competency.

In a highly competitive world, destination care must be "worth it". Mayo Clinic is laser-focused on proving and improving its value to patients and payers. Simultaneously, leaders have been working with city and state officials to create a vibrant community that welcomes visitors from all over the world who need specialised medical care. People from 135 different countries seek treatment at Mayo Clinic each year.

In 2013, Mayo Clinic and its community partners announced Destination Medical Center (DMC), an innovative economic development initiative designed to grow both Mayo Clinic and Minnesota's status as a global destination for medical care. The DMC strategy calls for more than $5 billion investment in Mayo Clinic and other private investment in Rochester over the next 20 years. In the 2012-13 session, the Minnesota Legislature committed $585 million to support infrastructure needs for the expansion.

"Ten years from now, there will emerge just a few specialised medical centres with the reputation for healthcare excellence and patient-focused outcomes that will attract patients from all over the world," Dr Noseworthy predicts. "Mayo Clinic intends to be one of them."

But Dr Noseworthy notes that complex care also must be integrated seamlessly with the other sections of the pyramid. Healthcare reform – with its focus on providing capitated, accountable care for a population – is also nudging healthcare organisations to integrate among and between the levels of care.

Part of Mayo Clinic for two decades, Mayo Clinic Health System (MCHS) is a family of clinics, hospitals and healthcare facilities serving more than 70 communities in Iowa, Georgia, Wisconsin and Minnesota. MCHS offers primary and intermediate healthcare services to local communities. This community care expertise complements Mayo Clinic's destination medical care. Of the one million unique patients seen each year by Mayo Clinic, half of them are seen in the health system. Today, Mayo Clinic and MCHS are working more closely together to supply the right care to each patient at the right time.

"Prior to 2008, the MCHS regional practices were always respected for what they did, but they were not considered strategically essential for Mayo," says Robert Nesse, MD, CEO of Mayo Clinic Health System. "The organisation now recognises the important contributions that MCHS makes.

"In the future, five things will be required for healthcare providers to succeed," he continues. "A network of providers, alignment of purpose, coordinated delivery mechanisms, aligned finances and easily assessable data to help us improve care. All of this depends on our ability to collaborate, integrate and think of Mayo Clinic as a knowledge platform and a system of care instead of a collection of sites."

The single practice: As previously mentioned, another goal is to build a single, integrated, high-value practice across all of Mayo Clinic – sites, departments, specialty service lines and care delivery platforms (for example, hospital, outpatient and e-health). This translates into meeting the needs of patients at the right place and time, with the appropriate level of care.

The new single operating entity model supported integrated planning and practice standardisation by creating a single budget for a central Clinical Practice Committee (CPC). In order to get approval for more people, space or equipment, project proponents must now seek approval and funding from this central CPC. Requests are prioritised against the Mayo Clinic operating plan, and proponents must report progress toward goals using the discipline of project management.

Another integrating force is the Practice Convergence Council. Composed of clinical practice and information technology leaders, this group has the authority and responsibility to facilitate the convergence of IT systems, data and core processes across Mayo Clinic.

In addition to these efforts, more than 50 cross-site specialty councils comprised of the chairs of clinical departments from across the four sites were formed to enhance Mayo's ability to share knowledge and ensure that patients receive affordable, high-quality care – no matter what campus their care provider calls home. Typically, specialty councils work on convergence of IT systems data and processes; quality and process improvement; and content for knowledge management systems such as AskMayoExpert (AME), a provider-to-provider application that captures and organises the breadth and depth of Mayo's medical knowledge and delivers it at the point of care. All content in AME is written and vetted by Mayo Clinic specialists and is a culmination of best-practice advice on hundreds of medical conditions.

Practice transformation through research: As part of transforming the clinical practice, Mayo Clinic recently created three cross-disciplinary centres to speed the translation of discoveries from research into new therapies and approaches. Discoveries made in these centres will support the clinical practice and have direct impact on patients.

> **The Center for Regenerative Medicine** uses various types of native and bioengineered cells, assistive devices and engineering platforms to design and develop a new generation of reparative solutions for patients with diabetes; heart, liver and lung diseases; neurological disorders; hand, face and other injuries; and congenital anomalies. This centre is closely linked with Mayo Clinic's transplantation practice.

> **The Center for Individualised Medicine** creates and uses advances in genomic and clinical science to further tailor healthcare to each patient. Mayo Clinic physicians and scientists are working together not only to make new genomic discoveries, but more importantly to translate these breakthroughs into new ways to predict, diagnose and treat disease more quickly.

> **The Center for the Science of Health Care Delivery** focuses on how patients actually receive care. From using engineering principles to determine the most efficient way to schedule patient appointments, to research focusing on the most successful, cost-effective means for delivering treatment, this discipline's aim is to enhance the patient's experience by improving quality, outcomes and cost.

The centres are funded from a variety of sources including Mayo Clinic funds, benefactors, grants, contracts, intellectual property and new businesses.

◎ Health Guidance and Health Information

Mayo Clinic typically treats one million patients each year face-to-face, but there are some limits on how large the practice can grow. The organisation is constrained by walls, infrastructure and currently available information systems. A 2011 Mayo Clinic study confirmed that many more people want access to the clinic. These people are not limited to those with a serious illness, but include people wanting increased access to the knowledge and expertise of Mayo Clinic in their everyday lives.

"Modern technology makes this possible," says Dr Noseworthy. "People can be part of Mayo Clinic without ever coming here, and we're building an array of products and services from which physicians, patients and other people can choose. By reaching out in this way, we hope to leverage Mayo Clinic's collective knowledge to make a meaningful impact on the lives of millions of people."

Historically, Mayo Clinic has operated in the health guidance arena through the following initiatives:

- **Mayo Clinic Health System** regional practices and clinical outreach.

- **Global Business Solutions**, which produces and sells Mayo Clinic products that centre around healthy living (i.e. books and newsletters), care management (Ask Mayo Clinic Telephone Nurseline) and health plan management (third-party administration).

- **Mayo Medical Laboratories,** a global reference laboratory consulting service that provides esoteric tests to clients in more than 130 countries.

In developing new offerings in both health guidance and health information, the organisation continues to evaluate market segments, geographic locations, distribution channels, partnerships, differentiation opportunities, and the timing and sequencing of activities. Newly-launched initiatives include the **Mayo Clinic Care Network** (MCCN) and the **Center for Social Media**.

MCCN is a non-owned affiliate network of like-minded organisations, which share a common commitment to improving the delivery of healthcare in their communities. MCCN members are selected based on a rigorous set of clinical excellence, patient care and quality criteria. "Creating an affiliated provider network was a huge step for Mayo, and a big new initiative to come out of the 2020 work," remarks David Hayes, MD, medical director of MCCN. "This strategy is driven by clinically meaningful activity to improve patient care at local sites and facilitate integrated care with Mayo Clinic as appropriate."

MCCN provides healthcare providers across the United States with access to Mayo Clinic expertise and resources. With two international and 22 domestic members, this growing network offers Mayo Clinic expertise without requiring travel to one of its facilities. The network achieves this goal by developing closer relationships with community medical providers through formal collaboration and information-sharing tools, including eConsult, a rapid turnaround, non-visit consultation which adds the expertise of a Mayo medical specialist without the need for an additional appointment or travel; Ask-MayoExpert, a Web-based information system that allows doctors to quickly connect with expert clinical information on hundreds of medical conditions at any hour of the day or night; and business consulting, which provides access to peers, tools and expertise in business processes and integrated clinical practice models.

Social media and social networks allow people to play an active role in their healthcare. An early adopter of social media tools, Mayo Clinic's Public Affairs team has been using "new media" tools such as podcasts and blogs since 2005. In July 2010, Mayo Clinic created the Center for Social Media to accelerate the effective application of social media tools and to spur broader and deeper engagement in social media by Mayo Clinic employees and students, healthcare organisations, medical professionals and patients. The centre now supports a YouTube channel, 12 different blogs and maintains more than one million connections via Facebook and Twitter.

"Mayo Clinic believes individuals have the right and responsibility to advocate for their own health, and that it is our responsibility to help them use social media tools to get the best information, connect with providers and with each other, and inspire healthy choices," explains Dr Noseworthy. "Social platforms give us opportunities to connect on a previously unimaginable scale."

Offering consultation, training and infrastructure, the Center for Social Media is a catalyst to help Mayo's 58,000 employees and students explore ways to work more effectively to accomplish the mission. The centre has also established a Social Media Health Network, which includes more than 140 like-minded organisations on four continents wanting to harness social tools to promote health, fight disease and improve healthcare globally.

Mayo Clinic is also actively creating software applications (apps) to reach key audiences via smartphone or tablet. Examples include:

> The Mayo Clinic app for *patients* offers health news and information, online appointments, secure access to personal health information and help finding accommodation at Mayo Clinic locations.

> The Anxiety Coach, an app for *consumers*, is a self-help tool that assists people in reducing a variety of fears and worries ranging from extreme shyness to obsessions and compulsions.

> Mayo Medical Laboratories is connecting with *clients* through two new apps that provide guidance on test selection and result interpretation as well as quick access to reference values, cautions, testing algorithms, and clinical and interpretive information for each test.

Mayo Clinic plans to offer an integrated set of health and medical services such as these by partnering with technology companies and distribution networks which increase the opportunity to scale for greater patient use.

◎ Broader Scaleability

Over time, Mayo Clinic has sporadically disseminated pockets of knowledge, services, and products to the world as a result of organic service line growth, academic collaboration, and the occasional entrepreneurial business opportunity. Historically, each of these offerings has been a scaleable outgrowth of existing work or intentional next steps. Meanwhile, US-based healthcare competitors have leapfrogged Mayo Clinic's international market position with bold, highly visible deployment strategies to build global relevance.

Recognising the opportunity internationally, Mayo Clinic is embracing a more coherent, cohesive, and coordinated approach to international expansion. While this expansion will be focused on selected regions initially, the infrastructure of its knowledge delivered through the destination clinical practice, the physician and provider network, and global business and laboratory service offers a platform for scaleability.

Mayo Clinic is focusing on offering a trusted and valued suite of authentically Mayo Clinic offerings, leveraging its strength in healthcare, health guidance and health information, and delivering those products and services in an integrated way, to be truly differentiated in the marketplace.

◎ Mayo Clinic Ventures

Mayo Clinic Ventures is dedicated to quickly bringing answers to the people who need them most. With backgrounds in science, business and law, staff use their expertise to connect Mayo Clinic inventions with companies willing to commercialise them. For example, a psychiatric genomic test developed by Mayo Clinic experts is now available nationwide through AssureRx Health, which offers genetic tests that guide doctors in prescribing medication to patients with psychiatric disorders. Test results are displayed in personalised reports that suggest which medications to prescribe, which to prescribe with caution, and which not to prescribe.

◎ Planning and Execution

Leaders developed Mayo Clinic's single operating plan by focusing on its newly defined core business – creating, connecting and applying integrated knowledge to deliver the best healthcare, health guidance and health information ("knowledge to delivery"). Using the Balanced Scorecard to translate the vision and strategy, physicians and their administrative partners categorised operational activities into three major areas: People, Processes and Outcomes.

People: Create the healthcare workforce of the future that sustains Mayo's values. With this operating principle, the organisation acknowledged that staff will continue to be the most critical factor in its future success. Lifelong learning, professionalism and dedication to a positive work environment will ensure the recruitment and retention of the best and the brightest. The organisation also created a new Office of Leadership and Organizational Development, providing focused structure to strengthening leadership and staff development. Seven measureable objectives fall within this area. For example, one objective is to increase the number and skill of physicians and clinical/ basic scientists engaged in generating new knowledge. Each of the objectives has a tactical plan and measures in place to drive focused, improved performance and results.

Processes: Transform Mayo Clinic's knowledge management and healthcare delivery process. Processes define how Mayo Clinic will accomplish its core aim – translating knowledge to delivery. This portion of the operating plan will refine care models for different practice settings – destination medical care, intermediate care, community healthcare and e-health. Transformation extends to payment models, the research and education activities that support the practice, and the expansion of products and services offered to patients and customers.

Six objectives are part of the "Processes" category. One example is to standardise, improve effectiveness and reduce costs in all practice settings, core clinical processes and core business processes.

Outcomes: Deliver highest-value care and achieve mission-advancing financial performance. The Mayo Clinic Operating Plan outlines desired outcomes from the perspective of both the patient and the organisation. The outcomes are a direct result of the activities in the "People" and "Processes" objectives. To deliver the highest-value patient care, the operating plan expects outstanding outcomes in quality, safety and service. From Mayo Clinic's perspective, a certain level of financial return is required to sustain the mission of integrated practice, education and research. In this context, one objective is to reinvest a portion of net operating income in research and development for new products and services, practice transformation and strategic growth.

Mayo Clinic's single operating plan – flowing from the common mission, vision and values – allows the organisation to focus and achieve its interwoven goals. The operating plan contains a total of 22 objectives with performance targets and measureable outcomes; aligned and prioritised portfolios of projects; and fiscal responsibility and individual accountability. Together with the site-, business- and mission-specific plans, the Mayo Clinic Operating Plan is reviewed and modified quarterly. Leaders expect the plan to be recalibrated many times as new trends appear, threats emerge and flaws in directional assumptions become apparent.

To create awareness and engagement in this new strategic and operational direction, internal experts in Public Affairs, Planning and Media Support Services assembled a strategic plan communications team and developed a comprehensive communications programme to help spread the word. The messaging platform – "The Mayo Effect" – highlighted how each Mayo Clinic employee would contribute to achieving the mission. "The Mayo Effect" used bold graphics with a look that was fresh and different for Mayo, making strategic plan-related communications instantly recognisable. The team also gave the communication programme the voice of real staff and real work-experience stories – underlining the concept of "the Power of One" in accomplishing great things. Dr Noseworthy and Ms Weis conducted 50 meetings with staff from campuses in Minnesota, Florida and Arizona to communicate this message.

From an operational standpoint, the Enterprise Portfolio Management Office (EPMO) supports leadership with the efficient execution of the Mayo Clinic Operating Plan, objectively assessing ideas for their business value, alignment with operational direction and risks/benefits. Assessment results dictate resource allocation to activities of the greatest value. The office manages portfolios of projects that directly relate to key strategic priorities, goals and objectives. It also coordinates and integrates similar projects and ideas to ensure optimal synergy and provides measurement reports. The organisation has more than 200 projects that directly relate to each objective of the operational plan.

RESULTS

Mayo Clinic uses a Balanced Scorecard as a tracking mechanism for implementing strategic objectives and measuring results. The scorecard tracks organisational progress on leading indicators – the input objectives in the "People" and "Processes" categories – as well as more commonly measured lagging indicators, such as financial results. This enables more proactive decision-making that links to overall strategy and drives high performance.

Each of the 22 objectives in the Mayo Clinic Operating plan is given a status on a quarterly basis – green (on target to meet plan), yellow (moderate risk of not meeting plan) and red (high risk of not meeting plan). Status is determined by a number of quantitative measures that are tied to each objective, as well as progress on key projects that are managed through EPMO. For example, achieving the highest level of outcomes, safety and service for patients is central to Mayo Clinic's mission. The 2012 scorecard shows a green status for this objective, based upon a global quality index score comprising six dimensions: improving patient survival, preventing harm, coordinating care, improving the patient experience, and managing cost and utilisation. Broadly, the organisation has made significant progress in all three objective areas, meeting or exceeding plan in the following categories:

People
- Staff satisfaction with Mayo Clinic
- Capacity and skill in comparative effectiveness and healthcare delivery research
- Deployment of individual provider scorecards

Processes
- Specialty Council formation
- Value projects implemented at all sites
- Use of Mayo-vetted knowledge through the AskMayoExpert tool
- Patients involved in clinical trials
- Core measures for acute myocardial infarction, pneumonia and surgical care improvement
- Wellness products and services available for consumers
- Mayo Clinic Care Network affiliates

Outcomes (for patients and Mayo Clinic)
- High levels of outcomes, safety and service for patients
- Net Operating Income (NOI) from strategic business development
- Reinvestment of NOI in new products and practice transformation

The scorecard also points out areas for improvement – specifically in developing a diverse staff, improving leadership training and mentoring, reducing costs and fees, and meeting NOI targets from practice operations. Results are reported quarterly and depict a snapshot in time, allowing leaders to manage short-term operations while moving the organisation towards fulfilling its long-term vision. From an external viewpoint, Mayo Clinic is consistently recognised for high-quality patient care more often than any other academic medical centre in the United States.

CONCLUSIONS

The 2020 initiative and subsequent strategic and operational planning conveys a vision of Mayo Clinic as a single, integrated, high-value medical practice as well as a global knowledge resource for physicians, patients and people everywhere. The strategy has been in place for three years, and results show steady progress toward transforming Mayo Clinic's healthcare delivery process. "Our vision is what we aspire to be," says Dr Noseworthy. "We're not there yet – it's not 2020 – but we're working very hard together across Mayo Clinic to achieve it." Several lessons have emerged from the transformation process that is under way at Mayo:

External environment: Environmental factors that create the case for change help build momentum and urgency within the organisation.

Iteration: Organisational change is an iterative undertaking. It is never finished. Flexibility is required for success.

Business discipline: Harry Harwick, Mayo Clinic's first administrator, remarked that the organisation "must be able to find a practical, harmonious balance between medical ideals and philosophies on the one hand and reasonably sound business methods on the other." Mayo Clinic's 2020 visioning and strategic planning process strikes this balance by applying best business practices and principles to develop a shared vision, mission, strategy and operational plan. The discipline of project management guides the plan's execution.

Governance and management: The consolidation and realignment of governance and management structures have been essential. Ms Weis commented that progress toward the 2020 vision would have been nearly impossible without moving from a holding company model to a single operating entity. The new structure also allows for more calculated risk-taking, quicker decision-making, and swifter execution while conserving the organisation's commitment to a consensus management model.

Alignment tied to resource allocation: All business units within the organisation must align their work, innovations and ideas to help execute the single operating plan. A single budget allocates resources centrally in a fair, open and transparent way so that proponents know what they can accomplish if they align tightly with the operational plan.

Leadership style: Leading change requires both visionary and participative leadership. Top-down leadership is not most effective. Instead, leaders must enthusiastically set the new strategic direction and continue to communicate clearly and openly. Leaders must use integrated communications methods – from face-to-face meetings to social media – to establish two-way communication with frontline staff. Mayo Clinic continues to embrace the model of servant leadership, in which the desire to serve supersedes the desire to lead.

To be successful, expect some failures: Not every project within the strategic plan has been successful. For example, Mayo Clinic opened a healthy living store at the Mall of America with the goal of reaching out and engaging patients beyond "the doctor's office". Although the store closed within two years, Mayo learned a great deal about delivering health and wellness offerings in the retail setting and will apply those lessons to other initiatives.

Culture: Mayo's strong culture of teamwork and commitment to common values has helped to create the trust required for significant organisational change. Conversely, change can be difficult to manage and implement in a successful, 150-year-old organisation with many longtime employees. An ingrained, risk-averse culture can slow progress toward the vision.

Staff engagement: The nearly 60,000 employees of Mayo Clinic own the 2020 vision and will make it a reality. Execution of the strategy is truly about the Mayo Effect – the power of each staff member to deliver Mayo Clinic's knowledge and expertise to patients and people. Embracing and including a diverse staff of professionals is critical in achieving this goal.

Pace: As a physician-led, consensus-driven organisation, Mayo Clinic has traditionally made decisions slowly and deliberately. To accomplish the new vision, the pace of all Mayo Clinic activities must accelerate.

In the coming years, Mayo Clinic will continue to work toward its 2020 vision, advancing the science and art of medicine through the generation, integration and management of knowledge. Its experts will gather, interpret and apply information on a massive scale, offering hope not only to the patients who seek care at Mayo Clinic, but also to millions throughout the world who may have previously had little hope. With this bold direction, the organisation will overcome current environmental challenges, further refining its high-quality, integrated group practice of medicine and creating new ways to deliver health and healthcare by building upon the model it pioneered.

CHAPTER 17

HEALTHCARE INNOVATION IN PRACTICE

This chapter describes the strategy of the Noaber Foundation to develop an unorthodox approach to force breakthroughs in healthcare innovation. One of the first steps in this approach was the start of a separate network for healthcare bringing together a broad range of stakeholders. The Noaber Foundation established VitaValley, a network for innovation in healthcare. We describe the original ideas and visions that underlie this approach and show how, in a process that started with utopian dreaming and much trial and error, we built a network of stakeholders of knowledge, clinical experience, technology and capital, to develop and implement new innovations in medicine and healthcare delivery. Research innovation was connected to investment, business and implementation. A strategic alliance with the Mayo Clinic in the USA was established to strengthen the impact of basic research and clinical investigations, and to connect these to innovative solutions and investments. Later on, this resulted in the Alliance for Healthy Ageing, an international cooperation between Mayo, Noaber, VitaValley, and the University of Groningen. Our experiences have taught us that breakthroughs in innovation in healthcare can only be realised by the effective use of networks to develop eco-systems with a shared vision – and that innovation has to be driven with a focus on impact.

THE QUALITATIVE ANALYSIS FOR THIS CHAPTER
IS ON PAGE 393 OF THE ANNEX

WITH PAUL BAAN AND NICHOLAS LARUSSO.
TEXT BY MAARTEN VERKERK

INTRODUCTION

In Western countries healthcare faces enormous challenges. Rising costs make strong demands on economies, the rise of individualism undermines the idea of solidarity, and the dominance of the medical approach clashes with the social and spiritual needs of patients. In addition, it appears an uphill battle to convince citizens to adopt healthier lifestyles, when increasing prosperity encourages new epidemics like obesity. One might get the impression that our healthcare system will collapse under the weight of its own success.

These observations have stimulated a number of scholars to analyse the state of healthcare and to propose new solutions. In *Redefining Health Care*, Michael Porter and Elizabeth Olmsted Teisberg argue for a radical re-orientation of healthcare policy. They conclude that "the combination of high costs, unsatisfactory quality, and limited access to healthcare has created anxiety and frustration for all participants."[1] They state that in a "normal market" the "competition drives relentless improvements in quality and cost."[2] But healthcare does not appear to be a normal market because "competition does not reward the best providers, nor do weaker providers go out of business."[3] They conclude that the market mechanism fails in healthcare. Porter and Teisberg believe that the problems of healthcare can only be cured by realigning "competition with value for patients", where *value for patients* is defined as "the health outcome per dollar of cost expended."[4]

The problems that Porter and Teisberg identify have been addressed by several American authors. Shannon Brownlee estimates in her book *Overtreated: Why too much medicine is making us sicker and poorer* (2007) that Americans spend between one fifth and one third of their healthcare dollars on care that does nothing to improve their health. Gilbert Welch shows in his book *Overdiagnosed: Making people sick in the pursuit of health* (2011) that paradigm changes in healthcare induce overdiagnosis, resulting in worse health, lower quality of life and increasing costs. In *Taming the beloved beast: How medical technology costs are destroying our health care system* (2009), Daniel Callahan states that the "reigning model of limitless medical progress and technological innovation"[5] should be rejected.

All these studies show that there are no simple recipes to cure healthcare of the problems of quality, limited access and rising costs. The main reason is that the crisis is not caused by a limited number of identifiable problems but is rooted in the behaviour of all stakeholders, the architecture of the system, and the values that drive individuals and underlie the whole system. As a consequence, old paradigms, old ways of thinking, and old values cannot solve current problems. Perhaps more radical innovations and changes are needed to develop sustainable, accessible and high-quality healthcare. System-wide problems require a system-wide analysis and a network to address them.

In this chapter we investigate the Dutch example of "Healthcare innovation in practice" as developed by the entrepreneur and philanthropist Paul

Baan. His approach focuses on the foundations for changing behaviour and systems on a large scale. We try to identify distinguishing features and to judge his ideas in view of societal developments in developing a network for healthcare innovation.

Innovations are defined as new discoveries or inventive designs. For medicine, this includes the discovery of new medical treatments, new methods of delivery, new technologies, greater efficiency and management, and new arrangements for formal and informal care. The innovations apply to the whole range of visions, scientific discoveries and inventions, business models and applications, and also to the integration of various stakeholders. The story of VitaValley contains many lessons in the process from dreams to reality, in much trial and error, re-evaluations, and the development of new business strategies, initiatives and applications in order to create what is now a thriving network of partners.

BEGINNINGS: IDEAS AND VALUES

Concerned that ageing would become one of the major social problems in the Netherlands, Paul Baan was one of the first entrepreneurs to address these challenges. He worried that demographic developments would lead to an ageing society, the so-called grey wave, in which the growth of the number of retired elderly would greatly exceed the growth in the number of working adults. Consequently, the supply in healthcare would never keep up with the growth in demand. Without relevant measures, the costs of healthcare would explode. The Noaber Foundation, which Baan and his wife founded in 2000, believed that these type of problems could only be solved by broadly understood innovations—not only innovations that changed healthcare as such, but also the social and economic context in which healthcare operates.

At the time, the grey wave was not recognised by the government and insurance companies as a problem. Nor was it seen as a market opportunity by commercial enterprises. The Noaber Foundation decided to contribute to the solution of this problem by developing a network that brought these stakeholders together.

The challenge was: How to make a difference with a limited budget? How to develop innovations that result in breakthroughs? How to develop an authoritative network or coalition that could maximise societal impact? At that time, there were no solutions, but we started with several new ideas.

The first idea was that an unorthodox approach to innovation would be required to address the problems of the grey wave. In one way or another, the whole process of "vision" and "execution" had to be integrated. The second idea was that neither the government nor the market could solve the problems of the grey wave by themselves. These kinds of problems require intensive cooperation between all stakeholders. The third idea was that traditional ways of financing innovations, such as giving subsidies (governments) or donations (foundations), would never solve these problems because neither subsidies nor donations induce fundamental changes. They only make the recipients dependent on their sponsors.

Finally, these ideas were complemented by the fundamental values of solidarity, cooperation and entrepreneurship that motivate the founders of the Noaber Foundation. From the beginning they believed that the foundation alone could never make a difference. Not only its limited resources but also its position as a philanthropic organisation with a Christian identity would limit its ability to "change the world". Therefore, a separate foundation with a medical focus was established that would operate at arm's length. In December 2004, VitaValley was born.

THE FIRST CONCEPT: CONTOURS OF THE FUTURE

VitaValley defined itself as a "network of public and private parties in healthcare that cooperate intensively to develop, to validate, to market and to make accessible new innovative solutions for healthcare." In June 2005 VitaValley presented its first concept and strategic plan. It formulated the objective of facilitating the development of accessible and affordable healthcare in the light of a greying population. Its mission was defined as "to accelerate innovation in healthcare by means of information technology." VitaValley believed that its objectives could be realised by:

(1) Focus on prevention
(2) Focus on early diagnosis
(3) Use of telecare to support independent living
(4) Increase of capacity with use of personal networks and volunteers
(5) Use of modern technology and logistics.

The projects and their execution are at the nexus of healthcare, information technology, logistics and supply chains. The aim is to accelerate innovation: to realise its objectives three different types of activities were defined. The first activity was the *VitaValley Network*.

The objective of the network was to bring parties of different backgrounds together to cooperate in developing innovation in healthcare: healthcare organisations, technology companies and knowledge institutions. It was also expected that in the future international parties from Europe and the USA would join. VitaValley would facilitate joint innovation projects with project managers and experts.

The second activity was the *VitaValley Campus*, in the belief that a physical place was required for meeting and cooperating with each other. The campus was to function as a birthplace of new innovations with a knowledge centre, a validation centre, a demonstration centre, and a telecare centre. For every centre, services, target groups and added value were defined. As its location, the Noaber Foundation offered the beautiful Zonneoord country estate in Ede, the Netherlands.

The third activity was the *VitaValley Incubator*. At the time, it was believed that the development and implementation of innovations in healthcare had to be financed by the government. In practice, however, the government did not release enough subsidies with the result that most innovations did not move from the development stage to the implementation stage. This is known as the innovation gap.

CLOSING THE INNOVATION GAP

VitaValley proposed another approach to accelerate the development and implementation of innovations: social entrepreneurship and social investing. VitaValley believes that social entrepreneurship could be an excellent tool to speed up the innovation process. However, at the time, classical investors and banks did not invest in healthcare. Therefore an incubator fund had to be established. The different cogwheels were identified.

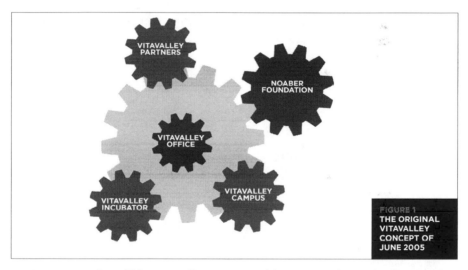

FIGURE 1
THE ORIGINAL
VITAVALLEY
CONCEPT OF
JUNE 2005

However, they did not really engage with one another. The interaction between the different parties was limited and the dynamics in the network were low. From June 2005 on, this concept was translated into strategies, plans and actions. In a process of trial and error, VitaValley began to learn how to close the innovation gap. Visions were challenged, concepts adapted and refined; new strategies, plans and actions were developed in an iterative process. In this process we fleshed out the original ideas and visions. Basically, the original ideas and visions did not change but understanding how to make them happen sharpened their meaning.

Looking back, we can identify four connecting threads that determined the evolution of VitaValley:

    (a) The development of the VitaValley Network and the VitaValley Campus as an ecosystem for innovation.

(b) The development of the VitaValley Incubator Fund into a range of investment funds: Vitality Ventures (pre-seed), Next Gen Ventures (seed) and Health Innovation Fund (growth fund).

(c) Development of the Alliance of Healthy Ageing with the Mayo Clinic to strengthen the authority of the network and to increase the impact of innovations.

The original idea was to develop a network of partners who would cooperate intensively and innovate actively to cope with the consequences of the grey wave. However, innovation is a difficult job. Most partners did not feel a sense of urgency, resulting in a passive attitude. Additionally, it was believed that VitaValley would easily develop a business model so that it would become independent of donors. This presupposition did not come true.

— **Dirk Jan Bakker**, co-founder of VitaValley

DEVELOPING AN ECOSYSTEM FOR INNOVATION

In the development of VitaValley we can distinguish four phases: utopian dreaming, a focus on business models, a focus on implementation, and a focus on societal impact. In all these phases, the original ideas and vision shaped and reshaped the mission, strategy and plans. Its trial-and-error history contrasts with its initial pure ideals and concept but the experience contains valuable lessons on how to create something new that has no precedent. Ideals do not realise themselves.

◎ Phase I: Ideas and ideals

With the wisdom of hindsight, we can characterise the first phase (2005-2007) as utopian dreaming. It was believed that the network would grow rapidly, that Zonneoord would become a centre of innovation, and that a number of social enterprises could be established to quickly roll out innovations all over the Netherlands.

In the start-up phase, we visited a large number of healthcare organisations, technology firms and knowledge institutions to discuss VitaValley's ideas and to invite them to become partners of the network. The basic idea was that every partner would contribute with an annual fee to fund the network and to stimulate innovations. These discussions showed that innovation in healthcare was extremely limited and that there was no awareness that innovation required a supporting ecosystem. Consequently, the growth of the number of paying partners did not meet expectations. In the period 2005-2007 the network grew from one (Noaber) to seven partners. It would take much longer to reach the critical mass of about forty partners.

In the original plan, Zonneoord would become a campus for innovation combining healthcare, knowledge and capital. Its rural location would facilitate the development of the estate into a big living lab in which innovations could be tested before being rolled out across the Netherlands. It consisted of small healthcare units, animation studios, piloting environments, exhibition rooms and so on. In the earliest workshops, we dreamt up and formulated ideas of what a new world of healthcare should look like.

In this period a large number of projects were launched at Zonneoord in the areas of telecare, healthcare portals, and independent living for the elderly. All these projects resulted in an enormous amount of knowledge about innovation in healthcare, but none of them led to a living lab or an environment for pilot studies. In the following years, it became clear that small-scale healthcare units could not be built in the countryside, and that living labs did not flourish in laboratory conditions but needed to be situated in real healthcare institutions.

Finally, it was thought that every year a number of successful projects developed by the network could be transferred to new social enterprises. It was also expected that VitaValley would acquire a substantial stake in these social enterprises, resulting in additional income.

In this period, the first social enterprise was set up: Vital Health Software, a company working in the field of internet portals and supply chain software for healthcare. The main investors in this company were the Mayo Clinic and the Noaber Foundation. However, the next successful investments were a long time in coming. In those years VitaValley learnt how difficult innovation in healthcare is.

At first, the whole sector had a conservative attitude so that both the development and the implementation of new innovations was difficult. In addition, the idea of a network in which parties developed new innovations together did not work smoothly. The classical methods did not work well and new methods had to be developed. Finally, it appeared that the whole Dutch healthcare financial system hampered innovation. The payment structure did not offer any incentives to innovate, with the result that the business case for many innovations was not made.

◎ Phase II: Business models

In the second phase (2008-2010), the network grew steadily, with the number of partners increasing from seven to twenty-five. The process of identifying and evaluating new innovations was restructured, and the execution of projects was professionalised. The most important development in this phase was the focus on business models.

In this period, VitaValley discovered that the most important problem in healthcare was not a shortage of good ideas, nor the development of good prototypes, but rather the question: "Who will pay for the innovation?" At the time, the follow-up of the implementation of innovations was not problematic. In other words, discovering the innovation was the focus and challenge but it was almost assumed that its application would happen by itself.

The government subsidised basic and clinical research. Universities and healthcare institutions focused their attention on acquiring knowledge and proving the feasibility of an innovation. It was believed that healthcare insurers would pay the costs for new innovations, which would then be rolled out across the healthcare system. These assumptions, however, turned out to be wrong.

Healthcare insurers rejected many innovations that resulted in a higher quality of care because the business case was negative: the costs were higher than the savings. Further, many innovations with a positive business case were rejected because of the so-called "substitution problem". For example, the business case of a self-management system for diabetes appeared to be positive because there would be fewer admissions to hospital. These savings, however, could not be realised because the resulting "empty beds" were filled with other patients (substitution). In other words, the overriding hospital rule that an "available bed is a filled bed" killed the innovation.

For that reason VitaValley redefined its strategy: from the development of new innovations to the development of business models that would facilitate the implementation of the innovations.

◎ Phase III: Implementation

In the third phase (2011–mid-2013), the implementation of innovations in the Netherlands was identified as a problem which required multiple strategies to solve. In the VitaValley network a few eHealth applications were developed and implemented, in the fields of prevention, informal care, self-management and mental health. But for all these applications the number of users fell well short of expectations. We learned to distinguish between phases of implementation, to reconfigure our strategies accordingly, and to appreciate that different approaches were needed for different types of stakeholders.

First, one of the most important lessons was that a distinction had to be made between primary, secondary and tertiary implementation. The primary implementation involves acceptance (and payment) by the healthcare institution or insurance company; the secondary implementation is the acceptance and initial use by doctors and patients; and the tertiary implementation is routine use in daily practice. It appeared that for all these implementations different conditions had to be fulfilled that had to be taken into account as early as the development phase.

For example, to overcome the "not-invented-here" syndrome it was of the utmost importance to build strong coalitions in the development phase in order to facilitate the implementation of the innovation.

Second, a new strategy for implementing innovations was developed. We found that the stakeholder configuration required to support the development of a new innovation is often different from the stakeholder configuration that is required to support its implementation. In addition, we learned that the stakeholders who are required in the implementation phase already have to be committed in the development phase, not only to prevent the "not invented here" syndrome but also with respect to the content. We learned about the different nature of research stakeholders and business stakeholders. Research stakeholders always believe that it is too early to launch the innovation and do not want to let go; whereas business partners believe that the innovation has to be snatched from the hands of the researchers. These problems require intensive dialogue between different partners.

Another step was to develop strategic partnerships with trusted parties in the Netherlands to roll out successful innovations over the whole country. The trusted parties were selected on the basis of their networks and strong brands. These partnerships were designed in such a way that a strong commitment from these parties was developed smoothly, especially by adapting the business model to that partner.

The executive power of the VitaValley board was strengthened by placing development and implementation in a separate social enterprise: Vital Innovators. This allowed the VitaValley board to focus on the identification and initiation of new innovations.

Third, implementation was greatly hindered by fragmentation in initiatives. At first, most initiatives had insufficient funds and an insufficient network to make a breakthrough. In addition, competing initiatives induced market uncertainty, resulting in delays in implementation. It became clear that successful implementation required a strategy to overcome fragmentation. That meant a strategy in which initiatives, funds and networks cooperated to enable a critical mass of stakeholders to concentrate their capabilities to realise a shared vision and mission. Such a strategy was applied in the field of internet tools for family carers and resulted in the initiative WeHelpen, an online portal for informal care.

Finally, the position of the Zonneoord estate was re-evaluated. Over time it had become clear that living labs could best be established in existing care facilities. So it was decided that the building would be renovated to facilitate joint development projects. Individual offices were replaced by an open-plan design in order to include partners in the innovation process as much as possible.

◎ Phase IV: Ecosystem for innovation

In mid-2013, VitaValley hit a crisis because a couple of partners resigned from the network. They explained that they appreciated VitaValley's mission, values and projects, but believed that they did not get value for their money. At the same time, the supervisory board questioned the sustainability of the innovation network itself. The discussion centred on VitaValley's business model. "Who is willing to pay for the network?" and "Why are they paying?" These events forced the VitaValley board to review its own business model.

In the recent past, the network had acquired the necessary experience with coalitions of partners starting innovation projects together. We learned that this way of working was very fruitful: financial means, human resources and risks were shared. Additionally, we learned that such coalitions could attract grants and investment money more easily. Gradually, the idea developed that VitaValley's business model had to be located in a joint development strategy that covered the interests of our partners as much as possible. As a result, both the mission and the strategy were redefined.

VitaValley now defined its mission in terms of an ecosystem: "The development of an open and independent network for initiating, designing, implementing and marketing sustainable innovations in healthcare."

The strategy was defined in terms of a strategic innovation programme that would cover the innovation needs of the partners. Four key themes were identified: vitality; the ability to live independently (self-management); the ability to care for others (mutual aid); and the quality and efficiency of healthcare. Two further supporting themes were defined: the structural conditions for innovation; and the ethics of innovation. For each theme, discussions have been initiated to determine what type of coalitions with influential external parties are required to generate impact.

VitaValley has started in-depth discussions with every partner to understand their strategy and their innovation needs. The objective is to define joint projects, to build coalitions to innovate, and join forces in implementation. Moreover, a couple of healthcare foundations are supporting this approach with grants. In their view, this approach increases the chance of development and implementation of innovations and lowers the risk of failures.

A RANGE OF INVESTMENT FUNDS

In 2008, four years after the founding of VitaValley, the (pre-)seed fund Vitality Ventures was established to close the innovation and commercialisation gaps. This fund consisted of a number of investors who agreed to invest in healthcare projects.

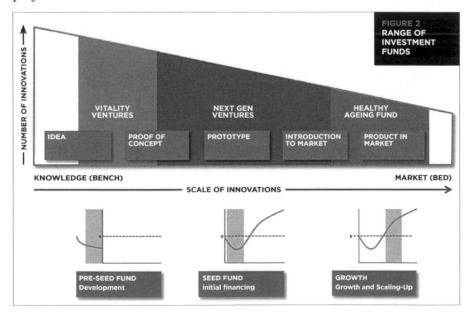

Basically, it was a group of investors who all agreed to invest a certain amount of money per year. They could decide whether or not they intended to invest in each project. The idea was to increase their commitment to the projects they invested in. It was also expected that each investor would support the start-up by using their own knowledge and network. Gradually, the deal flow started to increase. More and more initiatives outside the VitaValley network found their way to Vitality Ventures for (pre-)seed money.

In the period 2008-2012 three new social enterprises were established – Vital Health Software, MentalShare and Vital Innovators – and six enterprises were refinanced. However, three big problems became apparent. First, the idea of a circle of investors did not work. The process took too much time because of its two-stage decision mechanism, first by the fund management and then by individual investors.

In addition, too often only one investor wanted to invest with the result that not enough money was raised. Second, it was difficult to attract investors because the focus of the funds (pre-seed, seed and growth) was too broad. Some investors wanted to invest only in a seed fund and others only in a growth fund. Finally, the investments of the (pre-)seed fund were limited to about €500K. That meant growth capital for successful companies like Vital Health Software could not be provided.

It was concluded that Vitality Ventures had to be reshaped into a range of investment funds required to finance "spin-offs" (see figure 2):

- Vitality Ventures: pre-seed fund with investments of €25K-€75K;
- NextGen Ventures: seed fund with investments of €100K-€500K;
- Healthy Ageing Fund: growth fund with investments of €500K-€2,000K.

These three funds reflect the different focuses of phases II to IV of VitaValley (see previous section). In Vitality Ventures the main discussions are about the business model of the new innovation; in Next Gen Ventures about the implementation strategy; and in Healthy Ageing Fund about scaling up.

The main rationale behind this chain of investment funds is that it mimics the lifecycle of enterprises from bench to bedside, while allowing for the different characteristics of initiatives in each stage of development as well as the focus and risk-appetite of investors. Ideally, enterprises develop from bench to bedside with the support of the respective funds, but the funds' structure also allows for an outside-in strategy to engage meaningful innovations initiated outside VitaValley with the network. The arms-length relation between the respective funds also allows for validation of the innovations.

"In my opinion, it is very important to establish these types of funds with other investors. First, to enlarge the societal support for a new initiative; and second, to judge the viability of the new enterprise." **– Paul Baan**

The focus of Vitality Ventures is to facilitate the transition from project to enterprise. This is in line with VitaValley's objective of ensuring long-term sustainability. The focal points in this transition are the business models and entrepreneurs. Often, innovations lack either (or both) of these crucial ingredients, thereby disqualifying them from venture funding. In its reshaped form, Vitality Ventures is positioned as a pre-seed fund providing limited investment to develop and test a business model and to match the right entrepreneur to the innovation. In a period of approximately six months, this should result in a viable investment proposition for seed financing. Vitality Ventures' new style was established in 2012. Since then, more than twenty applications for pre-seed money have been evaluated and three applications approved. The shareholders of this fund are Noaber, VitaValley and the NDDO (New Drug Development Office, Amsterdam).

NextGen Ventures was established in October 2013 to provide seed financing for innovations in healthcare. NextGen Ventures is focused on initiatives with a certain level of promise but still not sufficiently proven that they can attract funding from traditional investors. This is known as the commercialisation gap. NextGen Ventures believes it can help initiatives overcome the commercialisation gap not only by providing them with capital but also by giving them access to content and clients. The fund management of NextGen Ventures combines universities, medical institutions, care organisations and healthcare insurers. Since its founding, more than forty applications for seed and early-stage financing have been evaluated and the fund is working towards its first investments. The shareholders of the fund are Noaber, Triade (linked to UMCG Groningen) and De Friesland Zorgparticipaties, an insurance company.

The Healthy Ageing Fund is still in the process of being established. The last development to support investment activities is the website www.zorginnovatie.nl, an interactive site in which innovations in healthcare are shared, discussed and ranked. Additionally, a network has been started for young entrepreneurs in healthcare, to support them by connecting them to experienced entrepreneurs and by offering guidance by executives in residence.

THE MAYO CLINIC AND THE ALLIANCE FOR HEALTHY AGEING

"In 2006 the first contacts were made with the Mayo Clinic. I was impressed by the professionalism of this organisation and their patient-friendly attitude. The patient really comes first. Mayo is one of the best hospitals in the United States. In my opinion, cooperation with such an authoritative hospital would strongly support innovation." — **Henk van den Breemen,** Co-founder VitaValley

From the beginning it was believed that strategic alliances between VitaValley and renowned international partners would facilitate the development of new innovations and speed up the implementation of proven innovations. The first contacts with the Mayo Clinic in Rochester, Minnesota, were made in 2006.

At the beginning of the 21st century, Mayo leadership has committed itself to having the same impact on medicine as the founders had a hundred years earlier. Mayo's aspiration of transforming healthcare delivery has many components, especially understanding the biology of ageing and accelerating transformative innovation in healthcare delivery.

The main motivation of VitaValley to partner with Mayo was to accelerate innovation by cooperation with a "best in class" organisation by:

- Increasing the impact of basic research by developing joint programmes between Mayo and Dutch universities
- Combining know-how and best practices to develop new innovations
- Closing the commercialisation gap for new innovations by an intelligent use of the network and funds of both organisations
- Enriching the portfolio of proven innovations by exchange of innovations between both organisations
- Facilitating funding of growth of innovative enterprises in healthcare

Dr Nicholas LaRusso, who led the development of Mayo's Department of Medicine's 2002 strategic plan and has led the Center for Innovation since 2007, noted that promoting innovation was one of the principal objectives: "It was decided to focus innovation efforts on the delivery of healthcare, where Mayo's most important innovations had been in the past. Although the science of medicine has been enormously innovative, particularly in the United States since the Second World War, the delivery models for making groundbreaking discoveries accessible and affordable were unchanged and increasingly obsolete."

Dr LaRusso added: "The first concrete manifestation of the commitment to the needs of the elderly was the Kogod Program on Ageing which began in the Department of Medicine in 2005 through the generosity of Robert and Arlene Kogod and under the leadership of myself and colleagues. The focus of this effort was the study of ageing from conception to death with the goal of applying these basic science discoveries to extending the duration (lifespan) and quality (healthspan) of American's citizens. With the generosity of Robert and Arlene Kogod and the support of the Noaber Foundation, the Kogod Program in Ageing was expanded to a Mayo-wide activity."

In 2007, Dr LaRusso was asked to lead the Center for Innovation, which focused on "discovering and implementing new ways to deliver better health" and whose methodology represented a fusion of design and the traditional scientific method. The contacts with Mayo Clinic were formalised with the Alliance for Healthy Ageing. The most important partners of this international cooperation were Mayo Clinic, the University of Groningen (the Netherlands), Noaber Foundation and VitaValley.

The international cooperation covered the whole field from bench (research) and bedside (clinical studies, implementation in hospitals and long-stay hospitals) to home (implementation in homes). It also implied a paradigm shift from lifespan to healthspan and from costs to benefits.

It was recognised that the challenge of healthcare was not just to lengthen human life but to lengthen the healthy part of life and to increase the quality of life during physical and psychic deterioration. It was also recognised that politics had to focus more on the societal added value of healthcare than on its costs.

"Our intention was not only to donate to Mayo but also to cooperate with them. In the course of the time it became clear that cooperation with Noaber and VitaValley was also beneficial for them. They realised that a large and consensus-driven organisation is like a large tanker: it is very difficult to change its course. They said to us: 'You are like a small towboat that can change the direction of a large tanker'."

– Paul Baan and Henk van den Breemen

In the Alliance the international cooperation in the field of the "bench" (research) is well-established. A number of joint articles have been written and there is an active exchange of researchers and students. International cooperation in the field of the "bedside" (clinical studies, implementation in long-term hospitals) and at home) has begun.

The first international project was the development of exercise games for the elderly. The main question was how to design the social environment so that the elderly can be persuaded to use an exercise game. Other projects in the field of the ethics of care for the frail elderly and the experience and delivery of care for the same age group are in the process of being started up.

IMPLEMENTATION: OUTCOMES

Today VitaValley has developed into an eco-system for innovation in healthcare with about forty partners and an impressive track record. The overall VitaValley ecosystem is depicted in Figure 3, showing the parnters, initiatives and project. VitaValley and its partners have now successfully initiated and implemented a large number of projects. The most important projects are:

◎ **Projects**

1. VitaValley participated in the **PAZIO consortium** from 2007-2011. The objective of this consortium was to set up a health portal within the new VINEX location of Leidsche Rijn, in west Utrecht (VINEX stands for the mass development of homes on the outskirts of big Dutch cities). PAZIO is currently involved in about twenty organizations and has a reach of about one million users. It is in the process of attracting investors to help it develop.

2. VitaValley initiated with TNO (the Netherlands Institute for Applied Scientific Research) and UMCG (the University Medical Centre Groningen) the **"Frail Elderly" programme** (2011). This presented a view on care for the

frail elderly and consisted of five pillars: prevention, early diagnostics, technology base set, medical intervention, and terminal phase. The programme resulted in a lot of follow-up projects within the network.

3. VitaValley initiated with Eleos, a Christian institution for mental healthcare, and Prolife (a Christian healthcare insurance company) the **Christian mental healthcare coalition** (2012). The objective of this coalition is to increase the accessibility and quality of Christian mental healthcare. It has decided to develop a joint internet portal to strengthen its market position, to support a "beyond fragmentation" policy in Christian healthcare, and to develop a joint innovation programme.

4. VitaValley started the **Vitaal Thuis coalition** in 2012, with the objective of achieving a breakthrough in technological support for independent living. The main problem is that home technology is not viable because of high costs (both initial and monthly) and the absence of standardisation and operability. In 2013 this coalition presented its view in the publication *Vitaal Thuis*. Standard specifications are now being developed and purchasing power is being organised to facilitate a transformation of the home technology market from a professional to a consumer market.

5. VitaValley set up a coalition of more than ten partners to investigate the possibilities and potential applications of applied gaming in the care of the frail elderly (2013).

6. VitaValley is supporting one of its partners, Dr Leo Kannerhuis, a mental healthcare professional specialising in patients with autism, to guide its **Quli portal** from the project phase to the commercialisation phase. Quli was originally developed for patients with autism to help them to manage their own lives. it is also suitable for patients with other mental health disorders and for the handicapped.

◎ Spin-offs

VitaValley and its partners have started a number of projects that resulted in spin-offs:

1. VitalHealth Software: a joint initiative of VitaValley, Noaber and Mayo Clinic to develop and implement solutions for collaborative health management, self-management applications and routine outcome monitoring. Since the inception of VitalHealth in 2005, the company has become the leading ehealth solution provider in the Netherlands and has significantly expanded its international business.

2. MentalShare: a joint initiative of the Trimbos Institute, Utrecht, and Noaber and supported by VitaValley to develop and implement web-based solutions in the field of mental health. This company was established in spring 2008.

3. VitaValley and Beteor, a consultancy firm, established the social enterprise **AnderZinzorg** (Different in Care) in 2010. Its objective was to implement the concept of "Hospitality in Health Care" in Dutch long-term care homes.

4. VitaValley initiated a project about internet tools for family carers in 2009. The main objective was to manage all organisational matters around informal (that is, non-professional) care in a more efficient way. Over time, cooperation with other projects and organisations was achieved. In 2012 the cooperative **WeHelpen** (WeSupport) was established: VitaValley was one of the founding fathers. By the beginning of 2014, more than 10,000 people were using this portal.

◎ Research and other activities

VitaValley also initiated several projects in research, consultancy, online innovation and enterpreneurship.

It set up the research project **Future-proof living with Guaranteed Care** in 2006. This project is focused on senior citizens aged 55 years and over who wish to stay in their own homes, living independently, for as long as possible, even if their physical and mental health is diminishing.

The project takes into consideration the specific needs the elderly have that may change over time, as well as the durable use of materials and energy-saving applications. It resulted in the Dutch publication *De zilverbouwwijzer* (a home design manual for the elderly).

It started a study of the ethics of care for the vulnerable elderly in 2012. The objective was to explore the field of overtreatment and to offer an ethical framework to prevent it. In 2013, it resulted in the book *Over-behandelen. Ethiek van de zorg voor kwetsbare ouderen* (Over-treatment: Ethics of care of the vulnerable elderly).

For consultancy, the social enterprise **Vital Innovators** was established in 2011 by VitaValley and Noaber. This objective of this consultancy group is to support VitaValley in managing and implementing innovations in healthcare. This enterprise also carries out assignments outside the VitaValley network.

For online innovation, VitaValley and Noaber established the internet platform www.zorginnovatie.nl in November 2013 to facilitate collaborative innovation processes online.

In March 2014 the network **Entrepreneurs in Healthcare** was established. One of its aims is support for young entrepreneurs by well-known executives in this field.

And in the Alliance for Healthy Ageing, the following projects have been succesfully initiated by VitaValley and Noaber in cooperation with other partners in the Alliance.

Noaber and VitaValley support **Professorships at Mayo Clinic** in the field of healthy ageing. An important element of these professorships is cooperation in their research with other partners of the Alliance of Healthy Ageing, such as the University of Groningen, that have resulted in groundbreaking publications in *Nature, Cell Reports* and *Nature Cell Biology*.

The HAIL Fellowship is a joint research programme between Mayo and TNO (a Vita Valley partner), with the support of Noaber, into the motivational factors of exergaming (exercise computer games), which laid the foundation for a broader cooperation between VitaValley partners for the integration of gaming in their care processes.

All of these initiatives and partnerships have resulted in a vastly expanded ecosystem. Figure 3 on the next page gives a summary of the present concept of VitaValley. When compared to the original 2005 concept of figure 1, the last figure shows the learning curve that this network has undergone.

CONCLUSION: IT'S ALL ABOUT IMPACT

In the beginning there were values, ideas and visions. There was also entre-preneurship, money and knowledge of ICT. All these elements were brought together and translated into an initial rough concept—and VitaValley was born. The history of VitaValley shows that original values, ideas and visions drove the development of this innovation network in healthcare. Above all, we feel we have effectively closed the innovation and commercialisation gaps by bringing stakeholders of research, business and delivery together.

In the course of time these values, ideas and visions were made concrete and the concept was fleshed out with tangible strategies, initiatives and projects. The original values, ideas and visions did not change, but their meaning was clarified and concretised. Looking back, I would like to draw two conclusions with respect to innovation in healthcare.

The first is that innovation in healthcare requires a strong network, with an integrated eco-system of partners to design, implement and market innovations. The main reason is that innovation in healthcare is complex, with many stakeholders involved. A "critical mass" of healthcare institutions is required to be able to scale up and (social) investors are required to finance design, implementation and growth. All these conditions cannot be realised by one commercial enterprise or by one healthcare institution, but require an active and integrated eco-system. A strong and dedicated network is the precondition for a breakthrough.

The second conclusion is that innovation in healthcare is all about impact. There is an African saying, "When you want to start quickly, go alone, but when you want to go far, go with others." The same holds for innovation. One enterprise or one healthcare institution can easily start the development of an innovation. But when you opt for broad implementation and high impact, then you need a network. The development of VitaValley, the close cooperation of VitaValley and Noaber, and the development of the Alliance for Healthy Ageing is all about impact.

The ideas of an eco-system and aiming for impact are also driving the latest developments. First, VitaValley is strengthening its strategic programme by intensive dialogues with all of its partners. These discussions should result in a limited amount of projects that make a difference. More and more partnerships are being agreed with other foundations and networks to increase the impact even more. Second, VitaValley and Noaber are fine-tuning their strategic innovation programmes. This process will not only focus on projects worth investing in but also on addressing the structural and financial conditions that can support them. Third, the idea of impact will reshape the cooperation between VitaValley and Noaber. In the Noaber network several foundations that are active in healthcare have been established, such as Ambitus, Eleven Flowers and The Owls Foundation. The eco-system developed by VitaValley is an important lever to increase the impact of these foundations' projects.

VitaValley has left its childhood and adolescence. Step by step, it is growing into maturity. Its main challenge in the years ahead is to develop its own business model to increase its impact and to become more financially independent.

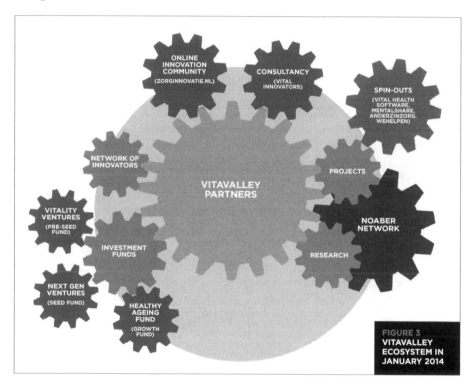

FIGURE 3
VITAVALLEY ECOSYSTEM IN JANUARY 2014

CHAPTER 18

THE AUGEO FOUNDATION:
TACKLING CHILD ABUSE

The Owls team met one afternoon with Gemma Kobessen and Mariëlle Dekker of the Augeo Foundation. They are a new charity with a broad vision, original concept and a wide-ranging strategy, seeking to force breakthroughs in tackling child abuse and neglect in the Netherlands. In confronting a difficult topic, they have shown how to analyse it, how to develop new public-private partnerships and educational programmes, while continually monitoring their impact and effectiveness. Their platform includes a concept and strategy for new partnerships, and a range of educational activities including a magazine and innovative e-learning modules targeted at professionals in medicine, education and social work. The Augeo Foundation has already made a demonstrable impact on how these professionals fulfil their responsibilities. While there has been a large increase in incident reporting, many challenges remain. Their innovative approach can be applied to many other sectors and may be introduced in other countries.

THE QUALITATIVE ANALYSIS FOR THIS CHAPTER
IS ON PAGE 394 OF THE ANNEX

WITH GEMMA KOBESSEN AND MARIËLLE DEKKER.
INTERVIEWS BY THE OWLS TEAM.
TEXT BY BENJAMIN BILSKI

INTRODUCTION: BACKGROUND

Child abuse and domestic violence are demanding problems, difficult to tackle, or even think about. They are not issues that national or local politicians like to spend a lot of time dealing with. Professionals who deal with children, especially in medicine and education, do not like to be confronted with them either. The problems surrounding tackling child abuse have been structural. It is an unattractive and multi-faceted problem; there is ignorance about facts and statistics, and about identifying and reaching vulnerable children; the organisation of the government and supporting institutions on this topic is diffuse; and most activity occurs on the level of discussion and paperwork with insufficient implementation to reach and help the target group.

Gemma Kobessen and Mariëlle Dekker of the Augeo Foundation, a Dutch charity founded in 2007, decided to tackle the problem and devote their time, energy and resources to these issues in the broader context of the protection of children. They decided to tackle the question on a large scale with a business approach to make a national impact. For this they formulated a committed vision, and developed a concept and strategy for implementation with four elements: a national analysis of the problem of bottlenecks in the system and how they were tackled; an innovative concept of public-private partnerships; a range of partnerships with professional associations; and continual follow-up analysis of the impact of their activities and educational products. Everything starts, however, with an idea. How did the idea to a new approach first emerge?

Gemma Kobessen: "I studied economics and developmental psychology. And I was astonished to read a study that 80,000 children [in the Netherlands] suffer child abuse or domestic violence. They weren't quite sure. In 2006-2007 new research was carried out and then they came up with 80,000-100,000 children. I read it and could not believe it. How was that possible, 100,000 children?"

Mariëlle Dekker adds, "And those are the actual cases. Every year 100,000 new cases."

GK: "For children in the Netherlands we are talking about neglect and all sorts of abuse. A large part is witness to domestic violence and neglect. And then there are 20,000-30,000 children who have experienced physical violence. And we are talking about serious physical violence. Not just spanking, but children who arrive at the general practitioner or the emergency room with significant and demonstrable injuries. And the psychological injuries are significant enough to affect their daily functioning. These are also between 20,000 and 30,000 cases each year. I simply could not believe it.

"This is why I started studying the problem more deeply. And the more you read about it, the more shocking were the numbers. I still find the numbers shocking. In the Netherlands there are 48,000 children in institutionalised care. That's huge. I was very surprised. Many of the children in institutions are our target group. Those are the children who experience these problems. And I was astonished how little was being done."

POLITICAL CONTEXT: WHO IS RESPONSIBLE?

If the problem occurs on such a scale, has it not been noticed? Has the government not developed policies to confront it, have activist groups not called attention to it, has it not been studied in academia? More broadly speaking, who has ownership over the problem and should take responsibility? If we start with the government, we can imagine for a moment the possibilities open to someone who wishes to tackle the problem from parliament or a government ministry. How can someone from within government unify policy and make a meaningful impact on professionals and families?

When a newly elected young parliamentarian, filled with idealism, enters the legislature, he soon discovers that the centre of decision-making lies elsewhere. Higher up on the party lists, budget priorities have been set and there is little room for manoeuvre. The young parliamentarian may succeed in booking time to debate the subject, but what will the outcome be? It can lead to support for a pilot programme, but who will implement it? Perhaps he should press for the passage of a law that mandates professionals who work with children, to educate themselves on the subjects to be able to report signs of abuse. The impact of a discussion and the passage of a law ultimately depend on others for implementation. The question of ownership arises again, when the parliamentarian wishes to call the executive branch to account. Which government minister is responsible? Responsibility for child abuse is currently spread between five ministries: Justice, Public Health, Social Affairs, Education and the Interior.

After twenty years, our young parliamentarian reaches the position of government minister, and will be able to create a new department taking responsibility for all matters pertaining to child abuse and domestic violence, a Ministry of Youth and Family. The minister intends to launch initiatives, but who will carry them out? The department's civil servants will remind him that while he can set policy, with a limited budget in times of austerity, he will not be able to do anything ambitious.

Reality did not differ much from this scenario. The history of the attempts by the Dutch central government to address child abuse and domestic violence is one of lack of focus and attention, ignorance about statistics, diffuse organisation and too much emphasis on generating paper rather than meaningful implementation on a national scale. Until 2007 there was little serious attention to the issue by the central government.

According to Mariëlle Dekker, "It was usually delegated away with a trial project. In 2007 the last government memo on this subject on the ministerial level was twenty years old. Hedy D'Ancona was the first to tackle it."

In 1982, in her capacity as Secretary of State, Hedy d'Ancona organised a conference on the sexual abuse of women and girls and launched pioneering academic studies on the subject. At the time, however, there were few procedures for reporting,, referral and care. In 1988, a committee was created to set out new and better guidelines. The United Nations International Convention of the Rights of the Child was adopted that year, broadening the concept of child abuse by framing it as a violation of a child's fundamental rights.

In her capacity as Minister of Public Health from 1989 to 1994, Hedy d'Ancona devoted attention to the subject, but the 1992 Youth Services Act shifted responsibility of the subject away from the central government to the fifteen provincial governments. Networks of care facilities and institutions were set up, but when this was done the issue was dropped from the central government's agenda.[1] A government minister, André Rouvoet of the Christian Union party, the junior partner in the 'Roman-Red coalition' with the larger Christian Democrat and Labour parties, brought it back onto the agenda in 2007.

This happened thanks to campaigning by Professor Andries van Dantzig of the University of Amsterdam, the most important scholar on the subject in the Netherlands and its strongest activist for many years. He launched a series of round-table discussions between academics, professionals and the government. Although Professor van Dantzig passed away in 2005, his efforts brought child abuse back on the agenda and up to ministerial level in 2007, the year the Augeo Foundation was founded.

MD: "It was André Rouvoet who started it again. There had been a gap of twenty years of little political attention until it was brought back on to the political agenda in 2007.

"The nice thing was that when we had André Rouvoet as Minister of Youth and Family, the theme was anchored with one person and one ministry. In Dutch politics it is very important for parliamentarians that they can call somebody into Parliament who is responsible for an issue.

"It was very nice when we had a Minister for Youth and Family, because everyone knew that if there was an escalation or if something went wrong with a troubled family, Rouvoet was the one whom parliamentarians could address."

Mariëlle Dekker notes: "The problem today is that the topic has become fragmented again, and no single party is responsible: the Ministry of Justice does a piece of safety and domestic violence; the Ministry of Public Health does a bit; the Ministry of Education does a bit; and the Ministry of the Interior has a portfolio on the subject. All these departments are working on it, but still in a fragmented way.

"They won't criticise each other and don't cooperate enough. Sometimes they do meet, and for a few cases the Ministries of Public Health and Justice work together especially with regard to domestic violence. Justice seems to be leading in this regard. The problem is if we meet parliamentarians in the lobby that there is no single address to call upon. We all ask: who is responsible in the end?"

When the central government delegated responsibility for child abuse to fifteen provincial governments in 1992, it was still relatively manageable to oversee the activities of fifteen institutions on the subject. But today the government has done something that will lead to even greater fragmentation. The governmental responsibility for child abuse and domestic violence has been passed down to the municipal level, where it will be fragmented between 440 municipalities, making oversight more difficult.

With the background of shocking statistics and fragmented action by government and parliament, Augeo was founded in 2007. How did the idea take shape and how was the decision taken to start a private foundation? Gemma Kobessen and Mariëlle Dekker found each other, "it clicked, and we decided to work together."

Gemma Kobessen has a background in economics and developmental psychology. Mariëlle Dekker is a child therapist and manager of a child protection team in the Dutch Public Healthcare system. They shared a disappointment with the lack of interest by the central government and the limited, small-scale experiments that had taken place. The narrow bureaucratic thinking of The Hague had to be reviewed, with a new emphasis on a clear vision and new conceptual thinking. Their ambitions were big from the beginning, as they sought to make an impact on a national scale.

The first step was to create a national analysis of what is known of abuse, what is done about it and by whom. The analysis would focus on the bottlenecks in the existing systems, identifying where they could make the greatest impact. This analysis would be combined with their platform, Augeo's innovative concept of partnership tiers, which would be realised with new public-private partnerships and cooperation with a broad range of professional associations. With this basic architecture in place, a range of educational and social activities could be carried out, which Augeo would continually monitor for impact. The first preparatory step was not unlike market research by a new business.

FIRST STEPS: THE VISION AND NATIONAL MAP

The first bottleneck analysis served to draw a national map of the problem of child abuse and domestic violence. The analysis concerned the conventional system of reporting and care, the effectiveness of programmes that had been carried out at the private and public level, and the efficiency of communication and referral channels. Above all, this overview was needed to determine where Augeo could contribute the most.

GK: "We needed to know: what does the map of child abuse look like? And where are the gaps?"

MD: "And which strings can we pull – as a private actor? With a new map of child abuse and domestic violence, as well as those involved, it led to the questions: 'Who are they, and what are they doing? And how can we make a difference?' If you look at where your heart lies, you see: are we going to care for these children? Are we going to do anything for the parents? We say, no: we are a private actor. But where can we help, what is within our reach? That involves going to the people who are closest to the children. That is the professionals."

As a result of this analysis, the foundation produced a fourteen-page document in 2007 that detailed the landscape of child abuse in the Netherlands and the bottlenecks in the system of reporting and treatment. The report articulated Augeo's vision, mission, concept and strategy for activities and partnerships, positioning itself in a place of greater independence than other non-profit organisations.[1]

The vision of the Augeo Foundation is defined as a non-profit devoted to ensuring a safe environment in which children can be raised. The initial goals were defined as outreach to strengthen those professionals who work with children; to promote the implementation of proven effective methods; to stimulate cooperation with parties in the youth sector to combat fragmentation; and to promote research and outcome-based innovation.

In the Netherlands, tens of thousands of children experience physical abuse, psychological or emotional abuse, neglect, sexual abuse or a combination of the above. The report estimated 50,000 to 80,000 children are victims of abuse, and approximately 100,000 children are witnesses to domestic violence. The consequences of child abuse include a range of physical injuries, disease, increased risk of smoking, drug abuse, and psychiatric problems, as well as permanent developmental and neurobiological problems. The direct and indirect societal cost of child abuse and its consequences in the Netherlands is estimated to be at least €965 million per year.[2]

Taking note of what has been done to counter child abuse in the Netherlands, the document concludes that these measures taken together do not come close to addressing the scale of the problem. The efforts include the establishment of reporting hotlines; the development of support networks to counteract domestic violence; the development of an integrated child health policy in the organisation of school doctors; Professor Dantzig's effort of trial projects in four regions; the development of law on reporting code; legal measures prohibiting physical and emotional abuse in upbringing; and the installation of André Rouvoet as Minister of Youth and Family.[4] The report next identified a number of bottlenecks.

Because of a lack of coordination and communication, existing efforts overlapped and their effectiveness was less than the sum of their parts. The level of interest in the problem did not match its scale, and money spent on counteracting it was not proportionate to the societal cost. Efforts were fragmented between provinces, municipalities and private initiatives. Professionals who work with children were not equipped to recognise child abuse, which was not a mandatory element in the curricula of medicine, paediatrics, teacher's colleges or social work. The chain of communications and referral in youth care was also noted to be too slow: a number of institutions, each with their own waiting lists, intake and research procedures that unnecessarily overlapped.

Above all, there was a lack of training and expertise in proven methods, no unity in their application, insufficient reach, and a lack of therapy and support for abused children. Because of the limited impact of face-to-face training and the limitations of the trial regions approach, it was crucial to increase the scale. And scaling up was a business challenge that required a business approach. The document then identified those areas where the Augeo Foundation could do the most.

Reiterating the vision of putting children's rights and safety at the core of its mission, the document stresses those areas that need improvement, including increasing the participation of parents with relevant institutions, shortening the chain of support, and increasing use and reach of internationally recognised evidence-based methods. Then they arrived at the first concrete programme for implementation.

FROM VISION TO CONCEPT: "THINK BIG, BUT ACT SMALL AND FAST"

Having determined all the bottlenecks of the existing system and the professionals involved, Gemma Kobessen noted: "Then we had to decide what to focus on: we wanted to focus on a part of the problem that we as a private actor could make a difference. As Henk van den Breemen once said: *think big, but act small and fast.*" Mariëlle adds: "We decided that our vision for the next five years would focus on the professionalisation of the people who work with parents and children: they should be able to recognise child abuse and neglect, and to be able to talk about it and act upon it."

The vision, mission and national map were next translated into a concept and strategy. After concluding the bottleneck analysis, Augeo's concept document continues to describe organisational model with four main elements: the platform, the projects, the facilities and the fund.

The platform is the model of partnerships, identifying three tiers of partners: core partners, network partners and strategic partners. The core partners are key figures, actively involved in the field, who can play a central role in the implementation of specific projects. These include leaders of associations that deal with children, including general practitioners, leaders in paediatrics and educators. Network partners include comparable non-profits with whom to exchange research and advice. The work with strategic partners is to maximise large-scale impact. These include client organisations, international partners and the government.

The document elaborates on the choice for a partnership model that gathers all parties together for the wellbeing of children, from the level of the individual teacher and social worker up to the government.[5] On all levels the same questions guide the partnerships: what are we going to create? Who is going to do it? What are our specific goals? Answers to these questions lead to very specific partnership agreements on each layer.[6]

In this way, the vision and mission are shared among all stakeholders, not merely to improve communication, coordination and exchange of expertise, but also to share responsibility. As we shall see, once the Augeo Foundation enters into partnership with another institution, their role and responsibility are redefined. It is notable how effectively Augeo would transform other institutions for the better.

STRATEGY: NEW PARTNERSHIPS

The vision and national map led to the development of the concept. The concept in turn contains what Augeo calls its platform, or partnership model. The next step was to reach out to government and professional associations, and more than fifty agreements have been signed at the time of writing. The activities that followed, in publications and the development of educational products, resulted from these partnerships.

Augeo's first public-private partnership would be of a new kind. It would require both a private initiative and the luck of timing with the right partner in government, when André Rouvoet became Minister of Youth and Families in 2007.

GK: "The minister who was responsible could think conceptually. Minister Rouvoet was very good at that. He understood immediately. We sat down with him, and we arranged cooperation within ten minutes. What had we agreed on? We said we want to focus on professionals who work with children and families. And he understood. They are the ones who first have to signal which children are at risk, who need to know what they must do next, how to talk about it, and how to offer treatment. Minister Rouvoet understood very well how essential this was."

The vision and concept concerned a large-scale approach with a national focus, starting with a magazine and by offering courses to professionals for recognition and reporting – not face-to-face teaching but e-learning. The Augeo Foundation would develop these courses, and work to place child abuse and domestic violence on the political agenda. Was the government not capable of launching a programme like this?

GK: "Personally I think a few things were important. The first is that we really embraced the topic and wanted to make an impact; for example, not simply to develop teaching programmes, but to really reach professionals with that knowledge, and to change their attitudes and behaviour in cases of child abuse. The minister wanted this too, but he needed partners who would be able to have an impact, while his possibilities and budget were limited. He needed to prove to the public and political parties that the measures he took were effective.

"We were independent. An independent organisation with a vision. This was also very good for him. Not just the independence, idea and vision, but also the financial means. Those three things came together and this was very useful for the minister. He could see that this could work: they can get it on the agenda with me and also have the means to support it. He had to arrange the conditions and we could make the impact. That combination made it possible for us to come to an agreement so quickly.

"We basically presented him with a ready-made solution to implement, because he couldn't do that. He could set policy, but he couldn't implement it from his position."

This combination of policy set by the government and the vision, concept and implementation by an independent private organisation, brought about a new kind of public-private partnership. Mariëlle adds: "We made it very concrete for [minister Rouvoet] where it was clear what we would provide and what he would provide.

"We would establish an e-academy focused on tackling child abuse and neglect. He arranged that the Dutch Youth Institute provided content. We arranged that six hospitals in the country started piloting the e-materials. He arranged that the results of the pilot were spread by his department as an example of good practice in all kinds of meetings of the Ministry of Health.

"As a young starting organisation we could convince hospitals to participate in the e-learning project. At that time this was a very innovative way of teaching, because we were able to say that the minister supported the project in a public-private partnership. On the other hand, the minister could convince parliament that he was really investing in tackling child abuse and neglect.

"So, we needed each other to achieve a certain outcome, but we also didn't need each other too much, in the sense that he – so to speak – had to pay for it. But of course we could only do so from a position of financial independence."

The organisations with which the Augeo foundation has signed partnerships include a Utrecht hospital group, the Dutch General Practitioners Association, the Royal Dutch Association of Physical Therapists and the Association of Mental Health Care institutions. Together with these major associations, Augeo focuses on every stage of development and implementation of agreements to create and distribute content for Augeo's e-learning products.

In addition, dozens of partnerships have been signed with other research institutes, branch organisations, and professional associations who contribute concretely to development and distribution of products. These include research organisations, expert groups, reporting centres, as well as organisations focused on support, parenting, childcare, paediatrics, nursing, mental health, disability and related areas.[7] Each partnership unifies an existing organisation to Augeo's vision and mission, counteracting the previous fragmentation. In each partnership at every level, responsibility is shared, tasks are divided and paper commitments made concrete.

But when Mariëlle and Gemma first spoke with minister Rouvoet, none of this had been realised yet. They promised to reach 40 per cent of emergency medical personnel and general practitioners. A very great challenge lay ahead.

The first priority was to focus on educating professionals who work with children on recognition and reporting of child abuse. Between the sectors of education and medicine, it was decided to first target medical professionals, especially doctors and nurses of emergency departments, and general practitioners. The ambition was to make a big national impact.

IMPLEMENTATION: EDUCATIONAL ACTIVITIES

If we compare the 2007 concept document to the activities and impact of the Augeo Foundation today, it is notable how consistently and methodically the concept and its strategy were carried out. The vision, mission and partnership concept were translated into a strategy. They reached out to a broad range of sectors to develop a broad spectrum of activities. The core vision remained the driving force and reference point in the process of planning and implementation, measuring results against the goals set out in the vision and concept. These results were not only measured in the sales of educational products, but also in impact analyses of the amount of sold courses actually completed and applied.[8]

The idea, concept and means were attached to expertise and technology. And once this worked well, the same model could be multiplied in other places. In the beginning, the focus was to do one thing well and accomplish a meaningful impact there, before reproducing the concept in other areas. Today the Augeo Foundation is a thriving organisation that dominates the debate on child abuse, but it had to start small.

Augeo's first initiative was to enter the small 'market' of professionals with an investment in a magazine on child abuse, *Tijdschrijft Kindermishandeling* (TKM) in late 2007. In less than a year they took over the magazine completely.

Gemma Kobessen: "We first started with the magazine and then with the [partnership] platform. We had to buy into the market. It sounds very strange, but it is true. We told each other that we have to start with something concrete."

MD: "And visible."

GK: "And tangible. There was a magazine on child abuse. It existed, but it was in financial trouble, and they came knocking on our door. And that's how we started. We said that we are willing to help finance the magazine, but we also would like to have a greater say in it. And gradually we took over the magazine, while keeping all the relationships with the participating research institutes and experts intact."

MD: "That was a real lesson. Actually it was a very good start. There we actually learnt how this works. It came down to it that everyone carried on doing what they were doing, while trying to give us the feeling that we are thinking along with them. We said no, this is not how it's going to work. We'll be the publisher and editor-in-chief ourselves. This was a good exercise for *The Next Page*, which followed. We saw that if we were active, it makes a difference."

GK: "Yes, you don't just sponsor but actively carry out work yourself. Some people will resent that you won't finance the project that occupies them every day. I understand that. But it was quite difficult for a lot of people to see that these people weren't just going to write a cheque, but they also had ideas. And they also wanted to participate in the whole story as a partner. The magazine was the first step, but to reach professionals at a national level more was needed in a way that was as clear and accessible as possible: an e-academy. The first category of professionals was the medics."

The Next Page was launched, an e-academy that offers courses and 'webinars' (web seminars) targeted at professionals on a variety of subjects. At that time, e-learning was still very new. Worldwide interactive e-courses on child abuse and neglect were rare. Most people thought that such a sensitive issue could not be taught digitally.

Today, has expanded to more than forty courses for general practitioners, emergency room doctors and nurses, schoolteachers, foster parents, professionals in child support, nurses in day care and ambulance services. The subjects include recognition and reporting of abuse and domestic violence; learning what questions to ask; how to communicate about abuse; learning how to act; and preventive strategies. In addition, there is a variety of general courses on parenting, sexual abuse, legal considerations, children and trauma, long-term consequences, forced marriage, teenage behaviour, and domestic violence against adults.[9]

The first concept document for the digital academy was issued in January 2008. It notes that additional schooling for working professionals usually reaches fewer than 10 per cent, and the digital academy aims to bundle high-quality, inexpensive and efficient e-learning modules on children's rights, tailored to professionals. The document also sets a number of efficiency goals: to halve the time it takes to complete an average course, with a 90 per cent reduction of the cost, and to increase the reach of professionals from 10 to 40 per cent in the period 2008-2011. They would invest in high-quality technology and maximum accessibility, both in content and cost. Content for each module was to be supervised by content groups of experts.[10] There was a measure of trial and error in approaching partners, but Augeo would only work with parties with whom they had concrete agreements for cooperation.

This document further specified how the digital academy fitted into the platform of public-private partnership. The document recalls that as a signatory of the 1989 Convention of the Rights of the Child, the government shares ownership over addressing child abuse. Announcing the cooperation with Minister Rouvoet, the Augeo Foundation would complement and strengthen government policy.[11]

Mariëlle Dekker: "We started with the partnership platform. I remember the brainstorming sessions where we sketched this out: who would provide the expertise, who would do the implementation, who would do this and that. But we eventually managed to sell it to partners with the e-academy. We approached hospitals, and we actually got them excited about the idea. And then, according to our idea, we attached the expertise and the technology.

"What was interesting for the hospitals, I believe, was not the platform itself. What was interesting is that we approached them and said: you can now do something. You can address child abuse in a way that you want. It is possible to train all your staff year after year on this topic within a reasonable amount of time and money. And then we will work together on making that happen. We had a solution for them."

Gemma Kobessen: "When we approached hospitals, the process took months. Six hospitals in Utrecht eventually wanted to join the project. We made very concrete agreements, that they would take doctors' hours and nurses' hours and put them in a content group. And then we would make sure that the context would eventually appear in an attractive computer module.

"We started with the course 'Identifying Child Abuse' for doctors and nurses in hospital emergency departments. This is a module of about three hours digital learning, where all sorts of methods are discussed, teaching medical staff how to identify abuse.

"We had it scientifically tested by the Wilhelmina Children's Hospital (*Wilhelmina Kinderziekenhuis*). They did a proper randomised control trial of a group of medics and nurses who had taken the course and a group who hadn't. They were made do to a case study and it revealed three things. Those who had taken our course ask parents more and better questions, their judgment is better, and their reasoning is better."

In a study published in *Archives of Childhood Diseases*, one of the journals of the British Medical Association, two groups of nurses were compared: those who had done a *Next Page* course and a control group who had not. The module covered recognition of child abuse, acting and communication with simulations of clinical cases, video animations and interactive elements. In the area of child abuse and neglect studies, this was the first internationally published randomised control trial that measured the effects of a course on child abuse and neglect on the level of performance of attendees, revealing a positive impact:

> The total performance during post-test of the intervention group was significantly better than that in the control group, indicating that more adequate questions were asked, resulting in a higher quality of history taking. (...) Nurses trained in this programme asked more adequate questions to determine suspicion on child abuse. This is a positive finding, which might lead to the identification of more abused children. Furthermore, asking more of the right questions might decrease the false positive rate. In our hospital only 40% of the initially screened positives for child abuse are eventually referred for an intervention, on the basis of a strong suspicion or confirmation of child abuse.[12]

GK: "With the hospitals it's a great success. Over 80 per cent of hospitals now train their emergency personnel with our modules. We rolled out the programme for hospitals in no time. Recognition and reporting of child abuse in hospitals has tripled. We cannot show that this is only due to us, but I dare to say that we had something to do with it. That is a very real impact. The general practitioners noticed it too.

"This is also where the role of the government is so essential. Government inspectors told hospitals: you have to teach yourselves about child abuse and domestic violence. This is not taught in the basic curriculum.

"But then the government inspectors told them: it cannot be true that abuse does not occur here, because of all the children who need emergency treatment. Something has to be done. I am convinced that without the standards set by the inspections, we would not have over 80 per cent of the hospitals."

It is notable that investment is made primarily for impact. The Augeo Foundation has a charitable mission, but does so as a business selling educational products to target audiences. Nonetheless, with the focus on impact, they do more than a typical e-learning company would do. They have increased financial risk to deepen impact, and also carried out a detailed follow-up analysis, comparing the number of sold course licences to the number of courses actually completed. Because social impact is the primary focus rather than the financial return, the iterative process resumes, with Augeo maintaining active working relationships with the professionals of their target audience.

Gemma Kobessen noted: "In the past year we were at about 70 per cent of the break-even figure. We hope this improves in the coming year, but the priority is still the social impact, not the financial return. If it is a choice between reaching 100,000 professionals and not reaching break-even, or being break-even and reaching 50,000 fewer, we choose the former. In that sense this is very much a mission of a charitable foundation."

NEW LAWS, WIDENING FOCUS

The political environment is changeable and the government is not a stable partner. After the fall of the Labour-Christian coalition of Balkenende IV in 2010, the issues of child abuse and domestic violence were divided again among several departments. In implementing austerity measures, the next government pushed the topic even further away from the centre. Whereas in 1992, responsibility for action was passed to fifteen provincial governments, today it has been passed down to 440 municipalities. This fragmentation makes it nearly impossible to create a shared vision on any level of government. Nonetheless, some key national legislation has recently come into force.

Together with the Ministry of Public Health, the Augeo Foundation developed products for professionals that would be implemented with the passage of the Law on Reporting Code for Child Abuse and Domestic Violence (*Wet meldcode voor huiselijk geweld en kindermishandeling*), which eventually passed in early 2013 and went into force in July 2013.

While the impact has been deep among hospitals and general practitioners, the one sector that has been harder to reach is education. When on average each classroom may have one or two children who are victims of child abuse or domestic violence, teachers have a very important role to play in recognition and reporting.

GK: "But teachers do not feel equipped to act on this subject. They think it's too complicated. They will say: but we have a relationship of confidentiality with this family. They don't see it as their responsibility to do something about it, but we show that it is possible with our courses to learn how to deal with these sorts of dilemmas.

"You notice that educational institutions are waiting for the government inspectors to start checking it. They are just waiting: 'If the inspectors start asking questions, and when we have the Law on Reporting Code, we will do it. But we are so busy with all our teaching responsibilities, so this is considered an extra.' This is true, but it's clearly a sector that was awaiting developments.

"But we saw with the hospitals – and they are all busy too – when the inspectors came and told them to educate themselves on the topic, they started doing a lot more than was required by law. And that is really the added value. Of course, the government created the incentive, but we caught the wave and offered the means to do it. And what we offered had a lot more than was mandated by law.

"Take the magazine, for example. There are now a lot of nurses who read it. And then there is professional embarrassment. You really notice that with this issue. When you start educating professionals on the topic, they start to feel embarrassed, because they really start seeing things. And then they want to know more about it."

Since our first interview with Gemma and Mariëlle, the Law on Reporting Code was passed and went into force. Immediately, had a number of modules ready specifically tailored for teachers in elementary schools explaining recognition of abuse in context of the new law. Gemma adds: "In certain sectors impact has gone up to 40 per cent. Other sectors, such as education, are still behind, but now that the Law on Reporting Code has passed, we can target different sectors specifically. When we reach 15,000, we will have crossed the 15 per cent threshold. So we are definitely making an impact. In a way if you are already working successfully with other sectors, that gives you the leverage to approach new sectors. So it is definitely a very useful law. There are 100,000 teachers in the Netherlands, so there is work to be done, but we can then take it the Ministry of Education."

And what has been the impact of the Law of Reporting Code in the first six months? GK: "More research is needed, but four out of ten professionals say that their institution works with the Law on Reporting Code, and of those three-quarters understand how the law works. That's a 13 per cent rise since the last survey." With three out of ten professionals understanding the law properly, there remains room for improvement. What have been the results so far?

GK: "As of October 2013, over 100,000 course licences have been sold to nearly 35,000 professionals. There are 28,000 online readers of the magazine, and 13,000 subscriptions. And although it's early days with the education sector, 15 per cent of Dutch teachers have started courses with . Close to 80 per cent of Dutch hospitals and 40 per cent of general practitioners are teaching themselves with Augeo's online modules. Over 83 per cent of those who have completed courses feel better equipped to handle situations of child abuse."

The target for *The Next Page* in the 2008 concept document was to break even by 2010. This goal has not been met, but with the passage of the Law of Reporting Code and expansion into the educational sector it might well be soon.

The business approach applies to the organisational structure and to measuring impact. The hybrid approach between business and charity sets social impact as its goal, not money. The e-learning products are sold to professionals in the most accessible manner.

GK: "Because it is a difficult theme, we understood we needed to introduce it with a threshold as low as possible. If a doctor needs to take a course on diabetes, it's normal for him to pay a few hundred euros for it. He understands that. But for child abuse a doctor won't do that. So when we first offered courses, they were 10 euros each. The idea is that they should pay something for it because the responsibility does lie with the professional. They have to feel they are invested in it.

"But we also realised that it's more difficult to get the books balanced, because we invest in high quality. We invested a lot in the technology. And we have created a quality company with educational experts and quality people.

"But if you tell a story that you are offering courses as an organisation with a vision, and not just a club that's producing modules to make money, it makes a big difference to people. Our account managers tell us it helps a lot.

"And therefore we are working to bring more together in our structure. We first started this company and said: this has to be run effectively and efficiently. Now we are bringing more and more parts of the foundation together, and in this way, we carry more weight."

EVALUATION: A DURABLE VISION AND CONCEPT

The Augeo Foundation's 2007 document that spelled out the vision, mission, bottleneck analysis, partnerships platform and strategy for implementation is still standing strong. The foundation took the time to do proper research and to set their goals carefully. The original concept is continually tested in application, and results are measured against the goals in an iterative process, before the same approach is multiplied to create more courses and programmes and more sectors are targeted. *The Next Page* is a remarkable portal, and Augeo are clearly very proud of it. The concept is not only well designed, but it also reflects a firm vision and a clear method for implementation. There is continual attention to evaluate how many sold courses have actually been started (41 per cent in 2013) and completed (32 per cent), revealing room for improvement.

This attention includes the magazine; follow-up courses; lobbying the government; and expansion to turn the portal into an online community. The e-academy is expanding to become its own social network. This will deepen the engagement of professionals not just as consumers of course materials, but also as a community actively engaged in shaping content and as ambassadors for the shared vision and mission to protect children.

◎ Partners

The platform is thriving and has expanded to more than fifty partners, with more partnerships added in all three tiers of core partners, network partners and strategic partners.

For the core partnerships, Augeo has also expanded to reach out for those apples still on the tree. It does not only offer courses for professionals in the field; it received a subsidy from the Ministry of Public Health to develop course materials to be used in a number of colleges where future professionals in education and social work are being trained. This too will be complemented with a digital portal with its own social network as a community of learning, to be launched in 2015.

Other core partners have been mentioned earlier: the Utrecht hospital group, the Dutch General Practitioners Association, the Royal Dutch Association of Physical Therapists and the Association of Mental Health Care institutions. Augeo has succeeded in turning partnerships with these organisations into an integral part of the development of its course content, outreach, distribution, implementation and follow-up. The second tier has expanded to more than forty network partnerships with research institutes, branch organisations and professional associations.

On the third level, the principal strategic partner has been the Dutch government. The legislature passed the Law on Reporting Code, and the Ministry of Public Health subsidises the abovementioned project. The Ministry of Education may be approached in the near future regarding materials for the educational sector.

Because the government has devolved responsibility of tackling child abuse to the 440 municipalities in the same year that the Law on Reporting Code was passed, a new pamphlet emerged, *A Safe Home: A municipal vision for tackling domestic violence and child abuse*, which explains the new law to local councils. The Augeo Foundation has been involved in the background to help ensure that all the information on the accompanying website is accurate.

On the strategic level, Augeo is looking at expanding abroad, but this remains challenging. There are cultural differences between countries about what constitutes abuse, and these are sometimes reflected in legal differences.

The Augeo Foundation also participated in the quadrennial track-two report *Treating the effects of child abuse*, which was released in 2011. This lengthy English-language report was prepared in parallel with a government report on the subject by the Health Council of the Netherlands (an NGO) presented to the United Nations in 2014.

◎ Vision for the Future

The vision is kept alive, and the concept is durable, both to expand operations and to keep their own staff motivated.

GK: "It is something we are proud of. This is something we keep telling our team: we are doing something very special here. We feel that our conceptual thinking matches the technology. We started with basic technology, but it still works beautifully for our modules. We are constantly thinking about a platform where all sorts of things happen.

"There is continual learning, for which you see a lot of triggers on the website. A few things are free, and then you get to a paid environment where you can learn about a number of areas. And if you really want to deepen your understanding, there are some very advanced professional modules as well.

"But we also notice in the organisation, both internally and outwardly, that the why – why we do it together – is very essential if you are constantly working on it. That makes you different from other organisations.

"People kept saying that also – and we almost forgot it in our daily work. Now we emphasise this often together. And they are very proud of the work they are doing. It gives us energy, and it shows outwardly: that's why they went to work for this company, or attached themselves to this foundation."

But other creative ideas are also circulating, concerning volunteers and people who may be close to vulnerable children: "Every weekend there are 300,000 volunteers with a million children on sports fields, and we can provide something for that group, to give them a grasp of how to be more of a supporting figure for children, say Augeo's founders." In this way the same concept is expanding more deeply into new sectors, with a new focus on using the exisiting family and local support networks to signal and tackle cases of child abuse when they occur. In November 2014, they launched their first outreach to the general public with the magazine *KIND* (*Child*), which was inserted into the *Volkskrant*, the highest-circulation daily in the Netherlands reaching half a million people.

The goal of this outreach is to help realise a new goal of Augeo: to encourage children who have experienced abuse to find a support figure from their immediate environment, such a grandparent, aunt, neighbour or teacher. Mariëlle adds: "Much scholarship on this subject agrees that having a support figure can be one of the decisive factors for recovery from traumatic childhood experiences. *KIND* magazine provides the public with information about childhood traumas, their consequences and the positive effects of social support. Depending on the outcomes of this, we are considering publishing a sequel. In 2015 we will launch additional projects to stimulate social support for children who have experienced abuse."

CONCLUSION

And how do they feel about all that has been accomplished so far? Mariëlle answers: "I think that we are blessed with a continual sense of dissatisfaction – in the positive sense of the term. We are just not there yet. We really want to mean something for those children and for those parents. It's still amazing to us that we don't yet have a hundred thousand professionals doing this. Our targets are set very high, but then you look back and think: I would never have imagined we would come this far five years ago. In my last job I was happy with each general practitioner who came to take a course. Now they all flock online. I'm actually very happy, but at the same time there is always more to accomplish."

Gemma adds: "I want to do something out of the box again. I'm very happy with what we have created, and it's substantial. We were awarded the [biannual] Van Dantzig Prize [in 2010], which had also been awarded to Minister Rouvoet [in 2008]. This was recognition from the world of tackling child abuse that our approach was appreciated. I am very proud of that."

The Augeo Foundation and their activities are a good example of innovation tied to a process which is gradually forcing a breakthrough in the Netherlands on a difficult subject. The vision and mission to make a meaningful change for children on a national scale was made possible by a combination of key factors. These are a clear vision and mission to help children on a national scale, a vision that energises a highly motivated team and which must be shared to enter into a partnership with Augeo. This shared vision is the precondition for creating a genuine shared responsibility. A well-balanced shared vision can overcome differences in roles.

The original 2007 concept document articulates the vision, mission, partnership platform, and strategy for implementation. It contained a very comprehensive national map of every aspect of the recognition, reporting, treatment and follow-up capacities of child abuse and domestic violence in the Netherlands, identifying the bottlenecks in the system and with a level of business professionalism that is rare for NGOs.

The vision and mission lead to partnerships. The platform concept that categorises three levels of partners (core, network and strategic) contains the strategy. In this way, the vision leads to a partnership concept, which connects the vision of the foundation to expertise in the field. The next step is to turn these relationships into workshops that develop the content, which makes it into the magazine, or together with the technology of the e-learning portal, into high-quality digital course content.

Because each stage and each relationship is defined and planned in the concept, and because the concept is applied and expanded into each course, programme and initiative, the connection between the vision and each activity is maintained throughout. Augeo's modus operandi contains one of the most comprehensively structured iterative processes that we have come across in our studies for this volume. The principle of 'think big, but act small and fast' is central.

There is an iterative process in taking a business approach to measuring impact, which is continually measured against goals set and the means to attain them. It is not enough to have a good idea. It is not enough to have money. It is also not enough to have money and an idea, because a breakthrough will not be accomplished without a process where each stage is defined, described and planned.

The platform of partnerships not only categorises partners in three tiers, but spells out how responsibility is shared. What was remarkably consistent in each and every institution that Gemma and Mariëlle approached (or were approached by) is that they effectively changed other organisations for the better by genuinely sharing responsibility. This was not about throwing money at a problem, but supplying a vision, mission and strategy, and managing substance and the process of implementation themselves.

When the magazine *Tijdschrift Kindermishandeling* approached them for financial support, their condition was to have an active say and then they took over the magazine completely. When they approached the Association of General Practitioners, who were unwilling to participate in developing course content, they understood quickly that it was not going to work. When they developed the early courses for emergency personnel, they developed them with emergency personnel. In announcing partnership with the government, the document first emphasised that as a signatory of the Convention of the Rights of the Child, the government shares ownership of responsibility for this problem. Every partner that has the honour to work with the Augeo Foundation has to share responsibility and is transformed for the better by this process.

Assuming responsibility and reminding others of their responsibility about a difficult problem can be unpleasant if it disrupts the status quo. But that is precisely the point.

CHAPTER 19

IMPACT INVESTING AND SOCIAL RENEWAL

The global financial crisis and the accounting scandals of large companies have stimulated a new assessment of the contribution of enterprises and financial institutions to economic prosperity and the greater public good. This assessment has led to a re-evaluation of the relationship of businesses to their stakeholders and to underlying economic structures. It has also drawn attention to the ideas of social entrepreneurship and impact investing. In this chapter we explore these ideas by considering their philosophical basis in light of corporate social responsibility. We present six case studies: Grameen Bank, Tendris, two initiatives by the Noaber Foundation and two by DOB Equity for Africa. These social entrepreneurs and impact investors are distinguished by their social objectives, values and worldview, with a focus on the justified interests of all stakeholders. In the next decade, social entrepreneurs and impact investors will become a growing new investment sector and play an increasing role in global development.

THE QUALITATIVE ANALYSIS FOR THIS CHAPTER
IS ON PAGE 395 OF THE ANNEX

WITH PIETER DE RIJCKE AND PAUL BAAN.
TEXT BY MAARTEN VERKERK

INTRODUCTION

In 2008 the world economy was shaken to its foundations. The bankruptcies of Bear Stearns and Lehman Brothers marked the beginning of a financial crisis that spread across the world. Many people lost their jobs, large banks went bust, and several countries and cities came close to bankruptcy. The crisis also increased injustice in the world. A price was paid in rich countries by members of the lower classes who lost jobs, savings, pensions and homes; and by poorer countries whose economies collapsed. In retrospect, the financial crisis cannot be seen as an isolated incident. It was preceded by a number of accounting scandals and bankruptcies that indicated that something was going wrong: Waste Management in 1998, Enron in 2001, WorldCom in 2002, HealthSouth in 2003, Freddie Mac in 2003, and the American International Group (AIG), which had its own executive accounting scandal in 2005 and was at the centre of the financial crisis of 2008. Since the crisis, many measures have been proposed and executed to restore trust in the financial world, especially in new legislation and additional supervision. Opinions about the causes of the crisis vary.

Supporters of the free market believe that the present market is not free enough. They argue that regulation and interventions by governments and international institutions disturb the market. Others believe that the crisis was caused by flaws in our financial system and that the imperfections have to be repaired. Others believe that the fundamentals of our economy are wrong. They plead for a fundamental rethinking of our present economic order.[1] Even long before the crisis, Christian economists have argued for the development of a new paradigm based on Christian values like solidarity and justice.[2]

The aftermath of the financial crisis opened the door to a thorough assessment of the contribution of enterprises and financial institutions to the greater public good and economic prosperity. In this chapter we focus on one of the results of that assessment: a plea for social enterprises and impact investing. How are these terms defined?

Following concerns in recent decades that philanthropy was leading to dependency without fundamental improvements, the first steps were taken to combine philanthropy with business. This was first called 'active philanthropy', which later became 'venture philanthropy', making charities more business-like. With the introduction of the terms 'social venturing' and 'social enterprise', a greater emphasis was placed on the conduct of business with a positive social outcome. New company and charity structures to this effect are now recognised in the laws of several countries.[3] Today the expressions 'social enterprise', 'social entrepreneur' and 'social business' are fairly well established. From the investor's point of view, different expressions are used: 'impact investing', 'social finance', 'mission-related investments' and 'blended investments'. The term 'impact investing' is used most often today, and we prefer it because it most clearly expresses the intention of investors: to make a social and societal impact. The essence of impact investing is the manner in which it makes a social impact by connecting parties and stakeholders.

Social entrepreneurs and impact investors believe that social goals can go hand in hand with financial returns. Many of them think that the primary objective of an enterprise is to contribute to the public good and view profit as a means to guarantee a sustainable contribution. The Global Impact Investing Network defines impact investing as 'investments made into companies, organizations, and funds with the intention to generate social and environmental impact alongside a financial return (...) and target a range of returns from below market to market rate, depending upon the circumstances.'[4] This definition shows that social enterprises and impact investors are distinguished by having the intention to generate social and environmental impact with an eye on sustainability and the long term, by accepting short-term returns below a market to market rate. This network is expanding each year and combined assets designated for impact investing are projected to reach $1 trillion by the end of this decade.

The objective of this chapter is to explore the ideas of social enterprises and impact investors with the background of the financial crisis. I would like to answer three questions:

a) What are social enterprises and how do impact investors act?

b) Do social enterprises and impact investors represent a new paradigm?

c) Can social enterprises and impact investors effectively address economic and social problems in Western society and the wider world?

This chapter has three parts, starting with an analysis of the financial crisis. With philosophical considerations about the relationship of business to the economy and society, we consider the financial crisis and the accounting scandals to get a deeper insight into what went wrong. We argue that the problems in the financial sector are not an isolated incident but symptoms of a wider societal problem in which financial standards replace all social values and people are reduced to instruments rather than ends in themselves. In the second part, we consider several case studies of social enterprises and impact investors. In the final part, we examine the nature of social enterprise in relation to the problems that underlie the financial crisis. Are social enterprises a viable solution? We explore the role and potential of social enterprises and impact investors for the future of global development.

PART I: THE FINANCIAL CRISIS AS MORAL CRISIS

What went wrong in the world of finance? Why did so many CEOs take such huge risks? Why did so many directors engage in fraud? A detailed analysis of the financial crisis and the accounting scandals goes beyond the objective of this chapter. But in order to judge whether social enterprises and impact investing embody a fundamental rethinking we have to understand some of the main characteristics of the financial crisis and the different accounting scandals. Many books have been written on these, but I will base my analysis on three authoritative sources: the documentary *Inside Job* about the financial crisis, the book *Too Big to Fail* about the fall of Lehman Brothers and its consequences, and the book *The Smartest Guys in the Room* about Enron.

In *The Smartest Guys in the Room: The Amazing Rise and the Scandalous Fall of Enron*, Bethany McLean and Peter Elkind provide an inside view. It starts in 1984 when Ken Lay becomes the CEO of Houston Natural Gas and ends with the collapse of Enron in 2001. Along the way it describes the development of new financial products; the method of mark-to-market accounting that led to overrating; the fraudulent financial constructions of hiding debt in subsidiary companies; the corporate culture of vicious competition; and the hubris of its main characters. Finally, it tells the story of an enterprise that abandoned its roots, which lay in providing society with good services.[5] Enron is not an isolated scandal but a "symptom of a system that fails on all points". [6]

The international bestseller *Too Big to Fail* by Andrew Ross Sorkin gives an inside view of Wall Street and the bankruptcy of the Lehman Brothers investment bank. It reveals what happened behind closed doors and describes the actions of the leading figures in this financial drama. It tells the story of the "fallibility of people who thought they themselves were too big to fail". Sorkin provides an in-depth insight into their personalities, their hunger for power and their greed.[8]

The 2010 documentary *Inside Job* by Charles Ferguson provides a staggering report on financial malpractices. It tells the story of new financial products with large risks that drove companies, shareholders and customers to the abyss. Deregulation of financial service industries led to high-risk investments with customers' savings and to large-scale lending, where in some cases the leverage ratio of lending exceeded thirty times the assets of a bank; or in the case of Iceland, loans taken out in excess of ten times the size of the country's GDP. These were margin levels comparable to the prelude of the crash of 1929. It shows that deregulation enabled the creation of a chain where all risk was passed on and exposure was maximised, but no one was responsible: the homeowner's mortgage and debts to the local lender were bought up by large investment banks, who bundled debts to create derivative investment products.

These products in turn were sold to investors, but also insured, swapped and passed on as new insurance investments. The same investment bank would simultaneously sell a product to clients while betting on its failure. Very few understood the complexity of this increasingly unstable system, in which CEOs and traders rewarded themselves with short-term premiums and bonuses while passing losses on to others. They lost sight of long-term risks and isolated themselves from the wider economy, society and even their own companies. They eventually gambled not only with their clients' and investors' funds, but also with their own firms and the entire financial system. The cover of the DVD ironically notes that the film cost over $20,000,000,000,000 to make!

"The core of the problem of the financial crisis is the single-minded pursuit of shareholder value. As a result, banks have abandoned their core objective: to fund enterprise." — **Pieter de Rijcke**

We can draw on the so-called 'practices model' to understand the financial crisis and accounting frauds. This model was developed by the philosophers Jochemsen, Glas and Hoogland.[9] A big advantage is that it encourages us to understand professional practices and institutions from three different perspectives: the intrinsic nature and purpose of the enterprise (*structure*), its roots in society (*context*), and the basic beliefs that motivate its actors and their culture (*direction*).[10]

◎ Structure

The *structure* of a practice refers to the intrinsic nature of a practice and the formal aspects of an organisation. It has to do with the nature of the primary process, its organisational structure, procedures and code of conduct. The discussions induced by the crisis and the accounting scandals focused on the 'rules of the game': statutory regulations, internal procedures, and supervision. Better rules and more supervision are required to prevent new crises and scandals. Consequently, in the whole of the Western world accounting principles for business and the regulation of banks are being extended and sharpened, and supervision has been intensified.

In general, I agree with the call for more rules and supervision. However, this call can easily lead the conversation away from the core issue—namely, that practices and their structures primarily concern their 'internal goods', 'essence' or 'excellence', as defined by the philosopher Alasdair MacIntyre, who in turn draws upon Aristotle.[11] The idea of 'internal goods' refers to the values that are realised specifically by those practices.

The internal goods concern the legitimacy of an enterprise's 'licence to operate' or 'right to exist'. The internal goods of healthcare are cure and care for patients, and the internal goods of banking are financial services for citizens and enterprises. For Plato in *The Republic*, the essence of a physician is the extent to which he is a healer. As a corollary to his work, the doctor makes money; but being a money-maker is not an essential part of the definition of a physician.[12]

The idea of 'internal goods' is contrasted with the idea of 'external goods', which are those goods that are external to the aims realised by the practice, e.g. prestige, status and money. Being a rich or famous doctor is not a part the essence of the practice of medicine, which serves to benefit the patient. The private benefit to the physician is the external good.

The idea of 'excellence' emphasises that practices are not about average performance but about excellent performance according to the aim of the pursuit and the standards in the sector. MacIntyre emphasises that the realisation of excellence in internal goods requires virtues that are characteristic of that practice. That means, in his modern reinterpretation of Plato's and Aristotle's philosophy, 'excellence' and 'virtues' are directly related.[13]

Additionally, in the ethics of Aristotle the idea of 'happiness' (*eudaimonia*) is not a short-lived emotion, but a term that implies a lifelong 'living well' and 'faring well' according to fulfillment of the potential and highest abilities of human nature.[14] The ideas of 'internal goods', 'excellence', and 'virtues' clearly show where business institutions failed. The focus was shifted from 'internal' goods to 'external' goods. The primary purpose of a business is to provide excellent goods and services, to which profits are a corollary. Losing sight of the primary purpose means replacing excellence with profits, and reducing virtues to targets.[15] In addition, long-term sustainability was replaced by short-term focus on profits and bonuses.[16] Robert Solomon describes this financial focus as 'abstract greed' because in his view it has nothing to do with 'real wants, real needs, or real expectations'.[17]

◎ Context

The *context* of a practice refers to the influence of the environment on professional practices and the organisations in which they are embedded. It refers to the network of stakeholders that exert influence on the organisation.

In business ethics there are two approaches with respect to stakeholders. Milton Friedman argues that business corporations have only one social responsibility: to increase their profits.[18] Consequently, a corporate executive should focus on only one stakeholder: the owners or shareholders. Friedman believes in the free market, denies social responsibilities other than increasing profits, understands society as a 'collection of individuals' and of the various groups they 'voluntarily form', and states that business has to stay 'within the rules of the game' (legislation). On the other hand, R. Edward Freeman argues for a broader stakeholder approach. In his view, stakeholders whose interests are affected by an enterprise have a right to make a claim.[19] That means that a corporate executive has to balance the multiple claims of (conflicting) stakeholders.

He acknowledges that business has a normative core that reflects 'liberal notions of autonomy, solidarity, and fairness as articulated by John Rawls, Richard Rorty and others'. The financial crisis and accountancy scandals show that the Friedmanian approach dominates in many organisations.[20] From a philosophical point of view, a 'double reduction' takes place. First, the broader societal context of stakeholders is reduced to shareholders. Second, the interests of shareholders are reduced to short-term financial interests.

◎ Direction

The *direction* refers to the basic beliefs that underlie the professional practices and institutions in which they are embedded. *Inside Job, Too Big to*

Fail and *The Smartest Guys in the Room* clearly show that many financial institutions and industrial corporations believe in the idea of the free market, deregulation by governments, maximisation of profits, and fierce competition. John Gray goes one step further. He describes the present business climate as a utopia that spurs its followers to a blessed future and legitimates any action to realise that future.[21] John Cassidy describes the rising influence of what he calls 'utopian economics' that is blind to how real people act and denies the many ways an unregulated free market can produce disastrous unintended consequences.[22] From a philosophical point of view, I would like to emphasise the direction component of a practice in general and the values and beliefs that underlie organisations in particular. Worldviews, values and basic beliefs not only determine the way we observe the world but also guide our understanding of reality and even steer the way we shape the world.[23] The idea of the financial world as a 'professional practice' was very helpful in analysing the financial crisis and its features. I draw three preliminary conclusions.

First, regarding *structure*, the financial industry has lost sight of its primary calling. This industry focuses its attention on maximising turnover and profits instead of delivering excellent financial products that serve customers and contribute to society's long-term prosperity.

Second, regarding *context*, the financial industry has lost its roots in society. It concentrates its efforts on serving the financial interests of shareholders instead of the financial and non-financial interests of all stakeholders.

Third, regarding *direction*, the financial industry is in the firm grip of the ideology of the free market. A worldview or ideology functions not only as a guide for action but also as a pair of glasses with which to observe society and to legitimate its ideas. The analysis of the financial crisis and accounting scandals showed that key players in the business and financial world were profit-driven, focused on the interests of the shareholders, believed in the free market, and rejected control by the government.

INCIDENT OR SYMPTOM?

"The financial crisis finds its origin in 'self-interest'. The financial world and the business community had created their own world. They forgot that they were part of a larger whole. They forgot that 'shareholder value' and 'profit' are only means to reach societal goals (...) Short-term profit was at the expense of long-term sustainability (...) Perhaps the most devastating development was a new split between the public and the private. The public sector became responsible for the common goods and so the private sector could narrow its focus to individual needs. This new split made the public sector into a 'cost area' and the private sector a 'profit area'. All the problems in the field of common goods (social security, healthcare, environment) can only be solved by cooperation between the public and the private sectors." — **Paul Baan**

"There is a big difference between enterprises quoted on the stock exchange and enterprises that are owned by families. Generally, the former have a short-term orientation and the latter a long-term orientation." — **Pieter de Rijcke**

How should we understand the problems in the financial world? Are they limited to this sector or are they a symptom of a wider problem? There is a lot of evidence that the problems of the financial sector are not an isolated incident but a symptom of a more general societal problem. We noted that the financial crisis was preceded by a number of accounting scandals in the industry, revealing that fraud, violation of laws and the disregard of the justified interests of stakeholders were widespread. Another signal is the large number of environmental disasters caused by major companies who had cut corners on safeguards, such as the Gulf of Mexico oil spill (BP), the Niger Delta (Shell), Bhopal (Union Carbide), Love Canal (Hooker Chemical), Minamata Bay (Chisso Corporation), Exxon Valdez (Exxon), and Three Mile Island (General Public Utilities Corporation). Although every scandal, fraud and disaster has its own characteristics, analysis shows that in nearly every case maximising short-term profit while neglecting the justified interests of stakeholders can play a dominant role.

Critical scholars warn that the ideology of a market economy penetrates other sectors of our society. For example, in *What Money Can't Buy: The Moral Limits of Markets*, Michael Sandel argues that market values are penetrating every aspect of our lives. He illustrates by a number of examples how personal and social goods like health, education, family life, nature, art and civic duties, as well as national security and public safety, are being turned into commodities that can be priced and traded, corroding their intrinsic meaning and value. He signals that Western society "drifted from *having* a market economy to *being* a market society."[24]

Sandel's warning is confirmed by Michael Porter and Elizabeth Olmsted Teisberg in the field of healthcare. *In Redefining Health Care: Creating Value-Based Competition on Results* (2006), they present an analysis of the healthcare system in the USA. They note that healthcare has lost its primary calling: it is not focused on value for patients. Further, they show that healthcare institutions concentrate on their own financial outcomes instead of the interests of all stakeholders involved. Consequently, they plead for a radical re-orientation of healthcare. They write: "Ironically, the solution to the crisis lies in refocusing the healthcare system on health."

The problems in the financial sector are not an isolated incident but a symptom of a wider societal problem in which people are viewed instrumentally. If people are not considered ends in themselves, but only as a means to profit or prestige, then it leads to the three fundamental problems that underlie the financial crisis: a loss of the primary calling of businesses to provide excellent goods or services; a loss of societal embedment; and a loss of non-financial values.

To return to Plato's example of the physician: the loss of his primary calling will reduce the role of the physician to that of technician and moneymaker, in which the patient is a means to serve the doctor or the business that is the hospital. In a sense, this instrumental treatment of the patient also leads to a loss of identity of the physician, who would have ceased to focus on the inherent excellence of the art of medicine. In the case of businesses, the sacrifice of excellence for short-term profit can lead to indifference, a loss of identity of the company, and ultimately to collapse.

If companies lose the connection to the society in which they are embedded, they will neglect their responsibility to all stakeholders except the shareholder. Banks judge people by abstractions without knowing them; companies are indifferent to the wider society in which they operate, and do not see the connection between their own profitability and the wider social and public good of a prosperous society.

These are related to the third problem: the loss of non-financial values, when the drive for profit erases any sense of justice. In other words, the financial values that govern the economy (economic prosperity) and the social values that build society (public good) are disconnected. These three losses are the long-term moral causes of the financial crisis and accountancy scandals that we have described above.

In the next section, I consider six initiatives by social enterprises and impact investors, who are driven by a concern for the public good and combine business objectives with the aim of a sustainable social impact. The objective is to investigate whether these initiatives and organisations provide a fundamental solution to the problems revealed by the financial crisis.

PART II: SOCIAL ENTERPRISES AND IMPACT INVESTING

Social enterprises have the potential and capability to reconnect financial values with the public good. It is possible for impact investors to address pressing societal problems that are not addressed effectively either by the government or by the market.[25] If our analysis of the financial crisis makes sense, then social entrepreneurs and impact investors focus on excelling in adding value to society ('internal goods', 'excellence'); recognition of the justified interests of all stakeholders; and values like sustainability, stewardship, justice and peace.

In this section we will consider six varied examples of social enterprises and impact investing in the areas of finance, sustainability, health and agriculture. Each of these is an example of a profitable business, but also motivated by a desire to make a lasting positive social impact: Grameen Bank (microfinance) and Tendris (sustainability), two projects by the Noaber Foundation (healthcare) and two by DOB Equity for Africa (food). Paul Baan founded and leads the Noaber Foundation; and Pieter de Rijcke's family founded the *Stichting De Oude Beuk*, renamed the DOB Foundation, which trades under

DOB Equity for Africa. With pioneering initiatives, they put social ventures and impact investing on the map in the Netherlands. They also took the initiative of endowing a chair in Social Venturing Economics at Tilburg University in the Netherlands.

◎ Grameen Bank and Tendris

"I am in favour of strengthening the freedom of the market. At the same time, I am very unhappy about the conceptual restrictions imposed on the players in the market. This originates from the assumption that entrepreneurs are one-dimensional human beings, who are dedicated to one mission in their business lives—to maximise profit. This interpretation of capitalism insulates entrepreneurs from all the political, emotional, social, spiritual and environmental dimensions of their lives. This was done perhaps as a reasonable simplification, but it stripped away the very essentials of human life."
– Muhammad Yunus, 2006 Nobel Lecture

The world's most famous social enterprise is the Grameen Bank, founded by the Nobel laureate Muhammad Yunus. He launched a research project in Bangladesh to study how to provide banking services to the rural poor. This research resulted in a bank that delivers small loans (microcredits) to the impoverished without requiring collateral. A group-based approach is applied to use pressure from the other members of the group to stimulate a responsible use of the money and to ensure repayment. The Grameen Bank gives small loans to the poorest of the poor, many of them women. In October 1983 the Grameen Bank was authorised by national legislation to operate as an independent bank. In the period from 1976 to 2009, the cumulative disbursement was $8.7 billion with nearly 8 million borrowers, of whom 97 per cent were women. In the year 2009, the total disbursement was $1.15 billion, with an end-of-year outstanding loan book of $790 million. The loan recovery rate is an impressive 96.7 per cent.[26]

The second example is Tendris, established in the Netherlands in 2002 by a group of entrepreneurs concerned with sustainability. Tendris believes that the big issues of our era like climate change, depletion of raw materials, hunger and drought can be solved by thinking and acting differently. Tendris also believes that people can be invited to adopt a sustainable lifestyle by offering real solutions that increase the quality of life by using a commercial approach. Its mission is 'to make the world a better place' by offering 'relevant products that contribute to this way of life'. Tendris has established among others Lemnis, a company producing LED lamps, and Innolumis, a company that offers public lighting solutions. One of Tendris's new projects focuses on pumps based on disc stream technology to develop less expensive and more fuel-efficient pumps for developing countries. Its mission focuses on supporting the development of commercially viable and environmentally sustainable solutions.[27]

⊚ The Noaber Foundation: VitalHealth Software and the Netherlands Institute for Prevention and Early Diagnosis

"Classical charitable foundations are limited, because the method of donating often does not result in a sustainable impact on society. It was decided to create a combination of a classical foundation and a commercial enterprise. This way of thinking was quite innovative: both the government and the business community were not used to it. The classical foundation hides a tension: it is fiscally and legally designed for the long term, but donating is mainly a short-term act. We wanted to run the foundation in such a way that it could make a long-term impact on society. However, in the financial world the word 'social venturing' did not come across. It was interpreted as a 'soft' way of investing. Later on, we used the term 'impact investing' and framed this way of investing as a new asset class."   **– Paul Baan**

The Noaber Foundation pioneered impact investing in the Netherlands, and aims to achieve structural transformations in healthcare by encouraging innovation, especially in the nexus of healthcare and information technology. The objective is to contribute to sustainable healthcare, in view of demographic changes and the increase in costs.[28] Our healthcare system's current activities are mainly triggered by the occurrence of symptoms. Our knowledge of risk factors that lead to life-threatening diseases is increasing, and preventive measures to influence specific risk factors have been shown to prevent or slow down relevant disease processes.

The increased acknowledgement of the importance of risk reduction and disease prevention has renewed a focus on developing effective prevention and health maintenance strategies. The Noaber Foundation was closely associated with the establishment of two social enterprises: VitalHealth Software and the Netherlands Institute for Prevention and Early Diagnosis (NIPED).

Together with the Mayo Clinic, the Noaber Foundation launched VitalHealth Software in 2006.[29] The key idea was to combine the best medical expertise of Mayo Clinic with the information technology and entrepreneurial experience of the Noaber Foundation by developing cloud-based eHealth solutions for managing chronic diseases such as diabetes, chronic obstructive pulmonary disease, heart failure, cancer, Alzheimer's and depression. Its headquarters is in Ede, the Netherlands, and it has locations in the US, India and Germany.

VitalHealth defines itself as an *impact-driven enterprise*. The idea of 'impact' determines its mission, vision, business processes and reporting. VitalHealth defines its mission as 'improving the health of millions of people through eHealth solutions'. This mission is made concrete for patient empowerment (2016 target: 10 million impacted patients), medical professional empowerment (2016 target: 50,000 impacted professionals), and number of diseases (2016 target: 10 impacted diseases).

Social Impact Indicators are reported quarterly and are part of the bonus and incentive system at all levels. Such a social return on investment calculations plays an increasingly leading role in sales pitches and development priorities.

The Netherlands Institute for Prevention and Early Diagnosis was established in 2004.[30] It has forged an alliance of physicians, scientists, social investors, corporate partners and government agencies to develop and launch an evidence-based knowledge and decision support (KDS) system for personalised prevention. This system was marketed under the name PreventionCompass and developed in accordance with stepwise care principles and the Chronic Care Model. It is based on evidence-based algorithms, test and treatment thresholds, scientific guidelines and best practices.

To raise awareness and inspire individuals to take specific actions to promote their health, design and communication is based on behavioural frameworks, including motivational interviewing, protection motivation theory, stage theories and social cognitive theory. The PreventionCompass links a personal risk profile to a tailored health maintenance programme, including self-management modules, best-practice lifestyle services and medical follow-up.

The knowledge and decision support system also allows for regional adaptations. It has a modular structure that integrates risk profiling for various chronic diseases, including cardiovascular diseases, diabetes, kidney disease, common mental disorders, chronic obstructive pulmonary disease, musculoskeletal disorders and some frequently occurring cancer types for which early detection is meaningful. The risk profiling includes a web-based questionnaire (medical and family history, lifestyle, motivation, personality), biometrics (blood pressure, body mass index, waist circumference) and laboratory evaluation of blood, urine and faeces. The application of the PreventionCompass supports the following goals:

a) To organise quality-assured multi-disease prevention without labour-intensive involvement of professionals;

b) To stimulate and facilitate behaviour risk intervention and surveillance;

c) To facilitate scientific research and dynamic guideline development.

The PreventionCompass was first implemented and evaluated in the occupational health field where it has been shown to be feasible and to stimulate individuals to undertake health-promoting action resulting in a healthier lifestyle, a decreased cardiovascular risk profile and a 20 per cent reduction in absenteeism.[31] In 2010 the NIPED developed with a number of medical organisations the so-called PreventionConsult.[32] This is a web-based health risk assessment of cardio-metabolic risk and lifestyle management.[33] A large-scale feasibility and cost-effectiveness study of primary care was carried out.

This initiative was received with a lot of enthusiasm. However, the times appeared not to be ripe for preventive healthcare: the turnover of the enterprise did not meet expectations. The worsening economic conditions appeared to be the last straw: turnover dropped further and the company went bankrupt in May 2013. At the same time, a new marketing strategy was developed and new implementation plans were made. The Noaber Foundation was one of the impact investors who made a relaunch of this important social initiative possible. The new approach is gradually beginning to pay off: the company is now making a profit.

◎ DOB Equity: Tanga Fresh and Prothem

"De Oude Beuk evolved over the years into DOB Equity. The objective of this foundation is to provide growth capital to enterprises in East African countries. Among others we invest in Burundi, Kenya and Tanzania. In these types of countries, particular initiatives and entrepreneurship are required to support economic development. We learned that investments could only be successful when there is a solid entrepreneur involved and when the activities are well embedded in the local context. We do not select entrepreneurs who offer the highest financial return on investment but entrepreneurs who focus their attention on sustainable businesses that contribute to the development of the local population. In other words, we pursue both financial and non-financial values."   **– Pieter de Rijcke**

DOB Equity is an independent, long-term investor in companies in East Africa.[34] It invests in companies that will contribute positively to a more social and sustainable society while delivering long-term profitability. The fund is evergreen, with all proceeds from investments reinvested, making it a true long-term growth partner to portfolio companies. Here we highlight two of DOB Equity's Africa projects: tea growing in Burundi and milk production in Tanzania. Both cases show how the programmes provide stability and continuity for smallholders who were otherwise at the mercy of either state-based or private monopolies. This cup of milky tea is designed to change the social and economic context.

In Tanzania, the climate is divided between the wet season and the dry season: milk production is abundant in the wet season and low in the dry. Together with others, DOB Equity invested in Tanga Fresh, the main dairy processor in Tanzania, founded in 1996. Tanga Fresh is co-owned by Tanzania Dairy Cooperative Union (TDCU), a cooperative of more than 4,000 smallholders who are guaranteed that their milk will be bought by Tanga Fresh whatever the season. This continuity guarantees the income of smallholders, which allows them to invest with an eye on the long term. New mechanisms have emerged, with auctions allowing farmers to buy a cow on credit while paying it off with milk earnings.

Tanga Fresh has built and improved the whole supply chain of milk from the Tanga region production area to market in the capital, Dar es Salaam. The DOB Equity investment was used to develop a new processing plant with a capacity of at least 50,000 litres per day. The combination of ownership by the supplying smallholders and a private investor, in combination with independent management, was the key to the success of Tanga Fresh. There is a relationship between revenue, profits and the price of milk: when profits rise, these can be passed on to the farmer. And the farmers, in turn, are shareholders in the company; they share in the profits and participate in decisions. The impact of this cooperative was has been great: the amount of money paid to smallholders in the Tanga region increased from TSH 2,800,000,000 (3,000 smallholders) in 2007 to TSH 9,500,000,000 (4,500 smallholders) in 2013.

Prothem is a private company in Burundi that buys, processes and sells tea, procuring it from over 10,000 smallholders and providing them with agricultural advice as well as payment and extension services. Prothem existed before DOB Equity became involved and was the first privately owned tea factory in Burundi to enter into competition with government-owned plants. Its example of paying its farmers market prices has led to a doubling of income compared to what government-owned tea factories were paying. This combination of better business practice and increased transparency set a positive example that made a nationwide impact: now all government-owned factories also pay market prices to their smallholders.

Today, DOB Equity is focused on further improving efficiency, quality and the implementation of automation in payment-processing mechanisms and operations, which will also be carried out by government-owned tea factories. It is also working on achieving higher quality certifications, which in turn will enable a greater revenue to be passed on to farmers.

Prothem and Tangafresh provide stability and continuity by guaranteeing purchase and a fairer distribution of revenue. Both cases address the legitimate interests of all stakeholders—investors, entrepreneurs, government and farmers. The pitfalls of a monopoly market that would leave smallholders at the mercy of the state or a conglomerate are avoided—whether in a public monopoly where too much money disappears into the pockets of the civil service, or a private monopoly where the maximum is squeezed out for the benefit of a few.

The very nature of milk and tea means that they have to be moved fresh to the processing plant within four hours of harvesting or milking. This ensures a continual stream of process, and a continual stream of income to the farmers. In the case of durable products like coffee or chocolate, large quantities are produced and hoarded and a buyer appears once a season to make a large, market-disrupting purchase. Prothem's tea is processed continually and the entire sector benefits. DOB Equity is working to enable its produce to enter the European market.

PART III: EVALUATION: IMPACT INVESTING AND SUSTAINABILITY

◉ The social enterprise versus the profit-driven organisation

We considered the financial crisis and its moral causes in the loss of three elements: primary calling, societal embedment, and non-financial values. We next considered six cases of social enterprises that placed the social impact and public good at the heart of their business strategy. The moral and economic problems that caused the financial crisis do not occur here. Social entrepreneurship is a very young field that has not yet stood the test of time: it is too early to say whether it presents universal solutions. The specific character of social enterprises (and impact investments) comes into focus when they are compared with profit-driven organisations.[35] The main characteristics of a profit-driven organisation as revealed in part I are:

(1) **External goods**. Profit-driven organisations focus on external goods like profits. Excelling in business does not aim to excel in the values that are inherent to the business: the only objective is to increase profits.

(2) **Shareholders**. Profit-driven organisations pursue the interests of one stakeholder: the shareholders. The justified interests of other stakeholders are only taken into account when they contribute to the interests of the shareholders or when they are legally required.

(3) **Worldview**. Profit-driven organisations advocate a worldview that considers the individual as both starting and end point, emphasising the free market and rejecting regulation by the government. If these elements are considered the most important, it can lead to the three losses of direction, context and non-financial values.

Social enterprises and impact investors differ fundamentally with respect to these three characteristics. First, the objective of social enterprises is to realise the *internal goods* that are inherent to a practice. The Grameen Bank focuses on good financial services for the poor, Tendris on sustainable solutions in poor and rich countries, the Noaber Foundation develops long-term healthcare services mainly in Western countries,[36] and DOB Equity invests (inter alia) in the production of high-quality food. In the view of social enterprises the legitimacy of their 'licence to operate' or 'right to exist' lies in the added value for the societies in which they operate: a positive impact on the lives of individuals, families, villages and rural areas.

One of the main challenges in this field is to make the impact of a social enterprise transparent and explicit.[37] This requires that we understand the micro-mechanisms and pre-existing bonds that underlie the success and impact of social enterprises. For example, the Grameen Bank is very successful in granting microcredits to impoverished people without requiring collateral. The 'secret' of this success is a group-based approach that ensures a responsible use of the money which guarantees repayment of the loan. DOB Equity is very successful in East Africa with Tanga Fresh and Prothem. The most important factor in its success was the existing local cooperation between farmers and the fact that the farmers became co-owners of the company. When these micro-mechanisms are understood, transparency about the impact of social entrepreneurship can be created. One way is the so-called social return on investment (SROI).[38] This method makes the social impact of an initiative explicit, determines the indicators that characterise this impact, and translates them into financial parameters. For example, a social return on investment calculation for the main projects of VitalHealth Software showed a social return ratio of two to five. That means that every euro invested in this cooperative resulted in total social impact of between two and five euros. For the PreventionCompass of NIPED a SROI ratio of 3.2 was calculated.

Second, social entrepreneurs believe that every stakeholder has justified interests that have to be addressed. They also believe that cooperation with every stakeholder is required to develop solutions that work. The projects of the Noaber Foundation and DOB Equity are examples in which different stakeholders are involved to address innovation in healthcare and food production. The role that stakeholders play also comes to the fore in the process to determine the impact of an initiative. In the *social return on investment method*, not only is the contribution of every stakeholder to the solution valued, but the impact of the initiative on every stakeholder is also calculated. For example, the calculation of the social return of the PreventionCompass of NIPED showed that the employer benefits greatly from this initiative. It is important to note that involvement of stakeholders and maximising societal impact is a normative characteristic of the idea of the social enterprise and impact investing, and is in agreement with the stakeholder approach and the idea of relational economics.[39]

Third, social entrepreneurs and impact investors do not believe that the free market is the highest value, but pursue social and environmental values. For a PhD dissertation, Henk Kievit interviewed social entrepreneurs and impact investors and found that their activities were inspired by religious beliefs, the good example of their parents, or the feeling of a need to put something back into society.[40] These inspirations drive them not only to pursue social and environmental objectives (first characteristic), but also to involve relevant stakeholders (second characteristic). Additionally, these inspirations motivate social entrepreneurs and social impact investors to accept a below market-to-market rate. The whole field of social entrepreneurship and impact investing shows that the world of business and financial services is not morally neutral, but is driven by a certain worldview and motivated by fundamental values.

◎ The social enterprise and the idea of corporate social responsibility

Corporate social responsibility is now a catch-all term that recognises the societal responsibility of companies. The main idea is that companies have to consider the impact of their actions on society and should pursue the welfare of society as a whole along with their own interests. There are four components:[41]

(1) Economic responsibility: be profitable.

(2) Legal responsibility: obey the law.

(3) Ethical responsibility: be ethical. An obligation to do what is right, just and fair, and to avoid doing harm.

(4) Philanthropic responsibility: be a good corporate citizen. Contribute resources to the community and improve the quality of life.

Another well-known version of corporate social responsibility is the so-called Triple-P approach as formulated by John Elkinton.[42] In this approach social responsibility is summarised in three parameters: People (social justice), Profit (financial returns) and Planet (ecological limits). The basic idea of this approach is that a sustainable development of our society requires a social, economic, and environmental bottom line. In the last decade these ideas of corporate social responsibility have gained a firm footing in the business world. Many enterprises publish a corporate social responsibility report that covers its various responsibilities. In addition, several institutions publish lists of the ten, fifty or hundred organisations they rate as the most socially responsible.

The ideas of social entrepreneurship and corporate social responsibility have a lot in common. In both approaches economic, social and environmental values are acknowledged. In both approaches it is believed that the responsibility of the organisation goes beyond legal regulations and that the legitimate interests of stakeholders have to be taken into account. The main difference between these approaches is that social entrepreneurship is first and foremost concerned with social and environmental objectives, whereas corporate social responsibility aims for a balance between social, environmental and economic values. This difference is (partly) rooted in the worldview of the main participants. For social entrepreneurs profit is a 'tool' to achieve the mission of an organisation and a condition of gaining access to the capital of impact investors. Impact investors will accept a below-market rate when social or environmental goals have to be met. Corporate social responsibility, on the other hand, defines profit as one of its objectives and the commitment of the shareholders and investors depends on this objective; generally, a below-market rate will not be accepted.

◎ Social enterprises, impact investing and the future of global society

Social entrepreneurship and impact investing have gained significant momentum in recent years. Estimates indicate that impact investing can become a new asset class or investment style that will grow to $1 trillion by 2020. In the same period, the total amount of financial assets will grow to about $900 trillion. This means that by 2020 impact investing will still only represent 0.1 per cent of all financial assets. However, the impact of social entrepreneurship and impact investing may be much larger than suggested by this figure.

The most important reason is that these approaches have a larger influence on local and international development than the mere size of the outstanding loans would suggest.[43] Why can impact investing have a larger influence than its size suggests? Maximilian Martin states that impact investing is a sufficiently proven concept that governments can use as leverage to change the world.[44] He sketches four fields of global problems or 'megatrends', in which social entrepreneurship and impact investing will play a key role:

1) Massive pent-up demand at the bottom of the pyramid, i.e. the 4 billion people with annual incomes below $3,000 in local purchasing power.

2) Driving green growth. Environmental risks, shortage of raw materials, and ecological scarcities threaten humanity. A changeover to a green economy is required to support sustainable growth.

3) Reconfiguration of the welfare state. In many countries the welfare state is threatened by financial problems. The expenditures of government on healthcare, education, and welfare are higher than the revenues. A reconfiguration of the welfare state is required to guarantee a sustainable future.

4) Emerging 'lifestyles of health and sustainability' (LOHAS) consumers. In many countries, the awareness of consumers is growing that a paradigm shift is required with respect to lifestyle, health and sustainability. LOHAS consumers are willing to spend more on products designed to be environmentally sustainable and socially responsible.

The social initiatives presented in Part II all belong to these categories: the Grameen Bank, DOB Equity at the bottom of the pyramid, Tendris in green growth and LOHAS consumers, and the Noaber Foundation in the reconfiguration of the welfare state and LOHAS consumers.

Martin concludes that businesses shifting sustainability to the core of their business model "will see their ability to create value enhanced" and countries with a coherent and realistic embrace of impact investing will "see the lives of their citizens improved."[45] It goes without saying that investments in these fields have a big impact on the development of the global world. Their impact is much larger than might be expected based on the amount of money involved. The examples of Grameen Bank, Tendris, the Noaber Foundation and DOB Equity speak volumes.

CONCLUSION

The financial crisis has provoked a thorough assessment of the contribution of enterprises and financial institutions to the greater public good and economic prosperity. One of the results of this assessment is a demand for social enterprises and impact investing. The objective of this chapter was to explore the social enterprise and the impact investor against the background of the financial crisis. This is a very promising field but still at an early stage. More research is needed on the long-term viability of these approaches. But it does appear that social entrepreneurship represents a serious attempt to build business on new moral and social foundations.

The first conclusion is that social enterprises and impact investors have a focus on the long term with the intention of solving social and environmental problems. They believe that business principles can address these problems in a financially sustainable way.

The second conclusion is that social enterprises and impact investors embody a new paradigm. They differ from profit-driven enterprises in every aspect: focus, managing shareholders, and worldview and basic beliefs. They differ from the idea of corporate responsibility in their main objectives: social and environmental problems.

The third conclusion is that social enterprises and impact investors may be a key in addressing several difficult problems facing Western society and the world such as the bottom of the pyramid, green growth, reconfiguration of the welfare state, and consumers focused on sustainable behaviour. The amount of money involved in this field is relatively low but its impact is expected to be relatively large.

Interestingly, Maximilian Martin shows that the financial returns of impact investments are in fact larger than the financial returns of 'normal' investments.[46] This has a lot to do with the focus on the long term and the sustainable development of thriving communities. Much earlier, Collins and Porras have also shown that value-driven organisations are—in the long term—more profitable than profit-driven organisations.[47] This data suggests that values, beliefs and fundamental motives make a big difference. It is a challenge for economists and philosophers to understand the mechanisms that underlie this difference—but a sound economic analysis must also learn to look at what cannot be counted.

REFLECTIONS BY HENK VAN DEN BREEMEN

One of the main goals of the Owls Project is to contribute to an ongoing discussion on innovations and breakthrough processes. We do this through the transfer of knowledge and experiences of key leaders and by our research. In so doing, we also intend to contribute to the development of stimulating environments for innovations in order to enable genuine breakthroughs and impact.

We are very proud that we were able to engage actively with so many highly qualified and experienced figures from our network. This is one of the distinguishing features of this book. These remarkable people were generous with their time and thought hard to reflect on their experiences in terms of the generic factors that we identified. They were asked to recall or write down how the process stages were related to each other, and to reflect on what role the factors of leadership, environment and window of opportunity played in their specific activity and in general. All the chapters tell their own story. The form was semi-structured and left total freedom in composition and tone of voice, thus enhancing accessibility and authenticity. But we were also aware that this would make the assessments in the qualitative analysis more challenging.

The stories are remarkable and cover an extraordinarily wide range of activities across the world. The subjects were selected in this way because the aim of our project is broad. We live in a world of great interdependency where no country, institution or business can operate and succeed on its own. And indeed, no innovation will arise on its own either. What we also see is that cross-over activities between different disciplines are increasing, for example in health and logistics, sectors which are both seeking to overcome similar challenges of delivery and efficiency.

The Owls Project wanted not only to go for a broad overview of subject areas, but also to dig deeper in order to get a better understanding of the underlying mechanisms of innovations. By doing so, we also could get deeper insights into the possibilities of enhancing impact. Therefore we looked for generic factors.

These are factors which we assumed to be present in all our cases. Coming from our practical background, we wanted them to be closely linked to the real practice of innovation. Therefore we linked and modelled them in the stages of an implementation process, bearing in mind that each innovation process starts with a *creative phase*, which might be an invention, a brilliant *idea* or a great *vision*. The first challenge is to transfer this creative impulse into reality by developing a proper *concept*.

In the *concept* the thinking is transferred to the concrete sub-targets, which lead to *strategy*, *planning* and *execution*. We call this the *operational phase*. In that phase the *iterative process* also plays a role in continuously checking to ensure that execution and targets are kept in sync. As a result of a pre-test we added to the six original factors (*innovation/breakthrough, idea/vision, concept, mission/strategy, planning/execution, iterative process*) three additional factors: *human factors*, *environmental factors* and the *window of opportunity*. This practical approach turned out to be very effective and enlightening.

We selected different types of innovations and breakthroughs. Some innovations and breakthroughs are driven from within the organisation itself, of which the Mayo Clinic is a good example. As one of the most advanced healthcare institutions in the world, it has developed a vision and long-term plan that includes managing internal innovation processes. In the case of the Arctic it is quite literally the environment that is forcing businesses, countries, indigenous peoples and international organisations to innovate. In the energy sector, innovations are driven by scarcity. In logistics they are driven by global demand and the pursuit of efficiency and cost reduction. In agriculture, breakthroughs are driven by scientific discovery and by individuals and institutions devoted to promoting a scientific concept as national and international policy.

We found that in all these and the other cases of our research generic factors were present and that their role can differ case by case. It is fascinating to see how factors can work towards success or failure. For example, German Unification was *enabled* by geopolitical and social change (*environmental factor*), but achieved by leadership (human factor) which seized the opportunity (*window of opportunity*). The establishment of Al Jazeera is also a good example of the importance of the *window of opportunity* and leadership. Both cases were followed up by a very smooth *execution* (operational factor). The Oslo Accords case is an example where it was difficult to transfer the *concept* into achievable sub-targets.

These examples show that generic factors help to understand the underlying mechanisms of innovation and breakthrough processes. What can we do with that? How can we benefit? First, the generic factors play an important role in the overall results of the research in each chapter. Together they form a very useful reference bank for anyone who wants to start or is in the middle of an innovation or breakthrough process. Each chapter holds valuable lessons for individuals, companies, institutions and governmental entities.

This knowledge can be beneficial for multidisciplinary and cross-over activities which are of great importance in today's globalised world. It is very helpful if you are able to see and understand the mechanisms involved in the different activities we describe. For example, health and logistics are both adapting to consumer-driven markets (*concept, planning* and *execution*). Different countries have different cultures, and the factor of the *environment* may be very important for the success or failure of a process.

We also did qualitative overall research on all the chapters. It showed that there are some really dominant factors which play an important role in all of our case studies. They are the *creative* factors—*innovation/breakthrough, idea, vision* and *concept*—as well as the *enabling, human* and *environmental factors* and *window of opportunity*. Our study shows that the *operational* factors scored less highly.

The generic factors that we identified turned out to be more than an analytical tool. They can also be used as 'buttons' to improve the chance of success. For example, if the *environment* is not ready, you can work on creating a better one by promoting awareness of opportunities. The Responsibility to Protect case is a good example of a *vision* and *concept* making a diplomatic breakthrough in the United Nations, after the *environment* had been steadily prepared for it over a period of several years with discussions, pamphlets and advocacy. In other cases—whether in business, healthcare or diplomacy—if you wish to bring a diverse set of stakeholders together, then you will need to show leadership (*human factor*) and to 'press the button' of *vision*, because only a clear *vision* with a shared goal by leaders can translate into institutional partnerships between diverse stakeholders.

Very often an implementation gets stuck in the *concept* stage. If there is no proper transformation of 'the thinking to the doing', the result is that there is no proper *executive* follow-up. The same applies in a situation where there are plenty of new *ideas*, but no proper capacity to *execute*. Another important factor is the role played by the *environment*, which includes society and governments. They can be decisive stumbling blocks, and understanding their role requires attention beforehand.

These examples show that generic factors can contribute to a stimulating *environment* for innovation and breakthrough in which there is keenness to seize opportunities for innovations, and welcome, stimulate and implement them quickly. If this is done, we will achieve the impact we want.

In our qualitative analysis, we examined each of the cases, focusing on the presence and role of these factors. We did also an overall analysis of the data. The results of our qualitative research were assessed by a software programme and an assessment team. Thanks to the software analysis it was possible to examine large data sets in a short period of time. The results of both analyses stand on their own and are extremely useful. However, this project did not aim to determine absolute truths, but to provide insightful information on the mechanism of innovations and breakthroughs.

We elaborate extensively on the research method and results of the qualitative analysis in the Annex, which starts on page 373. The results are graphed for each case. These graphics will also be linked to the website we are developing, to begin the wide-ranging discussions that we hope will follow.

QUALITATIVE ANALYSIS

In this section we present our research methods and the qualitative analyses and graphs for all nineteen case studies.

RESEARCH METHOD

The underlying research of the Owls Project is a study of the generic factors that play a role in innovation and breakthrough processes. By processes we mean the trajectory in stages from idea to realisation. In this research project we seek to determine whether generic factors played a part in the successful execution of these innovation and breakthrough processes, and if so which ones.

We carried out nineteen case studies by descriptive and semi-structured research, and analysed them with additional qualitative research. Our starting hypothesis was that the assumed generic factors exist and that their role in an innovation and breakthrough can be observed and tested.

The case studies are the result of desk and field research, with the field research carried out in qualitative semi-structured interviews. We carried out an additional qualitative analysis for each study with the aid of software. For these analyses, the theories of Juliet Corbin and the late Anselm Strauss (2008) were used, as well as QI Macros® software (KnowWare International, Inc). By applying this specific software, it was possible to unambiguously examine large data sets in a short period of time. For this it was important to make use of an open and proper coding of the data.

To ensure that the semi-structured interviews for each case study were carried out with the same qualitative approach, they were guided by a template that focused the interview on the generic factors involved. This template provided a structure for the desk and field research (interviews) with open questions. Therefore, the template did not influence the content of the research.

Our starting point and hypothesis was to use the elements of a conventional production/implementation process as the generic factors. In the first version of the hypothesis, six generic factors were chosen for the research: innovation and breakthrough; idea and vision; concept; planning and strategy; implementation; and the iterative process. In order to make sure that the correct choices were made, five cases were tested and it turned out that the defined generic factors worked well. In the course of the research, it also became apparent that three additional factors also play a frequent role. We call these the enablers: human factors, environmental factors, and the window of opportunity. The generic factors were grouped into three parts: the creative phase, the operational phase and the enabling factors.

SOFTWARE ANALYSIS AND THE ASSESSMENT GROUP

On the basis of open and axial coding the generic factors were enriched with related terms, so that all case studies could be equivalently analysed by the software. Next, the chapters and complete interview transcripts were inserted and analysed by the software. To ensure the integrity of the interpretations, three case studies were analysed on the basis of either the chapter or the interview transcripts. This comparison showed similar patterns and no significant differences in the results. We could therefore assume that the write-ups of the case studies were faithful representations of the interviews.

The software analysis measured the presence of generic factors (enriched with related key terms) as described in the case studies and interviews. This analysis computes the extent to which the factors are named and discussed, which implies the presence or importance of a given generic factor. To compare the different case studies, the software examined the extent to which a given generic factor, including the related key terms, occurs in each case study per 1,000 words.

The advantage of this is that all case studies are analysed in the same way and are comparable, regardless of the length of the chapters and transcripts. The extent of the impact of each factor, however, is not fully demonstrated in this way. The software analysis supplements a human qualitative analysis by an assessment group who assessed the case studies with understanding of their full context.

An assessment group of six members analysed the cases for the extent to which the generic factors have influenced the innovation and breakthrough process. This analysis reflects the averaged assessment from the members of the assessment group. In principle, this was a subjective interpretation: each member judged the extent of influence that each generic factor had in each innovation and breakthrough process case study by entering a number on a scale from 1 to 5. The different assessments were compared and discussed and the members strove to arrive at a shared assessment.

The results of the software analysis and the final judgment of the assessment group are translated to a graphical model in which these results are represented separately. These two different research methods have produced two separate data sets, which in turn can be compared. In this graphical comparison between the software analysis and the assessment group, we can observe some correlations in the patterns of the generic factors, which imply their importance or influence in the innovation and breakthrough process.

The results of both the research and the analysis of the data are verifiable. All data has been stored and analyses have been carried out unambiguously, and can be made available for review to anyone interested.

The project does not aim to determine absolute truths, but to provide information on and insights into the development of innovation and breakthrough processes in which the defined generic factors have played a part. The generic factors we chose to focus on are not meant to be exhaustive, but they emerge from a process-centric analysis of innovations and breakthroughs. These analyses offer some universal insights into the role that the generic factors played in each process, without prejudice. The aim of this project is to stimulate further discussion around innovation and breakthrough processes and to make organisations aware of their importance so they can use this to their benefit..

◎ Graphical model

For the graphical representation of the results we made use of two models. In one model we placed the generic factors on the horizontal axis, and on the vertical axis the extent to which each generic factor played a role in the innovation and breakthrough process. Both the software analysis and the analysis by the assessment group are overlaid on the same scale, so that they can easily be compared.

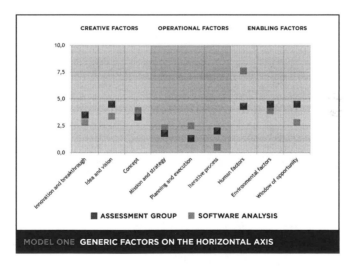

The second model is based on a web-diagram, in which we compared the groups of generic factors: the creative phase, the operational phase and the enablers. By placing the total outcomes per cluster on specific axes, we obtain a graphical model that shows to what extent a cluster of generic factors has greater or lesser impact on each given innovation or breakthrough process. This three-axis diagram of the Oslo breakthrough immediately reveals to what extent the creative and enabling factors weigh more heavily, while the opera-

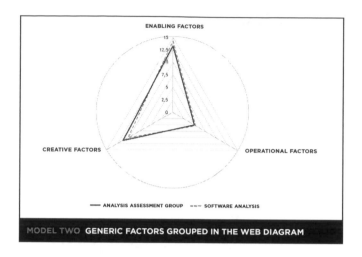

ENABLING FACTORS

15
12,5
10
7,5
5
2,5
0

CREATIVE FACTORS

OPERATIONAL FACTORS

⎯⎯ ANALYSIS ASSESSMENT GROUP   ⎯ ⎯ SOFTWARE ANALYSIS

MODEL TWO **GENERIC FACTORS GROUPED IN THE WEB DIAGRAM**

tional factors were less prominent—an observation on which the software and human analysis agree. Our website is currently under development, and willl have additional graphical materials of the case studies.

CHAPTER ANALYSIS

Chapter 1 The Creation and Impact of the Cyber Domain Page 1

This case describes two breakthroughs of the creation and the public release of the cyber domain. These breakthroughs each occurred in two very different environments; in the first phase of government and military, and the second phase the commercial market and society. The turning point of the privatization of packet-switched information technology, the internet protocol, was accompanied by a vision expressed in President Bush's speech when he signed the concept of the 'Gore Bill' into law. It was the release of an open system to the public – a system that everyone could connect to and which could not be shut down. The two breakthroughs have had a major impact on society, security, stability and governance. In this successful innovation and breakthrough process, the factors innovation/breakthrough, vision, concept, human factors (leadership) and the environment played an important role to its success using the window of opportunity.

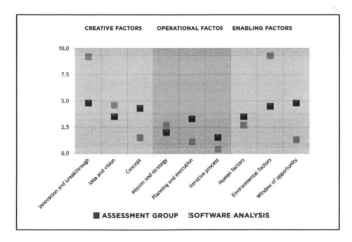

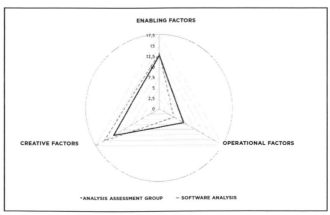

This chapter presents examples of on-going innovations, in an overview of the main innovations in logistics of the last 200 years up until the near future. This is driven mostly by demand and cost reduction. To cope with this, an overarching vision is needed. In this breakthrough, many players have developed – unorchestrated – an overarching environmental vision that goes hand-in-hand with good business practice: a reduction of carbon emissions is a reduction of energy cost. This vision has its own dynamic and on the sub-level has led to many different visions, concepts, business strategies and activities. In this case the factors of continuous innovation, vision, environment and execution (delivery), play the biggest roles. It is quite literally the space of operations, where innovation is driven by external factors, such as demand in an international context.

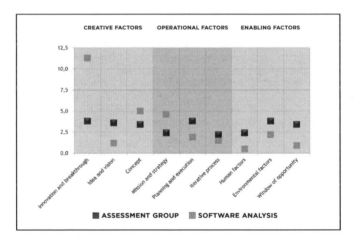

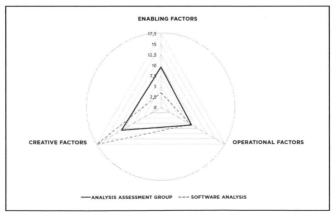

Chapter 3 **The Silent Revolution in Agriculture** Page 39

This is a case about the gradual breakthrough of the global influence of a concept of agricultural optimization. Innovations from German agricultural science were picked up, refined and continually developed at the agricultural University of Wageningen in the Netherlands. From the 1960s onwards, scientific outcomes were rapidly implemented in programmes that unified research with public information and education campaigns. This iterative process enabled the scientists at Wageningen to refine the concept and determine its universality. When the concept was elevated to national policy in the 1980s, Dutch agricultural output was further optimised. A gradual global breakthrough followed as the concept became the new standard of agricultural practice around the world. The key factors in this case are the long-term vision, the scientific concept, the iterative process, and the environment of global demand. Key leaders and institutions promoted the concept as policy.

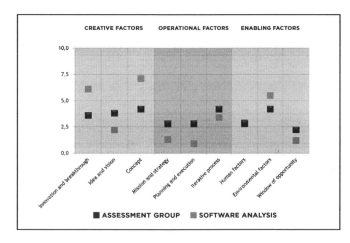

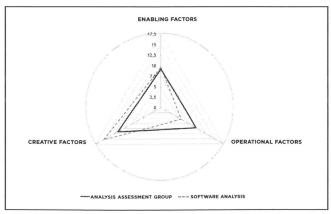

The Far North represents an on-going natural breakthrough forced by nature, driving international and national breakthroughs at several levels – international, bilateral, national and corporate. Innovation is literally forced by nature and to deal with this, leadership is needed to formulate an overarching vision. We have seen expressions of international vision, most notably in the establishment of the Arctic Council and the Ilulissat Declaration. These visions pointed to international concepts for cooperation, environmental protection, resource sharing, settlement of disputes, and safety. On the sub-level, all countries have arctic policy concepts and strategies where the general principles of the international visions are echoed and have clearly filtered down. The national concepts and strategies, however, are fragmented and vary among each other. The most important factors are the overarching international vision and national visions, concepts, strategies and the role of the natural and political environments. Leadership is needed to overcome fragmentation on all levels.

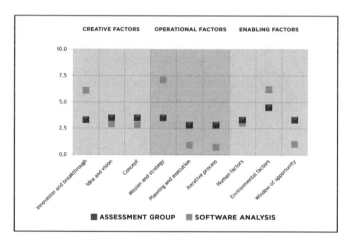

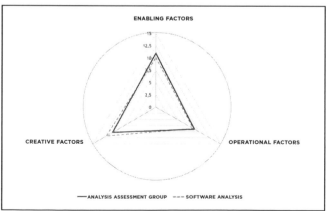

Chapter 5 **Europe's Energy Impasse** Page 81

The author argues that due to global trends of economics, energy demand and environmental change Europe will run into an impasse on energy unless there is a genuine course change to develop new innovations. The financial crisis also had a debilitating effect on energy policy, which contributes to a lack of vision in Europe and a 'dramatic indecision' in France. The author notes the promising innovations of shale gas, carbon capture technology, hydrogen technology, which have economic potential, but that leadership and a vision is needed for Europe to re-evaluate energy mixes on the basis of new principles, and to launch a powerful medium-term research effort on renewables. The lack of a common vision and leadership currently leads to short-term policy concepts and sub-optimal processes. It is not unlikely that the sub-optimisations are so bad that current policies will do real damage over the long term. The key factors to help overcome the energy impasse are innovation & breakthroughs, vision, leadership and the role of the environment.

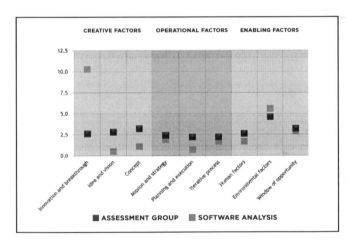

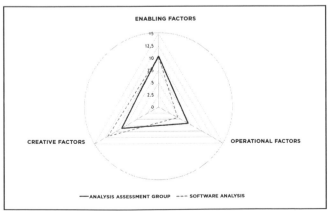

This case is an example of a technology-driven innovation, with great promise of decentralising electricity generation. The concept of the smart grid is the key innovation under discussion, which offers opportunities to overcome sub-optimalisations and to fulfil new standards of durable energy. The development of smart grids means a transition from bulk generation systems, and the transmission of their energy over long distances, to production and consumption of local energy in micro-grids where consumers also participate as producers. Leadership is a requirement for the development of smart grids, and this is currently present, but it is fragmented. Smart grids will be a growing area of interest, and effective systems can become genuine breakthroughs for sustainable energy in the future. The key factors here are innovation, concept and the role of the environment, where planning and execution can lead to breakthroughs – but where further implementation is needed in the near future.

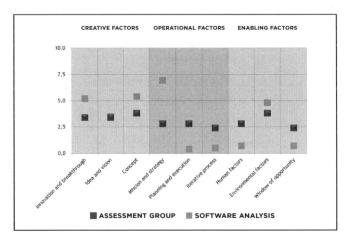

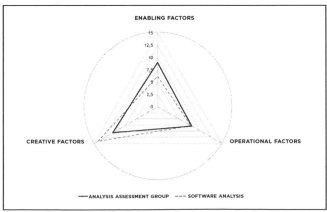

Chapter 7 **Postscript on the Future of Energy** Page 119

This case tells a story how a breakthrough could be achieved, but in fact is obstructed by a lack of international governmental vision and political will. Jeroen van der Veer notes that meeting carbon emissions targets in a world where energy demand will double over the next few decades will be impossible without key innovations and breakthroughs. One priority is to make renewable energy sources economically viable, but this requires investment in research and development rather than subsidies in currents generations of machinery that are not market-viable. Van der Veer proposes new iterative solution to this problem by investing in several cycles of research and development. To realise this requires a new shared long-term vision and new public-private partnerships. Several factors of the environment – government, public opinion, environmentalism – are all key. A real breakthrough in the energy policy of Europe requires above all leadership with a strong vision, to boost the creative and operation factors.

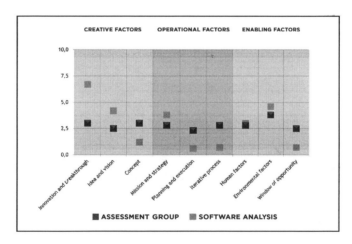

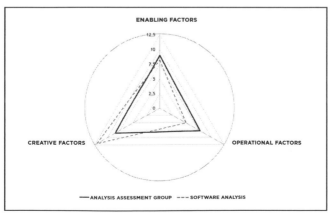

The Responsibility to Protect at the United Nations represents a breakthrough by creation. It is a great case study for this project, not least because the language of the official discourse so closely matches the language of our project. The progression and development from vision, concept, adoption of concept, strategy and implementation are all visible. A clear vision lead to a clear concept. By continually rolling it out and *frappez toujours* – and with good preparation to seize an opportunity when it presented itself at the World Summit of 2005 to elevate the concept to an international principle. If you seed an idea and concept for a long time, then you can create your own opportunity. The key factors in this case are the innovation & breakthrough, vision, concept, strategy, leadership and the window of opportunity. Planning and execution also very important, because implementing R2P is not just about the internal reform of the UN building and policies in New York, but it will ultimately be judges on its effectiveness to protect vulnerable civilians around the world.

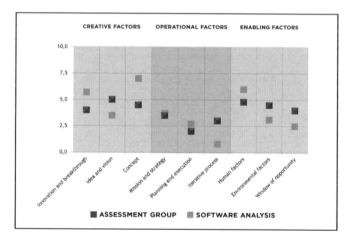

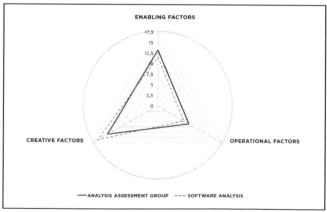

Chapter 9 An Unexpected Success: The Rapid Unification of Germany Page 159

This case describes the breakthrough of the political, legal and military unification of two countries separated by the Cold War. Decisive in this case was the leadership, especially of Chancellor Helmut Kohl and President George H.W. Bush, who overcame German domestic, European and Russian opposition to the idea, and seized a narrow window of opportunity when events forced them to accelerate the plan. There were competing visions and concepts of the future of Germany and Europe, but the overriding factor why this breakthrough occurred in the manner that it did was the environment, in the speed of developments and the willingness of leaders to seize the opportunities when they arose for Germany to determine its own fate. The most important factors are the role of innovation & breakthrough, vision, environment, human factors (leadership) and a successful execution in a narrow window of opportunity.

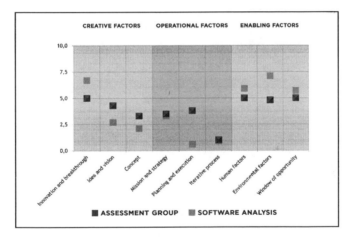

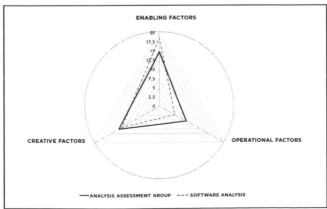

The Olso Accords represent an initial diplomatic and political breakthrough between two parties in a protracted conflict. The shared idea and vision, good will and chemistry of the negotiators was successfully translated into an initial joint concept, which was a genuine breakthrough of new relations between Israel and the Palestinians, but its lack of substance meant it could not be translated to a joint strategy and plan for joint execution. The human factors score high in the analysis, but the operation factors lower. The leadership was key to initiate the process, but this was also its vulnerability. The implementation was also too dependent on personalities, rather than on strong institutions. The most important factors were the innovative idea, vision, concept, planning & execution, leadership and window of opportunity. This case is a good example to illustrate all our process elements.

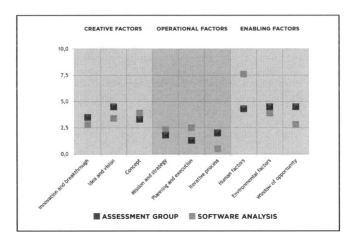

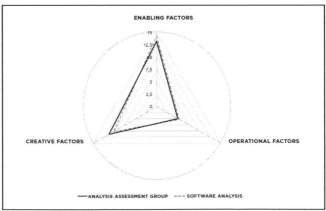

Chapter 11 China in the Age of Accelerating Change:
A Positive Approach Page 201

This chapter concerns the innovative breakthrough of the geo-economic trans-fer from the transatlantic to the transpacific region, and more specifically, from the USA to China. This change in environment has been crucial to create conditions to stimulate innovation. The environment in China is now very open to innovation and her economic growth is fuelled by the combination of foreign direct investment and inexpensive labour. In his positive approach, the author highlights economic opportunities and mutual benefits of a pos-itive-sum gain for both the USA and China that derive from a new mutual dependence – and a mutual desire for growth and stability. Change is accel-erating and a healthy long-term view, concept and grand strategy are needed with an eye on innovation. The factors of the innovation/breakthrough, idea, vision, concept, and the enablers all play their part.

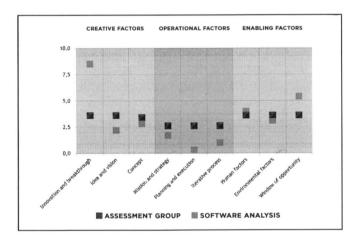

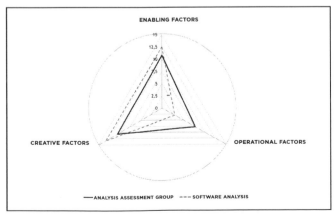

This case describes the breakthrough of creating a new space for a national public debate on democratic values. It is an example of pioneering individual leadership to successfully change the environment of public sentiment, where public opinion and political correctness initially resisted an open debate on Islam as taboo. It is a breakthrough of initiating a public debate. The most important factor was the innovative vision, leadership and courage of Frits Bolkestein who spoke and published repeatedly on this subject. The most mportant factors are innovative vision, environment and the human factor of leadership.

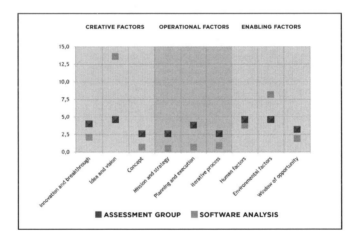

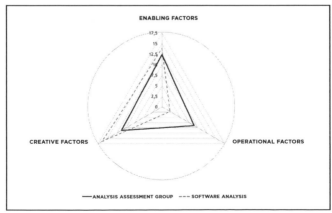

Chapter 13 **Privatisation as Breakthrough?** Page 227

This case study traces the political decision-making of privatisation policies in Europe in the 1980s and 1990s, and their consequences. This is not so much a breakthrough or innovation on a specific case, but a reflection of a more general political process and its consequences. The author argues that the transfer of public industries to private ownerships has had a mixed record, which has not always served the public interest or innovation. The relationship between a market-driven and an innovative economy is not automatic, because it also concerns cultural factors, such as liberty, education and partnerships. To create genuinely stimulating environments for innovation, requires leadership to create new partnerships between public institutions, private industry and academia. The most important factors in this case are innovation, vision, concept and human factors, including leadership.

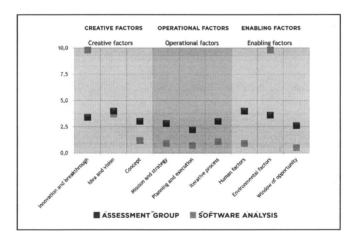

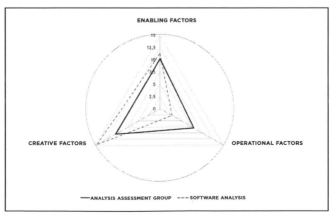

This case represents breakthroughs in communications in the creation of a broadcast station and its impact. The decisive factors were window of opportunity, vision, leadership, together with means and a ready-made plan for execution. The concept was 'ready-made', insofar that the BBC unintentionally prepared both trained journalistic manpower and a model to emulate. The introduction of a state-supported and editorially independent pan-Arab station was a first, and an innovation and breakthrough for all.

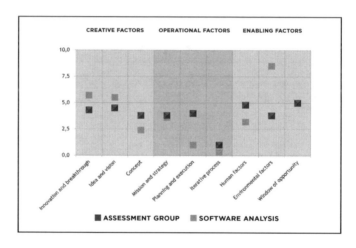

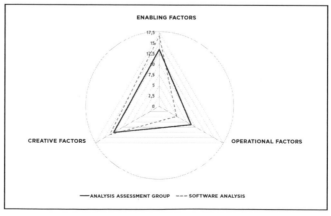

Chapter 15 High-Value Healthcare For All: Innovative Approaches in the United States and the Netherlands Page 257

This chapter reflects an overarching vision between many parties in the Netherlands and the United States to deliver high value health Eight civil society organisations are considered who represent innovative approaches to healthcare delivery – four service line innovators and four network facilitators. Each of the cases reflects their own, innovations and breakthrough process, visions, concepts and practices – and the authors find valuable lessons in each of them. The authors emphasise that the goal of achieving high-value healthcare depends heavily on having a shared vision and goals. The lesson of this case is that, while you need innovation on the level of government, the healthcare system and in healthcare financing, these kinds of bottom-up innovations in the field should also be stimulated. The most important factors are innovative vision and concept, strategy (cooperation and collaboration), execution, human factors, stimulating environments for bottom-up approaches.

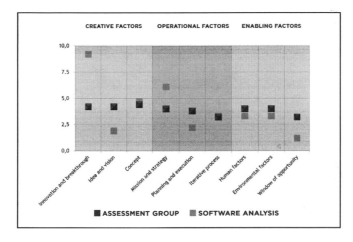

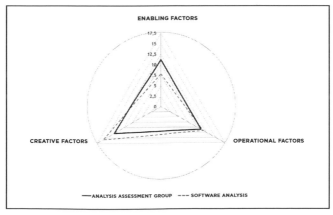

The Mayo Clinic is an example of a large organisation that is forcing itself to innovate by imposing and developing a long-term vision. They do this by developing their own internal innovation processes, together with a mechanism for high quality implementation. Mayo also strives for high quality (a human factor) in all its activities. The organisation stimulates innovation by its internal structure, planning process, management and communication flows, where doctors and nurses on the ground process feedback and ideas back to a Center for Innovation (iterative process). Within the Mayo Clinic all factors of an innovation and breakthrough process are strongly present and integrated. Their internal mechanisms are formally structured to stimulate innovations and to connect these to processes. The following factors all score highly: innovation, vision, concept, strategy, long-term planning and the human factors (highly quality practitioners and leadership).

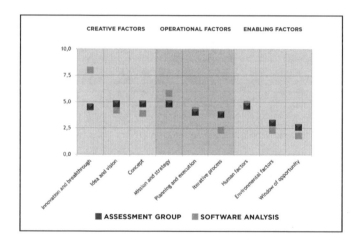

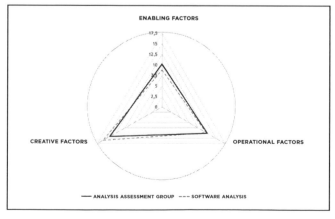

Chapter 17 **Healthcare Innovation in Practice** Page 311

VitaValley represents a breakthrough in bringing parties together in health care in an unorthodox way, to stimulate innovations and their implementation to achieve scalability, multi-disciplinarity and internationality. Its focus is on connecting innovations to processes, which is a separate art. VitaValley focuses on creating the bridge between innovations, the academy and technology on one side; and investors, business, hospitals and government on the other. It does so as a strategy and planning organisation, with an emphasis on the executive and operational side. It is an organisation of partners, where the network organisation is the innovation. This is a functional network with a clear division of tasks. The creative, operational and enablers, especially human factors, all score very high in this case study.

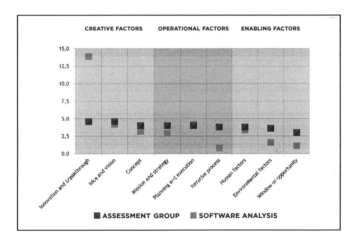

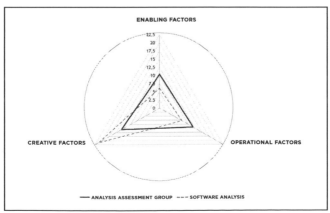

The Augeo Foundation represents a breakthrough in the creation of an organisation that develops new partnerships with a range of institutions focused on improving professional practice. They succeed in gradually winning over the environment of stakeholders and the government, in drawing attention and forcing a breakthrough on the difficult problems of child abuse and domestic violence. The combination of a vision, concept, resources, partnerships and personal involvement create a power to realise results more than a typical foundation. The most important factors are: innovation, vision, concept, planning, execution and leadership.

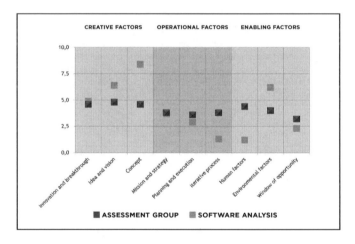

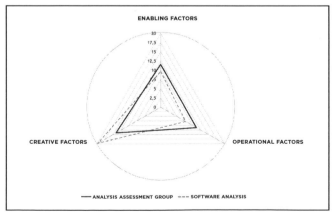

Chapter 19 Impact Investing and Social Renewal Page 349

Impact investing and social venturing represent a new concept of doing business with shared value to make a positive social impact. A new vision was driven by a reaction to an irresponsible economic environment, where the main actors – in both corporations, financial institutions and states – had lost sight of long-term shared value. The case studies of impact investing in this chapter represent the first steps of a new approach to structuring economic activity that take the legitimate interests of all stakeholders into account, including the impact on society. A large number of foundations and corporations have signed on to support social entrepreneurship in the future. The most important factors are idea & vision, mission & strategy, leadership and the window of opportunity.

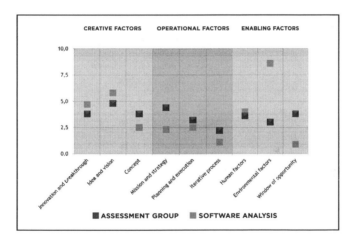

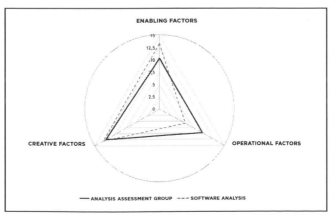

For both analytical methods the scores of all the cases are presented in a single graphic. The highest and the lowest score per generic factor and average overall score are shown. For both the software analysis and that of the assessment group, it is interesting to note that the operational factors are less present than the other clusters. The software analysis is the most striking result. It underlines what this book is all about: how to make innovations work and how to create impact by implementing them. The analyses show which factors are most important if we want to improve implementation.

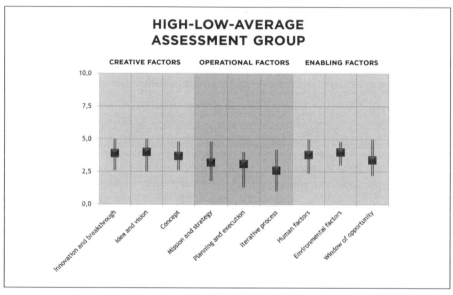

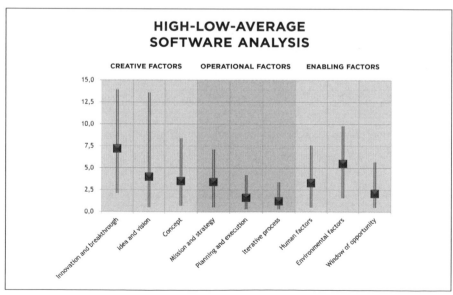

CONTRIBUTORS

FRANCES ABELE is Professor of Public Policy and Aboriginal people of the Arctic at Carleton University, specialised in circumpolar political economy, Aboriginal-Canada relations, northern development policy, public participation and democracy.

SIMON ADAMS is the Executive Director of the Global Centre for the Responsibility to Protect. He has worked with governments and civil society organisations in South Africa, East Timor, Rwanda, Mozambique and elsewhere. Between 1994 and 2002 Dr Adams worked on the Northern Ireland peace process. He is also a former anti-apartheid activist and member of the African National Congress.

MANFRED AUSTER is the Minister-Counsellor, Deputy Ambassador and the Head of the Political and Public Affairs Section of the delegation of the European Union to Canada. He previously served as counsellor and head of economics at the Embassy of Germany to Canada; head of division for Germany's relations with the European Parliament; and counsellor for political affairs, permanent representation of Germany to NATO.

PAUL BAAN is the founder and Chairman of the Noaber Foundation and a Board Member of the Owls Foundation. He was the co-founder of the Baan software company, a large ERP vendor. He is a pioneer in the areas of social venturing and impact investing.

DIRK BARTH is the former Secretary General of the Dutch Ministry of Defence. He is a member of the Advisory Council on International Relations for the Dutch Ministries of Foreign Affairs and Defence.

YOSSI BEILIN is the President and founder of Beilink, a business consultancy. He has served as Chairman of Meretz, and as Member of the Knesset for Meretz and Labour, and has held four ministerial posts in the Israeli government. In his capacity as Deputy Minister of Foreign Affairs, he coordinated the Oslo negotiations with the Palestinians.

MARTHA HELENA BEJAR is CEO and Board Director of Flow Mobile in Seattle, WA. She is also a founding partner of the Red Bison Advisory Group, which specialises in furthering business relations between the US and China. Prior to joining Flow Mobile, Martha was the Chair and CEO of Wipro Infocrossing Cloud Services.

JYOTI BHARGAVA is a circumpolar analyst at the Department for Aboriginal Affairs and Northern Development of Canada's Federal Government.

BENJAMIN BILSKI is author and editor with The Owls Project, the Executive Director of the Pericles Foundation and a doctoral candidate in legal philosophy at the University of Leiden. He has studied and taught in the US, the UK and the Netherlands, and has degrees in philosophy, biochemistry and philosophy of science. He has co-authoured four books, including *Towards a Grand Strategy for an Uncertain World* (2008).

JAMES BLAKER is a former Defense Department official, where he served as Deputy Assistant Secretary of Defense; Deputy Undersecretary of the Air Force and the Senior Advisor to the Vice Chairman of the Joint Chiefs of Staff. He was also Department Director at Science Applications International Corporation; and the Vice President and Director of Research of the Hudson Institute.

MATTHIJS BLOKHUIS is the Managing Director of the Noaber Foundation and Noaber

Ventures in the Netherlands. He also serves as a non-executive board member at Ecolane, Vital Health Software and other ventures on behalf of Noaber Ventures.

FRITS BOLKESTEIN is a retired Dutch politician. In his public life he was Party Leader and Parliamentary Leader of the VVD party; Minister of Defence; and European Commissioner for Internal Market and Services. He is the author of eighteen books.

HARRY BORLASE is the Director of Non-Renewable Resources for Nunatsiavut Government in the province of Newfoundland and Labrador, Canada. In this capacity he works to promote sustainable resource development in northern Labrador; and he works with mining and oil and gas industry to meet expectations of beneficiaries for development on Labrador Inuit Lands.

THEO BOSTERS is the Director and owner of Corpos, a consultancy that specialises in strategic communication management and research. He also lectures on strategic communications and research at the Avans University of Applied Sciences in the Netherlands.

HENK VAN DEN BREEMEN is the Chairman of the Owls Foundation. He holds several advisory and board memberships with large and small institutions, specialising in development of strategies for innovation and their implementation. He is a retired General and the former Chief of Defence of the Netherlands, who carried out a far-reaching modernisation and professionalisation of the Dutch armed forces after the fall of the Berlin Wall. He organised and co-authored *Towards a Grand Strategy for an Uncertain World* (2008).

HAAKON BRUUN-HANSSEN is an Admiral of the Royal Nowegian Navy and the Norwegian Chief of Defence since 2013. He was educated at both the Norwegian Naval Staff College and the Netherlands Staff College. He has served as Chief of Staff and Inspector General of the of the Norwegian Navy.

FRANÇOIS CHABANNES is the President of the ALCEN Foundation for the Understanding of Energy, and the President of Technochabs. He is the Former Delegate-General of the Council of French Defence Industries (CIDEF), the Group of Telecommunication and Professional Electronics Industries (GITEP-EDS) and General Manager of the Industrial Laser Company (CILAS).

DENIS A. CORTESE, MD is Foundation Professor at Arizona State University; Director of ASU's Healthcare Delivery and Policy Program; and President of the non-profit Healthcare Transformation Institute based in Phoenix, AZ. He is an Emeritus President and CEO of the Mayo Clinic.

JED COLT COWDELL is Resident Physician at the Mayo Clinic in Rochester, MN. Prior to this he was Assistant Supervisor at Arizona State University Medical School.

MARTIJN DADEMA is Mayor of the city of Raalte in the Netherlands. He was previously the Deputy Head of the Political Section at the Netherlands Permanent Mission to the United Nations in New York.

JACKIE DAWSON is Chair of the Environmental Studies Program, and Canada Research Chair in Environment, Society and Policy at the Department of Geography in the University of Ottawa, Canada. Professor Dawson's academic research focused on climate change in the Far North.

MARIËLLE DEKKER is Director of the Augeo Foundation and Editor-in-Chief of its magazine Tijdschrift Kindermishandeling. In the Augeo Foundation and in her prior work in developmental psychology, she is devoted to tackling child abuse and promoting good parenting.

FRANCIS DENG is the first Permanent Representative of South Sudan to the United Nations. He was previously the Special Adviser to the UN Secretary General on the Prevention of Genocide. He has held posts in various think tanks, was a Minister in Sudan, and is the author and editor of dozens of books and policy briefs, as well as the novel *The Cry of the Owl*, on the crisis of Sudanese identity.

SVERRE DIESEN is a retired General and researcher at the Norwegian Defence Research Establishment (NDRE), Analysis Division, and is engaged on a number of projects supporting Norwegian long-term defence planning, including cyber warfare, network enabling capabilities and the future security environment. He was educated at the Norwegian and British Army Staff Colleges and was the Norwegian Chief of Defence from 2005 to 2009.

GERT VAN DIJK is Professor of Cooperative Business Administration and Management at Nyenrode Business Universiteit. He is also an external Professor at the Universities of Wageningen and Tilburg. He serves on the advisory board of the Noaber Foundation. With specialties in agriculture, animal husbandry, social venturing and developmental economics, he has dozens of publications on agricultural science and economics.

KEN FLEMING is the CEO of Eyefreight Transport Management Systems. Before joining Eyefreight, he was the President and Founder of Fleming & Partners Management Consulting; President and COO of Transora, where he was responsible for global technology and operations functions; and VP of Global Product Marketing at Kewill Systems, a European ecommerce supply chain management solution provider.

BERNARD FUNSTON is President of Northern Canada Consulting, which provides policy and strategic advisory services on northern Canadian and Arctic affairs. He was previously Chair of the Canadian Polar Commission; served as Executive Secretary of the Arctic Council's Sustainable Development Working Group; and was Special Adviser to the Government of the Northwest Territories.

COLUM GORMAN, M.B., B.Ch., Ph.D., now retired, was Chair of Endocrinology at Mayo Clinic, a member of Mayo's Board of Governors and President of the American Thyroid Association. He has authored more than 100 scientific papers on thyroid diseases, diabetes and information technology. He played an instrumental role in establishing the Alliance for Healthy Aging between the Mayo Clinic, the Noaber Foundation, the University of Grongingen, the VitaValley Group and the Dutch pension organisation PGGM. He was made an Officer of the Dutch Royal Order of Orange-Nassau for his life's work and for fostering long-standing research partnerships with the Netherlands.

CARRIE GRABLE is the Research and Development Manager of Inuit Qaujisarvingat: Inuit Knowledge Centre, a Canadian research institute devoted to increasing Arctic knowledge and to promoting the Inuit contribution to research, science and policy. She has been with Inuit Qaujisarvingat since its founding in 2010.

JOHN GROFFEN is the Ambassador of the Netherlands to Nigeria, and formerly Ambassador to Qatar and Slovenia. He has held a number of positions in the Netherlands Ministry of Foreign Affairs.

STEVEN GRUNAU serves in the International Trade Division at the Department of Foreign Affairs, Trade and Development of the Federal Government of Canada. He has an MA from the Norm Paterson School of International Affairs at Carleton University.

PETER HARRISON is the Director of the School of Policy Studies at Queen's University in Kingston, Ontario, Canada. Dr Harrison has served as Senior Associate Deputy Minister of Indian and Northern Affairs Canada, responsible for Northern Affairs and Inuit Relation; as well as Deputy Minister of Fisheries and Oceans Canada.

STEPHEN HENDRIE is the Executive Director of Inuit Tapiriit Kanatami, a nonprofit organisation devoted to the wellbeing of the Inuit. He has worked as communications officer at the Makivik Corporation to raise awareness of Inuit issues in the Nunavik region of Northern Quebec, and as an announcer on CBC Radio Canada.

HANS HILLEN is the former Minister of Defence of the Netherlands, and has served as a Member of the Dutch Parliament and Senate for the Christian Democratic party. He was made an Officer of the Order of Orange-Nassau.

FENNIGJE HINSE is Senior Political Officer at the Embassy of the Netherlands in Ottawa. She holds a Master of Laws from the London School of Economics and Political Science.

ANNA HOUCK is a Political Trainee at the Embassy of the Netherlands in Ottawa. She holds a Master of Arts in international relations from the University of Groningen in the Netherlands.

TOINE HUIBERS is Finance and Investment Manager at DOB Equity. He served on the Board of Directors of Tanga Fresh Ltd, a dairy company in Tanzania; and serves on the Board of Barefoot Power. Before joining DOB Equity Toine was General Manager of Caripro Engineering BV, and worked as a General Manager at the Brinkmans Advies Groep.

PETER INGE, retired Field Marshal, was Chief of Staff of the British armed forces from 1994 to 1997. After his military career, he was made a life peer with the title of Baron Inge of Richmond in the County of North Yorkshire. He is also a member of the Privy Council and a Knight of the Garter.

NIGEL INKSTER is the Director of Transnational Threats and Political Risk at the International Institute of Strategic Studies in London. He served for 31 years in the British Secret intelligence Service (SIS), with postings in Asia, Latin America and Europe. He was Assistant Chief and Director for Operations and Intelligence of MI6.

ROBERT KADAS is Deputy Director of the Circumpolar Division at the Department of Foreign Affairs, Trade and Development of the Federal Government of Canada. His responsibilities include implementing the Northern Dimension of Canada's foreign policy. Between 1992 and 2000, he served as Special Assistant to Lloyd Axworthy, Minister for Foreign Affairs.

AB KLINK is a former Minister of Health of the Netherlands. He has served as member of the Dutch parliament and Senate for the CDA party. He was also the Director of the Research Institute of the CDA party. Today he is member of the Board of the insurance company cVGZ (the second-largest health plan in the Netherlands) and Professor at the Free University in Amsterdam.

GEMMA KOBESSEN is the Founder and active Chair of the Board of the Augeo Foundation, a foundation in the Netherlands devoted to tackling child abuse and domestic violence and promoting good parenting.

MARY KORICA is a Policy Officer at Canada's Department of National Defence where she has worked on policy development, public policy, speechwriting and parliamentary affairs. She studied at York University, Canada's School of Public Service and the University of Zagreb.

MOHAMED KRICHEN is a Tunisian journalist and senior presenter at the Al-Jazeera News Network (Arabic).

CHRISTEN KROGH is the Deputy Head of Mission and Counsellor at the Embassy of Denmark in Ottawa. He has served in the Danish Ministry of Foreign Affairs as the Deputy Head of Department for Northern Europe; and as the Head of Section for Nordic Countries, Greenland and the Faroe Islands.

ROEL KUIPER is a historian and philosopher, member of the Dutch Senate and Professor of Christian Philosophy at the Erasmus University in Rotterdam. He is the author and editor of dozens of books. As Senator, he chaired a committee that reviewed the history of privatisation policies and their consequences in the Netherlands. In 2013 he published *De Terugkeer van het algemeen belang (The Return of Public Interest)*.

PHILIPPE LAFORTUNE is Policy Officer and Program Manager at the Department of National Defence in the Federal Government of Canada.

NATALIE LANDMAN is the Associate Director for Projects of the Healthcare Delivery and Policy Program at Arizona State University. Natalie joined ASU after three years at McKinsey & Company, where she served numerous clients in the healthcare and high tech sectors on a range of strategic topics including business unit and corporate growth strategy, product development, marketing and brand management. She holds a PhD in Neurobiology and Behavior from Columbia University.

JACQUES LANXADE is a retired Admiral. After a long career in the French Navy, has been appointed as strategic adviser of the Président de la République in 1989-1991 before to be Chief of defense until 1995. Then he became Ambassador to Tunisia until 2000. He is the author of two books, including Towards a Grand Strategy for an Uncertain World (2008).

NICHOLAS F. LARUSSO, M.D., is the Charles H. Weinman Endowed Professor of Medicine. He is the former Chair of Medicine and the former Director for the Center for Innovation at Mayo. Prior to this he was the Program Director at the Department of Hepatology and Internal Medicine at the Mayo Graduate School of Medicine, at the Mayo Clinic in Rochester, MN.

DAVID LENARCIC is a Policy Officer in the Directorate of Cabinet Liaison and Assistant Deputy Minister for Policy in the Department for Aboriginal Affairs and Northern Development in the Federal Government of Canada.

AMNON LIPKIN-SHAHAK (1944-2012) was the Chief of Defence of Israel from 1995 to 1998. After retiring from the IDF, he was Minister of Tourism and Minister of Transportation. He was awarded the Medal of Courage twice for his leadership and bravery during the 1967 Six Day War and the 1973 October War.

DAVID LUNDERQUIST is a Counsellor and the Deputy Head of Mission of the Swedish

Embassy to Canada. He was previously the Deputy Director of the EU Department in the Swedish Ministry of Foreign Affairs.

ALAN MCKINNON is Professor and Head of Logistics at Kühne Logistics University in Hamburg, Germany, and Emeritus Professor at Heriot-Watt University in Edinburgh, Scotland. He has been lecturing, researching, publishing and advising on logistics and transport for 35 years. He was the first chairman of the World Economic Forum's Logistics and Supply Chain Council and has worked closely with other international organisations including the European Commission and OECD. In 2003 he was awarded the Sir Robert Lawrence prize, the highest distinction of the UK Chartered Institute of Logistics and Transport.

STEPHANIE MEAKIN is owner of Meakin Consultants, which specialises in Environmental Science and Research Services. She has worked as a Science Adviser with the Inuit Circumpolar Council for 17 years. She holds a degree in molecular biology from Carleton University.

JEANETTE MENZIES is Head of the Canadian International Centre for the Arctic Region, in the Department of Foreign Affairs, Trade and Development. Her portfolio includes formulating Canada's Arctic foreign policy; working on the Arctic Council chairmanship; conducting outreach to foreign embassies in Ottawa; managing a leading role in scientific research; and encouraging business and investment in Canada's North.

JAMES MITCHELL is a founding partner of the policy consulting firm Sussex Circle in Ottawa. After several years as a university lecturer, he began his government career in 1978 in the Department of Foreign Affairs before moving to the Privy Council Office in 1983. He later served as Assistant Secretary of the Treasury Board and, from 1991 to 1994, as Assistant Secretary to the Cabinet. He holds a PhD in philosophy from the University of Colorado.

DOUGLAS MURRAY is Associate Editor of the *Spectator* magazine and Associate Director of the Henry Jackson Society. He is an award-winning author of a number of books, most recently of *Bloody Sunday*, which won the Ewart-Biggs memorial prize for promoting peace and reconciliation.

KLAUS NAUMANN was the Chief of Defence of the German armed forces from 1991 to 1996,

and the Chairman of the NATO Military Committee from 1996 to 1999. In his capacity of Chief of Staff, he oversaw the dismantling of the East German armed forces and the reintegration of East German Non-Commissioned Officers into the united German army. He is the author of three books, including *Towards a Grand Strategy for an Uncertain World* (2008).

JOHANNA NOOM is the Project Manager of the Owls Foundation. She is specialised in communications, project management and international executive support. She has completed a Masters degree in communications, focused on strategic business communications.

JOHN H. NOSEWORTHY, M.D., is president and chief executive officer of Mayo Clinic, a not-for-profit, healthcare leader that has been dedicated to clinical practice, research and education for 150 years. During his tenure as CEO, Dr. Noseworthy and his leadership team have created a strategic plan to ensure that Mayo Clinic remains a trusted resource for patients amid a rapidly changing healthcare environment – extending Mayo's mission to new populations, providing care through more efficient delivery models, and increasing personalized healthcare for everyone.

WILLIAM A. "BILL" OWENS is a retired Admiral of the US Navy and former Vice Chairman of the Joint Chiefs of Staff. He has served as President, Chief Operating Officer and Vice Chairman of Science Applications International Corporation (SAIC); and has served as CEO of Nortel; and Chairman and CEO of AEA Holdings Asia.

WILLIAM PACE is the Convenor of the Coalition for the ICC; Executive Director of the World Federalist Movement, and Executive Director of the International Coalition for the Responsibility to Protect. He has pioneered the coalition of NGOs to support the development and adoption of the R2P concept.

MIRIAM ELANA PADOLSKY is the Associate Director of the Strategic Policy and Integration Directorate, at the Northern Policy and Science Integration Branch of the Department of Aboriginal Affairs and Northern Development of the Canadian Federal Government. She holds a PhD in Sociology from the University of California at San Diego, on the science and participation of Canadian and Australian climate change campaigns.

SHIMON PERES was the ninth President of the State of Israel from 2007 to 2014. In a political carreer spanning six decades, he has served as Member of Knesset, Prime Minister, Minister of Defence, Minister of Finance and Minister of Transportation. He is the author of ten books.

SHELLY PLUTOWSKI is a senior communications professional in Mayo Clinic's Department of Public Affairs, with more than 20 years of experience in the field. She worked in the Mayo Clinic Health Policy Center, which successfully established Mayo Clinic as "the voice" for patient-centered healthcare reform both regionally and nationally. In the last several years, she has collaborated with Mayo Clinic's CEO, CAO and other executive leaders on a variety of speeches and academic papers.

HENK POLINDER is Associate Professor at the Technical University of Delft in the Netherlands. He is an electrical engineer and main research interests are design aspects of electrical machines for renewable energy and mechatronic applications. He is author and co-author of over 100 academic articles.

WIM POST is programme manager at the Noaber Foundation in the Netherlands. He has worked as a consultant to guide innovation in the Dutch education system. Before the Noaber Foundation, he managed a center of innovation for the Baan Company, a large ERP vendor.

ROCHUS PRONK is the Deputy Head of Mission of the Embassy of the Netherlands in Ottawa, Canada. Prior to this, he headed the Afghanistan Task Force in the Dutch Ministry of Foreigh Affairs. He has studied at the University of Oslo, the Universiy of Utrecht and at American University in Washington, D.C.

RON PUNDAK (1958-2014) was an Israeli historian and journalist, and co-Chairman of the Israeli-Palestinian Peace NGO Forum. He was Director-General of the Peres Center for Peace from 2001 until 2011. Together with Professor Yair Hirschfeld, he initiated the Oslo negotiations with the Palestinians.

AHMED ALI MOHAMMED QUREI, also known as Abu Ala'a, is a former Prime Minister of the Palestinian Authority. In his capacity as the Senior Economist in the PLO, he was the key figure in the Oslo Peace negotiations with Israel.

HASSAN RACHIDI is a Moroccan journalist and the Director of Al Jazeera in Morocco.

PAULO F. RIBEIRO is Professor at the Center of Excellence in Smart Grinds at the Federal University of Itajubá, Brazil and an adjuct Professor at Calvin College in Minnesota. He has served at numerous universities around the world (co)authored over 200 academic publications. Professor Ribeiro has degrees in electrical engineering, business and theology.

PIETER DE RIJCKE is the chairman of De Hoge Dennen, the investment fund of the de Rijcke family. He is involved in several philanthropic foundations and social investment activities, and is a member of the Board of the Owls Foundation.

JELLE ROODBEEN is the Financial Director at De Hoge Dennen, an investment firm in the Netherlands. Prior to this he worked with AS Watson, KPMG and was educated at Nyenrode Business School in the Netherlands. He currently serves on the boards of Eyefreight, e-Traction and VitalHealth Software.

GERT ROSENTHAL is Ambassador and the Permanent Representative of Guatemala to the United Nations. In October 2012, he served as the President of the United Nations Security Council. He was Director of the United Nations Economic Commission for Latin America and the Caribbean; and a member of the Oversight Commission of the Guatemalan Peace Accords.

URI SAVIR is the President of the Peres Center for Peace, the President of the Glocal Forum and the Founder of Yala Young Leaders. He has served as a diplomat, Member of Knesset and Director General of the Israeli Ministry of Foreign Affairs.

HERMAN SCHAPER is a retired Dutch Ambassador and was the Permanent Representative of the Netherlands to the United Nations from 2009 to 2013. Prior to this he has served as the Dutch Ambassador to NATO. He has served in Parliament for the D'66 party, followed by a distinguished carreer the Dutch foreign service.

AHMED SHEIKH is a Palestinian journalist and the Editor-in-Chief of the Al Jazeera News Network.

ALEXANDER SHESTAKOV is the director of the Global Arctic Programme of the World Wildlife Fund in Canada. A specialist in environmental management and conservation, he has consulted for the Russian Parliament on environmental law, and is the author of over seventy publications.

GERTIE SMEDTS is Corporate Adminstratie Manager at Irdeto in Canada. Prior to this she was Executive Assisant at the Embassy of the Netherlands.

ROBERT K. SMOLDT, MBA is the Associate Director of the Healthcare Delivery and Policy Program at Arizona State University; and the Emeritus CAO of the Mayo Clinic in Rochester, MN.

ARNE SOLLI is a retired General and was the Norwegian Chief of Defence from 1994 until 1999. He was awarded the title of Commander of the Royal Norwegian Order of St. Olav in 1995.

MOSTEFA SOUAG is the Director General of the Al Jazeera News Network (Arabic). He had held various positions within the network, including Director of News of Al Jazeera (Arabic) and Media Advisor to the Chairman of the Board of Al Jazeera. He also served as Director of the Al Jazeera Centre for Studies, and was based in London as Editorial Bureau Chief. Before joining Al Jazeera, he worked at the BBC World Service and at the MBC media group. Souag holds a PhD in literary studies.

HORST TELTSCHIK is a German politician and business manager, who served as the Head of International Affairs and national security adviser under Chancellor Helmut Kohl. In this capacity, he played an instrumental role in the negotiations surrounding the unification of Germany. He has also served as CEO of the Bertelsmann Foundation and has led the Munich Security Conference.

CLIVE TESAR is the Head of Communications and External Relations of the Arctic Program of the World Wildlife Fund in Ottawa, Canada. Prior to joining WWF, he worked throughout the Arctic as a communications consultant for NGOs, Indigenous peoples' organisations and governments.

JEROEN VAN DER VEER is the former CEO of Royal Dutch Shell until 2009, and remains on the Board of Directors. He joined Shell in 1971, and served as Managing Director of Shell Nederland, as President of Chief Executive of Shell Chemical Company in the US, and as Group Managing Director. In all these functions he has led Shell through major changes. Mr. van der Veer has served on many advisory boards, including Madeleine Albright's expert group who advised the development of the new NATO strategic concept of 2010.

MAARTEN VERKERK is Professor of Reformational Philosophy at the Technical University of Eindhoven, the Netherlands; and member of the Board of the VitaValley Network. With a background in chemistry, physics, and philosophy, he has published over a dozen books and hundreds of articles on subjects ranging from chemistry, theoretical physics and applied economics, to ethics, feminism and philosophy.

MARIA LUIZA RIBEIRO VIOTTI is the Ambassador of Brazil to Germany. From 2007 to 2013 she was the Permanent Representative of Brazil to the United Nations, and in February 2011 President of the United Nations Security Council. She has served the Brazilian Ministry of External Relations in various capacities, focusing on human rights and international organisations.

NILS WANG is Rear Admiral in the Royal Danish Navy and one of Denmark's leading experts on Arctic Security issues. In 2011, the Danish Minister of Foreign Affairs included him as a special advisor on Arctic Security during the finalization of the Kingdom of Denmark's Arctic Strategy. Prior to his present position as Commandant of the Royal Danish Defence College, he was Head of the Royal Danish Navy from 2005 to 2010.

SHIRLEY WEIS is the former Chief Administrative Officer, Vice President Emerita and Board Member Emerita of the Mayo Clinic in Rochester, MN. She has served on many boards in health care business, was named among the Top 25 Women in Healthcare in 2007 and 2013, and named Woman of the Year by the National Association of Women in 2011.

NICK XENOS is the Director of Arctic Science Policy at the Department of Aboriginal Affairs and Northern Development of the Federal Government of Canada. He oversees Canada's Economic Action Plan and the construction of the Canadian High Arctic Research Station, which is a year-round multi-disciplinary facility bringing together the academic, private and public sectors.

JORDAN ZED is a manager in the Department of Foreign Affairs Trade and Development of the Federal Government of Canada. He is also President of The Panel, a Canadian civil society platform.

FOOTNOTES AND SOURCES

CHAPTER 1
The Creation and Impact of the Cyber Domain

FOOTNOTES

1 President George H.W. Bush, 'Remarks on Signing the High-Performance Computing Act of 1991', (9 December 1991).
2 N. B. Ellison et al, 'The Benefits of Facebook "Friends:" Social Capital and College Students' Use of Online Social Network Sites', *Journal of Computer-Medicated Communication* 12 (4), July 2007, pp. 1143-1168.
3 David Kilcullen, *Out of the Mountains* (2013), p. 65.
4 *Ibid*. p. 170.
5 *Ibid*. p. 55-56.
6 Evgeny Morozov, *The Net Delusion: How Not to Liberate the World* (2011), pp. 33-56.
7 *Ibid*. p. 83.
8 All 49 volumes of the *"Documents from the US Espionage Den"* are accessible at archive.org/details/documentsfrom theu.s.espionageden
9 *Estimating Illicit Financial Flows Resulting from Drug Trafficking and Other Transnational Organized Crimes*, UN Office on Drugs and Crime Research Report (2011), p. 5.
10 'DOD Needs Industry's Help to Catch Cyber Attacks, Commander Says', *American Forces Press Service*, 27 March 2012.
11 projects.washingtonpost.com/top-secret-america/articles/a-hidden-world-growing-beyond-control/
12 *2012 Report on Security Clearance Determinations*, Office of the Director of National Intelligence (2012), p. 3.
13 Eric Schmidt and Jared Cohen, *The New Digital Age* (2013), p. 109
14 Richard Clarke, *Cyber War, The Next Threat to National Security and What to Do About it* (2012).
15 Morozov, p. 86.
16 'China Tightens Censorship of Electronic Communications', *NY Times*, 21 March 2011.
17 opennet.net/country-profiles
18 Alexander Klimburg, 'The Internet Yalta', *CNAS* (5 February 2013), p. 1.

SOURCES

With thanks to David Nordell for comments.

○ President George H.W. Bush, 'Remarks on Signing the High-Performance Computing Act of 1991' (9 December 1991).
○ David Kilcullen, *Out of the Mountains* (2013).
○ *Tweets from Tahrir: Egypt's Revolution as it Unfolded, in the Words of the People Who Made it* (2011).
○ Evgeny Morozov, *The Net Delusion: How Not to Liberate the World* (2011).
○ 'DOD Needs Industry's Help to Catch Cyber Attacks, Commander Says', *American Forces Press Service*, (27 March 2012). (www.defense.gov/news/newsarticle.aspx?id=67713)
○ *2012 Report on Security Clearance Determinations*, Office of the Director of National Intelligence (2012).
○ Eric Schmidt and Jared Cohen, *The New Digital Age* (2013).
○ Richard Clarke, *Cyber War, The Next Threat to National Security and What to Do About it* (2012).
○ China Tightens Censorship of Electronic Communications', *NY Times*, 21 March 2011.
○ Alexander Klimburg, 'The Internet Yalta', *CNAS*, 5 February 2013.

CHAPTER 2
Innovations in Global Logistics

FOOTNOTES

1 M. C. Christopher, *Logistics and Supply Chain Management* (2003).
2 Oxford Illustrated Dictionary, 2nd edition (1975).
3 J. P. Roth, *The Logistics of the Roman Army at War (264 BC–AD 235)*, p. 1(n2).

4   *Ibid*. pp. 1(n2), 2.
5   This section on military history is based on passages from a forthcoming PhD dissertation by Benjamin Bilski.
6   D. Bennet, 'Risk Ahoy: Maersk, Daewoo Build the World's Biggest Boat', *Bloomberg Businessweek*, 5 September 2013; M. Levinson, *The Box, How the Shipping Container Made the World Smaller and the World Economy Bigger* (2006).
7   'How much bigger can container ships get?', *BBC World Service*, 19 February 2013.
8   A. McKinnon, 'The economic and environmental benefits of increasing maximum truck weight: the British experience', *Transport Research 10* (2005), pp. 77-95.
9   A. McKinnon, 'Integrated Logistics Strategies', Chapter 10 in *Handbook of Logistics and Supply Chain Management*, ed. A. M. Brewer et al. (2001), pp. 157-159.
10 *Ibid*. p. 159.
11 The just-in-time concept has also been referred to as the 'Toyota production system' and as 'lean manufacturing'.
12 S. Wagner, 'Innovation Management in the German Transportation Industry', *Journal of Business Logistics 29* (2), (2008), pp. 215, 224.
13 Although in the conclusion, the author admits, "Further research could examine innovation adoption or innovation diffusion in the transportation industry." (*Ibid*. p. 227)
14 *RFID Journal* and IDTechEx Research.
15 *RFID Journal*: www.rfidjournal.com/faq/show?85
16 'Tesco ends trial of CCTV spy chip on razor blades', *The Guardian*, 22 August 2003; 'Gillette shrugs off RFID-tracking fears', *cnet.com*, 14 August 2003; 'Privacy groups protest RFID tracking of razors', *zdnet.com*, 15 August 2003.
17 M. Kückelhaus, *DHL Logistics Trend Radar*, Dinalog conference, 1 April 2014.
18 www.gartner.com/newsroom/id/2575515
19 www.piggybee.com, www.zipments.com, www.bringbuddy.com, www.shipees.com.
20 Wible, B., Mervis, J. and Wigginton, N.S. 'Rethinking the Global Supply Chain' Science, vol. 344, issue 6188 (2014)
21 B. Montreuil, 'Towards a Physical Internet: Meeting the Global Logistics Sustainability Grand Challenge', *CIRRELT*, January 2011, p. 3.
22 B. Montreuil, *Physical Internet Manifesto* (2012).
23 www.modulushca.eu
24 *Eyefreight TMS – Solution Overview* (www.eyefreight.com), p. 2.
25 Interview Jelle Roodbeen.
26 Additional comments by Ken Fleming.
27 *Ibid*.
28 Interview Matthijs Blokhuis.
29 Americans with Disabilities Act, Title II.
30 D. Bennet, 'Risk Ahoy: Maersk, Daewoo Build the World's Biggest Boat', *Bloomberg Businessweek*, 5 September 2013.
31 www.maerskline.com

32 N. Magnusson, 'Maersk CEO Says Balancing Supply of Ships to Demand Is Years Off', *Bloomberg Businessweek*, 13 November 2013.

CHAPTER 3
The Silent Revolution in Agriculture

FOOTNOTES

1   G. van Dijk, 'Collaborating, surviving and thriving in farming', *2007*, p. 301.
2   H.H.F. Wijffels, G. van Dijk et al, (2001), 'The Future of Livestock Production, agenda for the restructuring of the sector.' *Report to the Minister of Agriculture, Nature management and Fisheries*, 2001; G. van Dijk, 'Collaborating, surviving and thriving in farming'. In: T. Rehman and T. Giles (eds.), *2008: Twenty-five years of the Edith Mary Gayton Memorial Lectures 1984-2008*. Farm Management Unit (2008), Univ. of Reading, pp. 294-295.

CHAPTER 4
Driven by Nature: The Future of the Arctic

FOOTNOTES

1   Special Report 'The melting north', *The Economist*, 16 June 2012, p. 3-4.
2   J. Mazo, *Climate Conflict*, IISS Adelphi 409 (2010), p. 12; J. Mazo and C. Le Mière, *Arctic Opening: Insecurity and Opportunity*, IISS Adelphi 440 (2013), p. 41.
3   The two main feedback loops that accelerate Arctic heating are the albedo effect, and the release of methane gas. The albedo effect occurs when light-coloured reflective snow and ice is replaced by dark-coloured heat trapping land, and warming accelerates more warming. Also, in the thawing of large quantities of permafrost, underlying biomass will release more carbon dioxide, and especially methane – a much more potent greenhouse gas. (*The Economist*, Arctic Special Report, pp. 4-5.)
4   Interview Arne Solli and Sverre Diessen, 7 August 2012.
5   D. Cressey, 'The next land rush', *Nature*, vol. 451(3), 2008, pp. 12-15.
6   *Declaration of the Establishment of the Arctic Council*, 1(a), Ottawa, Canada, 19 September 1996.
7   The Arctic Athabaskan Council, the Aleut International Association, Gwich'in Council International, the Inuit Circumpolar Council, the Russian Association of Indigenous Peoples of the North, and the Saami Council.
8   China, France, Germany, India, Italy, Japan, Republic of Korea, the Netherlands, Poland, Singapore, Spain, and the United Kingdom.
9   Interview Bernard Funston, Chairman of the Canadian Polar Commission, 17 July 2013.

10 Arctic Council Secretariat, *The Vision for the Arctic*, Kiruna, Sweden, 15 May 2013.

11 It was also noted, however, that the "downside of this development, is an increasingly state-centric Arctic Council that might unintentionally reduce the influence of the NGOs representing the indigenous people from the region.", cf. N. Wang and D. Degeorges, 'Greenland and the New Arctic: Political and security implications of a state-building project', *RDDC Brief* (2014), p. 5.

12 *The Ilulissat Declaration*, Arctic Ocean Conference, Ilulissat, Greenland, 27-29 May 2008.

13 It was a remarkable diplomatic accomplishment for the Danish Foreign Minister to persuade the United States to agree to this, because the UN Convention of the Law of the Sea still remains un-ratified in the US Senate, although the US recognises and remains bound by any provisions of customary international law. Per Stig Møller had "woken up with a nightmare" that Greenpeace, WWF and other actors were clamouring for an Arctic Treaty that was modelled on the Antarctic Treaty. One study suggested that the US felt they owed the Danes something for their support for the missions in Iraq and Afghanistan, cf. Interview Nils Wang.

14 The 2009 Tromsø Declaration created a working group, which prepared a Search and Rescue instrument for the Arctic: The *Aeronautical and Maritime Search and Rescue in the Arctic*', 21 April 2011. This agreement was made in accordance with the 1979 International Convention on Maritime Search and International Civil Aviation. The *Agreement on Cooperation on Marine Oil Pollution Preparedness and Response in the Arctic*, 15 May 2013

15 Interview Nils Wang, 12 December 2012; Interview members of Canadian Departments, 17 July 2013; Interview Haakon Bruun-Hanssen, 6 August 2013.

16 *Arctic Opening*, p. 40.

17 Interview Haakon Bruun-Hanssen.

18 *Ibid.*

19 *Arctic Opening*, p. 96.

20 www.imo.org/mediacentre/hottopics/polar/Pages/default.aspx

21 *Canada's Arctic Council Chairmanship 2013-2015* (brochure).

22 According to the Spitsbergen Treaty, "Norway has sovereignty over the archipelago, but citizens from other countries are allowed equal (but not unrestricted) access to fisheries and mineral resources on the islands and in territorial waters. Oslo's position is that the treaty provisions are restricted to these areas, and do not apply to areas between 12nm and 200nm offshore, which it considers part of Norway's EEZ [exclusive economic zone] under UNCLOS. Russia argues that Norway has no rights beyond the territorial sea, while other signatories acknowledge that Svalbard has an EEZ and continental shelf but that the provisions of the treaty apply in those zones." cf. *Arctic Opening*, pp. 38-39; cf. Interview Arne Solli and Sverre Diessen, 7 August 2012.

23 *Treaty between the Kingdom of Norway and the Russian Federation concerning Maritime Delimitation and Cooperation in the Barents Sea and the Arctic Ocean*, signed 15 September 2010; Annex I on 'Fisheries Matters' monitoring by a joint Russian-Norwegian Fisheries Commission to monitor fish stocks and set quotas; Annex II on 'Transboundary Hydrocarbon Deposits' specifies rules on apportionment and share of revenues in oil and gas fields that straddle the maritime boundary.

24 Interview Haakon Bruun-Hanssen, 6 August 2013.

25 These include include iron, nickel, gold, silver, zinc, lead, tin, palladium, platinum, palladium, apatite, cobalt, tungsten, titanium, molybdenum, gypsum, rare earths, diamonds, other gemstones, ceramic raw materials and mica.

26 Barents Sea Treaty, pp. 5, 14; Interview Nils Wang; *Arctic Opening*, p. 55.

27 Donald. L. Gautier et al., 'Assessment of Undiscovered Oil and Gas in the Arctic', *Science*, vol. 324, no. 5,931, 29 May 2009, pp. 1175-9; and 'Circum-Arctic Resource Appraisal: Estimates of Undiscovered Oil and Gas North of the Arctic Circle', USGS Fact Sheet 2008-3049.

28 *The Economist*, Arctic Special Report, p. 10.

29 Interview Nils Wang.

30 Interview members of Canadian departments, 17 July 2013.

31 *Arctic Opening*, p. 61.

32 Speech by R. Admiral David Titley, 'Climate Change and National Security', *AMS Briefing*, 28 May 2010.

33 Interview Haakon Bruun-Hanssen; Interview Arne Solli and Sverre Diessen.

34 Interview Nils Wang; N. Wang, 'Arctic Security - An Equation with Multiple Unknowns', *Journal of Military and Strategic Studies* 15(2) (2013), p. 29: "As a major consumer of energy and mineral resources, China will prefer the Arctic to remain a stable region where it is possible to conduct business. Consequently, China will not have any immediate interest in being militarily present in the region. However, if the relationship between China and the US deteriorates as a result of differences in the South China Sea for instance, it cannot be ruled out that this would provoke a Chinese military presence in the Arctic. By invoking the same principles of freedom of navigation as the United States, China will, when it becomes technologically and operationally ready, be able to deploy nuclear submarines to the Polar Seas, thus becoming a member of a very exclusive group of nations."

35 Interview Nils Wang.

36 The treaty specifies the delimitation of the maritime boundary and exclusive economic zones, and also cooperation on fishing rights and sharing trans-boundary energy resources, cf. *Treaty between the Kingdom of Norway and the Russian Federation concerning Maritime Delimitation and Cooperation in the Barents Sea and the Arctic Ocean*, signed in September 2010, ratified by the Norwegian Storting on 8 February 2011, by the Duma on 25 March 2011 (and by the Upper House on 30 March). The instruments of ratification were exchanged in a ceremony in Murmansk on 7 June 2011, and the treaty entered into force on 7 July 2012.

37 Denmark and Norway have concluded an agreement on the delimitation of the bilateral maritime boundaries in 1965, and resolved the delimitation of the boundary between Greenland and the small volcanic island of Jan Mayen, which was adjudicated by the International Court Justice in the 1988 case, and formalised in a treaty in 1995. In 2006, the states concluded an agreement to settle the boundary between Greenland and Spitsbergen establishing the delimitation of the continental shelf and fisheries zones: ICJ Case of *Maritime Delimitation in the Area between Greenland and Jan Mayen* (1988-1993); *Agreement between the Kingdom of Denmark and the Kingdom of Norway concerning the Delimitation of the Continental Shelf in the Area between Jan Mayen and Greenland and concerning the Boundary between the Fishery Zones in the Area* (1995). Norway and Iceland had already settled the boundary between Iceland and Jan Mayen in the *Agreement between Norway and Iceland concerning Fishery and Continental Shelf Questions* (1980).

38 *Agreement between the Government of the Kingdom of Denmark and the Government of Canada to the Delimitation of the Continental Shelf between Greenland and Canada* (1973).

39 'Rules of Procedure of the Commission on the Limits of the Continental Shelf', CLCS/40/Rev.1 (17 April 2008), Article XI, Rule 45.

40 'Danish Mission to gather data for North Pole claim', *Barents Observer*, 30 July 2012.

41 Interview Admiral Nils Wang; Interview Generals Solli and Diessen (December 2012)

42 *Основы государственной политики Российской Федерации в Арктике на период до 2020 года и дальнейшую перспективу* (*Principles of State Policy of the Russian Federation in the Arctic for the period up to 2020 and Beyond*), (September 2008); *The Norwegian Government's High North Strategy*, (2006, revised 2009); *Canada's Northern Strategy: our North, our heritage, our Future* (2009); *Kingdom of Denmark Strategy for the Arctic 2011—2020* (2011); 'Arctic Region Policy', *National Security Presidential Directive* NSPD-66 (White House, 2009); *Arctic Opening*, p. 120.

43 Interview Arne Solli and Sverre Diessen, July 2012.

44 Interview with Aleksander Shestakov, 17 July 2013; Interview with Bernard Funston, 17 July 2013; Interview with Haakon Bruun-Hanssen.

45 Interview Nils Wang.

46 *Основы государственной политики Российской Федерации в Арктике на период до 2020 года и дальнейшую перспективу* (*Principles of State Policy of the Russian Federation in the Arctic for the period up to 2020 and Beyond*), September 2008. www.scrf.gov.ru/documents/98.html

47 *Ibid*. 4(d).

48 *Ibid*. IV, V, VI.

49 *Ibid*. 6(b).

50 'Arctic Special Report', *The Economist*, p. 5.

51 S. J. Blank (ed.), *Russia in the Arctic*, SSI Monograph (July 2011), p. 100.

52 *Энергетическая политика*, (*Energy Strategy of Russia for the Period up to 2030*) (2010); 'Putin Urges Shift in Response to Shale Gas', *Wall Street Journal*, 24 October 2012; 'Russia's New Asia Strategy: Assessing Russia's Eastward Pivot', CSIS roundtable, 14 November 2012.

53 Interview Adm. Bruun-Hanssen.

54 Interview Generals Solli and Diessen, July 2012.

55 Interview Generals Solli and Diessen, July 2012.

56 Interview Generals Solli and Diessen December 2012.

57 Interview Generals Solli and Diessen December 2012.

58 *The Norwegian Government's High North Strategy*, Norwegian Ministry of Foreign Affairs (2006). pp. 7-9.

59 *Ibid*. pp. 19-20.

60 *Norwegian Defence*, Norwegian Ministry of Defence (2008), p. 7.

61 Interview Arne Solli and. Sverre Diessen, December 2012.

62 Interview Haakon Bruun-Hanssen.

63 *Pomors* were the Russian hunters who carried out expeditions to Spitsbergen in the 18th century, where they competed fiercely with Norwegian hunters. By naming the joint-military exercises, initiated in 2010, the *Pomor*-series, both countries point to cooperation replacing past competition.

64 *Arctic Opening*, p. 96.

65 Interview Haakon Bruun-Hanssen.

66 Legal status of Eastern Greenland (Denmark v Norway), *PCIJ Judgment* 20 (5 September 1933), para. 165.

67 The uses of rare earth elements include the development of smart phones, electronic displays, nuclear batteries, special lamps, magnets, lenses, enamels, lasers, x-ray machines, hi-tech weapons systems and many other products of the clean-tech industry.

68 *Ibid*. p. 9; Interview Nils Wang.

69 N. Wang, 'Råstoffer, rigdom og realpolitik', *Politiken* (12 June 2012).

70 *Ibid*; *Mineral Strategy 2009: Update of objectives and plans for mineral exploration activities in Greenland*, Naalakkersuisut, Government of Greenland (2009).

71 The Nuclear Suppliers Group; and the The Wassenaar Arrangement on Export Controls for Conventional Arms and Dual-Use Goods and Technologies.

72 N. Wang and D. Degeorges, 'Greenland and the New Arctic – Political and security implications of a statebuilding project', *RDDC Brief* (2014), p. 12 (quote); Interview Admiral Nils Wang (December 2012); 'China stockpiling rare earths for strategic reserves', *The Telegraph* (5 July 2012); 'Rare minerals dearth threaten global renewables industry', *The Guardian* (27 January 2012); 'Shortages of rare minerals: China's strategic control over terbium, yttrium, dysprosium, europium and neodymium', *Global Research* (2 February 2012); *Arctic Opening*, p. 57.

73 N. Wang, 'Råstoffer, rigdom og realpolitik', *Politiken* (12 June 2012).

74 N. Wang and D. Degeorges, *Greenland and the new Arctic*, p. 8-9.

75 Interview Admiral Nils Wang, December 2012.

76 N. Wang and D. Degeorges, *Greenland and the new Arctic*, p. 10-11.

77 N. Wang and D. Degeorges, *Greenland and the new Arctic*, p. 13.

78 *Ibid*. p. 15.

79 A. Hammond and M. Rosing, 'Grønlands fremtid er et fælles ansvar', *Kroniken*, 7 May 2014.

80 *Denmark Strategy for the Arctic 2011–2020*, p. 20.

81 *Ibid*. pp. 20-21; *Danish Defence Agreement 2010–2014*, pp. 12-13; Additional comments by Nils Wang.

82 Interview with members of Canadian departments, 17 July 2013.

83 *Report of the Special Rapporteur on the situation of human rights and fundamental freedoms of indigenous people, Mission to Canada,* Commission on Human Rights (E/CN.4/2005/88/Add.3), p. 2.

84 *Canada's Arctic Council Chairmanship 2013–2015* (brochure).

85 *Ibid*.

86 *Arctic Opening*, p. 91.

87 *Ibid*. p. 92.

88 *Ibid*. p. 105.

89 'Canada renames Northwest Passage', *Barents Observer*, 4 December 2009.

90 This move, as a precursor to extracting the higher premiums of a northern Suez, also reflects disputing interpretations of the Law of the Sea. Canada is claiming sovereignty on the basis of its status as an 'archipelagic state' according to UNCLOS Article 46. The EU and US in turn would point to Article 37, arguing that EEZs that connect international seas are a transit passage or an 'international strait' (comparable to Denmark) and may not be blocked by the state bordering the strait, cf. J. Kraska, 'The Law of the Sea Convention and the Northwest Passage', *The International Journal of Marine and Coastal Law* 22(2), pp. 260-262.

91 Interview with members of Canadian Departments.

92 *Canada's Northern Strategy: Our North, Our Heritage, Our Future* (2009), p. 16.

93 Interview Admiral Nils Wang, December 2012.

94 'Canada island visit angers Danes', *BBC News* (25 July 2005).

95 The flag now hangs as a souvenir in the office of Thomas Winkler, the senior international law adviser of the Danish Ministry of Foreign Affairs, cf. Interview Admiral Nils Wang, December 2012.

96 'Arctic Region Policy', *National Security Presidential Directive NSPD-66 / Homeland Security Presidential Directive HSPD-25*. www.fas.org/irp/offdocs/nspd/nspd-66.htm

97 Interview Nils Wang.

98 *National Strategy for the Arctic Region*, White House (May 2013); *Arctic Strategy* (November 2013).

99 greenfleet.dodlive.mil/climate-change/

100 *US Navy Arctic Roadmap* (October 2009); *US Navy Climate Change Roadmap* (April 2010).

101 *National Strategy for the Arctic Region*, White House (May 2013), p. 8.

102 *Arctic Strategy*, Department of Defense (November 2013), p. 2.

103 *Ibid*. p. 8.

104 The *European Union and the Arctic Region*, Communication from the European Commission to the European Parliament and Council (20 November 2008).

105 'Norway invites EU to 'update' its mental map', EurActiv.com, 23 March 2012. www.euractiv.com/global-europe/norway-invites-eu-update-mental-news-511725

106 S. Weber & I. Romanshyn, 'Breaking the Ice: The European Union and the Arctic', *International Journal* (Autumn 2011), pp. 857-858. 'Growing Importance of the Arctic Council', *IISS Strategic Comments* 19 (16), June 2013.

107 Interview Nils Wang, December 2012.

108 Interview Arne Solli and Sverre Diessen, December 2012.

109 The largest scientific facility on Spitsbergen at Ny-Ålesund is Chinese.

110 Interview with Aleksander Shestakov and Clive Tesar of the WWF Arctic Group, 17 July 2013.

111 Interview with Canadian academics, 17 July 2013.

112 *Ibid*.

113 President John F. Kennedy, Speech at Rice University, Houston, Texas, 12 September 1962.

SOURCES

The interviews were conducted by The Owls Team: Henk van den Breemen, Johanna Noom and Benjamin Bilski.

With many thanks to Ambassador Rochus Pronk and the staff of the Dutch Embassy, Canada.

- Generals Arne Solli and Sverre Diesen, Oslo, 7 August 2012 and 13 December 2012.
- Admiral Nils Wang, Copenhagen, 12 December 2012.
- Interview with members of Canadian Departments, Ottawa, 17 July 2013.
  - Department of Foreign Affairs, Trade and Development (Jeanette Menzies, meeting chaired by Robert Kadas)
  - Department of National Defence.
  - Department of Aboriginal Affairs and Northern Development Canada (Frances Abele, David Lenarcic, Nick Xenos and others)
- Interview with Canadian academics, Ottawa, 17 July 2013.
  - Jackie Dawson, Professor of Public Policy at University of Ottawa, 17 July 2013.
  - Bernard Funston, Chair of the Canadian Polar Commission, 17 July 2013.
- Admiral Haakon Bruun-Hanssen, Bodø, 6 August 2013.

WRITTEN SOURCES

Articles and Books
- Special Report 'The melting north', *The Economist*, 16 June 2012.
- J. Mazo, *Climate Conflict*, IISS Adelphi 409 (2010).
- J. Maxo and C. Le Miere, *Arctic Opening: Opportunities and Challenges*, IISS Adelphi 440 (2013).
- D. Cressey, 'The next land rush', *Nature*, vol. 451(3), 2008.
- D. Avango, et al. 'Between markets and geo-politics: natural resource exploitation on Spitsbergen from 1600 to the present day', *Polar Record* 47(240) (2011).
- Torbjørn Pedersen, 'Norway's rule on Svalbard: tightening the grip on the Arctic islands', *Polar Record* 45(233) (2009).
- Donald. L. Gautier et al., 'Assessment of Undiscovered Oil and Gas in the Arctic', *Science*, vol. 324, no. 5,931, 29 May 2009, pp. 1175–9.
- 'Circum-Arctic Resource Appraisal: Estimates of Undiscovered Oil and Gas North of the Arctic Circle', *USGS Fact Sheet* 2008-3049.
- 'Danish Mission to gather data for North Pole claim', *Barents Observer*, 30 July 2012.
- S. J. Blank (ed.), *Russia in the Arctic*, SSI Monograph (July 2011).
- 'Putin Urges Shift in Response to Shale Gas', *Wall Street Journal*, 24 October 2012.
- 'Russia's New Asia Strategy: Assessing Russia's Eastward Pivot', CSIS roundtable, 14 November 2012.
- 'China stockpiling rare earths for strategic reserves', *The Telegraph* (5 July 2012).
- 'Rare minerals dearth threaten global renewables industry', *The Guardian* (27 January 2012).
- 'Shortages of rare minerals: China's strategic control over terbium, yttrium, dysprosium, europium and neodymium', *Global Research* (2 February 2012).
- N. Wang, 'Råstoffer, rigdom og realpolitik', *Politiken* (12 June 2012).
- J. Kraska, 'The Law of the Sea Convention and the Northwest Passage', *The International Journal of Marine and Coastal Law* 22(2), pp. 260-262.
- 'Canada island visit angers Danes', *BBC News* (25 July 2005).
- Norway invites EU to 'update' its mental map', *EurActiv.com*, 23 March 2012.
- S. Weber & I. Romanshyn, 'Breaking the Ice: The European Union and the Arctic', *International Journal* (Autumn 2011), pp. 857-858.
- 'Growing Importance of the Arctic Council', *IISS Strategic Comments* 19(16), June 2013.

Speeches
- R. Admiral David Titley, 'Climate Change and National Security', *AMS Briefing*, 28 May 2010.
- President John F. Kennedy, Speech at Rice University, Houston, Texas, 12 September 1962.

Treaties and Cases
- *Treaty between the Kingdom of Norway and the Russian Federation concerning Maritime Delimitation and Cooperation in the Barents Sea and the Arctic Ocean*, signed 15 September 2010.
- *Maritime Delimitation in the Area between Greenland and Jan Mayen*, ICJ (1988–1993).
- *Agreement between the Kingdom of Denmark and the Kingdom of Norway concerning the Delimitation of the Continental Shelf in the Area between Jan Mayen and Greenland and concerning the Boundary between the Fishery Zones in the Area* (1995).
- *Agreement between Norway and Iceland concerning Fishery and Continental Shelf Questions* (1980).
- *Agreement between the Government of the Kingdom of Denmark and the Government of Canada to the Delimitation of the Continental Shelf between Greenland and Canada* (1973).

Arctic Council
- *Declaration of the Establishment of the Arctic Council*, 1(a), Ottawa, Canada, 19 September 1996.
- Arctic Council Secretariat, *The Vision for the Arctic*, Kiruna, Sweden, 15 May 2013.
- *The Ilulissat Declaration*, Arctic Ocean Conference, Ilulissat, Greenland, 27-29 May 2008.

Canada
- *Canada's Northern Strategy: Our North, Our Heritage, Our Future* (2009).
- *Canada's Arctic Council Chairmanship 2013–2015* (brochure).

Russia

- *Основы государственной политики Российской Федерации в Арктике на период до 2020 года и дальнейшую перспективу* (*Principles of State Policy of the Russian Federation in the Arctic for the period up to 2020 and Beyond*), (September 2008).
- *Энергетическая политика* (*Energy Strategy of Russia for the Period up to 2030*), (2010).

Norway

- The Norwegian Government's High North Strategy, Norwegian Ministry of Foreign Affairs (2006).
- Norwegian Defence, Norwegian Ministry of Defence (2008).

Denmark and Greenland

- *Kingdom of Denmark Strategy for the Arctic 2011–2020.*
- *Danish Defence Agreement 2010–2014.*
- *Mineral Strategy 2009: Update of objectives and plans for mineral exploration activities in Greenland*, Naalakkersuisut, Government of Greenland (2009).

Unites States of America

- 'Arctic Region Policy', *National Security Presidential Directive* NSPD-66/Homeland Security Presidential Directive HSPD-25.
- *U.S. Navy Arctic Roadmap* (October 2009).
- *U.S. Navy Climate Change Roadmap* (April 2010).
- *U.S. Navy Arctic Roadmap* (October 2009).
- *U.S. Navy Climate Change Roadmap* (April 2010).
- *National Strategy for the Arctic Region*, White House (May 2013).
- *Arctic Strategy*, Department of Defense (November 2013).
- *Arctic Strategy*, US Coast Guard (May 2013).

European Union

- 'The European Union and the Arctic Region', *Communication from the European Commission to the European Parliament and Council* (20 November 2008).

CHAPTER 5

Europe's Energy Impasse

SOURCES

Climate and Energy Package, European Union (2008): ec.europa.eu/clima/policies/package/index_en.htm

Total Energy, LACQ project: total.com/en/society-environment/environment/climate-carbon/carbon-capture-storage/lacq-pilot-project

Z. Barlow, 'Breakthrough in hydrogen fuel production could revolutionize alternative energy market', *Virginia Tech* (Press release 4 April 2013)

CHAPTER 6

Sustainable Energy and Smart Grids

REFERENCES

- CEN-CENELEC-ETSI, 2012, *CEN-CENELEC-ETSI Smart Grid Coordination Group. Smart Grid Architecture.*
- Chabannes, F., 2013, 'Fessenwind. Une centrale éolienne terrestre pour remplacer Fessenheim?', internal publication.
- Dooyeweerd, H., 1969, *A New Critique of Theoretical Thought*, The Presbyterian and Reformed Publishing Company.
- European Commission (EC), 2010, 'Energy 2020: A strategy for competitive, sustainable and secure energy', COM (2010) 639 final.
- European Commission (EC), 2011, 'Smart Grid Projects in Europe: Lessons Learned and Current Developments', European Commission, Institute of Energy, Netherlands, 2011.
- European Electricity Grids Initiative (EEGI), 2010, 'Roadmap 2010–2018 and detailed implementation plan 2010–2012'.
- Energy Information Administration (EIA), 2013, International Energy Outlook 2013, July 2013.
- International Energy Agency Wind (IEA Wind), 2012, Annual Report 2012.
- Jochemsen, H., 2006, 'Normative practices as an Intermediate between Theoretical Ethics and Morality', *Philosophia Reformata* 71:96-112.
- Litos Strategic Communication (LSC), 2010, *The Smart Grid: An Introduction*, prepared for the US Department of Energy.
- Loster, M., 2010, retrieved December 16th, 2013, www.ez2c.de/ml/solar_land_area/.
- MacKay, D.J.C., 2009, *Sustainable Energy – without the hot air*, UIT Cambridge, Cambridge.
- National Renewable Energy Laboratory (NREL), 2013, *Renewable Electricity Futures Study*, July 2013.
- Naess, A., 1973, 'The Shallow and the Deep. Long-Range Ecology Movement. A Summary', *Inquiry* 16: 95-100.
- Pike Research, 2011, 'Smart Grids in Europe', Pike Research Cleantech Market Intelligence, available at: www.pikeresearch.com/research/smart-grids-in-europe, accessed February 2011.
- Ribeiro, P.F., Polinder, H., and Verkerk, M.J., 2012, 'Planning and designing smart grids: philosophical considerations', *IEEE Technology and Society Magazine*, Fall 2012, 34-43.
- Sandia Report, 2013, DOE/EPRI 2013 Electricity Storage Handbook in Collaboration with NRECA, July 2013.
- Technische Universiteit Eindhoven (TUE), 2012, www.tue.nl/fileadmin/content/faculteiten/ee/Onderzoek/Technologische_centra/Centre_for_Wireless_Technology/1_-_Peter_Baltus_-_intro_and_vision.pdf
- Verkerk, M.J., Hoogland, J., Stoep, J. van der, and Vries, M.J. de, Thinking, Designing, Making (in Dutch), Boom, Amsterdam.
- Vuuren, D.P. van, Nakicenovic, N., Riahi, K.,

Brew-Hammond, A., Kammen D., Modi V., Nilsson, M., and Smith, K.R., 'An energy vision: the transformation towards sustainability – interconnected challenges and solutions', *Current Opinion in Environmental Sustainability* 2012, 4:18–34.

CHAPTER 7
Postscript on the Future of Energy

FOOTNOTES

1 Sociaal-Economische Raad, *Energieakkoord voor duurzame groei (Energy agreement for Sustainable Growth)*, (2013). This report is a consensus of more than 40 Dutch interest groups, which include employers' organisations, insurers, trade unions, environmental groups, the national rail company, social organisations, financial institutions, housing associations, car owners' associations and the central and provincial governments. From the energy industry, there are electricity providers, but no representatives from oil or natural gas.
2 While the *Energieakkoord* has announced €3.7 billion investment for offshore wind energy, the real number remains contentious as critics have noted that the cost of wind energy had risen. The government had admitted that it has risen to €14 billion, but not as high as over €40 billion as some critics alleged, cf. Letter by Minister Kamp to Parliament 11 November 2013 (*Kamerbrief over hernieuwde doorrekening Energieakkoord*) www.rijksoverheid.nl/documenten-en-publicaties/kamerstukken/2013/11/11/kamerbrief-over-hernieuwde-doorrekening-energieakkoord.html

CHAPTER 8
The Power of Ideas:
Responsibility to Protect

FOOTNOTES

1 Interview with Francis Deng (18 July 2012).
2 Francis Deng and Roberta Cohen, 'Normative Framework of Sovereignty', *Sovereignty as Responsibility: Conflict Management in Africa* (1996), pp. 1-33; Lloyd Axworthy, *Navigating a New World: Canada's Global Future* (2004), pp. 177-199, 414-416; Gareth Evans et al, *The Responsibility to Protect* (2001); Gareth Evans, *The Responsibility to Protect: Ending Mass Atrocities Once and For All* (2009); Kofi Annan, *Interventions* (2012), pp. 83-135.
3 Interview Francis Deng.
4 Francis Deng et al, *Sovereignty as Responsibility* (1996), p. xvi.
5 *Ibid.* p. xvi.
6 *Ibid.* Chapter 1, 'Normative Framework of Sovereignty', p. 1.

7 *Ibid.* p. 7
8 *Ibid.* p. 9.
9 *Ibid.* p. 15.
10 A/63/677, Report of the Secretary-General, *Implementing the responsibility to protect* (January 2009).
11 *Sovereignty as Responsibility*, pp. 31-32.
12 Kofi Annan, *Interventions*, p. 119.
13 Interview Ambassador Herman Schaper, 15 January 2013.
14 *The Kosovo Report*, Independent International Commission on Kosovo, Executive Summary.
15 Kofi Annan, 'Two Concepts of Sovereignty', *The Economist*, 18 September 1999.
16 Interview Francis Deng; Lloyd Axworthy, *Navigating a New World: Canada's Global Future* (2004), p. 414-415.
17 The Dutch had also attempted to develop similar ideas, with several workshops taking place in the Netherlands around the same time, "but the Canadians were quicker and did it better." (Interview Ambassador Herman Schaper).
18 "Between Ottawa and Geneva roundtables, Gareth Evans came up with the idea of reframing the debate in terms of a 'responsibility to protect'. The phrase was aired as a way of reconciling sovereignty and human rights and of resolving four problems, set out in a discussion paper put before the 31 January 2001 Geneva roundtable." Alex Bellamy, *Responsibility to Protect: The Global Effort to End Mass Atrocities* (2009), p. 43; Interview Simon Adams. When one of the authors of this chapter asked Evans about the origin of the phrase, he answered that he thought about combining words for a time, starting with 'Responsibility' from Deng's concept. When he first presented 'Responsibility to Protect' to the working group, they were taken aback. (Gareth Evans and Alex Bellamy, speeches at House of Commons, London, 15 May 2013).
19 Gareth Evans, *The Responsibility to Protect* (2009), p. 42.
20 Gareth Evans et al, *The Responsibility to Protect* (2001), p. 13.
21 *Ibid.* p. 15.
22 Interview Ambassador Schaper.
23 *The Responsibility to Protect* (2001), pp. 57-64.
24 *Ibid.* pp. 39-45.
25 *Ibid.* p. XIII.
26 Bellamy, pp. 70, 72-73.
27 *Ibid.* p. 71.
28 Today William Pace's International Coalition for the Responsibility to Protect has over 65 NGOs as institutional members (www.responsibilitytoprotect.org/index.php/about-coalition/current-members).
29 Interview William Pace.
30 Bellamy, p. 72.
31 *Ibid.* p. 73-76.
32 *Ibid.* p. 76: But "rather optimistically, the HLP hoped that members would be reluctant to

declare publicly their opposition to collective action in conscience-shocking cases and that this would reduce the threat of veto."

33 Interview Ambassador Schaper.

34 G. Mitchell and N. Gingrich, *American Interests and UN Reform*, Report on the Task Force on the United Nations (2005).

35 Bellamy. pp. 77-81.

36 Interview William Pace; Gareth Evans, *The Responsibility to Protect* (2009), p. 47.

37 *Ibid.* pp. 83-97.

38 UN General Assembly, World Summit Outcome 2005, A/RES/60/1, 24 October 2005.

39 S/2007/721, 'Letter dated 31 August 2007 from the Secretary-General addressed to the President of the Security Council'.

40 In accordance with Article 140 of the World Summit Outcome of 2005: "We fully support the mission of the Special Adviser of the Secretary-General on the Prevention of Genocide."

41 Passing the budgetary vote for these offices in the 5th committee was the first major victory for R2P after the World Summit Outcome. On 24 December 2007, the vote was approved; it, also identified the opponents of R2P: Cuba, Venezuela, Pakistan, China, Egypt, Nicaragua, Iran, and India.

42 A/63/677, *Implementing the responsibility to protect* (2009), para 32.

43 A/64/864, *Early warning, assessment and the responsibility to protect* (2010), para 7.

44 Statement by Edward C. Luck, 'Informal Interactive Dialogue on Early Warning, Assessment, and the Responsibility to Protect', UN GA 9 August 2010.

45 A/65/877–S/2011/39, *The role of regional and sub-regional arrangements in implementing the responsibility to protect* (2011), para 24.

46 Interview Simon Adams.

47 Interview with Ambassador Gert Rosenthal, 18 July 2012.

48 Interview Gert Rosenthal.

49 A/Res/63/308, 7 October 2009.

50 The personal friendship between the Canadian and Dutch ambassadors led to this arrangement; cf. Interview Ambassador Schaper.

51 S/PRST/2013/2 (12 February 2013).

52 S/PRST/2013/4 (15 April 2013).

53 United Nations High Commissioner for Refugees, the International Committee for the Red Cross and the Office for the Coordination of Humanitarian Affairs.

54 S/2012/376, para 21.

55 The UN Development Programme, the Department of Political Affairs, and the Department for Peace Keeping Operations.

56 www.stanleyfoundation.org/preview. cfm?ContentType=Article&ID=750

57 *Report of the Secretary General's Review Panel on United Nations Action in Sri Lanka*, November 2012, para 76, p. 27

58 Darfur Consortium (www.darfurconsortium.

org/darfur_crisis/background.html); and International Coalition for the Responsibility to Protect (responsibilitytoprotect.org/index. php/crises/crisis-in-darfur)

59 The EU Parliament, Resolutions on the situation in Darfur: 2006/2553(RSP) (6 April 2006); 2006/2625(RSP) (28 September 2006); 2007/2514(RSP) (15 February 2007); 2007/2589(RSP); On Sudan and the ICC: 2008/2580(RSP) (22 May 2008); and The expulsion of NGOs: 2009/2556(RSP) (12 March 2009).

60 S/Res/1706 (2006); S/Res/1769 (2007); S/res/1935 (2010).

61 'Warrant of Arrest for Omar Hassan Ahmad Al-Bashir', ICC-02/05-01/2009 (4 March 2009); and 'Second Warrant of Arrest for Omar Hassan Ahmad Al-Bashir' (12 July 2012)

62 responsibilitytoprotect.org/index.php/ component/content/article/129-africa/1501-violence-in-kenya-statement-made-by-french-foreign-and-european-affairs-minister-bernard-kouchner

63 www.un.org/apps/news/story. asp?NewsID=25189&Cr=kenya&Cr1#. UYDSRivwKD0

INTERVIEWS

Interviews conducted by the Owls Team: Henk van den Breemen, Johanna Noom and Benjamin Bilski.

○ Francis Deng, 18 July 2012
○ Ambassadora Maria Luiza Ribiero Viotti, 18 July 2012
○ Simon Adams, 18 July 2012
○ William Pace, 19 July 2012
○ Ambassador Gert Rosenthal, 19 July 2012
○ Ambassador Herman Schaper, 15 January 2013

BOOKS AND ARTICLES

○ Kofi Annan, Interventions (2012).
○ Kofi Annan, 'Two Concepts of Sovereignty', *The Economist*, 18 September 1999.
○ Lloyd Axworthy, *Navigating a New World: Canada's Global Future* (2004).
○ Alex Bellamy, *Responsibility to Protect: The Global Effort to End Mass Atrocities* (2009).
○ Francis Deng et al, *Sovereignty as Responsibility: Conflict Management in Africa* (1996).
○ Gareth Evans et al, *The Responsibility to Protect* (2001).
○ Gareth Evans, *The Responsibility to Protect: Ending Mass Atrocities Once and For All* (2009).
○ G. Mitchell and N. Gingrich, *American Interests and UN Reform*, Report on the Task Force on the United Nations (2005).

UNITED NATIONS

○ A/63/677, Report of the Secretary-General, *Implementing the responsibility to protect*

(January 2009).
- *The Kosovo Report*, Independent International Commission on Kosovo (2001)
- UN General Assembly, *World Summit Outcome* 2005, A/RES/60/1, 24 October 2005
- S/2007/721, 'Letter dated 31 August 2007 from the Secretary-General addressed to the President of the Security Council'.
- A/63/677, *Implementing the responsibility to protect* (2009).
- 43A/64/864, *Early warning, assessment and the responsibility to protect* (2010).
- A/64/864, *Early warning, assessment and the responsibility to protect* (2010).
- Edward C. Luck, 'Informal Interactive Dialogue on Early Warning, Assessment, and the Responsibility to Protect', UN GA, 9 August 2010.
- A/65/877–S/2011/39, *The role of regional and sub-regional arrangements in implementing the responsibility to protect*, (2011).
- A/Res/63/308, 7 October 2009.
- S/PRST/2013/2 (12 February 2013).
- S/PRST/2013/4 (15 April 2013).
- S/2012/376
- *Report of the Secretary General's Review Panel on United Nations Action in Sri Lanka*, November 2012
- S/Res/1706 (2006)
- S/Res/1769 (2007)
- S/res/1935 (2010)

EUROPEAN UNION

- The EU Parliament, Resolutions on the situation in Darfur: 2006/2553(RSP) (6 April 2006); 2006/2625(RSP) (28 September 2006); 2007/2514(RSP) (15 February 2007); 2007/2589(RSP);
- On Sudan and the ICC: 2008/2580(RSP) (22 May 2008).
- The expulsion of NGOs: 2009/2556(RSP) (12 March 2009).

INTERNATIONAL CRIMINAL COURT

- *Warrant of Arrest for Omar Hassan Ahmad Al-Bashir*, ICC-02/05-01/2009 (4 March 2009).
- *Second Warrant of Arrest for Omar Hassan Ahmad Al-Bashir* (12 July 2012).

CHAPTER 9

An Unexpected Success:
The Rapid Unification of Germany

FOOTNOTES

Additional research and interview with Horst Teltschik (29 January 2014) by Benjamin Bilski.

1 Interview Horst Teltschik, 29 January 2014
2 G. H. W. Bush and Brent Scowcroft, *A World Transformed* (1998), p. 299.
3 'Taking Lyon on the Ninth Day? The 1964 Warsaw Pact Plan for a Nuclear War in Europe

and Related Documents' *Parallel History Project on NATO and the Warsaw Pact*, PHP Publications Series Washington (May 2000).
4 Interview Horst Teltchik.
5 *A World Transformed*, pp. 186-187.
6 *A World Transformed*, p. 185.
7 Interview Horst Teltschik.
8 *A World Transformed*, p. 188.
9 Interview Horst Teltschik; *Joint Declaration signed by Federal Chancellor Kohl and President Gorbachev*, 13 June 1989; Helsinki Final Act (1975), Article VII (2): "By virtue of the principle of equal rights and self-determination of peoples, all peoples always have the right, in full freedom, to determine, when and as they wish, their internal and external political status, without external interference, and to pursue as they wish their political, economic, social and cultural development."
10 Interview Horst Teltschik.
11 Interview Horst Teltschik.
12 Horst Teltschik, *329 Tage*, p. 42.
13 *Ibid*. p. 43
14 *Ibid*. p. 44; Interview Horst Teltschik.
15 Interview Horst Teltschik.
16 *A World Transformed*, p. 194; Helmut Kohl's Ten-Point Plan for German Unity, November 28, 1989, (germanhistorydocs.ghi-dc.org).
17 *A World Transformed*, p. 191.
18 *Ibid*. p. 192.
19 *Ibid*. p. 197.
20 Interview Horst Teltschik.
21 'Mitterrand, in Kiev, Warns Bonn Not to Press Reunification Issue', *New York Times*, 6 December 1989.
22 A world transformed, p. 246.
23 'The last day of the Stasi', *Die Welt* (dw.de), 15 January 2005.
24 *Ibid*. 232.
25 *Ibid*. pp. 232-233.
26 *Ibid*. p. 239.
27 Horst Teltschik, *329 Tage*, p. 173.
28 *Ibid*. p. 176.
29 *A World Transformed*, p. 259.
30 *Ibid*. 282.
31 *A World Transformed*, p. 299.

CHAPTER 10

The Oslo Breakthrough

FOOTNOTES

1 Arab League, Khartoum Declaration, 1 September 1967, Art 3: "This will be done within the framework of the main principles by which the Arab States abide, namely, no peace with Israel, no recognition of Israel, no negotiations with it, and insistence on the rights of the Palestinian people in their own country."
2 UN Security Council Resolution 242 (22 November 1967), Art 1(ii).
3 Interview Shimon Peres, 26 June 2012.

4   The chief Oslo negotiator and our interviewee Uri Savir recently considered movements to revive the Jordanian option, but argues that such a regional arrangement only makes sense after the establishment of a Palestinian state, cf. Uri Savir, 'A Palestinian-Jordanian Confederation', *Jerusalem Post*, 10 January 2013.

5   The Jordanian move entailed cutting off all administrative ties and stripping all West Bank   Palestinians of Jordanian citizenship. It meant dissolving the Jordanian parliament, removing all West Bank representatives, and cutting salaries to tens of thousands of civil servants. An ad-hoc Executive Committee was to be formed, and the Jordanians instructed the Palestinian leadership to "agree on the principle of declaring a Palestinian state and forming a government"; where the leadership was to be a combination of the PLO and the "Unified Leadership of the Intifadah"; who were to form a government, which must agree on the "relationship between the government and the PLO"; and finally, a "host county" should be found for the "government of Palestine". ('VI Declaration Process Started', *Palestine Yearbook of International Law*, Vol. IV (1987/88), p. 321.)

6   Following the expulsion of the PLO from the West Bank, Arafat led a rebellion against the Jordanian kingdom in the February 1970 to July 1971 civil war – where the PLO was decisively crushed. The PLO's tactics then shifted from attempting a military challenge against Israel or Jordan, but to seeking international recognition, coupled with some spectacular acts of international terrorism. Their reward came in the Arab summit in Rabat in October 1974, where the formula was adopted that the PLO was the "sole and legitimate representative of the Palestinian people", cf. A. Bligh, 'Jordanian-Israeli Strategic Partnership in Historical Perspective', *ACPR Policy Paper* No. 24 (1998), pp. 2-6.

7   Track-II Diplomacy, p. 32; '396. Palestinian National Council political statement and declaration of independence - 14 November 1988', *Israel Ministry of Foreign Affairs*, vol. 9-10 1984-1988.

8   *Ibid*: The preamble on the intifada: "Thus did the struggle of the children of the RPG outside our homeland and the struggle of the children of the sacred stones inside it blend to a single revolutionary melody. (…) By standing firm, continuing their revolution and escalating their intifada, our people have proved their determination to press ahead regardless of the sacrifices". And the operative decisions included: "A: to provide all means and capabilities needed to escalate our people's intifada", and "C: To bolster and develop the Popular Committees and other specialized and trade union bodies, including the attack groups and the popular army, with a view of expanding

their role and increasing their effectiveness."

9   '397. Foreign Ministry Statement on the PNC Decisions - 15 November 1988', *Israel Ministry of Foreign Affairs*, vol. 9-10, 1984-1988.

10   Interview Abu Ala'a, 27 June 2012.

11   Speech by President George H. W. Bush before a Joint Session of Congress on the Cessation of the Persian Gulf Conflict, 6 March 1991.

12   Boris Pankin and James Baker, 'U.S.-Soviet Invitation to the Mideast Peace Conference in Madrid', October 18, 1991.

13   Interview Amnon Shahak, 18 November 2011.

14   Interview Yossi Beilin, 31 May 2011.

15   Interview Amnon Shahak.

16   Interview Uri Savir, 31 May 2012.

17   'After the Gulf War: Israeli Defense and its Security Policy', Address at Begin-Sadat Center for Strategic Studies, Bar Ilan University, 10 June 1991, cf. Efraim Inbar, *Rabin and Israel's National Security* (1999), pp. 172-178.

18   Interview Uri Savir.

19   Interview Uri Savir; Yossi Klein Halevi and Michael Oren, 'Contra Iran', *The New Republic*, 26 January 2007; Shimon Peres, *The New Middle East* (1993), p. 34.

20   Interview Uri Savir.

21   Interview Shimon Peres.

22   Shimon Peres, The New Middle East (1993), p. 30.

23   *Ibid*. Chapters 4-11.

24   Interview Uri Savir; Interview Yossi Beilin; Interview Ron Pundak.

25   Interview Shimon Peres.

26   Interview Amnon Shahak.

27   Interview Yossi Beilin.

28   Interview Yossi Beilin; Interview Shimon Peres.

29   Interview Ron Pundak.

30   Interview Abu Ala'a.

31   Interview Ron Pundak.

32   Mahmoud Abbas, *Through Secret Channels* (1995), p. 113.

33   Interview Ron Pundak.

34   Interview Uri Savir; Interview Ron Pundak.

35   These include: reference to UN resolutions 242 and 338; the extent of the Palestinian authority; Security; Elections; and a variety of committees to deal with development, water, refugees, environment, and security.

36   Interview Amnon Shahak; Interview Uri Savir; Interview Yossi Beilin.

37   Interview Uri Savir; Interview Yossi Beilin.

38   Other track-II conversations had taken place between Ephraim Sneh and Nabil Shaath, and Haim Ramon initiated meetings as well, but none of them took off like the Oslo track.

39   Interview Yossi Beilin.

40   Shimon Peres, *Battling for Peace: Memoirs*, p. 329.

41   Yossi Beilin, *Touching Peace*, p. 84.

42   Interview Yossi Beilin.

43   Interview Uri Savir.

44   Uri Savir, *The Process*, p. 64.

45   Interview Ron Pundak; Interview Uri Savir.

46 Uri Savir, *The Process* (1998), pp. 94-96.
47 *Ibid*. p. 69.
48 Interview Abu Ala'a.
49 Ahmed Qurie, *Beyond Oslo, The Struggle for Palestine* (2008), p. 16.
50 Uri Savir, *The Process* (1998). pp. 69-77.
51 Interview Amnon Shahak.
52 Interview Amnon Shahak.
53 In our interviews, Amnon Shahak and Ron Pundak agreed that this was the maximum that was attainable at the time. Yossi Beilin disagreed: he wanted to move straight from his ideological vision to final status, skipping any process stages in between.
54 Old and new countries in the post-Soviet space established and restored diplomatic ties with Israel that had been broken off since the 1967 War, following the end of the Cold War in 1990-1992. A great number of African countries had broken off diplomatic relations with Israel after the 1973 war, and restored these following the Oslo agreements in 1993-1995.
55 The 'Interim Agreement on West Bank and Gaza Strip', also known as "Oslo II" was signed on 24 and 28 September 1995. It bundled and superseded three prior agreements that were planned in the 1993 Declaration: the 'Gaza–Jericho Agreement' of 4 May 1994, that included the 'Protocol on Economic Relations'; the 'Agreement on Preparatory Transfer of Powers and Responsibilities Between Israel and the PLO at Erez Crossing' was signed on 29 August 1994; and the 'Protocol on Further Transfer of Powers and Responsibilities' was signed in Cairo on 27 August 1995.
56 Declaration of Principles on Interim Self-Government Arrangements, Article 3(1).
57 Interview Yossi Beilin.
58 Uri Savir, *The Process* (1999), p. 94: "Abu Mazen's response was, in effect, to seclude himself in his Tunis home for over a year. Abu Ala, who was interested in strengthening the Palestinians' ties with their immediate Arab neighbors, plunged into negotiations for an economic treaty with Jordan."
59 *Ibid*. p. 96.
60 *Ibid*. pp. 93-98.
61 Later Ambassador to the Netherlands.
62 Uri Savir, *The Process*, p. 99-100.
63 *Ibid*. p. 114.
64 *Ibid*. pp. 121-134; Interview Uri Savir.
65 Yossi Beilin, *Touching Peace*, p. 144: "I had a feeling that if such a meeting were possible, anything was possible, and I took a deep breath and asked why he didn't change out of his military gear into civilian clothes, now that he had finally entered a political phase. Silence. After a long pause, Hannan replied on his behalf: 'That's how his people see him, how they know him. Without the uniform he'd be a different person.' There was no response from Arafat but eventually, after another long and awkward pause, we moved to a corner of the room for a more private conversation."
66 Uri Savir, *The Process*, p. 140.
67 Declaration of Principles, Article 3.
68 The largest donor was the United States with $500 million. Arab States, who had supported Palestinian struggle against Israel, refrained from supporting Palestinian peace-building, in part because they had not forgiven Arafat for his support for Saddam Hussein's conquest of Kuwait (Uri Savir, *The Process*, pp. 145-146)
69 Declaration of Principles, Article 13.
70 Daniel Polisar, 'Arafat and the Myth of Legitimacy', *Azure* (Summer 2002), pp. 32-35.
71 *Ibid*. p. 45-46, cf. Gaza-Jericho Agreement, Article 7(9): "Laws and military orders in effect in the Gaza Strip or the Jericho Area prior to the signing of this Agreement shall remain in force, unless amended or abrogated in accordance with this Agreement."
72 Polisar, pp. 47-48: "In Jericho, Saeb Erekat appointed a PLA colonel with no experience in the laws of the West Bank to head the Civil Court: According to a senior official of the International Commission of Jurists, this judge generally based his decisions on "personal views rather than on the letter of the law."
73 Drafts of a Palestinian Basic Law code were drafted 1994 and 1995, but failed to pass in those years. The Palestinian Legislative Council passed the Basic Law in 1997, and this was ratified by Arafat in 2002.
74 To illustrate, a UK-based Arab Organization for Human Rights published a report in December 2012, showing that 96% of Palestinians in Palestinian prisons have experienced torture, among them women and old people, cf. 'UK-based Arab HR group accuses PA of abuse', *Jerusalem Post*, 30 December 2012.
75 Gaza-Jericho Agreement, Article 1(6).
76 Polisar, pp. 26, 35-37, 55.
77 *Ibid*. pp. 58-62.
78 Thomas Friedman, *From Beirut to Jerusalem* (2nd ed. 1995), p. 563.
79 *Ibid*. pp. 563-564.
80 Interview Uri Savir.
81 Sara Roy, *Hamas and Civil Society in Gaza* (2011), pp. 34-35.
82 Interview Amnon Shahak.
83 *Hamas and Civil Society in Gaza*, p. 36.
84 Peres was leading in the polls, but Netanyahu narrowly won – surprising all concerned. "Went to bed with Peres, woke up with Netanyahu," went the saying.
85 After Netanyahu was first elected Prime Minister in 1996, his office produced a list of all the major PLO violations of the Oslo Accords. These included: opening fire on Israeli forces; failure to confiscate illegal arms and disarm and disband militias; failure to extradite suspected terrorists to Israel; incitement to violence against Israel; failure to change the PLO Covenant; recruiting terrorists to serve in the Palestinian police; abuse of human rights and the rule of law; and violations in the conduct of foreign relations.
86 Interview Amnon Shahak.

87 Interview Shimon Peres.
88 Interview Abu Ala'a.
89 Interview Shimon Peres.

SOURCES

Interviews conducted by the Owls Team: Henk van den Breemen, Johanna Noom and Benjamin Bilski.

∘ General Amnon Shahak, 18 November 2011
∘ Uri Savir, 31 May 2012
∘ Ron Pundak, 31 May 2012
∘ Yossi Beilin, 31 May 2012

Interviews by Henk van den Breemen and Johanna Noom.

∘ President Shimon Peres, 26 June 2012
∘ Ahmed Qurie (Abu Ala'a), 27 June 2012

MEMOIRS

Mahmoud Abbas, James Baker, Yossi Beilin, Thomas Friedman, Ephraim Halevy, Henry Kissinger, Aaron David Miller, Shimon Peres, Ahmed Qurie, William Quandt, Condoleezza Rice, Dennis Ross, Uri Savir.

OTHER SOURCES

∘ Track-II Diplomacy: Lessons from the Middle East (2004)
∘ Daniel Polisar, 'Arafat and the Myth of Legitimacy', Azure (Summer 2002)
∘ Benny Morris, Righteous Victims (2001)
∘ Palestine Yearbook of International Law, vol. IV (1987/88)
∘ Israel Ministry of Foreign Affairs, vol. 9-10 (1984-1988)

CHAPTER 11

China in the Age of Accelerating
Change: a Positive Approach

FOOTNOTES

1   Traditionally, the portion of a population in poverty – using "purchasing power parity" to adjust for differences in national currencies – has been the basic means of measuring material wellbeing. When applied to China, it indicates that in 1981 (several years after the government began economic reforms) about 63 per cent of the population of China was in poverty. By 2008 that percentage had dropped to close to around 10 per cent. In three decades more than 500 million Chinese climbed out of poverty. Material well-being, however, is only one of the dimensions associated with "happiness", "satisfaction", or other psychological aspects [of well-being] that can affect political events and governmental policy. Surveys and different assessments of these dimensions indicate China's dramatic improvement in material well-being has been accompanied by, among other things, a growing concern and dissatisfaction with growing disparities in wealth within the population.

2   One iteration –"the Great Leap forward" – undertaken in the 1950s produced four years of negative economic growth, famine, and tens of millions of excessive deaths. Another – the Great Proletarian Cultural Revolution in the 1960s – was similarly highly disruptive economically and socially, and probably triggered the "Great Opening" which is now generally credited with China's economic rise.

3   The allusion here is to speculation by Martin Jacques (among others). See Jacques, *When China Rules the World: The End of the Western World and the Birth of a new Global Order*, (NY: Penguin Press, 2009).

4   James Fallows, *The $1.4 Trillion Question*, www.theatlantic.com/magazine/archive/2008/01/the-14-trillion-question/6582/

5   C. Fred Bergsten, Nicholas R. Lardy, et al, *China: The Balance Sheet* (New York: Public Affairs, 2006), p. 89.

6   For a review of the official dialogue, see Shirley A. Kan, U.S.-China Military Contacts: Issues for Congress (Washington: Congressional Research Service, Report RL32496), March 19, 2013. www.fas.org/sgp/crs/natsec/RL32496.pdf

7   By "better technology", I include greater information security, which would have resulted from the procedures and inspections that Huawei was willing to accept.

CHAPTER 12

Opening National Debate:
Islam and the Netherlands

FOOTNOTES

1   'On the collapse of the Soviet Union', Speech at the Liberal International conference in Luzern, Switzerland, 6 October 1991.

2   F. Bolkestein, 'De integratie van minderheden', *De Volkskrant*, 12 October 1991.

3   Wetenschappelijke Raad voor het Regeringsbeleid, *Etnische Minderheden* (1979), p. xxii.

4   Wetenschappelijke Raad voor het Regeringsbeleid, *Allochtonenbeleid* (1988), p. 44.

5   F. Bolkestein, 'De integratie van minderheden', *De Volkskrant*, 12 October 1991.

6   Frits Bolkestein, *The Intellectual Temptation: Dangerous Ideas in Politics* (2013), pp. 286-289.

7   'Polderen', a verb in Dutch that derives from the word 'polder', which is the low-lying arable land that has been reclaimed from water. The verb 'polderen', however, refers to the 'polder model', which is the method by which labour disputes have been resolved in the Netherlands since the 1990s, by creating a mechanism for negotiations between unions, employers and

government. 'Polderen' can also refer to ongoing circular negotiations in general.

8 Speech by A. J. van der Staay, Director of the Netherlands Institute for Social Research, 16 February 1996.
9 Paul Schnabel, *De multiculturele illusie: een pleidooi voor aanpassing en assimilatie* (2000 as book).
10 Frits Bolkestein, *Islam & Democratie* (1994); Frits Bolkestein, *Moslim in de polder* (1997); Paul Scheffer, 'Het multiculturele drama', *NRC Handelsblad*, 29 January 2000; Afshin Ellian, 'Leve de monoculturele rechtsstaat', *NRC Handelsblad*, 30 November 2002
11 President Marie François Carnot of France in 1894; Prime Minister Antonio Cánovas of Spain in 1897; Empress Elisabeth of Austria in 1898; King Umberto of Italy in 1900; President William McKinley of the United States in 1901; and another Prime Minister of Spain, José Cana Lejas, in 1912.
12 *Weerstand en Tegenkracht: Actuele trends en ontwikkelingen van het salafisme in Nederland*, AIVD Rapport (2009), pp. 1, 7, 11.
13 'Toenemende integratie bij de tweede generatie?', Chapter 14 in *Sociaal en Cultureel Rapport* 2010, p. 298.
14 Ahmed Marcouch, 'Marokkanen: pak je eigen tuig aan', *De Volkskrant*, 19 July 2011.

SOURCES

○ Frits Bolkestein, De Goede Vreemdeling (2011)
  – 'De Goede Vreemdeling', speech, 6 September 2011
  – 'On the collapse of the Soviet Union', speech in Luzern, Switzerland 6 September 1991
  – 'Integratie van minderheden', De Volkskrant, 12 September 1991
○ Frits Bolkestein, The Intellectual Temptation (2013).

OTHER SOURCES

○ *Integratiekaart 2006*, Centraal Bureau voor de Statistiek Cahier 2006-8.
○ *Weerstand en Tegenkracht: Actuele trends en ontwikkelingen van het salafisme in Nederland*, Algemene Inlichtingen en Veiligheidsdienst (2009)
○ *Sociaal en Cultureel Rapport 2010*, Sociaal en Cultureel Planbureau (2010)
  – 14. 'Toenemende integratie bij de tweede generatie?', pp. 297-324.

CHAPTER 13
Privatisation as Breakthrough?

FOOTNOTES

1 Ruchir Sharma, *Breakout Nations, In Pursuit of the Next Economic Miracles* (2012).
2 Sharma, *Breakout Nations*, p. 254.
3 Arjan Vliegenthart, *Transnational Forces and*

Corporate Governance Regulation in Postsocialist Europe (Amsterdam, 2009).
4 See my book (in Dutch): *De terugkeer van het algemeen belang. Privatiseringsverdriet en de terugkeer van het algemeen belang* (Amsterdam: Van Gennep, 2014).
5 John Campbell, *The Iron Lady. Margaret Thatcher. From Grocer's Daughter to Iron Lady* (Vintage Books: London, 2012), p. 114
6 Campbell, *The Iron Lady*, p. 169.
7 Richard Vinen, *A History in Fragments. Europe in the Twentieth Century* (London: Abacus, 2000), p543. See also: David Butler and Gareth Butler, *Twentieth Century British Political Facts* (London, 2000), pp. 430-433.
8 The book that reflected this approach is: David Osborne and Ted Gaebler, *Reinventing Government. How the Entrepreneurial Spirit is Transforming the Public Sector* (New York: Plume, 1993).
9 Massimo Florio, *Network Industries and Social Welfare. The Experiment that Reshuffled European Utilities* (Oxford University Press, 2013), p. 217.
10 Florio, *Network Industries*, p. 330.
11 "Planning our Electric Future: a White paper for Secure, Affordable and Low-carbon Electricity" (Department for Energy and Climate Change, July 2011). Florio, *Network Industries*, p. 177.
12 www.atp-israel.com/mission.html
13 Jeffrey Sachs, *The Price of Civilization. Economics and Ethics after the Fall* (2011), p. 246.
14 Niall Ferguson, *The Great Degeneration. How Institutions Decay and Economies Die* (Penguin Books: London, 2012), p. 34.
15 This is also what John Ralston Saul wanted to express by his book *The Collapse of Globalism and the Reinvention of the World* (2005).

SOURCES

○ Niall Ferguson, *The Great Degeneration: how institutions decay and economies die* (2012)
○ Roel Kuiper, *De Terugkeer van het Algemeen Belang: privatiseringsverdriet en de toekomst van Nederland* (2014)
○ John Ralston Saul, *The Collapse of Globalism and the Reinvention of the World* (2005)
○ Jeffrey Sachs, *The Price of Civilization. Economics and Ethics after the Fall* (2011)
○ Ruchir Sharma, *Breakout Nations: In pursuit of the next economic miracles* (2013)

CHAPTER 14
The Al Jazeera Breakthrough

FOOTNOTES

1 H. Miles, *Al-Jazeera* (2005), Ch. 1-2.
2 Interview Ahmad Rachidi.
3 Interview Mohamed Kichen; Interview Ahmad Rachidi.

4   *BP Statistical Review of World Energy*,
    June 2013.
5   Interview Ambassador John Groffen.
6   H. Miles, *Al-Jazeera*, Ch. 1.
7   Interview Dr Mostefa Souag.
8   H. Miles, *Al Jazeera*. Ch. 1.
9   Constitution of the Emirate of Qatar, Article 47:
    Freedom of expression of opinion and scientific
    research is guaranteed under the conditions
    and circumstances set forth in the Law; Article
    48: Freedom of the press and media, shall be
    guaranteed in accordance with the Law.
10 Interview Ahmed Sheikh.
11 *Ibid.*
12 Interview Ahmed Sheikh.
13 Interview Dr Mostefa Souag.
14 Interview Ahmed Sheikh.
15 *Ibid.*
16 Interview Ahmed Sheikh.
17 *Ibid.*
18 *Ibid.*
19 'Code of Ethics', *Aljazeera.com*, Nov 2010.
20 'Al Jazeera: No apology to Rabat', Aljazeera.
    com, 28 June 2008; 'Al Jazeera for Morocco
    trial delay', *Aljazeera.com*, 28 June 2008; 'Al
    Jazeera Morocco trial to resume', *Aljazeera.
    com*, 4 July 2008; 'Al Jazeera Morocco chief
    fined', *Aljazeera.com*, 12 July 2008.
21 Interview Ahmed Sheikh.
22 H. Miles, *Al Jazeera*, Ch. 2.
23 *Ibid.* Ch. 2.
24 Tareq Ayyoub (April 8, 2003, in Baghdad, Iraq);
    Rashid Hamid Wali (May 21, 2004, in Karbala,
    Iraq); Ali Hassan al-Jaber (March 13, 2011, in
    an area near Benghazi, Libya); Mohamed al-
    Mesalma (January 18, 2013, in Daraa, Syria).
    Source: *Committee to Protect Journalists* (www.
    cpj.org/killed).
25 'Al Jazeera journalists arrested in Egypt',
    Aljazeera.com, 30 December 2013; 'Egypt
    to try Al Jazeera journalists on terror
    charges', *Committee to Protect Journalists*
    (29 January 2014).
26 Interview Dr Mostefa Souag.
27 H. Miles, *Al Jazeera*, Ch. 1.
28 Interview Ahmed Sheikh.
29 H. Miles, *Al Jazeera*, Ch. 2.
30 *Ibid.* Ch. 2.
31 Interview Hassan Rachidi.
32 Interview Hassan Rachidi.
34 Interview Ahmed Sheikh.
33 Interview Ahmed Sheikh.
35 Interview Mohamed Krichen.
36 Interview Ambassador John Groffen.
37 Interview Hassan Rachidi.
38 H. Miles, *Al Jazeera*, Ch. 2.
39 Additional comments by Ambassador
    John Groffen.
40 Comments by Admiral Jacques Lanxade, Dirk
    Barth and Ambassador John Groffen.
41 'Unprecedented Tension Between Qatar And
    Saudi Arabia/UAE/Bahrain Threatens To Break
    Up Gulf Cooperation Council', *MEMRI* Inquiry
    & Analysis Series, Report 1075, 14 March 2014.
42 Interview Ahmed Sheikh.

43 *Ibid.*
44 Interview Ahmed Sheikh.

BOOKS AND ARTICLES

◦ Hugh Miles, *Al Jazeera, How Arab TV News
  Challenged the World* (2005).

INTERVIEWS

The interviews were carried out by Henk van
den Breemen and Johanna Noom of the Owls
Team. Ambassador John Groffen, former
Ambassador of the Netherlands to Qatar (2009-
2013), 30 May 2013.

◦ Ahmed Sheikh, former Editor in Chief,
  Al Jazeera, 28 May 2013.
◦ Hassan Rachidi, former Morocco station chief,
  Al Jazeera, 28 May 2013.
◦ Dr Mustafa Souag, Acting Director General,
  Al Jazeera, 29 May 2013.
◦ Mohamed Krichen, Senior presenter, Al Jazeera,
  30 May 2013.
◦ Additional comments by Dirk Barth,
  Ambassador John Groffen and Admiral Jacques
  Lanxade.

CHAPTER 15

High-Value Healthcare For All:
Innovative Approaches in the
United States and the Netherlands

FOOTNOTES

1   Cortese, DA and RK Smoldt. 2006. Healing
    America's ailing health care system. *Mayo
    Clinic Proceedings*, 81(4): 492-496
2   Squires et al. International Profiles of
    Healthcare Systems, 2012. The
    Commonwealth Fund, November, 2012.
3   Buchmueller, TC and AC Monheit. April 2009.
    Employer-sponsored health insurance and the
    promise of health insurance reform. *NBER*,
    working paper number 14839
4   Cortese, DA and RK Smoldt. 2006. Healing
    America's ailing health care system. *Mayo
    Clinic Proceedings*, 81(4): 492-496
5   Cutler, D. 2010. Where are the health care
    entrepreneurs? The failure of organizational
    innovation in health care. NBER, working
    paper 16030, May.
6   Emanuel, EJ. "Saving by the bundle." *The New
    York Times*, November 16, 2011.
7   The Dutch healthcare system is a dual system:
    long-term care and acute care. Longterm
    care, which involves the permanent (in and
    outpatient) care for the elderly and the mentally
    and/or physically handicapped, is covered by a
    tightly state-controlled mandatory insurance.
    The premium is income-related and is collected
    in a national long-term care fund. Regionally
    private insurance companies execute the
    insurance: they function as public bodies

directed and controlled by the Ministry of Health, Welfare and Sports. Activities are governed by the *Algemene Wet Bijzondere Ziektekosten* (General Law on Exceptional Healthcare Costs), which first came into effect in 1968. The costs of long-term care are approximately 4 per cent of Dutch GDP, significantly higher than those of other European countries.

8 The first payment system reform was initiated in 2009, when the Minister of Health redefined reimbursement for pharmacy services. Specifically, pharmacists would now be paid for dispensing medication, and not keeping patients healthy through medication reviews or insuring therapy adherence. Thus reimbursement for services was redesigned in a way that would reward volume instead of value.

9 Klink, A. *Toerusting in de arena van de gezondheidszorg*, Amsterdam, 2012.

10 Porter, ME. 2010. "What is value in health care?" *NEJM*, 363:2477-2481

11 Case study based on interviews with and content provided by: Nico Moleman, MD; nico.moleman@ molemann.nl; Eerste Weteringplantsoen 6, 1017 SK, Amsterdam, the Netherlands.

12 Case study based on interviews with and content provided by: Hugo Wijnen, MD; hwijnen@rijnstate.nl; Wagnerlaan 55, 6815 AD Arnhem, the Netherlands.

13 Parker, MJ and CR Palmer. 1995. Prediction of rehabilitation after hip fracture. *Age Ageing*, 24:96-98

14 Broos et al.1990. Hip fractures in elderly: mortality, functional results and probability of returning home. Ned Tijdschr Geneeskd, 134:957-961.

15 Gullberg et al. 1997. Word-wide projections for hip fracture. *Osteoporos Int*, 7:407-413.

16 Saltzherr et al. 2006. Proximal femur fractures in the elderly in the Netherlands during the period 1991-2004: incidence, mortality, length of hospital stay and an future. Ned Tijdschr Geneeskd, 150: 2599- 2604

17 Friedman et al. 2009. Impact of a comanaged geriatric fracture centre on short-term hip fracture outcomes. Arch Intern Med, 169(18):1712-1717.

18 Case study based on interviews with and content provided by: Bruce Leff, MD, founder of Hospital at Home®; bleff@jhmi.edu; Melanie Van Amsterdam, MD, lead physician; mvanamste@phs.org

19 www.phs.org/about-us/Pages/default.aspx. Accessed November 4, 2014

20 Cryer et al. 2012. Costs for 'Hospital at Home' patients were 19 percent lower, with equal or better outcomes compared to similar inpatients. Health Affairs, 31(6): 1237-1243

21 *Ibid*

22 Case study based on interviews with and content provided by: Sheldon Zinberg, MD, CareMore founder; sheldon.zinberg@ niftyafterfifty.com; Donald Furman, MD,

former CareMore CMO & executive advisor; donaldsfurman17@gmail.com

23 Main, T. and A. Slywotzky."The Quiet Health-Care Revolution." The Atlantic. N.p., Nov. 2011. Web. 12 Dec. 2012

24 "Our Mission." CareMore. November 9, 2012. www.caremore.com/en/About/ Mission.aspx

25 Do, H. 2010. Medical "extensivists" care for high-acuity patients across settings, leading to reduced hospital use. AHRQ Health Care Innovations Exchange; www. innovations. ahrq.gov/content.aspx?id=2903

26 WellPoint completes acquisition of CareMore Health Group. Press release, August 22, 2011. ir.wellpoint.com/phoenix. zhtml?c=130104&p =irolnewsArticle& ID=1598772&highlight.

27 Case study based on interviews with and content provided by: Jos de Blok, CEO of Buurtzorg Foundation; j.deblok@buurtzorg.com

28 Case study based on interviews with and content provided by: Arnold Romeijnders, GP, medical director of PoZoB; A.Romeijnders@ pozob.nl Victor Pop, MD, PhD, professor of Primary Care, Tilburg University, scientific adviser to PoZoB; v.j.m.pop@uvt.nl

29 Case study based on interviews with and content provided by: James L. Reinersten, MD, former CEO of Park Nicollet and first chair of ICSI; jim@reinertsengroup.com

30 Reinertsen, JL. 1995. Collaborating outside the box: When employers and providers take on environmental barriers to guideline implementation. Jt Comm J Qual Improv, 21(11):612-618

31 "Institute for Clinical Systems Improvement" in Regional Health Improvement Collaboratives: Essential Elements for Successful Healthcare Reform, pp. 19-21, www. iha.org/pdfs_documents/resource_library/ RegionalHealthImprovement Collaboratives. pdf, Accessed November 4, 2014

32 Reinertsen, JL. 1994. Living guidelines. Healthcare Forum Journal, November/ December: 57-61

33 www.icsi.org/about_icsi/. Accessed November 4, 2014

34 Godfield, AG and JL Reinertsen. 2010. Achieving clinical integration with highly engaged physicians. www.ihi.org/resources/ Pages/Publications/Achieving ClinicalIntegrationHighlyEngagedPhysicians. aspx; Accessed November 4, 2014

35 Reinertsen, JL. 1994. Living guidelines. Healthcare Forum Journal, November/ December: 57-61

36 www.icsi.org/about_icsi/our_history/. Accessed November 4, 2014

37 "Institute for Clinical Systems Improvement" in Regional Health Improvement Collaboratives: Essential Elements for Successful Healthcare Reform, pp. 19-21, www. iha.org/pdfs_documents/resource_library/ RegionalHealthImprovement Collaboratives. pdf, Accessed November 4, 2014

38 *Ibid*

39 Reinertsen, JL. 1995. Collaborating outside the box: When employers and providers take on environmental barriers to guideline implementation. *Jt Comm J Qual Improv*, 21(11):612-618

40 Case study based on interviews with and content provided by: Diana Resnik, B.S., President and CEO Shoal Creek Hospital and Community Care; DResnik@seton.org

41 kff.org/state-category/health-coverage-uninsured/. Accessed November 4, 2014

42 Harrington et al. 2006. A community partnership to improve access and quality of care for medically indigent uninsured patients. icc-centex.org/wp-content/uploads/2012/07/Overview_of_ICC.pdf; Accessed November 4, 2014

43 *Ibid*

44 icc-centex.org/. Accessed November 4, 2014

45 ICC asthma program evaluation: 2007-2009. icc-centex.org/wp-content/uploads/2012/ 07/FINAL-ICCAsthma-Report-1.pdf. Accessed November 4, 2014

CHAPTER 16

Mayo Clinic in the 21st Century: Reinventing a Health Care Icon

FOOTNOTES

1 Nelson, Clark W. *Mayo Roots: Profiling the Origins of Mayo Clinic*. Rochester, MN: Mayo Foundation for Medical Education and Research, 1990. Print.e

2 *Celebrating a Century of Integrated, Patient-centered Practice*. Mayo Alumni Fall 2010: 2-4. Web. <www.mayo.edu/mayo-edu-docs/alumni-documents/mc4409-1110.pdf>.

3 "Mayo Clinic Facts and Statistics - 2012." Web.

4 Wang, Haidong. "Age-specific and Sex-specific Mortality in 187 Countries, 1970-2010: A Systematic Analysis for the Global Burden of Disease Study 2010." *The Lancet*, Volume 380, Issue 9859 (15 December 2012): 2071-094. Print.

5 Trustees' Report Summary. Social Security: The Official Website of the US Social Security Administration. Social Security Administration, Web. 26 June 2013

6 Rivard, Chris. "The 5 Mega-Trends That Are Changing the Face of Health Care." *The Atlantic* 9 May 2012: Web.

7 Congress of the United States. Congressional Budget Office. *Technological Change and the Growth of Health Care Spending*. By Peter Orszag.2008. Print. Ser. 2764.

8 Susannah, Fox. Health Online 2013. Publication. Pew Research Center's Internet & American Life Project, 15 January, 2013. Web. 26 June 2013.

9 Keckley., Paul H. *The New Health Care Workforce: Looking Around the Corner to Future Talent Management*. Issue brief. Deloitte Center for Health Solutions, 2012. Print.

10 Spoerl, Bob. "6 Trends in an Era of Consumer-Driven Healthcare." *Becker's Hospital Review*. ASC Communications, 6 June 2012. Web. 26 June 2013.

11 *Summary of the Affordable Care Act*. Publication no. 8061-02. Kaiser Family Foundation, 2013.

12 Farndale, Nigel. "Lehman Brothers Collapse: How the Worst Economic Crisis in Living Memory Began." *The Telegraph* [London] 23 December, 2008, Finance sec. Print.

13 *Experience*. Rep. Rochester, MN: Mayo Foundation for Medical Education and Research, 2008. Print.

14 *Bringing Light through Hope and Healing*. Rep. Rochester, MN: Mayo Foundation for Medical Education and Research, 2009. Print.

15 *Mayo Clinic: Governance and Management Structure*. Rep. Mayo Clinic, Web. 9 July 2013. <www.mayoclinic.org/governance/pdfs/governance-management-structure.pdf>.

16 Kaplan, Robert S., and David P. Norton. "Using the Balanced Scorecard as a Strategic Management System." *Harvard Business Review*, January-February, 1996: Print.

17 Trewin, Karen. *Using Social Media to Promote "The Mayo Effect" at Mayo Clinic*. Case Study. Melcrum: Connecting Communicators, July-Aug. 2011. Web. 10 July 2013

18 Harwick, Harry J. *Forty-Four Years with the Mayo Clinic, 1908-1952*. Rochester, MN: Whiting, 1957. Print.

CHAPTER 17

Healthcare Innovation in Practice

LITERATURE

° Brown Lee, S. (2007), *Overtreated. Why too much medicine is making us sicker and poorer*. Bloomsbury, New York.

° Callahan, D. (2009), *Taming the Beloved Beast. How Medical Technology Costs are Destroying our Health Care System*. Princeton University Press, Princeton.

° Porter, M.E. and Teisberg, E.O. (2006), *Redefining Health Care. Creating Value-Based Competition on Results*. Harvard Business School Press, Boston.

° Welch, H.G. (2011), *Overdiagnosed. Making people sick in the pursuit of health*. Beacon Press, Boston.

CHAPTER 18

The Augeo Foundation: Tackling Child Abuse

FOOTNOTES

1 *Treating the effects of child abuse*, Health Council of the Netherlands (2011), pp. 22-23.

2 'WeCare: Samen voor veilig opvoeden, samen tegen kindermishandeling'. *Concept*

Startnotitie WeCare, Augeo Foundation (April, 2007).
3   *Ibid.* p. 3.
4   *Ibid.* pp. 3-4.
5   *Ibid.* p. 8.
6   Additional comments by Gemma Kobessen and Mariëlle Dekker.
7   Documentation supplied by Augeo Foundation.
8   'Cijfers Augeo foundation, Verkoop en bereik', presentation 3 January 2014.
9   www.thenextpage.nl
10 'Informatie Project "Kinderrechten e-Academie", *Augeo Foundation* (January 2008), p. 1.
11 *Ibid.* p. 2.
12 A E F N Smeekens, D M Broekhuijsen-van Henten, J S Sittig, et al. 'Successful e-learning programme on the detection of child abuse in Emergency Departments: a randomised controlled trial', *Arch Dis Child* (2011) doi:10.1136/adc.2010.190801, pp. 3-4.
13 'Cijfers Augeo foundation, Verkoop en Brereik', *Augeo Foundation*, 3 January 2014.
14 *Een veilig thuis: Gemeentelijke visie voor de aanpak huiselijk geweld en kindermishandeling*, (20 June 2013).
15 Treating the effects of child abuse, Health Council of the Netherlands (2011).

INTERVIEWS

° Interview with Gemma Kobessen and Mariëlle Dekker, conducted by Henk van den Breemen, Johanna Noom and Benjamin Bilski (24 January 2013).
° Interview with Gemma Kobessen and Mariëlle Dekker, conducted by phone by Johanna Noom and Benjamin Bilski (30 September 2013).
° Additional comments by Gemma Kobessen and Mariëlle Dekker (27 February 2014)

SOURCES FROM AUGEO

° www.augeo-foundation.nl/www.thenextpage.nl/ www.tkmnieuws.nl
° 'WeCare: Samen voor veilig opvoeden, samen tegen kindermishandeling'. Concept Startnotitie WeCare, Augeo Foundation (April, 2007).
° 'Informatie Project "Kinderrechten e-Academie", Augeo Foundation (January 2008),
° Augeo's vision, mission and approach (English-language brochure).
° Cijfers Augeo foundation, Verkoop en bereik (January 2014).

ADDITIONAL SOURCES

° A. Smits, M. Dekker, M. Haagmans, 'Identifying, Treating and Preventing Child Abuse and Neglect (CAN)', Pediatric Research (2010) 68, 40-41; doi:10.1203/00006450-201011001-00074.
° A E F N Smeekens, D M Broekhuijsen-van Henten, J S Sittig, et al. 'Successful e-learning programme on the detection of child abuse in

Emergency Departments: a randomised controlled trial', Archives of Disease in Childhood (2011) 96, 330-334; doi:10.1136/ adc.2010.190801.
° Treating the effects of child abuse, Health Council of the Netherlands (2011).
° Een veilig thuis: Gemeentelijke visie op de aanpak van huiselijk geweld en kindermishandeling, Netherlands Ministry of Public Health (20 June 2013).

CHAPTER 19
Impact Investing and Social Renewal

FOOTNOTES

1   A. Nicholls, *Social Entrepreneurship; New Models of Sustainable Social Change* (2006); M. Kelly, *Owning Our Future; The Emerging Ownership Revolution* (2012); M. Martin, *Making Impact Investible* (2013); P. Mills and M. Schluter, *After Capitalism: Rethinking Economic Relationships* (2012).
2   B. Goudzwaard, Kapitalisme en vooruitgang (1976), N. Wolterstorff, *Until Justice and Peace Embrace* (1983).
3   For example, mixed structures like 'Social Enterprise' and 'Community Interest Company' have been introduced into English Company and Charity Law in 2006.
4   Website Global Impact Investing Network: www.thegiin.org.
5   R. C. Solomon, *Ethics and Excellence; Cooperation and Integrity in Business* (1993).
6   R. A. M. Pruijm, *Appropriate governance. Lessons from accounting scandals* (2003) (In Dutch).
8   The central bank of the Netherlands, De Nederlandse Bank (DNB), has also written a report and analysis of the financial crisis under the title *In the track of the crisis. Backgrounds of the financial crisis* (2010). This analysis is in agreement with the accounts of A. Sorkin, *Too Big to Fail; Inside the Battle to Save Wall Street* (2009); J. Cassidy, *How Markets Fail. The Logic of Economic Calamities* (2009); and B. McLean and J. Nocera, *All the Devils are Here. The Hidden History of the Financial Crisis* (2010).
9   Jochemsen, H. and G. Glas, *Verantwoord medisch handelen; Proeve van een christelijke medische ethiek* (1997); Hoogland, J. and H. Jochemsen, 'Profesional Autonomy and the Normative Structure of Medical Practice', *Theoretical Medicine and Bioethics 21*(2000), pp. 457-475;
10 Practices are always embedded in institutions. The specific relation between practices and institutions will not be investigated in this paper.
11 A. MacIntyre, After Virtue (1981).
12 Plato, *The Republic*, Book 3.
13 The Greek word 'arete' is both translated as 'virtue' and 'excellence'.

14 Aristotle, *The Nichomachean Ethics*, Book I
15 Sorkin (2009), Cassidy (2009), McLean and Nocera (2010).
16 Pruijm (2003), McLean and Elkind (2004), Sorkin (2009).
17 R. Solomon, *Ethics and Excellence; Cooperation and Integrity in Business* (1993) pp. 36-37.
18 Milton Friedman, *Capitalism and Freedom* (1961); 'The Social Responsibility of a Business Is to Increase Its Profits', *New York Times Magazine* (13 September 1970).
19 R. E. Freeman, 'The Stakeholder Theory of the Modern Corporation', in *Ethical Theory and Business*, 6th edition, edited by T. L. Beauchamp and N. E. Bowie (2001).
20 Pruijm 2003, McLean and Elkind 2004, Sorkin 2009, Cassidy 2009, McLean and Nocera 2010.
21 John Gray, *Black Mass; Apocalyptic Religion and the Death of Utopia* (2007).
22 John Cassidy, *How Markets Fail. The Logic of Economic Calamities* (2009).
23 K. E. Weick, The Social Psychology of Organizing (1979).
24 M. Sandel, *What Money Can't Buy* (2012), p. 10.
25 M. Martin, 'Making Impact Investible', *Impact Economy Working Papers* 4 (2013).
26 See www.grameen-info.org.
27 www.tendris.nl/home/
28 www.noaber.com/
29 www.vitalhealthsoftware.com/
30 check.preventiekompas.nl/nl/
31 See: www.preventiekompas.nl
32 These organisations were: Dutch Societies of General Practitioners (NHG and LHV), the Dutch Association for Occupational Health, the Dutch Heart Foundation, the Diabetes Federation, and the Kidney Foundation.
33 www.testuwrisico.nl and www.testuwleefstijl.nl
34 www.dobequity.nl/
35 Schematically, the whole field of philanthrophy and investing is often represented in the following way. The poles are formed by philanthrophy (social impact only) and profit-driven (financial impact only). The social enterprise/impact investing is located in the middle (social and financial impact). The well-known approach of CSR (corporate social responsibility) and Triple P (People, Planet, Profit) can be located between social entrepreneurship and profit-driven.
36 VitalHealth Software also has customers in Argentina, the Middle East, India and China.
37 Maximilian Martin, *Making Impact Investible* (2013).
38 See www.socialevaluator.eu.
39 P. Mills and M. Schluter, *After Capitalism: Rethinking Economic Relationships* (2012), R. E. Freeman, 'The Stakeholder Theory of the Modern Corporation' (2001).
40 H. Kievit, *Social Venturing Entrepreneurship; Een plaatsbepaling*. Dissertation Nijenrode (in Dutch) (2011).
41 A. K. Buchholtz, and A. B. Carroll, *Business and Society*, pp. 44ff
42 J. Elkington, *Cannibals with Forks: The Triple Bottom Line of 21st Century Business* (1997).
43 Martin, *Making Impact Investible* (2013), pp. 3-5.
44 *Ibid.* pp. 10ff.
45 Martin (2003), pp. 10ff.
46 Martin (2003), pp. 10ff.
47 J. C. Collins, and J. I. Porras, *Built to Last; Successful Habits of Visionary Companies*, (2000).

REFERENCES

○ Aristotle (1998), *The Nichomachean Ethics*, translated by W. D. Ross, Oxford University Press, Oxford.
○ Buchholtz, A. K. and A. B. Carroll (2009), *Business and Society*, 7th edition, South-Western, London.
○ Cassidy, J. (2009), *How Markets Fail. The Logic of Economic Calamities, Farrar, Straus & Giroux, New York.
○ Collins, J. C. and J. I. Porras (2000), *Built to Last; Successful Habits of Visionary Companies*, Random House, London.
○ De Nederlandse Bank (2010), In the track of the crisis. Backgrounds at the financial crisis (in Dutch) , De Nederlandse Bank, Amsterdam.
○ Dooyeweerd, H. (1975), *In the Twilight of Western Thought*, The Craig Press, Nutley NJ.
○ Elkington, J. (1997), *Cannibals with Forks; The Triple Bottom Line of 21st Century Business*, Capstone, Oxford.
○ Ferguson, Ch. (2010), documentary *Inside Job*.
○ Freeman, R. E. (2001), 'The Stakeholder Theory of the Modern Corporation', in *Ethical Theory and Business*, 6th edition, edited by T. L. Beauchamp and N. E. Bowie, Prentice Hall, New Jersey.
○ Friedman, M. (1961), *Capitalism and Freedom*, University of Chicago Press, Chicago.
○ Friedman, M. (1970), 'The Social Responsibility of a Business Is to Increase Its Profits', *New York Times Magazine*, September 13.
○ Goudzwaard, B. (1976), *Kapitalisme en vooruitgang*, Van Gorkum, Assen. Translated in 1979 as *Capitalism and Progress; A Diagnosis of Western Society*, Wedge Publishing Foundation, Toronto.
○ Gray, J. (2007), *Black Mass; Apocalyptic Religion and the Death of Utopia*, Penguin, New York.
○ Hoogland, J. and H. Jochemsen (2000), 'Profesional Autonomy and the Normative Structure of Medical Practice', *Theoretical Medicine and Bioethics* 21, 457-475.
○ Jochemsen, H. and G. Glas (1997), *Verantwoord medisch handelen; Proeve van een christelijke medische ethiek*, Buijten & Schipperheijn, Amsterdam (in Dutch).
○ Kelly, M. (2012), *Owning Our Future; The Emerging Ownership Revolution*, Berrett-Koehler Publishers, San Francisco.

- Kievit, H. (2011), *Social Venturing Entrepreneurship; Een plaatsbepaling. Dissertation Nijenrode*, Breukelen (in Dutch).
- MacIntyre, A.C. (1981), *After Virtue; A Study in Moral Theory*, Duckworth, London.
- Martin, M. (2013), *Making Impact Investible*, Impact Economy Working Papers 4. Retrieved 20 September 2013 from www.impacteconomy. com.
- McLean, B. and P. Elkind (2004), *The Smartest Guys in the Room; The Amazing Rise and Scandalous Fall of Enron*, Portfolio, New York.
- McLean, B. and J. Nocera (2010), *All the Devils are Here. The Hidden History of the Financial Crisis*, Portfolio/Penguin, New York.
- Mills, P. and M. Schluter (2012), *After Capitalism: Rethinking Economic Relationships*, Jubilee Centre, Cambridge.
- Nicholls, A. (editor) (2006), *Social Entrepreneurship; New Models of Sustainable Social Change*, Oxford University Press, Oxford.
- Porter, M.E. and Teisberg, E.O. (2006), *Redefining Health Care. Creating Value-Based Competition on Results*, Boston: Harvard Business School Press.
- Pruijm, R.A.M. (2003), *Appropriate governance. Lessons from accounting scandals* (in Dutch), Van Gorcum, Assen.
- Sandel, M. (2012), *What Money Can't Buy. The Moral Limits of Markets*, London: Allen Lane.
- Scott, A.O. (2010), 'Who Maimed the Economy, and How', *The New York Times*, October 7, 2010.
- Solomon, R.C. (1993), *Ethics and Excellence; Cooperation and Integrity in Business*, Oxford University Press, Oxford.
- Sorkin, A.R. (2009), *Too Big to Fail; Inside the Battle to Save Wall Street*, Penguin, New York.
- Verkerk, M.J., J. Hoogland, J. van der Stoep and M. J. de Vries (2007), *Denken, ontwerpen, maken; Basisboek Techniekfilosofie*, Boom, Amsterdam (in Dutch).
- M.J. Verkerk (2013), 'Social Entrepreneurship and Impact Investing', *Philosophia Reformata*, 78, nr 2, 209-221.
- Weick, K. E. (1979), *The Social Psychology of Organizing*, 2nd edition, McGraw-Hill, New York.
- Wolterstorff, N. (1983), *Until Justice and Peace Embrace*, Eerdmans, Grand Rapids.
- Yunus, M. (2003), *Banker to the Poor; The Story of the Grameen Bank*, Aurum Press, London.
- Zijlstra A. (2013), 'The Neoliberal Delusion; A Religious-Philosophical Critique', *Philosophia Reformata* 78, nr 2, 162-178.

uitgevers.
- Corbin, J. M., & Strauss, A. (2008). *Basic of Qualitative Research*. Thousand Oaks, California, USA: Sage Publications.
- Swanborn, P. G. (2013). *Case studies, Wat, wanneer en hoe?* Den Haag, Nederland: Boom|Lemma uitgevers.

QUALITATIVE ANALYSIS

SOURCES

Qualitative analysis and graphs produced by Theo Bosters of Corpos (www.corpos.nl).

- Boeije, H. (2008). *Analyseren in kwalitatief onderzoek*. Den Haag, Nederland: Boom|Lemma